Contents

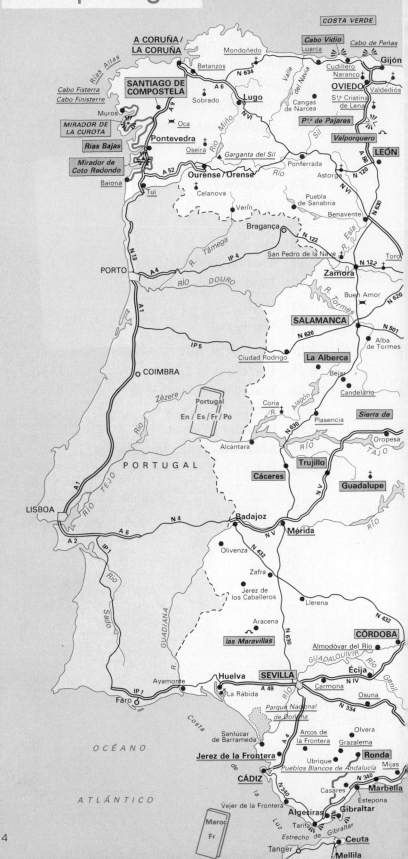

Touring programmes

★ Altas
Rías
Ferrol
★ A CORUÑA / LA CORUÑA
Betanzos ★   N 634   Ribadeo
A 9   A 6
★★★ SANTIAGO DE COMPOSTELA
R. Miño   N VI   R.
A 9
Pontevedra ★   C 536
Rías Bajas ★★
N 120
VIGO   Ourense / Orense
★ Baiona   R.
Tui ★
N 13
Bragança
PORTO   A 4   R. Tâmega   IP 4
RÍO DOURO
★★
IP 5   Ciudad Rodri
★ La Alb
COIMBRA   C 526
R. Zêzere   ★ Coria   R.
P O R T U G A L
★★ Cáceres
A 1   RÍO TEJO
LISBOA   N 4
A 6   N V   M
A 2   IP 1   N 630
Río Sado
RÍO GUADIANA
★★★ SEVILLA
A 49
RÍO   A 4
Faro
★ Jerez de la Frontera
OCÉANO
★ CÁDIZ   Pue
Me
Sie
ATLÁNTICO

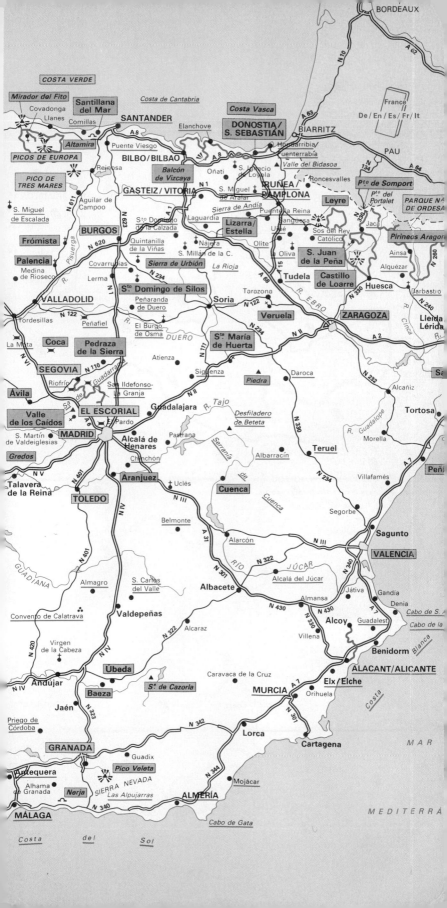

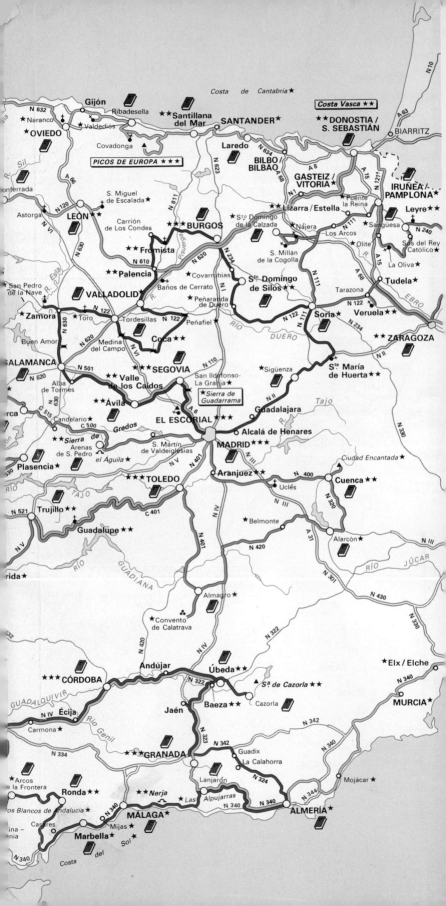

Overnight stop

Costa Brava ★★   Region described in the guide accompanied by a detailed map

0   100 km

Tour of Spain's main towns : 3 500 km-2 175 miles (3 weeks)

The northwest : 2 200 km-1 367 miles (17 days including one in Santiago de Compostela)

Aragón and Navarra : 1 100 km-684 miles (1 week)

Cataluña : 1 200 km-746 miles (9 days including two in Barcelona)

Castilla y Léon : 1 200 km-746 miles (2 weeks including two days in Madrid, one in Segovia and another in Salamanca)

Extremadura and Castilla-La Mancha : 1 600 km-994 miles (13 days including two in Madrid and one in Toledo)

Andalucía : 1 800 km-1 119 miles (15 days including two in Sevilla, one in Córdoba and another in Granada)

Life in Spain

EVERYDAY SIGHTS AND SOUNDS

Mealtimes – The morning (**mañana**) in Spain lasts until 2pm, when it is time for lunch (**almuerzo** or **comida**). After that there's the siesta, and the afternoon (**tarde**) begins at about 5pm. At 8pm people begin thinking about having a drink and so the evening (**noche**) begins. Dinner (**cena**) is served from 9pm and the evening may continue well into the night.

The Plaza Mayor – There's no town, large or small, no village in Spain, without its main square, lined, for the most part, by a covered arcade. This rarely serves as a main crossroads; rather it is enclosed and accessible from adjoining streets only through arches beneath one or more of the surrounding houses. It is the hub of community life (often acting as a forecourt to the *Ayuntamiento*, or Town Hall) and is the setting for public festivities and great occasions. In the 18C, entrances would be blocked so that the square could serve as a bullring – a practice still observed in villages without an arena but determined to hold a *corrida*.

The street – Large towns generally have an old quarter of pedestrian streets where shops have retained their charm and their old-fashioned fronts. This is where whole families go out for a stroll, where one can do one's shopping or buy a lottery ticket from one of the many ticket sellers working for the *Once* (an association for the blind). The great street event is the evening **paseo**. As the sun begins to set everyone meets in the main street to join the streams of people walking slowly up and down; one walks *(pasear)* to enjoy the last light and the cool of the evening. Groups of girls and boys saunter along the street, laughing and chatting, while the older generation looks on from pavement cafés.

Bars – Bars are popular meeting places where one goes for an aperitif (**chateo**) at lunchtime, a well established tradition, to drink a glass of wine with friends and try the **tapas** or **raciones** which may be anything from olives to seafood to chips with mayonnaise. Televisions are ubiquitous as are the one-arm bandits that invariably play the theme tune from *The Third Man*. Then it's time for coffee: black is *café solo* or simply *café*; white *café con leche* or *café cortado*.

After work comes the **tertulia** or virtually informal club hour when men gather and, over a glass, discuss the news, politics and football (the latest feats of teams like Atlético, Real Madrid or F.C. Barcelona) or tell jokes (**chistes**). The end of the afternoon is when people often have a *café con leche* or, in summer, a **horchata de chufas**, a refreshing cold drink made from the tiger-nut rhizome, and **churros**, delicious twisted fritters traditionally served with thick, hot chocolate.

National holidays – **Christmas** is a religious family holiday when *cestas de Navidad*, large traditional hampers containing bottles of wine, hams, sugared almonds, nougat *(turrón)* and marzipan, are given by friends. **New Year's Eve** is celebrated out of doors: in Madrid the crowds gather at the Puerta del Sol to eat a grape at each stroke of the clock at midnight – a custom observed in every Spanish home. At **Epiphany** there is a family exchange of presents and the Twelfth Night cake or **roscón** is eaten. (The person who draws the charm hidden in the cake is supposed to have a surprise that day).

POLITICAL AND ADMINISTRATIVE ORGANISATION

Under the terms of its constitution approved by the *Cortes* (Parliament) in 1976 and passed by referendum on 6 December 1978, Spain is a constitutional monarchy. The king holds important powers such as appointing the head of government and convening and dissolving the *Cortes*. Real power, however, ultimately lies with the Prime Minister.

The constitution has taken specific local requirements into account by creating 17 *Comunidades Autónomas* (each with its own government consisting of an executive and a legislature elected by universal suffrage). Certain regions such as Catalunya, Galicia and the País Vasco (Basque Country) enjoy a reinforced autonomy with, among other things, the recognition of their own regional language. Central government retains power over Defence, Foreign Affairs and economic policy for the whole country. Since 1983 the law on the Process of Self-government has given it a say in decisions taken by the Autonomous Communities.

(See the map on p 3 and the chapter on regions and landscape on p 12).

For a quiet place to stay
consult the annual Michelin Red Guide España Portugal
which gives a choice of pleasant hotels.

Introduction

Regions and landscape

The Iberian Peninsula (581 000km² - 224 325sq miles), which is separated from the rest of Europe by the Pyrenees, is made up of continental Spain and Portugal. Spain covers an area of 505 000km² - 194 980sq miles, including the Islas Canarias and Islas Baleares, and is the fourth largest European country after Russia, the Ukraine and France. The population is nearing 40 million. Spain's position in Europe is unique due to its geographical isolation, its contrasts of relief and extremes of climate. The southernmost tip of the country is less than 15km - 9 miles from Africa.

A mountainous country – The average altitude in Spain is 650m-2 100ft above sea level and one sixth of the terrain rises to more than 1 000m - 3 300ft. The highest peak is Mulhacén (3 482m - 11 424ft) in the Sierra Nevada.
The dominant feature of the peninsula is the immense plateau at its centre. This is the **Meseta**, a Hercynian platform between 600 and 1 000m - 2 000 and 3 300ft high, which tilts slightly westwards. The Meseta is surrounded by long mountain ranges which form barriers between the central plateau and the coastal regions. All these ranges, the **Cordillera Cantábrica** of the northwest (an extension of the Pyrenees), the **Cordillera Ibérica** in the northeast and the **Sierra Morena** in the south, were caused by Alpine folding. Other mountains rising here and there from the Meseta are folds of the original, ancient massif. They include the **Sierras de Somesierra, Guadarrama** and **Gredos**, the **Peña de Francia** and the **Montes de Toledo**. The highest massifs in Spain, the **Pyrenees** (Pirineos) in the north and the **Sierras Béticas**, including the **Sierra Nevada**, in the south, are on the country's periphery, as are Spain's greatest depressions, those of the Ebro and Guadalquivir rivers.

A varied climate – The great diversity of landscapes in Spain is partly due to the variety of climates that prevail over the peninsula. The Meseta has a **continental** climate with extremes of temperature ranging from scorching hot in summer to freezing cold in winter. On the north coast where mist often develops into drizzle, the climate is **mild and very humid**. The east and south coasts have a **Mediterranean** climate verging on a desert climate in the Almería region.

For each of the regions described below, the respective autonomous communities are given, together with the provinces when appropriate, or otherwise the capital. See the administrative map on p 3.

ATLANTIC SPAIN
País Vasco / Euskadi
Provinces: Álava, Guipúzcoa, Vizcaya
Area: 7 261km² - 2 803sq miles
Population: 2 109 009

Galicia
Provinces: La Coruña, Lugo, Orense, Pontevedra
Area: 29 500km² - 11 390sq miles
Population: 2 720 445

Principado de Asturias
Capital: Oviedo
Area: 10 565km² - 4 079sq miles
Population: 1 098 725

Cantabria
Capital: Santander
Area: 5 282km² - 2 039sq miles
Population: 530 281

País Vasco, Cantabria, Asturias: a kind of Switzerland by the sea – The mountain chain that borders the northern edge of the Meseta emerged in the Tertiary era and today runs through each of the coastal provinces. The **Montes Vascos**, secondary limestone ranges, continue westwards from the Pyrenean foothills and rise to 1 500m - 4 900ft. The **Cordillera Cantábrica** further west forms an imposing barrier which has given the province of Cantabria the name of La Montaña. The range rises above 2 500m-8 200ft in the **Picos de Europa**, less than 50km-31 miles from the sea.

A village in the Picos de Europa

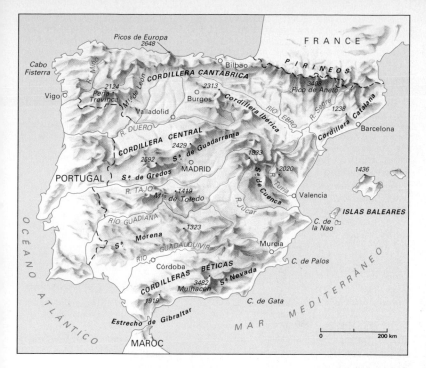

The **País Vasco** (Basque Country) is a markedly undulating region with little villages and isolated farms nestling in the valleys. Local architecture is very distinctive: half-timbered houses with broad whitewashed fronts. The middle land sandwiched between the mountains and the sea in **Cantabria** and **Asturias** is very hilly. Roads wind along valley floors hemmed in by lush meadows, cider apple orchards and fields of maize and beans. Dairy produce is a major source of livelihood, especially in Cantabria. Maize, originally imported from America, has since become an important crop, judging by the large number of *hórreos* or squat drying sheds, so typical of Asturian villages.
The coast is indented by deep inlets or *rías* and lined by low cliffs in many places. There are beautiful beaches, particularly in Cantabria.

Galicia – This remote region fronting the Atlantic on its northern and western borders is reminiscent of Ireland, Wales or Brittany. Galicia is an ancient eroded granite massif that was displaced and rejuvenated as a result of Alpine folding. Although peaks on the massif rise to 2000m - 6600ft (that of Peña Trevinca is 2124m - 6968ft high) the average altitude is less than 500m - 1600ft. Yet the overall impression of Galicia is that of a hilly and mountainous region.
The coast, cut by deep **rías**, is more densely populated than the interior. It is Spain's chief fishing region where most of the produce is used for canning. Other activities include the timber industry and shipbuilding in the *rías* of Ferrol and Vigo.
The interior is primarily an agricultural region where mixed farming is the norm: maize, potatoes, grapes and rye. Orense province produces beef for export.
The climate is strongly influenced by the sea: temperatures are mild and vary little (the annual average is 13°C - 55°F), and rainfall is abundant.

THE PYRENEES AND THE EBRO REGION

Aragón	Navarra	La Rioja
Provinces: Huesca, Zaragoza, Teruel	**Capital:** Pamplona	**Capital:** Logroño
Area: 47 669km² 18 405sq miles	**Area:** 10 421km²- 4 024sq miles	**Area:** 5 034km² - 1 944sq miles
Population: 1 221 546	**Population:** 523 563	**Population:** 267 943

The Pyrenees (Pirineos) – **Alta (Upper) Aragón** embraces the Pirineos Centrales, a region of mountain valleys and piedmont vales, spring waterfalls (Parque Nacional de Ordesa) and villages of rough stone houses with slate roofs. The main source of livelihood is farming around Huesca and stock-raising in the valleys. There are some industries in Zaragoza.
In **Navarra** the Pyrenees are watered by Atlantic rain. They rise regularly from the 900m - 2953ft of Mont La Rhune to the 2504m - 8215ft of the Pic d'Anie (both peaks just over the French border). East of Roncesvalles, the terrain becomes more mountainous and the harshness of the climate becomes visible in the ruggedness of the forest cover and the steeply-sloped slate roofs and stone fronts of the houses.

Resemblance to the Basque provinces is apparent west of Roncesvalles where small parcels of land grow alternate fields of pasture or maize and the houses have tiled roofs with half-timbered whitewashed fronts. Beyond the limestone range of the Andía, Urbasa, Navascués and Leyre *sierras* the land drops away to the Ebro basin.

The Ebro depression – This clay basin was formerly a gulf that has since been filled in. The terraces on either side of the river are deeply ravined, a feature even more pronounced in the Monegros desert in Aragón with its saline outcrops. In contrast, the lower valley has been transformed by irrigation into lovely green *huertas*.

Cereals predominate in the Cuenca region, also known as the Pamplona basin, in **Navarra**. Western **Ribera**, a continuation of the famous **Rioja**, is a wine-growing area, while the well-irrigated eastern part of the province around Tudela has become a prosperous horticultural region growing and canning asparagus, artichokes and peppers. Tall brick houses are typical of the architecture in this area.

Cordillera Ibérica – The clay hills bordering the Ebro basin in **Bajo (Lower) Aragón** around Piedra, Daroca and Alcañiz are planted with vineyards and olive groves. Brick villages and ochre-coloured houses merge in with the tawny shade of the deeply-scored hillsides. The plateaux surrounding Teruel form part of the massive spread of the **Montes Universales**, one of Spain's great watersheds where the Cabriel, Turia, Júcar and Tajo (Tagus) rivers rise. The climate is harsh.

THE MESETA

Castilla y León

Provinces: Ávila, Burgos, León, Palencia, Salamanca, Segovia, Soria, Valladolid, Zamora.
Area: 94 147km² - 36 350sq miles
Population: 2 562 979

Comunidad Autónoma de Madrid

Capital: Madrid
Area: 7 995km² - 3 087sq miles
Population: 5 030 958

Castilla – La Mancha

Provinces: Albacete, Cuidad Real, Cuenca, Guadalajara, Toledo.
Area: 79 226km² - 30 589sq miles
Population: 1 651 833

Extremadura

Provinces: Badajoz, Cáceres
Area: 41 602km² - 16 063sq miles
Population: 1 056 538

The Meseta accounts for 40% of the surface area of the Iberian Peninsula. Its horizons appear infinite, broken only here and there by a rock-brown village clustered at the foot of a castle, or by the indistinct ouline of **páramos** (bare limestone heights).

The northern Meseta – The Castilla y León region (Old Castile) in the north consists almost entirely of the Duero basin. This area is about 1 000m - 3 300ft high and is ringed by the Montes de León in the northwest, the Cordillera Cantábrica in the north, the Cordillera Ibérica in the east and the Cordillera Central in the southeast. As the Tertiary sediment on the Meseta resists erosion in different ways, there are different landscape features such as wide terraced valleys dotted with rock pinnacles, narrow defiles and gently rolling hills. In spite of these variations, the general aspect is one of a sparsely populated plateau with only the occasional village breaking the endless horizon. Cereal growing predominates everywhere; wheat on the better land, oats and rye elsewhere. Only the southwest peneplains near Salamanca are used for stock-raising; sheep on small properties and fighting bulls on larger ones of often over 500ha - 1 200 acres.

Countryside near Zamora (Castilla y León)

The southern Meseta – This comprises the whole of Madrid-Castilla-La Mancha (New Castile) and Extremadura. It is a vast tableland slightly tilted towards the west, watered by two large rivers – the Tajo (Tagus), which cuts a deep gorge through the limestone Alcarria region, and the sluggish Guadiana. The terrain is flatter than in Castilla y León and rises to an average altitude of less than 700m - 2300ft compared to between 800 and 1000m - 2600 and 3300ft in the north. The aridity of the region is particularly apparent in summer and the name La Mancha comes from the Arab *manxa* meaning 'dry land'. Despite this there is considerable cultivation and a sweeping look across the Meseta would take in wind-ruffled cereal fields, stretches of saffron turned purple in the flowering season, and straight lines of olives and vines. This is Spain's leading vineyard for popular modestly-priced wines, with vintages such as Manzanares and Valdepeñas. The famous La Mancha cheese known as *queso manchego* is also produced here.

The bare, eroded and virtually uninhabited Montes de Toledo separate the Tajo basin from that of the Guadiana, while the other massifs in the region ring the borders. The **Cordillera Central** runs along the northern edge (Sierras de Gredos and Guadarrama), the **Sierra Morena** is in the south, and the **Serranía de Cuenca**, a limestone plateau pitted with swallow-holes *(torcas)* and cut by gorges *(hoces)*, lies to the northeast. The **Alcarria** further north is a region of remote villages where the Tajo and its tributaries flow through deeply eroded gullies. Its upper mountain slopes grow aromatic plants such as thyme, rosemary, lavender and marjoram from which a well-known honey is produced.

The rural character of the region persists; small towns look more like large villages with the arcaded *Plaza Mayor* still acting as the nerve-centre.

Extremadura in the southwest is a schist and granite Hercynian platform that levels off at about 400m - 1300ft. The immense plateaux of the region are used for sheep grazing but lie deserted in summer when the animals are moved to higher pastures. Cork provides supplementary income as does traditional pig farming. The population is concentrated along the rivers that supply irrigation for a variety of crops including tobacco, cotton and wheat as well as market-garden produce. The Badajoz Plan that controls the flow of the Guadiana by means of a series of dams has made it possible to reafforest a large area and to develop high-yield crops such as maize, sunflowers, market-garden produce and above all animal fodder.

THE MEDITERRANEAN REGIONS

Catalunya/Cataluña

Provinces: Barcelona, Girona, Lleida,
      Tarragona
Area: 31930km² - 12328sq miles
Population: 6115579

Región de Murcia

Capital: Murcia
Area: 11317km² – 4369sq miles
Population: 1059612

Comunidad Valenciana

Provinces: Alicante, Castellón, Valencia
Area: 23305km² - 8998sq miles
Population: 3923841

Comunidad Autónoma de las Islas Baleares

Capital: Palma de Mallorca
Area: 5014km² - 1936sq miles
Population: 745944

Catalunya – Catalunya is a triangle of varied landscapes between the French border, Aragón and the Mediterranean. In the north, the eastern stretch of the Pyrenees, between Andorra and the Cabo de Creus headland, is a green wooded area with peaks over 3000m - 9800ft high. The **Costa Brava** between France and Barcelona is a rocky area with many bays and inlets. It has a Mediterranean climate as does the **Costa Dorada** (Gold Coast) in the south with its vast sandy beaches. The hinterland, separated from the coast by the Catalan *sierras*, is a drier region with harsh winters. The Pyrenean foothills resemble the *sierras* in Aragón and the houses here are like *mas*, the farmhouses in the south of France. The southern part of the triangle is composed of green hills sloping down to an intensively cultivated plain around the lower Ebro and its delta. Although fertile (cereals, vines, olives and market-garden produce), Catalunya is primarily an industrial region with its main activities centred around Barcelona.

Levante – The whole of the Levante, including Valencia and Murcia, comprises a narrow alluvial plain between the Mediterranean coast and the massifs of the interior (the Cordillera Ibérica in the north and the Sierras Béticas in the south).

The coast, called **Costa del Azahar** (Orange Blossom Coast) near Valencia and the **Costa Blanca** (White Coast) around Alicante and Murcia, consists of dunes and offshore sand bars which form pools and lagoons.

The climate is Mediterranean but drier than average in this area. Little rain falls except during the autumn months when the rivers flood. Thanks to an ingenious system of irrigation *(acequias)* developed since Antiquity, the natural vegetation, of olives, almond and carob trees and vines, has gradually been replaced, and the countryside transformed into **huertas** (irrigated areas), lush citrus orchards and market gardens, with orange trees between Castellón and Denia and lemons near Murcia. The prosperous *huertas* are among the most densely populated areas in Spain. There are palm groves around Elche and Orihuela in the south and rice is grown in swampy areas.

The region's industry, based on mineral deposits (lead, zinc and copper) and backed by its ports, is well-developed and includes metallurgy, steel, oil refining, paper and shoes. Finally, tourism is booming on the coast where there are resorts like Benidorm.

Islas Baleares (Balearic Islands) – The Balearic archipelago consists of two groups of islands: Mallorca and Menorca on the one hand, Ibiza and Formentera, known as **Pityuses** in Antiquity, on the other.

The limestone hills, none of which exceed 1500m - 4900ft, differ in origin. Ibiza and Mallorca are an extension of the Cordillera Bética in Andalucía while Menorca belongs to the submerged massif from which Corsica, Sardinia and the Catalan cordilleras rise. The lush vegetation produced by the autumn rains is one of the sunny islands' greatest attractions. Pines shade the indented shores, junipers and evergreen oaks cover the upper hillsides, while almonds, figs and olives cloak the plains.

The three larger islands differ considerably in character although they share the same contrast between the tranquillity of the hills inland and the bustling tourism along the coast. Their beaches are washed by a wonderfully calm, clear sea.

ANDALUCÍA

Andalucía: Junta de Andalucía

Provinces: Almería, Cádiz, Córdoba, Granada, Huelva, Jaén, Málaga, Sevilla.

Area: 87268km² - 33694sq miles
Population: 7040627

Andalucía was formerly known as *Baetica* by the Romans and *Al Andalus* by the Arabs. Although it comprises a wide variety of geographical regions, Andalucía's character has been strongly marked by its houses. Its villages and old quarters are usually lined by white houses adorned with wrought-iron grilles opening onto cool flowery *patios*.

Sierra Morena – This mountain chain separates the Meseta from Andalucía. It is rich in minerals and thickly covered by a scrub of oaks, lentisks (mastic trees) and arbutus (strawberry trees). Jaén province's extraordinary landscape consists of row upon row of olive trees as far as the eye can see.

The Guadalquivir depression – This Quaternary basin, a former gulf, opening broadly onto the Atlantic, is one of the richest agricultural areas in Spain. Cereals, cotton, olives and citrus fruit are grown on the plains, and rice and vines (around Jerez) on the coast where fighting bulls are also bred. The centre of the region is Sevilla, Spain's fourth largest city. The whole area is a vast tract of cultivated land divided into large properties known as **fincas**.

Cordilleras Béticas – The **Sierra Nevada**, which includes Spain's highest peak, Mulhacén (3482m - 11424ft), is continued westwards by the **Serranía de Ronda** and **Sierra de Ubrique**. The range's snow-capped heights dominate a series of basins like the wide *vega* plain of Granada.

In spite of a sub-desert climate, the extremely touristic **Costa del Sol** (Sun Coast) produces citrus and early fruit and vegetables which are grown on irrigated land.

1492

If there were only one important date to remember in Spanish history, it would be 1492. That year, after 781 years of Muslim occupation, the Reconquest ended with the fall of Granada *(qv)* on 2 January. This was also the year that the Jews were expelled, the Spaniard Rodrigo Borja (Borgia) became Pope Alexander VI and on 12 October, Christopher Columbus discovered America.

Christopher Columbus (Cristóbal Colón) (?1451-1506) and the discovery of America – Born in Genoa, the son of a weaver, Columbus began his seafaring career at an early age. He travelled to Lisbon in 1476 where he developed a passion for map-making on discovering Ptolemy's Geography and the Frenchman Pierre d'Ailly's Imago Mundi. Convinced that the Indies could be reached by sailing west, he submitted a navigation plan to João II of Portugal and to the Kings of France and England. He ultimately managed to gain the support of the Duke of Medinaceli and that of the Prior of the Monasterio de La Rábida *(qv)*, Juan Pérez, who was Isabel the Catholic's confessor. The Catholic Monarchs agreed to finance his expedition, and if he succeeded, to bestow upon him the hereditary title of Admiral of the Ocean and the viceroyship of any lands discovered. On 3 August 1492, heading a fleet of three caravels (the Santa María, under his command, and the Pinta and the Niña captained by the Pinzón brothers), he put out from Palos de la Frontera *(qv)*. On 12 October, after a difficult crossing, San Salvador (Bahamas) came into sight and a short time later Hispaniola (Haiti) and Cuba were discovered. On his return to Spain on 15 March 1493, Christopher Columbus was given a triumphant welcome and the means with which to organise new expeditions. This marked the beginning of the great Spanish discoveries of the New World.

Historical table and notes

From Antiquity to the Visigothic kingdom

11-5C BC	Phœnician and Greek trading posts founded on the eastern and southern coasts of Spain, inhabited by **Iberians** and **Tartessians** respectively. In the 9C, the central-European **Celts** settle in west Spain and on the Meseta, intermingling with the Iberians (forming **Celtiberians**).
3-2C BC	The **Carthaginians** take over the southeast after conquering the Greeks and Tartessians. The capture of **Sagunto** by Hannibal leads to the Second Punic War (218-201 BC). Rome expels the Carthaginians and begins the conquest of peninsular Spain (with resistance at **Numancia**).
1C BC-1C AD	Cantabria and Asturias are finally pacified in 19 AD. Spain is now known as *Iberia* or *Hispania*. Christianity spreads there during the 1C AD.
5-6C AD	Early Suevi (Swabian) and Vandal invasions are followed by those of the **Visigoths** (411) who estabish a powerful monarchy with Toledo as capital. The peninsula unites under King Leovigild (584).

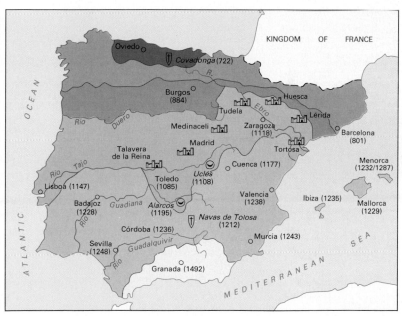

THE CHRISTIAN RECONQUEST OF THE IBERIAN PENINSULA

Kingdom of Asturias *c* 750

Recovered territory
rc
c 850
c 1040
c 1150
c 1270
Between 1270 and 1492

Christian victories   Muslim victories   Muslim strongholds

Muslim Spain and the Reconquest

8C	Moors invade and annihilate the Visigothic kingdom after the **Battle of Guadalete** in 711. Pelayo's victory at **Covadonga** in 722 heralds a 700 year long Christian War of Reconquest. The first Muslim invaders are subjects of the Umayyad Caliphate in Damascus. **Abd ar-Rahman I** breaks with Damascus by founding an independent emirate at Córdoba in 756.
9C	Settlement of uninhabited land by Christians.
10C	Golden age of the emirate of Córdoba, which is raised to the status of a caliphate (929-1021) by **Abd ar-Rahman III**. A period of great prosperity ensues during which the expansion of Christian kingdoms is checked. Fortresses are built in the north along the Duero river.
11C	Christian Spain now includes the kingdoms of León, Castilla, Navarra, Aragón, and the County of Barcelona. On the death of al-Mansur in 1002, the Caliphate of Córdoba disintegrates into about twenty *taifa* (faction) kingdoms (1031). Alfonso VI conquers Toledo (1085), and the Tajo river area is resettled by Christians. The *taifa* kings call upon the **Almoravids** (Saharan Muslims) for assistance and in a short time the tribe overruns a large part of Spain. Pilgrims begin to tread the Way of Saint James of Compostela. **El Cid** conquers Valencia (1094).

12C	Dissension stemming from a second age of *taifa* kingdoms assists the Reconquest, especially in the Ebro valley (Zaragoza is taken in 1118, Tortosa in 1148 and Lleida in 1149), but after Yacoub al-Mansur's victory in Alarcos (1195), the **Almohads** (who routed the Almoravids) recover Extremadura and check Christian expansion towards the Guadiana and Guadalquivir rivers. Sevilla, which has taken Córdoba under its control, enjoys a period of great prosperity. Great military Orders are founded, among them Calatrava, Alcántara, and Santiago. Unification of the kingdoms of Aragón and Catalunya (1150).
13C	The *taifa* kingdoms enter their third age. The decline of the Muslims begins with the **Battle of Las Navas de Tolosa** (1212). Muslim influence is reduced to the Nasrid kingdom of Granada (present-day provinces of Málaga, Granada and Almería) which holds out until its capture in 1492. Unification of Castilla and León under Ferdinand III, the Saint (1230). The Crown of Aragón under James I (Jaime I), the Conqueror (1213-1276), gains control over considerable territory in the Mediterranean.

The Catholic Monarchs (1474-1516) and the unity of Spain

1474	Isabel, wife of Ferdinand of Aragón, succeeds her brother Henry IV to the throne of Castilla. She has to contend with opposition from the supporters of her niece Juana la Beltraneja *(qv)* until 1479.
1478-1479	The court of the **Inquisition** is instituted by a special Papal Bull and **Torquemada** is later appointed Inquisitor-General. The court, a political and religious institution directed against Jews, Moors and later Protestants, survives until the 19C. Ferdinand becomes King of Aragón in 1479 and Christian Spain is united under one crown.
1492	The **fall of Granada** marks the end of the Reconquest. Expulsion of Jews. **Christopher Columbus** discovers America on 12 October *(p 16)*.
1494	The Treaty of Tordesillas divides the New World between Spain and Portugal.
1496	Juana, daughter of the Catholic Monarchs, marries Philip the Fair, son of Emperor Maximilian of Austria.
1504	Death of Isabel. The kingdom is inherited by her daughter Juana the Mad but Ferdinand governs as regent until Juana's son Charles (b 1500), future Charles V, comes of age.
1512	The Duke of Alba conquers Navarra, thus bringing political unity to Spain.

Spain's Golden Age

	16C Spain flourishes under the rule of the Habsburg House of Austria – **Charles V** (1516-1556) and **Philip II** (1556-1598). American colonies are conquered.
1516	On the death of Ferdinand, his grandson becomes Charles I of Spain. Through his mother, Charles inherits Spain, Naples, Sicily, Sardinia and American territories. Cardinal Cisneros governs until the new king arrives for the first time in Spain in 1517.
1519	On the death of Maximilian of Austria, Charles I is elected Holy Roman Emperor under the name of **Charles V**. He inherits Germany, Austria, the Franche-Comté and the Low Countries.
1520-1522	The Spanish, incensed by Charles V's largely Flemish court advisers and the increasing number of taxes, rise up in arms. The emperor quells **Comuneros** *(qv)* and **Germanías** revolts in Valencia and Mallorca.
1521-1556	Charles V wages five wars against France in order to secure complete control of Europe. In the first four he conquers François I (imprisoned at Pavia in 1525) and in the fifth he routs the new French king, Henry II, and captures Milan. The **conquistadores** move across America. **Núñez de Balboa** discovers the Pacific; **Cortés** seizes Mexico in 1521; **Pizarro** and **Diego de Almagro** subdue Peru in 1533; **Francisco Coronado** explores the Colorado river in 1535; **Hernando de Soto** takes possession of Florida in 1539, then Chile in 1541.
1555	Charles V signs a compromise – the Peace of Augsburg – with the Protestants in Germany after failing to suppress the Reformation.
1556	Charles V abdicates in favour of his son and retires to a monastery in Yuste. **Philip II** becomes king, inheriting Spain and its colonies, the Kingdom of Naples, Milan, the Low Countries and the Franche-Comté, but not Germany and Austria which are left by Charles to his brother Ferdinand I of Austria. Philip II turns his attention to Spain and the defence of Catholicism. He chooses Madrid as capital in 1561. Spain goes through a serious economic crisis.

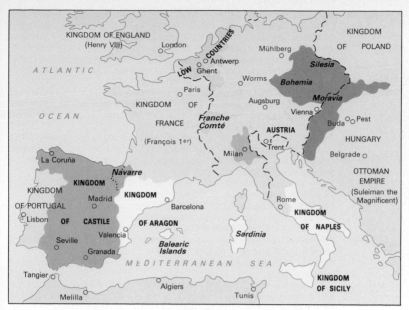

THE EMPIRE OF CHARLES V

▨ Burgundian inheritance	▨ Austrian inheritance	■ Other possessions
▨ Spanish inheritance	■ Charles V's conquests	– – – The Holy Roman Empire

1568-1570	Revolt of the *Moriscos* (Muslims who converted to Christianity) in Granada.
1571	The Turks are defeated in the **Battle of Lepanto** by a fleet of ships sent by the Pope, the Venetians and the Spanish, under the command of **Don Juan of Austria**, the king's natural brother. The victory seals Spain's mastery of the Mediterranean.
1580	The King of Portugal dies without an heir. Philip II asserts his rights, invades Portugal and is proclaimed king in 1581.
1588	Philip II sends the **Invincible Armada** against Protestant England, which supports the Low Countries. The destruction of the fleet marks the end of Spain as a sea power.
1598	Philip II dies, leaving an immense kingdom which, in spite of vast wealth from the Americas, is crippled by debt after 70 years of almost incessant war and the erection of monumental buildings like El Escorial.
1598-1621	**The decline** – The last of the Habsburgs, **Philip III** (1598-1621), **Philip IV** (1621-1665) and **Charles II** (1665-1700), lack the mettle of their forefathers. Paradoxically, Spain enjoys a **golden age** of art and culture. Philip III entrusts the affairs of state to the Duke of Lerma who advises him to expel the *Moriscos* in 1609. 275 000 Moors leave Spain with disastrous consequences for agriculture.
1640	Under Philip IV, the Count-Duke of Olivares adopts a policy of decentralisation which spurs Catalunya and Portugal to rebellion. The Portuguese proclaim the Duke of Braganza, King John IV, but their independence is not recognised until 1668.
1618-1648	Spain wastes her strength in the **Thirty Years War**. In spite of victories like that of Breda (1624), the defeat in the Netherlands at Rocroi (1643) signals the end of Spain as a European power. The **Treaty of Westphalia** gives the Netherlands independence.
1659	The **Treaty of the Pyrenees** ends war with France. Philip IV arranges the marriage of his daughter María Teresa to Louis XIV, King of France.
1667-1697	Spain loses strongholds in Flanders to France during the **War of Devolution** (1667-1668). The Dutch Wars (1672-1678) end with the **Treaty of Nijmegen**. The **Treaty of Ryswick** (1697) concludes the war waged by the Confederation of Augsburg (of which Spain is a member) against France.

The Bourbons; Napoleon and the War of Independence (1808-1814)

1700	Charles II dies without issue. He wills the crown to Philip, Duke of Anjou, grandson of his sister María Teresa and Louis XIV. Emperor Leopold, who had renounced his rights to the Spanish throne in favour of his son, the Archduke Charles, is displeased, but the appointment of the Bourbons to the Spanish throne stabilises the balance of power in Europe.

1702-1714	**War of the Spanish Succession** – England, the Netherlands, Denmark and Germany support the Archduke of Austria against France and Philip of Anjou. Catalunya, Valencia and Aragón also side with the Archduke and war spreads throughout Spain (1705). By the **Treaty of Utrecht**, Spain forfeits Gibraltar and Menorca (taken by the English) and many of her Italian possessions. **Philip V** is proclaimed King of Spain (1714-1745).
1759-1788	The reign of **Charles III**, an enlightened despot, is the most brilliant of those of the Bourbons. He is assisted by competent ministers (Floridablanca and Aranda) who draw up important economic reforms. Expulsion of the Jesuits in 1767.
1788	**Charles IV** succeeds to the throne. A weak-willed king, he allows the country to be governed by his wife María Luisa and her favourite, Godoy.
1793	On the death of Louis XVI, Spain declares war on France (then in the throes of the Revolution).
1796-1805	Spain signs an alliance with the French Directory against England (Treaty of San Ildefonso, 1796).
	Napoleon enters Spain with his troops on the pretext that he is going to attack Portugal. The renewed offensive against England in 1804 ends disastrously with the **Battle of Trafalgar** *(qv)*.
1805-1808	Napoleon takes advantage of the disagreement between Charles IV and his son Ferdinand to engineer Charles IV's abdication and appoint his own brother Joseph, King of Spain. The Aranjuez Revolt *(qv)* takes place in March 1808.
2 May 1808	The Madrid uprising against French troops marks the beginning of the **War of Independence** (The Peninsular War) which lasts until Napoleon is exiled by Wellington in 1814. During the war there are battles at Bailén (1808), Madrid, Zaragoza and Girona.
1812	The French are routed by Wellington in the Arapiles valley; King Joseph flees from Madrid. Valencia is taken by the French general, Suchet.
	Spanish patriots convene the Cortes (parliament) and draw up the liberal **Constitution of Cádiz** *(qv)*.
1813-1814	Anglo-Spanish forces expel Napoleon after successive victories.
	Ferdinand VII returns to Spain, repeals the Constitution of Cádiz and so reigns as an absolute monarch until 1820. Meanwhile, the South American colonies struggle for independence.

The 19C Disturbances

1820-1823	The liberals oppose the king's absolute rule but their uprisings are all severely quelled. The 1812 constitution is reinstated after a **liberal revolt** led by **Riego** in Cádiz in 1820, but only for three years.
	In 1823 Ferdinand VII appeals to Europe for assistance and a hundred thousand Frenchmen are sent in the name of St Louis to re-establish absolute rule (which lasts until 1833).
1833-1839	On the death of Ferdinand VII, his brother Don Carlos disputes the right to the throne of his niece Isabel II, daughter of the late king and Queen María Cristina. The traditionalist Carlists fight Isabel's liberal supporters who, after six years, win the **First Carlist War** (Convention of Vergara). In 1835, the minister **Mendizábal** has a series of decrees passed which do away with religious orders and confiscate their property **(desamortización)**.
1840	A revolutionary junta forces the regent María Cristina into exile. She is replaced by General Espartero.
1843-1868	Queen Isabel II comes of age. The **Narváez uprising** forces Espartero to flee. A new constitution is drawn up in 1845. The **Second Carlist War** (1847-49) ends in victory for Isabel II but her reign is troubled by a succession of uprisings on behalf of progressives and moderates.
	The **1868 revolt** led by General Prim puts an end to her reign. Isabel leaves for France and General Serrano is appointed leader of the provisional government.
1869	The Cortes passes a progressive constitution which however envisages the establishment of a monarchy. Amadeo of Savoy is elected king.
1873	The **Third Carlist War** (1872-1876). The king abdicates on finding himself unable to keep the peace. The National Assembly proclaims the **First Spanish Republic.**
1874	General Martínez Campos leads a revolt. The head of the government, Cánovas de Castillo, proclaims Isabel's son Alfonso XII, King of Spain. The Bourbon **Restoration** opens a long period of peace.
1885	Death of Alfonso XII (at 28). His widow María Cristina (who is expecting a baby) becomes regent.
1898	Cuba and the Philippines rise up with disastrous losses for Spain.
	The United States, which supports the rebel colonies, occupies Puerto Rico and the Philippines, marking the end of the Spanish empire.
1902	**Alfonso XIII** (born after the death of his father Alfonso XII) succeeds to the throne at 16.

Fall of the Monarchy; The Second Republic (1931-1936)

1914-1918 Spain remains neutral throughout the First World War. A general strike in 1917 is severely put down.

1921 Insurrection in Morocco. In 1927 General Sanjurjo occupies North Morocco.

1923 **General Miguel Primo de Rivera** establishes a **dictatorship** with the king's approval. Order is restored, the country grows wealthier but opposition increases among the working classes.

1930 In the face of hostility from the masses, Primo de Rivera is forced into exile and General Berenguer is appointed dictator.

1931 April elections bring victory to the Republicans in Catalunya, the País Vasco, La Rioja and the Aragonese province of Huesca. The king leaves Spain and the **Second Republic** is proclaimed.

June 1931 A constituent Cortes is elected with a socialist republican majority; a Constitution is promulgated in December. Don Niceto Alcalá Zamora is elected President of the Republic. Agrarian reforms, such as the forced purchase of large properties, meet strong opposition from the right.

1933 Founding of the **Falange Party**, against regional separation, by **José Antonio Primo de Rivera**, son of the dictator. The army plots against the régime.

Oct 1934 Catalunya proclaims its autonomy. Miners in Asturias spark off a revolt against the right-wing government and are brutally repressed.

Feb 1936 The Popular Front wins the elections and so precipitates a revolutionary situation. Anarchy invades the streets and the right promptly retaliates.

The Civil War (1936-1939)

17 July 1936 The Melilla uprising triggers off the Civil War. The army takes control and puts an end to the Second Republic.

Nationalist troops based in Morocco and led by **General Franco** cross the Straits of Gibraltar and make their way to Toledo which is taken at the end of September. Franco is proclaimed Generalísimo of the armed forces and Head of State in Burgos. Nationalists lead an unsuccessful attack against Madrid.

While Madrid, Catalunya and Valencia remain faithful to the Republicans, the conservative agricultural regions – Andalucía, Castilla and Galicia – are rapidly controlled by the Nationalists. These latter outnumber the Republicans tenfold and the Republicans themselves are torn by dissension between anarchists and communists within their own ranks. They do, however, receive assistance from International Brigades.

1937 Industrial towns in the north are taken by Nationalist supporters in the summer (Gernika is bombed by German planes). The Republican Government is moved to Barcelona in November. In the battle of **Teruel** in December the Republicans try to breach the Nationalist front in Aragón and thereby relieve surrounded Catalunya. Teruel is taken by the Republicans and recaptured by the Nationalists soon after.

1938 The Nationalist army reaches the Mediterranean, dividing Republican territory into two parts. The **Battle of the Ebro** lasts from July to November: the Republican army flees eastwards and Franco launches an offensive against Catalunya which is occupied by the Nationalists in February 1939.

1 April 1939 The war ends with the capture of Madrid.

The Franco Era

1939-1949 Spain becomes a monarchy with Franco as Head of State. Remains neutral in the Second World War. Period of diplomatic isolation.

1952 Spain joins UNESCO.

1955 Spain becomes a member of the United Nations.

1969 Prince Juan Carlos is appointed Franco's successor.

20 Dec 1973 Prime Minister Carrero Blanco is assassinated.

20 Nov 1975 **Death of Franco. Juan Carlos I** becomes **King of Spain.**

Democracy

15 June 1977 General elections – **Adolfo Suárez** is re-elected Prime Minister. A new constitution is passed by referendum in 1978. Statutes of autonomy are granted to Catalunya, the País Vasco (Euskadi) and Galicia.

1981-1982 Suárez resigns. There is an attempted military coup on 23 February 1981. The general elections on 28 October 1982 are won by the Socialist Party and **Felipe González** becomes Prime Minister.

1 Jan 1986 Spain joins the **European Economic Community.**

11 Mar 1986 Spain's continued membership of NATO is voted by referendum.

11 June 1986 General elections – Felipe González, leader of the Socialist Party (PSOE), is re-elected Prime Minister.

Oct 1989 General elections again won by the Socialists under Felipe González.

1992 Barcelona hosts the 1992 Summer Olympics, and Sevilla Expo 1992.

Art and architecture

FROM PREHISTORY TO THE MOORISH CONQUEST

Prehistoric art – Prehistoric inhabitants of the Iberian Peninsula have left some outstanding examples of their art. The oldest are the Upper Palaeolithic (40 000-10 000 BC) cave paintings in Cantabria (Altamira, Puente Viesgo) and the Levante (Cogull, Alpera). Megalithic monuments like the famous Antequera dolmens were erected during the Neolithic Era (7 500-2 500 BC) or Stone Age, while in the Balearic Islands strange stone monuments known as *talayots* and *navetas* were built by a Bronze Age people (2 500-1 000 BC).

The Dama de Elche
(in the Museo Arqueológico, Madrid)

First millennium BC – Iberian civilisations produced gold and silverware (treasure of Carambolo in the Museo Arqueológico in Sevilla – *qv*), and fine sculpture. Some of their work such as the Córdoba lions, the Guisando toros and, in the Museo Arqueológico in Madrid, the *Dama de Baza* and the *Dama de Elche* (*qv*), is of a remarkably high standard. Meanwhile, Phoenician and in turn Greek colonisers introduced their native art: Phoenician sarcophagi in Cádiz, Punic art in Ibiza and Greek art in Empuries.

Roman Spain (1C BC-5C AD) – Besides roads, bridges, aqueducts, towns and monuments, Roman legacies include the Mérida theatre, the ancient towns of Italica and Empuries, and the Segovia aqueduct and Tarragona triumphal arch.

The Visigoths (6-8C) – Christian Visigoths built small stone churches (Quintanilla de las Viñas, San Pedro de la Nave) adorned with friezes carved in geometric patterns with plant motifs. The apsidal plan was square and the arches were often horseshoe shaped. The Visigoths were outstanding gold and silversmiths who made sumptuous jewellery in the Byzantine and Germanic traditions. Gold votive crowns (Guarrazar treasure in Toledo), fibulae and belt buckles adorned with precious stones or *cloisonné* enamel were presented to churches or placed in the tombs of the great.

HISPANO-MOORISH ARCHITECTURE (8-15C)

The three major periods of Hispano-Moorish architecture correspond to the reigns of successive Arab dynasties over the Muslim-held territories in the peninsula.

Caliphate or Córdoba architecture (8-11C) – This period is characterised by three types of building: **mosques**, built to a simple plan consisting of a minaret, a courtyard with a pool for ritual ablutions and finally a square prayer room with a *mihrab* (prayer-niche marking the direction of Mecca); **alcazares** (palaces), built around attractive patios and surrounded by gardens and fountains; and **alcazabas** (castle fortresses), built on high ground and surrounded by several walls crowned with pointed merlons and dominated by a watch-tower or *Torre de la Vela* as in Málaga. The most famous monuments from this period are in Córdoba (the Mezquita and the Medina Azahara palace) and in Toledo (Cristo de la Luz) where, besides the ubiquitous horseshoe arch which virtually became the hallmark of Moorish architecture, other characteristics developed

A Visigothic column
(detail)

including ornamental brickwork in relief, cupolas supported on ribs, turned modillions, arches with alternating white stone and red brick voussoirs, multifoil arches and doors surmounted with blind arcades. These features subsequently became popular in Mudéjar and Romanesque churches.

The Umayyads brought a taste for profuse decoration from Syria. As the Koran forbids the representation of human or animal forms, Muslim decoration is based on calligraphy (Cufi inscriptions running along walls), geometric patterns (polygons and stars made of ornamental brickwork and marble) and lastly plant motifs (flowerets and interlacing palm leaves).

MICHELIN

Caliphate architecture
(The Mezquita In Córdoba)

Almohad architecture
(The Giralda in Sevilla)

Nasrid architecture
(The Alhambra in Granada)

Almohad or Sevilla architecture (12-13C) – The religious puritanism of the Almohad dynasty, of which Sevilla was the capital, was expressed in architecture by a refined, though sometimes rather austere, simplicity. One of the characteristics of the style consisted of brickwork highlighted by wide bands of decoration in relief, without excessive ornamentation (the Giralda tower in Sevilla is a good example.) The style was later used in the Mudéjar architecture of Aragón. Other features that emerged at this time include *artesonado* ceilings and *azulejos (qv)*. Arches of alternate brick and stonework disappeared, the horseshoe arch became pointed and the multifoil arch was bordered by a curvilinear festoon (ornament like a garland) as in the Aljafería in Zaragoza. Calligraphic decoration included cursive (flowing) as well as Cufic script to which floral motifs were added to fill the spaces between vertical lines.

Nasrid or Granada architecture (14-15C) – This period of high sophistication, of which the **Alhambra** in Granada is the masterpiece, produced less innovation in actual architectural design than in the decoration, whether stucco or ceramic, that covered the walls. Surrounds to doors and windows became focal points for every room's design and the spaces between them were filled by perfectly proportioned panels. Arch outlines were simplified – the stilted round arch became widespread – while detailed lace-work ornamentation was used as a border.

Mudéjar architecture – This is the name given to work carried out by Muslims while under the Christian yoke, yet executed in the Arab tradition. It was fashionable from the 11C to the 15C in different regions depending on the area recovered by the Reconquest, although some features, like *artesonado* ceilings, continued as decorative themes for centuries.

Court Mudéjar, developed by Muslim artists (in buildings ordered by Peter the Cruel in Tordesillas and Sevilla, and in synagogues in Toledo), was an extension of the Almohad or contemporary Nasrid style. Popular Mudéjar, on the other hand, was produced by local Muslim workshops and reflects marked regional taste: walls were decorated with blind arcades in Castilla (Arévalo, Sahagún, Toledo) and belfries were faced with *azulejos* and geometric strapwork in Aragón.

The decorative arts – Extremely rich and varied decorative artefacts from this period include geometric wood strapwork, brocades, weapons, ceramics with metal lustre decoration and small ivory chests.

PRE-ROMANESQUE AND ROMANESQUE ARCHITECTURE (8-13C)

Asturian architecture – A highly sophisticated style of court architecture, characterised by sweeps of ascending lines, developed in the small Kingdom of Asturias between the 8 and the 10C. Asturian churches (Naranco, Santa Cristina de Lena) followed the precepts of the Latin basilica in their rectangular plan with a narthex, a nave and two aisles separated by semicircular arches, a vast transept and an east end divided into three. Decoration inside consisted of frescoes, and borrowings from the east including motifs carved on capitals (strapwork, rosettes and monsters) and ornamental openwork around windows. Gold and silversmiths in the 9-10C produced rich treasures, many of which may be seen in the Cámara Santa in Oviedo cathedral.

Mozarabic architecture – This term is given to work carried out by Christians living under Arab rule after the Moorish invasion of 711. Churches built in this style, especially in Castilla (San Miguel de Escalada, San Millán de la Cogolla), brought back Visigothic traditions (horeshoe arches) enriched by Moorish features such as ribbed cupolas and turned modillions.

Illuminated manuscripts provide the earliest known examples of Spanish medieval painting (10C). They were executed in the 10 and 11C by Mozarabic monks and have Moorish features such as horseshoe arches and Arab costumes *(illustration, p 33)*. They portray St John's Commentary on the Apocalypse written in the 8C by the monk **Beatus de Liébana** *(qv)*, after whom the manuscripts were named.

Catalunya, home of the earliest Romanesque style in Spain – Catalunya was largely closed to Mozarabic influences but had intimate links with Italy and France and consequently developed an architectural style strongly influenced by Lombardy from the 11 to 13C. This evolved in the Pyrenean valleys, isolated from the more travelled pilgrim and trade routes. Sober little churches often accompanied by a separate bell-tower decorated with Lombard bands. Interior walls in the 11 and 12C were only embellished with frescoes which, in spite of their borrowings from Byzantine mosaics (heavy black outlines, rigid postures, and themes like Christ in Glory portrayed within a mandorla), proved by their realistic and expressive details to be typically Spanish. Altarfronts of painted wood, executed in bright colours, followed the same themes and layout.

European Romanesque art along the pilgrim routes to Compostela – Northwest Spain opened its gates to foreign influence during the reign of Sancho the Great of Navarra early in the 11C. Cistercian abbeys were founded and French merchants allowed to settle rate-free in towns (Estella, Sangüesa, Pamplona). Meanwhile, the surge of pilgrims to Compostela and the fever to build along the routes, brought about the construction of a great many religious buildings in which French influence was clearly marked (characteristics from Poitou in Soria and Sangüesa, and from Toulouse in Aragón and Santiago de Compostela). The acknowledged masterpiece of this style is the cathedral of Santiago de Compostela.

In Aragón, Romanesque art was particularly evident in sculpture. The artists who carved capitals in the manner of their leader, the Maestro de San Juan de la Peña, had a seemingly clumsy style because their emphasis was more on symbolism than realistic portrayal. Disproportionate faces with bulging eyes were the means by which the sculptor illustrated the soul, while gestures such as outstretched hands conveyed religious meaning.

In the early 12C, reform of the Cistercian order with emphasis on austerity brought an important change to architecture. The Transitional style which heralded the Gothic (intersecting ribbed vaulting, squared apses) was introduced and the profusion of Romanesque decoration disappeared. Examples of this style may be seen in the monasteries of Poblet, Santes Creus, La Oliva and Santa María de Huerta.

THE GOTHIC PERIOD (from the 13C onwards)

Architecture, the early stages – French Gothic architecture made little headway into Spain except in Navarra where a French royal house had been in power since 1234. The first truly Gothic buildings (Roncesvalles church, Cuenca and Sigüenza cathedrals) appeared in the 13C. Bishops in some of the main towns in Castilla (León, Burgos, Toledo) sent abroad for cathedral plans, artists and masons. An original style of church, with no transept, a single nave (aisles, if there were any, would be as high as the nave), and pointed stone arches or a wooden roof resting on diaphragm arches, developed in Valencia, Catalunya and the Islas Baleares (Balearic Islands). The unadorned walls enclosed a large, homogeneous space in which there was little carved decoration, and purity of line supplied a dignified elegance.

Civil architecture followed the same pattern and had the same geometrical sense of space, used with rare skill particularly in the *lonjas* or commodity exchanges of Barcelona, Palma, Valencia and Zaragoza.

Development of the Gothic style – During the 14 and 15C in Castilla, the influence of artists from the north such as **Johan of Cologne** and **Hanequin of Brussels**, brought about the flowering of a style approaching Flamboyant Gothic. As it adapted to Spain, the style developed simultaneously in two different ways: in one, decoration proliferated to produce the Isabelline style; in the other, structures were simplified into a national church and cathedral style which remained in favour until the mid 16C (Segovia and Salamanca).

The last of the Gothic cathedrals – Following the example of Sevilla, Gothic cathedrals became vast. Aisles almost as large as the nave increased the volume of the building, while pillars, though massive, retained the impression of thrusting upward lines. A new plan emerged in which the old crescendo of radiating chapels, ambulatory, chancel and transept was superseded by a plain rectangle, a vast space in which the only part that remained of the original cruciform plan was the transept crossing – set off by a lantern – between the *capilla mayor* and the *coro*. In contrast to this severity, specifically Gothic decoration accumulated around doors, on pinnacles and in elaborate star vaulting: a style echoed in some Andalusian cathedrals.

Painting – Artists in the Gothic era worked on polyptyches and altarpieces which sometimes reached a height of more than 15m - 50ft. The Primitives, who customarily painted on gold backgrounds, were influenced by the Italians (soft contours), the French and the Flemish (rich fabrics with broken folds and painstaking detail). Nonetheless, as they strove for expressive naturalism and lively anecdotal detail, their work came across as distinctively Spanish.

Gothic painting. Altarpiece by Pedro Serra

There was intense artistic activity in the states attached to the Crown of Aragón, especially in Catalunya. The Vic, Barcelona and Valencia museums contain works by **Ferrer Bassá** (1285-1348) who was influenced by the Sienese **Duccio**, paintings by his successor **Ramón Destorrents** (1346-1391), and by the **Serra** brothers, Destorrents's pupils. Among other artists were **Luis Borrassá** (*c*1360-1425) who had a very Spanish sense of the picturesque, **Bernat Martorell** (d 1452) who gave special importance to landscape, **Jaime Huguet** (1415-1492) who stands out for his extreme sensitivity and is considered to be the undisputed leader of the Catalan school, and finally **Luis Dalmau** and **Bartolomé Bermejo**, both influenced by Van Eyck (who accompanied a mission sent to Spain by the Duke of Burgundy).

In Castilla, French influence predominated in the 14C and Italian in the 15C until about 1450 when Flemish artists like **Roger Van der Weyden** arrived. By the end of the 15C, **Fernando Gallego** had become the main figure in the Hispano-Flemish movement in which **Juan of Flanders** was noted for his appealingly delicate touch.

Sculpture – Gothic sculpture, like architecture, became more refined. Relief was more accentuated than in Romanesque carving, postures more natural and details more meticulous. Decoration grew increasingly abundant as the 15C progressed and faces became individualised to the point where recumbent funerary statues clearly resembled the deceased. Statues were surmounted by an openwork canopy, while door surrounds, cornices and capitals were decorated with friezes of intricate plant motifs. After being enriched by French influence in the 13 and 14C and Flemish in the 15C, sculpture ultimately developed a purely Spanish style, the Isabelline.

Portals showed a French influence. Tombs were at first sarcophagi decorated with coats of arms, sometimes surmounted by a recumbent statue in a conventional posture with a peaceful expression and hands joined. Later, more attention was paid to the costume of the deceased; with an increasingly sure technique marble craftsmen were able to render the richness of brocades and the supple quality of leather. In the 15C, sculptors produced lifelike figures in natural positions, kneeling for instance, or even in nonchalant attitudes like that of the remarkable Doncel in Sigüenza cathedral. Altarpieces comprised a predella or plinth, surmounted by several levels of panels and finally by a carved openwork canopy. Choir-stalls were adorned with Biblical and historical scenes or carved to resemble delicate stone tracery.

The Isabelline style – At the end of the 15C, the prestige surrounding the royal couple and the grandees in the reign of Isabel the Catholic (1474-1504) provided a favourable context for the emergence of a new style in which exuberant decoration covered entire façades of civil and religious buildings. Ornamentation took the form of supple free arcs, lace-like carving, heraldic motifs and every fantasy that imagination could devise *(see Valladolid)*.

The diversity of inspiration was largely due to foreign artists: **Simon of Cologne** (son of Johan) – San Pablo in Valladolid, Capilla del Condestable in Burgos; **Juan Guas** (son of the Frenchman, Pierre) – San Juan de los Reyes in Toledo; and **Enrique Egas** (nephew of Hanequin of Brussels) – Capilla Real in Granada.

If you intend combining a tour of Spain
with a visit to one of the neighbouring countries,
remember to take the appropriate
Michelin Green Guide France or Portugal.

THE RENAISSANCE (16C)

In the 16C, at the dawn of its golden age, Spain was swept by a deep sense of its own national character and so created a style in which Italian influence became acceptable only when hispanicised.

Architecture – **Plateresque** was the name given to the early Renaissance style because of its finely chiselled, lavish decoration reminiscent of silverwork (platero: silversmith). Although close to the Isabelline style in its profusion of carved forms extending over entire façades, the rounded arches and ornamental themes (grotesques, foliage, pilasters, medallions and cornices) were Italian. The Plateresque style predominated during the reign of Charles V and was brought to a climax in the façade of the Universidad de Salamanca and that of the Convento de San Esteban (St Stephen's Monastery). Among architects of the time were **Rodrigo Gil de Hontañón** who worked at Salamanca (Palacios de Monterrey and Fonseca) and at Alcalá de Henares (university façade), and **Diego de Siloé**, the main

The Plateresque Style. Universidad de Salamanca

architect in Burgos (Escalera de la Coronería). Together with **Alonso de Covarrubias** (d 1570) who worked mainly in Toledo (Alcázar and Capilla de los Reyes Nuevos in the cathedral), Diego de Siloé marked the transition from the Plateresque style to the classical Renaissance. **Andrés de Vandelvira** (1509-1576) was the leading architect of the Andalusian Renaissance (Jaén cathedral). His work introduces the austerity which was to characterise the last quarter of the century.

The Renaissance style drew upon Italian models and adopted features from Antiquity such as rounded arches, columns, entablatures and pediments. Decoration became of secondary importance after architectonic perfection. **Pedro Machuca** (d 1550) who studied under Michelangelo, designed the palace of Charles V in Granada, the most classical example of the Italian tradition. Another important figure, **Bartolomé Bustamante** (1500-1570), built the Hospital de Tavera in Toledo.

The greatest figure of Spanish classicism was **Juan de Herrera** (1530-1597) who gave his name to an architectural style characterised by grandeur, austerity and geometric effect. He was the favourite architect of Philip II. The king saw in him the sobriety that suited the Counter-Reformation and in 1567 entrusted him with the task of continuing work on El Escorial *(qv)*, his greatest achievement.

Sculpture – Sculpture in Spain reached its climax during the Renaissance. In the 16C, a great many choir-stalls, mausoleums and altarpieces (also known as retables or reredos) were still being made of alabaster and wood. These latter were then painted by the **estofado** technique in which gold leaf is first applied, then the object is coloured and finally delicately scored to produce gold highlights. Carved altarpiece panels were framed by Corinthian architraves and pilasters.

The sculptures of **Damián Forment** (c1480-1540), who worked mainly in Aragón, belong to the transition period between Gothic and Renaissance styles. The Burgundian **Felipe Vigarny** (d 1543) and the architect **Diego de Siloé**, who was apprenticed in Naples, both worked on Burgos cathedral. **Bartolomé Ordóñez** (d 1520) studied in Naples and carved the *trascoro* (choirscreen) in Barcelona cathedral, the mausoleums of Juana the Mad, Philip the Fair (Capilla Real in Granada) and Cardinal Cisneros (Alcalá de Henares).

The home of the Renaissance School moved from Burgos to Valladolid in the mid 16C by which time the Spanish style had absorbed foreign influences and Spain's two great Renaissance sculptors had emerged. The first, **Alonso Berruguete** (1488-1561), who studied in Italy under Michelangelo, had a style which drew closely on the Florentine Renaissance and reflected a strong personality. He sought strength of expression rather than formal beauty and his tormented fiery human forms are as powerful as those of his master (statue of San Sebastián in the Museo de Valladolid). The second, **Juan de Juni** (d 1577), a Frenchman who settled in Valladolid, was also influenced by Michelangelo and founded the Catalan school of sculpture. His statues, recognisable by their beauty and the fullness of their forms, anticipated the baroque style through the dramatic postures they adopted to express sorrow. Many of his works, such as the famous Virgen de los Siete Cuchillos (Virgin of the Seven Knives) in the Iglesia de las Angustias in Valladolid and the Entombments in the Museo de Valladolid and Segovia cathedral, were subsequently copied.

Most of the finely worked wrought-iron grilles closing off chapels and *coros* (chancels) were carved in the 15 and 16C. Members of the **Arfe** family, Enrique, Antonio and Juan, stand out in the field of gold and silversmithing. They made the monstrances of Toledo, Santiago de Compostela and Sevilla cathedrals respectively.

Painting – Under Italian Renaissance influence, Spanish painting in the 16C showed a mastery of perspective, a taste for clarity of composition and glorification of the human body. These features found their way into Spanish painting mainly through the Valencian School where **Fernando Yáñez de la Almedina** and **Fernando de Llanos** introduced the style of Leonardo da Vinci, while **Vicente Macip** added that of Raphael and his son **Juan de Juanes** *(qv)* produced Mannerist works. In Sevilla, **Alejo Fernández** painted the famous *Virgin of the Navigators* in the Alcázar. In Castilla, the great master of the late 15C was **Pedro Berruguete** (*c*1450-1504) whose markedly personal style drew upon all the artistic influences in the country. His successor, **Juan de Borgoña**, specialised particularly in landscape, architecture and decorative motifs. Another artist, **Pedro de Campaña** from Brussels, used chiaroscuro to dramatic effect while **Luis de Morales** (*c*1520-1586), a Mannerist, gave his work a human dimension through the portrayal of feelings. Ordinary people with religious sentiments responded favourably to the spiritual emotion expressed in his paintings. At the end of the 16C, Philip II sent for a great many Italian or Italian-trained artists to paint pictures for El Escorial. During his reign he introduced portrait painting under the Dutchman **Antonio Moro** (1519-1576), his disciple **Alonso Sánchez Coello** (1531-1588) and **Pantoja de la Cruz** (1553-1608). **El Greco**, on the other hand, was scorned by the court and settled in Toledo *(qv)*.

BAROQUE (17-18C)

Spanish art reached its apogee in the mid 17C. Baroque met with oustanding success in its role as an essentially religious art in the service of the Counter-Reformation and was particularly evident in Andalucía, then enriched by trade with America.

Architecture – Architects in the early 17C were still under the influence of 16C classicism and the Herreran style to which they added decorative details. Public buildings proliferated and many continued to be built throughout the baroque period.

Public buildings of the time in Madrid include the Plaza Mayor *(qv)* by **Juan Gómez de Mora**, built shortly before the Ayuntamiento (Town Hall), and the most significant building of all, the present Ministerio de Asuntos Exteriores (Ministry for Foreign Affairs) by **Juan Bautista Crescenzi**, the architect of the Panteón de los Reyes at El Escorial.

Church architecture of the period showed greater freedom from Classicism. A style of Jesuit church, with a cruciform plan and a large transept that served to light up altarpieces, began to emerge. Madrid has several examples including the Iglesia de San Isidro by the Jesuits Pedro Sánchez and **Francisco Bautista**, and the Real Convento de la Encarnación by Juan Gómez de Mora. In the middle of the century, architects began to look for alternatives to the austerity of El Escorial and so changed plans and façades, broke up entablatures and made pediments more elaborate. A good example of this Italian baroque style is the Iglesia Pontifica de San Miguel (18C) in Madrid. A new feature, the **camarín**, was introduced: at first simply a passage behind the high altar leading to the retable niche containing a statue venerated by the faithful, it developed into a highly ornate chapel. Decoration of this kind may be seen in Zaragoza's Basílica de Nuestra Señora del Pilar designed by **Francisco Herrera the Younger** (1622-1685). The Clerecía in Salamanca is a magnificent baroque creation with a patio that anticipates the audacity and super-abundant decoration characteristic of the Churrigueresque style.

The Churrigueresque style – In this style, named after the Churriguera family of architects (late 17C), architecture became no more than a support for dense concentrations of ornament covering entire façades. The style is typified by the use of *salomonicas* or barley sugar columns entwined with vines, and *estípites*, or pilasters arranged in an inverse pyramid. Early examples of this extravagance, the altarpiece of the Convento de San Esteban in Salamanca and the palace in Nuevo Batzán near Madrid, were by **José de Churriguera** (1665-1725) who was the instigator of the style but did not make any architectural changes. His brothers **Joaquín** (1674-1724) and especially **Alberto** (1676-1750) who designed the Plaza Mayor in Salamanca, took greater liberties in their work. **Pedro de Ribera** (1683-1742), a Castilian architect who worked mainly in Madrid, surpassed the Churriguera brothers in decorative delirium. The other great Castilian, **Narciso Tomé**, is remembered for the façade of the Universidad de Valladolid (1715) and particularly for the *Transparente* in Toledo cathedral (1720 to 1732).

Regional variations – The popularity of the baroque spread countrywide, differing from province to province. In **Galicia**, where the hardness of the granite precluded delicate carving, baroque took the form of bold lines and decorative mouldings. The best example of the style and the masterpiece of its designer, **Fernando de Casas y Novoa**, is the Obradoiro façade of Santiago de Compostela cathedral (1750).

In **Andalucía**, baroque attained its utmost splendour, especially in decoration. Undulating surfaces characterised the façades of palaces (Écija), cathedrals (Guadix) and the doorways of countless churches and mansions (Jerez) in the 18C. As well as sculptor and painter, **Alonso Cano** was the instigator of Andalusian baroque and designed the façade of Granada cathedral. The major exponent of the style was, however, **Vicente Acero**, who worked on the façade of Guadix cathedral (1714 to 1720), designed Cádiz cathedral and built the tobacco factory in Sevilla. Mention should also be made of **Leonardo de Figueroa** (1650-1730) for the Palacio de San Telmo in Sevilla and **Francisco Hurtado** (1669-1725) and **Luis de Arévalo** for La Cartuja in Granada; Hurtado worked on the monastery's Sagrario and Arévalo on the sacristy, the most exuberant baroque works in Andalucía.

In the **Levante**, baroque artists used polychrome tiles to decorate church cupolas and spires like that of Santa Catalina in Valencia. In the same town, the Palacio del Marqués de Dos Aguas by **Luis Domingo** and **Ignacio Vergara** is reminiscent of façades by Ribera, although its design is more like French rococo. The cathedral in Murcia has an impressive façade by **Jaime Bort**.

The Golden Age of Spanish painting – This was characterised by the rejection of the previous century's Mannerism and the adoption of naturalism. The starting point was Caravaggio's tenebrism, powerful contrasts of light and shade, and his stern realism. Painters took up portraiture and still life *(bodegón)*, while vanities (paintings showing the triviality of life) acquired a philosophical purpose by illustrating a symbolic link between wealth and death. Among 17C artists were two from the Valencian School – **Francisco Ribalta** (1565-1628), who introduced tenebrism into Spain, and **José de Ribera** *(qv)* (1591-1652), known for his forceful realism. Some of the greatest baroque artists worked in Andalucía. One was **Francisco Zurbarán** *(qv)* (1598-1664), master of the Sevilla School; light in his paintings springs from within

Detail from The Surrender of Breda by Velázquez
(in the Museo del Prado, Madrid)

Museo del Prado, Madrid / LAUROS-GIRAUDON

the subjects themselves. Other artists included **Murillo** *(qv)* (1618-1682), who painted intimate, mystical scenes, and **Valdés Leal** *(qv)* whose powerful realism clearly challenged earthly vanities. **Alonso Cano** (1601-1667), architect, painter and sculptor, settled in Granada and painted delicate, reserved figures of the Virgin.

The Castilian painters of the century, **Vicente Carducho** (1575-1638) and the portraitists **Carreño de Miranda** (1614-1685) and **Claudio Coello** (1642-1693), all excellent, pale beside **Velázquez** *(qv)*. His aerial perspective and outstanding sense of depth are beyond compare.

Sculpture – Spanish baroque sculpture was naturalistic and intensely emotive. The most commonly used medium was wood, softer than marble. To enhance their realism, sculptures were painted in oils, rather than *estofado*, and given crystal eyes and tears. While altarpieces continued to be carved with simpler designs, **pasos** or statues specially made for Semana Santa processions proved a great novelty.

The two major schools of baroque sculpture were in Castilla and Andalucía. **Gregorio Hernández**, Juni's successor, worked in Vallodolid, the Castilian centre. His style was a lot more natural than that of his master, and his Christ Recumbent for the Convento de Capuchinos in El Pardo was widely copied. Sevilla and Granada were the main centres for the Andalusian School. **Juan Martínez Montañés** (1568-1649) settled in Sevilla and worked exclusively in wood, carving a great many pasos and various altarpieces. Alonso Cano *(qv)*, Granada's illustrious artist, became famous for the grace and femininity of his Immaculate Conceptions while his best-known disciple, **Pedro de Mena** *(qv)*, produced sculptures of great dramatic tension which contrasted with his master's understated style. The statue of Mary Magdalene (Museo Nacional de Escultura Policromada, Valladolid), St Francis (Toledo cathedral) and the Dolorosa (Monasterio de las Descalzas Reales, Madrid) are telling examples of his work.

In the 18C, the great Murcian, **Francisco Salzillo** *(qv)* emerged as an imaginative sculptor, developing a spectacular, dramatic style inspired by Italian baroque.

Churrigueresque excess in sculpture took the form of immense altarpieces which reached the roof. These huge constructions surrounding a central tabernacle took on such grand proportions that they began to be designed by architects. Their statues seemed smothered by decoration, lost in an overabundance of gilding and stucco.

BOURBON ART

Austrian imperialism was succeeded by enlightened Bourbon despotism which resulted in artistic as well as political change in the 18C. Henceforth the rules of art were to be governed by official bodies like the Academia de Bellas Artes de San Fernando.

Architecture – During the first half of the century architecture still bore the stamp of Spanish baroque, itself influenced at the time by French rococo. The king and queen had palaces built in a moderate baroque style (El Pardo, Riofrío, La Granja and Aranjuez) and began work on Madrid's Palacio Real modelled on Versailles. These buildings sought to ally French classical harmony with Italian grace and to this end most of the work was entrusted to Italian architects who generally respected the traditional quadrangular plan of *alcázars*, so typically Spanish. The vast gardens were given a French design.

Excavations of Pompeii and Herculaneum contributed to the emergence of a new, neo-classical style which flourished between the second half of the 18C and 19C. It repudiated baroque excess and aspired to Hellenistic beauty through the use of Classical orders, pediments, porticoes and cupolas. The kings of Spain, Charles III in particular, set about embellishing the capital by building fountains (Cibeles, Neptune), gates (Alcalá and Toledo), and planting botanic gardens.

The first Spanish neo-classical architect, **Ventura Rodríguez** (1717-1785), who was actually apprenticed in Italian baroque, quickly developed an academic neo-classical style. His works include the façade of Pamplona cathedral, Paseo del Prado boulevard in Madrid and the Basílica de Nuestra Señora del Pilar in Zaragoza. **Sabatini** (1722-1797), whose style developed along similar lines, designed the Puerta de Alcalá and the building that now houses the Ministerio de Hacienda (Ministry of Finance) in Madrid. The leading architect was without doubt **Juan de Villanueva** (1739-1811), schooled in Classical principles during a stay in Rome. He designed the façade of the Ayuntamiento in Madrid, the Casita del Príncipe at El Escorial and most importantly, the Museo del Prado. Two notable town planners emerged during the 19C: **Ildefonso Cerdá** in Barcelona *(qv)* and **Arturo Soria** (1844-1920) in Madrid *(qv)*.

Painting – Bourbon monarchs took pains to attract the greatest painters to court and grant them official positions. In 1752 Ferdinand VI founded the Academia de Bellas Artes de San Fernando where it was intended that students would learn official painting techniques and study the Italian masters. Leading artists of the time were **Anton Raffael Mengs** (1728-1779) from Bohemia and the Italian **Gian Battista Tiepolo** (1696-1770), both of whom decorated the Palacio Real. There was also **Francisco Bayeu** (1734-1795) from Aragón, who painted a great many tapestry cartoons, as did his brother-in-law **Francisco Goya** (1746-1828) *(qv)*. Goya's work, much of which may be seen in the Prado, Madrid, was to dominate the entire century.

Painters working in the post-Goya period did not follow in the master's footsteps as academic neo-classical influences and romanticism took over; Goya's legacy was not taken up until the end of the 19C. The following stand out among artists of the academic romantic trend: **Federico de Madrazo**, representative of official taste in royal portraits and historical scenes, **Vicente Esquivel**, portrait-painter, and lastly **Leonardo Alenza**, and **Eugenio Lucas**, the spokesmen for **Costumbrismo** which had attained full status as a genre. (This was a style of painting illustrating scenes of everyday life which gradually developed from the simply anecdotal to a higher calling, the evocation of the Spanish soul.) Historical themes became very popular in the 19C with works by José Casado de Alisal, Eduardo Rosales and Mariano Fortuny.

Impressionist features began to appear in naturalist paintings by **Martí Alsina** and in post-romantic landscapes by **Carlos de Haes**. The style secured a definitive hold in the works of **Narciso Oller, Ignacio Pinazo**, the best Valencian Impressionist, **Darío Regoyos** and lastly, **Joaquín Sorolla**, who specialised in light-filled folk scenes and regional subjects. The Basque artist **Ignacio Zuloago** (1870-1945) expressed his love for Spain in brightly-coloured scenes of everyday life at a time when Impressionism was conquering Europe.

The decorative arts – Factories were built under Bourbon rule to produce decorative material for royal palaces. Philip V founded the Alcora tile factory in 1727, but this was soon superseded by the Buen Retiro works founded in 1760 by Charles III where ceramics for the famous Salón de Porcelana in the royal palaces of Aranjuez and Madrid were made. The factory was destroyed during the Napoleonic invasion. In 1720, Philip V opened the Real Fábrica de Tapices de Santa Bárbara (in Madrid), the equivalent of the French Gobelins factory in Paris. Some of the tapestries were of Don Quixote while others depicted scenes of everyday life based on preparatory cartoons by Bayeu and Goya.

20C ART

From Modernism to Surrealism – The barren period that Spanish art in general experienced at the end of the 19C was interrupted in Catalunya by a vast cultural movement known as **Modernism**. This was particularly strong in architecture, with outstanding work by **Antoni Gaudí** *(qv)*, **Lluís Domènech i Montaner** *(qv)* and **Josep María Jujol**. In the field of sculpture, **Pau Gargallo** broke new ground through the simplicity of his shapes, the attention he gave to volume and the use of new materials like iron.

Painting was varied and prolific. The following stand out among the many artists of the time: **Ramón Casas**, the best Spanish Impressionist, whose works are suffused with an atmosphere of grey melancholy, **Santiago Rusiñol, Isidro Nonell**, instigator of Spanish expressionism, and **Pablo Ruiz Picasso** (1881-1973), the dominant figure whose innovations were to mark the entire history of 20C painting.

Picasso's attention was first devoted to academic naturalism *(Science and Charity)*. He subsequently became a Modernist and social expressionist. Later, once he had moved to Paris (1904), his style developed through the successive 'blue' and 'rose' periods to Cubism *(Les Demoiselles d'Avignon)*, Surrealism and Expressionism *(Guernica)*, which in turn led to a totally personal and subjective lyrical style *(La Joie de Vivre)*.

In the 1920s a movement began to emerge that was influenced by Cubism and more particularly, by Surrealism. Its sculptors were **Angel Ferrant, Victorio Macho, Alberto Sánchez** and lastly **Julio González**, who strove towards abstract expressionism through the use of iron and simple shapes. Painters of the movement included **Daniel Vásquez Díaz**, Juan Gris, Joan Miró and Salvador Dalí. **Juan Gris** (1887-1927), the most faithful analytical Cubist, worked in Paris. The works of **Joan Miró** (1893-1983), champion of Surrealism, are characterised by childlike spontaneity and an original attitude to everyday objects. Miró used very bright colours and magic symbols in all his paintings. **Salvador Dalí** *(qv)* (1904-1989), a quasi-Surrealist, dreamed up his own creative method which he called the paranoic critical. Some of his best paintings were a result of his interest in the subconscious and his vision of a dream world. All his works attest to an excellent drawing technique and many show an attention to detail worthy of the best miniaturists.

Post-war art – Spanish art was crucially affected by the Civil War in two ways: firstly, the fact that several artists went into exile meant that the country suffered cultural loss, and secondly, official taste in architecture developed a penchant for the monumental. This is clearly apparent in a number of colossal edifices. Many government buildings, all in Madrid, were designed in the manner of El Escorial, including the Ministerio del Aire, the Museo de América, the Arco del Triunfo and the Consejo de Investigaciones Científicas. The most striking example is the monument of the Valle de los Caídos (Valley of the Fallen) *(qv)* outside Madrid. However, among exponents of the nationalist style, there were several innovative architects like **Miguel Fisac.**

In 1950 the first signs of a new style, based on rational and functional criteria, began to emerge. Examples abound in Barcelona – the Vanguardia building by **Oriol Bohigas** and **José María Martorell**, the residential block by **Ricardo Bofill** in Carrer de Nicaragua – and in Madrid – the Colegio Monfort by **A. Fernandez Alba** and the Maravillas secondary school *(gimnasio)* by **Alejandro de la Sota** and the Torres Blancas (White Towers) by **F. Javier Sáenz de Oíza.**

Post-war sculpture and painting are basically academic but there are some notable artists such as **José Gutiérrez Solana**, whose paintings are full of anguish, and the landscape painters **Benjamín Palencia**, who glorifies the country and light of Castilla, and **Rafael Zabaleta**, who is more interested in painting the region's country-folk.

Avant-garde painters also began to emerge after the war. The first post-war Surrealists are members of a group called **Dau al Set** including **Modest Cuixart, Antoni Tàpies** and **Juan José Tharrats**. Tàpies is a veritable pioneer, one of the major abstract artists. In the 1950s two abstract groups, with different qualities but with the common aim of artistic innovation, were formed. They are the **El Paso** group in Madrid with **Antonio Saura, Manuel Millares, Rafael Canogar, Luis Feito, Manuel Viola** and **Martín Chirino**, all representatives of what is known as action painting, and the **El Equipo 57** group in Cuenca with **Duart, Ibarrola, Serrano** and **Duarte**, who are more interested in drawing. Among the movement's sculptors are **Jorge Oteiza, Andréu Alfaro** and lastly **Eduardo Chillida**, who works in iron and wood and strips his sculptures of any figurative suggestion.

Guernica by Picasso (in the Museo Nacional Centro de Arte Reina Sofia, Madrid)

ARCHITECTURAL TERMS
(words printed in blue are Spanish)

Ajimez: paired window or opening separated by a central column.

Alfarje: wooden ceiling, usually decorated, consisting of a board resting on cross beams (a feature of the Mudéjar style).

Alfiz: rectangular surround to a horseshoe-shaped arch in Muslim architecture.

Alicatado: section of wall or other surface covered with sheets of ceramic tiles *(azulejos)* cut in such a way as to form geometric patterns. Frequently used to decorate dados (a Mudéjar feature).

Aljibe: Arab word for cistern.

Altarpiece: also retable. Decorative screen above and behind the altar.

Apse: far end of a church housing the high altar; can be semi-circular, polygonal or horseshoe.

Apsidal or radiating chapel: small chapel opening from the apse.

Arch:

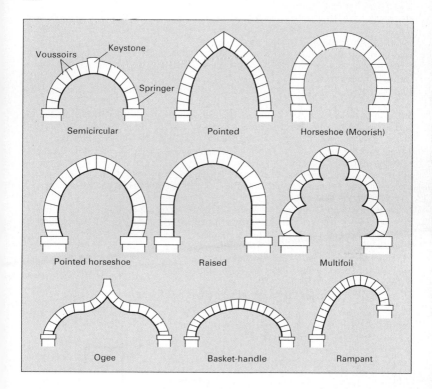

Voussoirs — Keystone — Springer

Semicircular — Pointed — Horseshoe (Moorish)

Pointed horseshoe — Raised — Multifoil

Ogee — Basket-handle — Rampant

Archivolt: ornamental moulding on the outer edge of an arch.

Artesonado: marquetry ceiling in which raised fillets outline honeycomb-like cells in the shape of stars. This particular decoration, which first appeared under the Almohads, was popular throughout the country, including Christian Spain, in the 15C and 16C.

Ataurique: decorative plant motif on plaster or brick which was developed as a feature of the Caliphate style and was subsequently adopted by the Mudéjar.

Azulejos: glazed, patterned, ceramic tiles.

Barrel vaulting: vault with a semicircular cross-section.

Caliphate: the architectural style developed in Córdoba under the Caliphate (8-11C) of which the finest example is the mosque in that town.

Churrigueresque: in the style of the Churrigueras, an 18C family of architects. Richly ornate baroque decoration.

Estípite: pilaster in the shape of a truncated inverted pyramid.

Gargoyle: projecting roof gutter normally carved in the shape of a grotesque animal.

Groined vaulting: vault showing lines of intersection of two vaults or arches (usually pointed).

Grotesque: typical Renaissance decoration combining vegetation, imaginary beings and animals.

Kiblah: sacred wall of a mosque from which the *mihrab* is hollowed, facing towards Mecca.

Lacerías: geometric decoration formed by intersecting straight lines making star-shaped and polygonal figures. Characteristic of Moorish architecture.

Lombard bands: decorative pilaster strips typical of Romanesque architecture in Lombardy.

Lonja: commodity exchange building.

Mihrab: richly decorated prayer-niche in the sacred wall *(kiblah)* in a mosque.

Minaret: tower of the mosque *(mezquita)*, from which the muezzin calls the faithful to prayer.

Minbar: pulpit in a mosque.

Mocárabes: decorative motifs of Muslim architecture formed by assembled prisms ending in concave surfaces. They resemble stalactites or pendants and adorn vaults and cornices.

Mozarabic: the work of Christians living under Arab rule after the Moorish invasion of 711. On being persecuted in the 9C, they sought refuge in Christian areas bringing with them Moorish artistic traditions.

Mudéjar: the work of Muslims living in Christian territory following the Reconquest (13-14C).

Naveta: megalithic monument found in the Balearic Islands, which has a pyramidal shape with a rectangular base, giving the appearance of an upturned boat.

Plateresque: term derived from *platero:* silversmith, and used to describe the early style of the Renaissance characterised by finely carved decoration.

Predella: the lower part of an altarpiece.

Sebka: type of brick decoration developed under the Almohads consisting of an apparently endless series of small arches forming a network of diamond shapes.

Seo or seu: cathedral.

Soportales: porticoes of wood or stone pillars supporting the first floor of houses. They form an open gallery around the *plaza mayor* of towns and villages.

Star vault: vault with a square or polygonal plan formed by several intersecting arches.

Stucco: type of moulding mix consisting mainly of plaster, used for coating surfaces. It plays a fundamental role in wall decoration in Hispano-Muslim architecture.

Talayot: megalithic monument found in the Balearic Islands, which takes the form of a truncated cone of stones.

Taula (*mesa* in the Mallorcan language): megalithic monument found in the Balearic Islands, which consists of a monolithic horizontal stone block placed on top of a similar vertical stone block.

Triforium: arcade above the side aisles which opens onto the central nave of a church.

Tympanum: inner surface of a pediment. This often ornamented space is bounded by the archivolt and the lintel of the doors of churches.

Venera: scallop-shaped moulding frequently used as an ornamental feature. It is the symbol of pilgrimages to Santiago de Compostela.

Yesería: plasterwork used in sculptured decoration.

Plan and furnishings of a Spanish church

The following are Spanish architectural terms and their translations used in the guide. Some words like coro *are kept in the original Spanish as there is no equivalent in English.*

Cabecera: the east or apsidal end of a church.

Camarín: a small chapel on the first floor behind the altarpiece or retable. It is plushly decorated and very often contains a lavishly costumed statue of the Virgin Mary.

Capilla Mayor: the area of the high altar containing the **retablo mayor** or monumental altarpiece which often rises to the roof.

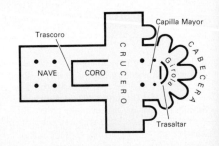

Coro: a chancel in Spanish canonical churches often built in the middle of the nave. It contains the **stalls** *(sillería)* used by members of religious orders. When placed in a tribune or gallery it is known as the **coro alto.**

Crucero: transept. The part of a church at right angles to the nave which gives the church the shape of a cross. It consists of the transept crossing and arms.

Girola (also *deambulatorio*): ambulatory. An extension to the aisles forming a gallery around the chancel and behind the altar.

Presbiterio: the space in front of the altar. (The presbytery is known as the *casa del Cura*).

Púlpito: pulpit.

Sagrario: chapel containing the Holy Sacrament. May sometimes be a separate church.

Sillería: the stalls.

Trasaltar: back wall of the *capilla mayor* in front of which there are frequently sculptures or tombs.

Trascoro: the wall, often carved and decorated, which encloses the *coro*.

Literature

Roman Spain produced great Latin authors such as **Seneca the Elder** or the Rhetorician, his son **Seneca the Younger** or the Philosopher, Quintilian, the satirist Martial and the epic poet **Lucan**. In the 8C, the monk Beatus wrote the Commentary on the Apocalypse which gave rise to a series of outstanding illuminated manuscripts known as **Beatus**. Arab writers won renown during the same period. Works written in Castilian began to emerge only in the Middle Ages.

The Middle Ages – The Reconquest provided material for epic poems, tales of adventure recited by wandering minstrels. In the 12C, the first milestone of Spanish literature appeared in the form of *El Cantar del Mío Cid*, an anonymous Castilian poem inspired by the adventures of **El Cid**. In the 13C, the monk **Gonzalo de Berceo**, drawing on religious themes, won renown through his works of *Mester de Clerecía*, the learned poetry of clerics and scholars. **Alfonso X, the Wise**, an erudite king who wrote poetry in Galician, decreed that in his kingdom, Latin should be replaced as the official language by Castilian, an act subsequently followed throughout Spain except in Catalunya where Catalan remained the written language. In the 14C, **Don Juan Manuel** introduced the use of narrative prose in his moral tales while Juan Ruiz, **Archpriest of Hita**, wrote a brilliant satirical verse work entitled *El Libro de Buen Amor*, which later influenced the picaresque novel.

A Beatus illuminated manuscript
(in the Monasterio de El Escorial)

Monasterio de El Escorial / H. Stierlin

The Renaissance – In the 15C, lyric poetry flourished under Italian influence with poets such as **Jorge Manrique** and the **Marquis of Santillana** *(qv)*. **Romanceros**, collections of ballads in an epic or popular vein, perpetuated the medieval style until the 16C when *Amadís de Gaula* (1508) set the model for a great many romances or tales of chivalry. In 1499, *La Celestina*, a novel of passion in dialogue form by Fernando de Rojas, anticipated modern drama in a subtle, well-observed tragi-comic intrigue.

The Golden Age (Siglo del Oro) – Spain enjoyed its greatest literary flowering under the Habsburgs (1516-1700), with great lyric poets such as **Garcilaso de la Vega**, disciple of Italian verse forms, **Fray Luis de León** *(qv)* and above all **Luis de Góngora** (1561-1627) whose obscure, precious style won fame under the name Gongorism. Pastoral novels became popular with works by Cervantes and Lope de Vega. The **picaresque** novel, however, was the genre favoured by Spanish writers at the time. The first to appear in 1554 was *Lazarillo de Tormes*, an anonymous autobiographical work in which the hero, an astute rogue (*pícaro* in Castilian), casts a mischievous and impartial eye on society and its woes. There followed Mateo Alemán's *Guzmán de Alfarache* with its brisk style and colourful vocabulary, and *La Vida del Buscón*, an example of the varied talents of **Francisco de Quevedo** (1580-1645), essayist, poet and satirist. The genius of the Golden Age, however, was **Cervantes** (1547-1616) *(qv)*, with his masterpiece, the universal **Don Quixote** (1650). Lope de Rueda paved the way for *comedia*, which emerged at the end of the 16C. Dramatists proliferated, among them the master **Lope de Vega** (1562-1635), who perfected and enriched the art form. This "phoenix of the mind" wrote more than 1,000 plays on the most diverse subjects. His successor, **Calderón de la Barca** (1600-1681), wrote historical and philosophical plays *(La Vida es Sueño or Life's a Dream* and *El Alcalde de Zalamea or The Mayor of Zalamea)* in which he brilliantly reflects the mood of Spain in the 17C. **Tirso de Molina** (1583-1648) left his interpretation of Don Juan for posterity while **Guillén de Castro** wrote *Las Mocedades del Cid* (youthful adventures of the Cid). Mention should also be made of works on the conquest of America by **Cortés** and **Bartolomé de las Casas** among others. Finally, the moralist **Fray Luis de Granada** and the mystics **Santa Teresa de Ávila** (1515-1582) and **San Juan de la Cruz** (St John of the Cross) (1542-1591) wrote theological works.

18 and 19C – The critical mode found expression in the works of essayists such as **Benito Jerónimo Feijóo** and **Jovellanos**, also a poet. Elegance dominated the plays of **Moratín**, while Ramón de la Cruz delighted audiences with his *sainetes*, or satiric comic interludes. The great romantic poet of the 19C was **Bécquer** (1836-1870) from Sevilla, while **Larra** was a social satirist, **Menéndez Pelayo** a literary critic and **Ángel Ganivet** a political and moral analyst. Realism was introduced to the Spanish novel by **Alarcón** *(The Three-Cornered Hat)* and **Pereda** *(Peñas Arriba)* who concentrated on regional themes. By the end of the 19C, the best realist was **Pérez Galdós** whose prolific, lively work *(National Episodes)* is stamped with a great sense of human sympathy.

20C – A group of intellectuals known as the Generation of '98, saddened by Spain's loss of colonies like Cuba, pondered over the future and character of their country and, more generally, the problems of human destiny. The atmosphere was reflected in the work of essayists such as **Miguel de Unamuno** (1864-1936) *(qv)* who wrote *El sentimiento trágico de la Vida (The Tragic Sense of Life)*, and **Azorín**, as well as the philologist **Menéndez Pidal**, the novelist **Pío Baroja** and the aesthete **Valle Inclán**, who created an elegant poetic prose style. Among their contemporaries were **Jacinto Benavente** (winner of the 1922 Nobel Prize for literature), who developed a new dramatic style, and the novelist **Vicente Blasco Ibáñez** *(qv)*. Henceforth Spain opened up to literary contributions from abroad. Some great poets began to emerge, including **Juan Ramón Jiménez** (Nobel Prize 1956), who expressed his feelings through simple unadorned prose poems *(Platero y Yo)*, **Antonio Machado** (1875-1939) *(qv)*, the bard of Castilla, and **Rafael Alberti**. **Federico García Lorca** (1898-1936) *(qv)*, equally great as both poet and dramatist *(Bodas de Sangre)*, was Andalusian through and through. His work was, perhaps, the most fascinating reflection of a Spain whose mystery **Ortega y Gasset** (1883-1925), essayist and philosopher, spent his life trying to fathom.

Post-war writing – Several years after the Civil War, writing rose from its ashes with works by essayists (Américo Castro), playwrights (Alfonso Sastre) and above all, novelists such as **Miguel Delibes**, **Camilo José Cela** *(La Familia de Pascual Duarte)* who won the Nobel Prize for Literature in 1989, **Juan Goytisolo**, **Ramón Sender** and Antonio Ferres, all preoccupied with social issues.

Among contemporary authors, mention should be made of novelists Juan Benet, Juan Marsé, **Manuel Vásquez Montalbán**, Terenci Moix, Javier Marías and **Eduardo Mendoza**, and playwrights Antonio Gala, Fernando Arrabal and Francisco Nieva.

In conclusion, the Spanish-speaking countries of Latin America are making enormous contributions to Spanish literature with works by Jorge Luis Borges, Gabriel García Márquez, Pablo Neruda and Miguel Ángel Asturias.

Music

Alongside its impressive wealth of folk music, Spain has developed an extraordinarily rich musical repertory since the Middle Ages, marked by a large number of influences including Visigothic, Arabic, Mozarabic and French. Polyphonic chants were studied in the 11C and the oldest known piece for three voices, the *Codex calixtinus*, was composed at Santiago de Compostela c1140. During the Reconquest, bishops in towns recaptured by Christians encouraged great musical creativity in the form of liturgical chants, church plays *(autos)* like the *Elche Mystery (p 105)* which is still performed today, and poetry like the 13C **Cantigas de Santa María** by Alfonso the Wise. As music was intimately linked with religion, it retained its sacred character for centuries.

At the end of the 15C, the dramatist **Juan de la Encina** composed secular songs thus proving that he was also an excellent musician. Music, like the other arts, however, reached its climax in the second half of the 16C, under the protection of the early Habsburgs. **Victoria** (1548-1611) was one of the most famous composers of polyphonic devotional pieces, while among his contemporaries, **Francisco de Salinas** and **Fernando de las Infantas** were learned musicologists and **Cristóbal de Morales** and **Francisco Guerrero** were accomplished religious composers. As for instruments, the organ became the invariable accompaniment to sacred music, while a favourite for profane airs was the *vihuela*, a sort of guitar with six double strings which was soon replaced by the lute and eventually by the five-string Spanish guitar. In 1629, Lope de Vega wrote the text for the first Spanish opera. **Calderón de la Barca** created the *zarzuela* (1648), a musical play with spoken passages, songs and dances, which, since the 19C, has based its plot and music on popular themes. The major composer of religious and secular music in the 18C was Padre **Antonio Soler**, a great harpsichord player.

In the 19C, the Catalan **Felipe Pedrell** brought Spanish music onto a higher plane and opened the way for a new generation of musicians. He was a prolific composer, the first to combine traditional tunes with classical genres. At the beginning of the century, while works by French composers (Ravel's *Bolero*, Bizet's *Carmen*, Lalo's *Symphonie Espagnole* and Chabrier's *España*) bore a pronounced Hispanic stamp, Spanish composers turned to national folklore and traditional themes: **Isaac Albéniz** (1860-1909) wrote *Iberia*, **Enrique Granados** (1867-1916) became famous for his *Goyescas* and **Joaquín Turina** (1888-1949) for his *Sevilla Symphony*. This popular vein culminated in works by **Manuel de Falla** (1876-1946) including *Nights in the Gardens of Spain, El Amor Brujo* and *The Three-Cornered Hat*.

Among the best-known classical guitar players of our day, **Andrés Segovia** (1894-1987), **Joaquín Rodrigo** (b 1902) and **Narciso Yepes** (b 1927), have shown that this most Spanish of instruments can interpret a wide variety of music. Another Spaniard, **Pablo Casals** (1876-1973), was possibly the greatest cellist of all time. Spain holds a leading position in the world of opera with singers such as Victoria de los Ángeles, Montserrat Caballé, Plácido Domingo, Alfredo Kraus, José Carreras and Teresa Berganza.

Cinema

Spanish cinema dates back to a short film in 1897 which shows people leaving the Basílica de Nuestra Señora del Pilar in Zaragoza after Mass. Studios for silent movies were later set up in Barcelona.

In the 1920s, several Surrealists tried their hand at the new art form. Among them were **Dalí** and above all **Buñuel**, the master of Spanish cinema, who made *Un chien Andalou (Un Perro Andaluz)* in 1928 and *L'Age d'Or (La Edad de Oro)* in 1930. When talking films appeared in the 1930s, Spain was in the throes of a political and economic crisis and so her studios lacked the means to procure the necessary equipment. At the end of the 1930s, when films like *Sister Angelica (Sor Angélica)* by Gargallo tended to address religious themes, Juan Piqueras launched a magazine called *Nuestro Cinema* which was strongly influenced by Russian ideas and gave star billing to films which could almost have been qualified as propaganda. One of these, *Las Hurdes - Land without Bread (Las Hurdes - Tierra Sin Pan*, 1932) by Buñuel, showed poverty in a remote part of Spain.

During the Civil War and the ensuing Franco era, films were heavily censored and the cinema became one of the major vehicles for the ideology of the time, with historical and religious themes glorifying death and the spirit of sacrifice. One such success was *Marcelino, Bread and Wine (Marcelino, Pan y Vino*, 1955) by Ladislao Vajda. Change came with works by **Juan Antonio Bardem** like *Death of a Cyclist (Muerte de un Ciclista*, 1955) and with **Berlanga's** *Welcome Mr. Marshall (Bienvenido, Mr. Marshall*, 1953) and *The Executioner (El Verdugo*, 1964).

The 1960s enjoyed a period of renewal with directors like **Carlos Saura**, whose first film, *The Scoundrels (Los Golfos)*, came out in 1959. More than ever before, the 1970s saw a new wave in Spanish cinema with outstanding directors and films. These were mainly concerned with the problems of childhood and youth marked by the Franco régime. Saura's *Ana and the Wolves (Ana y los Lobos*, 1973) shows a young girl arriving as an outsider in a family in which three fifty-year-old brothers personify the all-powerful hold of the army and religion during the Franco era. Mention should also be made of *Cría (Cría Cuervos*, 1975) also by Saura, *The Spirit of the Beehive (El Espíritu de la Colmena*, 1973) and *The South (El Sur*, 1983) by **Víctor Erice**, *The Beehive (La Colmena*, 1982) by **Mario Camus**, and films by **Manuel Gutiérrez Aragón** such as *Demons in the Garden (Demonios en el Jardín*, 1982) and *The Other Half of Heaven (La Otra Mitad del Cielo*, 1986) which illustrate the economic changes between Spain under Franco and Spain as a democracy. **Pedro Almodóvar** breaks with this serious, nostalgic type of cinema so critical of the Franco era. His films are of a completely different, modern Spain in which the *Movida* (a fashionable, progressive anti-establishment movement in the arts during the 1980s) in Madrid is shown in a comic light, as in *Women on the Edge of a Nervous Breakdown (Mujeres al Borde de un Ataque de Nervios*, 1988).

Death of a Cyclist by Juan Antonio Bardem

Handicrafts

Spain has always had a rich tradition of arts and crafts reflecting the character of each region as well as the influence of the various civilisations – Iberian, Roman, Visigothic, and Muslim – that have marked the country's history. Traditional wares such as pottery, ceramics, basketwork and woven goods are produced countrywide.

Ceramics and pottery – The variety and quality of these crafts give them pride of place in Spain. In Castilla, pottery is mainly made by women who use a primitive technique. Among their specialities are kitchen utensils, jars and water pitchers. The basic items of crockery used in farm houses – dishes, soup tureens and bowls made of glazed earthenware *(barro cocido)* – appear in villages and on stalls in every market. The technique, patterns and colours of ceramics in many parts of Spain have been influenced by Islamic art. There are two large pottery centres in the Toledo region. The first, **Talavera de la Reina** is famous for its blue, green, yellow, orange and black ceramics while the second, **El Puente del Arzobispo**, mainly uses shades of green. Pottery from **La Bisbal d'Empordà** in Catalunya has a yellow background with green decorative motifs. The Mudéjar tradition is evident in Aragón and the Levante region where blue and white pottery is made in **Muel**, green and purple ceramics in **Teruel** and lustreware in **Manises** (Valencia). Most of the figurines used as decoration for cribs at Christmas are produced in **Murcia**. Spain's richest pottery region is Andalucía with workshops in **Granada** (glazed ceramics with thick green and blue strokes), **Guadix** (red crockery), **Triana** in Sevilla, (polychrome animal figures, glazed and decorated), **Úbeda**, **Andújar** (jars with cobalt blue patterns) and in **Vera** (white pottery with undulating shapes). In Galicia, porcelain and earthenware goods with contemporary shapes and designs are factory-made at the **Sargadelos** centre in the province of La Coruña, but there is also a craft industry at **Niñodaguia** in Orense (where the yellow glaze only partially covers the objets) and at **Bruño** (where yellow motifs set off a dark brown background). Mention should be made of the famous *Xiruels* whistles decorated in red and green in the Islas Baleares.

Ceramic tiles from Talavera de la Reina

Lace, woven and embroidered goods – The textile industry was very prosperous under the Muslims and several workshops still thrive today. Brightly coloured blankets and carpets are woven in the Alpujarras region, la Rioja, the area around Cádiz **(Grazalema)** and at **Níjar** near Almería (where *tela de trapo* carpets are made from strips of cloth). Blankets from Zamora, Palencia and Salamanca are well known.
In some villages in the province of Ciudad Real (particularly in **Almagro**) women lacemakers may still be seen at work in their doorways with bobbins and needles. Lacework from **Camariñas** in Galicia is also famous. The most popular craft, however, is embroidery, often done in the family. The most typical, geometrically patterned embroideries come from the Toledo region **(Lagartera** and **Oropesa)**. Embroidery has been raised to the level of a veritable art in two thoroughly Spanish domains: firstly, in the ornaments used for pasos during Holy Week and secondly in bullfighters' costumes.

Gold, silver and ironwork – Iron forging, a very old practice in Spain, has produced some outstanding works of art like the wrought-iron grilles and screens that adorn many of the country's churches. Blacksmiths continue to make the grilles for doors and windows so popular in architecture in the south of Spain (La Mancha, Extremadura and Andalucía).
Copper smelting continues to this day at **Guadalupe** in Extremadura where pots, boilers, braziers and stills are made. Damascene weapons (steel inlaid with gold, silver and copper) are still being produced today, in **Eibar** (País Vasco) and in **Toledo** particularly, according to pure Islamic tradition. Traditional knife-making is centred around **Albacete**.

Gold and silver smithing, of which outstanding treasures may be seen in Spain's archaelogical museums, was developed in Antiquity and throughout the Visigothic period and has retained some of its traditional methods. An example is filigree ornamentation (soldered, intertwined gold and silver threads) crafted in **Córdoba** and **Toledo**. Salamanca, Cáceres and Ciudad Rodrigo specialise in gold jewellery.

Leather goods – Leather-making has always been an important trade, especially in Andalucía, and has become industrialised in some areas. (Fine leather goods and shoes are made in Andalucía, in the Alicante area and in the Islas Baleares). The production of the famous **Córdoba** leather *(guadameciles)*, embossed polychrome leatherwork which was once highly prized throughout Europe, has retained its craft status.

Typically Spanish gourds and wineskin containers are made in the provinces of Bilbao, Pamplona and Burgos and in other wine-growing areas.

Basketwork – Basket-making remains one of the most representative of Spanish crafts. Although carried out countrywide, it is particularly rich on the Mediterranean coast and in the Islas Baleares.

The type of product and the material used vary from region to region. Baskets, hats and mats are made of reeds, willow, esparto grass, strips of olive-wood and birch and chestnut bark, while furniture may be rush or wickerwork. Willow is used in Andalucía and in the Levante, hazel and chestnut in Galicia and in the Asturias, and straw and esparto grass on the island of Ibiza.

Tradition and folklore

The main festivals in Spain are listed in the Calendar of Events at the end of the guide.

A DEEPLY RELIGIOUS COUNTRY

The people's deeply-rooted Catholic faith and their ability to express their feelings freely, combined with their love of spectacle and devotion to traditional ceremonies make religious festivals in Spain incredibly splendid occasions. Festivities vary according to the region – bucolic in Galicia, exuberant in Andalucía, reserved in Castilla – and are generally mixed with local folklore and purely profane rejoicings.

Epiphany, Corpus Christi and Holy Week are celebrated throughout the country while each town and region also has its own saint's day. The main festivals take the form of processions and *romerías*.

Romerías – These are pilgrimages made to an isolated shrine or hermitage by a procession of people grouped in brotherhoods or guilds or by town quarter or even whole villages. Most *romerías* are to chapels of the Virgin famous for their statues, which are usually held in deep veneration. The best known are those of Pilar (Zaragoza), Guadalupe, Montserrat and Rocío.

Pilgrims may dress in local costume and sing folksongs along the way. A *romería* is a good opportunity to get together, picnic and dance. Some *romerías* in the northern *rías* take place at sea, on boats bedecked with flowers.

C. et J. Lenars/EXPLORER

Penitents in Sevilla

Processions – Every religious occasion, whether it is an important Christian festival or the feast day of a local saint, is accompanied by a procession. **Semana Santa** (Holy Week) is without doubt the festival which inspires the most fervent display of devotion throughout Spain. It begins on Palm Sunday with the blessing of palm fronds followed by demonstrations of mourning. Rich church ornaments are veiled in black while processions of **pasos** or floats bearing groups of lifesize wooden statues illustrate the different stages of the Passion. The most spectacular of these slow solemn processions is that of Sevilla with its hooded penitents. In Catalunya, the villagers themselves act out the scenes of the Passion. Among other major religious festivals are the processions of **Nuestra Señora de Monte Carmel**, patron saint of sailors, and of **Corpus Christi** when streets are carpeted with flower petals and the Holy Sacrament is carried inside a gold or silver monstrance.

Ferias – *Ferias* or agricultural fairs, often held in conjunction with religious festivals, are very popular events, especially in Andalucía. Those of Sevilla and Jerez de la Frontera attract large crowds in Andalusian costume.

REGIONAL TRADITIONS AND FOLKLORE

Andalucía – The **flamenco**, derived from gypsy and Arab sources, is a befitting expression of the Andalusian soul. It is based on the *cante jondo* or deep song which describes the performer's profound emotions in ancient poetic phrases. The rhythm is given by hand-claps, heel-clicks and castanets. The **sevillana**, from Sevilla, is a more popular type of dance. Sevilla and Málaga are the best places to see **tablaos** or performances of Andalusian music. Flamenco and Sevillana owe much of their grace to the Andalusian costume of brilliantly coloured flounced dresses for women and close-fitting short jacketed suits, wide flat hats and heeled boots for men.

Aragón – No general rejoicing here goes without a **jota**, a bounding, leaping dance in which couples hop and whirl to the tunes of a *rondalla* (group of stringed instruments), stopping only for the occasional brief singing of a *copla* by a soloist.

Catalunya and the Comunidad Valenciana – The **sardana** dance is still very popular in Catalunya where it is performed in a circle in main squares on Sunday. The **Xiquets**, who form daring human pyramids, may be seen in festivals at El Vendrell and Valls. In the Levante, the rich local costume notable for its colour and intricate embroidery is worn during lively, colourful festivals. Valencia's **Fallas** in March are a veritable institution which Alicante's **Fogueres** try to rival. The citizens indulge their taste for decoration, parody and exuberance by making giant pasteboard figures, which are set alight amidst noisy rejoicings and fireworks displays. Lastly, the *Moros y Cristianos* festivals – those of Alcoy are the best known – give a colourful replay of the confrontations between Moors and Christians during the Reconquest.

The Cantabrian coast and Galicia – *Romerías* in Asturias and Galicia are always accompanied by the shrill tones of the **gaita**, a type of bagpipe, and sometimes by drums and castanets. The *gaita* is played during events in honour of cowherds, shepherds, sailors and others who work in the country's oldest occupations. The most typical festivals are those held in summer for *vaqueiros* or cowherds in Aristébano and others for shepherds near the Lago de Enol. Common dances in Galicia include the *muñeira* or dance of the miller's wife, the sword dance performed only by men, and the *redondela*.
Bowls *(bolos)* is a very popular game.

País Vasco and Navarra – These regions have preserved many of their unusual traditions. Men dressed in white with red belts and the famous red berets dance in a ring accompanied by **zortzicos** (songs), a **txistu** (flute) and a *tamboril*. The most solemn dance, the *aurresku*, is a chain dance performed by men after mass on Sunday. The **espata-dantza** or sword dance recalls warrior times while others, like the spinners' dance or another in which brooms are used, represent daily tasks. The Basques love contests, such as trunk cutting, stone lifting and pole throwing. But by far the most popular sport is *pelota*, played in different ways: with a **chistera** or wickerwork scoop, or with the very similar **cesta punta** in an enclosed three-walled court *(jai alai)*, or with a wooden bat or **pala** or, finally, simply with the hand, **a mano**. There is a famous Pelota university at Markina in Vizcaya.
The most important festival in Navarra is the **Sanfermines**, held in Pamplona *(qv)*.

Castilla – Few regions in Spain are as mystical or as strictly moral as Castilla. Traditional dances include the **seguidilla** and the **paloteo**, also known as the **danza de palos**, which is accompanied by flute, tambourine, and sometimes by a bass drum or the most typical of Castilian instruments, the local reed-pipe or **dulzaina**. Peasant costumes around Salamanca are richly embroidered with precious stones, silk thread and sequins.

Islas Baleares – Mallorca's traditional dances include the *copeo*, the *jota*, the *mateixes* and the *bolero*. Dances and festivals are accompanied by a *xeremía* (local bagpipes) and a tambourine. In Menorca, a festival dating back to medieval times and calling for about a hundred horsemen in elegant costumes, is held at Ciutadella on Midsummer's Day. Popular dances in Ibiza have a poetical accompaniment to guide the performers' movements.

BULLFIGHTING

The bullfight was performed on horseback from the Middle Ages to the 18C. It subsequently became a popular form of entertainment and was carried out on foot. Present-day rules governing bullfighting were established during the 18 and 19C by the **Romero** family and the toreros **Costillares, Francisco Montes «Paquiro»** and **Juan Belmonte** (1892-1962). **Pepe Hillo** (1754-1801) created the spontaneous, graceful Sevillian style which contrasts with the solemnity and sobriety of that of Ronda. He was succeeded by the Córdobans **Lagartijo** (1841-1900), **Guerrita** (1862-1941), **Joselito** (1895-1920), **Manolete** (1917-1947) and **El Cordobés**.

The stock – Bulls are reared in almost total freedom on properties in Andalucía and in Castilla between Salamanca and Ciudad Rodrigo. When they are about two years old, their fighting ability is judged during a **tienta**, or test of bravery. Each stock farm acquires its own qualities which are analysed by connoisseurs or **aficionados**.

The corrida – The programme starts at 5pm and is made up of two kills each by three *matadores*. (The six 4-year-old bulls each weigh around 450 kilos-992 pounds). The action begins, to the tune of a *paso doble*, with the **paseo** or grand entry led by two mounted *alguazils* (servants of the *corrida* president) in 17C costume. These are followed by the *toreros* or ring contestants: the three *matadores*, each in what is known as his costume of lights, leading his *cuadrilla* or team. The contests **(lidias)** are divided into three acts **(tercios)**, marked by trumpet calls. As the action unfolds, the *matador* should progressively gain domination over the bull.

1: Arrival and appraisal of the bull – The peones attract the bull's attention with the aid of a cape. The matador enters and plays his wide pink cape in front of the bull to make it turn swiftly so that he can judge its behaviour. This exercise comprises various formal figures including the famous *verónica* pass. Next the *picadores* on their padded, caparisoned horses, wait with pikes for the bull to charge, when they thrust their weapons into its withers.

2: The banderillas – To allow the bull to regain its wind and to rouse it further, the *banderilleros* thrust beribboned darts *(banderillas)* into the back of its neck.

3: The kill – Deft work with the *muleta*, a red serge cloth bound to a stick which is smaller and easier to handle than the cape, opens the last act. After saluting the president and dedicating the bull to a particular person or to the crowd, the *matador*, with his sword in his right hand and the *muleta* in his left, attracts the attention of the bull. He controls it through a series of passes which, by their elegance and daring, may win him triumphant applause.

At the final *estocada* stage, the bull stands still. The *matador* advances, his sword straight before him, and aiming between the shoulder blades thrusts to the bull's heart as his body brushes the right horn of the animal still fascinated by the *muleta*. If the *matador* has fought well, he may be awarded one or both of the bull's ears and sometimes also its tail.

Other types of fight – **Capeas** are popular festivals during which young amateurs match their skills against bulls in village squares, as at the well-known Ciudad Rodrigo contests. At **novilladas,** young 3-year-old bulls or *novillos* are fought by apprentice bullfighters known as *novilleros*. A **rejoneador** is a mounted bullfighter who takes part in the traditional three-act corrida.

The Verónica Pass

J. L. Barde/SCOPE

Food and wine

See wine map in the current Michelin Red Guide España Portugal

Spanish food is distinctively Mediterranean: it is cooked with an olive oil base, seasoned with aromatic herbs and spiced with hot peppers. It nevertheless varies enormously from region to region. Among dishes served throughout the country are garlic soup, **cocido** or a type of stew accompanied by beans in the north and by chickpeas in the south, omelettes with potatoes, like the famous **tortilla**, typical pork meats like **chorizo** (a kind of spicy sausage) and delicious lean *serrano* hams. Fish and seafood are also used in a great many dishes.

No description of Spanish food should be complete without mentioning the ubiquitous **tapas**, the hors d'œuvres which appear on the counters of most bars and cafés just before lunch and dinner. This often vast array of colourful appetizers comes in two different forms, *tapas* (small saucer-size amounts) or *raciones*, more substantial portions. A selection of 2 or 3 *tapas* or 1 or 2 *raciones* makes for a very pleasant lunch accompanied by a glass of draught beer *(caña)*.

Northern regions – Galicia's cuisine owes its delicacy to the quality of its seafood: octopus, hake, gilt-head, scallops *(vieiras)*, mussels *(mejillones)*, goose-barnacles *(percebes)*, prawns *(gambas)*, king prawns *(langostinos)* and mantis shrimps *(cigalas)*. There is also **el caldo gallego**, a local stew, **lacón con grelos** (hand of pork with turnip tops) and another common traditional recipe, **pulpo gallego** (Galician-style octopus), often served as a *tapa* or *ración*. All these dishes may be accompanied by local wines such as red or white Ribeiro or white Albariño.

In **Asturias** fish and seafood are also important but the main speciality is a casserole dish called **fabada** made with white beans, pork, bacon and spicy sausages. As far as cakes and pastries are concerned, mention should be made of **sobaos**, delicious biscuits which originated in Cantabria and are cooked in oil. Cider is often drunk at meals.

Cooking in the **País Vasco** (Basque country) has been raised to the level of a fine art and requires laborious preparation. There are a good many meat dishes cooked in a sauce, and fish stews in which cod or hake are accompanied by a green parsley sauce *(salsa verde)* or by peppers. *Chiperones en su tinta* is a dish of baby squid in their own ink. *Marmitako*, a typical fishing village dish, is composed of tunny, potatoes and red peppers, and is often served with a good *txacolí*, a tart white wine.

The Ebro region – Navarra and La Rioja *(qv)* are the regions for game, excellent market-garden produce and the best Spanish wines, especially reds. The food is varied and refined, with partridge, quail and woodpigeon competing with trout for pride of place in local dishes. Navarra has noteworthy rosés and fruity white wines. Delicious Roncal cheese is made in the valleys from ewe's milk.

Aragón is the land of **chilindrón**, a savoury tomato and red pepper sauce served with meat and poultry, and also of **ternasco** or roast kid or lamb. These dishes may be washed down with heavy red Cariñena wines.

Paella

Meseta regions – Castilian specialities from local produce include roast lamb **(cordero asado)**, suckling-pig **(cochinillo tostón** or **tostado)** and the ubiquitous **cocido**, all of which may be accompanied by a light fresh Valdepeñas red.

Rueda wines from southern Valladolid province are fresh fruity whites, while those from Ribera del Duero are generally acidic reds.

The Meseta is also a cheese-producing region with a ewe's milk speciality from Burgos and many varieties of *manchego*, Spain's best known cheese. Among local sweets are the famous marzipans from Toledo.

Mediterranean regions – Catalunya and the Levante have a typically Mediterranean cuisine. Look out in particular for Catalan *pan con tomate* (bread rubbed with a cut tomato and occasionally garlic and sprinkled with olive oil), red peppers cooked in oil, and wonderful fish dishes with a variety of sauces such as *all i oli* (crushed garlic and olive oil) and *samfaina* (tomatoes, peppers and aubergines). Among pork meats are **butifarra** sausages, various kinds of slicing sausage and the *fuet* sausage from Vic. Dried fruit is used in a great many dishes or may be served at the end of a meal. The most widespread dessert is **crema catalana**, a kind of custard cream mould with a thin layer of caramel. Catalunya is home to *cava*, a sparkling wine. Excellent light wines are made in the Empordà region, fruity whites in Penedés and reds in Priorato.

The Levante is the kingdom of the famous **paella** which is cooked with a saffron rice base and chicken, pork, shellfish, squid, shrimps and king prawns. As for sweets, **turrón** (made of almonds and honey or castor sugar, rather like nougat) is a Levantine speciality.

Soups are specialities in the **Islas Baleares** (Balearic Islands); Mallorca's *mallorquina* has bread, leeks and garlic, while other soups are made with fish. **Tumbet** is a well-known casserole of potatoes, onions, tomatoes, courgettes and peppers. **Sobrasada**, a spicy sausage, flavours many local dishes. **Cocas**, pastries with sweet or savoury fillings, and **ensaimadas**, light spiral rolls, make delicious desserts.

Andalucía – The region's best known dish is **gazpacho**, a cold cucumber and tomato soup made with oil and vinegar and flavoured with garlic. Andalusians love their food fried, especially fish and seafood. Pigs are reared in the Sierra Nevada and Sierra de Aracena for the exquisite *serrano* ham. Among local desserts, *tocino del cielo* is as sweet as an Oriental pastry.

The region is especially well-known for its dessert wines: the famous **Jerez** or sherries *(more about these under Jerez de la Frontera)*, **Manzanilla** and **Málaga** *(qv)*.

Gazpacho

On a gastronomic level, Andalucía is renowned mainly for its fried fish dishes, and also its *gazpacho*, a cold soup which is particularly refreshing and tasty during the hot summer months.

Ingredients: tomatoes, peppers (red or green), chillies, garlic, olive oil, vinegar, seasoning, breadcrumbs, stock.

Method: Grind the chillies, garlic and a little salt in a large pestle and mortar. The traditional method would be to add the diced peppers and tomatoes and the breadcrumbs and pound by hand until well mixed – but these days, most people liquidize everything with the help of a food processor! Slowly pour the oil onto the mixture stirring all the time. Leave to soak for a while, then add some cold stock and strain the mixture through a sieve. Add a little vinegar and seasoning. Serve well chilled, with croutons, diced cucumber, red peppers and raw onion sprinkled on top.

Paella Valenciana

Ingredients *(serves 4):* small cup of olive oil, 2 cloves of garlic (crushed), 1 green pepper (finely sliced), half a cup of tomato puree, 100 g chicken (diced into medium-sized pieces), 100 g pork (diced into medium-sized pieces), 250 g arborio or long grain rice, 1 tsp saffron, salt and pepper, 500 ml fish stock, 500 ml chicken stock, 100 g clams, 100 g mussels, 100 g prawns, 50 g squid (cut into thin slices), 50 g sweet red peppers (cut into thin slices), 25 g frozen peas.

Method: Heat the olive oil in a large frying pan or paella dish. Add the garlic and green peppers and fry for 2 minutes. Add the chicken, pork and squid and cook, stirring, for a further 5 minutes. Add the rice, saffron and tomato puree, followed immediately by the fish and chicken stock and salt and pepper. Cook for 10 minutes, stirring occasionally. Once the rice is almost cooked, add the mussels, clams, prawns, sweet red peppers and green peas. Cook for a further 3 to 5 minutes or until shellfish is cooked through. Garnish with slices of lemon. ¡Que aproveche!

The Mezquita. Córdoba

Sights

AGUILAR DE CAMPÓO

Castilla y León (Palencia)
Population 7 594
Michelin map 442 D 17 – Michelin Atlas España Portugal p 12

The landscape in this region on the northern edge of the Meseta is broken by limestone escarpments thrust up by the folding which formed the Cordillera Cantábrica. From its position on one of these high outcrops Aguilar castle has withstood time as it looks down on the old town which still possesses rampart gateways with pointed arches, in some cases surmounted by a carved figure or crest, and mansions emblasoned with coats of arms.

The vast **Aguilar reservoir** 2km - 1.5 miles to the west is a water sports centre.

Monasterio de Santa María la Real ⊘ – *On the edge of town towards Cervera de Pisuerga.*
This fine transitional Romanesque Gothic (12-13C) monastery is known for its historiated capitals inside the church, its cloister and chapter house. It is presently undergoing extensive restoration.

Colegiata de San Miguel ⊘ – The church at the end of the long, porticoed Plaza de España shelters within its vast Gothic aisles two fine mausoleums: the first, 16C, of the Marquises of Aguilar praying, the second, in the north apsidiole, carved in a surprisingly realistic manner, of the archpriest García González.

Parque Nacional de AIGÜESTORTES and LAGO DE SANT MAURICI★★

Catalunya (Lleida)
Michelin map 443 E 32-33 – Local map under PIRINEOS CATALANES

This national park in the Catalan Pyrenees covers an area of 10 230 hectares - 25 279 acres at an altitude between 1 500 and 3 000m - 4 900 and 9 800ft. This particular range consists of granite and slate, a very different terrain from that of the limestone Pyrenees in the Ordesa national park. The glacially eroded landscape in Aigüestortes national park has a harsh type of beauty with U-shaped valleys and high mountain lakes. It is a well-watered area abounding in waterfalls and rushing streams. The 'twisting' waterways or *aigües tortes* that have given the park its name wind gently through valleys between moss-covered meadows and wooded slopes. The vegetation consists of a variety of coniferous trees such as firs and Scots pines but there are also birch and beech trees which change colour in autumn. Herds of light brown cows graze the pastures while ibex roam the peaks and ridges and capercaillies still haunt the woods.

EXCURSIONS

The park ⊘ may be reached from the east via Espot or from the west via Boí.

Lago de Sant Maurici – *Reached by road from Espot.* The lake is surrounded by forest and dominated by the peaks of the Sierra dels Encantats.

Aigüestortes – Reached by a branch off the Barruera-Caldes de Boí road. The track *(5km - 3 miles)* is practicable for private vehicles although there are also organised jeep tours. The road leads into Aigüestortes where a stream winds its way through rich pastures. There is a path to Estany Llong lake *(3 hours Rtn on foot)*.
There are a number of signposted paths, including the one that crosses the park, and four mountain refuges where hikers may spend the night.

ALARCÓN★

Castilla-La-Mancha (Cuenca)
Population 245
Michelin map 444 N 23 – Michelin Atlas España Portugal p 54

Alarcón stands atop a mound of brown earth almost completely encircled by a meander of the Júcar river. The 13-14C castle, now a parador, is one of Spain's best examples of medieval military architecture. This fortress, a square construction of gold-coloured stone, is guarded by two rows of fortifications and adds considerably to the melancholy beauty of the **site★★**.

Alarcón, meaning Alaric's town, was founded by the son of the Visigothic king of the same name. It was reconquered from the Muslims in 1184 by Alfonso VIII, then ceded to the Knights of Santiago and eventually came into the hands of the Infante **Don Juan**

Manuel (1284-1348) who wrote many of his cautionary tales while living there. In the 15C, the castle became the object of bloody battles between its owner, the Marquis of Villena, and the Catholic Monarchs who wished to put an end to feudal power.
The Alarcón dam, 3km - 2 miles away, controls the Júcar's variable flow.

The village – Roughcast obscures many a fine stone house front in the modest country village.
Apart from its elegant Plateresque (16C) west door, the church of **Santa María** possesses a vast Gothic interior and a remarkable carved altarpiece dating from the same period.
The parish church of San Juan stands on the **Plaza de Don Juan Manuel** as does the porticoed town hall (Ayuntamiento).

The diagram on the back cover shows the Michelin Maps *covering the Guide; the chapter headings specify the appropriate map for the locality.*

ALBACETE

Castilla-La Mancha
Population 135 889
Michelin map 444 O 24, P 24 – Michelin Atlas España Portugal p 67
Town plan in the current Michelin Red Guide España Portugal

Albacete (*Al Basite* meant the Plain to the Arabs), the capital of the south of La Mancha, stands on a plateau which forms an arid Castilian promontory jutting into the fertile greenery of the huerta country between the Beatic chains and the Iberian Cordillera.
Albacete has specialised in the manufacture of knives and scissors since the Muslim era.

Museo de Albacete ⊘ – The museum, a modern building on the edge of Abelardo Sánchez park, was designed to display finds from excavations in the province.
The archaeological section houses a rich collection of Iberian and Roman artefacts. Examples of the former include a **sphinx from Haches** and sculptures from the sanctuary at Cerro de los Santos. Amongst Roman finds note the **dolls with movable joints** ★ – four dolls made of ivory and one of amber – and some of the funerary items discovered in a 4C burial-ground at Ontur in 1946.

EXCURSION

★ **Alcalá del Júcar** – *50km - 31 miles northeast. Take the AB 891, the A 892 and then the road through Villavaliente.*
The village spreads between its castle tower and church over a **site** ★ equally magnificent by day or night. It has been built into the very face of the cliff which is circled below by the Júcar. A walk through the steep alleys is well worthwhile. Most of the dwellings hollowed out of the rock have long corridors leading to balconies overlooking the other side of the cliff. Some of these dwellings, like the Masagó, can be visited.
A visit to Alcalá could well be followed by a drive along the Jorquera road which snakes its way beside the Júcar through steep-sided **gorges**.

ALBARRACÍN ★

Aragón (Teruel)
Population 1 164
Michelin map 443 K 25 – Michelin Atlas España Portugal p 55

Hidden away in the Sierra de Albarracín, this medieval city tinged with pinkish hues stands in an exceptional **site** ★, perched on a cliff above the Guadalaviar river. The ramparts extending up the hill behind the town were built by the Moors in the 10C then restored to a large extent by the Christians in the 14C. The Sierra de Albarracín has been inhabited since the Upper Palaeolithic era, as can be seen from the many **rock engravings** in prehistoric sites at Callejón del Plou and Cueva del Navaza *(5km - 3 miles southeast towards Bezas and Valdecuenca).*

The spirit of independence – In the 11C the Almoravid Beni Razin dynasty, from which the town took its name, founded a small *taifa* kingdom on the spot. A defensive wall was built against Almohad incursions and help sought from Navarra. In the mid-12C the town was ceded to the Azagras, Christian nobles from Estella in Navarra. The lords of Albarracín refused submission to the powerful Kingdom of Aragón for 50 years until James II was able to bring the fief within the royal domain in 1300.

★**THE VILLAGE** *time: 45 min*

A random wander through the narrow, steep and winding, cobbled streets will reveal a different aspect of the town at every corner. Starting out from the **Plaza Mayor**, you come to a quarter where the houses have ground floors built of limestone and overhanging upper storeys faced with rose-coloured roughcast. Fine woodwork balconies, wrought-iron grilles at the windows and the occasional coat of arms add character to the façades. The covered roof galleries are quite different from those to be found on houses elsewhere in Aragon.

Catedral ⊘ – The belfry, crowned by a smaller lantern, marks the position of the cathedral slightly south of the town centre. One of the chapels off the vast 16C nave contains a small wooden altarpiece (1566) carved with scenes from the life of St Peter. The chapter house is well worth a visit for its **treasure** which includes gold and silverwork as well as some 16C **tapestries**★, of which seven were woven in Brussels and recount the life of Gideon.

La ALBERCA★★

Castilla y León (Salamanca)
Population 958
Michelin map 441 K 11 – Michelin Atlas España Portugal p 37

La Alberca lies at the heart of the Sierra de la Peña de Francia. The region is an isolated one, traversed by few roads, and consequently has kept its character.

The village – The village exudes charm with its winding streets and unusual old houses. These are built of stone up to first floor level and surmounted by overhanging half-timbered upper storeys. The main square, known here as the **Plaza Pública** in recognition of its active community life, has an irregular shape and is partly arcaded.

Traditionally religious, the community fervently celebrates the 15 August, Assumption, with the ancient mystery play or *Loa* relating the triumph of the Virgin over the devil. Intricately-embroidered costumes are worn for the occasion.

Plaza Pública, La Alberca

EXCURSIONS

★★ **Peña de Francia** – *15km - 9 miles west.* The Peña, a shale crag of 1 732m - 5 682ft and the highest point in the range, can be distinguished from a considerable distance. The approach road is spectacular, affording wide **panoramas**★★ of the Hurdes mountains, the heights of Portugal, the Castilian plain and the Sierra de Gredos. There is a Dominican monastery with a dependent hostelry *(open in summer only)* at the top.

★ **Carretera de Las Batuecas** – This road climbs imperceptibly to the Portillo pass (1 240m – 4 068ft) before plunging through 12km - 7 miles of sharp bends into a deep, green valley in which the Batuecas monastery lies hidden. It continues beyond Las Mestas, to the desolate and long isolated **Las Hurdes** region of Extremadura, the setting in 1932 for Buñuel's film *Land without Bread*.

Miranda del Castañar – *15km - 9 miles east.* The narrow alleys of the village are lined with houses with widespread eaves and flower-filled balconies.

ALCALÁ DE HENARES

Madrid
Population 162780
Michelin map 444 or 442 K 19 – Michelin Atlas España Portugal p 40

Under the Romans the city was an important centre known as *Complutum* but the history of Alcalá is mainly linked to that of its university, founded by Cardinal Cisneros in 1498. It became famous for its language teaching and in 1517, Europe's first Polyglot Bible was published with parallel texts in Latin, Greek, Hebrew and Chaldean. The university was moved to Madrid in 1836. Today, Alcalá once again has a university and benefits from extensive industrial development.

Alcalá was the birthplace of **Cervantes, Catherine of Aragon**, daughter of the Catholic Monarchs and first wife of Henry VIII, and the Renaissance architect **Bustamante** *(qv)*.

Cervantes – Adventure and storytelling are the words that best sum up the life of **Miguel de Cervantes Saavedra** who was born in Alcalá in 1547. As a young man he spent four years in Italy after which he enlisted and fought at the Battle of Lepanto (1571) where he was wounded. In 1575 he was captured by the Turks, taken off to Algeria as a slave and rescued only after five years by Fathers of the Holy Trinity. In 1605 he published the first part of **Don Quixote** which was an immense and immediate success. In this tragi-comic masterpiece an elderly gentleman sets out as a doughty knight errant in search of adventure, hoping to redress wrongs in the terms of the storybooks he loves; he is accompanied by his simple but astute squire, Sancho Panza. The interaction of the ideal and the real, the true and the illusory, reveals the meditations of a man of 58 deeply involved in philosophy, life and the Spain of his day. His writing continued with *Exemplary Novels* or humorous stories of adventure and intrigue, comedies, *entremeses* or one-act prose farces, novels and, in 1615, the second part of *Don Quixote*. He died a year later, on 23 April 1616 – the same day as Shakespeare.

Antigua Universidad or **Colegio de San Ildefonso** ⊘ – The old university building, now used to house the university Education Offices, stands on the Plaza de San Diego. Its beautiful **Plateresque façade★** (1543) is by Rodrigo Gil de Hontañón. The **Patio Mayor**, known as the Santo Tomás de Villanueva *patio*, with its three-storeyed buildings, has a certain dignity; at the centre is a well-head with a swan motif, the emblem of Cardinal Cisneros. Across the Patio de los Filósofos stands the delightful **Patio Trilingüe** (1557) where Latin, Greek and Hebrew were taught. The **Paraninfo**, a small room formerly used for examinations and degree ceremonies, is now the setting for the solemn opening of Alcalá University terms. The decoration includes a gallery delicately ornamented in the Plateresque style, and an **artesonado** ceiling.

San Ildefonso ⊘ – This 15C chapel houses the richly carved **mausoleum★** of Cardinal Cisneros by Fancelli and Bartolomeo Ordóñez. Note the fine **artesonado** ceiling.

ALCÁNTARA

Extremadura (Cáceres)
Population 1948
Michelin map 444 M 9 – Michelin Atlas España Portugal p 49

Alcántara stands in a countryside of ancient shale rocks through which the river Tajo has cut its course, watching over the old Roman bridge which once brought it renown and from which it took its name (*Al Kantara* is the Arabic for bridge).

The Order of Alcántara – The Knights of San Juan de Pereiro changed the name of their order to Alcántara when they were entrusted with the defence of the town's fortress in 1218. Like the other great orders of chivalry in Spain – Calatrava, Santiago and Montesa – the Order of Alcántara was created to free the country from the Moors in the 12C. Each order, founded as a military unit under the command of a master, lived in a communuity bound by the Cistercian rule. These religious militias, always prepared for combat and capable of withstanding long sieges in their fortresses, played a major role in the Reconquest.

★ El Puente Romano – *2km - 1 mile northwest of Alcántara on the road to Portugal.* This magnificent construction was thrown across the Tajo, slightly below its junction with the Río Alagón, by the Romans under Emperor Trajan in 106 AD. The bridge is made of massive granite blocks held together without mortar. It is 194m - 636ft long with a central arch 70m - 230ft high, built to withstand the most formidable floodwaters. More damage, however, has been caused by man and it has had to be restored several times. The small temple at one end and the central triumphal arch are both Roman.

Convento de San Benito ⊘ – The old headquarters of the Military Order of Alcántara stands high above the Tajo. The 16C monastery buildings, now restored, include a richly decorated Plateresque church with star vaulting, a Gothic *patio* and outside, a graceful arcaded Renaissance gallery used as the backdrop for plays.

ALCAÑIZ

Aragón (Teruel)
Population 12 820
Michelin map 443 I29 – Michelin Atlas España Portugal p 44

Alcañiz, set amidst orchards and fertile olive groves, is the capital of Lower Aragón. The region is famous for its Holy Week ceremonies accompanied by incessant drum playing known as *tamborrada*.
The film director **Luis Buñuel** (1900–1983) was born in Calanda, 17km - 10.5 miles southwest of Alcañiz.

Plaza de España – Two memorable façades meet at one corner of the square: the tall Catalan Gothic arcade of the **Lonja**, where a market was once held, and the Renaissance town hall (Ayuntamiento). Both buildings are crowned by the typical Aragón gallery with overhanging eaves.

Colegiata ⊘ – A rhythmic interplay of vertical lines and curves marks the upper part of the façade of the collegiate church, rebuilt in the 18C, while below is an exuberantly baroque **portal★**. The spacious interior is divided by massive columns with composite capitals reaching up to a noticeably projecting cornice.

Castillo – The castle standing on the hilltop was the seat of the Aragón commandery of the Order of Calatrava *(qv)* in the 12C. Most of the buildings now used as a parador date from the 18C. At the far end of the courtyard are the Gothic chapel, with its single aisle of equilateral arches, and on the first floor of the keep, 14C wall paintings.

ALCARAZ

Castilla-La Mancha (Albacete)
Population 2 087
Michelin map 444 P 22 – Michelin Atlas España Portugal p 66

Alcaraz stands isolated upon a clay rise tinted with the wine colour typical of the region, in the middle of the sierra of the same name. The town, which grew rich manufacturing carpets, retains a Renaissance character marked by the style of the architect Andrés de Vandelvira who was born here in 1509.

Plaza Mayor – Among several elegant, porticoed buildings overlooking the square are the 18C **Lonja** which abuts the **Torre del Tardón** (clock tower), the 16C **Pósito**, a former municipal granary, the 16C **Ayuntamiento** (Town Hall) with a coat of arms and the 15C church of **La Trinidad** with a Flamboyant Gothic portal.
The main street or Calle Mayor, off which run stepped alleys, is fronted by old houses, testaments to the past importance of the town. Note the façade with the two warriors and the **Casa Consistorial** with its Plateresque doorway (Puerta de la Aduana).
The path leading out of the village to the cemetery affords an attractive **view** of the brown rooftops and the surrounding countryside.

EXCURSION

Nacimiento del Río Mundo – *62km - 39 miles south*.
The road passes through a wooded valley to emerge onto the Sierra de Alcaraz. 6km - 4 miles after Ríopar, take the turning left to Cueva de los Chorros. The Río Mundo, a tributary of the Segura, rises in a bubbling spring in a cave half hidden by vegetation at the foot of the steep Sierra del Calar.

ALHAMA DE GRANADA

Andalucía (Granada)
Population 5 783
Michelin map 446 U 17-18 – Michelin Atlas España Portugal p 85

Alhama is scarcely more than an overgrown village in a gently rolling, cereal-covered plain. The twisting streets and alleys leading to the well-proportioned church of golden stone are lined with white houses roofed with brown tiles.
Alhama's outstanding feature, which can best be seen from the esplanade below the public gardens, is its cliff face **site★★**. The houses are built into the steep rock below which the Río Alhama pours through a cleft, driving a series of waterwheels.
Outside the village, a path *(3km - 2 miles)* follows the ravine to a spa set in the heart of a mass of greenery beside a gurgling stream.

Water is a precious resource in drought-ridden Spain and is often carefully rationed.

ALICANTE/ALACANT★

Comunidad Valenciana

Population 275 111

Michelin map 445 Q 28 – Michelin Atlas España Portugal p 79

Plan of the conurbation in the current Michelin Red Guide España Portugal

In this friendly, typically Mediterranean town, unhurried provincial calm mixes pleasantly with the bustle of a major tourist centre.

Alicante has always been enjoyed for its remarkably luminous skies – the Greeks called it *Akra Leuka* (the white citadel), the Romans *Lucentum* (the city of light). The town came under Arab domination in 711 and was not reconquered until 1296 when James II incorporated it into the kingdom of Aragón.

The town stretches out below the Castillo de Santa Bárbara, along an immense bay between the capes of Huertas to the north and Santa Pola to the south.

Tourism and port activity – Its mild climate and proximity to vast beaches **(El Postiguet, La Albufereta** and **San Juan)** have made Alicante the tourist capital of the Costa Blanca *(qv)*. Seaside resorts such as **Santa Pola, Guardamar del Segura, Torrevieja** and **Campoamor** have sprung up all along the southern part of this flat, sandy coast.

Apart from its function as a tourist centre, Alicante plays an important role in the region's economy through its port which handles produce from the surrounding huerta (wine, almonds, dessert grapes) and from Murcia. Industry is also relatively important: metallurgy – particularly aluminum – and chemicals.

Hogueras – On 24 June, Midsummer's Day, Alicante gives itself over to the joys of the Hogueras festival. The creation of giant pasteboard figures which are set alight amidst noisy rejoicings beneath sparkling fireworks, gives citizens the chance to indulge their taste for display, satire, caricature and exuberance.

OLD TOWN

Follow the route marked on the town plan opposite

★ **Explanada de España (ABZ)** – This is the most pleasant promenade in the region with its multicoloured marble pavement adorned with geometric designs and its magnificent palms providing shade as you sit or walk beside the pleasure boat harbour. Concerts are held on the bandstand on Sundays.

Catedral de San Nicolás (AZ) ⊘ – The present building, which stands on the site of a former mosque, dates back to the beginning of the 17C. The nave, Herreran in style, is dominated by a well-proportioned cupola.

Ayuntamiento (Town Hall) (BZ H) ⊘ – This 18C palace of golden stone has a beautiful baroque façade flanked by two towers. Visit the rococo **chapel** decorated with azulejos from Manises, and two Romantic reception rooms with blue silk hangings.

Santa María (BZ) – The church stands in a picturesque square in the old town, just below Santa Bárbara castle. The façade is characteristic of 18C baroque with its wreathed columns, its pillars and the breaks in its cornices. Once a mosque, the church was rebuilt in the 14C and has since been altered several times inside, particularly in the 17C when the nave was enlarged and the sanctuary disfigured by heavy Churrigueresque decoration. Near the entrance are graceful Renaissance marble fonts and a painting on wood of John the Baptist and John the Apostle by Rodrigo de Osona the Younger.

★ **Museo de la Asegurada (BZ M)** ⊘ – Housed in an 18C palace, the museum contains an interesting collection of 20C painting and sculpture donated by the sculptor Eugenio Sempere. There are works by Spanish artists (Miró, Picasso, Gargallo, Tàpies, Saura, Genovés, Chillida and Dalí) and also by foreigners (Vasarely, Bacon, Braque, Chagall and Kandinsky).

Castillo de Santa Bárbara (BY) ⊘ – *Go up by lift and walk back down the path, either all the way (good views) or to the halfway stop.*

The fortress originally built, it is said, by the Carthaginian Hamilcar Barca, stands in a remarkable strategic position on the Benacantil hill and has played a major role in every episode of the city's history. There are three different sections; the first, the Plaza de la Torreta *(at the lift terminus)*, is surrounded by the oldest buildings, of which one houses the **Museu de Fogueras** with its exhibition of ninots or pasteboard figures burned on Midsummer's Day. A platform commands a fine **view** of the harbour, the town, Castillo de San Fernando on another hill, and of San Juan beach. The second section is 16C *(halfway point for the lift)* and the lowest, third perimeter dates back to the 17C. The footpath leads down into the narrow streets of the working-class Santa Cruz quarter of town.

EXCURSION

From Alicante to Alcoy – *70km - 43 miles north. Leave Alicante on the N 340* **(BZ)***. Take the Alcoy road at San Juan and then turn right.*

Cuevas de Canalobre ⊘ – 700m - 2 300ft up Mount Cabezón de Oro, the caves form a maze of stalactites and stalagmites, some shaped like candelabra *(canalobre)*.

**ALACANT
ALICANTE**

Alfonso X el Sabio (Av. de) ..	**AY**
Constitución (Av. de la)	**AZ** 24
Mayor..................................	**AZ**
Méndez Núñez (Rambla)	**AZ**
Abad Enalva	**AZ** 5

Ayuntamiento (Pl. del)	**BZ** 8
Capitán Meca.......................	**BZ** 12
Cervantes............................	**BZ** 15
Chapi (Pl.)............................	**AZ** 18
Chapuli	**AZ** 21
Doctor Gadea (Av. del)	**AZ** 25
Duque de Zaragoza	**AZ** 27
Elche (Portal de)	**AZ** 30
Gabriel Miró (Pl. de)............	**AZ** 33
Juan Bautista Lafora (Av. de)	**BZ** 41

López Torregrosa..................	**AY** 44
Manero Mollá	**AZ** 47
Rafael Altamira	**AZ** 53
Rafael Terol	**AZ** 56
Ramiro (Pas.)	**BZ** 58
San Fernando.......................	**AZ** 61
San José	**AZ** 63
Santa María (Pl.)	**BZ** 66
Teatre Chapi	**AZ** 67
Vicente Inglada	**AY** 69

H Ayuntamiento   M Colección de Arte del s. XX. Museo de "La Asegurada"

Return to the N340 and continue north.

The road crosses dry country dotted with fig and carob trees.

Jijona – The speciality of this small town is the manufacture of *turrón*, a sweet made of almonds and honey, exported worldwide. A small **museum** (El Lobo) and several factories are open to visitors.

Beyond Jijona the road threads its way through terraces of almond trees and up round a series of hairpin bends to a pass, the **Puerto de la Carrasqueta★** (1 024m - 3 360ft), which commands a view of the entire Torremanzanas valley with Alicante and the sea in the far distance.

Alcoy – Michelin map 445 P28. Alcoy is an industrial town (textiles, paper, metal-lurgy and confectionery) set in incredible mountain scenery at the confluence of the Serpis, Molinar and Barchell rivers.

At the end of April, Alcoy holds the **Moors and Christians** (Moros y Cristianos) **festivals** to commemorate an attack by the Moors in 1276 which ended with a Christian victory thanks to the intervention of St George.

Use Michelin Maps with Michelin Guides.

ALMAGRO ★

Bought Cuban cigar fresh Queso

Castilla-La Mancha (Ciudad Real)
Population 8 962
Michelin map 444 P 18 – Michelin Atlas España Portugal p 65

Standing in the middle of the vast La Mancha tableland, Almagro was the stronghold of the Military Order of the Knights of Calatrava *(qv)* from the 13C to the end of the 15C. The architectural wealth of the town's elegant, emblasoned façades may be explained by its distinguished past. The town had a university from 1574 to 1828 and many religious orders built convents and monasteries.
The explorer **Diego de Almagro** (1475-1538) was born here and later became Governor of Chile.
A 16C Franciscan monastery now houses the parador.
Almagro is known for its aubergines and lace.

Two bottles of wine (one great one tasted like grape juice) Beautiful Nativity scene at end of Plaza Mayor

Plaza Mayor, Almagro

B. Brillon / MICHELIN

SIGHTS

★★ **Plaza Mayor** – This elongated square is one of the most unusual in Castile. It has a continuous stone colonnade framing two sides, supporting two storeys of windows all with green surrounds. It was once the setting for bullfights and jousting tournaments.

★ **Corral de Comedias** ⊙ – This small 16C theatre *(no 17, Plaza Mayor)* with its wooden porticoes, oil lamps, stone well and scenery wall forms a charming composition in dark red and white. The International Festival of Classical Drama is held here every year.

The old streets – The walk described below takes you through cobbled streets lined with whitewashed houses where several convents and monasteries have fine stone carved doorways and grand coats of arms recalling the power of the Knights of Calatrava.

Suggested walk – Go to the end of the Plaza Mayor with the statue of Diego de Almagro and take Calle de la Nuestra Señora de las Nieves (which has some fine doorways) to the left. This leads to the triangular Plaza Santo Domingo, surrounded by mansions. Turn left into Calle de Bernardas and then take Calle de Don Federico Relimpio. Continue to the left along Calle de Don Diego de Almagro which is dominated by the imposing façade of the Dominican convent and its magnificent crest.

Convento de la Asunción (or Dominican Convent) ⊙ – The double-storeyed 16C cloisters have a fine Renaissance staircase and Plateresque doorways.

SPAIN: the Michelin Map Series at 1:400 000
When choosing a lunchtime or overnight stop
use the above maps as all towns listed in
the Red Guide España Portugal are underlined in red.
When driving into or through a town
use the map as it also indicates all places with
a town plan in the Red Guide España Portugal.
Common reference numbers make the transfer from map to plan easier.

ALMANSA

Castilla-La Mancha (Albacete)
Population 22 488
Michelin map 444 or 445 P 26 – Michelin Atlas España Portugal p 68

Almansa, once the Moorish *Al-Manxa*, spreads out around a steep limestone crag crowned by a medieval castle.

It was here that the battle of 1707, won by the Duke of Berwick against the English and their allies, secured the Spanish throne for the Bourbon king, Philip V (although peace was not signed until 1713).

Iglesia de la Ascunción – This church standing at the foot of the castle was completely transformed in the neo-classical period and retains a monumental Renaissance portal which is thought to be by Vandelvira *(qv)*.

The nearby seignorial mansion, the **Casa Grande**, has a fine 16C doorway with armorial bearings flanked by twin giants. Inside is a *patio* with superimposed galleries.

Castillo – The 15C ramparts (restored), perched precariously along the rock ridge, command a view of the plain and make a pleasant walk.

EXCURSION

Cueva de la Vieja ⊘ – *22km - 14 miles northwest via Alpera.*

This is one of the rare caves in the region that is easy to reach and still has clearly visible paintings. The elongated figures of men hunting stags with bows and arrows are typical of Levante cave painting. One of the figures has a plumed headdress, the women long robes.

ALMERÍA

Andalucía
Population 159 587
Michelin map 446 V 22 – Michelin Atlas España Portugal p 87
Town plan in the current Michelin Red Guide España Portugal

The white town of Almería spreads out between the sea and an arid hill upon which stands an impressive alcazaba. This Arab fortress is a reminder of the important role that *Al-Meriya* (meaning the Mirror of the Sea in Arabic) played in the 11C when it was the principal city of a *taifa* kingdom *(qv)*. Under the Almoravids, Almería became a den for pirates who raided as far abroad as Galicia. Determined to wipe them out, Alfonso VII captured the town in 1147 but on his death ten years later, it fell to the Moors again until the Reconquest in 1489.

Its especially mild winter climate has made it the centre of a rich farming region and an ideal tourist resort. The port exports fruit, vegetables and flowers produced by means of advanced technology in irrigation and greenhouse cultivation methods.

Life in the town centres on **Paseo de Almería**, an elegant tree-lined avenue bordered with shops, banks and cafés. The **Parque de Nicolás Salmerón** stretches out along the harbour beneath shading palms. **La Chanca**, to the west, is the fishermen's quarter, where the houses, each with its own terrace, stand in uneven lines like so many coloured cubes set into the living rock.

★ **Alcazaba** ⊘ – The Alcazaba, an Arab fortress dating back to the 8C, was badly damaged during an earthquake in 1522. However, its high, crenellated, ochre-coloured walls still dominate the town's white houses. A long wall, vestige of the old ramparts, links the fort to a second hill, the Cerro de San Cristóbal, which was formerly crowned by a castle.

Attractive **public gardens** have been laid out within the first walled enclosure where rivulets spring from fountains and flow between a variety of flower-beds. Excavations in the second enclosure, on the site of the royal apartments, have revealed sculptures and specimens of Arabic calligraphy, now displayed in the small **museum**. Immediately alongside is the former mosque, surmounted by a watchtower (Torre de la Vela). The keep with its incredibly thick walls was built by the Christians in the 15C.

The **view** from the battlements takes in the town, the Chanca district, the surrounding hills and the sea.

★ **Catedral** ⊘ – The cathedral was built in 1524 to replace the former mosque. Raids by Barbary pirates, however, decreed the construction of a fortified building – a rare necessity at the time.

In spite of its military character, the cathedral has two well-designed portals and, at the east end, a delicately carved sunburst. The spacious interior is homogeneous: the high altar and the pulpits of inlaid marble and jasper are 18C, the choir-stalls date from 1560 and the jasper *trascoro* with three alabaster statues is again 18C. The axial chapel contains the recumbent statue of the bishop who built the cathedral.

EXCURSIONS

The Almería countryside has a distinctive, desert-like appearance with cacti, aloes and prickly pears.

★**Cabo de Gata** – *29km - 18 miles east. Take the N344 then a signposted road to the right.*
The road crosses the salt flats of Acosta before reaching this desolate cape. The lighthouse on the rocky spur faces Mermaid Reef, a popular haunt for underwater fishing enthusiasts.
On the other side of the mountain is the small, pleasant summer resort of **San José** with its two beautiful beaches; los **Genoveses** and **Monsul**★ *(about 2km - 1 mile from the centre of the town).*

Níjar – *34km - 21 miles northeast. Take the N344.*
The old village, a fine example of popular architecture set high up off the road, carries on the traditional craft of jarapas or the weaving of thick hangings and bedspreads in pale colours. The wefts in the process are made of strips of already woven material *(trapo).*

★**The road northeast** – *55km - 34 miles along the N340.*
A tableland of sand dunes stretches for miles between Benahadux and Tabernas – it was used as the setting for *Lawrence of Arabia* and various westerns. Film sets are open to the public at **Mini-Hollywood**. Beyond Tabernas, the land is red and barren; pottery-making is the main occupation in the surrounding villages. **Sorbas** has an amazing **site**★ with its houses clinging to a cliff, circled below by a loop in the river course.

The road northwest – *71km - 44 miles along the N340 and N324.*
The road climbs to Guadix through a grandiose but desolate landscape of hills cut by great gorges. The aridity is occasionally relieved by a small green valley growing lemon and orange trees, or vines famous for their large sweet grapes. On 31 December, it is the Spanish custom to eat a grape at each stroke of midnight.

Castillo de ALMODÓVAR DEL RÍO★

Andalucía (Córdoba)
Michelin map 446 S 14 – Michelin Atlas España Portugal p 74

This imposing **castle** ⊙, its origins lost in history, is perched on an impressive hill dominating the wide expanses of the Cordoban countryside. The town sits at the foot of the hill on its southern side, by the Guadalquivir river. In the 8C, under Muslim domination, a large fortress already existed on this site, although its present construction dates mainly from the 14C. The castle was restored at the beginning of this century at which time a neo-Gothic mansion was added to the interior. The castle consists of two walled enclosures – one in the form of a barbican with eight different sized towers, while the larger of the two, known as the *torre del Homenaje* (keep), is in fact a turret. Once inside the castle, the narrow path behind the parapet, the parade ground and the towers are all well worth a pleasant stroll.

Las ALPUJARRAS★

Andalucía (Granada)
Michelin map 446 V 20 – Michelin Atlas España Portugal p 86

This mountainous region offering a variety of landscapes stretches across the southern slopes of the Sierra Nevada between the Gádor and Controviesa massifs. Because of its isolation from the rest of Spain it has managed to keep a traditional character.

Historical notes – In 1499 the Arabs who did not wish to leave Spain were forced to renounce their religion and to convert to Christianity. They were known as **Moriscos.** In 1566 Philip II forbade them their language and traditional dress, which sparked off a serious uprising, especially in Las Alpujarras where the Moriscos proclaimed as king Fernando Válor under the name Aben Humeya. In 1571 Philip II sent in the army under Don Juan of Austria who crushed the rebellion. However, a tense feeling of unrest remained, and in 1609 Philip III ordered the expulsion of all the Moriscos (who numbered about 275000) from Spain.

FROM LANJARÓN TO UGÍJAR *93km - 58 miles – time: half a day*

The High Alpujarras encompass the Guadalfeo river valley where the houses blend in perfectly with the landscape. The distinctive architecture of these dwellings recalls that of North Africa – white houses with a waterproof covering on their terraces made from *sierra* sand are built one against the other forming small rural settlements stepped neatly in rows up the mountainside.

Trevélez

From **Lanjarón**, a famous spa, the road climbs to the picturesque villages of **Pampaneira**, **Bubión** and **Capileira**. From here a track *(in poor condition and only open in summer)* goes up to Pico Veleta.
The route from Capileira to Pitres affords fine views of the deep valley and passes through woods of poplars, chestnuts and oaks to **Trevélez** which is famed for its hams. Beyond this point the valley begins to widen. **Yegen** is set high above the Eastern Alpujarras, while **Ugíjar**, a market town, is known for its cloth.

ALQUÉZAR★

Aragón (Huesca)
Population 215
Michelin map 443 F 30 – Michelin Atlas España Portugal p 47

Alquézar's **setting★★** is striking; at a bend in the road, the village seems to cling to a cliff dominated by a collegiate church built on the edge of the Río Vero canyon.
The village is a maze of uneven streets bordered by emblasoned house façades with rounded stone doorways. It has a charming little arcaded Plaza Mayor.

Colegiata ⊘ – The Moors built an *alcázar* on the site which later fell to Sancho Ramírez, King of Aragón. In the late 11C, early 12C, the still visible walls were constructed together with a church which was rebuilt in 1530. The north gallery of the Romanesque cloister has fine capitals carved in anecdotal archaic style illustrating the Sacrifice of Isaac, Balaam and his ass, Adam and Eve and the Last Supper. Inside the collegiate church is a beautiful Romanesque Christ dating from the 12C.

★ **Cañon del Río Vero** – The ascent of the river is quite spectacular. It takes at least a day, mostly on foot although some parts have to be swum. On the other hand, a walk to the Roman bridge at Villacantal *(time: 2 hours Rtn)* is enough to get a general impression of the canyon and its steep grey and ochre-coloured sides.

EXCURSION

Rodellar – *38km - 24 miles northwest. Take the HU 340, then turn right after Adahuesca and take the HU 343 and 341.*
This typically Aragonese village is set in the **Sierra de Guara**, a massif formed for the most part of limestone, consisting of barren plateaux through which rivers have cut impressive canyons. The best known are the Río Vero and the Mascún ravine *(barranco)* which may be reached from Rodellar. Both are popular with walkers and climbers.

Barranco de Mascún (Mascún ravine) – Natural relief features such as arches, monoliths and eroded cliff faces may be seen on a walk down into the gorges *(time: 3 hours Rtn)*.

Some hotels have their own gardens, tennis courts,
swimming pools, beach facilities;
consult the current Michelin Red Guide España Portugal.

Cuevas de ALTAMIRA★★

ALTAMIRA CAVES – Cantabria

Michelin map 442 B 17 – Michelin Atlas España Portugal p 12

The discovery of the cave – In 1879, the archaeologist **Marcelino de Sautuola**, noticed rock paintings on a cave roof which he eventually dated as prehistoric. These were the first such paintings ever to be discovered and as they were in such good condition there was widespread disbelief and scepticism in their authenticity. Only after 20 years and the discovery of similar paintings in the Dordogne Valley in France was the amazing pictorial art of Palaeolithic man fully recognised.

GUIDED TOUR ⊙

The Altamira caves consist of several galleries containing black outlines and very ancient engravings dating back to 25 000 BC, the Aurignacian Age at the beginning of the Upper Palaeolithic Period, but it is the chamber with the painted bison that has made the site famous. Known as the Sistine Chapel of Quarternary Art, this 18m - 59ft long and 9m - 30ft wide cave has an outstanding **ceiling★★★** painted during the Magdalenian Period (15 000-12 000 BC) like the Lascaux cave paintings in the Dordogne (France). Polychrome bison are shown asleep, crouched, stretching and galloping with extraordinary realism. The natural bulges on the rock face have been used with great skill to bring out body shape and to give the impression of movement. Other beasts include a wild boar running at speed and a stocky, primitive horse with a doe inside. The drawings are huge – 2m - 6 1/2ft doe at the far end of the cave, though the average is nearer 1.60m - 5ft.

The artists – who must have been in a crouched position to paint (the floor level has been lowered recently) – used natural pigments, chiefly ochre, yellow, red and brown which they reduced to a powder and mixed with animal fat. They outlined their subjects in black (with the use of charcoal) to give a firm edge to their colourwork.

Muséo ⊙ – The three sections of the museum, beside the caves, have exhibitions on the Palaeolithic Period and the importance of the discovery of Altamira, as well as a video film of the paintings on the ceiling. There is an excellent copy of the bison ceiling at the Museo Arqueológico in Madrid *(qv)*.

ANDÚJAR

Andalucía (Jaén)

Population 35 803

Michelin map 446 R 17 – Michelin Atlas España Portugal p 75

Many of Andújar's old houses and chapels date back to the 15C and 16C. The region, with Martos *(some 55km - 34 miles south)*, is Spain's major olive-producing area.

Santa María – Plaza de Santa María. El Greco's painting *Christ in the Garden of Olives*, hangs in a north chapel closed by a fine Bartolomé **grille★**. An *Assumption of the Virgin* by Pacheco can be seen in the north apsidal chapel.

EXCURSION

Santuario de la Virgen de la Cabeza – *32km - 20 miles north on the J501.*
There are good **views★★** through pines from the *corniche* road after Las Viñas. On an August night in 1227, the Virgin appeared to a shepherd on the rocky head – *cabeza* – where not long afterwards a commemorative chapel was built. In the 16C this was replaced by a monastery. Four centuries later, when civil war broke out, guards, their families and a thousand Nationalists sought refuge on the lonely rock. From September 1936 to May 1937, under their captain, Cortés, they held out against an enemy which outnumbered them tenfold. When they surrendered the sanctuary was in ruins. It has since been restored and is now a popular place of pilgrimage, particularly at the end of April.

ANTEQUERA★

Andalucía (Málaga)

Population 38 827

Michelin map 446 U 16 – Michelin Atlas España Portugal p 84

The white-walled town, a small industrial centre in the heart of a fertile valley, successfully integrates old and new buildings. Its cobblestone alleyways, windows with wrought-iron grilles, unusual roofs with coloured tiles and the many churches help to preserve its individuality. The San Sebastián belfry has fine brick Mudéjar decoration.

Museo Municipal ⊙ – The museum is housed in the 18C **Palacio de Nájera** and exhibits sacred and archaeological artefacts. The most outstanding item is the **Ephebus of Antequera★**, a bronze Roman sculpture dating from the 1C.

Santa María – Go through the 16C **Arco de los Gigantes** (Arch of the Giants) to the far end of Plaza Alta, beside the castle. The church, dating from 1514, has a façade decorated with cleverly composed geometric motifs, one of the earliest examples of Renaissance architecture in Andalucía.

Castillo – This was the first fortress captured by the Christians during the reconquest of the Kingdom of Granada (1410). It could not be held, however, as the position was encircled by the Moors. Today, there is a pleasant garden within its walls and from the towers, a fine **view**★ over Antequera's roofs and church towers to the plain and the Torcal plateau beyond.

Iglesia del Carmen ⊘ – The interior decoration of the church is entirely baroque with wavy shapes and bold colours in the wall scrollwork, the coffered ceiling and the gilded altarpieces.

EXCURSIONS

★ **Los Dólmenes** ⊘ – *On leaving town, turn left off the Granada road.*
The **Menga, Viera** and **El Romeral dolmens**, prehistoric constructions dating from 2500 to 1800 BC, take the form of funerary chambers beneath tumuli noteworthy for their Cyclopean size. Menga, the oldest and largest of the three, is an oblong chamber divided by a line of pillars supporting enormous stone slabs. The walls of Romerol, the most recent chamber, consist of small flat stones so laid as to produce a trapezoidal section in the corridor.

★ **El Torcal** – *16km - 10 miles south. Leave Antequera on the Málaga road. Bear right after 12km - 7 1/2 miles for El Torcal.*
Signposted paths lead to a monumental group of strangely shaped limestone rocks *(red arrows: 3 hours; yellow: 1 1/2 hours). For further information apply at the Refugio de El Torcal.*

★ **From Antequera to Málaga** – *62km - 39 miles south along the N331, C340 and C345.*
These pleasant well-planned roads, always within sight of majestic hills, afford splendid **views**★★ beyond the Puerto del León (Lion Pass, 960m - 3150ft) of Málaga and the Mediterranean.

ARACENA

Andalucía (Huelva)
Population 6739
Michelin map 446 S 10 – Michelin Atlas España Portugal p 72

Aracena is an attractive town set at a high enough altitude to soften the harshness of the Andalusian climate. It rises in tiers up a hillside crowned by the remains of a Templar's castle. The tower abutting the church is a former minaret and is decorated on the north side in the style of the Giralda of Sevilla *(qv)*.

★★ **Gruta de las Maravillas (Cave of Marvels)** ⊘ – Underground rivers below the castle have hollowed out vast caves covered in concretions which mirror their size in limpid pools. The series of high chambers and increasingly narrow passages follows the line of rock faults. The concretions consist of draperies, pipes and coral formations coloured by iron and copper oxide or brilliant white calcite crystal as in the first chamber discovered, which is known as El Pozo de la Nieve (Snow Well).

★SIERRA DE ARACENA

The western part of the Sierra Morena is refreshingly green; drives along winding roads between cork and eucalyptus trees are especially pleasant. The road from Aracena passes through a dense pine-wood to reach Minas de Riotinto *(35km - 22 miles south of Aracena)*, near the Campofrío reservoir.
As you approach **Minas de Riotinto**, the oldest working opencast mines in the world come into view. Although copper production stopped in 1986, gold and silver are still mined here. The landscape becomes drier to the south.
Serrano ham, which comes from this area, is considered a delicacy in Spain, especially that from Jabugo.

Information in this Guide is based on data provided at the time of going to press. Improved facilities and changes in the cost of living make alterations inevitable.

ARANJUEZ★★

Madrid
Population 35 872
Michelin map 444 or 442 L19 — Michelin Atlas España Portugal p 53

Aranjuez appears like an oasis at the centre of the harsh Castilian plain (particularly if you approach it from the south), green with shrubs and leafy avenues around the royal palaces. The shaded walks described by writers, sung by composers (Joaquin Rodrigo's famous *Concierto de Aranjuez*) and painted by artists (the Catalan, Rusiñol) are now popular with Madrileños, especially for Sunday strolls.

El motín de Aranjuez (The Aranjuez Revolt) – In March 1808, Charles IV, his queen and prime minister, Godoy, were at Aranjuez. They were preparing to flee (on 18 March) first to Andalucía, then to America, as Godoy had allowed Napoleon's armies free passage to Portugal through Spain the year before. In Portugal, the French were fighting the Portuguese who were strongly supported by the British. The Spanish people, however, had objected to the passage of the French and Godoy had advised his king to follow the Portuguese royal house (which had fled from Lisbon to Brazil) into exile. On the night of 17 March, Godoy's mansion was attacked by followers of the heir apparent, Prince Ferdinand; Charles IV dismissed his minister and was compelled to abdicate in favour of his son. This was not enough, however: Napoleon summoned both to Bayonne and made them abdicate in his own favour (5 May).

These intrigues and the presence of a French garrison in Madrid stirred the Spaniards to the revolt of May 1808 which marked the beginning of the War of Independence.

★★ROYAL PALACE AND GARDENS

The Catholic Monarchs enjoyed staying in the original 14C palace, then the Emperor Charles V enlarged the domain, but the present palace is mainly the result of an initiative by Philip II who called on the future architects of the Escorial to erect a new palace surrounded by gardens.

In the 18C, the town became one of the principal royal residences and was considerably embellished under the Bourbons. It was, however, ravaged by fire in 1727 and, no sooner was it rebuilt in 1728, it burned again. Most of the palace was then reconstructed, including the present frontage. Ferdinand VI built the town to a grid plan; Charles III added two wings to the palace and Charles IV erected the delightful Labourer's Cottage.

Palacio Real, Aranjuez

★ Palacio Real ⊘ – This classical style royal palace of brick and stone dates from the early 18C. In spite of many modifications it retains considerable unity of style and symmetry. The court of honour, overlooking a vast outer square, is framed by the main building with wings at right angles on either side; domed pavilions mark the angles.

The apartments have been left as they were at the end of the 19C.

The grand staircase was designed by the Italian Giacomo Bonavia during the reign of Philip V. The bust of Louis XIV by Coysevox recalls Philip V's French ancestry. In María Luisá's apartments, in an antechamber, are paintings by the Neapolitan artist Luca Giordano, and in the music room, a piano presented by Eugenia de Montijo to Isabel II.

The **Salón del Trono** (Throne Room), with crimson velvet hangings and rococo furnishings, has a ceiling painted with an allegory of monarchy — ironically it was in this room that Charles IV signed his abdication after the attack on 17 March 1808.

The **Salón de Porcelana★★** (Porcelain Room) is the palace's most appealing and gracefully appointed room. It is covered in white garlanded porcelain tiles, illustrating in coloured high relief scenes of Chinese life, exotica and children's games, all made in the Buen Retiro factory in Madrid in 1763. They are enhanced by carved and painted wood doors, a chandelier and a marble floor.

In the king's apartments a music room precedes the smoking or Arabian Room – a diverting reproduction of the Hall of the Two Sisters in the Alhambra in Granada. A fine Mengs Crucifixion hangs in the bedroom, and the walls of another room are decorated with **203 small pictures** painted on rice paper with Oriental style motifs.

★ **Parterre and Jardín de la Isla (Parterre and Island Garden)** – The **Parterre** extending along the palace's east front is a formal garden laid out by the Frenchman Boutelou in 1746. The fountain of Hercules brings a mythological touch to the balanced display of flower-beds and trees (cedars and magnolias).

The **Jardín de la Isla** was laid out on an artificial island in the River Tajo in the 16C. Cross the canal which once drove mill wheels to reach the park and its many fountains hidden amongst copses of chestnut, ash and poplar trees and banks and hedges of boxwood.

★★ **Jardín del Príncipe (The Prince's Garden)** – *Entrance in Calle de la Reina.* The garden beside the Tajo is more a vast gracefully laid-out park (150 ha - 371 acres). It has a surrounding grille and four monumental gateways by Juan de Villanueva. In 1763, called upon by the future Charles IV, the Frenchman Boutelou landscaped the park according to the romantic vision of nature fashionable at the end of the 18C. Within its bounds were a model farm, greenhouses with tropical plants and stables for exotic animals.

★★ **Casa del Labrador (The Labourer's Cottage)** – The so-called cottage, named after the peasant farm which originally stood on the site, stands at the eastern end of the Jardín del Príncipe and is a Versailles type Trianon built on the whim of Charles IV in a neo-classical style similar to that of the Royal Palace but with more luxurious decoration. The wrought-iron grille and balustrade surrounding the courtyard entrance are surmounted by 20 Carrara marble busts of figures from Antiquity. The interior, a reflection of Spanish Bourbon taste, is an excellent example of sumptuous 18C decoration: Pompeian style ceilings, embroidered silk hangings, mahogany doors, marble floors, furniture and lamps, canvases by Bambrilla, clocks and porcelain.

The billiard room on the first floor has a ceiling by Maella illustrating the Four Elements and magnificent embroidered silk hangings showing views of Madrid. The statue gallery is embellished with Greek busts and a marble floor covering inlaid with Roman mosaics from Mérida. The French clock in the middle of the gallery incorporates a reproduction of Trajan's column. The María Luisa room has remarkable embroidered hangings made up of 97 small pictures of Spanish towns. In the centre of the ballroom stand a magnificent malachite table and chair given to Charles IV by the Czar Alexander III. The Platinum Room or Gabinete de Platino is decorated with gold, platinum and bronze inlays while the figure of a bird in the anteroom is carved from a single piece of ivory.

Casa de Marinos (The Sailors' House) – A museum beside the former landing-stage contains the **falúas reales★★** (*royal vessels*) which once made up the Tajo fleet of launches that ferried the royal family and guests to the Labourer's Cottage. The vessels belonged to six sovereigns: Isabel II, Charles IV (whose ship has paintings by Maella), Alfonso XII (whose ship is made of mahogany), María Cristina (whose ship has paintings resembling woven hangings), Alfonso III and finally Philip V, whose vessel, a gift by a Venetian count, is remarkable for its ornate decoration in gilded, finely-carved wood.

EXCURSION

Tembleque – *47km - 29 miles south on the NIV.*
The picturesque 17C **Plaza Mayor★** in this La Mancha village is a very large quadrilateral, which must have once been used as a bullring. It is framed by a graceful three-storey portico in which the lowest arches are of stone, the upper of wood. An unusual cobweb style roof crowns one of the entrances to the square.

ARCOS DE LA FRONTERA★

Andalucía (Cádiz)
Population 26 466
Michelin map 446 V 12 – Michelin Atlas España Portugal p 83
See PUEBLOS BLANCOS DE ANDALUCÍA

Arcos has a remarkable **site**★★ atop a crag overlooking a loop in the Guadalete river. The best views are from the narrow road that crosses the dam east of Arcos and joins the N 342 to Bornos. The old town, right at the top of the rock, is huddled against the formidable crenellated castle walls and those of the two churches.
Holy Week processions are known for their fervour.

Park the car below the village in Paseo de Andalucía and walk up through the narrow alleys to Plaza del Cabildo (following the signs to the parador).

Plaza del Cabildo – One side of the large square overhangs the deep river precipice. The **view**★ extends to a wide meander of the Guadalete which encloses fields of cereals and fruit trees.

Iglesia de Santa María ⊙ – The **west face**★ of this church is a good example of Plateresque. The interior, with its mixture of Gothic, Mudéjar, Plateresque and baroque, has some fine star-vaulting and a late Renaissance altarpiece. An alley, Callejón de las Monjas, runs along the north side beneath the church's flying buttresses.
A charming maze of narrow alleys leads to the other side of the cliff and the **Iglesia de San Pedro** with its baroque bell tower.

ASTORGA

Castilla y León (León)
Population 13 802
Michelin map 441 E 11 – Michelin Atlas España Portugal p 10

In Roman times, *Asturica Augusta* (as Astorga was then known), was a major road junction; in the Middle Ages it was famous for its fairs and as a halt for pilgrims on their way to Santiago de Compostela *(qv)*.
Food lovers will relish Astorga's **mantecadas** or light bread rolls.

La Maragatería – Long ago an ethnic group of unknown origin, but possibly of mixed Gothic-Moorish blood, settled in this part of the Astorga region. These Maragatos led an isolated existence in the heart of an inhospitable region where they became muleteers. They may still be seen at religious festivals or weddings in their national costume of voluminous knee breeches, shirt front and wide embroidered belt. Jacks in full Maragato dress can be seen striking the hours on the clock of the **Ayuntamiento** on the **Plaza Mayor**.

SIGHTS

★ **Catedral** ⊙ – Building began with the east end of the church in a Flamboyant Gothic style in the late 15C and was not completed until the 18C, which explains the rich Renaissance and baroque work on the façade and towers. The front **porch**★ low reliefs illustrate specific events in the Life of Christ such as the Expulsion of the Moneylenders from the Temple and the Pardoning of the Adulterous Woman. Above the door is a beautiful Deposition.

Interior – The nave is large, with an impressive upsweeping effect created by the innumerable slender columns soaring from the pillars. Behind the high altar is a **retable**★ by three artists named Gaspar – Gaspar de Hoyos and Gaspar de Palencia were responsible for the painted, gilt decoration, and **Gaspar Becerra** (1520-1570), an Andalusian, for the low reliefs. After studying in Renaissance Italy, Gaspar Becerra developed a personal style of humanist sensitivity far removed from the baroque expressionism of the Spanish sculptors.

Museo de la catedral ⊙ – The cathedral museum contains a rich collection of gold and silver plate, including a 13C gold filigree Holy Cross reliquary and a 10C reliquary of Alfonso III, the Great. There is also a beautiful 13C Romanesque painted wood chest.

Palacio Episcopal ⊙ – This fantastic pastiche of a medieval palace was dreamed up by Gaudí *(qv)* in 1889. The original, brilliant interior decoration, especially that in the neo-Gothic chapel on the first floor, is a profusion of mosaics, stained glass and intersecting ribbed vaults.
The palace houses the **Museo de los Caminos** (Museum of the Way of St James) ⊙, a collection of medieval art reflecting the theme of pilgrimage.

The scallop shell, the attribute of St James the Great, became the emblem of pilgrims to Santiago de Compostela.

ÁVILA★★

Castilla y León
Population 49 868
Michelin map 442 or 444 K 15 – Michelin Atlas España Portugal p 38

Ávila, "Ciudad de cantos, ciudad de santos" *(city of stones, city of saints)*, stands within magnificently preserved 12C walls. It is Spain's highest provincial capital, situated on one of the plateaux of the Meseta at 1 131m - 3 710ft. The Castilian climate at such an altitude is extreme – winters are long with bitingly cold winds. Ávila, the birthplace of St Teresa, has long been marked by the saint's strong personality; her spirit pervades the entire town. Even the local speciality **yemas de Santa Teresa** or candied egg yolk, bears her name.

The city of St Teresa – St Teresa of Jesus (1515-1582), whose visions deeply affected her contemporaries, is one of the greatest mystics of the Roman Catholic Church. Living at a time when the Reformation was gaining adherents throughout Western and Central Europe, and the monastic orders, grown rich in power and possessions, were relaxing their discipline, she succeeded in widely re-establishing the strict observance of the Carmelites, gaining converts and founding convents.

Her letters are famous, particularly those to her spiritual director, St John of the Cross, as are her mystical writings and her autobiography, *Life*, published in 1588. She was canonised in 1622 and made a Doctor of the Church in 1970.

Several buildings in Avila preserve the memory of the saint, including two museums, one in the **Convento de San José (Las Madres)** (**B R**), the other in the **Convento de La Encarnación** (**B**). The **Convento de Santa Teresa (La Santa)** (**A B**) was built on the site of the house where she was born. The remains of the saint, however, are not in Ávila but in Alba de Tormes *(qv)*.

The walls of Ávila

SIGHTS

★★ **Murallas (City walls)** – The ramparts are complete and form one of Europe's most vivid examples of medieval fortifications. The best place for a general **view** of them is a spot known as **Cuatro Postes** or Four Posts on the Salamanca road. The crenellated walls punctuated by advanced bastions and towers (88 in all) enclose a quadrilateral area of 900m x 450m - 2 953ft x 1 476ft. The greater part dates from the 11C and has managed to keep an overall impression of unity in spite of modifications in the 14C. The sentry path along the top is open to the public.

★★ **Catedral** (**B**) ⊙ – The fortified **east end** of the cathedral serves as an advanced bastion in the ramparts and is crowned with a double row of battlements. The use of granite and the church's defensive stance give the exterior an austere appearance which window tracery, portal carvings and a ball decoration along the upper outlines of the tower, buttresses and pinnacles do little to mellow. The 14C **north doorway** with French Gothic decoration, unfortunately in stone too friable to resist erosion, originally stood in the **west front** but was removed in the 15C by Juan Guas when he redesigned the main entrance there. This was remodelled in the 18C in an unusual style more suitable for a palace.

The **interior** is a total contrast to the exterior with its high Gothic nave, its chancel with sandstone patches of red and yellow and its many **works of art★★**. These include the **trascoro** (1531) which has many beautifully detailed Plateresque statues (from left to right: the Presentation of Jesus in the Temple, the Adoration of the Magi and the Massacre of the Innocents) which blend into a harmonious whole, the **choir-stalls** from the same period, and two delicately worked wrought-iron **pulpits** – one Renaissance, the other Gothic.

ÁVILA

Alemania	B 2	Caballeros	B 6	Ramón y Cajal	A 19
Generalísimo Franco	B 14	Calvo Sotelo (Plaza de)	B 8	San Segundo	B 22
Reyes Católicos	B 21	Cardenal Pla y Deniel	B 10	San Vicente	B 24
Alférez Provisional (Av. del)	B 4	Esteban Domingo	B 12	Santa (Pl. la)	A 25
		General Mola (Plaza)	A 13	Sonsoles (Bajada de)	B 27
		Jimena Blázquez	A 15	Telares	A 28
		Lope Núñez	B 16	Tomás Luis de Victoria	B 30
		Marqués de Benavites	AB 18	Tostado	B 31

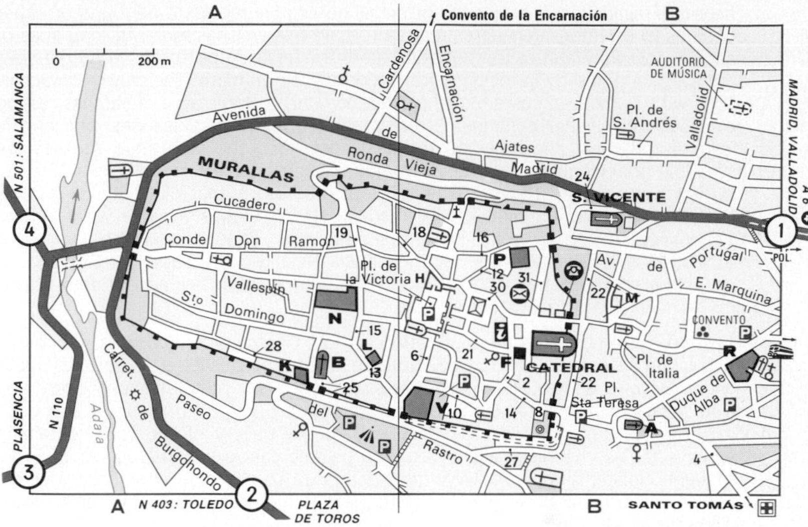

A Iglesia de San Pedro	**K** Palacio de Núñez Vela	**P** Palacio de los Verdugos
B Convento de Santa Teresa	**L** Torre de Guzmán	**R** Convento de San José (Las Madres)
F Palacio de Valderrábanos	**N** Palacio de Polentinos	**V** Palacio de los Dávila

At the end of the apse, in which the windows are still Romanesque – the cathedral's construction lasted from 1135 to the 14C – is a large painted **altarpiece** (*c*1500) by Pedro Berruguete and Juan de Borgoña. It has a gilt wood surround with Isabelline features and Italian Renaissance style pilasters. Against the back and sides of the high altar which face onto the double ambulatory are five carved Renaissance panels: those on the sides show the four evangelists and the four holy knights (Hubert, George, Martin and James). In the centre of the ambulatory is the sculptor Vasco de la Zarza's masterpiece: the alabaster **tomb**★★ of Don Alonso de Madrigal, theologian and prolific writer, who was Bishop of Ávila in the 15C and nick-named El Tostado or The Swarthy. He is shown writing before a beautiful Epiphany. The embroidery on the chasuble has been rendered with particular delicacy.

Museo ⏲ – Preceding the museum is a 13C ante-sacristy followed by a **sacristy**★★ from the same period which has a remarkable eight-ribbed vault, a massive 16C alabaster altarpiece and, in place of windows, wood sculptures of the four scenes of the Passion in imitation alabaster.

In the museum are a head of Christ by Morales painted on a tabernacle door, a portrait by El Greco, a monumental Isabelline grille, late 15C antiphonaries and a colossal monstrance 1.70m-5ft 8in high made by Juan de Arfe in 1571. The Gothic **cloisters** have recently been restored.

In the Plaza de la Catedral the former **Palacio de Valderrábanos** (**B F**), now a hotel, has a fine 15C doorway surmounted by the family crest.

★★ **Basílica de San Vicente** (**B**) ⏲ – This vast Romanesque basilica, which took from the 12C to the 14C to build, and, therefore, has ogive vaulting, stands on the alleged site of the 4C martyrdom of St Vincent of Zaragoza and his sisters, Sabina and Cristeta. The 14C south gallery with its slender columns clustered and ringed, the carved cornice extending the full length of the nave, the tall porch added to the west front and the two incomplete towers, all combine to form a harmonious whole.

The **west portal**★★ is outstanding for the statue columns beneath the richly decorative cornice and covings which seem so lifelike that they might almost be gossiping at the church entrance. The style of their clinging robes recalls that of sculptures in Vézelay, France. Inside, beneath the 14C **lantern**★ is the **martyrs' tomb**★★, a late 12C masterpiece under an unusual 15C Gothic canopy with a pagoda shaped top. The martyrdom of St Vincent and his sisters is depicted on the tomb so masterfully, both technically and evocatively, that it has been attributed to the same unknown sculptor as the west portal. The scenes of the martyrs' capture below the walls of Ávila, their stripping and torture, are particularly powerful.

★ **Monasterio de Santo Tomás** (B) ⊘ – This Dominican monastery founded at the end of the 15C and embellished with gifts from the Catholic Monarchs, who on occasion made it their summer residence, was also the university and the seat of the Inquisition.

The **church** façade incorporates the principal decorative motifs to be found on other buildings in the monastery: architectural details are emphasised with long lines of balls – a common feature throughout Ávila but here used profusely – and the yoke and fasces adopted by Ferdinand and Isabel as their emblem. The church, in accordance with Dominican custom of the time, has only a single aisle, its arches resting on clusters of slender columns. A rare feature are the two galleries, one on the west for the choir, the other on the east containing the high altar. As they are accessible only from the cloisters, the monks alone had access.

The fine **mausoleum**★ (1512) in the transept crossing is that of Prince Juan, only son of the Catholic Monarchs, who died at 19. Its alabaster table with delicate Renaissance carving is by the Florentine, Domenico Fancelli who also carved the Catholic Monarchs' mausoleum in the Capilla Real (Royal Chapel) in Granada. In one of the north chapels another fine Renaissance tomb belongs to Juan Dávila and his wife, the prince's tutors.

Claustro (Cloisters) – Beyond the unadorned 15C **Claustro de los Novicios** is the **Claustro del Silencio**★, small enough to be intimate and generously carved on its upper gallery. Beyond is the **Claustro de los Reyes** (Catholic Monarchs' Cloister), larger and more solemn with spectacularly bare upper arching.

From the Claustro del Silencio, stairs lead to the gallery of the *coro* containing beautiful 15C Gothic **choir-stalls** carved with pierced canopies and arabesques. From the same cloister's upper gallery, more stairs go to the high altar gallery where one can see in detail Berruguete's masterpiece in high relief, the **retable of St Thomas Aquinas**★★ (*c*1495).

Iglesia de San Pedro (B A) ⊘ – Standing on the vast **Plaza Santa Teresa**, this fine Romanesque church shows early Gothic influence in its pointed arches and especially in the delicate rose window in the façade. A lantern lights the transept.

Palacio de los Verdugos (B P) – The façade of this Gothic Renaissance palace, emblasoned above the entrance and window with the family crest, is flanked by two stout square towers.

Palacio de Polentinos (A N) – This palace, now a barracks, has a finely decorated Renaissance entrance and *patio*.

Torre de Guzmán (A L) – The Oñates' palace is distinguished by this massive square corner tower, complete with battlements, dating from the early 16C.

Palacio Núñez Vela (A K) – Now the Law Courts, the former residence of the viceroy of Peru is a Renaissance palace with windows framed by slender columns surmounted by coats of arms. There is a beautiful inner *patio*.

Palacio de los Dávila (AB V) – The palace consists of several seignorial mansions: two 14C Gothic buildings embellished with coats of arms give onto Plaza Pedro Dávila and two others, belonging to the Episcopal Palace, give onto Plaza de Rastro.

BADAJOZ

Extremadura
Population 130 247
Michelin map 444 P 9 – Michelin Atlas España Portugal p 61
Town plan in the current Michelin Red Guide España Portugal

If possible, approach Badajoz from the north so as to be able to appreciate the majestic entrance afforded by the alignment of the **Puente de Palmas**, a Herreran style granite bridge, and the 16C crenellated gateway of the same name. The town rises in tiers up a hill dominated by the walls of an Arab fortress.

An eventful history – Badajoz, in Roman times a modest town dependent on Mérida, became capital, in the 11C, of a Moorish kingdom or *taifa* (qv). In the 16C it held a key position in peninsular strategy and was caught up in the Wars of Succession between Spain and Portugal, which meant that it was often besieged and pillaged.

For centuries, the embattled town was shut away in narrow streets, protected by the Moorish fortress and medieval ramparts.

Today, the modern quarters stretching beyond the old town are a reminder that Badajoz is the capital of Spain's largest province. It is emerging economically as a result of the Guadiana Valley development scheme.

Manuel Godoy Álvarez de Faria (1767-1851) – Godoy, son of a modest provincial hidalgo, left his family at 17 for the Court where he enlisted in the Guards. Favours from Queen María Luisa assisted him in a meteoric career in politics; by the age of

25 he had been appointed Prime Minister. His rapid success earned him little sympathy from the Court, or from the common people who, outraged, accused him of being in Napoleon's pay. They insisted on his leaving the country. After the Aranjuez uprising *(qv)*, he followed the royal family into exile at Bayonne where he drew up Charles IV's act of abdication which was to deliver Spain to Napoleon. He died, unknown, in Paris in 1851.

SIGHTS

Catedral ⊙ – The cathedral, built in the 13C in the Gothic style, was considerably remodelled at the Renaissance and is consequently full of contrasts: it has a fortress type tower as well as a delicate Plateresque decoration of friezes and window surrounds. Inside, in the middle of the nave and masking the general view, is an impressive *coro* for which the stalls were carved in 1557.
In the sacristy to the right of the chancel hang six fine 17C Flemish tapestries.

Museo arqueológico provincial ⊙ – The 16C Palacio de la Roca inside the alcazaba now houses a modern museum with rich collections of local archaeological finds. These include prehistoric and proto-historic stelae and figurines; Roman mosaics and tools made of bronze; beautiful Visigothic **pilasters** carved with plant and geometric motifs; medieval artefacts and exhibits of work from the Islamic civilisation.

BAEZA★★

Andalucía (Jaén)
Population 17 691
Michelin map 446 S 19 – Michelin Atlas España Portugal p 76

Baeza, once a prominent frontier town, stands peacefully surrounded by olive groves on the Andalucía-La Mancha border. Its many seignorial mansions and other buildings of golden stone give an idea of its days as a *taifa* capital *(qv)*, of its importance as the first town to be reconquered in Andalucía (1227) and its position as a march in the Kingdom of Castilla until the 15C. Peace allowed the city to develop and intellectual interests to emerge: in 1551 a printing press was established and in 1595 a university was founded (disbanded in the 19C).

★★ ARCHITECTURAL CENTRE *time: 1 hour*

Route marked on plan overleaf

★ **Plaza del Pópulo** (**Z**) – Standing in the centre of the small, irregular square is the **Fuente de los Leones** (Fountain of the Lions), built with antique remains. The former **Carnicería** (Abattoir) (**A**), on the left, is a building of noble appearance considering its function (1550-1962); the blason over the first floor portico represents the imperial coat of arms.
The **Casa del Pópulo** (former court), at the end of the square, has decorative Plateresque windows and medallions. The six doors once opened on six notaries' offices; court hearings were held on the first floor. An attractive quarter-circle balcony projects onto the **Puerto de Jaén**, which, along with the Villalar arch, was dedicated to Charles V. The Jaén gate was erected to mark the emperor's visit on his way to Sevilla for his marriage to Isabel of Portugal on 12 March 1526. The **Arco de Villalar** was dedicated as a gesture of submission to the king after his victory, in 1521, over the Comuneros *(qv)* whom the town had supported.

Plaza de Santa María (**Z**) – On the left the walls of the 1660 Seminary are covered with inscriptions – the ancient custom having been to inscribe in bull's blood one's name and date on graduation. Behind the **Fuente de Santa María**, a triumphal arch adorned with atlantes, is the Gothic façade of the **Casas Consistoriales Altas** (**F**), emblasoned, between twin windows, with the arms of Juana the Mad and Philip the Fair.

★ **Catedral** (**Z**) ⊙ – The **interior** ★ was almost entirely remodelled by Vandelvira and his followers between 1570 and 1593. Some of the chapels are outstanding: the Gold Chapel beside the fonts has a delicate Italianate relief; St James's has a

Plaza Santa María, Baeza

F. Bouillot / MARCO POLO

BAEZA

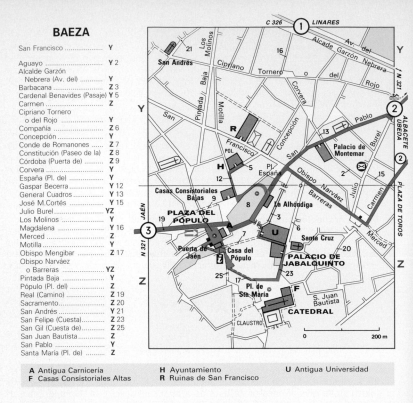

A Antigua Carnicería
F Casas Consistoriales Altas
H Ayuntamiento
R Ruinas de San Francisco
U Antigua Universidad

fine antique setting and St Joseph's is flanked by caryatids. The graceful door to the sacristy is adorned with scrollwork and angels' heads. A monumental iron grille by Bartolomé closes the first bay in the nave while a pulpit of painted beaten metal (1580) stands in the transept crossing. At the end of the north aisle, behind a grille and a metal curtain, is a gold and silver monstrance (1714) which is carried in procession on Corpus Christi.

The arches in the cloisters are from the former mosque.

★ **Palacio de Jabalquinto** (Z) – The palace's **façade**★, a perfect example of the Isabelline style, is best seen in the morning when the finials cast impressive shadows and the sun accentuates the Gothic decoration of the windows and pinnacles beneath slanting armorial bearings. The **patio**, built *c*1600, is of more sober style, the only informal feature being the two lions guarding the great baroque stairway.

Opposite the palace is the Romanesque church of **Santa Cruz**, the only one to remain of those built immediately after the town's reconquest.

Antigua Universidad (Z U) – The plain façade and elegant patio of this former university were built between 1568 and 1593. A fine Mudéjar ceiling can be seen in the large lecture hall.

La Alhóndiga (Z) – The old Corn Exchange features a frontage of arches and porticoes (1554).

Casas Consistoriales Bajas (Z) – This was built in 1703 as a gallery for officials attending celebrations held in the square.

★ **Ayuntamiento (Town Hall)** (Y H) – The façade of the former prison stands transformed by magnificent Plateresque windows, the armorial bearings of Philip II and of the town, and a wide cornice embellished with portraits of important persons carved on modillions.

ADDITIONAL SIGHTS

Iglesia de San Andrés (Y) ⊙ – Delicate Plateresque sculpture ornaments the south entrance of this church. The sacristy contains a group of nine Gothic paintings★.

Ruinas de San Francisco (Ruins) (Y R) – Only the vast transept and apse, with majestic carved stone altarpieces, remain to give an idea of the beautiful 16C church that once stood here.

Palacio de Montemar (or **Palace of the Counts of Garcíez**) (Y) – Beautiful Gothic windows and a Plateresque style *patio* adorn this early-16C nobleman's palace.

BAIONA / BAYONA★

Galicia (Pontevedra)

Population 9 690

Michelin map 441 F 3 – Michelin Atlas España Portugal p 20 – Local map under RÍAS BAJAS

The port of Baiona at the mouth of the Vigo inlet or *ría* faces out across its vast bay and is protected from ocean storms to the north and south by the Monte Ferro and Monterreal rock promontories. On 10 March 1493, the caravel *Pinta* – one of the three vessels in Christopher Columbus's fleet – captained by **Martín Alonso Pinzón**, sailed into Baiona bringing news of the discovery of the New World. In the 16 and 17C, the town developed considerably through sea trade.

The old town – Baiona has grown into a lively summer resort with a harbour for fishing boats and pleasure craft fronted by a promenade of terrace cafés. In the old quarter houses may still be seen with coats of arms and glassed-in balconies. The **Excolegiata** (former collegiate church) ⊙ at the top of the town was built in a transitional Romanesque-Gothic style between the 12 and 14C. Symbols on the arches of chisels, axes and knives represent the various guilds that contributed to the building of the church. Note also the stone pulpit dating from the 14C.

Monterreal ⊙ – The Catholic Monarchs had a defence wall built around Monterreal promontory at the beginning of the 16C. The fort within, which became the governor's residence, has been converted into a parador, surrounded by a pleasant pine-wood. A **walk round the battlements**★ *(about 1/2 hour)*, rising sheer above the rocks, is well worthwhile for the splendid **views**★★ of the bay, Monte Ferro, the Estela islands and the coast with its sandy coves stretching south to the Cabo Silleiro headland.

THE BAIONA-A GARDA ROAD *30km - 19 miles – time: about 1 hour*

The coast between the two towns is a flat, semi-deserted area indented by the sea.

Oia – The houses in the fishing village are clustered around the former Cistercian abbey of **Santa María la Real** with its baroque façade. On the other side of the road are the outlying slopes of green hills where wild horses roam. Festivals known as *curros*, during which the wild foals are rounded up for branding, are held in the hills on certain Sundays in May and June.

A Garda – This small fishing village stands at the extreme southern end of the Galician coastline. To the south, **Monte Santa Tecla**★ (341m - 1 119ft) rises above the mouth of the Miño, affording fine **views**★★ from the top. On the slopes are the extensive remains of a **Celtic city**, testimony to habitation by man from the Bronze Age to the 3C AD. Two round huts with stone walls and thatched roofs have been reconstituted on the side of the road.

BARBASTRO

Aragón (Huesca)

Population 15 827

Michelin map 443 F 30 – Michelin Atlas España Portugal p 57

Barbastro lies at the centre of the Somontano, a fertile plain into which two long, rugged Pyrenean valleys descend. The first leads down from the Parque de Ordesa *(qv)*, the second incorporates a canyon, the Congosto de Ventamillo *(qv)*. The town was a substantial market centre at the time of the Moors and later became and still is an episcopal see, a mark of its regional importance. On 11 August 1137, Barbastro was the setting for the marriage of Princess Petronila and Ramón Berenguer IV, a match sealing the union of Aragón and Catalunya.

★ **Catedral** ⊙ – The cathedral is a typical Spanish hall-church of the 16C but has particularly slender columns. While the capitals are plain, the network vaulting is ornate with abundant relief work. The side chapel doors are decorated in Churrigueresque style with an incredible quantity of stucco. An **altarpiece** with an alabaster base by Damián Forment decorates the high altar. The first north chapel contains a fine early-16C painted altarpiece.

EXCURSION

Torreciudad ⊙ – *24km - 15 miles north on the N 123 and A 2211.*
In 1804, an 11C Romanesque statue of Our Lady of Torreciudad was placed in a small shrine and venerated by the local people. In 1975 a church, now a place of pilgrimage, was built for the statue under the auspices of Monsignor José María Escrivá de Balaguer, founder of Opus Dei (1928). Preceding the brick buildings is a vast esplanade affording beautiful **views**★★ of the Pyrenees and, in the foreground, the El Grado dam. The church itself has a large nave and a modern alabaster altarpiece with relief work illustrating scenes from the Life of the Virgin. The statue of Our Lady of Torreciudad stands in the lower part of the altarpiece.

BARCELONA★★★

Catalunya

Population 1 681 132

Michelin map 443 H36 – Michelin Atlas España Portugal p 32

Plan of the conurbation on Michelin map 443 and in the current Michelin Red Guide
España Portugal-Michelin town plan Barcelona, scale 1:12 000, 41

Barcelona, the capital of Catalunya and the second largest city in Spain, stretches along the Mediterranean shore between the hills of Montjuïc, Vallvidrera and Tibidabo. It is a most attractive, stimulating city, especially from an architectural point of view.

The growth of the city – The city was founded by the Phoceans. It grew in the Roman era and was known as **Barcino** in the 1C BC. The Romans settled on Mount Taber (the site of the present cathedral) and a fortified wall was built in the 3C. In the 12C, Barcelona took control of most of the former Catalan earldoms and became the capital of Catalunya and the seat of the joint kingdom of Aragón-Catalunya as well as a very important market centre. It conquered considerable territories in the Mediterranean. At the same time, the Catalan Gothic style of architecture blossomed, many new buildings were erected and the city spread beyond its walls.

During the War of the Spanish Succession (1701-1714), Catalunya took sides with Charles, Archduke of Austria. After the victory of the Bourbons (on 11 September 1714) Barcelona lost its municipal government and its historical independence. Montjuïc hill was then fortified, a citadel, Ciutadella, was built and the district of Barceloneta was developed. The townspeople were not allowed to build beyond the walls within a radius of 2km – 1.2 miles, a distance corresponding to the range of cannon fire. The town then grew upwards inside the ramparts, with an extraordinarily high population density. The ban on building was not lifted until the middle of the 19C when a decision was taken to urbanise all the no-man's land around the old city. To this end the Cerdà plan *(p 75)* was chosen. Over a period of thirty years, Barcelona grew quickly and substantially, rapidly incorporating small neighbouring villages such as Grácia, Sants, Horta, Sarrià and Pedralbes. Industrialisation made Barcelona one of the most active towns in Europe and two International Exhibitions were held here, one in 1888 (on the site of the Ciutadella) and the other in 1929 on Montjuïc hill. There was an explosion of Modernist architecture during this period.

Barcelona present and future – More dynamic than ever, Barcelona is not only a large industrial centre with a very busy port, it is also a university town and the seat of the Generalitat de Catalunya. It is an important cultural centre with an opera-house and many museums, theatres and concert halls.

•••••••••••••••• **Barcelona today** ••••••••••••••••

- For a real taste of the atmosphere in Barcelona, one should begin with a stroll along the **Rambla** *(qv)* and Passeig de Gràcia, the city's most representative avenues, and also explore the maze of small streets in the Gothic quarter.

- **Cafés and restaurants** – *For restaurants see the Michelin Red Guide España Portugal.* The area around Eixample has a great many cafés and restaurants, some with Modernist decor, others very avant-garde. In the Gothic quarter and the area around the port the restaurants are more traditional, while the small ones in **Barceloneta** which serve paella and sea food have become very popular because of their proximity to the sea.

- **Shopping** – Barcelona's smartest shops – fashion, furniture design and antiques – are in and around Passeig de Gràcia, in the Rambla de Catalunya, Diagonal and either side of Plaça de Joan Carles I. There's another important shopping area on the seabord side of Plaça de Catalunya – itself dominated by the *El Corte Inglés* department store – in Avinguda Portal de l'Angel (with *Las Galerias Preciados*, another department store) and around the Rambla

- **Entertainment** – Barcelona has two famous concert halls: the Liceu (**LY**) opera-house *(destroyed by a fire in January 1994. A reconstruction project is being planned)* and the **Palau de la Mùsica Catalana** (**MV Y**). There is also a wide choice of theatres and cinemas. *Guía de Ocio*, an entertainment guide, is on sale in all news-stands.

- **Amusement Parks** – Barcelona's two famous amusement parks are both on hills. The first, Montjuïc (**CT**) may be reached by cable-car from the port, and the second, **Tibidabo** (**AR**), is approached by road or by funicular railway served by trams and buses. From the top of the 532m - 1 745ft hill there are excellent **panoramic views**★★ of Barcelona, the Mediterranean and the hinterland.

- **Transport** – Barcelona's black and yellow taxis are easy to find but if you prefer public transport the city's four underground lines serve most districts. A bus network covers the whole town. Booklets of tickets valid for ten journeys are available.

The Olympic Games, held in Barcelona in 1992, brought about the development of large-scale planning projects which have had an enormous impact on the city's appearance. These included the extension of the Diagonal, the building of a ring-road in the north of the city, and the reconstruction of part of the seafront which was converted from a free port zone into a residential area.

Catalan identity – Barcelona is above all a Catalan town. This is evident in the use of Catalan which is considered the official language along with Castilian Spanish. The Catalan people are proud to speak their own language which was banned for many years under the Franco regime. A simple stroll around the city will reveal that all the street names and signs are in Catalan. The same goes for the literature, as a glance at a bookshop window will show.

A thriving centre for artists – Barcelona has been and still remains a thriving city and place of residence for great artists. Among the best-known modern artists are the painters Picasso (p 73), Miró (p 75), Dalí, Tàpies (p 76), the sculptor Subirachs and the architects Gaudí (p 75), Josep Lluis Sert, Bofill and Bohigas.

★★ BARRI GOTIC (THE GOTHIC QUARTER) (MX)

Time: 3 hours including museum visits. See town plan p 71.

The Gothic quarter, so named on account of its many buildings constructed between the 13 and 15C, is, in fact, far older. There are traces of the Roman settlement as well as of the massive 4C walls built after barbarian invasions.

Plaça Nova (128) – This is the heart of the Gothic quarter. The Romans built a rectangular site with walls 9m - 30ft high and attendant watch-towers of which the two that guarded the West Gate remain to this day. In the Middle Ages when the town expanded beyond the walls, the gateway was converted into a house.

Opposite the cathedral, the **Collegi d'Arquitectes** (College of Architects) (**L**) stands out as an architectural surprise amongst the old buildings. Its modern façade has a decorative band of cement engraved by Picasso.

★★ Catedral ⊙ – The present cathedral, dedicated to St Eulalia and the Holy Cross, was built to replace a Romanesque church. Construction began at the end of the 13C, ending only in 1450. The west face and spire are modern (19C) reconstructions of the original designs by a builder from Rouen in France (hence the French influence in the gables, pinnacles and crockets).

The Catalan Gothic style **interior** has an outstanding elevation due partly to the delicate, slender pillars. The nave is clearly lit by a fine lantern above the first bay but the vista is unfortunately broken by the *coro*. This contains double rows of beautifully carved 15C **stalls**. The painted armorial bearings are those of the chapter of the Knights of the Order of the Golden Fleece who used to meet here under Charles V. Note also the humorous, delicately carved little scenes decorating the misericords.

The white marble **choirscreen ★** was sculpted in the 16C after drawings by Bartolomé Ordóñez, one of the greatest Renaissance artists in Spain. It illustrates the death of St Eulalia, 4C virgin and martyr, who was born in Barcelona and became patron of the town. Her relics lie in the **crypt** in an alabaster sarcophagus carved in the Pisan style in the 14C.

The Capilla del Santo Sacramento (Chapel of the Holy Sacrament), to the right as you enter the main door, contains the 15C Christ of Lepanto which is believed to have been mounted on the prow of the galley belonging to Don Juan of Austria during the Battle of Lepanto.

The side chapels, rich in Gothic altarpieces and marble tombs, include a retable to St Gabriel in the central ambulatory chapel; another of the **Transfiguration ★** by Bernat Martorell is in St Benedict's chapel, the second one south from St Gabriel's; and the retable in the following chapel depicts the Visitation.

Outside, across from the cathedral, is the **Casa de l'Ardiaca** (Archdeacon's House) (**A**) with a charming patio.

Claustro – The cloisters, built in 1448, form an oasis of greenery with their palms and magnolias and are enlivened by a flock of geese. Only one of the immense bays has the stone tracery and the slender columns intended for each.

A museum (**museu** ⊙), located in the chapter house off the west gallery, displays a *Pietà* (1490) by the Cordoban, Bartolomé Bermejo and altarpiece panels by the 15C artist, Jaime Huguet.

When you leave the cloisters, take Carrer Montjuïc del Bisbe opposite.

Plaça Sant Felip Neri (163) – The Renaissance houses surrounding this small square were moved here when Via Laietana was being built, to make room for the new street.

Leave the square on Carrer Sant Sever and turn right into Carrer del Bisbe Irurita.

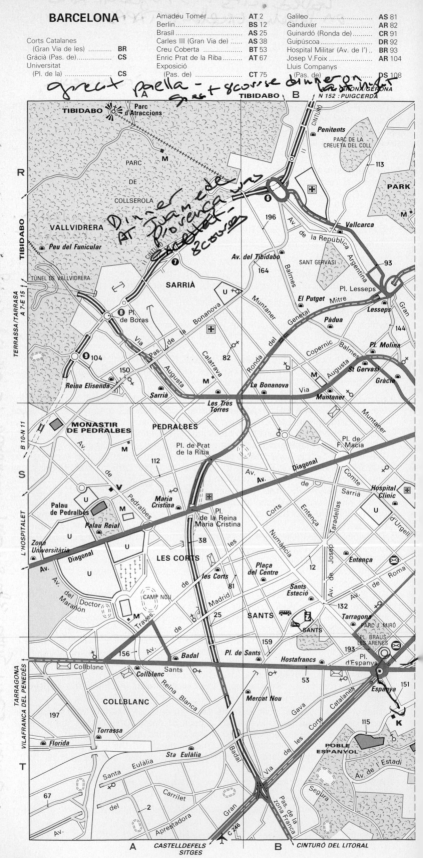

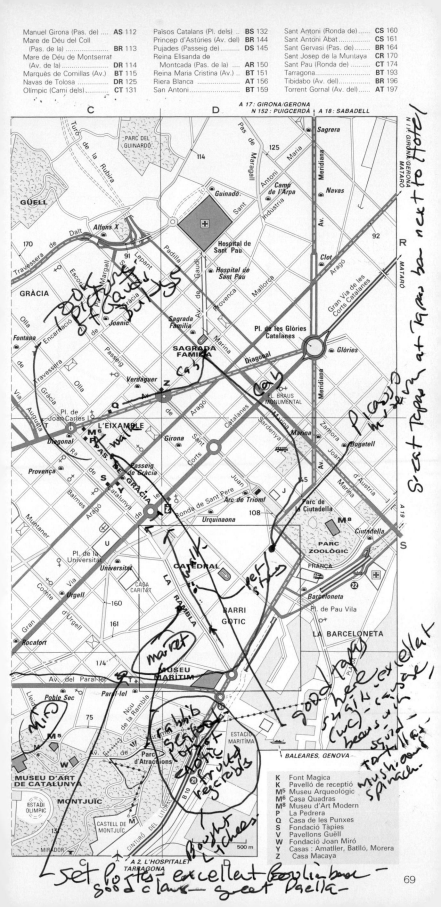

BARCELONA

A   Casa de l'Ardiaca
B   Casa dels Canonges
C   Saló del Tinell
E   Palau del Lloctinent
F   Capella Sta-Agata
H   Ajuntament
K   Mirador del Rey Martí
L   Collegi d'Arquitectes
M¹ Museu d'Història
        de la ciutat
M⁷ Castell dels tres Dragons
R   Palau de la Virreina
Y   Palau de la Mùsica
        catalana

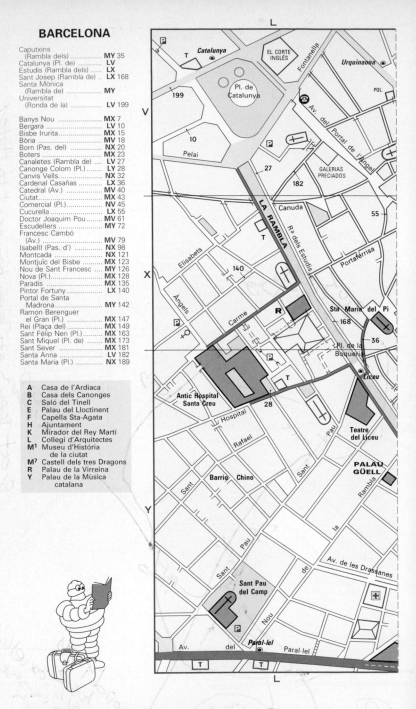

Carrer del Bisbe Irurita (**15**) – The right of the street is bordered by the side wall of the Palau de la Generalitat (Provincial Council). Above a doorway is a fine early-15C medallion of St George by Pere Johan. The left of the street is bordered by the **Casa dels Canonges** (Canons' Residence) (**B**), now the residence of the President of the Generalitat. A neo-Gothic covered gallery (1929), over a star-vaulted arch, spans the street to link the two buildings.

Palau de la Generalitat (Provincial Council) ⊘ – This vast 15 to 17C edifice is the seat of the Autonomous Government of Catalunya. It has a classical style façade on the Plaça Sant Jaume. The Generalitat has a set of bells; concerts are given on Sundays at midday.

Ajuntament (Town Hall) (**H**) – The Town Hall façade on Plaça Sant Jaume is neo-classical while that on Carrer de la Ciutat is an outstanding 14C Gothic construction.

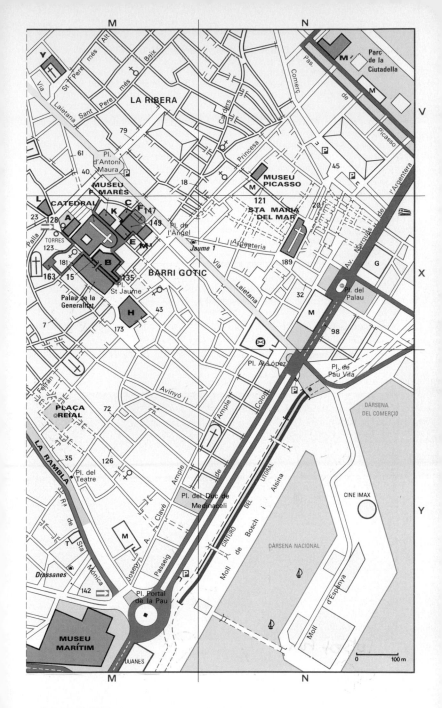

Carrer del Paradís (**135**) – At no 10 stand four Roman columns, remains of the **Temple of Augustus**.

Carrer del Paradís leads into Carrer de la Pietat which is bordered on the left by the Gothic façade of the **Casa dels Canonges** (Canons' Residence) (**B**). The cathedral cloister doorway opposite is adorned with a wooden 16C sculpture of a *Pietà*.

★**Plaça del Rei** (**149**) – Two sides of the square are bordered by buildings of the Royal Palace which include the Talaia or **Mirador del Rey Martí** (**K**), a tall five-storey watch-tower, the **Saló del Tinell** (**C**) (credence room), a former refectory with six Roman arches supporting a wooden ceiling with a 17m - 56ft span, and lastly, the 14C **Agueda** (or St Agatha Chapel) (**F**), built in the pure Catalan ogival style, which houses the large **altarpiece of the Constable** or the **Epiphany** by Jaime Huguet. The third side of the square is bordered by the **Palau del Lloctinent** (Vice Regal Palace) (**E**), a Renaissance building which contains regional archives, and the Casa Padellàs which houses the Museu d'Història de la Ciutat (City History Museum).

Museu d'Història de la Ciutat (City History Museum) (**M¹**) ⊘ – Casa Padellàs, a beautiful 15C home with a fine Gothic *patio*, was moved here when Via Laietana was being built in 1931. Substantial remains of the Roman city discovered at the time may be seen from the museum basement. The excavations spread underground beneath Plaça del Rei and the cathedral to include foundations of Roman houses, water channels, a store for wine jars and traces of a palaeo-Christian basilica.

★★ **Museu Frederic Marès** ⊘ – The sculptor Frederic Marès donated the collections to the city of Barcelona. The museum is in the Royal Palace, the residence of the Counts of Barcelona who were crowned kings of Aragón in 1137. The collections (on three levels) are rich in polychrome wood statues and demonstrate the development, continuity and variety of Spanish art.

Basement: stone sculpture, Romanesque and Gothic capitals and Romanesque portals including a most unusual primitive doorway from the 12C Tubilla del Agua monastery.

Ground floor: Iberian ex-votos, Punic terracottas, a 4C palaeo-Christian sarcophagus, a 12C stone sculpture of a group scene illustrating the Calling of St Peter by the Master of Cabestany and an impressive **collection**★ of polychrome wood sculpture of Crucifixes, Calvaries and Romanesque Virgins, including the 12-13C pewter covered wood statue of the **Virgin of Plandogau**.

1st floor: following on from Jaime Huguet's altarpiece of the Way of the Cross is a sculpture section showing works through the ages from the 14C to the 19C, including in particular a 16C **Entombment**★ of six separate figures and a 17C Adoration of the Magi by the sculptor Pedro de la Cuadra.

Museu Sentimental – *On the 2nd floor.* This is a large collection of objects used in everyday life including fans, pipes, snuffboxes and parasols.

Plaça Ramon Berenguer el Gran (**147**) – A section of the Roman city wall has been incorporated into the palace precincts.

lotsof fun –

La Rambla, Barcelona

★ **LA RAMBLA** *time: 1 1/2 hours*

The most famous street in Barcelona, La Rambla, made up of five different sections, follows the course of an old river-bed bordering on the Gothic quarter. La Rambla forms a long exuberant promenade between Plaça Portal de la Pau where the Columbus monument rises near the harbour, and Plaça de Catalunya which separates the Eixample district from the old quarter. At all times of the day and night a colourful crowd of locals, tourists and down and outs moves along the street beneath the plane trees, passing the bird and flower sellers and the newsstands that sell papers and magazines in every language. Various monuments can be seen on either side of the street.

★★ **Drassanes** (Shipyards) **and Museu Marítim** (**MY**) ⊘ – The former shipyards near the Monument a Colom (Columbus monument), consist of ten sections, seven dating from the 14C and the other three, beside La Rambla, from the 17C. They provide a perfect setting for the maritime museum with their long timber roof supported on a series of arches. Among the many models of sailing boats and steamships is the life-size copy of the Real, the galley in which Don Juan of

Austria sailed at the Battle of Lepanto. The map room contains a copy of the 1375 Catalan atlas by Abraham and Jafudra Cresques (the original is in the Bibliothèque Nationale in Paris) as well as some portulans (13-16C navigation charts) of the Mediterranean Sea.

★ **Plaça Reial (MY)** – This vast pedestrian square shaded by palm trees and lined with cafés is surrounded by neo-classical buildings constructed between 1848 and 1859. With its shoe-shiners and other small tradespeople it has kept its picturesque air. The fountain in the middle is flanked by lampposts designed by Gaudí. A stamp and coin market is held here on Sunday mornings.

The **Xines** (Barrio Chino) **(LY)** on the other side of La Rambla has inspired many writers. Although renovation has begun in this notorious working-class district where the bars and nightlife are typical of any large port, some streets are still risky.

Palau Güell ★ (Güell Palace) **(LY)** ⊘ in Carrer Nou de Rambla was built in 1888 and is now a theatre museum. It is one of the buildings designed by Gaudí *(qv)* and has a very interesting interior in terms of both architecture and furniture.

Further up La Rambla, on the left, the 1845 opera-house or **Teatre del Liceu (LY)** (its interior destroyed by fire in January 1994) is held by some to be one of Europe's most beautiful concert halls.

Turn right from Plaça de la Boqueria into Carrer Cardenal Casanas.

Iglesia de Santa Maria del Pi (LX) ⊘ – This 14C Catalan Gothic church is striking for its simplicity and the size of its nave. It stands in an attractive square (that bears its name) in which a flea market is held on Thursdays.

Return to Plaça de la Boqueria and take Carrer del Hospital opposite.

Antic Hospital de la Santa Creu (LY) – This complex of Gothic, baroque and neo-classical buildings is a veritable haven of peace in the middle of a very lively district. This former hospital now houses the Library of Catalunya. The former courtyard has been converted into a public garden. A charming *patio* can be reached through a hall decorated with *azulejos*.

As you leave the complex in Carrer del Carme, you will be able to see the future Museo de Arte Contemporáneo (Museum of Contemporary Art) at the end of Carrer dels Angels opposite. Part of the museum will be housed in the former Casa Caritat hospital.

Return to La Rambla on Carrer del Carme.

Palau de la Virreina (Palace of the Vicereine) (LX R) – This graceful 1778 palace was built for the vicereine of Peru.

Continue up La Rambla to Plaça de Catalunya.

★**CARRER DE MONTCADA (NX 121)**

Time: 1 1/2 hours including a visit to the Museu Picasso – plan of old city pp 70-71

The street, which takes its name from the powerful Montcada family, is in the Ribera district, east of the Gothic quarter. Its Gothic mansions housed originally the aristocracy and then, until the 18C, the wealthy bourgeoisie. Some of the residences are open to the public. Behind the unadorned façades are minute patios, their pure lines conforming perfectly to the golden rule of medieval Catalan architecture. Along one side, a single flight of steps, supported by a rampant arch, leads to the first floor, often with the added elegance of an arcaded gallery.

The following is a selection of small palaces with beautiful *patios:* the 15C Palau de Berenguer de Aguilar, now the Museu Picasso, the 14C Palau del Marqués de Lió which houses the Museu Tèxtil i d'Indumentària (Textile and Costume Museum), the 17C Palau Dalmases at no 20 with baroque frieze decorations on the staircase, and the 16C Palau Cervelló at no 25, now the Maeght Gallery, with a fine flight of steps.

★**Museu Picasso (NV)** ⊘ – The Gothic palaces of Berenguer de Aguilar and Baron de Castellet provide a wonderful setting for the museum. Many of Picasso's (Málaga 1881 - Mougins 1973) works are displayed, dedicated, in most cases, to his friend Sabartès of whom there are several portraits (including an abstract painting of him wearing a ruff).

Picasso's advanced genius is evident in work from his youth: portraits of his family, *First Communion* and *Science and Charity* (1897). Among examples of his early work in Paris are *La Nana* and *La Espera*, while *Los Desemparados* (1904) is from his Blue Period and the portrait of *Señora Casals* from his Rose Period. His *Las Meninas* series painted in 1959 consists of liberal variations on the famous picture by Velázquez.

Picasso's skill as an engraver may be seen in his outstanding etchings of bullfighting and his talent as a ceramist in the many vases, dishes and plates (donated to the museum by Jacqueline Picasso) that he made in the 1950s.

★**Santa Maria del Mar** (NX) ⊘ – The recently restored church is one of the most beautiful examples of the Catalan Gothic style. It was built in the 14C by local sailors who in spite of their modest means, wanted to compete with the wealthy townspeople who were building the cathedral. The result is a gracefully proportioned church, outstanding in its simplicity. The walls are unadorned in the Catalan manner and the west front decorated only by a portal gable and the buttresses flanking the Flamboyant rose window. The interior gives the impression of harmonious spaciousness due to the elevation of the nave and the side aisles divided only by slender octagonal pillars. *(man Jweck)*

★**MONTJUÏC** (CT) *time: 1 day, including museum visits – see general plan*

The 'mountain of the Jews' is a 213m - 699ft hill overlooking the city. When the citizens of Barcelona rose in revolt against Philip IV in 1640 they built a fort (**CT**) on the hill (now home to a military museum). The castle terraces command extensive **views★** of the city and the harbour to the south. Montjuïc hosted the International Exhibition in 1929 and since then **Plaça de Espanya** (**BT**), the gateway to the exhibition, has remained a major centre for World Fairs. Among the many remaining monuments and pavilions built for the event are the illuminated **fountain** (**BT K**) or *Font Magica* by Carles Buïgas, at the end of Avinguda de la Reina Maria Cristina, the recently reconstituted **pavilion** by Mies van der Rohe, outstanding for its simplicity, modernity and the variety of materials used, and the Spanish Village (Poble Espanyol in Catalan, Pueblo Español in Castilian). A Frenchman, Forestier, designed the gardens in the midst of which now stands a large amusement park (**CT**).

★★★**Museu d'Art de Catalunya** (**Museum of Catalonian Art**) (**CT**) ⊘ – The museum is in the National Palace that was built for the 1929 exhibition. The **Romanesque and Gothic departments** ★★★ contain beautiful items from many small churches in Catalunya and Aragón.

Romanesque period: a highly expressive popular art of extraordinary maturity developed in the 12C and 13C, particularly in the Pyrenean valleys, as can be seen in the displays of frescoes and wood altarfronts and carvings.

The **frescoes** are beautifully displayed in large rooms which recreate the size of their original churches. Like Byzantine mosaics, they have heavy black outlines, a superimposed frieze composition, lack of perspective and rigidity of stance. Their subjects too, remain in the Byzantine tradition (Christ or the Virgin in Majesty in a mandorla). But the addition of realistic or expressive details transforms the paintings into something wholly Spanish. Among the most outstanding are the frescoes from Boí (rooms 3 and 4) with the stoning of St Stephen, others from Pedret and Santa Maria de Aneu (room 10), from Sant Climent de Taüll (rooms 14 and 15) of which the apse has a remarkable Christ in Majesty, and from Santa Maria de Taüll (room 16).

The **altarfronts** of painted wood take up the same subjects and style. They divide into two main types: those painted on a single panel like that from the cathedral at Seo de Urgel, and those carved in relief, such as that from Santa Maria de Taüll.

Gothic period: from the 14C, altarpieces proliferated, becoming the main form of church decoration. Painting, at the time, was strongly influenced by the Italian style (as in the Santa Coloma de Gramenet altarpiece by **Juan de Tarragona**); relief also began to be used increasingly. By 1400 Catalan art had become a mainstream on its own, assimilating foreign influences, with leaders such as **Luis Borrassá** and his followers **Raimundo de Mur** (painting *c*1400-1415) and **Bernat Martorell** (painting *c*1430-1450), whose works are delicate in the extreme. Flemish naturalism eventually predominated, as can be seen in the famous *Retable of the Councillors* (1445) by **Luis Dalmau**, ultimately combining with a supreme elegance in works by such painters as **Jaime Huguet**, whose many works include the 1445 retable dedicated to St Michael in Santa Maria del Pi, and **Bartolomé Bermejo**.

Romanesque altarfront in the Museu d'Art de Catalunya

H. Sterlin.

[handwritten: mobils by Calder were fascinating - neat fountain with mercury.]

★ **Poble Espanyol (Spanish Village)** (BT) ⊘ – The village was built for the 1929 exhibition to illustrate regional styles in Spanish architecture. A walk through it will reveal a picturesque variety of local features ranging from a small Castilian square, a street in an Andalusian village with white-walled houses set off by flowering geraniums, to a Mudéjar tower from Aragón. There are also restaurants, old shops (a chemist's and a perfume shop) and craftsmen at work making traditional Spanish wares. *[handwritten: really enjoyed. Bought Miro print]*

★ **Fundació Joan Miró** (CT W) ⊘ – The foundation was created by the Barcelona artist Joan Miró (1893-1983) in 1971 and inaugurated in 1976. Miró's personality has left its mark on the town through his very original work which may be seen everywhere, from the wall ceramics in the airport to the ground mosaics in La Rambla. His work, a reflection of the artist himself, is a mixture of playfulness, humour, buoyancy and grace *(see the video films on the artist)*.

The museum is a well-proportioned modern building designed by Josep Lluis Sert (1902-1983), a Catalan architect who also planned the Maeght Foundation in St-Paul-de-Vence in France. The collection includes a great many of Miró's paintings and sculptures, especially those from the last twenty years of his life, as well as works by other artists such as Matisse, Tanguy, Max Ernst and Chillida.

Sculptures by contemporary artists may be seen in the museum grounds.

★ **Museu Arqueològic (Archeological Museum)** (CT M⁵) ⊘ – The museum has excellent presentations of megalithic civilisation in Spain (dolmens from Antequera, *talayots* from the Balearics and Punic art from burial-grounds in Ibiza) as well as Roman and Hellenistic collections excavated at Empúries, the antique Barcino and Badalona. Other exhibits include small bronze Roman statues, a rotunda (room 22) painted with delicate motifs after the Centenarian's House in Pompeii and the mosaics entitled *Circus Games* in the large central gallery.

EIXAMPLE AND MODERNIST ARCHITECTURE *see general plan*

The word *Eixample* (in Catalan) or *Ensanche* (in Castilian) means enlargement. Barcelona's Eixample district was added to the town as a result of the Cerdà Plan in the 19C.

The Cerdà Plan – 1859. The plan adopted for Eixample consists of a grid pattern of streets, some parallel to the sea, others perpendicular to it. The streets circumscribe blocks of houses (called *mançanes* in Catalan or *manzanas* in Castilian, also meaning apples) which are octagonal in shape because the right-angled corners have been trimmed off. This plan is crossed by two wide diagonal avenues, Avinguda Diagonal and La Meridiana, which meet on Plaça de les Glòries Catalanes. One of the great attractions of the Eixample district is its wealth of Modernist architecture.

Modernist architecture – This developed between 1890 and 1920 alongside similar movements in other parts of Europe, such as Art Nouveau in France, Modern Style in Great Britain (and in the United States), Sezession in Austria and Jugendstil in Germany. Modernist architecture sprang from artistic exploration that combined new industrial materials with modern techniques, using decorative motifs like curve and counter-curve and asymmetrical shapes in stained glass, ceramics and metal. It enjoyed great success in Catalunya at a time when large fortunes were being made as a result of industrialisation. The most representative architects of the style were Antoni Gaudí, Domènech i Montaner, Puig i Cadafalch and Jujol. A parallel movement in Catalan literature known as Renaixença also flourished during this period.

Gaudí (1852-1926) – Antoni Gaudí, born in Reus, studied architecture in Barcelona. His style was influenced first by Catalan Gothic architecture with its emphasis on large areas of space (wide naves, the effect of airy spaciousness) and subsequently by the Islamic and Mudejar styles. He also studied nature, observing plants and animals which inspired his shapes, colours and textures. He gave full rein to these images – liana-like curves, the rising and breaking of waves, rugged rocks and the serrations on leaves and flowers – when designing his fabulous buildings. Part of his great originality lay in his use of parabolic arches and spirals (as can be seen in the chimneys of Casa Milá). An intensely religious man, Gaudí drew upon a great many symbols for his buildings, especially for the Sagrada Familia (Church of the Holy Family) on which he worked for over forty years. He spent his last years here, hidden away in a small room in the middle of the site, until his tragic death when he was run over by a tram.

Gaudí worked a great deal for the banker **Eusebi Güell**, his patron and admirer, who asked him to design his private houses.

Gaudí's main works: Sagrada Familia, Casa Batlló, La Pedrera, Casa Vicens, Palau Güell, Pavellons Güell and Parc Güell.

Lluís Domènech i Montaner (1850-1923) – He attained his highly decorative style through extensive use of mosaics, stained glass and glazed tiles.

His main works: Palau de la Mùsica Catalana, Casa Lleó Morera, Castell dels Tres Dragons, Hospital de Sant Pau and Casa Montaner i Simó.

Josep Puig i Cadafalch (1867-1956) – The mixture of regional and foreign architectural tradition in his work reflects the Plateresque and Flemish styles.
His main works: Casa de les Punxes, **Casa Macaya** (1901) (**DR Z**) and Casa Quadras (1904).

★★ **La Sagrada Familia** (**Church of the Holy Family**) (**DR**) ◷ – The project begun by Francisco de P. Villar in 1882 was taken over by Gaudí in 1883. He planned a church shaped like a Latin Cross with five aisles and a transept with three aisles. On the outside, three façades were each to be dominated by four tall spires representing the Twelve Apostles and, above the transept crossing, a central spire flanked by four other spires were to represent Christ and the Evangelists. The nave was planned to look like a forest of columns. In his lifetime, only the crypt, the apsidal walls and the Nativity façade were finished. The Nativity façade comprises three doorways, Faith, Hope and Charity, richly decorated with statues and groups of carved figures. Just one spire was completed. After Gaudí's death, work resumed in 1940 and today there are eight spires together with the Passion façade which was completed in 1981. The Sagrada Familia is still a vast building site which can be disappointing to visitors if they have not been warned. From the top of the East spire there is a good overall view of the work on the church as well as of Barcelona beyond. One of Domènech i Montaner's main works, **Hospital Sant Pau** (**DR**), with its remarkable glazed tile roofs, may be seen at the end of Avinguda de Gaudí.

★★ **Passeig de Gràcia** (**CS**) – This luxurious street, adorned with elegant wrought-iron street lamps by Pere Falqués (1906), contains the finest examples of Modernist architecture in Barcelona. The styles of the three most famous Modernist architects can be compared in the block of houses known as the **Manzana de la Discordia** (Apple of Discord): no 35 **Casa Lleó Morera** (1905) (**Y**) by Domènech i Montaner, no 41 **Casa Amatller** (1900) (**Y**) by Puig i Cadafalch and lastly no 43 **Casa Batlló** ★ (1905) (**Y**) by Gaudí, with its extraordinary mosaic façade and its undulating roof covered in scales. From the street corner, in Carrer d'Aragó, you can see Domènech i Montaner's Casa Montaner i Simó

J. L. Bohin/EXPLORER

Gaudí's Casa Batlló, Barcelona

which now houses the Tàpies Foundation *(see Fundació Antoni Tàpies below)*. A little further along Passeig de Gràcia on the right, Gaudí's **La Pedrera** ★ ◷ or quarry (1905) (**CS P**), also known as **Casa Milá**, resembles an underwater cliff face. A visit to the roof-top, with its chimneys and ventilation funnels arrayed like some weird, wild army, is an eerie experience.

Turn right from Plaça de Joan Carles I into Avinguda Diagonal.

Avinguda Diagonal - **Casa Quadras** (1904) (**CS M⁶**) on the right, by Josep Puig i Cadafalch, houses the **Museu de la Mùsica** ◷, which has a remarkable collection of instruments from all over the world. A little further along on the left, **Casa de les Punxes** (**CR Q**), by the same architect, bears the stamp of Flemish influence.

★★ **Parc Güell** (**BC R**) ◷ – The park is the most famous of Gaudí's undertakings commissioned by Güell. Gaudí's extraordinary imagination is particularly evident here; the visitor has the impression of entering an enchanted world with mushroom-like houses, undulating benches and a mosaic dragon on a flight of steps. The covered walks seem intended for some initiation ritual, as they turn into caves and alcoves surmounted by cacti.

★ **Palau de la Mùsica Catalana** (**MV Y**) ◷ – *Carrer de Sant Pere Mès Alt*. The palace of Catalan music is Domènech i Montaner's most famous work. The façade is richly adorned with mosaics while the concert hall has extraordinarily sumptuous decoration and an inverted cupola of stained glass.

★ **Fundació Antoni Tàpies** (**CS S**) ◷ – The foundation was created by the artist himself – who was born in Barcelona in 1923 – and set up in a former publishing house in the Modernist Montaner i Simó building designed by Domènech i Montaner. The brick building is crowned by a large aerial sculpture by Tàpies called *Núvol i Cadira* (cloud and chair), the emblem of the museum. It is a fitting example of the painter's symbolic universe.

The interior, a vast bare sober space where everything is painted in colours favoured by Tàpies (brown, beige, grey and ochre), is lit by skylights (a cupola and a pyramid) and sets off the artist's work remarkably well. The collection of over 300 paintings and sculptures tracing the development of Tàpies' work since 1948 is displayed on a rota basis. The foundation is also a research centre and the wooden bookshelves that once belonged to the publishing house have been kept for a library.

ADDITIONAL SIGHTS

★**Monastir de Pedralbes (Pedralbes Monastery) (AS)** ⊘ − Although the village of Pedralbes has been incorporated into a residential quarter of Barcelona, it still preserves its rustic charm.

Founded in the 14C by King James II of Aragón and his fourth wife, Doña Elisenda de Montcada, the monastery has a fine Catalan Gothic church which houses the sepulchre of the foundress. The vast three-storey cloisters surrounded by cells and oratories are sober and elegant. St Michael's chapel is adorned with beautiful **paintings★** by Ferrer Bassá (1346), a Catalan artist strongly influenced by Italy.

The **Thyssen-Bornemisza collection★** *(access via the cloisters)* is on display in the former monk's dormitory and in the Sala de la Reina (Queen's Room). It contains 72 paintings and 8 sculptures (from the Middle Ages to the 18C) which were part of the large collection (over 800 works) on show at the Museo Thyssen-Bornemisza in Madrid. Among the numerous works with a religious theme, **Fra Angelico's** magnificent *Virgin of Humility* and **Zurbarán's** Santa Marina stand out, as do several paintings of the *Virgin and Child* (B. Daddi, 14C and L. Monaco, 15C). Another room worthy of special mention is the **Sala de los Retratos** (Portrait Room) which contains some fine examples of various 15C and 18C schools.

Palau de Pedralbes (Pedralbes Palace) (AS) ⊘ − The palace is located in the university quarter.

Between 1919 and 1929 the city of Barcelona built a residence for King Alfonso XIII which was influenced by palaces of the Italian Renaissance. The palace interior is noteworthy for its decoration and some fine art objects including tapestries, furniture and Murano chandeliers. The recently acquired collection of ceramics in the **Museu de Cerámica★** ⊘, previously in the Museu d'Art de Catalunya, comprises a diverse panorama of Spanish ceramic art with special emphasis on 18C *azulejos*, in particular *plafones* or large decorative panels.

Pavellons Güell (Güell Lodge) (AS V) − The entrance to the grounds has a particularly remarkable wrought-iron grille by Gaudí *(qv)*, decorated with a dragon.

La Ciutadella (The Citadel) (DS) ⊘ − The citadel − which could hold a garrison of 8 000 soldiers − was built on the orders of Philip V in 1716 to enable closer surveillance of Catalan rebels. It was razed in 1868 and replaced by public gardens. Several of the buildings erected in the park for the 1888 International Exhibition remain, including the **Castell des Tres Dragons (NV M⁷)** by Domènech i Montaner. It is a castle-like brick building which now houses a zoological museum. Boating is possible on a lake in the park. The monumental fountain near the lake was planned by Gaudí while still a student.

★**Parc Zoològic** (Zoo) **(DS)** ⊘ − The zoo takes up a large part of the Parc de la Ciutadella. It has a rich collection of animal species from all over the world and its star attraction is an albino gorilla. The Aquarama gives shows featuring dolphins.

Museu d'Art Modern (Museum of Modern Art) **(DS M⁸)** ⊘ − The museum is housed in a building of the former citadel which escaped demolition and contains works by Catalan artists from the 19C and the early 20C including Fortuny, Ramón Casas, Nonell, Regoyos, Gargallo and Sert.

Sant Pau del Camp (St Paul in the Fields) (LY) − The church was built as part of a Benedictine monastery at the end of the 10C and has preserved some of its original pavement and capitals on the portal. It has a charming little 11-12C **cloister★**.

The current **Michelin Red Guide España Portugal** *offers a selection of pleasant hotels in convenient locations. Each entry specifies the facilities available (gardens, tennis courts, swimming pool, beach facilities) and the annual opening and closing dates. There is also a selection of establishments recommended for their cuisine - well-prepared meals at moderate prices; stars for good cooking.*

BÉJAR

Castilla y León (Salamanca)
Population 17 027
Michelin map 444 or 441 K 12 – Michelin Atlas España Portugal p 50

Béjar's hill site is seen to best advantage when you approach the small town from the northwest. The town (known for its sheets and woollen fabrics) stretches out along a narrow rock platform at the foot of the Sierra de Béjar.

EXCURSIONS

★ **Candelario** – *4kms - 2 1/2 miles south.*
The picturesque village of Candelario is a maze of very steep, unevenly paved alleys lined with whitewashed houses. These have exposed grey stone window surrounds and tie-beams as well as flower-filled upper galleries of wood beneath spread eaves. An unusual feature is the waterproofing by means of upturned tiles on whole sections of walls. Similarly, house entrances are protected by gates to combat the rushing torrents in the streets when the mountain snows melt.

Baños de Montemayor – *17km - 11 miles southwest on the N 630.* The thermal spa retains its old quarter with the wooden balconies typical of houses in the sierra.

Hervás – *23km - 14 miles southwest on the N 630.* The bustling **judería** or old Jewish quarter with its winding alleyways has a lively atmosphere reminiscent of the Middle Ages.

BELMONTE★

Castilla-La Mancha (Cuenca)
Population 2 601
Michelin map 444 N 21 – Michelin Atlas España Portugal p 54

Belmonte, the native town of the 16C prose writer **Fray Luis de León** *(qv)*, retains some monumental gateways and part of the perimeter which linked town and castle.

Enter through one of the gateways and head towards the Plaza Mayor where there is a tourist information office.

Antigua Colegiata – This 15C collegiate church contains an interesting collection of altarpieces made by local artists in the 15, 16 and 17C. The 15C **choir-stalls★**, from Cuenca cathedral, illustrate, with stark realism, scenes from Genesis and the Passion. The font in which Fray Luis de León was christened has been preserved.

Castillo ⊙ – This hexagonal fortress, flanked by circular towers, was built in the 15C by Juan Pacheco, Marqués de Villena, as part of the defences of his vast domain. It was subsequently abandoned until the 19C when it was restored, although it had lost all its furnishings. In 1870 the triangular *patio* was disfigured by a brick facing ordered by the new owner, Eugenia de Montijo. All that remains in the empty rooms are beautiful Mudejar **artesonado★** ceilings – the audience chamber is outstanding – and delicately carved stone window surrounds. Follow the curtain walls for the stepped merlons for a view of the village and the austere La Mancha countryside beyond.

EXCURSION

Villaescusa de Haro – *6km - 4 miles northeast.*
The 1507 **Capilla de la Asuncíon** (Chapel of the Assumption) ★ belonging to the parish church is a magnificent late Gothic construction. It has crenels, a Gothic-Renaissance altarpiece and a wrought-iron screen with a flowery Gothic design of three arches.

BETANZOS★

Galicia (La Coruña)
Population 11 871
Michelin map 441 C 5 – Michelin Atlas España Portugal p 3

Betanzos, a onetime port now silted up, stands at the end of its *ría*. It was once the flourishing market for the rich Las Mariñas valley which provided wheat for the whole La Coruña province. At the centre of the town a substantial reminder of this former prosperity may be seen, in the form of three Gothic churches remarkable for their pure lines and rich ornamentation. The precincts with steep streets and old houses with glassed-in balconies maintain the old-world atmosphere.

★ **Iglesia de Santa María del Azogue** ⊙ – The name of the 14-15C church comes from *suk* or market-place in Arabic. The gracefully asymmetrical façade is given character by a projecting central bay pierced by a rose window and a portal with sculptured covings. Niches on either side contain archaic statues of the Virgin and the Archangel Gabriel, symbolising the Annunciation. Inside, three aisles of equal height, beneath a single timber roof, create an effect of spaciousness.

★ **Iglesia de San Francisco** ⊘ – This Franciscan monastery church, in the shape of a Latin Cross embellished with a graceful Gothic east end, was built in 1387 by the powerful Count Fernán Pérez de Andrade, Lord of Betanzos and Puentedeume. It is chiefly remarkable for the many tombs aligned along its walls, the carved decoration on its ogives and chancel arches and the wild boar sculpted in the most unexpected places. Beneath the gallery to the left of the west door is the monumental **sepulchre** ★ of the founder, supported by a wild boar and a bear, his heraldic beasts. Scenes of the hunt adorn the sides of the tomb; his hounds lie couched at his feet, while at his head an angel greets his soul.

Santiago – The church, built in the 15C by the tailors' guild, stands on higher ground than the two mentioned above. Its interior resembles that of Sta María. Above the main door is a carving of St James *Matamoros* or Slayer of the Moors, on horseback. The 16C **Ayuntamiento** (Town Hall) abutting the east end is embellished with an arcade and a fine sculpted coat of arms.

BILBAO / BILBO

País Vasco (Vizcaya)
Population 372 054
Michelin map 442 C 21 – Michelin Atlas España Portugal p 13
Local map under COSTA VASCA
Town plan in the current Michelin Red Guide España Portugal

Bilbao, capital of Vizcaya Province, 14km - 9 miles from the sea at the end of the Bilbao *ría* which forms the Nervión estuary, stands at the centre of a vast industrial area. Local industry began to develop in the middle of the 19C when iron mined from the surrounding hills was shipped to England in exchange for coal. Iron and steelworks were subsequently established.

The old city, founded in the early 14C, stands on the right bank of the Nervión river, up against the mountain on which stands the Santuario de Begoña (Begoña Sanctuary). It was originally named *las siete calles*, or seven streets, on account of its layout.

The modern *El Ensanche*, a business centre, stands on the left bank of the river on the other side of Puente del Arenal. Like other new areas that developed around large towns in the 19C, it was named *ensanche*, meaning enlargement. The town's rich residential area spreads around Doña Casilda Iturriza park.

Bilbao's main annual festivity takes place during **Semana Grande** in August with bullfights and Basque *pelota* championships.

Bilbao was the birthplace of the great writer and humanist **Miguel de Unamuno** (1864-1936).

Greater Bilbao and the ría – Since 1945 Greater Bilbao has included all the towns along the *ría* to the sea, from Bilbao itself to Getxo. Industrial works (iron and steel, chemicals and shipbuilding) are concentrated along the left bank in **Baracaldo, Sestao, Portugalete** with its **transporter bridge** built in 1893, and in **Somorrostro** where there is a large oil refinery. **Santurtzi,** a fishing port, is well-known for its fresh sardines.

Algorta, a residential town on the right bank, provides an attractive contrast to the heavy industry, while **Deusto** is famous for its university.

The *ría* is a vast river port, the largest commercial port in Spain. Only ships of less than 4 000 tons can navigate it although the large quays at the *ría* mouth can accommodate ships of 500 000 tons.

SIGHTS

★ **Museo de Bellas Artes** (Fine Arts Museum) ⊘ – The museum is housed in two buildings in Doña Casilda Iturriza park.

★★ **Ancient Art** – *Old building, ground floor.* Pride of place is given to the Spanish school from the 12C to the 17C. Noteworthy Romanesque works include a 12C Crucifixion from the Catalan school and fragments of frescoes from Urgel cathedral, while the section on 16-17C Spanish classical painting has canvases by Morales (known as the Divine), El Greco, Valdés Leal, Zurbarán *(St Catherine, St Isabel* and *Mother and Child)* and Ribera, with one of his most outstanding works, *Martyrdom of St Sebastian.*

15-17C Dutch and Flemish painting is also well represented with *The Usurers* by Quentin Metsys, a *Pietà* by Ambrosius Benson and a *Holy Family* by Gossaert.

In the left wing, the three magnificent portraits by Goya of Martín Zapata, the writer Fernández de Moratín and María Luisa de Parma show his perfect mastery of the art and his often merciless perception of his subjects.

Basque Art – *Old building, first floor.* This section houses the great Basque painters: Regoyos, Echevarría, Zuloaga, Iturrino, Arteta and Ucelay.

Contemporary Art – *New building.* This is a rich collection of works by artists both Spanish – Solana, Vázquez Díaz, Sunyer, Gargallo, Blanchard, Luis Fernández Otieza, Chillida and Tàpies – and foreign – Delaunay, Léger, Kokoschka, Vieira da Silva and Bacon.

Museo Arqueológico, Etnográfico e Histórico Vasco (Basque Archaeological, Ethnographical and Historical Museum) ⊘ – The museum is housed in the former **Colegio de San Andrès** in the heart of the old town. In the cloisters, coats of arms, tombs, carved stonework and the primitive, animal-like **idol of Mikeldi** may be seen. At the foot of the stairs is a copy of the Kurutriaga Crucifix (the original is in Durango). Basque decorative arts – statuary, superbly carved wooden furniture – are displayed on the 1st and 2nd floors together with an interesting exhibition of Basque traditions – linen weaving, ceramics, arts and crafts, fishing and ironwork. On the top floor is an immense relief model of Vizcaya province and rooms devoted to the Consulado de Bilbao.

Santuario de Begoña (Begoña Sanctuary) ⊘ – *You can drive up along the San Sebastián road (Avenida de Zumalacárregui) but it is easier to take the lift from Calle Esperanza Ascai.* There is an interesting view of Bilbao from the upper terminus footbridge. *On leaving the public gardens, take the 2nd street on the right.* The church contains the venerated figure of Nuestra Señora de Begoña, patron of the province, in a silver *camarín* in the chancel.

El BURGO DE OSMA★

Castilla y León (Soria)
Population 5 054
Michelin map 442 H 20 – Michelin Atlas España Portugal p 26

Approaching from the west you can see the tall baroque tower of El Burgo cathedral. The town is 18C with porticoed streets and squares and elegant baroque institutional buildings such as the San Agustín Hospital on the Plaza Mayor.

★ Catedral ⊘ – The Gothic sanctuary was built in 1232 as a result of a vow taken by a Cluniac monk, Don Pedro de Osma, to replace the former Romanesque cathedral which had stood on the site. The east end, transept and chapter house were completed in the 13C; the late-Gothic cloisters and the chancel were embellished with Renaissance decoration in the 16C, while the large sacristy, royal chapel and 72m – 236ft belfry were built in the 18C.

The Gothic decoration on the late-13C **south portal** includes on the splays, statues of (left to right) Moses, Gabriel, the Virgin, Judith, Solomon and Esther; on the lintel, a Dormition of the Virgin and on the pier, Christ displaying his wounds (late 15C).

The interior is remarkable for the elevation of the nave, the finely wrought-iron **screens** (16C) by Juan de Francés, the **high altar retable** by Juan de Juni with scenes from the Life of the Virgin and the 16C white marble **pulpit** and **trascoro altarpiece**.

The 13C polychrome limestone **tomb of San Pedro de Osma ★** may be seen in the west arm of the transept. In the **museum**, amongst the **archives** and **illuminated manuscripts ★** are a richly illustrated 1086 **Beatus** *(qv)* and a 12C manuscript with the signs of the Zodiac.

EXCURSION

Berlanga de Duero – *28km - 17 miles southeast on the C 116 and the SO 104.* Berlanga still appears protected in medieval fashion with stout ramparts below the massive walls of its 15C castle – the town was a strongpoint in the fortified line along the Duero. In the Gothic **Colegiata** ⊘, a monumental 16C hall-church, are two chapels containing altarpieces carved and painted in the Flamboyant style and two 16C recumbent alabaster statues.

8km - 5 miles southeast in **Casillas de Berlanga** is the **Iglesia de San Baudelio de Berlanga** ⊘, an isolated 11C Mozarabic chapel with a highly original layout. At the centre of the square nave is a massive pillar on which descend the eight flat ribs supporting the roof. The gallery rests on a double line of horseshoe-shaped arches and like the rest of the building, was covered with frescoes in the 12C. Some hunting scenes and geometric patterns may still be made out.

The Michelin Motoring Atlas to España-Portugal
provides the motorist in Spain and Portugal
with the best possible information
for route-planning and choosing where to go.
Scale 1:400 000. Spiralbound.

BURGOS★★★

Castilla y León

Population 169 111

Michelin map 442 E 18-19 – Michelin Atlas España Portugal p 25

Burgos, known as the cradle of Castilla, stands on the banks of the Río Arlanzón with the slender, openwork spires of its famous cathedral rising high into the sky. It has an exposed position on a windswept plateau at an altitude of 900m - 2 953ft.
Local industry (textiles and food products) has increased over the last few decades.

Historical notes – Burgos was founded by Diego Rodriguez in 884 and selected capital of the united kingdom of Castilla and León in 1037, a title it relinquished in 1492, on the fall of Granada, when the royal court moved to Valladolid. However, the loss of political involvement appears to have released energy for commercial and artistic enterprises: the town became a wool centre for the sheep farmers of the Mesta *(see under Soria)*; architects and sculptors arrived, particularly from the north, and transformed monuments into the currently fashionable Gothic style. Burgos became Spain's Gothic capital with outstanding works including the cathedral, the Monasterio de las Huelgas Reales (Royal Convent of Las Huelgas) and the Cartuja de Miraflores (Carthusian Monastery). Yet, the end of the 16C brought the decline of the Mesta and a halt to the town's prosperity.
Burgos was chosen by Franco to be the seat of his government from 1936 to 1938.

The Land of El Cid (1026-1099) – The exploits of Rodrigo Díaz, native of Vivar *(9km - 5 1/2 miles north of Burgos)* light up the late-11C history of Castilla. The brilliant captain first supported the ambitious King of Castilla, Sancho II, then Alfonso VI who succeeded his brother in somewhat dubious circumstances. Alfonso, irritated at Díaz's suspicions and jealous of the prestige he had won following an attack on the Moors in 1081, banished the warrior hero although he was, by then, married to the king's cousin, Ximena.
Díaz, as a soldier of fortune, entered service first with the Moorish king of Zaragoza and subsequently fought Christian and Muslim armies with equal fervour. His most famous enterprise came when at the head of 7 000 men, chiefly Muslims, he captured Valencia after a nine-month siege in 1094. He was finally defeated by the Moors in an exploit at Cuenca and died soon afterwards (1099). His widow held Valencia against the Muslims until 1102 when she set fire to the city before returning to Castilla with the Cid's body which was buried first in the San Pedro de Cardeña monastery *(10km - 6 miles southeast of Burgos)* before finally being interred in Burgos cathedral in 1921.
Legend has transformed the stalwart but often ruthless 11C warrior, the Campeador or Champion of Castilla, El Cid (Seid in Arabic), into a chivalrous knight of exceptional valour. The first epic poem **El Cantar del Mío Cid** appeared in 1180 and was followed by ballads. In 1618 Guillén de Castro wrote a romanticised version of El Cid in his **Las Mocedades del Cid** (youthful adventures of El Cid) upon which Corneille, in 1636, based his drama *Le Cid.*

★★★ CATEDRAL (A) ⓘ *time: 1 1/2 hours*

The cathedral, the third largest in Spain after Sevilla and Toledo, is a remarkable example of the transformation of French and German Flamboyant Gothic into a style that is typically Spanish through the natural exuberance of its decoration. The many works of art adorning the interior of the cathedral make it an outstanding showcase of European Gothic sculpture.
Ferdinand III laid the first stone in 1221 and there followed two principal stages of building which corresponded with distinct periods in the Gothic style. In the first, in the 13C, under the aegis of Maurice the Englishman, then Bishop of Burgos, who had collected drawings during a journey through France (at that time very much influenced by the Gothic style), the nave, aisles and portals were built by local architects.
The second period in the 15C saw the building of the west front spires and the Capilla del Condestable (Constable's Chapel) as well as the decoration of other chapels. These were directly influenced by foreigners from the north, through the architects and sculptors from Flanders, the Rhineland and Burgundy, whom another great Burgos prelate, Alonso de Cartagena, had brought back on his return from the Council of Basel.
These artists, from a Europe in which Flamboyant Gothic was beginning to wane, found new inspiration in Mudéjar arabesques and other elements in Spanish art. The most outstanding amongst them, **Felipe Bigarny**, the Fleming **Gil de Siloé**, the Rhinelander **Johan of Cologne**, integrated rapidly and with their sons and grandsons – Diego de Siloé, Simon and Francis of Cologne – created virtually a Burgos school of sculpture.
The cloisters were built in the 14C, while the magnificent lantern over the transept crossing – which collapsed after daring work by Simon of Cologne – was rebuilt by Juan de Vallejo in the mid-16C.

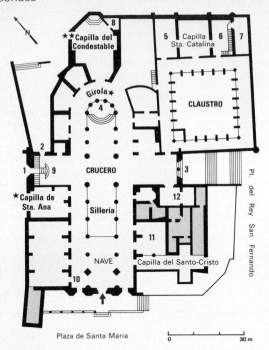

N

★★ **Capilla del Condestable**

8

5 **Capilla Sta. Catalina** 6 7

CLAUSTRO

Girola ★

4

2

1 9 **CRUCERO** 3

Pl. del Rey San Fernando

★ **Capilla de Sta. Ana**

Sillería 12

11

NAVE **Capilla del Santo-Cristo**

10

Plaza de Santa Maria   0   30 m

Exterior

A walk round the cathedral will reveal how the architects took ingenious advantage of the sloping ground (the upper gallery of the cloisters is level with the cathedral pavement) to introduce delightful small precincts and closes cut by stairways.

West front – The ornate upper area, with its frieze of Spanish kings and its two openwork spires, pinnacled and crocketed, is the masterwork of Johan of Cologne.

Portada de la Coronería (Coronería Doorway) (**1**) – The statues at the jambs have the grace of their French Flamboyant Gothic originals, although the folds of their robes show more movement. The Plateresque **Portada de la Pellejería** (**2**) or Skinner's Doorway in the adjoining transept wall was designed by Francis of Cologne early in the 16C.

As you continue round by the east end it becomes obvious that the Constable's Chapel, with its Isabelline decoration and lantern with pinnacles, is one of the cathedral's later additions.

Portada del Sarmental (Sarmental Doorway) (**3**) – The covings are filled with figures from the Celestial Court, while the tympanum is an incredible sculpture in which each of the four Evangelists sits in a different position as he writes.

Interior

The design of the interior is French inspired while the decoration bears an exuberant Spanish stamp.

★★ **Crucero, Coro and Capilla Mayor** (Transept crossing, choir stalls and chancel) – The splendid star ribbed lantern of the transept crossing rises on four massive pillars to a height of 54m - 177ft above the funerary stones of El Cid and Ximena, inlaid in the crossing pavement.

The imposing unit of 103 walnut choir-stalls, carved by Felipe Vigarny between 1507 and 1512, illustrates Biblical stories on the upper, back rows and mythological and burlesque scenes at the front. The handsome recumbent statue of wood plated with enamelled copper, on the tomb at the centre, dates from the 13C and is of Bishop Maurice.

The high altar (**4**) retable is a 16C Renaissance work in high relief against an intrinsically classical background of niches and pediments.

Claustro – The 14C Gothic cloisters present a panorama of Burgos sculpture with stone, terracotta and polychrome wood figures.

The **Capilla de Santiago** (St James's Chapel) (**5**) contains the cathedral treasure, a rich collection of church plate and liturgical objects.

In the **Capilla de Santa Catalina** (St Catherine's Chapel) are manuscripts and documents, including the marriage contract of El Cid. Note the 15C carved and painted consoles showing Moorish kings paying homage to the King of Castilla.

The **sacristía** (sacristy) (**6**) houses the *Christ at the Column* by Diego de Siloé, a supreme example of Spanish expressionism in post-16C Iberian sculpture. The **sala capitular** (chapter house) (**7**) displays, besides 15C and 16C Brussels tapestries symbolising the theological and cardinal virtues, a Hispano-Flemish diptych, a *Virgin and Child* by Memling and above, a painted wood Mudéjar *artesonado* ceiling (16C).

★ **Girola** (ambulatory) – The *trasaltar* (at the back of the high altar), carved partly by Felipe Vigarny, includes an expressive representation of the Ascent to Calvary.

★★ **Capilla del Condestable** (Constable's Chapel) – A magnificent grille closes off the area. The Isabelline chapel founded by Hernández de Velasco, Constable of Castilla, in 1482 and designed by Simon of Cologne, is lit by a lantern surmounted by an

BURGOS

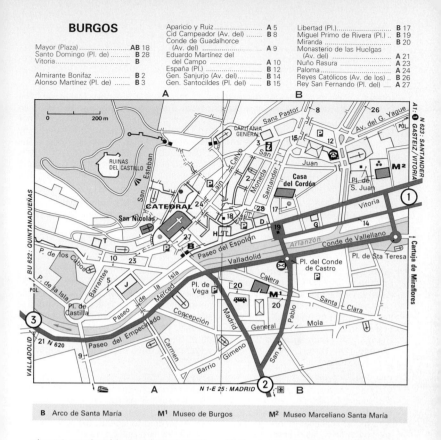

B Arco de Santa María **M¹** Museo de Burgos **M²** Museo Marceliano Santa María

elegant cupola with star-shaped vaulting. All the great early Renaissance sculptors of Burgos cooperated in the subsequent decoration of the walls and altarpiece. The heraldic displays in the chapel are striking. On either side of the altar, the constable's escutcheon, held by male figures, appears to be suspended over the balustrades of the tribune.

Statues of the constable and his wife lie on their tomb, carved in Carrara marble, and beside them is an immense garnet-coloured marble funerary stone for the names of their descendants. On the right side of the chapel is a Plateresque door to the sacristy (1512) **(8)** where there is a painting of *Mary Magdalene* by Leonardo da Vinci.

Escalera Dorada or **de la Coronería** (Golden or Coronation Staircase) **(9)** – The majestically proportioned staircase was designed in the pure Renaissance style by Diego de Siloé in the early 16C. The twin pairs of flights are outlined by an ornately elegant gilded banister by the French master ironsmith, Hilaire.

Capillas – Each of these side chapels is a museum of Gothic and Plateresque art: Gil de Siloé and Diego de la Cruz cooperated on the huge Gothic altarpiece in the **Capilla de Santa Ana★** which illustrates the saint's life. In the centre is a Tree of Jesse with at its heart, the first meeting of Anne and Joachim and at the top, the Virgin and Child.

At the beginning of the cathedral nave, high up near the roof, is the **Papamoscas** or **Flycatcher Clock (10)**, with a jack which opens its mouth on the striking of the hours. In the **Capilla del Santo Cristo** (Chapel of Holy Christ) is a Crucifixion with the particularly venerated figure complete with hair and covered with buffalo hide to resemble human flesh.

The **Capilla de la Presentation** (Chapel of the Presentation) **(11)** contains the tomb of the Bishop of Lerma, carved by Felipe Vigarny and the **Capilla de la Visitación** (Chapel of the Visitation) **(12)**, that of Alonso de Cartagena by Gil de Siloé.

★★REAL MONASTERIO DE LAS HUELGAS
(ROYAL CONVENT OF LAS HUELGAS) ⊙

1.5km - 1 mile west of Burgos; take Avenida del Monasterio de las Huelgas

Las Huelgas Reales, originally a summer palace of the kings of Castilla, was converted in 1180 into a convent by Alfonso VIII and his wife Eleanor, daughter of Henry II of England. The religious were Cistercians of high lineage; the abbess all-powerful; by the 13C the convent's influence, both spiritual and temporal, extended to more than 50 towns and it had become a common place of retreat for members of the house of Castilla and even the royal pantheon.

Rearrangement over the centuries has resulted in a heterogeneous and somewhat divided building in which, although the Cistercian style of the 12C and 13C predominates, there are Romanesque and even Mudéjar features (13-15C) as well as Plateresque furnishings.

Iglesia – The clean lines of the exterior of this church are pure Cistercian. The interior is divided into two by a screen: from the transept, open to all, you can see the revolving pulpit (1560), in gilded ironwork, which enabled the preacher to be heard on either side of the screen. Royal and princely tombs, originally coloured, rich in heraldic devices and historical legend, line the aisles, while in the middle of the nave, the nuns' *coro*, is the double sepulchre of the founders, Alfonso VIII and Eleanor of England. The rood-screen retable, delicately carved and coloured in the Renaissance style, is surmounted by a fine 13C Deposition. The altar is flanked on each side by two handsome 13C and 14C tombs.

Claustro – 13-15C. Enough fragments of Mudéjar vaulting stucco remain in these Gothic cloisters to give an idea of the delicacy of the strapwork inspired by Persian ivories and fabrics.

Sala Capitular – This chapter house contains the **pendón★**, a trophy from the Battle of Las Navas de Tolosa *(qv)*, decorated with silk *appliqué*.

★★ **Museo de Telas Medievales (Museum of Medieval Materials)** – The fabrics, court dress and finery displayed in the former loft provide a vivid review of royal wear in 13C Castilla. Of the clothes, (mainly tunics, pelisses and capes) found in the tombs, the most valuable items come from that of the Infante Fernando de la Cerda (who died in 1275), son of Alfonso X, the Wise. This tomb, one that was not desecrated by French troops in 1809, contained a long tunic, *pellote* (voluminous trousers with braces) and a very large mantle, all made of the same material embroidered with silk and silver thread. There is also a *birrete*, a silk crown adorned with pearls and precious stones.

Claustro – Late 12C. In these Romanesque cloisters, slender paired columns, topped by highly stylised capitals, combine to create an effect of elegance. Several rooms in this part of the building, Alfonso VIII's former palace, were decorated by the Moors. The **Capilla de Santiago** (Chapel of St James) retains an *artesonado* ceiling with its original colouring and stucco frieze. According to legend, the statue of the saint with articulated arms, dubbed the princes of royal blood, knights.

CARTUJA DE MIRAFLORES

(MIRAFLORES CARTHUSIAN MONASTERY) (B) ◷ *4km - 2 1/2 miles east of Burgos*

This former royal foundation, entrusted to the Carthusians in 1442, was chosen by Juan II as a pantheon for himself and his second wife, Isabel of Portugal. The church was completed in full Isabelline Gothic style in 1498.

★ **Iglesia** – The sobriety of the façade, relieved only by the buttress finials and the founders' escutcheons, gives no indication of the richness inside. This appears in the church's single aisle with its elegant vaulting and gilded keystones and particularly in the magnificent apse.

★★★ **Sculptured unit in the Capilla Mayor** (apse) – This was designed by the Fleming, Gil de Siloé at the end of the 15C and comprises the high altarpiece, the royal mausoleum and a funerary recess. The polychrome wood **altarpiece**, the work of Siloé and Diego de la Cruz, has a striking design: the usual rectangular compartments have been replaced by circles, each crowded with Biblical figures.

The white marble **mausoleo real** (royal mausoleum) is in the form of an eight-pointed star in which can be seen

Detail of the altarpiece
in the Cartuja de Miraflores, Burgos

M. Babey / ARTEPHOT

the recumbent statues of the founders, Juan II and Queen Isabel, parents of Isabel the Catholic. Dominating the exuberant Flamboyant Gothic decoration of scrolls, canopies, pinnacles, cherubim and armorial bearings, executed with rare virtuosity, are the four Evangelists. In an ornate **recess** in the north wall is the tomb of the Infante Alfonso, whose premature death gave the throne of Castilla to his sister Isabel the Catholic. The statue of the young prince at prayer is technically brilliant but impersonal (compare with that of Juan de Padilla, *see below*).

Also in the church are a 15C Hispano-Flemish triptych (to the right of the altar) and Gothic choir-stalls carved with an infinite variety of arabesques.

ADDITIONAL SIGHTS

★ **Museo de Burgos** (B M¹) ⊘ — Two sections, housed in separate buildings:

Prehistoric and Archaeological Department – Housed in the Casa de Miranda, a Renaissance mansion with an elegant *patio*, this section contains finds discovered in the province covering the Prehistoric to Visigothic periods.

Note the rooms devoted to Iron Age sites, to the Roman settlement of Clunia and the collection of Roman funerary steles.

Fine Arts Department – The Casa de Angulo houses works of art from the Burgos region covering the period from the 9C to the 20C. There are two precious items from the Santo Domingo monastery at Silas: an 11C **Hispano-Moorish casket★**, delicately carved in ivory in Cuenca and highlighted with enamel plaques, and a 12C **altarfront★** in beaten and enamelled copper.

In the section on 14-15C funerary sculpture is the **tomb★** of Juan de Padilla on which Gil de Siloé has beautifully rendered the countenance and robes of the dead man.

The collection of 15C painting contains a *Christ Weeping* by the Fleming, Jan Mostaert.

★ **Arco de Santa María** (A B) – The 14C gateway once defended the city walls. In the 16C it was modified to form a triumphal arch for Emperor Charles V and embellished with statues of the famous: below, Diego Porcelos Rodriguez is flanked by two semi-legendary judges said to have governed Castilla in the 10C, and above, Count Fernán González and El Cid (right) are shown with Charles V.

Iglesia de San Nicolás (A) ⊘ The **altarpiece★** of this church, carved by Simon of Cologne in 1505, is both large and ornate with more than 465 figures. The upper part shows the Virgin crowned at the centre of a circle of angels; St Nicholas in the central part is surrounded by scenes from his life – note the voyage by caravel to Alexandria – and below, there is a back view of the Last Supper.

Casa del Cordón (B) – The recently restored palace of the Constables of Castilla was built in the 15C (and presently houses the Caja de Ahorros savings bank). Still decorating its façade is the thick Franciscan cord motif which gave the palace its name. It is interesting historically as the place where Columbus was received by the Catholic Monarchs on his return from his second voyage to America and also where Philip the Fair died suddenly of a chill after a game of *pelota*, reducing to despair his already much disturbed wife, Juana the Mad.

Plaza Mayor (AB 18) – This delightful circular main square, typically lined by a portico, is the setting for all public festivities.

Museo Marceliano Santa María (B M²) ⊘ – The museum, built in the ruins of the former Benedictine Monastery of San Juan, displays Impressionist type canvases by the Burgos painter Marceliano Santa María (1866-1952).

CÁCERES★★

Extremadura
Population 84 319
Michelin map 444 N 10 – Michelin Atlas España Portugal p 49
Plan of the conurbation in the current Michelin Red Guide España Portugal

Cáceres, the capital of an agricultural province (cereals and stock rearing), is a lively town with a remarkable historical centre that dates back several centuries.

★★★ CÁCERES VIEJO (OLD CÁCERES) *time: 1 1/2 hours*

Within its defensive walls and towers built by the Moors, this old quarter includes a group of Gothic and Renaissance seignorial mansions beyond compare in Spain. The unadorned, ochre coloured façades of the residences belonging to the noblemen of the 15C and 16C bear no ostentatious flourishes as they reflect the nature of their owners, the Ulloas, the Ovandos and the Saavedras, proud warriors all, who in their fight against the infidel – Moor or American Indian – won more in prestige than in wealth. Minimal decoration consists of a narrow fillet around the windows, a sculptured cornice or a proud coat of arms. The fortified towers which once stood guard over the mansions and proclaimed their owners' power were lopped on the command of Isabel the Catholic in 1477.

Follow the route marked on the plan, setting off from Plaza del General Mola, the former Plaza Mayor. An evening visit is highly recommended.

Pass beneath the **Arco de la Estrella** (Star Arch) which was built into the wall by Manuel Churriguera in the 18C.

★ **Plaza de Santa María** – This irregularly shaped square forms the monumental heart of the old city; rising on all sides are attractive golden ochre façades. The front of the **Palacio Mayoralgo** (Mayoralgo Palace) (**B**), now restored, has elegant paired windows while the **Palacio Episcopal** (Bishop's Palace) (**C**) has a 16C bossed doorway with medallions of the Old and New Worlds on either side (left and right respectively).

Iglesia de Santa María ⊙ – This nobly styled church, completed in the 16C, serves as the city cathedral. The three Gothic aisles of almost equal height, have lierne and tierceron vaulting from which the ribs descend into slender columns engaged around the main pillars. The carved retable at the high altar (16C) is difficult to see but with its high standard of workmanship is well worth the effort.

By continuing round to the left of Santa María to the top of Calle de las Tiendas, you will see the **Palacio de Carvajal** (Carvajal Palace) ⊙ flanked by a 15C tower. The chambers, *patio* and chapel of this nobleman's residence are open to the public.

★ **Palacio de los Golfines de Abajo** (Lower Golfines Palace) – This rich mansion, twice honoured by visits by the Catholic Monarchs, has a rough stone façade, Gothic in style with the Plateresque traits characteristic of civil architecture of the late 15C. The paired window derives from the Moorish *ajimez*, while the fillet, delicately framing the two windows and the door, recalls the *alfiz (qv)*. To lighten the front, a Plateresque frieze with winged griffons was added to the top of the central area in the 16C, while medallions and the Golfines coat of arms – a *fleur-de-lys* and a tower – complete the decoration.

Plaza San Jorge (**31**) – The square is dominated by the austere 18C façade of the Jesuit church of **San Francisco Javier**.

San Mateo – The church's high Gothic nave, begun in the 14C, was abutted in the 16C by a *coro alto* resting on an arcade with basket vaulting. The interior is bare except for the baroque altarpiece and the side chapels containing tombs with decorative heraldic motifs.

Continuing round the church by the north wall you come, in succession, on two 15C towers both of which have lost their battlements but have retained unusual parapets – they are respectively the **Torre de la Plata** (Silver Tower) (**P**) and the **Casa del Sol** (Sun House) (**Q**) which owes its name to the elegant crest of the Solis family boldly carved over the arch.

Casa de las Cigüeñas (The House of the Storks) – The house, now occupied by the military, proudly sports a battlemented tower – the only one to escape the lopping decreed in the late 15C.

Casa de las Veletas (The Weather Vane House) – The mansion, with its fine 18C façade emblasoned with baroque family crests, was built over a Moorish *alcázar* of which the cistern still remains. Today, it houses the **Museo de Cáceres** ⊙ containing collections of archaeology (engraved Bronze Age steles, Celtiberian statues of wild boar known as *verracos*, Roman remains) and ethnology (local dress, arts and crafts).

Old Cáceres

CÁCERES

B   Palacio Mayoralgo
C   Palacio episcopal
P   Torre de los Plata
Q   Casa del Sol
V   Casa de la Generala

The 11C **aljibe** (Arab cistern) is still fed by a trickling stream of water from the roof and sloping square outside. It is covered by five rows of horseshoe-shaped arches supported by granite capitals with carving which is unfortunately barely noticeable.

Casa del Comendador de Alcuéscar (Commander of Alcuéscar's House) – The palace, now a *parador*, has a fine Gothic tower, delicate window surrounds and an unusual corner balcony.

By taking the alley alongside the ramparts you reach the **Palacio de los Golfines de Arriba** (Upper Golfines Palace) with an austere, imposing façade and an attractive *patio*. The **Casa de la Generala** (V) a little further on, houses the law faculty.

Go through the door in the ramparts opposite.

The steps leading down to the Plaza Mayor del General Mola afford an interesting view of the walls, particularly high at this point, and the Torre del Horno.

ADDITIONAL SIGHTS

Casa de los Toledo-Moctezuma – The mansion, its imposing façade surmounted by a gallery, was built by Juan Cano de Saavedra with the fabulous dowry brought him by his wife, none other than the Aztec princess, Montezuma's daughter (Moctezuma in Spanish).

Torre de los Espaderos (Tower of the Armourers) – This was truncated along with the other towers in the late 15C.

Iglesia de Santiago (St James's Church) ⊘ – The Romanesque church, rebuilt in the 16C, is traditionally held to be the birthplace of the Military Order of the Knights of Cáceres who in turn founded the Order of the Knights of St James. Inside, the altarpiece carved by Alonso Berruguete in 1557 bears scenes from the Life of Christ. These surround a vigorous, finely portrayed St James *Matamoros* or Slayer of the Moors.

The **Palacio de Godoy** opposite has an impressive coat of arms on the corner and a fine inner *patio* with decorative *azulejos*.

EXCURSIONS

Santuario de la Virgen de la Montaña (The Mountain Virgin) ⊘ – *3km - 2 miles east.* A 17C baroque shrine, built on a hill cloaked in olive trees, shelters a famous statuette of the Virgin. A picturesque *romería* to the shrine is held on the first Sunday in May. The esplanade affords an extensive **view★** across the Extremadura plateau.

Garrovillas – *36km - 22 miles northwest on the N 630 and the C 552.* In this typical Extremadura town, the Plaza Mayor is lined by arcades in which, in a delightfully artless way, fantasy has run rife with every pillar askew!

Arroyo de la Luz – *20km - 12 miles west on the N 521 and C 523. To find the Iglesia de la Asunción, take the tower as a bearing and proceed along the widest street.* The church has a 15-16C Gothic nave. The altarpiece is worth looking at for the 16 **pictures★** and 4 medallions it comprises which were painted on the spot by **Morales the Divine** *(qv)* between 1560 and 1563. As the artist's paintings are scattered, the collection here provides an opportunity to appreciate more fully than usual his gentle and noble style.

CÁDIZ★

Andalucía

Population 157 355

Michelin map 446 W 11 – Michelin Atlas España Portugal p 8

Cádiz, a bastion ringed by the sea, is attached to the mainland by a narrow sand isthmus. Its outstanding site and vast sheltered bay have attracted settlers since earliest times. It was founded by the Phoenicians in 1100 BC and subsequently came under Roman and Moorish rule. In the 18C, Cádiz became one of Europe's greatest ports once it had acquired trading rights with Spanish America, hitherto the monopoly of Sevilla.

On 21 October 1805, Admiral Villeneuve sailed out of Cádiz harbour with his Franco-Spanish fleet to confront the English off the **Cabo de Trafalgar** headland under Nelson. His ships were ill-equipped and poorly manned; after heroic combat his fleet was destroyed and he was taken prisoner. Nelson had been mortally wounded during the course of the battle but England's supremacy at sea was established.

During the French occupation and siege of 1812, Spanish patriots convened the Cortes which promulgated the famous liberal constitution of March 1812, known as the **Constitution of Cádiz** *(qv)*.

Cádiz today – Cádiz is an industrial town and port with shipbuilding and naval dock-yards. It is also an important fishing centre and a strategic hub for tourism to the Canary Islands and other parts of Spain.

SIGHTS

★**Seaside promenades** – The south and west promenades look out over the sea while those to the north and east with their public **gardens**★ (Parque Genovés, Alameda Marqués de Comillas and Alameda de Apodaca), some of the most attractive places in the city, look across to the far shore of the bay.

★**Museo de Cádiz** (**BY M**) ⊘ – *Access by Calle Antonio López.* The museum is housed in two buildings, one modern and the other a former Franciscan convent, and comprises three sections: archaeology, fine arts and ethnology.

Archaeological department – The wealth of the displays confirms the city's long history. One of the rooms is devoted to Roman necropolises and various funeral rites. There is a collection of vases, oil lamps and jewellery. The colossal statue of Trajan was found near Tarifa.

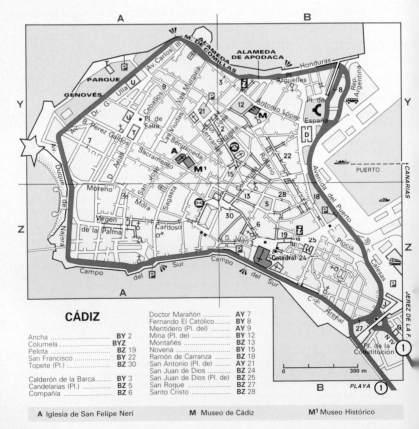

CÁDIZ

Ancha	**BY** 2
Columela	**BYZ**
Pelota	**BZ** 19
San Francisco	**BY** 22
Topete (Pl.)	**BZ** 30
Calderón de la Barca	**BY** 3
Candelarias (Pl.)	**BZ** 5
Compañía	**BZ** 6

Doctor Marañón	**AY** 7
Fernando El Católico	**BY** 8
Mentidero (Pl. del)	**AY** 9
Mina (Pl. de)	**BY** 12
Montañés	**BZ** 13
Novena	**BY** 15
Ramón de Carranza	**BZ** 18
San Antonio (Pl. de)	**AY** 21
San Juan de Dios	**BZ** 24
San Juan de Dios (Pl. de)	**BZ** 25
San Roque	**BZ** 27
Santo Cristo	**BZ** 28

A Iglesia de San Felipe Neri	**M** Museo de Cádiz	**M¹** Museo Histórico

The most outstanding exhibits are the two 5C BC **Phoenician sarcophagi ★**; that of the man was discovered in 1887 and that of the woman in 1980. They were copied by Greek artists after Egyptian models.

Fine Arts department – This presents a rich collection of 17C Spanish painting with works by Morales the Divine, Murillo, Ribera and in particular, **Zurbarán ★**. His canvases, brought from La Cartuja (Carthusian monastery) in Jerez, were painted when he was at the height of his glory between 1630 and 1640.

Ethnological department – Cádiz folklore since the 18C is represented by the Tía Norica puppet theatre, with its props and characters, including the popular Tía and her nephew Batillo.

Museo Histórico (AY M¹) ⊘ – The museum contains an outstanding ivory and mahogany **model ★** of the town in Charles III's reign (18C).

Iglesia de San Felipe Neri (AY A) ⊘ – It was in the oval-shaped interior of this church with its vast cupola that the Cortes gathered in 1812 to proclaim the constitution. Above the high altar is a Virgin by Murillo.

Catedral (BZ) ⊘ – The neo-classical church, after plans by Vicente Acero, took from 1720 to 1838 to build. The great composer **Manuel de Falla** (1876-1946) is buried in the crypt.

Museo – The rich collection of **church plate ★** in this museum includes a processional cross by Enrique de Arfe, a monumental silver tabernacle (5m - 16ft high) and the 1721 "million monstrance", so called since its decoration is said to comprise nearly a million jewels.

EXCURSION

Medina Sidonia – *44km - 27 miles east on the N IV, N340 and C346.*
The road from Cádiz follows an offshore bar with beaches on one side and the **San Fernando salt-pans** on the other.
Medina Sidonia is a hilltop village with beautiful views of the surrounding plain; one may see as far as the coast on clear days.
The Gothic church, **Santa María** ⊘, at the top of the village, has an outstanding Renaissance **altarpiece ★** by the sculptor Juan Bautista Vázquez the Elder.

Castillo - Convento de CALATRAVA★

CALATRAVA CASTLE-MONASTERY
Castilla-La Mancha (Ciudad Real)
Michelin map 444 P 18 – Michelin Atlas España Portugal p 64

The Castillo de Calatrava, a ruined citadel with its crumbling walls crowning a high hill, still inspires a feeling of awe. It conveys, as no other site, the lonely ordeals undergone by the Knights of the Reconquest.

Soldiering monks – In the mid-12C, the Campo de Calatrava plain was the scene of unceasing warfare between Christians and Muslims. The old Fortaleza de Calatrava, a fortress built originally by the Moors on the banks of the Guadiana, was captured and subsequently abandoned by the Templars, before being taken over by Raimundo, Abbot of Fitero. A soldier before he became an abbot, he installed a garrison in the castle where in 1158 he founded the **Orden Militar de Calatrava**, the first of Spain's military orders. Al-Mansur, however, captured the castle which remained in Muslim hands until the victory of Las Navas de Tolosa (1212) when the knights regained control of the region. They determined to build a new fortress in an impregnable position; it was completed by 1217.

Castillo-convento ⊘ – *7km - 4 miles southwest of Calzada de Calatrava, turn right into a 2.5km - 1 1/2 mile long surfaced uphill road.*
There are three stout perimeters, the second actually built into the rock.
The **church**, restored and lit by an immense rose window, has fine brick vaulting, described as swallow's nest in design and probably the work of Moorish prisoners.
The ruins of the **Castillo de Salvatierra** are visible from the fortress towers.

Each year
the Michelin Red Guide España Portugal
revises its selection of hotels and restaurants
in the following categories
– pleasant, quiet, secluded
– with an exceptionally interesting or extensive view
– with gardens, tennis courts, swimming pool, beach facilities.

CANGAS DE NARCEA

Asturias
Population 19 083
Michelin map 441 C 10 – Michelin Atlas España Portugal p 4

Cangas, gateway to the upper Narcea valley, is a meeting place for trout fishermen, excursionists and hunters.

EXCURSIONS

Corias – *3km - 2 miles north.*
The large monastery (**monasterio** ⊙) re-erected in neo-classical style after being burned down in the 19C, was founded in the 11C and occupied for 800 years by Benedictines. There are ornate Churrigueresque altars in the **church**.

Tineo – *30km - 19 miles northeast.*
The town perched 673m - 2 208ft up the mountainside commands an immense **panorama** ★★ of the surrounding sierras.

CARAVACA DE LA CRUZ

Murcia
Population 21 238
Michelin map 445 R 24 – Michelin Atlas España Portugal p 78

Caravaca stretches around the foot of a hill crowned by castle ramparts. In May each year, the town celebrates the miracle which took place within its walls in 1231. Then, it is said, a priest named Chirinos was celebrating mass before the Moorish king who had taken him prisoner, when the Cross, which had been missing from the altar, suddenly reappeared; the Moor was moved to immediate conversion and the Cross, believed to be part of the True Cross, became an object of great popular veneration. It was stolen in 1934.

Castillo - Iglesia de la Santa Cruz ⊙ – The restored ramparts of the 15C castle enclose the church which for so long sheltered the Holy Cross *(Santa Cruz)*. The 1722 doorway in local red marble has a surprisingly bold baroque character. *Estípites* or inverted balusters and delicately twisted pillars add to the vertical effect of the entrance without detracting from the robustness and, in fact, give it something of a Latin-American appearance. Inside there is a strictly Herreran elegance. From the battlements at the top of the building there is an interesting **view** of the surrounding town.

CARDONA

Catalunya (Barcelona)
Population 6 402
Michelin map 443 G 35 – Michelin Atlas España Portugal p 32

The Castillo de Cardona, an 11C hill citadel, was rebuilt in the 18C and today serves as a *parador*.
Of the 11C construction there remain a half-demolished round tower and the collegiate church, a jewel of Romanesque Lombard architecture. The top of the citadel commands a view of a **salt mine**, worked since Roman times, with some galleries more than 1km - 1/2 mile deep.

★ **Colegiata** ⊙ – The collegiate church was built in 1040 and has several features from the Lombard style of architecture which flourished at the time in Catalunya. The smooth, unadorned walls, the lantern over the transept crossing, the different types of vaulting – barrel in the nave with its impressive elevation and groined in the aisles – all testify to a skilful mastery of the art. Below, the vaults in the crypt rest on graceful columns. Outside, the charming Gothic cloisters date from the 15C.

Castillo de Cardona and the Colegiata

F. Bouillot / MARCO POLO

CARMONA★

Andalucía (Sevilla)
Population 23 516
Michelin map 446 T 13 – Michelin Atlas España Portugal p 73

The ancient walls of Carmona rise up on the edge of the plateau overlooking the vast cereal-growing plain of the Guadalquivir.

CIUDAD VIEJA (OLD TOWN) *time: 1 hour*

Park the car near the Puerta de Sevilla in the lower part of town.

The Puerta de Sevilla, its double Moorish arch a striking contrast to the baroque tower of the Iglesia de San Pedro opposite, opens onto the old town with its convents, white-walled alleys and stone gateways leading to the *patios* of former noble residences.

Calle Prim leads to Plaza San Fernando which is lined by 17 and 18C houses. The **Ayuntamiento** (Town Hall) *(in Calle de San Salvador)* retains a large Roman mosaic in its *patio*.

Continuing along Calle Martín López, you come to the **Iglesia de Santa María** ⊙ which is preceded by the former mosque's ablutionary courtyard. A little further along, in the church of **Convento de Santa Clara**, the walls of the nave are hung with portraits of 17C women. The style of the paintings recalls that of Zurbarán. The street continues to the **Puerta de Córdoba** which was built into the Roman wall in the 17C.

Calle de Calatrava and Calle G. Freire lead uphill to the **Alcázar del Rey Don Pedro** (Alcázar of King Peter I, the Cruel), which is now a *parador*.

ADDITIONAL SIGHT

Necrópolis Romana ⊙ – *Access to the Roman necropolis is indicated on the road to Sevilla.* More than 800 1-4C tombs have been discovered. Most comprise a vaulted funerary chamber with niches for the urns. The most interesting are the Tumba del Elefante (so called on account of the statue of an elephant) with three dining rooms and a kitchen, and the Tumba de Servilia, which is the size of a patrician villa.

CARTAGENA

Murcia
Population 173 061
Michelin map 445 T 27 – Michelin Atlas España Portugal p 79

Cartagena, a major naval base, lies in a unique position in the curve of a deep bay sheltered by fortified promontories.

Cartago Nova – In 223 BC the settlement was captured by the Carthaginians who named it *Cartago Nova*. Subsequently, it developed into a prosperous colony under the Romans (traces of the *forum* have been discovered beneath Plaza de los Tres Reyes); it was neglected in preference for Almería by the Arabs and Murcia by the Christians who also removed its bishopric. It returned to favour, however, in the reign of Philip II who fortified the surrounding hilltops and that of Charles III who built the Arsenal.

The construction of an oil refinery at Escombreras, 9km - 6 miles away, together with the export of lead, iron and zinc, have brought the town renewed prosperity.

Dramatic processions take place in the city during Semana Santa (Holy Week).

SIGHTS

City life centres around Calle Mayor, the main street. Near Plaza del Ayuntamiento is the early **submarine** invented by a native of the city, Lieutenant Isaac Peral, in 1888.

From the top of the **Castillo de la Concepción**, a former fort which is now a public garden (Parque Torres), there is a good general **view** of the harbour and the ruins of the former Romanesque **Catedral de Santa María la Vieja**.

Museo Nacional de Arqueología Marítima ⊙ – *Navidad dike, in the harbour. Take the Algameca road and when you reach the Empresa Nacional Bazán, turn into the road on the right and follow it to the end.*

This museum of maritime archaeology displays finds from various underwater excavations, notably a rich collection of Phoenician, Punic and Roman amphorae. Seafaring activity during Antiquity is illustrated by maps, small-scale models of vessels (galleys, biremes and triremes) as well as a model of the Mediterranean sea bed.

EXCURSION

Mar Menor – *35km - 22 miles east on the N 332.*
Mar Menor, or Little Sea, is a lagoon separated from the open Mediterranean by the **Manga**, a sand bar 500m – 1 640ft wide which extends northwards for 20km-12 miles from the eastern end of the rocky Cabo de Palos headland. Gilt-head, mullet and king prawns are fished from its shallow saltwater. The low-lying hinterland is cloaked in almond trees with here and there a palm or a windmill.
La Manga del Mar Menor is a large, elongated seaside resort with surrealistic tower blocks stretching for miles along the sand bar. Its sandy beaches and calm water are ideal for sailing, windsurfing and water-skiing.
In **Santiago de la Ribera,** where there is no natural beach, pontoons with changing cabins line the seafront. **San Javier,** nearby, is the seat of the Academia General del Aire (General Air Academy).

Sierra de CAZORLA★★

Andalucía (Jaén)
Michelin map 446 R 21-S 21 – Michelin Atlas España Portugal p 76

The Sierra de Cazorla is part of the **Parque Nacional de las Sierras de Cazorla, Segura y Las Villas,** a national park covering 214 336ha - 529 646 acres which was created in 1986 to protect the natural resources of the region.
The Baetic ranges in this sierra reach an altitude of more than 2 000m - 6 562ft. Springs rise in abundance, one of which eventually becomes Andalucía's greatest river, the Guadalquivir. At first the stream flows northeastwards before, at length, finding a passage west and finally south to the Atlantic. Altitude and rainfall produce an upland Mediterranean type vegetation, with thyme, lavender and other aromatic shrubs.
The forest, the most extensive woodland area in Andalucía, is open to the public along marked paths. There is a good variety of wildlife – deer, moufflons or wild mountain sheep, golden eagles, ospreys and vultures. The Sierra de Cazorla is a hunting preserve.

NORTH TO SOUTH ACROSS THE SIERRA

1. *110km - 68 miles including the ascent to the parador; allow 4 hours along winding roads*

9km - 6 miles north of Villacarrillo the road enters the Guadalquivir **gorges** *(gargantas)* which lead to the Tranco dam, one of Andalucía's biggest reservoirs which, in turn, provides water for the irrigation of the Úbeda region. When you come within sight of the picturesque **setting**★ of the perched village of **Hornos,** turn right into a road which skirts the lake and from which you will get good **views**★★ of the mountains and, at certain times of the day, of deer drinking at the water's edge. The Sierra del Pozo can be seen on the horizon.

Parque Cinegético (Game Reserve) – *Beyond Bujaraiza.* You may observe some of the typical wildlife in the sierra from lookout points. The call of stags echoes throughout the reserve in late summer.
A little further on you come to the **Centro de Interpretación Torre del Vinagre** which has a hunting museum.

★**Road up to the parador** – The steep road through the pines leads to the *parador* set in a splendidly isolated position. It is popular with hunters.
Return to the Cazorla road.

From a lookout a little further on there is a good **view**★★ of the upper valley of the Guadalquivir. An impressive mountain crest section precedes the Puerto de Las Palomas (1 290m - 4 232ft), a pass marking the dividing line between fertile green mountainsides and ochre-coloured hills. There are magnificent **views**★★ over an immense sweep of olive groves.

La Iruela – Turn right in the village square for the **carretera de los miradores** *(an unsurfaced but car-worthy forest track)* where three successive lookouts command steep **views**★★ of the town and the Castillo de Cazorla. A little further on there are fine **views** of the mountain circus.

Cazorla – The town is dominated by its castle *(photograph p 11).* Cazorla's steep and sometimes stepped alleys are full of character as are its two large squares, framed by old houses.

With this Green Guide
use the Michelin Maps no 441 to 446 at 1:400 000 (1 cm:4 km)
The maps provide both road and tourist information.

CELANOVA

Galicia (Orense)
Population 5 902
Michelin map 441 F 6 – Michelin Atlas España Portugal p 21

During the Middle Ages Celanova was an important halt on the pilgrim route from Portugal to Santiago de Compostela.

Monasterio ⊘ – The large, imposing monastery on the Plaza Mayor was founded in 936 by San Rosendo, Bishop of San Martín de Mondoñedo *(qv)*.

Church – The **façade** of this monumental late-17C edifice displays hints of classicism. The coffered vaulting is decorated with geometrical designs, the cupola with volutes. An immense altarpiece (1697) occupies the back of the apse. Note also the choir-stalls, baroque in the lower part and Gothic in the upper, as well as the fine organ.

★★ **Claustro** – The construction of these cloisters began in 1550 to plans by a monk from Celanova and took until the 18C to complete. The cloisters are among the most beautiful in Galicia: light and shade contrast brilliantly in the interplay of lines and ornamental relief.

Capilla de San Miguel (St Michael's Chapel) – This is one of the monastery's earliest buildings (937) and one of the rare Mozarabic monuments still in good condition.

EXCURSION

Santa Comba de Bande – *26km – 16 miles south on the N540.*
The small 7C Visigothic **iglesia** ★ ⊘ overlooks the lake. Inside the church, the plan is that of a Greek cross, lit by a lantern turret. The apse is square and is preceded by a horseshoe-shaped triumphal arch resting on four pillars with Corinthian capitals. Pure lines and perfect wall masonry add a rich quality to this unique building.

Avoid visiting a church during a service.

CEUTA★

North Africa
Population 73 208
Michelin map 959 folds 5 and 10

Ceuta, the closest African port to the Iberian Peninsula, occupies a strategic position dominating the Straits of Gibraltar. The city, with its typically European style architecture, is situated on the isthmus linking Monte Hacho with the African continent. Conquered by the Portuguese in 1415, the port passed into the hands of the Spanish in 1580, when Philip II annexed the Kingdom of Portugal.

★MONTE HACHO

10km - 6 miles – about half an hour. Best done in the morning.

Calle Independencia and Calle Recintor Sur, running parallel to the seafront, lead to the foot of Monte Hacho which has a citadel at its summit. The *corniche* road encircling the peninsula offers beautiful **views** of the Western Rif coastline to the south and the Spanish coast and the Rock of Gibraltar to the north.
Before reaching the lighthouse (no entry), bear left.

Ermita de San Antonio – *Leave your car in the car park.* At the end of a charming square is the 16C Capilla de San Antonio (Chapel of St Anthony). From the platform of the monument commemorating the passing through of General Franco's troops in 1936, there is a magnificent **view**★★ of, to the left, the town spread out on its slightly curved isthmus around the port, and to the right, far off views of the peninsula coastline.

ADDITIONAL SIGHTS

Museo Municipal ⊘ – This municipal museum houses a white marble Roman sarcophagus, Punic and Roman amphorae, a collection of coins and old weapons as well as various items of ceramic ware.

Other places worthy of interest are the **Iglesia de Nuestra Señora de África** (Church of Our Lady of Africa), housing the statue of the patron saint of the town, the 18C **Catedral** and the **Foso de San Felipe**, an old Portuguese fort where San Juan de Dios, the founder of the Orden de los Hospitalarios (Order of the Hospitallers of St John), worked in 1530.

CHINCHÓN★

Madrid
Population 3 994
Michelin map 444 or 442 L19 – Michelin Atlas España Portugal p 53

The name Chinchón has been made famous by its aniseed spirit and more importantly by the Countess of Chinchón to whom the west owes quinine. The countess, wife of a 17C viceroy of Peru, was cured of tropical fever by an Indian medicament prepared from tree bark; having proved the remedy she brought it back to Europe. In the 18C, Linneas, the Swedish botanist, named the bark-bearing tree chinchona, in the vicereine's honour.

★★**Plaza Mayor** – The uneven but picturesque arcaded square, dominated by its church, is surrounded by three-storeyed houses with wooden balconies. Bullfights are held here in summer.
The brick buildings of the former Augustinian monastery beside the square now house a *parador*.
Aniseed, gin and other spirits are distilled in the old castle at the top of the town.

CIUDAD RODRIGO★

Castilla y León (Salamanca)
Population 14 973
Michelin map 441 K 10 – Michelin Atlas España Portugal p 36

Ciudad Rodrigo appears high on a hilltop, guarded by the square tower of its 14C Alcázar (now a *parador*) and medieval ramparts and, if you are coming from Portugal, on the far side of the Río Agueda spanned by a Roman bridge. After the Moorish invasion it was re-established in the 12C by Count Rodrigo González from whom it takes its name; later it became a stronghold on the Spanish-Portuguese border and was involved in all the conflicts between Castilla and Portugal. Wellington's success in the bloody battle against the French in 1812 won him the title of Duke of Ciudad Rodrigo and Grandee of Spain.
The surrounding region is given over to large estates of ilex trees beneath which graze black pigs and fighting bulls.

★**Plaza Mayor** – Two Renaissance palaces stand on the city's lively main square: the first, now the **Ayuntamiento** (Town Hall), has a façade with two storeys of basket arcading forming a gallery and a loggia, while the second, the **Casa de los Cueto**, has a decorative frieze separating its first and second storeys.

★**Catedral** ⊘ – The cathedral was built in two main stages, first from 1170 to 1230 and then in the 14C; in the 16C Rodrigo Gil de Hontañón added the central apse. The stiffness of the figures of the Disciples in a gallery in the upper part of the south transept façade contrasts with the delicate ornamentation of the surrounding blind arcades. The 13C **Portada de la Virgen** (Doorway of the Virgin) ★, masked outside by a classical belfry which forms the cathedral narthex, has a line of apostles carved between the columns beneath the splayings and the covings.
In the interior, the Isabelline choir-stalls in the *coro* were carved by Rodrigo Alemán. The fine Renaissance **altar**★ in the north aisle is adorned with an alabaster Deposition, beautifully composed and carved in low relief, a masterpiece by Lucas Mitata.
The **cloisters**★ are made up of diverse architectural styles. In the west gallery, the oldest part, Romanesque capitals illustrate man's original sin, while grotesques on the column bases symbolise greed and vanity. Opening off the east gallery is a Plateresque door in the pure Salamanca style decorated with medallions including one (on the right) of the architect Pedro Güemes.

Capilla de Cerralbo – *South of the cathedral*. The chapel, built between 1588 and 1685, is pure and austere but harmonious in the Herreran style. Adjoining the south side is the Plaza del Buen Alcalde, a quiet arcaded square.

Palacio de los Castros (or **Palacio del Conde de Montarco**) – *Access via the eastern arcade of Plaza del Buen Alcade*. This late 15C palace, on Plaza del Conde (Square of the Count), has a long façade and an interesting off-centre doorway surrounded by an *alfiz* and flanked by twisted columns.

Murallas (Ramparts) – The walls built on the remains of Roman foundations in the 12C, were converted to a full defensive system on the north and west flanks in 1710. There are several stairways up to the 2km - 1 mile long sentry path.

When driving in Spain
use the **Michelin Motoring Atlas España Portugal***. Scale 1:400 000.*

Castillo de COCA★★

Castilla y León (Segovia)

Michelin map 444 or 442 I 16 – Michelin Atlas España Portugal p 39

This fortress (**castillo** ⊘) (on the outskirts of Coca village) is the most outstanding example of Mudéjar military architecture in Spain. It was built in the late 15C by Moorish craftsmen for the archbishop of Sevilla, Fonseca, and consists of three concentric perimeters, flanked by polygonal corner towers and turrets with, at the centre, a massive keep. It is the epitome of all fortresses, but with the sun mellowing the pink brick and the interplay of shadows on battlements and watch-towers, it can be attractive as well as awesome.

The *Torre del Homenaje* (keep) and *Capilla* (chapel), which contains Romanesque wood carvings, are open to the public.

Castillo de Coca

EXCURSION

Arévalo – *26km - 16 miles southwest.*
Isabel the Catholic spent her childhood in the 14C **castle** with its massive crenellated keep that dominates the town. Of note also in the town are the Romanesque-Mudéjar churches built of brick and several old mansions.

Plaza de la Villa★, the former Plaza Mayor, is one of the best preserved town squares in Castilla with its half-timbered brick houses resting on pillared porticoes. They blend in perfectly with the Mudéjar east end of the Iglesia de Santa María and its blind arcading.

CÓRDOBA★★★

Andalucía

Population 310 488

Michelin map 446 S 15 – Michelin Atlas España Portugal p 74

Plan of the conurbation in the current Michelin Red Guide España Portugal

Córdoba stands at the halfway point on the right bank of the Guadalquivir where the ranches and farmlands of the Sierra de Córdoba plateau to the north meet the wheatlands and olive groves of the southerly Campiña plains. The city owes its fame to the brilliance of the civilisations which it has twice fostered and which each time raised it to the position of capital.

It could live on its past but has chosen to develop modern industries on its outskirts and maintain its longstanding crafts of silver filigree and tooled leatherwork in their traditional setting in the heart of the city. Mid-May is festival time, with competitions in decking crosses, *patios*, windows and balconies, streets and squares with flowers until the end of the month when the *feria* brings celebrations in Andalusian costume and *flamenco* dancing.

Between Montilla and Lucena, approximately 50km - 30 miles south of Córdoba lies a wine region known as **Montilla-Moriles** which produces excellent wines and spirits comparable to those of Jerez.

The Roman town – Córdoba, capital of Baetica, was the birthplace of **Seneca the Rhetorician** (55 BC - 39 AD), his son **Seneca the Philosopher** (4 BC - 65 AD), who became tutor to Nero, and **Lucan** (39-65 AD). Seneca the Philosopher's nephew and companion to Nero in his student days. His writing, particularly the poem *Pharsalia* which recounts the war between Caesar and Pompey, won him great acclaim.

MICHELIN

Calleja de Las Flores, Córdoba

The early Christian period was marked by the episcopacy of **Ossius** (257-359), counsellor to Emperor Constantine, protagonist of orthodoxy against Arianism and reorganiser of the Church in Spain.

The Córdoba Caliphate – Emirs from the Damascus Caliphate established themselves in Córdoba as early as 719. In 756 **Abd ar-Rahman I**, sole survivor of the **Umayyads** of Damascus who had been annihilated by the Abbasids, arrived to found the dynasty which was to rule over Muslim Spain for three centuries and bring untold prosperity and fame to Córdoba. In 929 **Abd ar-Rahman III** proclaimed himself Caliph, and Spain independent. In the 10C a university was founded which won high renown. The open-mindedness and tolerance alive at the time allowed the three communities – Christian, Jewish and Muslim – not only to live side by side but to enrich one another intellectually and culturally. On the accession, in 976, of the feeble **Hisham II**, power fell into the hands of the ruthless but remarkable **Al-Mansur** (the Victorious); his descendants, however, failed to prevent Al-Andalus from fragmenting into small warring kingdoms, the **reinos de taifas**. Córdoba itself became part of the Kingdom of Sevilla in 1070. Political decline in no way diminished intellectual life, however. There lived in the city from 1126 to 1198 the Moor **Averroës**, a universal scholar – physicist, astrologer, mathematician, doctor and philosopher – who, although he was prevented from teaching by the doctrinaire Almohad leader, Yacoub al-Mansur, who opposed his theories, did much to bring the learning of Aristotle to the west. A contemporary of Averroës, the Jew **Maimónides** (1135-1204) was famed for his learning in medicine, theology and philosophy, but had to flee to Morocco and later Egypt to escape persecution.

Eventually reconquered by the Christians in 1236, the city's prosperity waned until the 16C and 17C, when Córdoba leatherwork, embossed, tooled and coloured, became the fashion for wall and seat coverings.

Some famous Córdobans – Among the city's sons are Gonzalo Fernández de Córdoba, the **Gran Capitán** (1453-1515) born in the nearby town of Montilla, who conquered the Kingdom of Naples in 1504, and **Luis de Góngora** (1561-1627), the great baroque poet and major exponent of *culteranismo*, a school of poetry characterised by its cultured verse. His main works include the *Fábula de Polifemo y Galatea*, and *Soledades*.

The Sephardic Jews

No history of Spain is complete without a mention of the Jews whose presence may still be felt in juderías (old Jewish quarters) and synagogues. The main Jewish towns in the past were Toledo, Córdoba, Sevilla, Palma de Mallorca and Girona.

The Sephardim or Sephardic Jews (Sefarad is the Hebrew word for Spain) came to the Iberian Peninsula in Antiquity at the same time as the Greeks and Phoenicians. In the 8C during the Arab occupation, they welcomed the Muslims who regarded them as sympathetic allies. The Muslims put them in charge of negotiating with the Christian community. As merchants, bankers, craftsmen, doctors and scholars, Jews played an important economic role and influenced the domains of culture and science. Some became famous, like Maimónides of Córdoba *(qv)*.

The Jews were particularly prosperous under the Caliphate of Córdoba (10-11C). However, at the end of the 11C, Jews from Andalucía moved to Toledo (qv) and Catalunya, especially Girona *(qv)*, as a result of intolerance and persecution under the Almohads. They were often persecuted by Christians during the Reconquest (a royal decree forced them to wear a piece of red or yellow cloth). In the end they were expelled by the Catholic Monarchs in 1492. Some chose to convert, others (known as Marranos), in spite of having publicly converted, continued practising their Jewish faith in hiding, while most emigrated to other parts of the Mediterranean, to the Netherlands, to England and America.

Today the Sephardic Jews represent 60% of the Diaspora. Some of them have kept their language, Ladino, which is pure 15C Castilian.

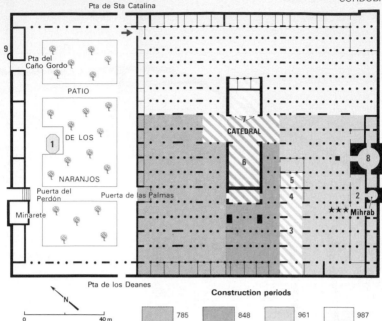

Pta de Sta Catalina

9

Pta del
Caño Gordo

PATIO

DE LOS

1

NARANJOS

Puerta del
Perdón

Minarete

Puerta de las Palmas

CATEDRAL

6

7

5

4

8

2

3

★★★ **Mihrab**

Pta de los Deanes

N

0   40 m

Construction periods

785   848   961   987

★★★ THE MEZQUITA AND THE JUDERÍA *time: 3 hours*

Córdoba's three faiths are represented in this quarter of the city: Islamic with its outstanding *mezquita* (mosque), Christian with its cathedral strangely incorporated into the mosque, and Jewish with its synagogue.

★★★ **Mezquita-Catedral (Mosque-Cathedral) (BZ)** ⊘ – Each part of the heterogeneous edifice must be admired separately.

Mezquita – The overall plan is the traditional Muslim one of a crenellated square perimeter enclosing the Patio de los Naranjos (Orange Tree Court) with a basin for ritual ablution – in this case that of Al-Mansur (**1**) – a hall for prayer and a minaret. The mosque was built in several stages. The first Muslims to arrive in Córdoba were content to share the Visigothic church of St Vincent with the Christians. Soon, however, this proved insufficient and Abd ar-Rahman I (758-788) purchased their part of the site from the Christians. He razed the church and around the year 780 began the construction of a splendid mosque with 11 aisles each opening onto the Patio de los Naranjos. Marble pillars and stone from former Roman and Visigothic buildings were re-used in the mosque which became famous for an architectural innovation: the super-imposition of two tiers of arches to give added height and spaciousness.
The mosque was enlarged over the years: in 848 Abd ar-Rahman II had it extended to the present-day Capilla de Villaviciosa (Villaviciosa Chapel), in 961 El Hakam II built the *mihrab*, and lastly, in 987, Al-Mansur gave it its present size by adding 8 more aisles (recognisable by their red brick pavement).
The interior is a forest of columns (about 850) and the horseshoe-shaped arches consist of alternating white (stone) and red (brick) voussoirs.

Make your way to the Puerta de las Palmas.

The aisle off the doorway, wider than the others and which served as the main aisle of the original mosque, has a beautiful *artesonado* ceiling. It leads to the **mihrab** ★★★ before which the faithful, led by the imam, would pray. What is nor-mally a simple niche is in this case a sumptuously decorated room preceded by a triple **maksourah** (**2**) or enclosure reserved for the caliph. The enclosure is roofed by three ribbed domes which rest on a most unusual series of apparently inter-weaving multifoil arches, as striking as the cupolas themselves which are faced with mosaics against a background of gold. Decoration throughout adds to the richness of the architecture: on the mosaics, alabaster plaques and stucco are ornate arabesques and palm-leaf motifs sometimes framed by Cufic script.
In the 13C, conversion of the building to Christian use brought certain physical alte-rations: the aisles (except that off the Puerta de las Palmas) were walled off from the court; a few columns were removed and pointed arches substituted for the Moorish ones when the first cathedral was built (**3**) – fortunately nothing was done which destroyed the perspectives in the mosque. Alfonso X was responsible for the chancel in the **Capilla de Villaviciosa** or **Lucernario** (**4**) and built the **Capilla Real** ★ (**5**) deco-rated in the 13C with Mudéjar stucco which harmonised with the whole.

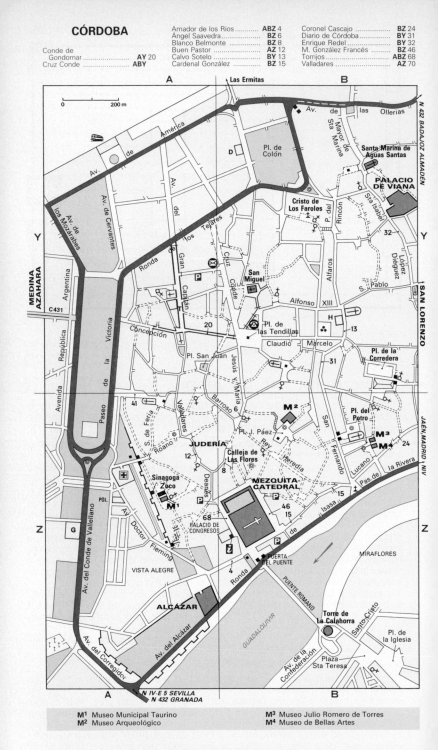

CÓRDOBA

M¹   Museo Municipal Taurino
M²   Museo Arqueológico
M³   Museo Julio Romero de Torres
M⁴   Museo de Bellas Artes

Catedral – In the 16C the cathedral canons desired more sumptuous surroundings. They began by cutting away the centre of the mosque to erect loftier vaulting. In spite of the talent of the architect Hernán Ruiz and his followers, Emperor Charles V was far from pleased with the result: "You have destroyed something unique", he said, "to build something commonplace". The search for grandeur led to a Gothic style transept and apse (1523-1547); Renaissance style decorative figures in medallions in the apsidal vaulting (1560); and dense Italian style stucco crowded with cherubim decorating the nave vaulting (1598) and in the coffered dome over the transept (1600). Additional enrichments are the baroque **choir-stalls★★** (**6**) by Pedro Duque Cornejo (c1750) and two **pulpits★★** (**7**) of marble, jasper and mahogany.

Tesoro – The treasury, built by the Baroque architect Francisco Hurtado Izquierdo, can be found in the **Capilla del Cardenal** (Cardinal's Chapel) **(8)**. A monumental C 16 **monstrance** by E. Arfe and an exceptional baroque figure of Christ in ivory stand out in this collection of liturgical objects.

Exterior features of the complex include the **minaret** (267 steps, fine **views**), from the top of which the muezzin called the prayer. In the 17C the minaret was enveloped in a baroque tower. At its foot, giving onto the street, is the 14C Mudéjar **Puerta del Pardón** (Pardon Doorway) which is faced with bronze. A little further on is a small chapel to the deeply venerated **Virgen de los Faroles** (Virgin of the Lanterns) **(9)**.

★★ **Judería (Old Jewish Quarter) (ABZ)** – Narrow streets, white walls spilled over with brilliant flowers, doors half open onto cool *patios*, delicate window grilles, bars where a group of Córdobans may burst into song to the accompaniment of a guitar, snapping fingers or sharp handclaps – such are the features of the old Jewish quarter, a colourful maze northwest of the cathedral.

Sinagoga (AZ) ⊙ – The Córdoba and Toledo synagogues are the only major synagogues which remain in Spain today. Built in the early 14C, this one consists of a small square room with a balcony on one side for the women. The upper parts of the walls are covered in Mudéjar stucco.

Not far away is the **Museo Municipal Taurino** or Bullfighting Museum *(see below)* and the **Zoco** or suk, where craftsmen work around a large *patio* which in summer is the setting for *flamenco* dancing.

ADDITIONAL SIGHTS

★★ **Palacio de Viana (BY)** ⊙ – Viana palace, a fine example of 15C Cordoban civil architecture, has 12 *patios* and an attractive garden. The city is famous for the beauty of its *patios* and those in this palace, with their charm and sensitivity are, without doubt, worthy of their renown.

The interior is lent a sense of harmony by its rich furnishings. On the ground floor are precious collections of porcelain, 17-19C side-arms and tapestries. The staircase to the first floor has a beautiful Mudéjar *artesonado* ceiling made of cedar. Of the many rooms open the most interesting are the gallery of Córdoban leather with magnificent 15-18C work, the room hung with tapestries made in the royal workshops after cartoons by Goya, the library and the main room adorned with a rich *artesonado* ceiling and tapestries illustrating the Trojan War and various Spanish tales.

The old stables are also open.

★ **Museo Arqueológico Provincial (BZ M²)** ⊙ – The archaeological museum is in the Palacio de los Páez, a 16C Renaissance palace designed by Hernán Ruiz. Displayed in rooms around the cool *patios* are prehistoric Iberian and particularly Roman collections of low reliefs, capitals, sarcophagi and mosaics, testifying to the importance of Córdoba at the time, as well as remains from the Visigothic period. The first floor galleries house examples of Córdoba's Muslim decorative arts: ceramics, a model of the mosque, capitals and bronze sculptures including the outstanding 10C work from Medina Azahara of a **stag★** or *cervatillo* decorated with plant motifs. Note also the Abad Samson bell and a large collection of well copings.

★ **Alcázar (AZ)** ⊙ – The Alcázar of the Umayyads stood at the centre of magnificent gardens facing the mosque on the site of what is now the Palacio Episcopal (Bishop's Palace). The present edifices were built under Alfonso XI in the early 14C. Of the palace there remain attractively cool Moorish *patios* with ornamental basins and pools, baths, a few rooms with Roman **mosaics★** and a fine 3C **sarcophagus★**. From the towers there is a **view** of the gardens, the Guadalquivir, the Roman bridge and the Torre de la Calahorra. The **gardens★**, in Arabic style, are terraced and refreshed with pools and fountains, and cypresses.

★ **Iglesias Fernandinas** – On 29 June 1236, Ferdinand III reconquered Córdoba. The arrival of the Christians had a large impact on the city's architecture with the construction of 14 parish churches under Ferdinand (Fernando). The beauty of these churches can still be seen today, particularly in **Santa Marina de Aguas Santas** (St Marina of the Holy Waters) **(BY)**, **San Miguel** (St Michael) **(BY)** and **San Lorenzo** (St Lawrence) **(BY)**. These late 13C and early 14C temples of stone, built in primitive Gothic style, are endowed with a sober yet rounded beauty by the purely structural elements. The addition of single trumpet-shaped doorways introduces the only lighter aspect to these edifices.

Torre de La Calahorra (BZ) ⊙ – The Moorish fortress was built in the 14C to defend the Roman bridge. It now houses a museum which, through audio-control techniques, traces the history of the Cordoban Caliphate, a period of great cultural, artistic, philosophic and scientific prosperity. Major trends in 12C Christian, Jewish and Muslim thought are illustrated through information on Alfonso X, Maimónides, Averroës and Ibn-Arabi respectively. There is also a fine **model★** of the mosque as it was in the 13C.

Museo Municipal Taurino (Municipal Bullfighting Museum) (**AZ M¹**) ⊘ – The museum, housed in a 16C mansion, has collections of items related to tauromachy including engravings, posters, bullfighters' costumes and documents on Córdoba's most famous matadors: Lagartijo, Guerrita, Manolete and Machaquito.

Plazuela del Potro (Square of the Colt) (**BZ**) – On this square, named after its fountain statue, stands the charming inn, **Posada del Potro** ⊘, described by Cervantes in *Don Quixote*. It now houses an interesting exhibition on Córdoban leatherwork.

On the far side of the square are the **Museo Julio Romero de Torres** (**BZ M³**) ⊘, a museum housing works by the early 20C Córdoban who painted beautiful women, and the **Museo de Bellas Artes** (Fine Arts Museum) (**BZ M⁴**) ⊘ with paintings by Spanish artists.

Cristo de Los Faroles (Christ of the Lanterns) (**BY**) – The Calvary surrounded by wrought-iron lanterns in a silent, austere square, is well known throughout Spain.

Plaza de la Corredera (**BY**) – The square, lined with 17C arcades, was formerly used for bullfighting.

EXCURSIONS

★ **Medina Azahara** (**AY**) ⊘ – *Leave Córdoba on the C 431. After 8km - 5 miles bear right into a road (3km - 2 miles) which ends on an esplanade.*
Excavations have revealed the remains of a sumptuous city built by Abd ar-Rahman III. Construction began in 936, however, hardly had the caliphs had time to complete the undertaking when it was sacked in 1013 by the Berbers, grown angry after aiding Al-Mansur's descendants who had not granted them power as expected. The city extended upwards in three tiers – a mosque below, gardens at the centre, and an *alcázar* at the top, of which two wings have been restored. In one of them the Abd ar-Rahman III room has gradually been reconstituted with the incredible floral decorations which once covered the walls, arches and capitals; whereas displayed on the floor are admirably carved stucco and marble pieces.

Las Ermitas (**BY**) – *13km - 8 miles west of Córdoba on the El Brillante road.*
Hermitages have stood on this site since as far back as the 6C.
There are lovely **views**★ of Córdoba and the Guadalquivir valley from the lookout.

CORIA

Extremadura (Cáceres)
Population 11 260
Michelin map 444 M 10 – Michelin Atlas España Portugal p 49

Coria stands at the centre of a tobacco growing region overlooking the Alagón valley. The city, once the Roman township of *Caurium*, still contains walls and gateways rebuilt on the ancient foundations in the Middle Ages. Coria has been the seat of a bishopric since the Reconquest.

★ **Catedral** ⊘ – The cathedral, a Gothic edifice embellished with elegant Plateresque decoration in the 16C, is crowned with a baroque tower and has a sculptured frieze on the top of its walls. Inside, the tall, single aisle has vaulting adorned with lierne and tierceron ribs which are typical of the region. Note the 18C altarpiece and, in the *coro*, the wrought-iron grilles and the Gothic choir-stalls.

La CORUÑA / A CORUÑA★

Galicia
Population 252 694
Michelin map 441 B 4 – Michelin Atlas España Portugal p 2
Plan of the conurbation in the current Michelin Red Guide España Portugal

The site of Galicia's principal city is a rocky islet, linked to the mainland by a narrow strip of sand. The lighthouse stands to the north, the curved harbour to the south and along the west side of the isthmus, sandy Riazor beach. Three distinct quarters testify to La Coruña's growth: the **City** (Ciudad), at the northern end of the harbour, a charming old quarter with its small peaceful squares and Romanesque churches, the business and commercial centre on the isthmus with wide avenues and shopping streets (**Avenida de Los Cantones** (**AZ 7** and **8**), **Calles Real** and **San Andrés**), and the **Ensanche** to the south, built up with warehouses and industrial premises, a reminder that La Coruña is the sixth largest commercial port in Spain as well as an important industrial and fishing centre.

A CORUÑA
LA CORUÑA

Cantón Grande .... **AZ** 7
Cantón Pequeño .... **AZ** 8
Real .... **AY**
San Andrés .... **AYZ**

Compostela .... **AZ** 13
Damas .... **BY** 14

Ferrol .... **AZ** 18
Finisterre (Av. de) .... **AZ** 19
Gómez Zamalloa .... **AZ** 20
Herrerías .... **BY** 23
Juan Canalejo .... **AY** 24
Juan de Vega (Av.) .... **AZ** 26
Maestranza .... **BY** 27
María Pita (Pl. de) .... **BY** 28
Padre Feijóo .... **AZ** 32
Payo Gómez .... **AZ** 36
Picavia .... **AZ** 37
Pontevedra (Pl. de) .... **AZ** 40
Riego del Agua .... **BY** 42

Rubine (Av. de) .... **AZ** 45
San Agustín .... **BY** 46
San Agustín (Cuesta de) .... **BY** 47
Sánchez Bregua .... **AZ** 50
Santa María .... **BY** 51
Santa Catalina .... **AZ** 52
Teresa Herrera .... **AZ** 55

E Colegiata de Santa María del Campo

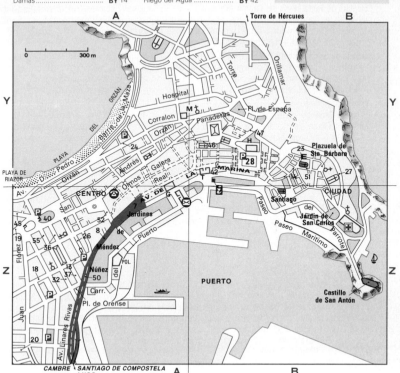

HISTORICAL NOTES

The town was already well developed in Roman times as can be seen from the old lighthouse, the **Torre de Hércules** (**BY**). The city walls date back to the 13C although they were constantly being rebuilt until, by the 18C, they formed a complete defence system to which was then added a castle, the **Castillo de San Antón** (**BZ**). General Sir John Moore, born in 1761 in Glasgow and mortally wounded in the Battle of Elviña in 1809, lies buried at the centre of the old city, in the **Jardín de San Carlos** (St Charles Gardens) (**BZ**).

It was from La Coruña (A Coruña in Galician) that Philip II's **Invincible Armada** set sail in 1588. The fleet of 130 men-of-war, manned by 10 000 sailors and transporting 19 000 soldiers, set out for England ostensibly to punish Elizabeth for the execution of Mary, Queen of Scots. The ill-fated expedition, however, dogged by bad weather and harassed by the smaller, more easily manœuvred English ships, was a failure. 63 ships and more than 15 000 men were lost. The defeat marked the end of Spanish sea power. A year later, in 1589, Elizabeth sent Drake to attack the Iberian coast. The invaders fired La Coruña but the town was saved by **María Pita** who seized the English standard from the beacon where it had been planted and gave the alarm.

Over two centuries later, during the Peninsular War, Marshal Soult led Napoleon's forces to a decisive victory over the English in the Battle of Elviña in 1809.

Throughout the latter years of the 19C, during the period of frequent liberal uprisings, La Coruña consistently supported the insurgents and in consequence suffered severe reprisals.

The town is proud of being the birthplace of the novelist **Émilia Pardo Bazán** (1852-1921) and to have been a home to the poet **Rosalía de Castro** (1837-1885).

SIGHTS

★ **Avenida de la Marina** (**ABY**) – The avenue, facing the harbour, is lined by tall houses with glassed-in balconies typical of La Coruña. Extending it on one side is the Paseo de la Dársena and on the other the attractively landscaped **Jardines de Méndez Núñez** (**AZ**), gardens with a variety of flowering trees.

Plaza de María Pita (BY 28) – The vast pedestrian square just behind Avenida de la Marina is named after the town's 16C heroine. It has a great many terrace cafés and is lined on three sides by arcades upon which rest houses with glassed-in galleries. On the fourth side stands the **Ayuntamiento** (Town Hall).

La Ciudad (The City) (BYZ) – La Ciudad is the original town with narrow cobbled streets and peaceful squares at the northern end of the harbour.

Colegiata de Santa María del Campo (BY E) ⏱ – A 15C Calvary stands in the small square between a fine baroque house and the Romanesque collegiate church of Santa María del Campo which has, beneath its rose window, a 13C or 14C portal and a tympanum carved with the Adoration of the Magi.

Plazuela de Santa Bárbara (BY) ⏱ – The small shaded square, a peaceful spot, is closely surrounded by old La Coruña houses and the high walls with iron grilles at the windows of the Convento de Santa Bárbara. On summer evenings concerts are given. A late-14C lintel above a doorway has a carving of the souls of the dead being weighed before Christ, the Father, St James, St Francis and St Dominic.

Iglesia de Santiago (Church of St James) **(BZ)** ⏱ – The church's three apses, which overlook Plaza de Azcárraga, and the north door are Romanesque. The west door is Gothic; Santiago *Matamoros* or St James Slayer of the Moors is shown on horseback below the tympanum while the figures of St John and St Mark are carved against the piers. The massive arches supporting the timber roof above the nave are also Gothic. The church contains a beautifully carved stone pulpit.

Torre de Hércules (Hercules Tower or Lighthouse) (BY) – This was built in the 2C AD and is the oldest lighthouse still functioning. In 1790 when Charles III modified the tower to its present square shape, the original outer ramp was enclosed to form an inner staircase. From the top (104m - 341ft), there is a **view** of the town and the coast.

EXCURSION

Cambre ⏱ – *11km - 7 miles south.*
The 12C Romanesque country church of **Santa María★** has a lovely façade, divided into three sections corresponding with the nave and two aisles inside. Multifoil arches, emphasizing the windows on either side, show Moorish influence as do the buttress capitals. The tympanum is carved with the Holy Lamb in a medallion supported by angels. The interior, with its great purity of style, has a feature often found in churches on the Santiago pilgrim route, an apse circled by an ambulatory with five radiating chapels.

COSTA BLANCA★

Comunidad Valenciana (Alicante, Murcia)

Michelin map 445 P 29-30, Q 29-30 – Michelin Atlas España Portugal pp 69 and 79

The Costa Blanca or White Coast stretches south from the shores of the Valencian province of Alicante to those of Murcia. It is mainly flat and sandy with the occasional area of high land where the *sierras* drop to the sea. The hot climate, low rainfall (350 mm - less than 14 inches a year), dazzling white light after which the coast is named, long beaches and turquoise water attract a vast number of Spanish and foreign tourists throughout the year.

FROM DENIA TO GUADALEST *165km - 103 miles – allow 1 day*

Denia – The former Greek colony was taken over by the Romans who named it *Dianium*. Denia today is a commercial port, fishing harbour, industrial centre specialising in the manufacture of toys, and a popular seaside resort. The fortress overlooking the town houses an archaeological museum.

The coast south of Denia becomes steep and rocky with pine forests.

★**Cabo de San Antonio** – From near the lighthouse on this headland, a last foothill of the Sierra del Mongó, there is a good **view★** towards Jávea and the Cabo de la Nao headland.

Jávea – The old quarter stands on high ground, its houses closely grouped around a fortified 14C Gothic church. The resort's modern quarter has grown up near its harbour, around the sandy beach where there is a *parador*.

★**Cabo de la Nao** – The climb affords views over Jávea at the foot of the Sierra del Mongó, before you enter thick pine-woods relieved only by villas standing in individual clearings. Cabo de la Nao is considered to be the eastern outpost of the Sierras Béticas (Baetic Cordillera) chain although in fact the formation continues under the sea to reappear as the island of Ibiza. There is a beautiful **view★** south from the point along the indented coastline to the Peñón de Ifach. Sea caves (approached by boat) and charming creeks such as **La Granadella** (south) and **Cala Blanca** (north) are excellent for underwater swimming.

Calpe – The **Peñón de Ifach★**, an impressive rocky outcrop 332m - 1 089ft high, pro- vides Calpe with a distinctive setting. A path leads to the top of the Peñón *(about 1 hour's walk)* from which, as you climb, you will get interesting views along the coast of Calpe and its salt-pans, of the darkish mountain chains, and northwards of the precipitous coast as far as Cabo de la Nao.

The Sierra de Bernia road twists and turns before crossing the spectacular Barranco de Mascarat (Mascarat Ravine) in the mountain hinterland to Cabo de la Nao.

Altea – Altea, white walls, rose coloured roofs and glazed blue tile domes, rises in tiers up a hillside overlooking the sea – a symphony of colour and reflected light below the Sierra de Bernia. A walk through the alleys to the church and then the view from the square over the village and beyond to the Penón de Ifach will reveal the attraction of so many painters towards Altea.

Benidorm – *Town plan in the current Michelin Red Guide España Portugal*. The excellent climate and two immense beaches (the Levante and the Poniente), curving away on either side of a small rock promontory, have provided the basic elements for Benidorm's incredible success as a tourist resort. It has grown from a modest fishing village in the fifties to a kind of Mediterranean Manhattan with modern tower blocks overlooking the sea, all manner of entertainment and a very lively nightlife.

From the lookout on **El Castillo** point, there are **views★** of the beaches and the Island of Plumbaria. The old quarter stands behind the point, close to the blue domed church.

An excursion inland from Benidorm to Guadalest is a must.

Take the road to Callosa de Ensarriá and from there head for Alcoy.

On the drive inland, you pass through small valleys cloaked in all sorts of fruit trees, including citrus and medlars. The village of **Polop** stretches up a hillside in a picturesque mountain setting. Beyond, the landscape becomes more arid but the views more extensive, the mountains more magnificent.

★Guadalest – Guadalest stands out from the terraced valleys of olive and almond trees to face the harsh limestone escarpments of the Sierra de Aitana. The **site★** is impressive with the village, in self-defence, forced halfway up a ridge of rock, a natural stronghold accessible only through an archway cut into the stone. Walk round the **Castillo de San José** (now the site of a cemetery) of which only ruins remain of the castle fortifications wrecked by an earthquake in 1744, to see the view over the green Guadalest reservoir with its reflections of the surrounding mountain crests, the amazing site of the old village, and beyond, the sea.

COSTA BRAVA★★

Catalunya (Girona)

Michelin map 443 E 39, F 39, G 38-39 – Michelin Atlas España Portugal pp 19 and 33

The Costa Brava or Wild Coast, comprising the entire coastline of the province of Girona, derives its name from its twisted, rocky shoreline. The Catalan mountain ranges form a line of cliffs which fall away to the sea. The beautiful inlets along the coast's entire length, its clear waters, picturesque harbours and fishing villages have given it an international reputation and attracted flocks of foreign tourists.

★THE ALBERES COASTLINE

⬚ From Portbou to Roses

66km - 41 miles – about 4 hours – local map overleaf

The last of the **Alberes** foothills form huge, enclosed bays, like those of Portbou and El Port de la Selva. The road twists up along the cliff tops from Portbou to Colera.

El Port de Llançà – The quiet village with a good flat beach has a harbour with little shelter from offshore winds like the *Tramontana*, or sudden Mediterranean storms that can be violent on this part of the coast.

El Port de la Selva – A natural harbour in a vast bay where fishing is an impor- tant occupation.

★★Sant Pere de Rodes ⊙ – *7km - 4 miles from El Port de la Selva then 1/4 hour's walk.*

The **monastery ruins** stand in a remarkable **setting★★** at the foot of the Sant Salvador crest from which the full sweep of the coast from Cerbère (France) to Cabo de Creus can be seen. Of the 10C conventual buildings erected by the Benedictines and protected by massive defensive walls surmounted by two tall towers, but aban- doned and pillaged in the 18C, the **church** remains best preserved. There are unusual architectural features in the interior including the two levels of columns (reminiscent of temples built in Antiquity) supporting the vaulting in the nave. The splendid **capitals** show Córdoban and Byzantine influence in the strapwork and acanthus leaf carving. Another rare feature for the time is the narrow ambulatory off which branch ovoid apses. Stairs from the north transept lead to a watch path built into the thickness of the walls above the ambulatory.

The coast between El Port de la Selva and Cadaqués is a series of beautiful creeks accessible only by sea (from El Port de la Selva). The road, meanwhile, continues through abandoned terraced hillsides covered in olive trees.

★**Cadaqués** – Last century Cadaqués was a simple fishing village; "discovery" by 20C writers and artists spread its name abroad (Salvador Dalí built a house by the *cala* or creek of Port Lligat). In spite of its popularity in the summer months, it remains a delightful place with white arcaded houses lining the main street that hugs the shoreline. Standing in the shaded old quarter is the parish church, which in contrast to its sober exterior, contains a richly decorated baroque altarpiece.

Once again, the road runs inland through the hills before descending to Roses bay.

Roses – This fishing village dates back to the ancient Greeks who founded a colony named Rhode on the site. The port developed in the 11C when the one at Castelló d'Empúries became silted up by the Fluvià.

THE EMPORDÀ PLAIN

② From Roses to Begur
65km - 40 miles – about 3 hours – local map opposite

This stretch of the Costa Brava, at the foot of the *cordillera*, is preceded by the fertile Empordà plain.

Empuriabrava – This "Venice", begun in 1973 for very wealthy, mainly German, sailing enthusiasts, is an enormous marina network of canals alongside which are villas, each with its own boat at the door.

Castelló d'Empúries –The **Iglesia de Santa María** ⊙ was built in the 13C when Castelló was at the height of its glory. It is flanked by a Catalan tower. In the 15C, the church was endowed with an imposing portal which has a carving of the Adoration of the Magi on the tympanum. Inside, the vast nave is separated from the aisles by slender columns. The high altar alabaster **retable**★ is carved with scenes of the Passion and crowned by conical pinnacles.

A rock formation between the rivers Fluvià and Ter divides upper from lower Empordà and forms the indented, though flat **coast**★ of the Golfo de Roses, a bay, ideal for water sports.

L'Escala – Two small promontories shelter the fishing harbour of which the speciality is salted anchovies. L'Escala has beautiful beaches, popular with swimmers.

★**Empúries (Ampurias)** – *See EMPÚRIES.*

★**Pals** – The medieval village with its pink stone houses has been restored. There are rampart remains, old houses and winding alleys with covered ways.

★★THE CORNICHE ROAD

③ From Begur to Blanes
98km - 61 miles – about 4 hours – local map above opposite

The coastline along this part of the Costa Brava varies between flat and rocky, with pine-woods giving way to a succession of long beaches and little coves and inlets.

The Costa Brava's most beautiful and best preserved creeks are around Begur: **Aiguafreda** and **Aigua Blava** are exclusive havens of luxury villas and hotels built amongst the pines. **Tamariu** creek is more popular.

Begur – The 18C castle above the village commands fine views. Some of the fine villas in Begur date from the beginning of the century and were built by returning emigrants from Spain's American colonies.

Calella de Palafrugell – This attractive fishing port, a pleasant combination of summer villas and fishermen's abodes, is known for its Festival de Habaneras (songs and dances of Afro-Cuban origin) held on the beach in July. The local **cremat**, a mixture of tafia rum, sugar and coffee, is drunk hot.

★**Jardín Botánico del Cap Roig** ⊙ – A road goes south from Calella to a farm at the entrance to these botanical gardens. Mediterranean shrubs and rare plants fill an attractively terraced park built out of the living rock, sheer above the sea. There are beautiful **views**★★ of Calella and the coast.

The road continues along the coast where beaches alternate with rocky inlets.

★ **S'Agaró** – S'Agaró is an elegant resort with luxurious villas in the middle of a pine forest. There are fine **views** ★ from the promenade on the seafront.

Sant Feliu de Guíxols – Sant Feliu lies encircled by hills in the curve of a bay. With its terrace cafés along the seafront, the resort is one of the most popular on the coast. It was founded in the 10C and grew up around its Benedictine monastery, of which a few traces can still be seen on the way out on the Tossa de Mar road. By the main square, marked at its centre by the 17C Arco de San Benito (St Benedict Arch), and abutting the old town wall, stands the church. The interior was modified in the 14C but the Romanesque façade was untouched and is preceded still by a curious arcade, Mozarabic in style below, Romanesque above.

Lay-bys enable one to enjoy the **corniche road** ★★ from Sant Feliu to Tossa de Mar which alternately skirts the sheer cliff top or descends into the **calas** ★ (rocky inlets) with their clustered houses.

Map labels:
PERPIGNAN · PERPIGNAN · FRANCE · N 114 · Cerbère · Le Perthus · Portbou · A 7 · N 260 · El Port de Llançà · El Port de la Selva · R. Muga · Llobregat · ★★ **Sant Pere de Rodes** · GE 613 · Cabo de Creus · San Salvador 670 · GE 614 · **Cadaqués** ★ · Figueres/Figueras · C 260 · Roses · **Castelló d'Empúries** · Empuriabrava · RIPOLL · N 260 · Golfo de Roses · R. Fluvià · **Empúries** ★ · L'Escala · RIPOLL · GE 632 · Banyoles · R. Ter · C 150 · Daró · **GIRONA/GERONA** · C 255 · ★ **Pals** · GE 650 · Aiguafreda · N 141 · **Begur** · Aigua Blava · Palafrugell · Tamariu · R. · Calella de Palafrugell · C 255 · **Cabo Roig** ★ · C 250 · Palamós · A 7 · C 253 · ③ · S'Agaró ★ · C 253 · GE 682 · **S'Agaró** ★ · **Sant Feliu de Guíxols** · N II · BARCELONA · ★ **Tossa de Mar** · R. Tordera · Lloret de Mar · **Blanes** · 0 · 15 km · ① · ② · ③ · P

★ **Tossa de Mar** – This major resort has a sand beach that curves around to the promontory on which stand the lighthouse and the 13C walls of the **Vila Vella**, the Old Town.

The **corniche road** ★ continues to Platja de Canyelles, then it drops down the hillside to the beaches.

Blanes – This is the southernmost resort on the Costa Brava.

★ **Jardín Botánico de Marimurtra** ⊘ – These beautiful botanical gardens are on a promontory high above the sea. There are more than 4 000 plant species from the five continents, in particular cacti and succulents from America and Africa. Twisting paths command wonderful **views** ★★ of Cala Forcanera and the coast.

COSTA DE CANTABRIA ★

CANTABRIAN COAST – Cantabria
Michelin map 442 B 16-20 – Michelin Atlas España Portugal pp 12 and 13

The Cantabrian coast stretches in a succession of gulfs, capes, peninsulas, splendid bays like those of Santander and Santoña, *rías* and long sandy beaches from Castro-Urdiales to San Vicente de la Barquera. The resorts of Santander and Comillas are especial favourites with Spanish holidaymakers while Laredo, San Vicente de la Barquera and Noja tend to attract foreigners. The hinterland, a very green wooded area, is given over to stock raising. In some places in the province summer hay-making is carried out according to age-old methods. Village houses often bear coats of arms, of which the finest examples are in Santillana del Mar.
Cantabria is rich in prehistoric caves with more than 20 bearing traces of human habitation in the Palaeolithic Age.

SIGHTS

Castro-Urdiales – The village, clustered round a Gothic church, a ruined castle and a lighthouse, stands on a promontory overlooking a vast bay. The annual Coso Blanco festival is held on the first Friday in July.

Laredo – The **old town** huddled around its church adjoins a long beach lined by modern buildings. It is a maze of narrow alleyways climbing up a hillside which shelters the fishing boat harbour below.

Limpias – The small fishing village on the banks of the Ría Asón is known for a miracle which occurred here in 1919. The local church contains the deeply venerated Crucifix said to have shed tears of blood, a wonderfully carved baroque figure attributed to Juan de Mena.

La Bien Aparecida – A winding uphill road leads to the baroque shrine of Nuestra Señora de la Bien Aparecida. Veneration for the patron of Cantabria province dates back to 1605. Splendid **panorama**★ of the Asón valley.

Santoña – The fishing port facing Laredo was selected as a military headquarters by the French in the Peninsular War. The **Iglesia de Nuestra Señora del Puerto** ⊘, which was remodelled in the 18C, has, in addition to Gothic aisles, Romanesque features including carved capitals and an old font.

Bareyo – The small **Iglesia de Santa María de Bareyo** ⊘ stands on a slope overlooking the Ría de Ajo. It retains interesting features from its original Romanesque design including slender, moulded arches and historiated capitals in the apse. The **font**★ is probably Visigothic.

★★**Peña Cabarga (view)** – A road with a 16% gradient (1 in 6) leads to the summit (568m - 1 863ft) on which stands a monument to the Conquistadores and the Seamen Adventurers of Castilla. From the top there is a splendid **panorama** of Santander bay and town.

★**Santander** – *See SANTANDER.*

★★**Santillana del Mar and Cuevas de Altamira (Caves)**★★ – *See SANTILLANA DEL MAR and ALTAMIRA.*

★**Comillas** – Comillas is a pleasant seaside resort with a delightful Plaza Mayor, a local beach and easy access to the extensive sands at Oyambre – 5km - 3 miles west. The town was a royal residence at the time of Alfonso XII. Buildings which catch the eye include, in the vast park surrounding the neo-Gothic **Palacio de los Marqueses de Comillas**, a freakish pavilion by Gaudí, **El Capricho** (now a restaurant) and, overlooking the sea from the crown of the hill, the Universidad Pontífica (Papal University).

★**San Vicente de la Barquera** – This resort has an unusual **site**★, a vast beach on the other side of the *ría* and interesting old houses. The **Iglesia de Nuestra Señora de los Ángeles** (Our Lady of the Angels) at the top of the partially fortified hill, has two Romanesque portals, Gothic aisles and several tombs dating from the 15C and 16C. If you are continuing to Unquera, look back after a few minutes for a pleasing **view**★ of San Vicente.

COSTA DE LA LUZ

Andalucía (Huelva, Cádiz)
Michelin map 446 U 7-10, V 10, W 10-11, X 11-13
Michelin Atlas España Portugal pp 82, 83 and 88

The Spanish coast from the Portuguese frontier to Tarifa on the Straits of Gibraltar is edged with beaches of fine sand interrupted by the Guadiana, Tinto, Guadalquivir and other river mouths. Although this Atlantic coast has attracted less tourism in the past than the Mediterranean coast of southern Spain, several resorts are being developed. Because of its dazzling white sand and translucent skies it is known as the Coast of Light.

THE HUELVA COAST

From Ayamonte to the Parque Nacional de Doñana
135km - 84 miles – about 1/2 day

Ayamonte – Ayamonte, bustling with cars crossing into Portugal, stands at the mouth of the Guadiana River which forms the Portuguese–Spanish border. It is a fishing port with picturesque alleyways.
The *parador* on the hill commands a beautiful **view**★ of the village, the Guadiana estuary and Portugal beyond.
Sand dunes, anchored by pines and eucalyptus trees, fringe the coast between Ayamonte and Huelva.

Secondary roads perpendicular to the coast lead to the resorts of **Isla Canela, Isla Cristina, La Antilla** and **Punta Umbría**.

Huelva – Population 127806. Town plan in the current Michelin Red Guide España Portugal. Huelva, a large port and capital of its province, has developed through the export of copper mined in the hinterland, oil refineries, canneries and chemical industry.

In the 16C, the Tinto estuary was one of the principal anchorages of the Conquistadores, and in particular of Christopher Columbus. A large **monument** to the navigator straddles the Tinto River, near the harbour at Punto del Sebo.

La Rábida – In 1484, the Prior of the Convento de la Rábida, Juan Perez, believed the theory put to him by Christopher Columbus, that the world was round and that it was therefore possible to sail to the Indies by a westerly route. The prior's support finally won Columbus the necessary commission from the Catholic Monarchs to set up his expedition.

Among the present buildings of the **monasterio** ⊘ are vestiges of a 15C church and its frescoes. A small, interesting museum contains models of the three ships used in the first voyage Columbus made, as well as navigation charts and old books.

Palos de la Frontera – It was from this port, now silted up, that Christopher Columbus sailed on 3 August 1492 and to which he returned on 15 March 1493 after having discovered the island of San Salvador (Bahamas) on 12 October, a day still celebrated annually throughout Spain as the Day of the Hispanidad.

It was also at this port that Hernán Cortés, conqueror of Mexico, disembarked in 1528. The 14C **Iglesia de San Jorge** (Church of St George) has a Mudéjar portal.

Moguer – Moguer was another port from which expeditions ventured to the unknown. Alabaster **tombs**★ of the navigators who founded the **Convento de Santa Clara** ⊘ can be seen before the altar and underneath the Isabelline and Renaissance style niches in the church.

In the main street, now named after him, a plaque marks the birthplace of the poet and 1956 Nobel prizewinner, Juan Ramón Jiménez (1881-1958).

Return to the N 442 which continues southeast along the coast.

Pine-covered sand dunes give way to endless beaches of fine sand dominated occasionally by cliffs as at **Mazagón** where there is a *parador*. Matalascañas is the main resort on this stretch of the coast.

★ **Parque Nacional de Doñana** – *See Parque Nacional de DOÑANA.*

THE CÁDIZ COAST

From Sanlúcar de Barrameda to Tarifa
168km - 104 miles – allow 1 day

The landscape is hillier south of the Guadalquivir and there are vineyards north of Cádiz.

Sanlúcar de Barrameda – The fishing port of Sanlúcar, at the mouth of the Guadalquivir, is the home town of Manzanilla, a sherry matured like Jerez Fino but which has a special flavour thanks to the sea air. The bodegas *(cellars)* are in the old quarter on the hill around the massive castle. The **Iglesia de Nuestra Señora de la O** close by has a fine Mudéjar doorway.

The **Iglesia de Santo Domingo** ★ ⊘, a church in the lower barrio, has the noble proportions of a Renaissance building and inside, beautiful coffered **vaulting**★ and cupolas.

Rota – The old town inside its ramparts has an almost medieval atmosphere, particularly in the streets leading to the castle and the church. Rota is an important American naval base.

El Puerto de Santa María – The harbour, in the Bahía de Cádiz, played an active role in trade with the New World. Today, fishing, the export of sherry (there are Terry *bodegas* in the town) and tourism (beaches and golf courses) make up the town's principal activities.

A palm-shaded promenade overlooking the quays along the north bank leads to the 12C **Castillo de San Marcos**, a castle which was once the seat of the Dukes of Medinaceli.

★ **Cádiz** – *See CÁDIZ.*

South of Cádiz there are good beaches at La Barrosa and Conil de la Frontera.

Vejer de la Frontera – Vejer, perched on a rocky crag, is one of the prettiest white villages of Andalucía. The approach is along a *corniche* road from the south. There is a **view**★ from the car park at the north end of the town, down into the winding Barbate valley.

The road runs through the foothills of the Baetic ranges between Vejer and Tarifa.

Tarifa – *See GIBRALTAR.*

COSTA DEL SOL★

Andalucía (Málaga, Granada, Almería)

Michelin map 446 W 14-16, V 16-22 – Michelin Atlas España Portugal pp 84-88

The Sunshine Coast stretches along Andalucía's Mediterranean shore from Tarifa in the Straits of Gibraltar to the Cabo de Gata, a headland east of Almería. Protected from the extremes of the inland climate by the Serranía de Ronda and the Sierra Nevada, it enjoys mild winters (12°C - 54°F), hot summers (26°C - 79°F) and sufficient rain in winter and spring to allow subtropical crops to grow in the small alluvial plains.

★THE WESTERN COASTLINE

From Estepona to Málaga *139km - 86 miles – allow 1/2 day*

This highly developed strip of land between the mountains and the sea is a succession of beach resorts, hotels and large residential buildings with all manner of tourist amenities including pleasure boat harbours, golf courses and tennis courts.

Estepona – Fishing port and pleasure boat harbour.

Casares, 24km - 15 miles inland on the MA 539, is a remarkable white-walled village clinging to its hilltop **site**★.

San Pedro de Alcántara – Fine beach.

★ **Marbella** – *See MARBELLA.*

Fuengirola – A large resort bristling with modern tower blocks.
Take the road left out of Fuengirola for Mijas.

★ **Mijas** – This village of appealing white houses decorated with iron grilles, which often turn out to be restaurants or cafés, is a market centre for Andalusian crafts (pottery, basketwork, woven goods). There are lovely **views** from the upper terraces of the coast.

Torremolinos – This has grown from a quiet fishing village in the fifties into an enormous tourist complex where high rise blocks have run wild. It is famous for its shopping arcades and entertainment facilities. There's a good sandy beach.

★ **Málaga** – *See MÁLAGA.*

★THE EASTERN COASTLINE

From Málaga to Almería *209km - 130 miles – allow 1/2 day*

This, at times, beautiful coast is punctuated along its entire length by the ruins of Moorish towers – defences built by local inhabitants after the Reconquest against attacks by Barbary pirates.
Market gardening, largely in greenhouses around Almería, sugar refining and the export of iron ore are the area's main economic activities.

Nerja – Its palm shaded terrace-promenade, washed on either side by small sea inlets is strangely known as the *balcón de Europa*.

★★ **Cueva de Nerja** ⊙ – *4.5km - 3 miles east along the Motril road.* This natural cave is remarkable for its size and the numerous concretions highlighted to full advantage. Traces of paintings, the discovery of weapons and tools, jewels and bones, indicate that the cave was inhabited in the Palaeolithic era.
An annual festival of music and dance is held in the Sala de la Cascada (Cascade Chamber).

★ **Road from Nerja to La Herradura** – The road follows a russet and purple coloured mountainside while the old scenic route commands delightful **views**★ of the coastline.

Almuñécar – The amenities of this cosmopolitan resort include a palm shaded promenade which skirts its pebble beach. Bananas, medlars, pomegranates and mangoes are grown on the small alluvial plain *(hoya)* behind the town.

Motril – This is a large market centre for sugar cane. Motril port is kept busy handling products from the local sugar refineries and produce from the Genil valley.

★ **Road from Calahonda to Castell de Ferro** – The road hugs the rocky coastline, offering views of the mountain and the sea.
After Balanegra the N 340 leaves the coast and turns inland through an immense sweep of greenhouses, a veritable sea of plastic around El Ejido, where flowers, vegetables and tropical fruit are grown.

Road from Aguadulce to Almería – Aguadulce was the pioneer beach for Almería's tourist industry. The sweeping view from the *corniche* road takes in Almería town, its bay, sheltered harbour and fortress.

Almería – *See ALMERÍA.*

COSTA VASCA★★

BASQUE COAST – País Vasco (Guipúzcoa, Vizcaya)

Michelin map 442 B 21-24, C 21-24 – Michelin Atlas España Portugal pp 13-14

The Basque Coast (Costa Vasca) stretches from the Golfo de Vizcaya (Bay of Biscay) to the pointed headland of the Cabo de Machichaco. The steep shoreline, lined by cliffs and indented by estuaries, is an almost uninterrupted line of small fishing villages nestling in inlets below green hills.

FROM SAN SEBASTIÁN TO BILBAO

184km - 114 miles – allow 1 day – see local map below

★★**San Sebastián** – *See SAN SEBASTIÁN.*

7km - 4 miles south of San Sebastián bear right into the Bilbao road (N 634).

Orio – Orio, a fishing village with some industry, lies at the end of the long Oria estuary. It has a picturesque old quarter behind the church. Its oarsmen *(arraunlaris)* are among the best in the Basque country.

As the road climbs, look back at Orio; further on there is a good **view**★ of Zarautz.

Zarautz – The resort has been fashionable since Queen Isabel II made it her summer residence in the 19C. The town is pleasantly situated in the centre of an amphitheatre of hills around a vast beach. Two **palaces** stand in the old quarter: the 16C property of the Marqués de Narros from which corner watch-towers look out over the beach, and the Luzea tower, on the Plaza Mayor, with its mullioned windows and a machicolated corner balcony.

Beyond Zarautz, the road rises to a picturesque **corniche section**★★ overlooking the sea. Getaria rock, known as "el ratón" *(the mouse)*, soon comes into sight.

Getaria – Getaria is a small fishing village known locally for its *chipirones* or squid and its rock – *el ratón*, or San Antón Island – to which it is linked by a narrow breakwater road *(car turning point on the island)*. From the rock you can see the harbour, the beach and Zarautz. Long ago fishermen sailed from Getaria harbour to hunt whales, and navigators like **Juan Sebastián Elcano** set out for the Indies. A native of Getaria, Elcano sailed with Magellan and after the navigator had been murdered in the Philippines, brought his only surviving ship home, the first sailor to actually circumnavigate the world (1522). A narrow street, lined with picturesque houses, leads to the 13-15C **Iglesia del Salvador** (Church of our Saviour). The chancel rests on an arch beneath which an underground alley passes, from which one can see into the crypt. Inside is a Flamboyant Gothic gallery.

Zumaia – Zumaia, a fishing port and seaside resort, lies below wooded hills at the mouth of the Urola. The house of the painter **Ignacio Zuloaga** (1870-1945) has been converted into a **museo** ⊙ showing his own works – realistic and popular themes illustrated by brilliant colours and strong lines – and his personal collection of paintings by El Greco, Goya, Zurbarán and Morales.

The **Iglesia de San Pedro** (Church of San Peter) contains a 16C altarpiece by Juan de Anchieto.

Iciar – The fortress-like church contains a Plateresque altarpiece in dark wood with, at the centre, a smiling 12C Romanesque Virgin, attired in a sumptuous mantle.

On the way to Deba there are several good views of the coast.

Deba – Deba, at the mouth of the Deva, is a fishing port and resort with a good beach. The **Iglesia de Nuestra Señora de la Asunción** (Church of our Lady of the Assumption), conceals beneath the porch in its fortified front, a Gothic portal decorated with extremely lifelike statues. The cloister galleries have intricate tracery.

There is a splendid **view**★ of the coast from the **corniche road**★ as it circles the promontory closing the Deva estuary and, increasingly, of Mutriku's enclosed **site**★ as you drive back towards the village.

Mutriku – Massive new buildings have affected the picturesque quality of this fishing village where tall houses overlook the harbour from the slopes of San Nicolás mountain.

Two belvederes afford **views**★ of Saturrarán beach, a wild strand at the foot of an immensely tall cliff, and Ondarroa, which you first see from a bend in the road.

Ondarroa – Ondarroa spreads over a spit of land between a hillside and a loop of the Río Artibay.

The church, upstanding like a ship's prow at one end, the tall Basque houses with washing at the windows and the encircling river, make an attractive **picture**★.

Canning and fish salting are the two main local activities.

The road between Ondarroa and Lekeitio is pleasant; on rounding a point you have a good **view**★ of Lekeitio, its beach and the island of San Nicolás, joined to the mainland at low tide.

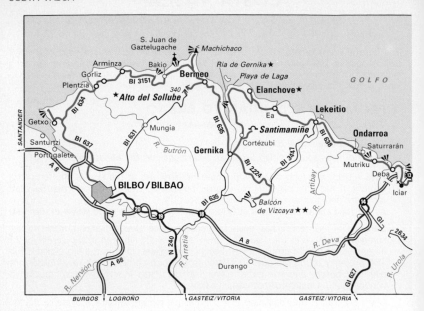

Lekeitio – A deeply indented bay at the foot of Monte Calvario, divided by the island of San Nicolás, serves as the harbour for Lekeitio's long-standing fishing industry. The town is a resort with good sand beaches. The 15C **iglesia** guarding the harbour has three tiers of flying buttresses and a tall baroque belfry.

Ea – Miniature harbour between two hills at the end of a quiet creek.

★ **Elanchove** – A peaceful village off the main road. Fishermen have long used the bay as a natural harbour and built their houses overlooking the water, against the steep side of Cabo Ogoño (300m - 1 000ft).

Once beyond **Playa de Laga**, a vast expanse of rose-coloured sand circling the foot of Cabo Ogoño, you can see along the coastline, the peaceful waters of the **Gernika Ría ★** (Estuary), the island of Izaro, the white outline of the town of Sukarrieta on the far bank and the island of Chacharramendi.

The resort of Playa de Laida, on the *ría*, is popular with Gernika residents.

Bear left at Cortézubi for the Cuevas de Santimamiñe.

Cuevas de Santimamiñe ⊙ – Wall paintings and engravings from the Magdalenian Period and interesting archeological deposits were discovered in these caves in 1917. Most of the paintings are in a small chamber where the walls are decorated with charcoal drawings of a horse, a bear and a goat, and on the ceiling six bison standing round a horse. To the right two bison stand upright in apparent confrontation. In a long gallery are splendid, brightly-coloured **limestone concretions ★**.

Return to the Gernika road.

Gernika – Picasso's famous painting, *Guernica (see p 171, photograph p 30)*, has immortalised the tragic event that took place in this little town during the Civil War: on 26 April 1937 a German air squadron bombed the town and local inhabitants who had come to the market, killing more than 2 000.

In the Middle Ages, the Gernika oak was one of the four places where newly created Lords of Biscay came to swear that they would respect the local *fueros* or privileges. Gernika was, on this account, visited by Queen Isabel in 1483. Today, the remains of the thousand-year-old tree are in the small temple behind the **Casa de Juntas** where representatives of the Biscay Provincial General Assembly meet.

Return to Gernika and take the Bermeo road north.

18km - 11 miles south on the BI 2224 and 3231, is the **Balcón de Vizcaya** (Balcony of Biscay) ★★, a remarkable viewpoint overlooking the mountainous Biscay landscape, a chequer-board of meadows and forests.

Two viewpoints built beside the road at the mouth of the inlet before you reach Mundaka, enable you to take a last look back along its still waters. As the road descends, you get a magnificent **view ★** of Bermeo.

Bermeo – Bermeo is an important inshore fishing port. The fishermen's quarter, still crowded onto the Atalaya promontory overlooking the old harbour, the Puerto Menor, was protected by the ramparts (traces remain), and the grim granite Torre de los Ercilla (now the Museo del Pescador, a fishermen's museum). In the Iglesia de Santa Eufemia, kings and overlords used to swear to uphold Biscay privileges.

Take the C 6313 southwest towards Mungia.

★ **Alto del Sollube (Sollube Pass)** – From the road up to the low pass (340m - 1 115ft) there is a good view of Bermeo's semicircular site.

Return to Bermeo, follow the coast road left for 3km - 1.8 miles then turn right.

Faro de Machichaco – From slightly left of this lighthouse there is a good view west along the indented coastline.

The road rises in a *corniche* to a **viewpoint** ★ overlooking the **San Juan de Gaztelugache** headland on which stands a hermitage *(pathway)*, the goal of a local *romería* (pilgrimage) each Midsummer's Day. Below, waves have eroded the rocks into flying buttresses.

There are extensive views from the **corniche road** ★ between Bakio and Arminza. A belvedere commands an interesting **view** ★ of the coast, Bakio, the valley farmlands and wooded hinterland.

Arminza – The only harbour along a wild section of high, inhospitable coast.

Gorliz – Attractive beach resort at the mouth of the Río Butrón. **Plentzia** nearby *(2km - 1 mile)*, once an important fishing harbour and commercial port, is now an oyster farming centre and a resort.

Getxo – A **Paseo Marítimo** or sea promenade overlooks the coast. From the road up to Getxo's well-known golf course there is an interesting view of the Bilbao inlet and on the far bank, Santurtzi and Portugalete.

Bilbao – *See BILBAO.*

COSTA VERDE★★★

Asturias

Michelin map 441 B 8-15 – Michelin Atlas España Portugal pp 4, 5 and 11

The Green Coast of Asturias, one of Spain's most beautiful, is so called on account of the colour of the sea, the pine and eucalyptus trees along the shoreline and the wooded pastures inland.

On a clear day the Picos de Europa, not far from the coast itself, lend a backdrop to the scene.

The coast from Unquera to Ribadeo is very rocky but follows an almost straight line due west except for where the Cabo de Peñas headland, west of Gijón, juts out to sea. The shore is lined by low cliffs interrupted by frequent sandy inlets; the estuaries are narrow and deep and although they are known locally as *rías*, bear little resemblance to those in nearby Galicia.

Three ports in this area handle Asturian coal and ore: San Esteban de Pravia, Gijón and Avilés. Other local ports are mostly small and go in for catching and canning fish. A plateau, never more than 20km   12 miles wide, follows the line of the shore, its far side bordered by high mountain ranges.

The coast from Cudillero westwards is steeper and more jagged; the coastal plain ends in a sheer line of cliffs overlooking small beaches tucked away in river mouths. There are fishing villages in the creeks.

SIGHTS – FROM EAST TO WEST

Llanes – A small peaceful fishing port (crayfish) and resort. The cliff top Paseo de San Pedro affords a good view of the old, once fortified town, the rampart ruins and castle and the squat Iglesia de Santa María. If you can, be there for the St Roch festival in August to see the dances (the *Pericote* and in particular the children's *Prima* dance) in brilliant local costume.

The shoreline between Llanes and Ribadesella is a succession of sandy beaches sheltered by rock promontories: **Celorio, Barro** and **Cuevas del Mar.**

Ribadesella – The town and port of Ribadesella are on the right side of the estuary while opposite, a holiday resort has grown along the beach.

Crowds of spectators come on the first Saturday in August every year to see the international kayak races down the Río Sella.

★ **Cuevas de Tito Bustillo** ⊘ − These caves are famous for their **wall of paintings**★ decorated by the Palaeolithic inhabitants of 20 000 BC (between the Solutrean and the
middle of the Magdalenian Periods). A few animals − a horse, two stags, a doe,
another stag and a horse − precede the smoothest area of rock, a sort of low
ceiling where, in the hollows of the stone, there are animal shapes 2m - 6 1/2ft
long, painted red or ochre and outlined in black.

La Isla − Squat drying sheds or *hórreos* stand beside the houses in the small,
attractive village built on a rock headland close to the road. The vast bay is lined
with beaches separated by rocks, one of which, lying offshore, gave the village its
name.

★★ **Mirador del Fito** − *12km - 7 miles southeast of La Isla on the C637.* This viewpoint commands a **panorama** of the Picos de Europa and the coast.

Lastres − Lastres is a typical fishing village built against the side of a steep cliff
between the beach and the harbour. It is known for its clams.

Priesca − The **Iglesia de San Salvador** has been restored. The chancel in this church
contains capitals resembling those at Valdediós *(see below)*.

Villaviciosa − It was in Villaviciosa that the future **Emperor Charles V**, aged 17 and
accompanied by a full escort of Flemish courtiers, landed in 1517 to take pos-
session of his newly inherited kingdom. The ships' intended destination was
Santander but by an error of navigation they sailed up the long *ría* to Villaviciosa
harbour.
Today's visitor will see a town with narrow streets, emblasoned houses and the
Iglesia de Santa María, its west front decorated with a Gothic rose window, its
Romanesque portal flanked by statue columns.
A short distance inland are Amandi and Valdediós with interesting churches.

Amandi − *3km - 2 miles south of Villaviciosa.* The bell gable of the **Iglesia de San
Juan** can easily be picked out as it stands perched on high ground at the centre of
the village. Though remodelled in the 18C the church still has its 13C portal and
apse of which the **decoration**★ shows a high degree of sophistication. Inside the
apse★, the frieze from the façade reappears to form a winding ribbon that follows
the curves of the intercolumniation. The capitals have been beautifully and imaginatively carved.

★ **Valdediós** − *7km - 4 miles south of Villaviciosa.* In the same valley are a small
Asturian church, full of character and ancient charm, and a monastery.
The **Iglesia de San Salvador** ⊘, which was consecrated in 893 and is known locally
as *El conventín* or the little monastery, dates from the end of the Asturian period
of architecture (8-10C). The raised nave is abutted by narrow aisles; the capitals
of the triumphal arch are decorated with the Asturian cord motif. The side portico
was intended to serve as a covered walk or cloister; the strapwork capitals, arcaded
windows and artistically sculpted *claustra* all show Mozarabic influence.
They monastery (**monasterio** ⊘) consists of a 13C Cistercian church and cloisters
dating from the 15, 17 and 18C.

Tazones − *12km - 7 miles north of Villaviciosa.* This is a delightful little fishing
village hidden away in a cove.

Gijón − *Town plan in the current Michelin Red Guide España Portugal.* Gijón is a
lively modern city with a population of over 250 000. It was originally built on the
narrow Santa Catalina headland between two inlets which today serve as harbour
(west) and beach, the vast Playa de San Lorenzo (east). **Plaza del Marqués**, near the
port, is surrounded by well-proportioned buildings, among them the late-17C
Palacio de Revillagigedo, with an elegant façade. The palace stands on the high Santa
Catalina side of the square adjoining the fishermen's quarter known as Cimadevilla.
Gijón was the birthplace of **Gaspar Melchor de Jovellanos** (1744-1811), one of Spain's
most eminent 18C men of letters. He was a poet, reformer, liberal economist,
author and politician.

Luanco − Luanco harbour lies in a bay sheltered by the Punta de Vaca. It has a
small beach and a sea promenade.

★ **Cabo de Peñas** − The road runs through moorland to this cape, the northernmost
point in Asturias. From the cliff and its large rock extension, all dominated by a
lighthouse, there are fine **views** of the coast on either side of the cape.

Salinas − This is a rapidly expanding resort bordered to the east by a pine forest.
The rock islet of La Peñona (footbridge) affords an overall **view**★ of the beach,
one of the longest on the Costa Verde. Waves crash against the jagged rocks
below.

Ermita del Espíritu Santo (Hermitage of the Holy Spirit) − As the road climbs there
are glimpses through the eucalyptus trees of the Nalón estuary also known as
Pravia Ría and of waves lapping the immense San Juan de la Arena beach. The
hermitage commands an extensive **view**★ west along the coastal cliffs.

View of Castropol from across the Ría Ribadeo

★ **Cudillero** – The fishing village surrounded by steep hills makes an attractive **scene**★ from the end of the jetty: tall houses on the hillsides, white cottages with brown tiled roofs leading down to the small harbour nestling between two rock points and a foreground of fishing boats, masts and nets drying in the sun.

Concha de Artedo – Superb beach.

★★ **Cabo Vidio** – From near the lighthouse, the **views**★ from this headland along the inhospitable coastline extend east to the Cabo de Peñas and west to Cabo Busto.

★ **Luarca** – Luarca has a remarkable **site**★ at the mouth of the winding Río Negro. The town, a distinctively attractive centre with its white houses and slate roofs, has seven bridges spanning the river, a sheltered fishing harbour and three beaches. At the end of the estuary, a lighthouse, church and cemetery stand on the headland once occupied by a fort. A narrow street leads to the top. For an interesting **view**★ of Luarca, take the lighthouse road left, then circle the church to the right and return to the harbour. On 15 August, the harbour fills with boats decked with flags.

Navia – See Valle del NAVIA.

Figueras – From the port of Figueras on the Ría Ribadeo you have a good view of Castropol, which from across the water, resembles an Austrian village casting its reflection in a lake.

Castropol – Castropol, the most westerly port in Asturias, lies along a promontory at the centre of a *ría* which marks the boundary with Galicia. The quiet village with an all-white square faces Ribadeo, its Galician counterpart *(see under RÍAS ALTAS)*.

Plan your route with the Michelin Atlas España Portugal.

COVADONGA

Asturias

Michelin map 441 C 14 – Michelin Atlas España Portugal p 11 – Local map under PICOS DE EUROPA

Covadonga, a famous shrine and landmark in Spanish history, is nestled in an impressive **setting**★★ at the bottom of a narrow valley surrounded by high mountains. It was from here that the Christian Reconquest began.

The cradle of the Spanish monarchy – The Muslims followed up the defeat of the Visigoths at the Battle of Guadalete in 711 AD by occupying the entire peninsula. **Pelayo**, a Visigothic nobleman, took refuge in Covadonga with his men to organise a revolt. When in 722, the Emir Alçama sent a military company from Córdoba to wipe out the rebellious force, Pelayo and his supporters won a resounding victory against the Muslims at Covadonga. Christians everywhere gained new heart and determined to re-establish a national monarchy: the Asturians elected Pelayo who set up his court at Cangas de Onís, thereby making Asturias the cradle of the Spanish monarchy and forever after a symbol of resistance.

SIGHTS

La Santa Cueva ⊙ – The Cave of Our Lady, Cova Dominica, is dedicated to the Virgin of the Battlefield and contains the deeply venerated 18C wood statue of the Virgin, patron of Asturias. It is known as **La Santina,** the centrepiece of a major procession on 8 September. Beside the statue are the tombs of Pelayo, who died in 747, and his son-in-law, Alfonso I.

Basílica ⊙ – The neo-Romanesque basilica built between 1886 and 1901 is preceded by a statue of Pelayo beneath the Cruz de la Victoria (Cross of Victory).

Museo de la Virgen ⊙ – This museum contains the gifts to the Virgin of Covadonga including the magnificent **crown**★ with more than 1 000 diamonds.

EXCURSION

★**Lagos de Enol and Ercina** – *See PICOS DE EUROPA: the road to Covadonga and the lakes.*

COVARRUBIAS★

Castilla y León (Burgos)
Population 629
Michelin map 442 F 19 – Michelin Atlas España Portugal p 26

Covarrubias, on the banks of the Arlanza, is partly surrounded by medieval ramparts guarded by the Doña Urraca tower, strangely shaped like a truncated pyramid. A Renaissance palace straddles the street to the picturesque old quarter where half-timbered houses supported by stone columns have been restored.

The town is the burial place of one of Castilla's great historic figures, **Fernán González,** who united several fiefs into a vast County of Castilla to fight relentlessly against the Moors and sweep them south. This gave the region a leading role in the Reconquest and so ultimately in the unification of Christian Spain.

★**Colegiata** ⊙ – This collegiate church, with a nave and two aisles and cloisters with ornamental vaulting, makes an impressive Gothic unit. It is also a pantheon, worthy of some twenty medieval tombs including those of Fernán González and the Norwegian Princess Cristina who married the Infante Philip of Castilla in 1258.

There is a very fine church organ.

Museo - Tesoro (Museum and Treasury) – A painting by Pedro Berruguete and another by Van Eyck stand out from the collection of Primitives; note especially the 15C Flemish **triptych**★ in which the central high relief of the Adoration of the Magi has been attributed to Gil de Siloé. There is also a splendid processional cross made by the goldsmiths of Calahorra in the 16C.

EXCURSIONS

Quintanilla de las Viñas – *24km - 15 miles northeast. Take the C 110 and the N 234 towards Burgos, then a small signposted road right.*

The road follows the Arlanza valley out of Covarrubias into pleasant wooded gorges. You will see, below and to the right, the ruins of the **Monasterio de San Pedro de Arlanza** with beautiful Romanesque apses.

★**Iglesia de Quintanilla de las Viñas** ⊙ – The church's great age – it is generally reputed to be 7C Visigothic – makes it interesting archaeologically. All that remains are the apse and transept, built of skilfully bonded blocks of stone. The outside walls are decorated with a frieze of bunches of grapes, leaves and birds as well as medallions and highly stylised motifs. The same foliated scrollwork is repeated inside on the keystones of the triumphal arch of which the imposts, on either side, are adorned with symbolic figures of the sun and moon.

Lerma – *23km - 14 miles west on the C 110.*

Lerma owes its splendour to the **Duke of Lerma,** Philip III's ambitious favourite who ruled the country from 1598 until he was usurped by his son, the Duke of Uceda, in 1618. The period was one of untold extravagance and corruption; the court, dizzied by celebrations and balls, divided its time between Madrid and Valladolid; the duke, once having feathered his own nest, turned his attention to his home town which as a result became one of Spain's rare examples of classical town planning.

The quarter built by the duke in the 17C, in the upper part of the town, retains its steep narrow cobbled streets and its houses, some of which are very old, with their wood or stone porticoes. The ducal palace, with its austere façade, stands on the spacious **Plaza Mayor** ★. The **Colegiata** ⊙ church has a 17C gilded bronze statue by Juan de Arfe of the Duke's nephew, the Archbishop Cristóbal de Rojas, shown at prayer.

CUENCA★★

Castilla-La Mancha

Population 46 047

Michelin map 444 L23 – Michelin Atlas España Portugal p 54

Cuenca stands in a spectacular **setting★★** at the heart of the Serranía de Cuenca in the western part of the Montes Universales range. Here, on the eastern edge of the Spanish Meseta, the limestone massif has been eroded into a rugged terrain dotted with fantastic rock formations.

Holy Week processions are considerably enhanced by the site; at dawn on Good Friday the slow ascent to Calvary is enacted along the steep alleys to the accompaniment of drums. A festival of sacred music is also held throughout Holy Week.

★★CIUDAD ANTIGUA (OLD TOWN) *time: 2 1/2 hours*

The old town clings to a rock platform high above the precipices of the Júcar and Huécar ravines. The winding streets are narrow and the houses tall for lack of ground space.

Go through the 18C Arco del Ayuntamiento (Town Hall Arch) and park in the Plaza Mayor de Pío XII.

Catedral ⊙ – The cathedral façade, rebuilt at the beginning of the century, fronts a 13C Gothic edifice, French and Norman in architectural style and Renaissance in decoration. Among the building's most outstanding features are the wrought-iron chapel **grilles**, a twin ambulatory, a triforium and an elegant Plateresque **door★** into the chapter house with carved walnut panels by Alonso Berruguete.

Walk along the cathedral south wall.

★ **Museo Diocesano** (Diocesan Museum) (**M¹**) ⊙ – The museum is housed in the Palacio Episcopal or Bishops' Palace. Among its key pieces are eight panels of an altarpiece by Juan de Borgoña (c1510), two El Greco paintings, a Calvary by Gérard David and an exceptional collection of gold and silver plate. One of the most outstanding works is a 13C **Byzantine diptych★** painted in a monastery on Mount Athos and covered in silver, pearls and precious stones. There is also the gilded bronze **Báculo de San Julián** (Crozier of St Julian) from Limoges (c1200) decorated with enamel. Tapestries and carpets are displayed on the first floor.

★ **Casas Colgadas** (Hanging Houses) – These famous 14C houses, now thoroughly restored, are home to a museum of abstract art and a restaurant. Go through an arched passageway beside the mesón to the Puente de San Pablo. From this bridge there is a **view★** of the most spectacular houses hanging over the Huécar ravine; an enchanting sight when the scene is illuminated in the evening.

On the far side of the bridge is the **Monastério de los Paúles.** Part of this former monastery now houses a *parador*.

★★ **Museo de Arte Abstracto Español** (Museum of Spanish Abstract Art) ⊙ – The museum was inaugurated in 1966. Its setting and the views it commands are such that some of the windows are veritable works of art in themselves. The collection, put together by Fernando Zóbel and enriched since its foundation, is a fine selection of Spanish abstract art including works by Chillida, Tàpies, Saura, Zóbel, Cuixart, Sempere, Rivera and Millares.

★ **Museo de Cuenca** (**M²**) ⊙ – The first floor of this museum displays prehistoric objects. The second floor has the most interesting exhibits: sculpture, numismatic items and ceramics found in the Roman excavations at Segóbriga, Valeria and Ercávica. Note the top of a Roman altar found at Ercávica illustrating items used in sacred rites.

Turn back to the cathedral and along Calle San Pedro; bear first left for the Plaza San Nicolás from which steps lead down to the Plaza de los Descalzos.

The Casas Colgadas (Hanging Houses) of Cuenca

F. Bouillot / MARCO POLO

CUENCA

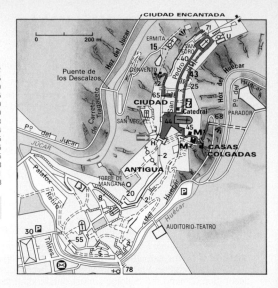

★ **Plaza de las Angustias (15)** – A Franciscan monastery and hermitage, known as the Virgin in Anguish, stands in the quiet, tree-lined square between the town and the Júcar ravine.

Return to the Calle San Pedro and continue to the church of the same name. Bear left into an alley which ends at the edge of the Júcar ravine (good view). Return to the church and walk down Calle Julián Romero.

Calle Julián Romero (43) – This delightful stepped alley with its small squares runs above the Huécar gorge and brings you back to the cathedral.

EXCURSIONS

Las Hoces (Ravines) – Roads which parallel the river on either side as it circles the bottom of the precipitous rock spur, afford amazing views of the hanging houses.

Hoz del Júcar – The Júcar is the shorter and more enclosed ravine. Poplars stand reflected in the green river waters below the ochre-coloured cliff.

Hoz del Huécar – *Round tour of 15km - 9 miles.* The Huécar course swings from side to side between less steep slopes as it drains a small valley given over to market-gardening. The Cuenca houses, seen from below, appear to defy gravity.

Turn left at the end of the ravine for Buenache de la Sierra and then left again for the Convento de San Jerónimo (monastery).

Shortly afterwards, in a right bend, there's a remarkable **vista**★ of the valley's tall grey rock columns, and, in the distance, of Cuenca. Enter the town through a gateway set in the ramparts of the old quarter.

★ **Las Torcas** – *Take the N420 then bear left after 11km.* The road passes through an attractive wood of conifers where the *torcas*, strange, circular depressions of earth which occasionally reach spectacular proportions, can be seen. The Torca del Lobo (Wolf's Hollow) is particularly interesting.

Serranía de CUENCA

Castilla-La Mancha (Cuenca)
Michelin map 444 K 23-24, L 23-24 – Michelin Atlas España Portugal pp 42, 54 and 55

The unusual landscapes of this limestone area have been formed over the centuries by the infiltration of river water and wind erosion. The whimsical rock formations, the pine groves and the numerous streams all combine to form a sierra of unquestionable beauty.

TOUR OF THE SIERRA *270km-168 miles – allow 1 day*

Ventana del Diablo (Devil's Window) – *25.5km-16 miles from Cuenca on the CU 921.* This overlooks the depths of the **Garganta del Júcar**★ (Júcar Gorges).

★ **Ciudad Encantada (Enchanted City)** – *Follow a detour signposted to the right of the CU 921.* The strange rock formations have been created by the shaping of the limestone by the natural elements. An arrowed circuit directs visitors through this dreamlike forest of rocks, the most interesting of which are the Tobogán (Toboggan Slope) and the Mar de Piedras (Sea of Stones).

To reach the **Mirador de Uña** *(2km-1 mile)*, continue along the road which leaves the car park. Enjoy the extensive **view** of the Júcar valley which is dominated along its entire course by towering cliffs, with, in the distance, Uña and its small lake.

Los Callejones (The Alleyways) – *3km-2 miles from Las Majadas, on the Uña road. Leave your car on the esplanade.* Although less spectacular than the Ciudad Encantada, this isolated geological spot is a strange natural sight with unusual shapes in a maze of eroded blocks, arches and the narrow alleyways which lend their name to the area.

★ **Hoz de Beteta (Beteta Ravine)** – Before reaching Priego *(3km - 2 miles)*, a road off to the right leads to the **Convento de San Miguel de las Victorias.** From its privileged **site**★ it dominates the entrance to the **Escabas river valley.** *(Return to the C202).* Continue along the valley for a few kilometres, the road then leaves the river and, having passed Vadillos, comes into the impressive gorge of the **Hoz de Beteta**★, through which the Guadiela river flows between towering vertical cliffs and lush vegetation.

★ **Nacimiento del río Cuervo (Source of the Cuervo)** – *30km-19 miles south-east of Beteta. Leave the car just after the bridge and walk up 500m.* A footpath leads to the **waterfalls**★ where water rushing through grottoes and out of moss-covered, hollowed out rocks forms the beginnings of the Cuervo river.

As you continue back towards Cuenca on the *CU921*, there are lovely **views** of the Embalse de la Toba (Toba Reservoir).

DAROCA★

Aragón (Zaragoza)
Population 2 630
Michelin map 443 I 25 – Michelin Atlas España Portugal p 42

Daroca is lodged between two ridges over which runs its 4km - 2 miles long perimeter of battlemented **walls**★. These were originally defended by more than a hundred towers and fortified gateways like the impressive **Puerta Baja** (Lower Gate) flanked by square towers.
The town was founded by the Muslims, freed from the Moors in 1120 and gained local independence in 1142.

The Milagro de los Sagrados Corporales – The miracle of the holy altarcloths took place in 1239, after the conquest of Valencia, when Christian troops in Daroca, Teruel and Calatayud were setting out to recover territory occupied by the Moors. Just as mass was being celebrated, the Moors attacked and the priest had to hide the conse-crated hosts between two altarcloths. Shortly afterwards, it was seen that the hosts had left bloodstained imprints on the linen. The three towns of Daroca, Tereul and Calatayud claimed the precious relic. To settle the dispute the holy cloths were placed upon a mule which was then set free. It made straight for Daroca, dying, however, as it entered the Puerta Baja.

SIGHTS

Colegiata de Santa María ☉ – This collegiate church, built in the Romanesque period as a repository for the holy cloths, was modified in the 15 and 16C. In the north wall beside the belfry is a Flamboyant Gothic portal.

Interior   The late Gothic nave includes several Renaissance features like the cupola above the transept crossing.
The **south chapels,** partly faced with locally manufactured 16C *azulejos,* contain a series of interesting altarpieces. To the right of the entrance is a 15C **altarpiece**★ in multicoloured alabaster which is believed to have been carved in England – note the anecdotal detail. Gothic tombs stand on either side of the nave. The 15C **Capilla de los Corporales** (Chapel of the Holy Relics) ★ is on the site of the original Romanesque apse. The altar, preceded by a kind of Flamboyant roodscreen and framed by scenes of the miracle on the walls, includes a shrine enclosing the holy altarcloths. All around stand statues in delightful poses carved out of multicoloured alabaster. The painted Gothic **retable**★ is dedicated to St Michael.

★ **Museo Parroquial (Parish Museum)** ☉ – Among the paintings on wood are two rare though badly damaged 13C panels and **altarpieces** to St Peter (14C) and St Martin (15C). All the gold and silver plate was made in Daroca except for the **reliquary** which formerly held the holy altarcloths, which was made by the 14C Catalan, Moragues. The figures are gold, the foundation silver. Most of the **chasubles,** many of them very old, were woven in the town, while others, dating from the 17C, are Mexican.

Iglesia de San Miguel ☉ – This church, equally outstanding in its fine appearance for the purity of its Romanesque east end and its 12C portal, has recovered its original design. The 13C wall paintings in the apse have, unfortunately, faded. Outside, a short distance below, you can see the restored Mudéjar style belfry of the **Iglesia de Santo Domingo** ☉.

Parque Nacional de DOÑANA★

Andalucía (Huelva, Sevilla)

Michelin map 446 U 10, V 10-11 – Michelin Atlas España Portugal p 82

Doñana National Park, created for the protection of its flora and fauna, stretches across the provinces of Huelva and Sevilla between the Atlantic Ocean and the mouth of the Guadalquivir river. Given its geographical position – the fact that it is close to Africa and is affected climatically by both the Atlantic and the Mediterranean – it is a rest stop for a great many African and European migratory birds. Doñana is Spain's largest wildlife reserve with a total protected area (inner and outer park) of 73 000ha - 180 390 acres. It is home to several animal species including lynx, wild boar, deer and a wide variety of birds: Spanish imperial eagle, flamingo, heron, wild duck and coot.

El Acebuche Information Centre, 2km - 1.2 miles north of Torre de la Higuera

Guided tours ⊙ in four-wheel-drive vehicles are organised by the information centre in El Acebuche. The park has a variety of ecosystems depending on the habitat; on the **moorland** (marisma) there are cork oak and pine forests (you may see branch covered hides still used by pine-kernel gatherers); the **lagoons** which form the largest part of the reserve, are home to numerous waterfowl in winter, while the **moveable sand dunes** advance inland from the beach an average 6m - 20ft every year.

El Rocío – El Rocío village, north of the Doñana reserve, has a shrine to Nuestra Señora del Rocío (Our Lady of the Dew) to which crowds of pilgrims from all over Andalucía flock annually at Whitsun. They arrive in flower decorated carts or riding horses saddled and bridled in rich Andalusian style; pilgrims from Cádiz take boats across the Guadalquivir and then cross Doñana national park. During the week of pilgrimage El Rocío is host to about a million people but the rest of the year it is a ghost town.

ÉCIJA

Andalucía (Sevilla)

Population 35 727

Michelin map 446 T 14 – Michelin Atlas España Portugal p 74

Écija, which was founded by the Romans, has a mild climate except in summer when it becomes so hot that it is known as the Frying-pan of Andalucía. The town lies in the Guadalquivir depression, its baroque belfries decorated with ceramic tiles visible at some distance across the plains. The most interesting tower, that of **San Juan★**, together with the belfries of San Gil and Santa Cruz, belong to churches now in ruins; Santa María *(to the left of the Ayuntamiento)* stands on a square of the same name lined by old houses.

SIGHTS

Park the car on Plaza de España.

The streets on either side of Avenida Miguel Cervantes still feature old palaces with beautiful façades: baroque for the 18C **Palacio de Benamejí** and Plateresque for the **Palacio de Valdehermosa.** The **Palacio de Peñaflor** front is concave and adorned with frescoes.

★ **Iglesia de Santiago (St James's Church)** ⊙ – The church is preceded by a pleasant 17C *patio*. Inside, the Mudejar windows of an earlier building were retained when the nave and side aisles were rebuilt after caving in, in 1628. The **retable★** at the high altar illustrates the Passion and the Resurrection.

ELCHE / ELX★

Comunidad Valenciana (Alicante)

Population 187 596

Michelin map 445 R 27 – Michelin Atlas España Portugal p 79

Plan of the conurbation in the current Michelin Red Guide España Portugal

Elche (Elx in Catalan), standing on the banks of the Vinalopó river, is famed for its *Dama*, its palm grove and its mystery play.

La Dama de Elche (The Lady of Elche) – Elche has been the site of several civilisations including that of the Romans when the town was known as *Illicis*. It was amongst Iberian and Roman ruins in **La Alcudia** *(2km - 1.2 miles south)* in 1897, that archaeologists discovered the great sculpture known as the Lady of Elche (4C BC), a masterpiece of Iberian art now exhibited in the Museo Arqueológico de Madrid *(qv, photograph p 22)*.

★★ **El Palmeral (Palm Grove)** – The grove, believed to have been planted by the Phoenicians, is the largest in Europe with more than 100 000 trees. The palms flourish in the mild climate, with the aid of a remarkable irrigation system. Dates

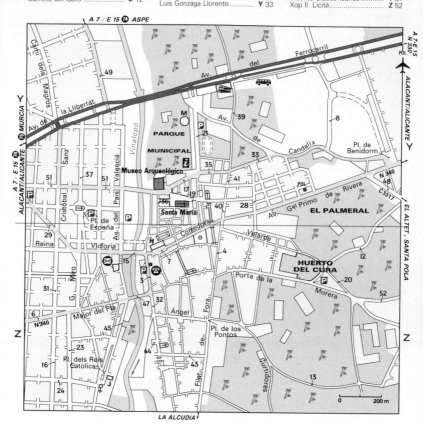

are cut in winter from the female trees and the fronds, after blanching, from the male trees for Palm Sunday processions and various handicrafts. Cereals and vegetables are grown beneath the trees outside the city limits.

El Misteri (Mystery Play) – The Elche Mystery, a medieval verse drama performed by an all-male cast, recounts the Dormition, Assumption and Coronation of the Virgin. It is played in the Basílica de Santa María on 14 and 15 August.

SIGHTS

★★ **Huerta del Cura** (Z) ⊘ – The *huerta* is a garden of bright flowers planted beneath particularly magnificent palm trees, including the Imperial Palm, with seven trunks, said to be 150 years old. There is also an interesting cactus section.

★ **Parque Municipal** (Y) – A pleasant garden set within the palm grove.

Museo Arqueológico (Y) ⊘ – The archaeological museum, housed in the Palacio de Altamira, displays finds taken mostly from excavations at La Alcudia. Among the most noteworthy items are sculpture and ceramics from the Iberian period and the *Venus of Illicis*, a delicately carved white marble Roman sculpture.

Basílica de Santa María (Y) – The monumental 18C baroque basilica, designed from the first as a setting for the mystery play, has an interesting portal by Nicolás de Bari.

For a quiet place to stay
consult the annual Michelin Red Guide España Portugal
which gives a choice of pleasant hotels.

119

EMPURIES / AMPURIAS

Catalunya (Girona)
Michelin map 443 F 39 – Michelin Atlas España Portugal p 19
Local map under COSTA BRAVA

The Graeco-Roman town of Ampurias (or *Emporion* as it was known to the Greeks, meaning market or trading station) was built on a striking **site**★★ beside the sea. Today, three centres can be distinguished: the old town, or **Palaiápolis**, the new town or **Neápolis**, and the Roman town.

In the mid-6C BC, the Phoceans (who had already settled in Marseille), founded Palaiápolis, a commercial port on the then offshore island now joined to the mainland and occupied by the village of Sant Marti d'Empúries. Some years later, a town began to develop on the shore facing the island, and so Neápolis came into being. As a Roman ally during the Punic Wars, it saw the arrival of an expeditionary corps led by Scipio Africanus Major in 218 BC. However, it wasn't until 100 BC that the Roman town was established to the west of Neápolis. The two centres coexisted independently until Augustus bestowed Roman citizenship upon the Greeks. The colony continued to grow but suffered severely from Barbarian invasions in the 3C AD. At one time, however, it was a bishopric as the basilica ruins discovered in Neápolis prove. It finally succumbed to the Moors in the 8C.

Neápolis ⊙ – The piling up of different edifices over a period of 1 000 years has made an analysis of the ruins difficult. Near the gate was the **Templo de Esculapio** (Aesculapius-god of healing) and a sacred precinct which contained altars and statues of the gods. Nearby stood the **watch-tower** and, at its foot, drinking water cisterns (a filter has been reconstructed). Another point of interest, the **Templo de Zeus Serapis** (a god associated with the weather and with healing), was surrounded by a colonnade. At the other end of the main street was the **Agora**, general meeting place and heart of the town, where the bases of three statues remain. A street ran from the agora to the sea, bordered on its left by the **stoa** or covered market formed of alleyways and shops. Behind the stoa are the clearly distinguishable ruins of a 6C **palaeo-Christian basilica** with a rounded apse.

Museo – A section of Neapolis is displayed together with models of temples and finds from the excavations including a mosaic of the sacrifice of Iphigenia, a Hellenistic work from the 2 or 1C BC, a mosaic of a partridge and yet another of a mask.

The Roman town – This stands on a hill behind the museum and unlike Neápolis, is a vast, geometrically laid out town. It has been but partially excavated, with restorations to some of the walls. **House no 1** (entrance at the back) has an atrium or inner courtyard with six columns. Around this are the residential apartments, the peristyle or colonnaded court, and the impluvium or basin for catching rainwater. The reception rooms are paved in geometric, black and white mosaic. At the house's northern end are the private baths.

Next door, **house no 2 B** has rooms paved with their original mosaic. One of these, near the atrium, has been reconstituted in clay (by the rammed earth method in use at the time) with its walls resting on stone foundations.

The **forum**, a large square lined by porticoes and to north and south respectively by temples and shops, was the centre of civic life in the town. A porticoed street led to the city gate and beyond the walls to the oval **amphitheatre** which is still visible.

Monasterio de El ESCORIAL★★★

The impressive monastery of San Lorenzo el Real, or El Escorial, stands at the foot of Monte Abantos on the southern slopes of the Sierra de Guadarrama at an altitude of 1 065m - 3 494ft. The massive building is a monument to King Philip II who commissioned it, the architect, Juan de Herrera, and 16C Spain.

There is a good **view**★ of the monastery and the surrounding countryside from **Silla de Felipe II** (Philip II's Seat). *Turn left beyond the monastery into the road marked Entrada Herrería-Golf and follow the signs to Silla de Felipe II.*

The feast day of San Lorenzo (St Lawrence), patron of the village and monastery, is celebrated annually on 10 August.

The building of the monastery – On 10 August 1557, St Lawrence's Day, Philip II's forces defeated the French at the memorable battle of St Quentin. In commemoration the king decided to build a monastery and dedicate it to the saint. It would be consigned to the Hieronymites and would also serve as royal palace and pantheon.

The project was stupendous – there are nearly 1 200 doors and 2 600 windows; it required 1 500 workmen but was completed in a mere 21 years (1563-1584) which is why the building has an exceptional unity of style.

The general designs of the first architect, Juan de Toledo, were followed, after his death in 1567 by his assistant **Juan de Herrera**, who, however, is responsible for the final overall elegance. Reaction to sumptuous ornateness fashionable in Charles V's reign produced from the architects a sober monument with cleancut, majestic lines. It is said that the monastery recalls St Lawrence's martyrdom with its gridiron plan. It measures 206m x 161m - 676ft x 528ft and is built of grey granite – the austerity of the stone serving to emphasise, if anything, the severity of the architecture. When the king commanded an increase in height to accommodate a larger religious community, Herrera took the opportunity to position the rows of windows asymmetrically to lessen the monotony of horizontal lines which, otherwise, are only relieved by the pointed corner towers. The edifice finally has the grandeur of a great palace, the austerity of a dedicated monastery.

TOUR ⏲ *time: 1/2 day*

★★ **Palacios (Royal Apartments)** – While Philip II and the Spanish Habsburgs remained on the throne, El Escorial was a place of regal splendour: the king resided in apartments encircling the church apse, other royal apartments extended around the Patio de los Mascarones (Mascaroon Courtyard). The Bourbons, who in fact preferred the palaces of La Granja, El Pardo and Aranjuez to El Escorial, when nevertheless in residence, occupied suites on the north side of the church. The palace took on renewed glory in the 18C in the reigns of Charles III and IV but lost its position as a centre of court life again later. A staircase built in the time of Charles IV goes up *(3rd floor)* to the **Palacio de los Borbones** (Bourbon Apartments). These are sumptuous with Pompeian ceilings and fine **tapestries ★**. The hangings include many made in the Real Fábrica (Royal Tapestry Works) in Madrid after cartoons by Spanish artists, notably Goya, as in the series on popular subjects and pastimes. In later rooms are Flemish tapestries – a *Neptune* (from the Telemachus series) and several (in the last room) in realistic style by Teniers.

The style of decoration changes, introducing the austerity of the Habsburgs. The large **Sala de las Batallas** (Battle Gallery) contains frescoes (1587): on the south wall, of the Victory at Higueruela in the 15C against the Moors and on the north wall, the Victory at St-Quentin against the French.

The restraint of the **Habitaciones de Felipe II** (Philip II's apartments) *(2nd floor)* is all the more striking after the luxury of the Bourbon rooms. Those of the Infanta Isabel Clara Eugenia, like those of her father, comprise a suite of relatively small rooms in which the principal decoration derives from dados of Talavera ceramic tiles. The king's bedroom, where he died in 1598, aged 71, is directly off the church. A communicating door allowed him to walk in at any time in the early years and at the end, when he was dying of gangrene caused by advanced gout, to be present during services and contemplate the high altar from his bed. The paintings in the apartments include a *St Christopher* by Patinir and a portrait of the king in his old age by Pantoja de la Cruz. Facing the gardens and the plain, the Salón del Trono (Throne Room) is hung with 16C Brussels tapestries, the Sala de los Retratos (Portrait Gallery), which follows, with royal portraits. Finally, one is shown Philip's sedan chair in which he was carried when no longer able to walk.

★★ **Panteones (Pantheons)** – Access is through the Patio de los Evangelistas (Evangelists' Courtyard) in which the walls are painted with frescoes by Tibaldi (east wall) and his followers.

Monasterio de El Escorial

A marble and jasper staircase leads down to the **Panteón de los Reyes**★★★ (Royal Pantheon) which lies beneath the chancel. It contains the mortal remains of all the Spanish monarchs from the time of Emperor Charles V, with the exception of Philip V, Ferdinand VI and Amadeus of Savoy who are buried respectively in La Granja, Madrid and in Italy.

The chapel, which is octagonal in shape, was begun in 1617 in the reign of Philip III and completed in 1654. The main architect was Juan Bautista Crescenci. Facing the door is the jasper altar; on either side stand the 26 marble and bronze sarcophagi in wall niches. The kings are on the left and the queens whose sons succeeded to the throne, on the right. The sumptuous decoration is completed by an ornate chandelier, the work of an Italian artist.

The 19C **Panteón de los Infantes**★ (Infantes' Pantheon) includes not only children but also queens whose children did not succeed to the throne. The decoration includes delicately carved sculptures. Climatic conditions are such that the room has been well preserved.

★ **Salas Capitulares (Chapter houses)** – Two fine rooms, with ceilings painted by Italian artists with grotesques and frescoes, form a museum of Spanish (16 and 17C) and Italian (16C) religious painting.

The first room contains canvases by El Greco and Ribera, a *St Jerome* by Titian and *Joseph's Tunic* painted by Velázquez in Rome. The second room has works from the 16C Venetian School, including paintings by Tintoretto, Veronese and Titian *(Ecce Homo)*. A room at the back contains works by Bosch and his followers: the *Haywain*, an example of his unbounded imagination, and the *Crown of Thorns (Los Improperios)*, his satirical verve.

★★ **Basílica** – Herrera based his final plan for the basilica on Italian drawings, introducing an architectural novelty, a flat vault, in the atrium. The church's interior owes much to St Peter's in Rome with a Greek cross plan, a 92m - 302ft high cupola above the transept crossing supported by four colossal pillars and barrel vaulting in the transept. The frescoes in the nave vaulting were painted by Luca Giordano in Charles II's reign. Wide, red marble steps lead to the sanctuary which has paintings on the vaulting of the Lives of Christ and the Virgin by Cambiasso. The massive **retable**, designed by Herrera, is 30m - 100ft tall and is composed of 4 registers of jasper, onyx and red marble columns between which stand 15 bronze sculptures by Leone and Pompeo Leoni. The tabernacle is also by Herrera. On either side of the chancel are the royal mausoleums with funerary figures at prayer by Pompeo Leoni. Charles V is shown with his Queen, Isabel of Portugal, their daughter María and her two sisters, while Philip II is portrayed in company of three of his wives, and his son, Don Carlos. The door at the end on the right is the one communicating with Philip II's room.

In the first chapel off the north aisle is the *Martyrdom of St Maurice* by Rómulo Cincinato, which Philip II preferred to that of El Greco *(see below)*. In the adjoining chapel is a magnificent sculpture of Christ carved by Benvenuto Cellini in 1562.

Patio de los Reyes (Kings' Courtyard) – One of the three classical gateways in the palace's principal façade opens onto this courtyard. The court is named after the statues of the Kings of Judea which adorn the majestic west front of the church.

★★ **Biblioteca (Library)** – *2nd floor.* The gallery is 54m - 177ft long and richly decorated; the shelving, designed by Herrera, is of exotic woods; the ceiling, sumptuously painted by Tibaldi, represents the liberal arts with Philosophy and Theology at each end. There are also magnificent portraits of Charles V, Philip II and Philip III by Pantoja de la Cruz and one of Charles II by Carreño.

Philip II furnished the library with over 10 000 books of which many suffered in the 1671 fire and the ravages of Napoleon's army. It is now a public library with over 40 000 books and some 2 700 manuscripts dating from the 5-18C. The unusual presentation of the books on the shelves, with the spine facing inwards, is for preservation purposes.

In the cases, on the marble tables, are precious manuscripts including some in Arabic, autographs of St Teresa, the finely illuminated *Cantigas de Santa María*, a poem by King Alfonso the Wise, and an 11C Beatus *(photograph p 33)*.

★★ **Nuevos Museos (New Museos)** – The **Museo de Pintura** (Picture Museum) contains an interesting collection of works illustrating religious themes.

1st room: canvases by Italian artists mainly from the 16C Venetian School (Titian, Veronese and Tintoretto). 2nd room: among others, two works by Van Dyck and a small painting by Rubens. 3rd room: works by Miguel de Coxcie, Philip II's Court Painter. 4th room: Rogier Van der Weyden's outstanding *Calvary*, a sober and expressive painting, is flanked by an *Annunciation* by Veronese and a *Nativity* by Tintoretto. 5th room: canvases by Ribera including *St Jerome Penitent*, the philosopher *Chrysippus* and *Aesop*, all with the artist's characteristic style of portraying especially vivid faces, together with two paintings by Zurbarán – *St Peter of Alcántara* and the *Presentation of the Virgin* – examples of his marvellous approach to light and subject matter. Last room: two paintings by Alonso Cano and various works by Luca Giordano.

The **Museo de Arquitectura** (Architectural Museum) in the vaulted basement outlines the construction of the monastery with biographies of the principal men involved, including craftsmen, as well as account books, Herrera's designs and so on.

On the ground floor, a continuation of the painting section, El Greco's **Martyrdom of St Maurice and the Theban Legionary**★ is given pride of place. The work, commissioned by Philip II but too original in composition, too acid in colouring to suit his taste, was rejected by the king. Nevertheless, this picture of the martyrdom of the legionary who refused to sacrifice to the gods, and of St Maurice trying to convince his companions that he should be executed in the other's place, is now considered one of El Greco's greater works.

ADDITIONAL SIGHTS

★ **Casita del Príncipe (Prince's Pavilion)** ⊘ – *Southeast along the road to the station.* Charles III commissioned Juan de Villanueva to build a leisure lodge for the future Charles IV in the Prince's Gardens, which stretch out below Philip II's apartments. Its exquisite decoration makes it a jewel of a palace, in miniature. There are painted **Pompeian**★ style ceilings by Maella and Vicente Gómez, silk hangings, canvases by Luca Giordano, chandeliers, porcelain and a beautiful mahogany and marble dining room.

Casita del Arriba (Upper Pavilion) ⊘ – *3km - 2 miles southwest beyond the golf-course.* Like the Prince's Pavilion, this lodge, also known as the Casita del Infante (Infante's Pavilion), was designed by Villanueva. It was built for the Infante Gabriel, Charles IV's younger brother. The interior is furnished in the style of the period; the first floor was arranged as apartments for Prince Juan Carlos before his accession to the throne.

ESTELLA / LIZARRA★★

Navarra

Population 13 569

Michelin map 442 D 23 – Michelin Atlas España Portugal p 14

Local map under SANTIAGO DE COMPOSTELA

Estella spreads over hilly ground on either side of the Río Ega and is divided into parishes which have grown in size without losing their local character. The nobility of the brick and rough stone façades recalls the destiny intended for the city selected in the 12C by the Kings of Navarra as their centre and in the 19C by the Carlists. On the first Sunday in May, the Carlists gather in remembrance.

"Estella la Bella" – Such was the name pilgrims gave the town in the Middle Ages on their way to Santiago. As Estella was a major halt on the pilgrim road, it was endowed with several artistic buildings which date mainly from the Romanesque period. Moreover, in 1076, King Sancho Ramírez granted the town certain privileges which attracted tradesmen and innkeepers most of whom were freemen who settled on the right bank of the Ega.

Pilgrims stopped to venerate Our Lady on the Hill whose shrine, now a modern church, stands on the site on which, according to tradition, on 25 May 1085, shepherds, guided by a shower of stars, found a statue of the Virgin. Of the town's many medieval hospices, the leper hospital of St Lazarus became the most famous.

SIGHTS

Plaza de San Martín The small square was originally at the heart of the freemen's parish, bustling with the comings and goings around its shops and inns; today nothing, apart from the splashing fountain, disturbs the peace. On one side stands the **former Ayuntamiento** (Town Hall) with an emblasoned front dating from the 16C.

★ **Palacio de los Reyes de Navarra (Palace of the Kings of Navarra)** – The building is a rare example of 12C Romanesque civil architecture. Its long front is punctuated by arcades and twin bays with remarkable capitals.

Iglesia de San Pedro de la Rúa ⊘ – The church stands facing the royal palace on a cliff spur formerly crowned by the city castle. It retains outstanding 12 and 13C features.

There is an unusual **doorway**★ at the top of a monumental flight of steps, in the north wall. The door's originality, with richly sculpted capitals and covings, lies in its equilateral scalloped arch, Caliphate influenced. Similar portals can be seen in Navarra at Puente la Reina and Cirauqui *(qv)* and in the Saintonge and Poitou regions of France.

Inside are three Romanesque apses, with, at the centre, a column of intertwined serpents.

The Romanesque **cloisters**★ lost two galleries when the nearby castle was blown up in the 16C. The loss becomes all the more regrettable as one discovers the skill and invention of the masons who carved the remaining capitals; the north gallery series illustrates scenes from the Lives of Christ and Sts Lawrence, Andrew and Peter, while plant and animal themes enliven the west gallery where the architect unexpectedly included a group of four slanting columns.

Calle de la Rúa – The pilgrim road. Note the **Palacio de Fray Diego de Estella**, at no 7, a palace with an emblasoned Plateresque façade.

Iglesia del Santo Sepulcro (Church of the Holy Sepulchre) – The church is remarkable for its portal which is purely Gothic. Superimposed above the door are the Last Supper, the three Marys at the Holy Sepulchre and Hell, and Calvary. The niches framing the doorway contain somewhat mannered figures of saints.

Take the Puente de la Cárcel (rebuilt in 1973) across the river.

Iglesia de San Miguel – The church stands in a quarter that was lived in by natives of Navarra at the end of the 12C and which still has a medieval atmosphere about its narrow streets. The **north portal**★ seems almost to have been designed as a challenge to the "foreigners" on the opposite bank of the river. On the tympanum is a figure of Christ surrounded by the Evangelists and other mysterious personages. Sculptures in the covings show censer-bearing angels, the Old Men of the Apocalypse, prophets and patriarchs, martyrs and saints, and scenes from the Gospels. The capitals illustrate the childhood of Christ and some hunting scenes. On the upper register of the walls are eight statue columns of the Apostles while on the lower register, two **high reliefs**★★, the most accomplished and expressive of the doorway show, on the left, St Michael slaying the dragon, and on the right, the three Marys coming from the Sepulchre. The noble bearing, the elegance of the draperies and the facial expressions, make the carving a masterpiece of Romanesque art.

EXCURSIONS

★**Monasterio de Irache** ⊙ – *3km - 2 miles southwest.*
A Benedictine abbey was founded on the site as far back as the 10C. Later, Irache, a major halt on the Santiago pilgrim road, was a Cistercian community before becoming a university under the Benedictines, in the 16C, which was to close in 1833.

★**Iglesia** – This church's pure Romanesque style apse lies directly in line with the original intersecting ribs of the nave vaulting. During the Renaissance the dome on squinches was rebuilt and the *coro alto* added to the original structure. The main façade and most of the conventual buildings were rebuilt in the 17C.

Claustro – The Renaissance cloisters are decorated with brackets and capitals illustrating the Lives of Christ and St Benedict.

★**Sierras de Andía and Urbasa** – *Round tour of 94km - 58 miles – about 3 hours.*
The pleasure of this tour lies in driving through beechwoods and, as you rise to the top of a pass, getting an extensive view over the countryside.

Leave Estella on the NA120 north towards the Puerto de Lizarraga (Lizarraga Pass).

Monasterio de Iranzu ⊙ – *9km - 5 1/2 miles north of Estella. Signposted from the NA120.*
The Cistercian monastery, built in lonely isolation in a wild **gorge**★ at the end of the 12C, is now a college. It is a good example of the Cistercian transitional style from Romanesque to Gothic in which robustness and elegance combine.
The cloister bays, where they have not been given a later florid Gothic fenestration, are typical, with Romanesque blind arcades, oculi and wide relieving arches. The church, with somewhat primitive vaulting, has a flat east end decorated with a triplet, or three windows, symbolising the Trinity, a feature found in many Cistercian churches.

★**Puerto de Lizarraga Road** – On emerging from the tunnel (alt 1090m - 3576ft) pause briefly at the **viewpoint**★ overlooking the green Ergoyena valley before beginning the descent through woods and pastures.

Continue to Etxarri-Arantaz where you take the N240 west to Olatzi and then turn left towards Estella.

★★**Puerto de Urbasa Road** – The fairly steep climb between great free-standing boulders and clumps of trees has a beautiful wildness in total contrast to the wide and lushly wooded valley which follows. Beyond the pass (alt 927m - 3041ft) tall limestone cliffs add character to the landscape before the road enters the series of gorges through which the sparkling Río Urenderra flows.

*Spain's most important religious festivals and pilgrimages
are listed in the Calendar of events,
in the Practical Information section at the end of the Guide.*

Catalunya (Girona)
Population 35301
Michelin map 443 F38 – Michelin Atlas España Portugal p 19

Figueres, capital of Alt Empordà, is a commercial centre and strategic road link between French and Spanish Catalunya. It is the birthplace of **Salvador Dalí** (1904-1989) *(qv)*, the famous Surrealist artist.

★ **Teatre-Museu Dalí** ⊙ – The Dalí theatre-museum, a world of folly and caprice which may charm or exasperate but never fails to impress, is a good reflection of the artist himself who said this of his creation: "The museum cannot be considered as such; it is a gigantic surrealist object, where everything is coherent, where nothing has eluded my design." It is housed in the former local theatre (1850) which was burnt down during the Civil War and restored in 1966. Dalí added an immense glass dome (beneath which he is now buried) and a vast *patio*, and decorated everything with fantasy objects: giant eggs, bread rolls – which cover the façade like the shells all over the Casa de las Conchas in Salamanca – basins and gilt dummies. He gave his eccentricity full rein in the squares around the museum where there are figures perched on columns of tyres, and inside, for instance in the Mae West sitting room where there is a lip-shaped sofa, a nose-chimney and eye-frames. Some of his canvases are exhibited in the museum (including a series showing him painting his wife Gala) as well as works by other artists such as Pitxot, Duchamp and Fortuny.

Iglesia de FRÓMISTA★★

FRÓMISTA CHURCH – Castilla y León (Palencia)
Michelin map 441 or 442 F16 – Michelin Atlas España Portugal p 25

Many pilgrims on the way to Santiago de Compostela *(qv)* halted at Frómista with its four hospices and the opportunity of making a pious offering at the Monasterio benedictino de San Martín. Of this, only the church remains at the centre of a large square.

★★ **Iglesia de San Martín** ⊙ – The church, built in 1066 with beautifully matched rough hewn stone blocks of considerable size, marks a climax in the development of Romanesque architecture in Castilla: after earlier essays in Palencia, Jaca and León (San Isodoro), it demonstrates the achievement of perfect ordinance in this particular style. Outside, the eye travels over the classic east end, rising from the apses up over the transept walls, almost imperceptibly to the **cupola** squinches and finally to the lantern. The decorative features are all there – billets outlining the windows, engaged columns and cornices with ornately carved modillions. The **interior** has a perfect basilica design with a nave, two aisles and a transept which does not project outside. The pure Romanesque lines of the exterior are apparent inside, in the barrel vaulting, apsidal oven vaults, the dome on squinches and double ribbed arches. The richly carved **capitals** with human figures or plant motifs provide indispensable decorative relief.
The church suffered a somewhat over-zealous restoration in 1904.

FUENTERRABÍA / HONDARRIBIA★

País Vasco (Guipúzcoa)
Population 13974
Michelin map 442 B24 – Michelin Atlas España Portugal p 14

Fuenterrabía (Hondarribia in Basque), now a popular seaside resort and large fishing port, was for centuries the target of attack by the French on account of its strategic position on the frontier. The old stronghold with its steep streets built on high ground above the Bidasoa river is still encircled by ramparts. As a reminder of its history, annually on 8 September, Fuenterrabía celebrates with a military parade *(alarde)* a festival to the Virgen de Guadalupe who is said to have delivered the town from a two-month siege by the French in 1638.
On the outskirts of the town near the harbour, the **Marina**, a bustling fishermen's quarter with characteristic wood balconies, is popular for its pavement cafés.

CIUDAD VIEJA (OLD TOWN) *time: 1 hour*

Puerta de Santa María – The gateway through the 15C ramparts is surmounted by the town's arms and twin angels venerating the Virgen de Guadalupe.

Calle Mayor – The narrow main street is picturesquely lined with old houses with wrought-iron balconies and carved wooden cornices.

Iglesia de Santa María – The impressive Gothic church, remodelled in the 17C when it was given a baroque tower, is supported round the apse by massive buttresses. It was in this church, on 3 June 1660, that the proxy wedding took place between the Spanish minister, Don Luis de Haro, on behalf of Louis XIV, and the Infanta María Teresa, six days before the solemnisation of the marriage in France.

Castillo de Carlos V – According to legend, the 10C founder of this austere fortress was Sancho Abarca, King of Navarra. The fortress served a key role as strongpoint throughout the history of the Kingdom of Navarra. Charles V restored it in the 16C; it has now been transformed again – this time into a *parador*.

EXCURSIONS

★**Cabo Higuer** – *4km - 2 1/2 miles north. To reach this headland, leave Fuenterrabía on the road to the harbour and beach.* Turn left and as the road climbs, you will get a good **view**★ of the beach, the town and the quayside and from the end of the headland, the French coast and the town of Hendaye.

★★**Ermita de San Marcial (Hermitage)** – *9km - 5 1/2 miles east. Leave Fuenterrabía on the Behobia road and take the first right after the Palmera factory; bear left at the first crossroads.*
A narrow road leads up to the wooded hilltop (225m - 738ft). The **panorama**★★ from the hermitage terrace includes Fuenterrabía, **Irún** and the **Isla de los Faisanes** (Pheasant Island) in the mouth of the River Bidasoa which marks the frontier and has been the setting for several historic events including, in 1659, the signing of the Treaty of the Pyrenees which stipulated the marriage between Louis XIV and the Infanta María Teresa. In the distance you can see San Sebastián and Hendaye beach.

★★**Jaizkibel Road** – *West of Fuenterrabía.*
The **drive**★★ is glorious at sunset. After 5km - 3 miles you reach the Capilla de Nuestra Señora de Guadalupe (Chapel of our Lady of Guadalupe) where there is a lovely **view**★ of the mouth of the Bidasoa and the French Basque coast. The road overlooks the sea as it rises through pines and gorse to reach the Hostal de Jaizkibel at the foot of a 584m - 1 916ft peak and a lookout with a superb **view**★★ *(viewpoint indicator).* The road down to Pasai Donibane affords **glimpses**★ of the indented coastline, the Cordillera Cantábrica range and the three mountains which dominate San Sebastián-Ulía, Urgull and Igueldo.

Pasajes (Pasaia) – *17km - 11 miles west along the Jaizkibel road.*
Pasajes, in fact, comprises three villages around a sheltered bay connected with the open sea only by a narrow channel; **Pasai Antxo** is a trading port, **Pasai Donibane**★ and **Pasai San Pedro** are both deep-sea fishing ports, processing cod in the town. They hold the highest catch value along the Cantabrian coast. To get to **Pasai Donibane**, either park the car at the entrance to the village or take a motorboat from San Pedro. The **view** from the water is picturesque – tall houses with brightly painted wooden balconies. The one and only village street winds between the houses and beneath arches offering glimpses of boats and landing-stages. A path runs alongside the harbour to the lighthouse *(3/4 hour).*

GANDÍA

Comunidad Valenciana
Population 52 000
Michelin map 445 P 29 – Michelin Atlas España Portugal p 69
Town plan in the current Michelin Red Guide España Portugal

Gandía lies on the Costa Blanca south of Valencia at the centre of a *huerta* which produces large quantities of oranges. These are exported from nearby **El Grao de Gandía**. A seaside resort has developed near the harbour along an immense sand **beach**.

The Borja fief – Gandía became the fief of the Borja family, better known under its Italian name, Borgia, when in 1485, the Duchy of Gandía was given by Ferdinand the Catholic to Rodrigo Borgia, future Pope Alexander VI. The pope is chiefly remembered for his scandalous private life and for his children – Lucretia, renowned for her beauty and culture, and Caesar who for political ends had his brother murdered and served as a model for Machiavelli's *The Prince*. However, the fourth duke and great-grandson of Alexander VI, who became **St Francis Borja** (1510-1572), was to redeem the family name. He served as equerry to Queen Isabel at the court of Emperor Charles V; and on her death, after having opened her coffin and seen her decomposed body, he resolved that if his own wife should die, he would devote himself to God. His wife did indeed die; he joined the Society of Jesus and became vicar-general.

Palacio Ducal (Former Palace of the Dukes of Borja) ⊘ – The mansion in which St Francis was born, now a Jesuit college, underwent considerable modification between the 16 and 18C. Only the *patio* remains Gothic in appearance and typical of those along the east coast of Spain. The tour includes richly decorated apartments with painted or coffered ceilings, *azulejos* and marble floors. Several rooms have been converted into chapels. The last room off the golden gallery has a beautiful floor, a Manises mosaic representing the four elements.

GIBRALTAR

Population 30 000
Michelin map 446 X 13
Town plan in the current Michelin Red Guide España Portugal

The self-governing British dependent territory of Gibraltar ⊘ lies at the northeastern entrance to the Straits of Gibraltar and is only 24km - 15 miles distant from the north African coast. For many, the first contact with Gibraltar is most likely to be the incredible landing strip – over which the road passes – which links the territory geographically to mainland Spain.

The Rock – This rocky promontory, linked to mainland Spain in the north, pushes southwards into the straits *(see below)*. The **Rock** is 4.5km long×1.4km at its widest point – (2.8×0.9 miles) – and has an area of 6.3km – 2 1/2sq miles. The highest point is Mount Misery at 423m – 1 388ft. The east side presents a sheer rock face plunging into the sea; the reclaimed land at the foot of the less abrupt west side forms the site of the town.

Key to the Mediterranean – The history of Gibraltar, one of Hercules' Antique pillars marking the end of the Classical world, begins in 711 AD with the invasion of the Moors under **Tarik-ibn-Zeyad.** He seized the Rock and named it Gibel Tarik (the mountain of Tarik) after himself, then built a castle upon it – now in ruins but still known as the Moor's Castle. It was recaptured by Spain on 20 August 1462, feast day of St Bernard, who was thereupon created patron of the town. In the War of the Spanish Succession *(qv)*, the British, in alliance with Holland, Austria and the Holy Roman Empire, captured Gibraltar with a naval force under **Admiral Rooke** (1704). The taking of Gibraltar was formally recognised by the Treaty of Utrecht signed in 1713. The citadel commanding the straits has remained in British hands ever since, in spite of Spanish and French attacks. The most notable attempt was the **Great Siege of 1779-1783,** when the garrison under General Elliot resisted all efforts to bomb or starve them into submission. Gibraltar became a Crown colony in 1830, and served as a naval base during both world wars. In 1967 the colony voted in a referendum by 12 138 to 44 in favour of retaining its connection with Britain. The frontier was re-opened in 1985 following a 15-year border blockade by Spain and is open 24 hours for those with valid identification (see Practical Information section). In 1973 Gibraltar became a member of the European Community along with Britain.

The Barbary Apes – The origin of the apes is unknown. Legend has it that the British will remain as long as the apes survive; when there seemed a danger of them becoming extinct in 1944 Churchill sent a signal ordering reinforcements. The colony has flourished ever since. The apes are actually tailless monkeys and are the protégés of the Gibraltar Regiment.

Gibraltar today – The colony's economy is based on a growing financial services sector and tourism. Gibraltar has retained its free port status and trade is based on transit and refuelling activities.

The west side of the Rock shelters the naval and commercial ports as well as the town with its English and Spanish style houses, its pubs and shops. Arabic architecture still persists, notably in the cathedral which has the plan of a mosque.

Tour of the Rock – The top of the Rock may be reached by car or cable-car. Drive down Main Street and follow the signs to Upper Rock. The road leads first to **St Michael's Cave** ⊘, – a natural cavern which has fine concretions. From here you may walk to the top *(1 hour Rtn)* where there are good **views★** of both sides of the Rock and the Spanish and African coasts. The road continues to **Apes' Den,** home to the Barbary Apes *(see above)*.

Straits of GIBRALTAR

Andalucía (Cádiz)
Michelin map 446 X 13 – Michelin Atlas España Portugal pp 88-89

The straits, gateway to the Mediterranean and a mere 14km - 9 miles wide at the narrowest point, have always played an important strategic role in the history of the local towns.

Algeciras – Population 86 042. Town plan in the current Michelin Red Guide España Portugal. The Arabs arrived in Algeciras from Africa in 711 and remained until 1344, naming the town Al Djezirah, the "island", after the Isla Verde, the Green Island, now joined to the mainland. The Bahía de Algeciras has always served the dual purpose of safe anchorage and vantage point overlooking the Straits of Gibraltar. Algeciras is Spain's busiest passenger port with crossings to Tangier and Ceuta several times a day (3.5 million passengers annually).

It is from across the bay that you get the world famous **views★★** of the Rock of Gibraltar.

Tarifa – Population 15 220. Tarifa stands on the most southerly point of the Iberian Peninsula. Atlantic and Mediterranean air masses converge over the area giving Tarifa the sea breezes ideal for windsurfing. It has become one of Europe's major centres for the sport.

Castillo – In 1292 this fortress, which had been taken by the Christians, was under the command of Guzmán el Bueno whose son was captured by the Moors. When Guzmán had to choose between the death of his child and the surrender of his town, he replied by throwing his dagger to the enemy for the execution.

The Muralla Sur (south wall) commands a fine **view**★ of the Straits of Gibraltar and the coast of Morocco only 13.5km - 8 miles away.

GIRONA / GERONA★★

Catalunya (Girona)
Population 70 409
Michelin map 443 G 38 – Michelin Atlas España Portugal p 33

Girona stands on a promontory at the confluence of the Ter and Onyar rivers. Its strategic site has been so coveted and its history so eventful that it has become known as the "city of a thousand sieges." Its ramparts were built and rebuilt by the Iberians, the Romans and throughout the Middle Ages. Charlemagne's troops are described, in the *Song of Roland (Canción de Rolando)*, as assaulting the city; in 1809, under General Álvarez de Castro's command, Girona resisted attacks from Napoleon's troops for more than seven months.

Girona and Judaism – Girona's Jewish community, in the old quarter around **Calle de la Força** (**BY**), became famous in the Middle Ages for its prestigious Cabalistic school. This past can be felt in atmospheric narrow alleyways like those of Cúndaro and Sant Llorenç. In this latter is the Centro Isaac el Cec (**BY A**) which is given over to the town's Jewish history (exhibitions, lectures, etc).

★★CIUTAT ANTIGA (OLD TOWN) *time: 3 hours*

From footbridges over the Onyar (**BY**), there are views of the picturesque orange and ochre-coloured buildings along the river banks, the cathedral tower and the spire of Sant Feliu.

Narrow alleys lead up to the cathedral which is preceded by a vast flight of 90 steps, known as the **Escaleras de la Pera**. The 14C **Pia Almonia** building (**BY N**) on the right is an elegant example of Gothic architecture.

★ **Catedral** (**BY**) ⊘ – The baroque façade has been designed like a stone altarpiece with a single huge oculus above. The rest of the building is Gothic: the chancel (1312) is surrounded by an ambulatory and radiating chapels; early in the 15C the decision was taken to add only a single **aisle**★★ but to make it outstandingly spacious (it is the largest Gothic nave in the world) and light. The two parts of the building have a similar, powerful, unadorned style, decoration having been restricted to the chapel arches, triforium niches and windows.

In the chancel, beneath a silver canopy symbolising the sky, is a silver-gilt embossed 14C **altarpiece**★, highlighted with enamelwork, which traces the Life of Christ. Among the chapels, many of which contain works of art, that of Sant Honorat (1st north chapel), is outstanding for the tomb, in a Gothic niche, with three superimposed registers, of Bishop Bernard de Pau (d 1457).

★★ **Tesoro** ⊘ – The treasury houses an extraordinarily rich collection of religious art, including one of the most beautiful copies of the **Beatus**★ *(qv)*, St John's Commentary on the Apocalypse, written in the 8C. These miniatures, dated 975, by the monk Emeteri and the nun Eude, are notable for the bright colours and lively expressions used to illustrate the series of fantastic beasts. They are Caliphate influenced and show traces of Visigothic decoration. There is a 12C Virgin of the Cathedral (de la Seu) in the same room. Splendid church plate is displayed in the rooms that follow, including a 14C enamel cross; of particular interest is the 10C embossed silver **Hixem Casket**, a fine example of Caliphate art. The end room contains the famous **Tapiz de la Creación** (Tapestry of the Creation) ★★★, a unique work dating from about 1100. It is a marvellously delicate embroidery with well preserved colours which shows Christ in Majesty in a circular area at the centre, surrounded by the different stages of creation. The four winds fill the corners.

★ **Claustro** – The 12-13C Romanesque cloisters, irregular in shape, with a double line of columns, date, like the 11C Torre de Carlomagno (Charlemagne Tower) which dominates them, from the former Romanesque cathedral. The beautiful friezes on the pillars at the gallery corners and centres, illustrate, in most cases, scenes from Genesis. Note the finely-drawn outlines, the delicate draperies and the serenity of the faces.

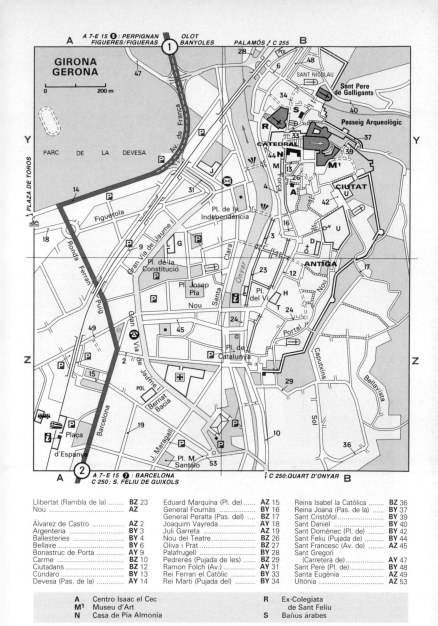

GIRONA GERONA

0 — 200 m

PARC DE LA DEVESA

★**Museu d'Art** (**BY M¹**) ⊘ – The museum is housed in the Palacio Episcopal and contains a comprehensive collection of art covering periods from the Romanesque to the 20C. The Romanesque section includes a 10-11C altar from Sant Pere de Rodes of wood and stone faced with silver, and a 12C beam from Cruïlles. The Gothic section has a lovely alabaster Virgin of Besalú dating from the 15C. Among the richly decorated altarpieces displayed in the Throne Room is that of **Sant Miquel de Cruïlles**★★ by Lluis Borrassá (15C), one of the most beautiful works of Catalan Gothic art. The Sant Feliu altarpiece by Juan de Borgoña marks the transition between the Gothic and Renaissance styles.

Ex-Colegiata de Sant Feliu (**BY R**) – This former collegiate church outside the town walls must originally have been a martyry built over the tombs of St Narcissus, Bishop of Girona, and St Felix, both patrons of the city. A Gothic church with a tall east end was later built on the Romanesque foundations. In the apse are eight early sarcophagi let into the walls. Two have outstanding carvings – on the right, the abduction of Prosperine, opposite, a spirited **lion hunt**★.

Banys Arabs (Arab Baths) (**BY S**) ⊘ – The late 12C baths consist of a **frigidarium**, a relaxation area with a pool surrounded by columns and lit by an unusual lantern, a **tepidarium** or warm room, a **hypocaust** for steam baths and a **caldarium** or hot room.

Passeig Arqueològic (Archaeological Promenade) (**BY**) – Steps opposite the baths lead to gardens at the foot of the ramparts from which you can look along the Ter Valley.

Iglesia de Sant Pere de Galligants (**BY**) ⊘ – Not far from Sant Nicolau, with its clover leaf apse, stands the Romanesque church of Sant Pere. It has been repeatedly fortified; its east end appears embedded in the town walls and the belfry once served as a watch-tower. The church and cloisters house the **Museu Arqueològic** ⊘ which has a collection of finds from excavations in the province. 13-14C Hebrew memorial plaques are displayed in the cloisters while in the former sacristy there is Roman art from Empúries and the magnificent 4C **tomb of Las Estaciones**★ (the seasons; autumn in particular).

FROM GIRONA TO OLOT *55km - 34 miles – about 2 hours*

Leave Girona on the N 11, marked ① on the town plan.

Banyoles (Bañolas) – This delightful town stands beside a bright blue **lake**★ full of fish. A road 8km – 5 miles long circles the water, passing, on the left bank, before the 12C **Iglesia de Porqueres** ⊘. Inside the church, a triumphal arch has most unusual carved human figures on the capitals and the upper parts of the columns.

B. Brillon / MICHELIN

Puente de Besalú

Besalú – In the Middle Ages, Besalú was the capital of a county which stretched from Figueres to the Ter valley. At the town entrance, spanning the Fluviá, is an impressive, angled, **fortified bridge**★ *(puente)*. The streets in the town centre have an ancient feel about them and many of the houses reveal attractive paired windows. The Romanesque **Iglesia de Sant Pere** has a fine window surrounded by lion carvings and, a rare feature for the region, an ambulatory.

As you continue west you enter the **Olot region** which is known for its volcanic relief. In the Tertiary Era, when the Pyrenees were being formed, a geological upheaval exposed the Olot basin to eruption which explains the presence of some fifty volcanic cones not far away from the city. The craters are, however, largely hidden from view by lush vegetation.

Castellfollit de la Roca – The village is interestingly poised on a high cliff, one of the typical basalt piles that punctuate the landscape.

Olot – The town stands on the slopes of a crater. In this agricultural centre, known chiefly for its cattle fairs, two traditional crafts are still practised: the carving and painting of sacred multicoloured wood figures and the manufacture of a red Catalan cap known as a *barretina*.

Admission times and charges for the sights described are listed at the end of the Guide.

Every sight for which there are times and charges is indicated by the symbol ⊘ *in the middle section of the Guide.*

GRANADA★★★

Andalucía
Population 287 864
Michelin map 446 U 19 – Michelin Atlas España Portugal p 85
Town plan of the conurbation in the current Michelin Red Guide España Portugal

Granada has everything: prestigious and exceedingly beautiful Moorish buildings, luminous skies and a luxuriantly green **setting★★** over which the city, built on three hills at the centre of a wide plain or *vega*, looks out to the snow-capped Sierra Nevada on the horizon. From the Albaicín, Sacromonte and Alhambra hills, there are also infinitely varied views, particularly from the first, of the red-walled Alhambra.
Religious festivals are lively, colourful events, especially those held in Holy Week and at Corpus Christi. The city also holds an annual Music and Dance Festival in June and July.

HISTORICAL NOTES

Granada began to gain importance in the 11C when the caliphate of Córdoba declined. It became the capital of a kingdom founded by the Almoravids who were ousted a century later by the Almohads. It was in the 13C, however, that Granada reached the height of its glory when Muslims from Córdoba, which fell to the Christians in 1236, sought refuge here. In 1238, a new dynasty, that of the **Nasrids**, was founded by Mohammed Ibn el-Ahmar who acknowledged allegiance to Ferdinand III. For the next two and a half centuries (1238 to 1492) the kingdom of Granada flourished, becoming a symbol of economic, cultural and artistic prosperity, with magnificent buildings like the Alhambra.

The fall of Granada – In the 15C, as more of the Muslim-controlled territory in Spain was being lost to the Christians, the Catholic Monarchs were looking to conquer Granada, one of its last bastions. A quarrel in the royal harem inadvertently assisted them: the Caliph became enamoured of a Christian girl, Zoraya, for whom he considered repudiating his queen, Aisha, by whom he already had a son, **Boabdil**. Aisha fled with her son but soon returned, to depose the infatuated monarch and set the Boy King – El Rey Chico – upon the throne. As the great Moorish families divided in allegiance, Ferdinand of Aragón seized the opportunity to capture the young king and force his submission. Intrigue and sieges followed for several months; the powerful **Abencerrajes**, accused of desiring the downfall of Boabdil and of having sold themselves to the Christians, were one of several families to see 36 of their leading members massacred at a palace reception.
By 2 January 1492, after a six-month siege, the Catholic Monarchs had entered Granada; Boabdil had given them the keys of the city and gone into exile. As he looked back on Granada from the Motril road his mother is said to have rounded on him: "You weep like a woman for what you could not hold as a man;"

The Alhambra, Granada, with the Sierra Nevada in the distance

the spot remains the Moor's Sigh – **Suspiro del Moro**. After 781 years the Moorish domination of Spain was ended.
Granada continued to flourish in the Renaissance which followed the Reconquest although the city's fortunes suffered an eclipse during the ruthless suppression of the Las Alpujarras revolt *(qv)* in 1570.

Great Granadines – **Alonso Cano** (1601-1667), architect, sculptor, painter, was the moving spirit behind the blossoming of art in 17C Granada. His art, eschewing Renaissance tradition, turned towards classicism; he banished pathos from his sculpture and was in favour of restrained emotion. **Pedro de Mena** (1628-1688), his follower, carved realistic sculptures on religious themes.
Eugenia de Montijo, future wife of Napoleon III (Empress Eugénie: 1853) was born in Granada in 1826, daughter of a grandee and, on her mother's side, granddaughter of William Kirkpatrick, Scots by birth, American by nationality and consul at Málaga.
Federico García Lorca, poet and dramatist, talented musician, friend of Dalí and Buñuel, was born 20km - 12 miles from Granada in Fuentevaqueros in 1899 (he died in 1936, shot by Franco's soldiers at the outbreak of the Spanish Civil War).

Granada today – Granada is the capital of an agricultural province (cereals, beet, fruit and beef) as well as an archbishopric and university town. Its main resource is tourism.

There is a striking contrast between the old quarters of the town east of **Plaza Nueva** (**BY**) on the green, peaceful Alhambra and Albaicín hills, and the noisy, bustling lower town with its network of commercial streets and the pedestrian quarter around the cathedral set between the city's two main avenues, **Gran Vía de Colón** (**ABXY**) and **Calle de los Reyes Católicos** (**BY**). Restaurants in the centre serve Granada's speciality – a dish of ham and beans called *habas con jamón*.

★★★ THE ALHAMBRA AND THE GENERALIFE *time: 1/2 day*

The architecture of Granada – Muslim architecture *(p 23)* in Spain reached its climax in Granada where it evolved as the pure expression of a sophisticated civilisation at its moment of decline. The Nasrid princes always built for the moment, not posterity: beneath the fabulous decoration are ill assorted bricks, plaster and rubble; each sovereign razed the monuments of his predecessor to provide a site for his own new palace which would retain only the architectural principle of grouping all rooms round a central *patio*.

Decoration was the prime factor. Although wall hangings and carpets have disappeared and there remains little furniture, the sculpture everywhere covering walls and ceilings reveals an art never since surpassed. This sculptural decoration is, in fact, stuccowork, both outside and in. The finely modelled plaster, sometimes pierced, is worked in patterns in a low relief of flat planes to catch the light; another decoration was accomplished by building up layers of plaster which were then cut away to form stalactites *(mocárabes)*. This type of ornament, brilliantly painted and even gilded, covered capitals, cornice mouldings, arches, pendentives and entire cupolas.

Ceramic tiles were used to provide a geometric decoration for most of the walls: *alicatados (p 31)* produced a colourful marquetry, lines of arabesque motifs forming star designs; *azulejos* colour, different hues being separated by a thin raised fillet or a black line *(cuerda seca)*. Calligraphic decoration employed the so-called Andalusian cursive which was particularly elegant; the more decoratively complicated Cufic was reserved for religious aphorisms which appear framed in scrollwork.

★★★ The Alhambra (CDY) ⊘

The beautiful Calat Alhambra (Red Castle) must be one of the most remarkable fortresses ever built. It stands at the top of a wooded hill commanding views of the town, the bleak Sacromonte heights, nearby hillsides and gardens.

The Alhambra's outer perimeter is entered through the Puerta de Las Granadas or the Pomegranate Gateway built by Emperor Charles V. A paved footpath leads through the **shrubbery★** to the massive **Puerta de la Justicia★** (Justice Gateway), built so that its tower forms part of the inner ramparts defending the castle terrace.

★★★ Palacios Nazaríes (Nasrid Palace)

Palacios Nazaríes (Nasrid Palace) – The Nasrid palace was built around the Patio de los Arrayanes (Myrtle Court) and the Patio de los Leones (Lion Court) in the 14C. Its richness and variety and the originality of its decoration defy description. The tour begins in the **Mexuar,** part of the first palace, which was used for government and judicial administration. After the Reconquest, it was converted into a chapel and lengthened by the addition of an oratory from which there is a good **view★** of the Albaicín. Cross the **Patio del Cuarto Dorado** (**1**) ⊘, in which the south wall, protected by a remarkable carved wood cornice, may be taken as an example of the essentials of Granada art: windows are surrounded by panels covered with every variety of stucco and tile decoration. Opposite is the **Cuarto Dorado** (Golden Room), a wide room with a tiled base, fine stucco work and a beautiful wood ceiling.

Adjoining is the beautiful oblong **Patio de los Arrayanes.** A narrow central pool banked by myrtles runs the length of the court and reflects the massive bulk of the **Torre de Comares** (Comares Tower) which contrasts sharply with the light, slender porticoes that give onto the **Sala de la Barca** (a name arising from the Arabic word barakha meaning benediction) and the Salón de Embajadores. The jewel of the Alhambra, the **Salón de Embajadores** (Hall of Ambassadors), was the audience chamber of the emirs. It has a magnificent domed cedarwood ceiling and is lit by bay windows offering remarkable **views★★** of the surrounding countryside. *Azulejos* and stucco bearing inscriptions, some from the Koran, others in honour of various princes, complete the decoration.

Another opening off the Patio de los Arrayanes leads to the second palace, the residence of the royal family, at the heart of which stands the justly famous **Patio de los Leones** built by Mohammed V. Twelve rough stone lions support an ancient low-lying fountain while delicate arcades of slender columns around the court lead to the main state apartments.

The **Sala de los Abencerrajes,** so called after Boabdil had ordered the family massacre and piled the heads into the room's central basin, has a stalactite ceiling and a splendid star-shaped lantern cupola. Adorning the end of the **Sala de los Reyes** (Kings' Chamber) are alcoves containing vaulting painted to illustrate the pastimes of

The Alhambra: Sala de las Dos Hermanas

Moorish and Christian princes – the style is so atypical that it is not known whether the artist was a Christian working for the sultan before the Reconquest or later. The **Sala de las Dos Hermanas** (Hall of the Two Sisters) (**2**), named after the two large white identical marble slabs in the pavement, is known for its honeycomb cupola vaulting. Beyond are the **Sala de los Ajmeres** and the **Mirador de Daraxa** (Daraxa Mirador), both equally resplendent. Leave the palace building and enter the Partal gardens through which you reach the green and silent Daraxa garden. A gallery leads to the **Patio de la Reja** (Window Grille Court) (**3**). Steps go down to the **Baños Reales** (Royal Baths) with their sumptuous multicoloured decoration where the light enters through small star-shaped apertures.

Cross the Daraxa garden to the Portal gardens.

★★ **Gardens and perimeter towers** – Spreading to the east of the royal palaces are the terraced Jardines de Partal which descend to the gracefully porticoed **Torre de las Damas** (Lady Tower). From this early 14C building, which is as ornately decorated inside as the royal palaces, there are views of the Darro directly below, of Albaicín and Sacromonte.

The Torre de Mihrab on the right, is a former Nasrid oratory – a rarity since the princes were not notably pious. The respectively Torre de la Cautiva and Torre de las Infantas (Captive's and Infantas' towers) are sumptuously decorated inside.

Enter the Palacio de Carlos V from the Partal gardens.

★ **Palacio de Carlos V** (Emperor Charles V's Palace) – The Nasrid palaces were not considered sufficiently majestic to serve as the imperial residence. In 1526, Pedro Machuca, who studied under Michelangelo, was charged with the design of a suitable palace to be financed from a tax levied on the Moors. Their uprising in 1568 interrupted the building and the palace was completed at a much later date. This

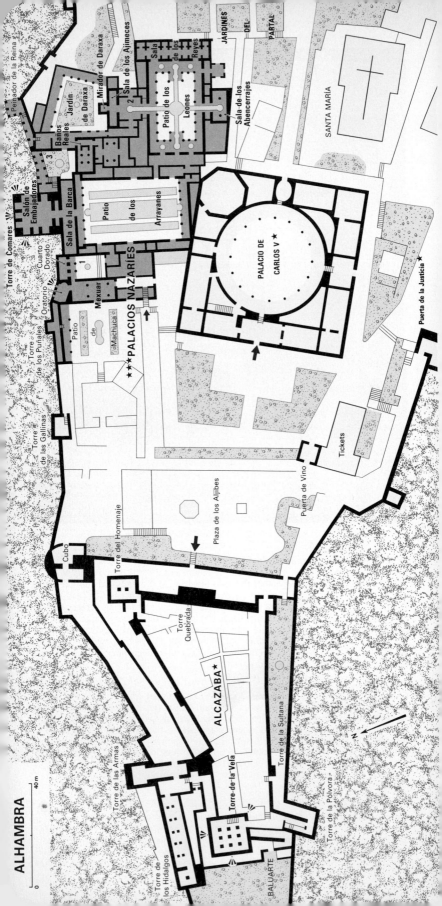

purely classical style building, always thought one of the most successful creations of the Renaissance period in Spain, is the only construction of Machuca's to remain. Although the contrast with the Nasrid palaces may at first appear unfortunate, the palace soon reveals its grandeur, so perfect are its lines, so dignified its appearance, so simple its plan of a circle within a square. It contains two museums:

Museo Hispano-musulmán (Hispano-Moorish Museum) – The museum is in rooms overlooking the Patio de los Arrayanes and the Patio del Cuarto Dorado and displays objects from the Alcázar: fragments of sculpture, perfume burners, braziers and vases. Outstanding objects include the famous **blue amphora★**, 1.32m - 52ins high, the Nasrid masterpiece which stood for years in the Sala de loas Dos Hermanas, and a 10C ablutions basin adorned with lions chasing stags and ibex.

Museo de Bellas Artes (Fine Arts Museum) – Religious sculpture and paintings of the 16 to the 18C predominate, with works by Diego de Siloé, Pedro de Mena, Vicente Carducho, Alonso Cano as well as a magnificent still life, **Thistle and Carrots★**, by Brother Juan Sánchez Cotán.

★ **Alcazaba** – The Alcazaba has existed since the 9C and is by far the oldest part of the Alhambra. The two towers overlooking the Plaza de los Aljibes (Cistern Court) date back to the 13C. The lofty Torre de la Vela (Watch Tower) commands a magnificent **panorama★★** of the palace, the Generalife, Sacromonte, Granada and the Sierra Nevada.

★★The Generalife (DX) ⊙

The 14C Generalife, the summer palace of the Kings of Granada, is particularly enjoyable for its cool, green, terraced water gardens. Both the Patio de los Cipreses (Cypress Alley) and the Patio de las Adelfas (Oleander), which are at their best in July and August, lead to the palace, a building of modest dimensions surrounding an elongated court, its axis marked by a narrow slit of water. This **Patio de la Acequia** (Canal Court), bordered by roses, has a graceful pavilion at either end. Linking these pavilions are, on the left, a gallery and on the right, the palace apartments. The *mirador* commands a fine **view** of Albaicín.

CATHEDRAL QUARTER *time: 3/4 hour*

★★ **Capilla Real (Chapel Royal) (BY)** ⊙ – The Catholic Monarchs wanted to be buried on the site of their definitive victory against the Moors and ordered the construction by Enrique Egas. It was begun in 1506 and completed under Emperor Charles V in 1521. The unity of style, richness of decoration and the art objects it contains, give a unique interest to the chapel. To enter *(by the south door)*, cross the courtyard of the old **Lonja** (Exchange) **(BY)**, also designed by Egas. The chapel's south front has an elegant Renaissance façade of two superimposed arcades with turned columns; opposite is the early 18C **Ayuntamiento** (Town Hall) **(BY)** in Granada baroque, built on the former 14C Muslim *madraza* or university of Yusuf I.

Every conceivable decoration of the Isabelline style is to be seen inside the chapel: ribbed vaulting, walls emblasoned with the arms of the Catholic Monarchs, the yoke and fasces (revived in 1934 by the Falange), a monogram of the initials of their first names, and the eagle of St John. Beautiful wrought-iron grilles close two chapels. The chancel, closed by a **screen★** by Master Bartolomé, contains the **mausoleums★★★** of the Catholic Monarchs, on the right, and of Philip the Fair and Juana the Mad, the parents of Charles V, on the left. The first was carved by Fancelli in Genoa in 1517, the second, which is magnificent in proportion and workmanship, by Bartolomé Ordoñez in 1519-1520 (the sarcophagi are in the crypt). The high altar **retable★** (1520) is one of the first to be free of all Gothic influence; the lower register of the predella depicts the siege of Granada.

Museo – *Access by the north arm of the transept.* Numerous objects of incalculable historical value can be seen in this museum which is situated in the sacristy. Among exhibits on display are **Queen Isabel's sceptre and crown, King Ferdinand's sword**, plus an outstanding **collection of paintings★★** by Flemish (Rogier Van der Weyden, Memling), Italian (Perugino, Botticelli) and Spanish (Bartolomé Bermejo, Pedro Berruguete) artists. In the rear of the museum can be found the famous **Triptych at the Passion** by the Fleming Dirk Bouts and two sculptures of the Catholic Monarchs at prayer by Felipe Vigarny.

★ **Catedral (BY)** ⊙ – *Enter from Gran Vía de Colón.* The cathedral illustrates the development of architecture in Granada between the 16 and 17C. Construction, in this case, was entrusted to Diego de Siloé in 1528 and continued after his death in 1563 according to his plans, apart from the façade (1667), overlaid by three tall arcades, which is by Alonso Cano.

The **Capilla Mayor★** is the first thing you notice inside, for its plan and decoration are surprising. Siloé designed a rotunda circled by an ambulatory, the whole cleverly linked to the nave and four aisles of the basilica. The rotunda combines two

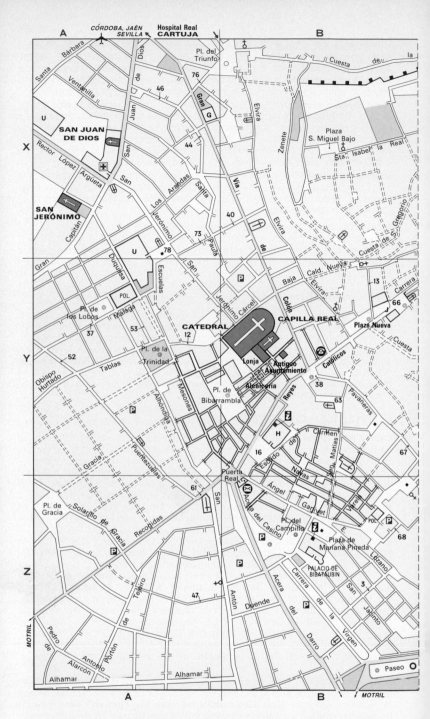

superimposed orders, the uppermost with paintings by Alonso Cano of the Life of the Virgin and beautiful 16C stained glass in paired windows. Marking the rotonda entrance on twin facing panels, are the figures at prayer of the Catholic Monarchs by Pedro de Mena and, in a medallion by Alonso Cano, those of Adam and Eve.

The impressive **organ** in the nave dates from about 1750 and was made by Leonardo of Ávila.

The finely carved Isabelline doorway in the south transept is the original **north portal★** of the older Capilla Real.

Alcaicería (BY) – The area, which has been reconstructed and is now a kind of *suk* or oriental bazaar with craft and souvenir shops, was a silk market in Moorish times.

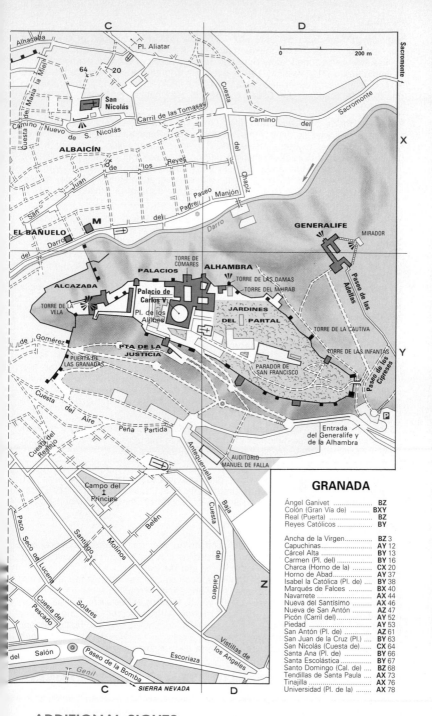

GRANADA

ADDITIONAL SIGHTS

★ **Cartuja (Carthusian Monastery)** (**AX**) ⊘ – Go through the cloisters into the church, exuberantly decorated with baroque stucco in 1662. At the back of the apse is the early 18C Holy of Holies (Sancta Sanctorum), inlaid with multicoloured marble; beneath the cupola, painted in false relief, is a marble Sagrario which contains the Tabernacle. The **sacristy** ★★ (1727-1764) is an outstanding example of late baroque. Some call it the Christian Alhambra on account of the intricate white stuccowork on the walls and vaulting, where straight lines and curves form never-ending patterns on mouldings and cornices. This stucco ornamentation contrasts sharply with the cupola paintings and the strong colours of the marble ogee moulding. The magnificent door and cedarwood furnishings inlaid with tortoiseshell, mother-of-pearl and silver, are by a Carthusian monk, Brother José Manuel Vásquez.

137

★**Iglesia de San Juan de Dios** (**AX**) ⊙ – The Church of St John of God is one of Granada's most important churches. The interior, access to which is through a beautiful carved mahogany doorway, is magnificent in both its richness and its stylistic uniformity. Behind the massive Churrigueresque altarpiece of gilded wood, is a lavishly decorated *camarín* which contains the funerary urn of **San Juan de Dios**. He founded the Order of Knights Hospitallers and died in Granada in 1550.

★**Monasterio de San Jerónimo** (**AX**) ⊙ – This 16C monastery was principally designed by Diego de Siloé. Fine Plateresque and Renaissance doorways lead on to its harmonious cloisters, characterised by their sturdy pillars. The church contains the tomb of Gonzalo Fernández de Córdoba, the Grán Capitán. The richness of its Renaissance style apse, magnificently illuminated by the transept windows and the roof with its superb coffers and vaulting adorned with saints, angels, animals, stands out. The **retable**★, worked on by a number of artists, is a jewel of the Granadine school. The paintings on the walls are from the 18C.

★**Albaicín** (**CX**) – The quarter, on the right bank of the Darro, covers a slope facing the Alhambra. It was here that the Moors built their first fortress, the refuge to which they retreated when the Christians reconquered the city. The alleys are lined by white-walled houses or the long walls that enclose luxuriant gardens of prosperous town houses called *cármenes*. Go to the **Iglesia de San Nicólas** (Church of St Nicholas) (**CX**) (*access by the Cuesta del Chapiz*, **DX**), if possible at sunset, for a really beautiful **view**★★★ of the Alhambra and the Generalife. The Sierra Nevada beyond is particularly spectacular in winter when covered in snow.

★**El Bañuelo (Moorish Baths)** (**CX**) ⊙ – The 11C baths are the best preserved in Spain. Star-pierced vaulting decorates a room surrounded by columns.

Hospital Real (Royal Hospital) (**AX**) ⊙ – The hospital, now the university rectorate, was founded by the Catholic Monarchs. The ground plan, similar to those in Toledo and Santiago de Compostela, is of a cross within a square and provides four spacious courtyards. Four Plateresque windows adorn the façade, while a Virgin and Child flanked by statues of the Catholic Monarchs at prayer, by Alonso de Mena, dominates the main doorway. Of interest in the interior are the two harmonious *patios* in the left wing, decorated with heraldic motifs.

Sacromonte (**DX**) – The hillside opposite the Generalife is covered by a network of paths which lead past clumps of Barbary figs to the gypsies' caves. Folk dances are performed in these troglodyte dwellings in the evenings.

Museo Arqueológico (**CX M**) ⊙ – The archaeological museum is housed in Casa Castril, a Renaissance palace with a fine **Plateresque doorway**★. It contains an outstanding collection of Egyptian alabaster vases found in a necropolis in Almuñecar, a bull figure from Arjona and a selection of decorative Roman and Moorish art.

SIERRA NEVADA

The Sierra Nevada lines Granada's horizon to the south: often snow-capped, massive, beautiful, and in season preceded by a wave of pink almond blossom. There is skiing in winter around Solynieve and the *parador*.
A road *(46km - 29 miles)*, which winds through an arid mountain landscape before it climbs to an altitude of 3398m - 11148ft, a feat which has earned it the name of the highest road in Europe – brings you to the **Pico de Veleta**★★. The panorama is wonderful, extending north to the Cordilleras Béticas, northeast to the Sierra de la Sagra, east to the wall of lofty summits dominated by the Mulhacén and Alcazaba, and south to the Mediterranean. Finally, in the west lie the jagged outlines of the Sierra de Tejeda and the Sierra de Almijara.

Palacio de La GRANJA DE SAN ILDEFONSO★

Castilla y León (Segovia)
Michelin map 444 or 442 J17 – Michelin Atlas España Portugal p 39
Local map under Sierra de GUADARRAMA

The palace of La Granja is a little Versailles at an altitude of 1192m - 3911ft at the foot of the Sierra de Guadarrama in the centre of Spain. It was built in 1731 by Philip V, grandson of Louis XIV, in pure nostalgia for the palace of his childhood.

Palacio ⊙ – Galleries and chambers, faced with marble or hung with crimson velvet, are lit, beneath painted ceilings and gilded stucco mouldings, by ornate chandeliers, made by the local royal workshops which became renowned in the 18C. A **Museo de Tapices** (Tapestry Museum) ★★ on the 1st floor contains principally 16C Flemish hangings, notably *(3rd gallery)* eight of the *Honours and Virtues* series and a 15C Gothic tapestry of *St Jerome* after a cartoon by Raphael.
Philip V and his Queen Isabel Farnese are buried in a chapel in the collegiate church.

Palace and gardens, La Granja de San Ildefonso

★★ Jardines (Gardens) ⊘ – Rocks were blown up and the ground levelled before the French landscape gardners (Carlier, Boutelou) and sculptors (Dumandré, Thierry) could start work in the 145ha - 358 acre park which is to a great extent inspired by the gardens and parkland of Versailles. The woodland vistas are more natural, however, the rides more rural, the intersections marked by less formal cascades. The chestnut trees brought from France at great expense, are superb. The **fountains★★** begin at the Neptune Basin, go on to the New Cascade (Nueva Cascada), a multicoloured marble staircase in front of the palace, and end at the Fuente de la Fama or Fame Fountain which jets up a full 40m - 131ft.

Sierra de GREDOS★★

Castilla y León (Ávila)

Michelin map 442 or 444 K-L 13-15 – Michelin Atlas España Portugal p 51

The granite massif of the Sierra de Gredos, which includes the Pico de Almanzor (2 592m - 8 504ft), the highest peak in the Cordillera Central, is bordered by four rivers: Tormes and Alberche to the north, Tiétar to the south and Alagón to the west. The contours of the *sierra* are dissimilar, the north face being marked by the remains of glacial features such as mountain cirques and lakes, the south, a steep granite wall, by eroded gullies. The valleys are fertile; those in the north produce fruit (mainly apples) and French beans (the speciality of Barco de Ávila); those in the south, sheltered by the *sierra*, grapes, olives and tobacco.

In order to preserve the trout in the Alberche and Tormes rivers, the deer and the *capra hispánica*, a type of mountain goat, which haunt the upper heights, the Reserva Nacional de Gredos was created.

SIGHTS

★ Cuevas del Águila (Águila Caves) ⊘ – *9km - 5 1/2 miles south of Arenas de San Pedro. Bear right immediately beyond the village of Ramacastañas and continue for 4km - 2 1/2 miles along the unsurfaced road.*
A single vast chamber is open to the public. Among the many concretions are lovely frozen streams of calcite, ochre crystals coloured by iron oxide and massive pillars still in process of formation.

★ Puerto del Pico Road – *29km - 18 miles northeast of Arenas de San Pedro.* The road cuts through the centre of the sierra. After crossing **Mombeltrán** (15C castle with well preserved exterior), the road rises to a corniche, paralleling the old Roman road, used for years as a stock route, which one can see below. From the pass (1 352m - 4 436ft) there is a good **view★** of the mountains and, in the foreground (south), of the Tiétar valley and, beyond, the Tajo. Beyond the pass the landscape becomes austere with granite boulders crowning the hilltops.
The **Parador de Gredos**, the first in Spain (1928), stands in a magnificent **setting★★** commanding extensive views.

★ Laguna Grande – *12km - 7 miles south of Hoyos del Espino. Park the car at the end of the road.*
A well-defined path leads up to Laguna Grande *(2 hours)*, a glacial basin fed by mountain torrents. Halfway along the walk, you have an unforgettable **panorama★** of the Gredos cirque.

GUADALAJARA

Castilla-La Mancha
Population 67 847
Michelin map 444 K 20 – Michelin Atlas España Portugal p 40

Guadalajara, which takes its name from the Arabic meaning river of stones, has developed into a satellite town on account of its proximity to Madrid.

The town became the fief of the **Mendozas** in the 14C, a name famous in Spanish history. It includes among its members Iñigo López de Mendoza, first **Marquis of Santillana** (1398-1458), poet and author of the pastoral *Serranillas*; his son, **Cardinal Pedro González de Mendoza** (1428-1495), adviser to the Catholic Monarchs; and the second Duke of Infantado, who built the palace at the north entrance to the town in the 15C.

★ **Palacio del Infantado (Palace of the Duke of Infantado)** ○ – The palace, built in 1483 by Juan Guas, is a masterpiece of civil Isabelline architecture in which the Gothic and Mudéjar styles combine. The magnificent **façade**★ is adorned with diamond stonework and a large crest, the Mendoza family coat of arms, above the doorway. The upper gallery consists of a series of paired ogee windows interposed between corbelled loggias. The effect of the whole is splendid in spite of the later windows, which were added in the 17C. The two-storey **patio**★ is just as remarkable with its multifoil arches resting on turned columns and its extremely delicate Mudéjar ornamentation. The decoration of the palace interior, equally sumptuous at the outset, was damaged during the Civil War.

When Francis I of France, captured at Pavia in 1525, was on his way to imprisonment in Madrid, he was received at the palace with the pomp due to his station.

EXCURSION

Pastrana – *42km - 26 miles southeast on the N 320*. This delightful town, once a ducal city, retains memories of the **Princess of Eboli**, favourite of Philip II. The **Palacio Ducal**, with its plain rough hewn stone façade, stands on Hour Square or Plaza de la Hora, so named because the duke, the princess's husband, confined her to the palace for the last five years of her life, allowing her to appear at the window for only an hour a day. The **Colegiata** ○, a collegiate church built by the dukes in the 16C, contains, in the sacristy, four Gothic **tapestries**★ woven in Tournai after cartoons by Nuno Gonçalves which illustrate the capture of Arzila and Tangier by Alfonso V of Portugal in 1471. They reveal the Portuguese painter's mastery of composition, love of detail (armour and costume) and talent for portraiture.

The Michelin Green Guide Portugal
presents a selection of the most interesting
and distinctive sights on the main tourist routes.

GUADALUPE★★

Extremadura (Cáceres)
Population 2 447
Michelin map 444 N 14 – Michelin Atlas España Portugal p 51

Suddenly before you as the road climbs, there is Guadalupe, set in a perfect **picture**★. The monastery, bristling with battlements and turrets, stands above the village which clusters around the foot of its austere ramparts. The road above the village commands a good **view**★ of the monastery.

The **old village**★ with its steeply pitched brown tile roofs is attractively picturesque, particularly in spring when flowers bring colour to the balconies. The traditional craft of copper smelting (jugs and pots) is still very much alive.

Patron of "Todas las Españas" (All the Spains) – The first shrine is believed to have been built following the discovery of a miraculous Virgin by a cowherd in 1300. Alfonso XI, having invoked the Virgin of Guadalupe, as she was known, shortly before his victory over the Moors at the **Battle of Salado** (24 October 1340) had a grandiose monastery built in gratitude and entrusted it to the Hieronymites. The pilgrimage centre, richly endowed by rulers and deeply venerated by the people, exercised a great influence in the 16 and 17C when it became famous for craftsmanship – embroidery, gold and silversmithing, illumination – and more importantly, situated as it was at the heart of the Kingdom of the Conquistadors, the symbol of the **Hispanidad** – that community of language and civilisation which links the Spanish of the Old and New Worlds. Christopher Columbus named a West Indian island after the shrine; the first American Indians converted to Christianity were brought to the church for baptism and Christians freed from slavery came in pilgrimage to leave their chains as votive offerings.

Solemn processions on 12 October celebrate the day of the Hispanidad.

★★ MONASTERIO ⊘
time: 1 1/4 hours

The monastery, abandoned in 1835, was taken over by Franciscans in 1908 and restored. The heart of the building dates from the Gothic period, late 14 – early 15C, but with rich donations, numerous additions were made in the 16, 17 and 18C. The resulting plan appears confused because the monks had to crowd ever more buildings within the fortified perimeter. The monastery contains artistic treasures of great value.

Façade – 15C. The façade, golden in colour, exuberant in its Flamboyant Gothic decoration, overlooks a picturesque square. It is set between tall crenellated towers of rough stone like the sombre defensive walls on either side. Moorish influence, characteristic of Mudéjar Gothic, can be seen in the exaggeratedly sinuous decoration in imitation of Moorish stuccowork. Bronze reliefs on the 15C doors illustrate the Lives of the Virgin and Christ.

Iglesia (Church) – 14C. The church was one of the first monastery buildings to be erected but in the 18C, additions were made such as the gilt baroque decoration on the vaulting and the pierced balustrade above the nave to take votive lamps in honour of the Virgin. An intricate iron grille, wrought at the beginning of the 16C by two famous Valladolid ironsmiths, closes the sanctuary which is ornamented with a large classically ordered retable carved by two 17C sculptors, Giraldo de Merlo and Jorge Manuel Theotocopuli, son of El Greco. The Virgin of Guadalupe stands in the middle of the altarpiece (1) but may be seen more clearly from the *Camarín.*

Sala Capitular (Chapter house) – The chapter house contains a remarkable collection of 87 **antiphonaries ★** by the monks of Guadalupe. The richly illuminated works cover a period from the 14 to the 18C, most of them dating from the 16C.

Claustro Mudéjar – 14-15C. The cloisters are remarkable for their great size and the two storeys of horseshoe-shaped arches. There is a small Mudéjar Gothic temple in the middle and in a corner, a lavabo faced with multicoloured tiles.

Museo de Bordados (Embroidery Museum) – The museum, in the former refectory, displays a fine collection of richly decorated **copes and altarfronts ★★**, skilfully embroidered by the monks between the 15 and 19C.

Monasterío de Guadalupe

B. Brillion / MICHELIN

Museo de Pinturas y Esculturas (Painting and Sculpture Museum) – The works include a 16C triptych of the *Adoration of the Magi* by Isembrandt, an ivory Christ attributed to Michelangelo, an *Ecce Homo* by Pedro de Mena, eight small canvases of the monks by Zurbarán, and another small painting by Goya, *Prison Confession*.

★★ **Sacristía (Sacristy)** – 17C. Canvases by Carreño de Miranda hang in the antechamber. The sacristy is a magnificently successful combination of classical style architecture and highly ornate baroque decoration. The unexpected harmony and rich colouring set off the well-known series of **paintings by Zurbarán**★★ to perfection. The 11 canvases, painted in a serene yet forceful style between 1638 and 1647, are of the Hieronymite monks and scenes from the Life of St Jerome including *The Temptation* in which he is shown resisting beautiful lady musicians.

Relicario (Reliquary Cabinet) – This contains a collection of the Virgin of Guadalupe's mantles and the crown, which is worn only in solemn processions.

★ **Camarín** – 18C. A chapel-like room where the Virgin of Guadalupe rests.
Riches of every description abound: jasper, gilded stucco and marble and precious wood marquetry frames for nine canvases by Luca Giordano. The Virgin herself sits on an enamelwork throne (1953), a small 12C figure carved in now darkened oak, almost obscured beneath a richly embroidered veil and mantle.

Claustro Gótico (Gothic Cloisters) – In the *hospedería* (hostelry). The cloisters were built in the 16C in an elegant Flamboyant Gothic style to serve as a dispensary for the four hospitals then in the monastery's care.

EXCURSION

Puerto de San Vicente (San Vicente Pass) – *40km - 25 miles east on the C401*. The **road**★ to the pass crosses the Las Villuercas mountain ranges. During the climb *(8km - 5 miles)* beyond the Guadarranque valley, there are wonderful **views**★ of green mountain ranges, their jagged crests aligned like the waves of the sea in the wild, moorland landscape.

Sierra de GUADARRAMA★

Madrid Castilla y León

Michelin map 444 J17-18 – Michelin Atlas España Portugal p 39

The Sierra de Guadarrama stretches for 100km - 62 miles from the Puerto de Malagón (Malagón Pass) to that of Somosierra, providing a northwest barrier for the province of Madrid. It is lower than the Sierra de Gredos of which it is a continuation, and its highest point, Peñalara, has an altitude of 2 429m - 7 970ft.
The range is part of the Hercynian massif uplifted by Tertiary earth movements. The countryside comprises granite and gneiss outcrops, steep slopes covered up to halfway in evergreen oaks and pine-woods but above, near the crests, are traces of glaciation, such as the Laguna de Peñalara, its waters covering the bottom of a glacial basin. Abundant rainfall in the upper heights gives rise to streams (Lozoya, Guadarrama, Manzanares and Jarama) which feed the province's many reservoirs (Pinilla, Navacerrada, Santillana and El Atazar).
The Sierra de Guadarrama is a green oasis in the desert of Castilla, so close to Ávila, Segovia and Madrid that you can see the range's snow-capped peaks from these towns in winter. Mountain and rural resorts have developed in the *sierra* to which Castilians flee in summer to escape the torrid heat of the Meseta: Navacerrada, Cercedilla, Guadarrama and El Escorial. Madrid's three ski resorts centre around the Puerto de la Navacerrada and the Puerto de los Cotos.

FROM MANZANARES EL REAL TO SEGOVIA

106km - 66 miles – allow 1/2 day excluding visits to Segovia, La Granja and Riofrío. See local map above opposite.

Manzanares el Real – The **castillo**★ standing at the foot of the Sierra de la Pedriza was built by the Duke of Infantado in the 15C. This gem of civil architecture is a well-proportioned fortress, the austerity of its lines relieved by bead mouldings on the turrets and the Plateresque decoration applied to the south front, which could be the work of Juan Guas.

Sierra de la Pedriza – This granite massif, foothill to the Sierra de Guadarrama, which presents by turns a chaos of rose-coloured rock and eroded screes with mountain streams, is popular with rock climbers, particularly in the Peña del Diezmo area (1 714m - 5 623ft).

Miraflores de la Sierra – Summer resort. Attractive view from a lookout on the village outskirts.

Puerto de la Morcuera
– As you reach the pass
(1 796m - 5 892ft), an
extensive view which
includes the El Vellón
reservoir, opens to the
south.

A descent through bare
moorland brings you to
the wooded Lozoya de-
pression. In the distance
by Lozoya town, is the
Pinilla dam, supplied by
the Río Lozoya, a well-
known trout stream.

★ **Real Monasterio de
Santa María de El
Paular** ⊘ – Castilla's
earliest Carthusian mo-
nastery stands in the
cool Lozoya valley. It

was founded in 1390 and was subsequently enriched by the Kings of Castilla and
those of unified Spain in the 15 and 16C. In 1954, the Benedictines began reconstruction of the complex, which comprises a monastery, church and a hotel (a former
palace). The **church** has a Flamboyant doorway by Juan Guas. Inside is a finely wrought
Gothic screen and a magnificent 15C alabaster **altarpiece**★★, illustrating the Lives of
the Virgin and Christ and which from its emphasis on the picturesque and detail in
costume and bourgeois interiors, is certainly Flemish. In contrast, the Tabernáculo
(Tabernacle), behind the high altar, is decorated in exuberant baroque.
The road continues through dense pine-woods.

Puerto de los Los Cotos – 1 830m - 6 004ft. The pass is the departure point for ski-
lifts to the slopes. From the upper chairlift terminus at Zabala, excursions may be
made in summer to the Laguna de Peñalara *(1/4 hour)*, the Picos de Dos Hermanas
(Summit of the Two Sisters) *(1/2 hour)* and Peñalara, the highest point *(3/4 hour)*.

★ **Puerto de Navacerrada** – 1 860m - 6 102ft. The pass, on the borders of the two
Castillas, commands a beautiful **view**★ of the Segovian plateau and the line of the
valley, hidden beneath dense pines, through which the road to Madrid runs.
The pass is a popular ski resort and is linked by train to Cercedilla.

★ **La Granja de San Ildefonso** – *See Palacio de La GRANJA DE SAN ILDEFONSO.*

★ **Riofrío** – *See SEGOVIA: Excursions.*

★★★ **Segovia** – *See SEGOVIA.*

GUADIX

Andalucía (Granada)
Population 19 534
Michelin map 446 U 20 – Michelin Atlas España Portugal p 86

Guadix, a farming centre, stands where the irrigated plain meets the dry plateau. The
plateau's soft stone has been deeply ravined into fantastic shapes by erosion.
The town's origins go back to prehistoric times; it became important under the
Romans and the Visigoths. Under the Moors, it was allowed to remain Christian. The
town's peaceful, modest air belies its eventful past which is nevertheless recalled by
the cathedral, the 15C Moorish fortress and the Plaza Mayor, which dates from the
reign of Philip II.

SIGHTS

★ **Catedral** ⊘ – The cathedral's baroque **façade**★ (1713) with its undulating lines
draws the eye even more than does the fine Renaissance belfry. The interior has
intricate star vaulting in the nave and aisles. The east end is by Diego de Siloé.

★ **Barrio Troglodita (Troglodyte Quarter)** – *Walk up the street which leads to the Iglesia
de Santiago.* Beyond the church is an area of dwellings which have been hollowed
out of the soft tufa hillside. The rocks round the entrances are whitewashed and
the homes have conical chimneys built to emerge on a level with the paths.

Iglesia de Santiago (St James's Church) – The church stands on a pleasant square.
Fine Plateresque decoration adorns its façade.

Alcazaba ⊘ – *In the street near the Iglesia de Santiago. Access through the
Saminario.* From the 15C crenellated walls there is a good **view**★ of Guadix, particularly of the troglodyte quarter and the Sierra Nevada beyond.

EXCURSIONS

Purullena – *6km - 4 miles northwest.* The **road**★★ winds through tufa rocks to reach the **troglodyte village**★ of Purullena. Pottery-making is a well-developed cottage industry as the many stalls along the roadside testify.
Beyond Purullena, the Granada road rises in a *corniche*, affording extensive **views**★ over the plateau, cut deep by canyons. It then enters a wild landscape to reach the Puerto de Mora (Mora Pass) at 1390m - 4560ft.

La Calahorra – *18km - 11 miles southeast.* La Calahorra stands in a vast plain which lies between the Sierra Nevada and the Sierra de Los Filabres. It is dominated by a **castillo** ⊙ imprisoned by four round towers with such an austere appearance that the graceful interior is completely unexpected. Park the car in the village and walk up to the castle. A heavy door opens onto a delightful Renaissance **patio**★★, a masterpiece of refinement. The design of the arcades and balustrade, the Italian style carving surrounding the windows and the skilful proportions of the staircase convey a highly sophisticated artistic style.

HUESCA★

Aragón
Population 50085
Michelin map 443 F 28 – Michelin Atlas España Portugal p 29 – Local map under JACA
Town plan in the current Michelin Red Guide España Portugal

Huesca, the capital of Alto Aragón (Upper Aragón), has a tranquil, provincial appearance which belies its turbulent historical past. In Roman times, the town was made capital of an independent state by praetor Sertorius, then became an important Moorish stronghold and was finally reconquered by **Pedro I of Aragón** in 1096. It was capital of Aragón until 1118 when Zaragoza was awarded the privilege.
"Resounding like the bell of Huesca" is a Spanish expression for describing a dire event with far-reaching effects. The saying goes back to the 12C, when the King, **Ramiro II**, angry at the insolence of his nobles, summoned them to his palace ostensibly to watch the casting of a bell *(compana)* which he promised would be heard throughout Aragón. When the lords assembled, the king had the most rebellious beheaded – thereby making the fame of the bell indeed resound throughout his kingdom.
During the Civil War, Huesca was besieged by the Republicans from September 1936 to March 1938. The devastation suffered by the upper part of the city was very great.

OLD QUARTER *time: 1 1/2 hours*

The old hilltop city is ringed by a belt of streets, among them the **Calle del Coso**, which run over the site of the former ramparts.

★**Catedral** ⊙ – The cathedral's façade is elegant, ornate Gothic and is divided unusually by a gallery and a typically Aragonese carved wood overhang. A narrow gable encloses a small rose window and the portal covings where the statues carved out of friable limestone are weatherworn. On the tympanum are the Magi and Christ appearing before Mary Magdalene. The late-Gothic (15-16C) church, on a square plan, is divided into a nave and two aisles covered by star vaulting. The high altar alabaster **retable**★★ dates from 1533. In this masterpiece by Damián Forment (one of Donatello's followers), three scenes of the Crucifixion appear in high relief in the middle of Flamboyant canopy and frieze decoration. Facing the cathedral is the Palacio Municipal Town Hall, a tastefully decorated Renaissance town house.

★**Museo Arqueológico Provincial** ⊙ – The museum is in the old university on an attractive old square. The university itself was built in 1690 as a series of eight halls round a fine octagonal *patio*. Parts of the former royal palace were incorporated in the building, including the gallery in which the "Compana de Huesca" massacre took place. The museum contains archaeological items (mainly from the prehistoric period) and paintings, in particular a **collection**★ of Aragonese Primitives. Among the most interesting works are several by the Maestro de Sigena (16C).

★**Iglesia de San Pedro el Viejo** ⊙ – Although restored, the 11C monastery's **cloisters**★, with their historiated capitals, remain a major example of Romanesque sculpture in Aragón. On the side facing the church, the tympanum of the cloister doorway has an unusual Adoration of the Magi with all the emphasis on the giving of gifts. The capitals in the east gallery are the least restored. A Romanesque chapel contains the tombs of Kings Ramiro II (Roman sarcophagus) and Alfonso I, the Battler, the only Aragonese kings not to be buried in the royal pantheon in San Juan de la Peña *(qv).*

EXCURSION

Monasterio de Monte Aragón – *5km - 3 miles east along the N240.*
The monastery ruins are visible from the road. It was originally built as a fortress by Sancho I Ramírez when investing the Moorish stronghold of Huesca.

JACA★

Aragón (Huesca)
Population 14 426
Michelin map 443 E 28 – Michelin Atlas España Portugal p 16 – Local map overleaf

Jaca stands on a terrace site in the Río Aragón valley, overlooked by the Peña de Oroel. Its strategic position is marked by a well-preserved 16C **ciudadela** (citadel). Jaca won renown early in its history by repelling the Moorish invasion (8C) and then by becoming the kingdom of Aragón's first capital city.

Jaca today, at the end of the road to the Puerto de Somport, serves as a busy gateway north to the Pyrenees, south to the rest of Spain and as a stopping place for hikers in summer and skiers in winter.

Many festivals are held in the town: in May, a pilgrimage of historic figures and local dancing commemorates the battle against the Moors and every other year, at the end of July or the beginning of August, there is an international folk festival.

★ **Catedral** ⊘ – This, Spain's oldest Romanesque cathedral, dates back to the 11C. Its carved decoration was to influence the Romanesque craftsmen who worked on the churches along the pilgrim route to Santiago de Compostela. Outside, note the **historiated capitals**★ of the south porch and behind it the south doorway where great attention has been given to the draperies on the figures in the Sacrifice of Isaac and in King David and his musicians.

Gothic vaulting, regrettably embellished with ornate keystones in the 16C, covers the aisles which are unusually wide for the period. The apse and side chapels are profusely decorated with Renaissance sculpture but the cupola on squinches over the transept crossing has retained its original simplicity.

Museo Episcopal (Episcopal Museum) ⊘ – The cloisters and adjoining halls contain Romanesque and Gothic **wall paintings**★ from village churches in the area: Urríes, Sorripas, de Ruesta, Navasa, Bagüés and a reconstitution of the Osia church apse. There is also a collection of Romanesque paintings of the Virgin and Christ.

EXCURSIONS

★★ **Round tour of 222km - 138 miles via Huesca, Castillo de Loarre and San Juan de la Peña** – *Allow 1 day. See local map overleaf. Leave Jaca on the southbound N 330 towards Huesca.*

★ **Embalse de Arguis** – The Arguis reservoir, deep green in colour against its mountain background, is the highlight of the Sabiñánigo–Huesca road.

★ **Huesca** – *See HUESCA.*

Continue northwest to Ayerbe, then follow the signs to Loarre.

★★ **Castillo de Loarre** ⊘ – As you approach the castle, the sheer beauty and peace of the place, a veritable eyrie, become ever more compelling. In the 11C, Sancho Ramirez, King of Aragón and Navarra, had this impenetrable fortress built at an altitude of 1100m - 3 609ft and then installed a religious community within it. The walls, flanked by round towers, command a vast **panorama**★★ of the Ebro depression. After the massive keep and fine covered stairway, turn to the **church** which was completed only in the 12C. Standing over a crypt are a tall nave, a cupola and an apse adorned with blind arcades, all in the purest Romanesque style. The capitals with stylised motifs are very beautiful.

Return to Ayerbe and continue northwest towards Puente la Reina de Jaca. After 9km - 5 1/2 miles take the Agüero road.

Agüero – The setting of the village with its tiled roofs is made spectacular by a background of upstanding *Mallos (see below)*. 1km - 1/2 mile before Agüero, a road leads off, right, to the Romanesque **Iglesia de Santiago** where the three aisles of the church are covered by three separate stone roofs. Note the carvings on the tympanum (Epiphany, Joseph Asleep) and the covings (Salome's Dance, left).

Return to the road and continue north.

The road becomes more enclosed. The Río Gállego soon comes into view, banked by tall crumbling cliffs, red ochre in colour. The **Mallos**★, as they are called, are a formation of rose pudding-stone, highly vulnerable to erosion which has here created sugar loaf forms – the most dramatic group stands to the right of the road, its flamboyant mass completely dominating the small village of **Riglos**. Further up the valley is the Peña reservoir.

Bear right, before Puente la Reina de Jaca, into the N 240, then, after 10km - 6 miles, right again for Santa Cruz de la Serós.

★ **Santa Cruz de la Serós** – *See under Monasterio de San Juan de la Peña: Excursions.* Beyond Santa Cruz de la Serós, the road rises through woodland into the Sierra de la Peña where the Monasterio de San Juan suddenly comes into view, nestled beneath an immense overhanging rock.

★★ **Monasterio de San Juan de la Peña** – *See Monasterio de SAN JUAN DE LA PEÑA.* The road continues past the upper monastery of San Juan de la Peña and then leads back to Jaca, commanding fine **views**★ of the Pyrenees along the way.

★**Roncal and Ansó Valleys** – *Round tour of 144km - 89 miles – about 4 hours. See local map right.*

These two high valleys played an important part in the Reconquest. They have for a long time lived self-sufficiently, preserving an ancient economy based on sheep rearing with common pastureland for grazing. Religious festivals are still celebrated in traditional costume.

Leave Jaca on the N 240, heading west.

The road runs along the Río Aragón valley between arid marl hills for 47km - 29 miles.

Turn right into the A 137 to the Roncal valley.

The road goes up the green **Roncal valley**★ watered by the Río Esca. A narrow humpbacked bridge precedes your arrival in **Burgui**.

1km - 1/2 mile south of Roncal, bear right into the Garde to Ansó road.

When it drops down towards **Ansó**, this spectacular **road**★ with high *corniche* sections affords a good bird's eye view of the town and church rising from a cluster of brown tile roofs. There is an interesting **Museo etnológico** ⊙ inside the church.

To return south, the road follows the winding Río Veral valley.

The river flows for 3km - 2 miles through the Veral's narrow gorge known as the **Hoz de Biniés**.

Somport Road – *95km - 59 miles north along the N 330. See local map above.*
The road leads north of **Canfranc-Estación**, an international rail link and summer mountain resort, to **Candanchú**, the most well-known ski resort in Aragón, 1km-1/2 mile from the Puerto de Somport.
The **Puerto de Somport**★★ (1 632m - 5 354ft) is the only pass in the Central Pyrenees which generally remains snow-free all the year round. Its history as a thoroughfare goes back to the Romans who built a road over it which was trodden by Pompey's legions, Saracen hordes and later cohorts of pilgrims on their way to Santiago de Compostela. Climb the mound to the right of the monument commemorating the building of the road for an extensive **panorama**★★ of the Spanish Pyrenees.

Siresa – *49km - 30 miles northwest. Leave Jaca on the N 240, west, to Puenta de la Reina de Jaca; there, take the A 176 north to Siresa. See local map above.*
The road runs along the Aragón Subordán river valley. The village of Siresa lies clustered at the end of a narrow valley, its stone houses with windows outlined in white, slate roofs and mountain-type chimneys a total contrast to the majesty of Iglesia de San Pedro. The Monasterio de San Pedro existed before the 9C since we are told that it was visited by **St Eulogus of Córdoba** who was martyred by the Infidels in 859. It was reformed at the end of the 11C and admitted Augustinian monks. The **church**★, which dates from the same period, has a fine elevation and walls decorated by the ornamental use of blind arcades and buttresses. The interesting **altarpieces**★ are principally 15C.

*Each year the **Michelin Red Guide España Portugal** revises its 130 town plans which show*
– through-routes and by-passes
– new roads, one-way systems and car parks
– the exact location of hotels, restaurants and public buildings.
This up-to-date information makes town driving less stressful.

JAÉN

Andalucía

Population 107 413
Michelin map 446 S 18 – Michelin Atlas España Portugal p 75
Town plan in the current Michelin Red Guide España Portugal

Jaén came under the domination of the Carthaginians, grew to importance under the Romans and, in the 11C, became a *taifa* capital *(qv)*.
The town stands open on one side to a plain covered with olive trees while the Sierra de Jabalcuz rises behind it and Cerro de Santa Catalina (St Catherine Hill) actually dominates it. The **view** from the Alameda de Calvo Sotelo gardens embraces the town, the never-ending sweeps of **olive groves★★** and the surrounding mountains.

★ **Museo Provincial** ⊘ – Of the museum's collections of fine arts *(first floor)*, and **archaeology★** *(ground floor)*, the latter is particularly interesting since there are such rare items as a fine Roman **mosaic** of Thetis, Iberian carvings from Porcuna and a 4C palaeo-Christian sarcophagus from Martos.

Catedral ⊘ – The architect most typical of the Renaissance in Andalucía, **Andrés de Vandelvira**, designed the cathedral in 1525, giving it a grandeur of classical proportions. The immense façade with its baroque decoration of statues, balconies and pilasters resembles that of a palace. Behind the high altar is a chapel containing the Santo Rostro relic, one of the veils used by St Veronica to wipe Christ's face.
The **choir-stalls★** are richly carved in the Berruguete manner.

★ **Museo** ⊘ – The cathedral treasure, displayed in three underground chambers, includes antiphonaries, paintings by Ribera, a delightful Flemish Virgin and Child and some large bronze candelabra modelled by Master Bartolomé.

Capilla de San Andrés (St Andrew's Chapel) – The **Capilla de la Immacula** (Chapel of the Immaculate Conception) **★★**, with a minutely decorated drum supporting its star vaulting, is a masterpiece of Plateresque art. The gilded wrought-iron screen which stands before the chapel, worked as delicately as a curtain of gold lace, is by **Maestro Bartolomé** (16C), a native son of Jaén.

Iglesia de San Ildefonso – Each of the portals of this church has a different style: Gothic, Renaissance and the third, neo-classical, by Ventura Rodriguez.

Baños Árabes (Moorish Baths) ⊘ – The baths, the largest in Spain (470m²-5 059 sq ft), are beneath the 16C palace of the Count of Villardompardo. They have been restored to their 11C appearance. The palace houses a **Museo de Artes y Tradiciones Populares** (Museum of Popular Art and Traditions).

Castillo de Santa Catalina (St Catherine's Castle) – *4.5km - 2 1/2 miles west*. The approach **road★** affords views of the blue tinged Sierra de Jabalcuz. The castle, now a *parador*, commands a vast **panorama★** of olive groves.

*The chapter on Practical Information
at the end of the Guide lists
– local or national organisations providing additional information
– admission times and charges.*

JÁTIVA / XÀTIVA

Comunidad Valenciana (Valencia)
Population 24 586
Michelin map 445 P 28 – Michelin Atlas España Portugal p 69

Játiva, set amidst vine and cypress covered hillsides, can be seen from a distance because of its crenellated ramparts which ring the two highest hills.
The town was the birthplace of two members of the Borja *(qv)* family who became popes, Calixtus III (1455-1458) and Alexander VI, and, in 1591, of the painter José Ribera.

El Españoleto – **José Ribera** studied in Valencia, probably with Ribalta before going to Italy where he settled in Naples in 1616. Lo Spagnoletto, or the Little Spaniard, as Italians called him on account of his small stature, became accredited to successive Spanish viceroys of Naples, notably the Duke of Osuna, and won early and equally widespread fame in Italy and Spain. He died in Italy in 1652.
A robust and realistic style, reminiscent of Caravaggio in its technique of chiaroscuro, characterises his early work: the religious figures, the monks and saints, have a somewhat coarse energy; the faces are portrayed with painstaking detail; the composition emphasises the dramatic, often dwelling upon the atrocious. However, some of his works, more serene and in mellower colours, reveal a different and surprisingly sensitive artist.

SIGHTS

Plaza de Calixto III – The 16C **cathedral**, modified in the 18C, faces the **hospital** which has an ornate Gothic and Plateresque style façade.

Museo ⊘ – The Almudín, which used to be a granary, now houses a collection of paintings.
In the *patio* is an 11C **Moorish fountain★** or *pila*, one of the most interesting remains of Moorish sculpture in Spain as it illustrates human figures, which is extremely rare in Islamic art.

Ermita de Sant Feliu (Sant Feliu Hermitage) ⊘ – *On the castle road*. A group of 15C Valencia **Primitives** hangs in the chapel. At the entrance is a white marble **stoup★** hollowed out of a former capital.

Castillo ⊘ – What remains of the castle – it was dismantled under Philip V – stands on the site of the original town. It commands extensive **panoramas** of the town, the surrounding countryside, the *huerta* and the sea in the distance. Among the Castillo Mayor's distinguished prisoners was the Count of Urgel, pretender to the throne of Aragón, who was defeated by his rival, Fernando I, in 1412.

JEREZ DE LA FRONTERA★

Andalucía (Cádiz)
Population 184 364
Michelin map 446 V 11 – Michelin Atlas España Portugal p 83

Jerez produces Spain's sherries and brandies. The town's proximity to the sea was one of the factors which brought about its rapid development in the 18C when English shippers were searching for alternatives to French wines. The name sherry, from the former English spelling of the town's name, Xeres, was first used in England in 1608.

Sherry – Sherry, a blended white wine, is divided into four main types: **Fino** (15-17°), or extra dry, the lightest in body and strawlike in colour; **Amontillado** (18-24°), or dry, fuller bodied and deeper in colour; **Oloroso** (18-24°), or medium, fragrant, full bodied and golden; and **Dulce**, or sweet. The grapes are picked when they have reached full maturity and sunned to concentrate their sugar content; the juice is fermented in 500-600 litre – 110-132 gallon casks and matured; in some cases a "flower" or yeast is allowed to develop at the top of the cask to impart a special flavour to the wine.
A visit to a **bodega★** (a wine storehouse) is an interesting experience: **Sandeman (AY B)**, **Williams (BY C)**, **Harvey's (BZ F)** and **González Byass (AZ A)**.

Ferias and festivals – Horses are no less important than sherry in Jerez and, in the region, locally bred mounts are equally famous. In the 16C, the Carthusian monastery (Cartuja) crossed Andalusian, Neapolitan and German breeds, giving rise to the famous **Cartujana** horse. Annually in early May there is the **Feria del Caballo** or Horse Show with racing as well as dressage and carriage competitions.
In September there is a **Fiesta de la Vendimia** (Wine Harvest Festival) which includes a cavalcade and a *flamenco* festival; the *cante jondo* is particularly alive and popular in Jerez (which is home to such famous singers as **Antonio Chacón** 1870-1929 and **Manuel Torres**).

SIGHTS

★★ Museo de los Relojes (Atalaya Clock Museum) (AY) ⊘ – The Palacio de Atalaya, set in a park, contains an outstanding collection of 300 English and French timepieces dating from the 17C to the 19C. They present a great variety of shape and decoration and are all in perfect working order. Everyday, at midday, their chimes ring out in a veritable concert.

★ Real Escuela Andaluza de Arte Ecuestre (Royal Andalusian School of Equestrian Art) (BY) ⊘ – The school, set in the Recreo de las Cardenas (park), was founded in 1973 by Álvaro Domecq Romero. Apart from training riders for dressage, it specialises in the famous Cartujana horses.
Visitors may tour the buildings and watch training sessions but the main attraction is the remarkable **show★★** by the Dancing Horses of Andalucía, an equestrian ballet performed by horse and rider in embroidered 17C costume.

Colegiata ⊘ **(AZ)** – The monumental 16 and 17C collegiate church, with five aisles, has well balanced Renaissance and baroque decoration, and is given added dignity by being placed at the top of wide baroque flights of steps. The transept crossing is covered by a dome.

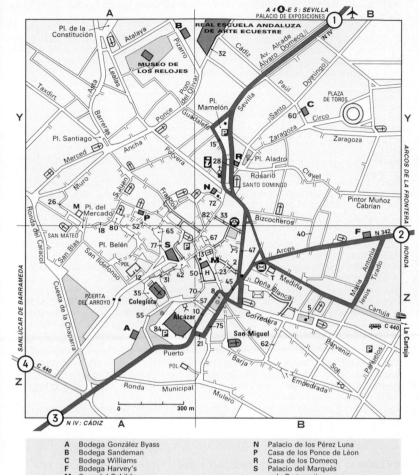

A Bodega González Byass	**N** Palacio de los Pérez Luna
B Bodega Sandeman	**P** Casa de los Ponce de Léon
C Bodega Williams	**R** Casa de los Domecq
F Bodega Harvey's	**S** Palacio del Marqués
M Casa del Cabildo	de Bertemati

Casa del Cabildo (Former Chapter) (**BZ M**) ⊘ – The Chapter's Renaissance front is the principal ornament of the attractive Plaza de la Asunción. Inside there is now a modest **Museo Arqueológico** which includes a 7C BC Greek casque.

Alcázar (**AZ**) ⊘ – Gardens now surround the walls of the old Moorish fortress.

Iglesia de San Miguel (**BZ**) ⊘ – The church has beautiful Isabelline portals in the side walls. The high altar retable was made by Martinez Montañés and José de Arce.

Casas Senoriales (Seignorial Mansions) – Interesting examples include the **Palacio del Marqués de Bertemati** (**AZ S**) with its baroque façade, the **Palacio de los Pérez Luna** (**BY N**), the **Casa de los Ponce de León** (**AY P**) with a Plateresque corner window and the **Casa Domecq** (**BY R**).

EXCURSION

La Cartuja (Carthusian Monastery) – *5km - 3 miles southeast*. The monastery, founded in 1477, has a Graeco-Roman style portal attributed to Andrés de Ribera. The Flamboyant Gothic church has a richly decorated baroque façade. Inside, the high altar was originally adorned with the famous canvases by Zurbarán which are now exhibited in museums in Cádiz and Grenoble (France).

JEREZ DE LOS CABALLEROS

Extremadura (Badajoz)
Population 10 295
Michelin map 444 and 446 R 9 – Michelin Atlas España Portugal p 72

Jerez stands in a fortified position on a hillside, its exuberantly baroque decorated belfries and towers pointing to the sky. On the summit is the even more ornate San Bartolomé with its façade and belfry faced with painted stucco, molten glass mosaics and azulejos. With its steep narrow streets lined by white-walled houses, Jerez gives a foretaste of Andalusian architecture.

The town's name, tradition and atmosphere stem from the Knights Templar – Caballeros del Temple – to whom the town was given by Alfonso IX of León on its recapture from the Moors in 1230. It is also the birthplace of the conquistador, **Vasco Núñez de Balboa** (1475-1517) who crossed the Darien Isthmus (now Panama) and in 1513 discovered the Southern Sea (the Pacific Ocean).

LEÓN★★

Castilla y León
Population 147 625
Michelin map 441 E 13 – Michelin Atlas España Portugal p 10
Local map see under SANTIAGO DE COMPOSTELA

León, one-time capital of the Kingdom of León, stretches along the banks of the Bernesga and is surrounded on all sides by the Meseta. The city was an important halt along the Way of St James and has preserved many fine monuments from its prestigious past, including masterpieces of Romanesque (San Isidoro), Gothic (cathedral) and Renaissance architecture (San Marcos).

The medieval town – In the 10C, as their territory expanded, the kings of Asturias moved their capital from Oviedo to León. They built a walled city on the site of earlier Roman fortifications and peopled it with Mozarabs, Christian refugees from Córdoba and Toledo; by the 11 and 12C León had become virtually the centre of Christian Spain.

The east part of the city recalls the early medieval period clearly in the still evident remains of the ramparts and the houses fronting alleys where peeling roughcast reveals brickwork façades. The most evocative quarter, known as the Barrio Húmedo (wet quarter or watering-hole) on account of its many small bars and restaurants, lies between the arcaded **Plaza Mayor** and **Plaza de Santa María del Camino** (B), a particularly attractive square with wooden porticoes, a fountain and church belfry.

The modern city – As León flourishes on its industry, the city limits are extending westwards along the river banks. Its development has depended on hydroelectric power from the Esla river basin, local mineral resources (iron and coal) and livestock farming.

León's artistic tradition has also been maintained, as can be seen in Gaudí's neo-Gothic palace, **Casa de Botines** (B) on Plaza de San Marcelo.

SIGHTS

★★★ **Catedral** (B) ⊘ – The cathedral, built mainly between the mid-13 and late 14C, is true Gothic in style even to the very high French-inspired nave with vast windows.

West face – The façade is pierced by three deeply recessed and richly carved portals separated by unusual, sharply pointed arches. The gently smiling Santa María Blanca *(a copy: original in the apsidal chapel)* stands at the pier of the central doorway in which the lintel carries a carving of the Last Judgment with graphic portraits of the blessed and the damned. The left portal tympanum illustrates scenes from the Life of Christ, while the right portal, the Puerta de San Francisco, includes the Dormition and the Coronation of the Virgin.

South face – The statues decorating the jambs of the central doorway are extremely fine.

Interior – The outstanding **stained glass windows**★★★ – 125 windows and 57 oculi with an area of 1 200m² - 12 917 sq ft – are unique in Spain but by their sheer mass are endangering the resistance of the walls (the last restoration was at the end of last century). The west front rose and the three central apsidal chapels contain the oldest, 13-15C glass; the Capilla de Santiago (St James's Chapel) has glass in which the Renaissance influence is already apparent while the nave windows, which were made much later, some are even considered modern, illustrate three major themes: the vegetable and mineral kingdom (below), historic personages and heraldic crests (behind the triforium) and, high up, the blessed. The Renaissance **trascoro**★ by Juan de Badajoz, includes four magnificent alabaster high reliefs framing Esteban Jordán's triumphal arch through which there is an attractive view down the length of the nave.

LEÓN

The high altar **retable**, painted by Nicolás Francés, is a good example of the 15C international style. To the left is a remarkable **Entombment★**, which shows a Flemish school influence and is attributed to the Master of Palanquinos. At the foot of the altar, a silver reliquary contains the relics of San Froilán, the city patron.

Several Gothic tombs can be seen in the ambulatory and transept, in particular that of Bishop Don Rodrigo – in the Virgen del Carmen chapel to the right of the high altar – which is surmounted by a multifoil arch.

★ **Claustro** – Before entering the cloisters, note the well-preserved, sheltered north transept doorway dedicated to the figure of the Virgin with the Offering, at the pier.

The galleries are contemporary with the 13-14C nave but the vaulting, with its ornately carved keystones, was added at the beginning of the 16C. The galleries are interesting for the frescoes by Nicolás Francés and the tombs dating from the Romanesque and Gothic periods.

Museo de la Catedral ⊙ – This museum collection includes a French-inspired 15C statue of St Catherine, a Christ carved by Juan de Juni in 1576 (proportioned in such a way as to be viewed from below), a Mozarabic Bible, with miniatures, from 920, an antiphonary dating from the same period, a 13C codex illustrated with engravings and the Plateresque staircase which formerly led up to the chapter house.

★ **San Isidoro (B)** – The basilica, built into the Roman ramparts, its belfry like a watch-tower overlooking the walls, was dedicated in 1063 to Isidore, Archbishop of Sevilla and Doctor of the Visigothic church, whose ashes had been brought north for burial in Christian territory since Sevilla was then under Moorish rule. Of the 11C church there remains only the pantheon. Construction of the present-day basilica began at the very end of the 11C and underwent modifications at a later date: the apse and transept are Gothic while the balustrade and the pediment on the south front were added during the Renaissance. The sculptures on the Romanesque portals, depicting Abraham's Sacrifice and the Descent from the Cross, are contemporary with those of the Iglesia de Frómista (Frómista Church).

★★ **Panteón Real** ⊙ – The Royal Pantheon is one of the earliest examples of Romanesque architecture in Castilla. The **capitals★** crowning the short, thick columns bear traces of the Visigothic tradition yet at the same time introduce great novelty into Romanesque carving in Spain. Some, with plant motifs, show influences from Asturian art, while others are fully historiated.

Oronoz/ARTEPHOT

The Panteón Real de San Isidoro, León

The beautifully preserved 12C **frescoes**★★ are outstanding. They illustrate not only classic themes from the New Testament but also scenes from country life; note, on the inside of an arch, a calendar of seasonal tasks.

The pantheon is the resting place of 23 kings and queens and many children.

★★ **Tresoro** – The treasury contains works of great artistic value. The 11C reliquary containing the relics of San Isidoro is made of wood, faced with embossed silver and covered in a Mozarabic embroidery. Other items include the famous **Cáliz de Doña Urraca**★ or Doña Urraca's chalice comprising two Roman agate cups mounted in the 11C in a gold setting inlaid with precious stones, the 11C **Arqueta de los Marfiles**★ (Ivory Reliquary) in which each finely carved plaque represents an apostle, and another reliquary decorated with Limoges enamelwork (13C). The library contains over 300 incunabula and a large number of manuscripts adorned with miniatures, including a Mozarabic Bible dating from 960.

★ **Antiguo Convento de San Marcos (Former Monastery of St Mark) (A)** – Part of the monastery has been converted into a *parador*. The site has been connected with the Knights of the Order of Santiago or St James since the 12C: first as that of the mother house of the soldier friars, protectors of pilgrims on the way to Santiago de Compostela and, three centuries later, when the Catholic Monarchs did away with the privileges of the Military Orders and became the Grand Masters themselves, as that of the monastery planned by Ferdinand as being worthy of the dignity and riches acquired by the Knights during the Reconquest. This resulted in the present sumptuous edifice, built finally at the height of the Renaissance. The church was completed in 1541 but work continued right up to the 18C.

The 100m - 328ft long **façade**★★ has a remarkable unity of style in spite of the addition of a baroque pediment in the 18C. It consists of two storeys of windows and niches set within a regular layout of friezes and cornices, engaged columns and pilasters. Medallions in high relief, of people from the Bible, Rome, or Spain, provide additional decoration: Lucretia and Judith flank Isabel the Catholic, Trajan and Augustus, Charles V. Carving above the main entrance traces St James's life from his slaying of the Moors to his apotheosis at the pediment apex.

The **church** front (on the extreme right), emblasoned with scallop shells, symbols of the pilgrimage to Santiago de Compostela, remains incomplete. The shell theme is repeated inside, on the wall behind the high altar.

★ **Museo de León** ⊘ – The first gallery of the museum, with its star vaulting, displays among its works of art from the Mozarabic to the late Gothic period, the 10C *Votive Cross of Santiago de Peñalba* and an outstanding 11C ivory crucifix, the **Cristo de Carrizo**★★★. A Byzantine influence is apparent in the small figure's great presence and penetrating gaze, the formally dressed hair and beard and the arrangement of the loincloth. Through a window can be seen the *artesonado* Renaissance ceiling of the old chapter house (now part of the *parador*). The **cloister** galleries, built between the 16 and 18C, now serve as a lapidary museum (note the fine medallions on the keystones). The northeast corner contains a low relief of the Nativity by Juan de Juni. (There is an interesting perspective from here).

The **sacristy**★, a sumptuous creation by Juan de Badajoz (1549), has ribbed vaulting decorated with scallop shells, ribands, cherubim and bosses carved as masks. Several works by Juan de Juni are displayed.

EXCURSIONS

★ **San Miguel de Escalada** – *28km - 17 miles by* ② *on the town plan.*
In the 11C, Alfonso III made a gift of an abandoned monastery to a group of monks who were expelled from Córdoba, enjoining them to rebuild. Of their work only the church remains (at the centre of a terrace) but even so, it is one of the few Mozarabic edifices in Spain and the best preserved. The **exterior gallery★**, built in 1050, has horseshoe-shaped arches resting on carved capitals at the top of smoothly polished columns. The main monastery (**monasterio★** ⊘) building is considerably earlier, dating from 913. The nave and two aisles, covered with wooden vaulting, are divided from the apses by a triple arched portico and a balustrade of panels carved with Visigothic (birds pecking seeds, bunches of grapes) and Moorish motifs (stylised foliage).

★★ **Cuevas de Valporquero (Valporquero Caves)** – *47km - 29 miles north* (**B**) *on the LE 311.* The caves hollowed out by underground streams are still in the process of formation *(be careful not to slip)*. The temperature is constant at 7°C - 45°F. Neutral lighting sets off the extraordinary shapes of the concretions – there is a stalactite "star" hanging from the roof of the large chamber – and the variety of tones – 35 have been counted – of red, grey and black – of the mineral oxide stained stone. The tour ends with a walk along a narrow passage 1 500m - 1 640yds long cut obliquely by subterranean waters through a 40m - 131ft thick layer of soft rock.

Monasterio de LEYRE★★

Navarra

Michelin map 442 or 443 E 26 – Michelin Atlas España Portugal p 15

A splendid **panorama★★** opens out at the end of a steeply winding approach road to the monastery, over the manmade Embalse de Yesa (lake); on all sides are marl hills, their limestone crests forming majestic ramparts while in the Sierra de Leyre itself, great walls of mixed ochre-coloured stone and local rock hang suspended, halfway up the the ridge face.

By the early 11C, the Abbey of San Salvador de Leyre had established itself as the uncontested spiritual centre of Navarra; Sancho III, the Great, and his successors made it their pantheon and gave their blessing to the building of a church which, with its crypt, was to be one of the earliest examples of Romanesque art in Spain (consecrated 1057). Bishops of Pamplona were, by tradition, former abbots of Leyre which held dominion over some 60 villages and 70 churches and monasteries.

In the 12C, however, when Navarra was joined to Aragón, the royal house neglected Leyre in favour of San Juan de la Peña; in the same period the Pamplona bishops sought greater authority and instituted a lawsuit which considerably reduced both the finances and the prestige of the old monastery. In the 13C, the monastery was home to the Cistercian order but by the 19C it had been abandoned. In 1954, however, a Benedictine community from Silos took it over. They restored the 17 and 18C conventual buildings which have now been converted into a hostelry.

★★ IGLESIA (CHURCH) ⊘ *time: 1/2 hour*

East End – 11C. Three apses of equal height, together with the nave wall surmounted by a turret and a further square tower with treble windows, make a delightful group. The beautiful smoothness of the walls and the absence of decoration, apart from several modillions, indicate the building's great age.

★★ **Crypt** – The crypt, built in the 11C to support the Romanesque church above (with which it shares the same ground plan), looks even older, so roughly robust and archaic is its appearance. The vaulting is relatively high but divided by arches with enormous voussoirs and, in some cases, double ribs, descending on massive capitals, incised only with the most rudimentary lines. Unusually these capitals stand on short shafts of unequal height, practically at ground level.

★ **Interior** – In the 13C when the Cistercians rebuilt the church's central aisle to include a bold Gothic vault, they nevertheless retained the first bays of the earlier Romanesque church as well as the chancel and semicircular apses. The three aisles which have come down to us intact have barrel vaulting with double ribs springing throughout from the same height. The decorative elegance arises from engaged pillars, finely designed capitals and beautifully assembled blocks of rough hewn stone. In the north bay a wooden chest contains the remains of the first kings of Navarra.

★ **West Portal** – 12C. The portal's rich decoration has won it the name of Porta Speciosa. Carvings cover every available space. On the tympanum are archaic statues – Christ *(centre)*, the Virgin Mary and St Peter *(on His right)* and St John *(on His left)*; the covings are alive with monsters and fantastic beasts. Above, the spandrels show *(on the right)* the Annunciation and the Visitation.

EXCURSIONS

★ **Hoz de Lumbier** – *14km - 9 miles west.* The gorge cut by the Irati through the Sierra de Leyre foothills between Lumbier and Liédana is a bare 5km - 3 miles long and so narrow that it appears at either end as a mere crack in the cliff face. There is a good **view** of the gorge from a lookout point on the N 240.

★ **Hoz de Arbayún** – *31km - 19 miles north on the N 240 and NA 211.* The Río Salazar is so steeply enclosed within the limestone walls of the Sierra de Navascués that the road has to diverge from the river course and the only way to see it is by going to the viewpoint north of Iso. From there a splendid **view ★★** opens onto the end of the canyon where the cliff walls are clad, at their base, in lush vegetation through which flows the sparkling stream.

LLEIDA / LÉRIDA

Catalunya
Population 119 380
Michelin map 443 H 31 – Michelin Atlas España Portugal p 31
Town plan in the current Michelin Red Guide España Portugal

Lleida was once a citadel, built on high ground to command a point where communications crossed. Caesar's and Pompey's legions stormed it savagely; the Moors occupied it from the 8 to the 12C. The ancient fortress, the Zuda or Azuda, sited like an acropolis, and occupied in the 13C by the Counts of Catalunya, was destroyed by artillery fire in 1812 and 1936 but the fortifications which surround it remain. The glacis has been converted into gardens. From the terraces there is an extensive view of the town, the green Segre plain and, to the southeast, the Sierra la Llena.

★ **Seu Vella (Old Cathedral)** ⊙ – The cathedral stands on a remarkable **site ★**, dominating the city from inside the walls. It was built between 1203 and 1278 on the site of a mosque; the tall, octagonal belfry was added in the 14C. Philip V converted it into a garrison fortress in 1707. Recent work, however, has restored the edifice to its original appearance.

Iglesia – The outstanding decoration in this transitional style church occurs in its great variety of **capitals ★**, many of which are historiated. Those in the apses and transept illustrate themes from the Old Testament, those in the nave and aisles, scenes from the New. Moorish influences can be seen in the exterior decoration, particularly in the carvings of the Puerta dels Fillols (Godchildren's Doorway) off the south aisle and in the Puerta de la Anunciata (Annunciation Doorway), in the corresponding transept. Above is a lovely rose window. The extremely delicate style of carving, reminiscent of Moorish stuccowork, on the capitals of the church doorways, has come to be known as the Romanesque School of Lleida and may be seen throughout the region, in particular on the superb portal from the Iglesia de **Agramunt** *(52km - 32 miles northeast).*

★ **Claustro** – The cloisters' unusual position in front of the church recalls that of a mosque forecourt or a Romanesque church narthex. The galleries, completed during the 14C, are remarkable for the size of the bays and the beautiful stone tracery, different in each case. The delicately carved decoration of plant motifs on the **capitals ★** and friezes is Moorish influenced. There is a fine view from the south gallery extending over the town and surrounding countryside.

LORCA

Murcia
Population 67 024
Michelin map 445 S 24 – Michelin Atlas España Portugal p 78

Lorca lies at the foot of a low mountain range crowned by a fortress, **Castillo,** in the fertile valley of the Guadalentín. It serves as agricultural market and main centre for the particularly arid southwest corner of the province of Murcia.

"Blancos" and "Azules" – Lorca is one of the cities of Spain where Holy Week is celebrated with full traditional panoply. Sumptuous embroideries, the pride of a local craftsmanship that is old and famous, adorn the *pasos.* Biblical and Imperial Roman characters in full costume join penitents in long processions, the brilliant colours of the former contrasting with the sombre robes of the latter. Finally, there is friendly competition between the White and Blue Brotherhoods who rival for solemnity and magnificence.

Plaza de España – The square is surrounded by the fine baroque façades of the **Ayuntamiento** (Town Hall), the palace, now the **Juzgado** (Law Courts) embellished with a corner sculpture, and the **Colegiata de San Patricio** (Collegiate Church).

Casa de los Guevara – The doorway, unfortunately in not very good condition, is, nevertheless, an outstanding example of baroque sculpture (1694).

LUGO★

Galicia

Population 87 605

Michelin map 441 C7 – Michelin Atlas España Portugal p 3

Under the Romans Lugo was a provincial capital and a major road junction. Now at the heart of an agricultural region specialising in cheese production, the town has taken on new life, building wide shopping streets such as Reina and Santo Domingo while also preserving a distinguished old quarter around the cathedral.

SIGHTS

★★ **Murallas (Town walls)** – The walls were built by the Romans in the 1 and 2C and modified during the Middle Ages. They are made of schist slabs levelled off at a uniform 10m - 33ft to form a continuous perimeter over 2km - 1 mile long with ten gateways into the old quarter. Steps from these gateways lead up to the sentry path which commands views of the town and surrounding countryside.

★ **Catedral (Z A)** – The Romanesque church (1129) was modified in later years by Gothic and baroque additions. The Chapel of the Wide-Eyed Virgin at the east end, by Fernando Casas y Novoa who built the Obradoiro façade in Santiago de Compostela, has a baroque rotunda enhanced by a stone balustrade. The north doorway, sheltered by a 15C porch, has a fine Romanesque **Christ in Majesty★**. The figure is above a capital curiously suspended in mid-air and carved with the Last Supper.

Inside, the Romanesque nave is roofed with barrel vaulting and lined with galleries, a feature common in pilgrim churches. There are two immense wooden Renaissance altarpieces at the ends of the transept – the south one is signed by the sculptor Cornelis de Holanda (1531). A door in the west wall of the south transept leads to the small but elegant **cloisters**.

City squares – The 18C **Palacio Episcopal (Z B)**, facing the north door of the cathedral on **Praza de Santa María (Z 74)**, is a typical *pazo*, one storey high with smooth stone walls, advanced square wings framing the central façade and decoration confined to the Gil Taboada coat of arms on the main doorway. Plays and concerts are given in the square in summer. **Praza del Campo (Z 8)**, behind the palace, is lined by old houses and has a fountain at its centre. Calle de la Cruz with its bars and restaurants, and Praza Maior or **Plaza de España (Z 45)** with its gardens and esplanade, are popular with the townspeople as places to meet and stroll.

Museo Provincial (Y M) ⊘ – Local and historical museum.

EXCURSION

Santa Eulalia de Bóveda – *15km - 9 miles southwest.* This attractive Galician village still has granite farm buildings with tile-stone roofs and drying sheds or *hórreos*. The **monumento paleocristiano** ⊘ discovered at the beginning of the century and excavated in 1924, consists of a vestibule (today open to the sky), a rectangular chamber with a basin and round arched niche and frescoes of birds and leaves, doubtless of Christian origin, on the walls. The dating and purpose of the monument continue to intrigue archaeologists.

LUGO

A	Catedral
B	Palacio episcopal
M	Museo Provincial

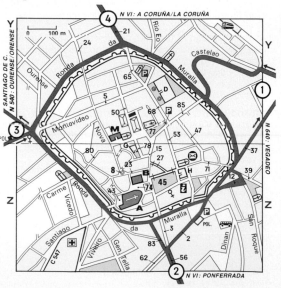

MADRID★★★

Population 3 084 673
Michelin map 442 or 444 K 18-19 – Michelin Atlas España Portugal p 53
Plan of the conurbation on maps 442 and 444 and in the current Michelin Red Guide
España Portugal

Madrid, Europe's highest capital (646m - 2 120ft), stands in the foothills of the Sierra de Guadarrama in the middle of the Meseta, right in the centre of the Iberian Peninsula. It is an hospitable city, known for the quality of its light, with a dry continental climate that is very hot in summer, and cold, yet sunny, in winter.

It became the capital in the 16C at a time when Spain ruled over a vast empire. The city's main monuments, classical and baroque in style, were built during the 17, 18 and 19C. Thanks to collections left by the Habsburgs and Bourbons, Madrid has an exceptional wealth of paintings which may be seen in the Prado, the Academia de San Fernando and the Museo Lázaro Galdiano, while the outstanding collections of the recently opened Museo Thyssen-Bornemisza have undoubtedly added to this wealth.

Madrid has undergone extraordinary development over the past few decades and now, renowned for its vitality, is a cosmopolitan centre with wide, busy thoroughfares.

Madrid in the past – Madrid, an unimportant village until the Moorish invasion, owes its name to the fortress *(alcázar)* of Majerit built under Mohammed I on the banks of the Manzanares in the 9C. In 1083 it was captured by Alfonso VI, who, it is said, discovered a statue of the Virgin by a granary *(almudín)* as he entered the town. He then converted the town mosque into a church, dedicating it to the Virgin of the Almudena who was declared the city patron. From the 14C the Kings of Castilla came regularly to Madrid; Emperor Charles V rebuilt the Muslim *alcázar* and in 1561 Philip II moved the court from Toledo to Madrid. The medieval town expanded rapidly and the population tripled. Its layout of winding streets can still be seen today around Plaza Mayor. The town really began to develop under the last of the Habsburgs, in the middle of Spain's Golden Age (16C). During the reign of Philip III, Juan Gómez de Mora undertook a series of reforms and from then on Plaza Mayor was to be the heart of the city. The town plan drawn up in 1656 by Pedro Texeira, gives a good impression of Madrid under Philip IV, when it had a large number of convents and churches. The king was an art lover who gave his patronage to many artists including Velázquez and Murillo, as well as men of letters such as Lope de Vega, Quevedo, Calderón and Tirso de Molina.

However, it was in the 18C under the Bourbons that the town underwent its greatest transformations. Philip V decided to build a royal palace, and Charles III, inspired by ideas from European courts, provided Madrid with a splendour hitherto unknown. This was the Prado and the Puerta del Alcalá, magnificent examples of neo-classical town planning. In turn, the nobility began building **palaces,** such as **Liria (KV)** and **Buenavista (MX)**, which they surrounded with gardens.

The 19C began with occupation by the French and the unfortunate events of 2 May 1808 *(p 168)*. In the second half of the 19C, Madrid underwent great alteration: in 1857 the remaining ramparts were demolished and a vast expansion plan *(ensanche)* gave rise to the districts of Chamberí **(BS)**, Salamanca **(CT)** and Argüelles **(AS)**, and, at the end of the century, **Arturo Soria's** *Ciudad Lineal* **(DS)**, a revolutionary town planning project, provided for a residential quarter for 30 000 inhabitants around today's Avenida de Arturo Soria.

At the beginning of the 20C, architecture was French-inspired, as can be seen in the Ritz **(NY)** and Palace **(MY)** hotels; the neo-Mudéjar style was also popular and brick façades so characteristic of Madrid went up all over the city **(Plaza de Toros de las Ventas,** *qv)*. The **Gran Vía,** a fast thoroughfare which crosses the centre of town to link Madrid's new districts, was inaugurated in 1910 and has since been popularised in an operetta *(zarzuela)*.

Madrid today – As capital, Madrid is Spain's leading town as far as banks, insurance companies, universities, administrative bodies and political institutions are concerned. It is also an important industrial centre with development in the suburbs for, among others, railway equipment, the metallurgical, food and textile industries and the building trade.

The business district, centred around the Puerta del Alcalá and Paseo de la Castellana, was modified extensively between 1950 and 1960 when traditional mansions were demolished to make room for new buildings. The city's most modern edifices may be seen in the **Azca (CS)** area, the result of one of Madrid's most revolutionary projects, designed to fulfil various administrative, residential and commercial functions. Among its most noteworthy buildings are the avant-garde Banco de Bilbao-Vizcaya and the Torre Picasso.

The town plans are easily interpreted
with the aid of the Key.

Cosmopolitan Madrid puts on a wide variety of exhibitions, shows, plays, films and concerts (*for details, see the weekly guide*, Guía del Ocio) and has an immense choice of places to spend an evening or simply have a drink (*ir de copas*), ranging from elegant, modern cafés in Chamberí (**BS**) and Salamanca (**CT**) frequented by the capital's "beautiful people" (*gente guapa*) to the more traditional coffee houses in the centre, some of which are veritable institutions, like the Gijón or the Oriente (opposite the Palacio Real) or the smaller, modest bars around Malasaña (**LV**) and Chueca (**MV**). Other possibilities include the Moncloa district (**AS**) with its university atmosphere and the area round the Santiago Barnabéu stadium (**CS**), in the north. Typical bistros and taverns are concentrated around Plaza Mayor and Calle de la Glorieta de Bilbao (**LV**), restaurants in the Old Town and the Salamanca and Castellana-Orense (**CS**) districts.

In summer, the capital is completely transformed when its pavement cafés come alive, in particular along the Paseos de la Castellana (**NV**), de Recoletos (**NV**) and del Pintor Rosales (**AT**) and in the Jardines de las Vistillas (**KYZ**).

Shopping – The whole of the centre of Madrid, around the Puerto del Sol, Plaza de Callao and Calle de Preciados, is a very popular, lively commercial area where traditional shops selling fans and lace stand side by side with modern establishments and department stores. Argüelles (**AS**) is another busy shopping district. Luxury boutiques and leading fashion houses are in Salamanca district (**CT**), around Calles de Serrano, Ortega y Gasset, Lagasca and Goya. This is a long-established shopping quarter with a great many jewellers, perfume shops and others specialising in interior design.

The most modern shops are in and around Calle Almirante (**MNV**).

Two major department stores, *El Corte Inglés* and *Galerias Preciados*, have branches in the following streets: Preciados, Carmen, Goya, Serrano, Arapiles, Raimundo Fernandez Villaverde and Princesa. Among Madrid's shopping malls are the Vaguada in the north, with cinemas, a hypermarket, cafeterias and bars, La Galería del Prado, opposite the museum, which is more exclusive and the Jardín de Serrano.

Antiques may be found in Calle del Prado (**MY**), the area around Plaza de las Cortes (**MY**), the market at Puerta de Toleda (**BU**) and on Sunday mornings, in the **Rastro** (**KZ**) *(qv)*, the famous flea-market where the most extraordinary variety of articles is sold. Good places for books are Cuesta de Claudio Moyano (**NZ**) and Calle Libreros (**KX**).

Art Galleries – There are a great many art galleries in the Salamanca district near Puerta de Alcalá and on the left-hand side of Paseo de la Castellana, in particular on the corner with Calle Génova.

Over the past few years there has been an increase in the number of new galleries which have opened in the Atocha district, home to the Centro de Arte Reina Sofia.

Theatres, Cinemas and Concert Halls – Madrid has a wide choice of cinemas, about twenty theatres, several concert halls and a casino. Performances of classical music are given in the *Auditorio Nacional* (National Concert Hall) (**CS**) which was inaugurated in 1988; *Zarzuelas* and ballets are performed in the **Teatro de la Zarzuela** (**MY**); the **Teatro Real** (**KX**) or Royal Theatre (19C) holds an annual opera season. Madrid has a particularly rich cultural programme during its Autumn Festival.

Parks – The **Retiro** *(qv)* is particularly lively on Sunday mornings with its open-air concerts and mime artists. A bandstand performance by the municipal orchestra is one of the capital's long-standing traditions.

Parque del Oeste *(qv)*, a peaceful, landscaped garden, is mainly enjoyed by people living in the immediate vicinity, while the **Casa de Campo** *(qv)*, Madrid's largest park, is wilder and wooded. Among other popular city parks are the Campo del Moro (**AT**), the **Jardín Botánico** (Botanical Gardens) (**NZ**) and the **Fuente del Berro** (**DT**).

Sports destinations outside Madrid – From December to March, Madrileños go to the snow slopes of the Sierra de Guadarrama (*1 or 2 hours from Madrid*) to ski, and in summer, to escape the searing heat in the capital, they head for one of the many nearby reservoirs, among them the **Mar de Castilla** (Sea of Castilla), to swim.

Touring Madrid – The following itinerary has been chosen to present Madrid in a historical context, respecting its development through the ages and starting with the original heart of the city, the **Viejo Madrid** (Old Madrid), around Plaza Mayor, with its maze of picturesque streets, its old-fashioned shops and small traders and the vitality typical of the Spanish character. The tour continues to the **Barrio de Oriente** (Eastern Quarter) around the Palacio real where the sumptuous Descalzas Reales and Encarnación convents may be seen. Finally, in **Bourbon Madrid** with its elegantly designed avenues, are two of the city's treasures: the **Museo del Prado**, one of the most famous picture galleries in the world, and the **Retiro** park.

★ VIEJO MADRID (OLD MADRID) *time: 2 1/2 hours – see town plan p 162*

The old town is best visited early in the morning or late in the afternoon when the churches are open.

★★ **Plaza Mayor** – This was built by Juan Gómez de Mora during the reign of Philip III (1619) and forms the architectural centre of **Habsburg Madrid**. On the north side, flanked by pinnacled towers, stands the **Casa de la Panadería** (a former bakery) which was reconstructed by Donoso in 1672. Its mural decoration, the third since it was built, is the work of the artist Carlos Franco. The 17C equestrian statue of Philip III in the middle of the square is by Giambologna and Pietro Tacca.

The vast square was the setting for *autos-da-fé*, mounted bullfights, and the proclamations of kings Philip V, Ferdinand VI and Charles IV.

Plaza Mayor, Madrid

F. Bouillot/MARCO POLO

A stamp and coin market is held under the arches on Sunday mornings while at Christmas, stalls are set up selling religious and festive decorations. The shops around the square, hatters in particular, have retained their look of yesteryear.

Pass through the **Arco de Cuchilleros** into the street of the same name, fronted by tall, aged houses with convex façades. This street, like its continuation, the **Cava de San Miguel**, is crowded with small restaurants *(mesones)* and bars *(tavernas)*. The name *cava* derives from the ditches or moats that once stood here.

By way of Plaza del Conde de Barajas, make for Plaza de San Justo or Puerta Cerrada, an old city gate. Continue right along the Calle de San Justo.

Pontificia de San Miguel ⊘ – The basilica by Bonavia is one of the rare Spanish churches to have been inspired by 18C Italian baroque. Its convex façade, designed as an interplay of inward and outward curves, is adorned with fine statues. Above the doorway is a low relief of saints Justus and Pastor to whom the basilica was previously dedicated. The interior is graceful and elegant with an oval cupola, intersecting ribbed vaulting, flowing cornices and abundant stuccowork.

Follow the north wall of the church to Plaza de la Villa.

★ **Plaza de la Villa** – The quiet pedestrian square is presided over by a statue of Álvaro de Bazán, hero of Lepanto, by Benlliure (1888). Several famous buildings are arranged around the square including the **Ayuntamiento** (Town Hall) (**H**), built by Gómez de Mora in 1617 and the **Torre de los Lujanes** (Lujan Tower), one of the rare examples of 15C civil architecture preserved in Madrid and in which Francis I was imprisoned after the battle of Pavia. Next door, the former **Hemeroteca Municipal** (**A**), which has a beautiful Gothic banister inside, contains in the vestibule the two fine Renaissance tombs of Beatriz Galindo and her husband. Finally, the **Casa de Cisneros**, built several years after the death of the cardinal of the same name, is adjoined to the Ayuntamiento by an arch. Of the original 16C edifice only an attractive window giving onto Plazuela del Cordón remains.

Plazuela del Cordón – The cord decoration surrounding the entrance to the Palacio de los Puñonrostro recalls that it was once a bishopric. Isidro, future patron saint of Madrid, lived as a servant in the **Casa de Juan de Vargas**.

Turn right immediately from Calle del Cordón into Calle del Conde.

Plazuela de San Javier (189) – A small square typical of old Madrid.

Return to Calle del Cordón and continue to Calle de Segovia.

Across the street rises the 14C **Mudéjar tower** of the **Iglesia de San Pedro** (Church of St Peter), which, apart from the Torre de San Nicolás, is the only example of the Mudéjar style in Madrid.

Go along Calle del Príncipe Anglona to Plaza de la Paja.

Plaza de la Paja – This was the commercial centre of Madrid in the Middle Ages. The Gothic **Capilla del Obispo**, a chapel built in the 16C by Gutiérrez Carvajal, bishop of Palencia, stands on one side of the square.

Go along Calle Redonilla and cross Calle del Bailén. The first street right leads to the Jardines de los Vistillas.

Jardines de las Vistillas (Vistillas Gardens) – The high ground commands a splendid panorama★, especially at sundown, of the Sierra de Guadarrama, Casa del Campo, the Catedral de la Almudena and the viaduct.

Iglesia de San Francisco El Grande ⊘ – The church's vast neo-classical façade is by Sabatini but the building itself, a circular edifice with six radial chapels and a large dome 33m - 108ft wide, is by Francisco Cabezas. The walls and ceilings of the church are decorated with 19C frescoes and paintings except those in the chapels of Sts Anthony and Bernardino which date from the 18C. The Capilla de San Bernardino, the first chapel on the north side, contains in the centre of the wall, a St Bernardino of Siena preaching before the King of Aragón (1781), painted by Goya as a young man. Some of the Plateresque stalls★ from the Monasterio de El Parral outside Segovia *(qv)* may be seen in the chancel. The 16C stalls★ in the sacristy and chapter house come from the Cartuja de El Paular, the Carthusian monastery near Segovia *(qv)*.

Walk along Carrera de San Francisco and Cava Alta to Calle de Toledo.

Calle de Toledo – This is one of the old town's liveliest streets. The popular **El Rastro** flea market *(qv)* sets up in neighbouring streets and along Ribera de Curtidores every Sunday morning and on public holidays.

Iglesia de San Isidro ⊘ – The church with its austere façade and twin towers is by the Jesuits Pedro Sánchez and Francisco Bautista. Formerly the church of the Imperial College of the Company of Jesus (1622), it was the cathedral of Madrid from 1885 until 1993. It contains the relics of Madrid's patron saint, Isidro, and those of his wife, Santa María de la Cabeza.

Plaza Provincia – Note the well-proportioned façade of the 17C **Palacio de Santa Cruz**, former court prison (Lope de Vega was incarcerated here) and present-day Ministry for Foreign Affairs.

Puerta del Sol – The itinerary ends at the Puerta del Sol, the liveliest and best-known square in Madrid. It has been a crossroads for historical events in the city over the ages although its present layout only dates back to the 19C. A small monument illustrating Madrid's coat of arms – a bear and an arbutus (strawberry) tree – stands on the point at which Calle del Carmen joins the square. The clock on the former Post Office (now the headquarters of the Presidencia de la Communidad de Madrid) chimes the traditional twelve strokes at midnight on New Year's Eve *(p 10)*. Kilometre Zero, on the ground in front of the building, marks the point from which all the main roads of Spain radiate and distances are measured.
The many streets leading into Puerta del Sol are crowded with small traditional shops with their colourful wood fronts where customers can just as easily find fans and mantillas as cooked delicacies.

★★BARRIO DE ORIENTE (EASTERN QUARTER) *time: 1 day*

The walk combines monumental buildings with panoramic views.

★★ **Palacio Real (Royal Palace) (KXY)** ⊘ – The best view of the palace, which overlooks the Manzanares river, is from Paseo de Extremadura (**AU**) and the Campo del Moro gardens.
The palace, an imposing edifice built by the Bourbons, was the royal family's official residence until 1931. Today, it is run by the Patrimonio Nacional (Spain's National Trust) and used by the king for state receptions.
On Christmas Day in 1734, while the royal family was staying at the Parque del Buen Retiro *(qv)*, a fire burnt the old Habsburg Alcázar to the ground. Philip V replaced it with a new palace, the present edifice, designed originally by the Italian architect, Felipe Juvara. When Juvara died, work continued under Sachetti, who modified his plans, and then under Ventura Rodríguez until completion in the reign of Charles III. It forms a quadrilateral made of Guadarrama granite and white stone, measuring some 140m - 459ft on the sides, on a high bossaged base. The upper register, in which Ionic columns and Doric pilasters alternate, is crowned by a white limestone balustrade. Colossal statues of the kings of Spain from Ataulf to Ferdinand VI were originally intended to be placed above this, but under Charles III they were put in the Plaza de Oriente and the Retiro gardens.
The north front gives onto the **Jardines de Sabatini**, the west the **Campo del Moro (AT)**. The **Plaza de la Armería** stands to the south between the west and east wings of the palace. The east façade gives onto **Plaza de Oriente** on which stand the Teatro Real (Royal Theatre) (1850) and the statues of Visigothic kings presided over by Pietro Tacca's equestrian statue of Philip IV.

Plaza de la Armería – The vast arcaded square is bounded to the south by the incomplete façade of the **Catedral de la Almudena**. This cathedral, which has taken over a century to complete (the first construction project began in 1879), has a

MADRID

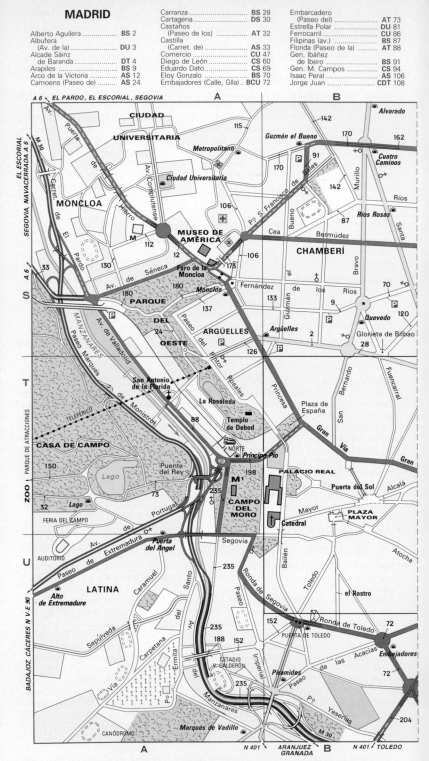

neo-baroque façade which is in complete harmony with the palace and the neo-Gothic interior. It was consecrated by Pope John Paul II in 1993.

The view from the west side of the square extends over the Casa de Campo and the Campo del Moro gardens which slope down to the Manzanares river.

★ **Palacio** (Palace) – A monumental staircase with a ceiling painted by Giaquinto leads to the **Salón de Columnas** (Column Room) in which the treaty for Spain's membership of the European Community was signed on 12 June 1985. The Gasparini antechamber, with a ceiling painted by Mengs, and Goya portraits of Charles IV and Queen María Luisa, is followed by the **Salón Gasparini** covered from floor to ceiling in pure rococo decoration.

The Alfonso XII **Comedor de Gala** or Banqueting Hall (for 145 guests) is adorned with 16C Brussels tapestries. In the chapel are frescoes by Corrado Giaquinto and paintings by Mengs, *Annunciation*, and Bayeu, *St Michael the Archangel*.

The antechamber leading to the apartments of Queen María Cristina contains a triptych by Juan of Flanders which belonged to Queen Isabel the Catholic.

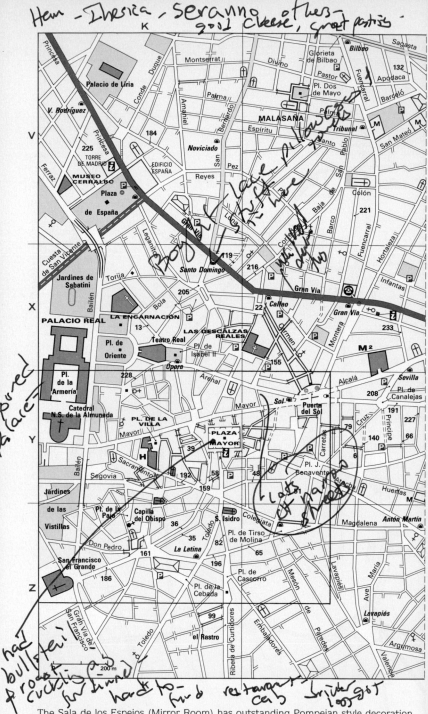

The Sala de los Espejos (Mirror Room) has outstanding Pompeian style decoration of low relief stuccowork.

The **Salón del Trono★** (Throne Room) is resplendent with crimson velvet hangings and a magnificent ceiling painted by Tiepolo in 1764. The consoles and mirrors are by Ventura Rodríguez, the gilded bronze lions by the Italian sculptor, Benicelli (1621). The music rooms contain a collection of instruments including several by Stradivarius.

Real Farmacia (Royal Pharmacy) – This consists of the distillation room where medicaments were concocted; note the glass and porcelain apothecary jars standing in neat rows.

★★ **Real Armería** (Royal Armoury) – The collection of arms and armour put together by the Catholic Monarchs, Emperor Charles V and Philip II, is outstanding. The key pieces of the display include Charles V's suit of armour and the weapons and

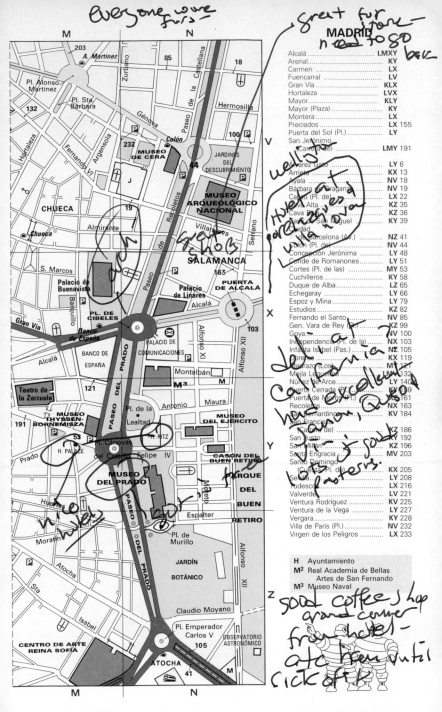

armour belonging to Philip II and Philip III. A vaulted hall in the basement contains an excellent collection of Bourbon shotguns, ranging from those made by Philip V's armourer to the Winchester given to King Alfonso XII by the President of the United States.

★ **Museo de Carruajes Reales** (Royal Carriage Museum) (**AT M¹**) ⊙ – A pavilion built in 1967 in the middle of the **Campo del Moro** ★ winter garden, which commands a good view of the palace, houses the old royal horse-drawn carriages, most of which date from the reign of Charles IV, in the late 18C. Among the exhibits are the late-17C Carroza Negra or Black Coach made of stained beech and ash, and some 18C berlins, including that used by the Marquis of the House of Alcántara. The coronation coach (drawn by 8 horses with accompanying footmen), was built in the 19C for Ferdinand VII and still bears marks of the assassination attempt made on Alfonso XIII and his bride, Victoria Eugenia, in May 1906.

★★ **Monasterio de las Descalzas Reales** (Descalzas Reales Convent) (**KLX**) ⊘ – Although the convent stands in one of the liveliest parts of Madrid, the moment one steps inside, one is taken right back to the 16C. It was Joanna of Austria, daughter of Emperor Charles V, who founded the convent of Poor Clares here in the palace in which she was born. For two centuries it served as a retreat for nobles who wished to live retired from the world. The nobility heaped gifts upon the order which has now put its rich collection of religious art on display in buildings abutting the conventual cloisters.

The magnificent grand **staircase**★, decorated with frescoes, leads to the upper cloister gallery where each of the **chapels** is more sumptuous than its precedent. Note the Recumbent Figure of Christ by the 16C sculptor Gaspar Becerra.

In the former nuns' dormitory are ten 17C **tapestries**★★ after cartoons by Rubens. Other convent treasures include, on the entresol, various portraits of the royal family and a *St Francis* by Zurbarán; in the chapter house, sculptures, a *Dolorosa* and an *Ecce Homo* by Pedro de Mena and a *Magdalene* by Gregorio Hernández; in the **Relicario** (Reliquary Chamber), a great many finely engraved chalices and caskets and, in the picture galleries, works by Titian, Bruegel the Elder and Rubens.

★ **Real Monasterio de la Encarnación** (Royal Convent of the Incarnation) (**KX**) ⊘ – The convent stands on a delightful square of the same name near the former Alcázar with which it was once connected by a passageway.

It was founded in 1611 by Margaret of Austria, wife of Philip III, and occupied by Augustines. The generosity of each successive Spanish monarch may be seen today in its impressive display of art works.

The collection of paintings from the 17C Madrid school is particularly rich and includes the historically interesting *Exchange of Princesses on Pheasant Island* in 1615 by Van der Meulen and a *St John the Baptist* by Ribera. There is a noteworthy polychrome sculpture of *Christ at the Column* by Gregorio Hernández on the first floor.

The **Relicario**★, with a ceiling painted by Vicencio Carducci, contains some 1 500 relics. Among the most notable are the Lignum Crucis and the phial containing the blood of St Pantaleon which is said to liquify each year on 27 July.

The church with its sober quasi-Herreran style portal was originally by Gómez de Mora (1611) but was reconstructed by Ventura Rodríguez in the 18C after the fire in the Alcázar.

Plaza de España (**KV**) – Every visitor to Madrid is bound to spend some time on the large esplanade during a tour of the city centre. The monument to Cervantes in the middle of the square, and the figures of Don Quixote and Sancho Panza, appear overwhelmed by the size of the skyscrapers built in the 1950s, in particular the Torre de Madrid and the Edificio España from the top of which there is a panoramic **view**★ of the town.

Starting from the square is the Gran Vía, a wide avenue lined by shops, cinemas and hotels, and Calle Princesa, popular with the young and with students, which leads towards the **Ciudad Universitaria**★ (University City) (**AS**).

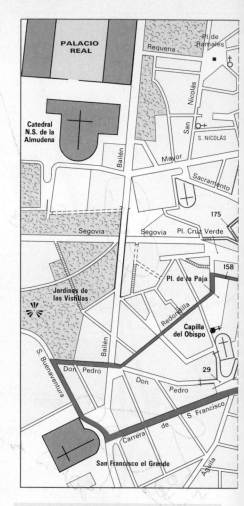

A   Hemeroteca Municipal
H   Ayuntamiento

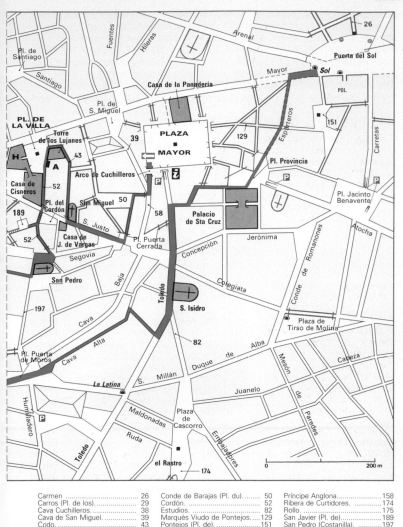

Faro de la Moncloa (Moncloa Beacon) (**AS**) ⊙ – Completed in 1992. From its 76m 250ft high **balcony**★★, there is a wonderful view of Madrid and its surrounding area. To the north-east, the outline of the sierra Madrileña can be seen.

★**Parque del Oeste (West Park)** (**AS**) – This delightful landscaped garden, extending across slopes overlooking the Manzanares, was designed at the beginning of the century. In the southern part, on Príncipe Pío hill, stands the small 4C BC **Egyptian Temple of Debod** (**AT**). It once stood beside the Nile in Nubia and was rescued from the waters when the Aswan Dam was being built. Note the hieroglyphs on the interior walls.

The **Paseo del Pintor Rosales** nearby, stretching northwestwards, acts as a balcony overlooking the park. Its pavilions and pavement cafés command wonderful views of Velázquez-like sunsets. **La Rosaleda**, a rose garden, holds flower shows in June. A **teleférico** (cableway) ⊙ links the Parque del Oeste to the **Casa de Campo**★ (**AT**), a vast natural expanse on the other side of the Manzanares. The park was reafforested under Philip II in 1559 and today is very popular with Madrileños who come to stroll, row on the lake, swim in the pools or visit the amusement park and the **zoo**★★ ⊙ where the main attraction is a panda born in captivity.

★★★THE MUSEO DEL PRADO (NY) ⊙ time: 3 hours

The museum is in the heart of Bourbon Madrid (see below).

The Prado is probably the greatest gallery of classical paintings in the world. The neo-classical building was designed by Juan de Villanueva under Charles III to house the Natural Science Museum. After the War of Independence (the Peninsular War), Ferdinand VII altered the project and instead installed the collections of Spanish painting made by the Habsburg and Bourbon kings which reflect the development of royal artistic taste over the centuries. The Prado also contains precious collections of work by Flemish painters, acquired by the Catholic Monarchs, as well as a great many paintings from the Italian school favoured by Emperor Charles V and Philip II.

Given the large amount of works in stock, some paintings are only displayed in temporary exhibitions. As the museum is presently being modernised, some of the rooms may be closed and their contents shown elsewhere in the museum.

The Spanish school holds pride of place for the quality and quantity of its works.

THE PRADO'S MAJOR WORKS

SCHOOL	ARTIST	PAINTING	FLOOR
Spanish 16-18C	Juan de Juanes	*Ecce Homo*	Ground
	El Greco	*Gentleman with his Hand on his Breast*	First
		Adoration of the Shepherds	First
	Zurbarán	*Still Life*	First
		St Isabel of Portugal	First
	Velázquez	*The Surrender of Breda*	First
		The Spinners	First
		The Maids of Honour (Las Meninas)	First
		Prince Baltasar Carlos on Horseback	First
		Infanta Doña Margarita of Austria	First
		The Forges of Vulcan	First
		Christ on the Cross	First
	Murillo	*Holy Family with a Little Bird*	First
		Immaculate Conception of Soult	First
		The Good Shepherd	First
	Goya	*Family of Charles IV*	First
		Maja Naked, Maja Clothed	First
		Executions at Moncloa	First
		The Second of May	First
		The Witches' Coven	Ground
Flemish 15-17C	Robert Campin	*St Barbara*	Ground
	Van der Weyden	*Deposition*	Ground
	Hans Memling	*Adoration of the Magi*	Ground
	Bruegel the Elder	*Triumph of Death*	Ground
	Hieronymus Bosch	*Garden of Earthly Delights*	Ground
	Rubens	*The Three Graces*	Ground
Italian 15-17C	Fra Angelico	*Annunciation*	First
	Andrea Mantegna	*Dormition of the Virgin*	First
	Botticelli	*Story of Nastagio degli Onesti*	First
	Titian	*Venus with the Organist*	First
	Tintoretto	*Washing of the Feet*	First
	Veronese	*Venus and Adonis*	First
German and Dutch 16-17C	Albrecht Dürer	*Self-portrait*	Ground
	Rembrandt	*Artemesia*	Ground

★★★ **Spanish School (15-18C)** – **Bartolomé Bermejo** *(Santo Domingo de Silos* – with his costume rich in gold) and **Yáñez de la Almedina**, who developed the style and technique of Leonardo *(Santa Catalina)*, stand out as two painters who cultivated an international style. Masip and his son **Juan de Juanes** *(The Last Supper)* are more associated with the style of Raphael, while Morales' favourite subject, a *Virgin and Child*, is also outstanding.

In those rooms devoted to the **Golden Age**, two painters stand out: **Sánchez Coello**, a disciple of the portrait painter Antonio Moro, and his pupil **Pantojo de la Cruz**, who was another portraitist at the court of Philip II. The personality of **El Greco**, who followed strong Byzantine traditions during his studies in Venice, stands apart within the Spanish School. Here, works dating from his early Spanish period *(Trinity)* through to his maturity *(Adoration of the Shepherds)* can be seen and the evolution of his style studied. Other works are proof that he was a great portraitist; pay particular note to the **Gentleman with his Hand on his Breast**.

Ribalta is the Spanish Baroque artist who first introduced tenebrism to Spain with its chiaroscuro technique already seen in Caravaggio's work. **José de Ribera**, also known as **Lo Spagnoletto**, is represented by his major work, the *Martyrdom of St Felipe –*

which was originally thought to be of St Bartholomew – in which the artist's vigorous use of chiaroscuro emphasizes the dramatic, horrifying nature of the scene. Both the portraits and still lifes of **Zurbarán** are peaceful compositions in which the use of chiaroscuro and realism are triumphant. In the Prado we discover the lesser known aspect of the style of this "Painter of Monks", both in the series of *The Labours of Hercules* which he painted for the Casón del Buen Retiro and in the portrait of *St Isabel of Portugal*. **Murillo**, who mainly painted Marian religious scenes, also cultivates popular subjects with delightful realism; note his enchanting child portraits (the *Good Shepherd* and *St John the Baptist Child*).

Velázquez (1599-1660) – The Prado possesses the greatest paintings of Velázquez. The artist of genius, born in Sevilla, was apprenticed first to Herrera the Elder and then to Francisco Pancheco whose daughter he married in 1618. He later moved to Madrid where he was called to the court by Philip IV in 1623 and subsequently painted a great many portraits. On the suggestion of Rubens he spent some time in Italy (1629-1631) where he painted **The Forges of Vulcan**. Influenced by Titian and Tintoretto he began to use richer, more subtle colours and developed his figure compositions as can be seen in his magnificent **Christ on the Cross**. On his return he painted **The Surrender of Breda** *(see Introduction under Art)* in which his originality emerges and where, as is borne out by the composition, the emphasis rests on the psychological relationship between the protagonists. The use of light in his pictures is crucial, setting off figures and objects yet also giving life to the space between them; on the strength of this Velázquez developed his famous aerial perspectives in which parts of the picture are left hazy in order to further highlight the central figures. He strove towards naturalism, as is shown in his royal hunting portraits of **Philip IV** and **Prince Baltasar Carlos, the Hunter** (1635, a wonderful rendering of a child) and his equestrian portraits of the royal family, in particular that of **Prince Baltasar Carlos on Horseback** with the *sierra* in the background. His predilection for realism is evident in his pictures of Aesop, as well as of buffoons and dwarfs, his favourite themes. In 1650 he returned to Italy where he painted two light, modern landscapes, the **Gardens of the Villa Medici**. During the last years of his life, when he was laden with honours and all manner of official functions, he portrayed the young princes and princesses very freely, as in the picture of the **Infanta Margarita of Austria** (1659) in tones of pink and grey. In his masterpiece, **The Maids of Honour (Las Meninas)** (1656), a magnificent display of light and colour, the Infanta Margarita is shown in the artist's studio accompanied by her maids and dwarves while the king and queen are portrayed in a mirror in the background. In **The Spinners** (1657), Velázquez has combined myth and reality in a wonderful interplay of oblique lines and curves.

Among the disciples of Velázquez was the court painter **Carreño de Miranda** *(Monstrua Naked* and *Clothed)*. Mention should also be made of **Alonso Cano** who painted scenes of the *Immaculate Conception*.

Goya (1746-1828) – Spanish painting maintained its supremacy in the 18 and 19C with Goya (born in Fuentedodos in 1746) who is magnificently represented in several rooms. His many portraits of the royal and famous, his war scenes, his depiction of everyday life which served as a model for tapestries, and finally his **Majas**, all widely illustrate his extraordinary realism and his enthusiasm for colour. The museum contains some 40 cartoons painted in oil between 1775 and 1791 for weaving at the Real Fábrica (Royal Tapestry Works). The colourful naturalness

Museo del Prado, Madrid/LAUROS-GIRAUDON

Detail of The Family of Charles IV by Goya (in the Prado, Madrid)

of the scenes gives a delightful picture of life in 18C Madrid. A little further on are the canvases of the **2 May** and the **Execution of the Rioters on 3 May 1808** painted by Goya in 1818. Here he was inspired by the rebellion in Madrid in 1808 against the French occupying forces when the people wished to prevent the departure of the queen and princes for Bayonne *(see Aranjuez, qv)*. The reprisal by Murat that ensued was terrible. Goya condemned the horror of that night and the execution that took place on Príncipe Pío hill. The two paintings bring out the violence and cruelty of war as do Goya's brutal etchings of the *Disasters Of War* (1808) and *La Tauromaquia*. The so-called *Black Paintings* (1820-1822) on the ground floor, which Goya made for his house, the Quinta del Sordo, are the anguished reactions of a visionary to the reality of life in Spain at the time *(The Witches' Coven, Cronus swallowing his Son)*.

★★★ **Flemish School (15-17C)** – *Ground floor.* The Prado has an exceptional collection of Flemish painting due to the close relations Spain developed with the Low Countries in the past.

Among the Flemish Primitives is the noticeable interest in interiors *(St Barbara* by Robert Campin known as the Master of Flemalle) to which **Van der Weyden** added great richness of colour, a sense of composition and the pathetic *(Descent from the Cross, Pietà).* The dramatic aspect is interpreted differently, through melancholy, by his successor, **Memling** *(Adoration of the Magi).*

There follow the weird imaginings of **Hieronymus Bosch,** known as El Bosco, *(The Garden of Earthly Delights)* which influenced his disciple Patinir *(Crossing the Stygian Lake),* and a painting by **Bruegel the Elder,** the *Triumph of Death.*

Notable in the collection of Flemish paintings from the 16 and 17C are **Ambrosius Benson's** religious pictures, the portraits of personalities at the court of Philip II by the Dutchman, **Antonio Moro** (16C), the series of the *Five Senses* by Brueghel the Younger (17C) and his and **David Teniers the Younger's** colourful scenes of everyday life.

The most baroque of painters, **Rubens** (who was born in Germany), breathed new life into Flemish painting *(The Three Graces).* There is a rich collection of his work in the museum completed by that of his disciples: **Van Dyck,** excellent portraits, **Jordaens,** everyday-life scenes, and animal paintings by their contemporaries, Snyders and Paul de Vos.

★★ **Italian School (15-17C)** – *First floor.* The Italian school is particularly well represented from the 15C and is especially rich in works by Venetian painters.

The Italian Renaissance brought with it elegance and ideal beauty as in paintings by **Raphael** *(The Holy Family, Portrait of a Cardinal),* Roman nobility and monumental bearing in the work of **Mantegna** *(Dormition of the Virgin)* and melancholic dreaminess in Botticelli *(Story of Nastagio degli Onesti).* On the other hand, the spirituality of the magnificent *Annunciation* by Fra Angelico belongs to the Gothic tradition. The collection also includes soft-coloured works by Andrea del Sarto, and others by Correggio, an artist from the Parma school who used chiaroscuro.

The triumph of colour and sumptuousness comes with the Venetian school: **Titian** with his exceptional mythological scenes *(Danae and the Golden Shower, Venus with the Organist)* and his admirable portrait of *Emperor Charles V;* **Veronese** with his fine compositions set off by silver tones; **Tintoretto's** golden fleshed figures springing from shadow *(Washing of the Feet)* and finally **Tiepolo's** paintings intended for Charles III's royal palace.

French School (17-18C) – The French are represented by **Poussin** landscapes and canvases by **Lorrain** (17C).

Dutch School (17C) – There are two interesting works by **Rembrandt:** a *Self-portrait* and *Artemesia.*

German School – This is represented by a selection of **Dürer's** figure and portrait paintings *(Self-portrait, Adam and Eve)* and two hunting scenes and a religious canvas by Cranach.

★ **Casón del Buen Retiro** (NY) ⊘ – *Entrance in Calle Alfonso XII, no 28.* This annexe to the Prado has an exceptional collection of the most innovative artistic trends in 19C Spain on exhibition (neo-classicism, Romanticism, Realism, Impressionism, etc.). The central **Gran Salón** (former Salón de Baile or Ballroom of the old Palacio del Buen Retiro) has preserved the beautiful roof decoration painted by Lucas Jordán. Exemplary works from Spanish historical painting hang from its walls, including *The Last Will and Testament of Isabel the Catholic* by Rosales, *Juana the Mad* by F. Pradilla and *The Execution of Torrijos and his companions on the beaches of Málaga* by A. Gisbert. Other artists represented elsewhere in the museum include José de Madrazo *(The Death of Viriato),* V. López *(Portrait of Goya),* E. Lucas, Alenza, Esquivel *(Contemporary Poets),* Federico de Madrazo, M. Fortuny *(The artist's children in the Japanese Hall),* Rosales, I. Pinazo *(Self-portrait),* Sorolla *(Children at the beach),* Regoyos, Rusiñol, Chicharro *(Pain),* Zuloaga, etc.

★★BOURBON MADRID *time: 3 hours*

This is the smart, residential part of Madrid with wide tree-lined avenues bordered by opulent-looking buildings, luxurious palaces and former mansions which now house museums. It's a pleasant area to stroll around in between a visit to the Prado and a walk in the Retiro.

★ **Plaza de la Cibeles** (MNX) – Standing in the centre of the square is one of the emblems of the city and Madrid's most famous fountain, the 18C Cybele, goddess of fertility who rides a lion-drawn chariot.

The square, nerve centre of tourist Madrid, stands at the junction of Calle de Alcalá, Gran Vía, Paseo del Prado and Paseo de Recoletos with its continuation, Paseo de la Castellana. Many an artist has been inspired to paint the perspectives opening from the square and the impressive buildings surrounding it such as the **Banco de España** (1891), the 18C **Palacio de Buenavista**, now the Ministry for Defence, the late-19C **Palacio de Linares**, now the home of the Casa de América and the **Palacio de Communicaciones** or Post and Telegraph Office (1919).

★ **Paseo del Prado** (MNXYZ) – This pleasant shaded avenue was part of Charles III's plan to develop an area of the city dedicated to both the sciences and the arts. The plan included a Science Museo, which later became the Prado, the Botanical Gardens and the Observatory. The area between the fountains of Cybele (Plaza de la Cibeles) and Neptune (Plaza Cánovas del Castillo) was designed as a promenade.

★★★ **Museo Thyssen-Bornemisza** (MY) ⊘ – The late 18C-early 19C neo-classical Palacio de Villahermosa has been magnificently restored by the architect Rafael Moneo to house an outstanding collection acquired by the Spanish state from **Baron Hans Heinrich Thyssen-Bornemisza**. The collection was assembled in the 1920s by his father, Baron Heinrich, and bears witness to what is considered to be one of the largest and most inspired collections ever brought together in the private art world. Its proximity to the Prado creates a magnificent focal point in the city for art-lovers.

The museum contains approximately 800 works (mainly paintings) from the late 13C to the present day. They are exhibited in chronological order on three floors (the visit should start on the second (top) floor where the collection's oldest exhibits are displayed), and provide an overview of the main schools of European art (Italian, Flemish, German, Dutch, Spanish, French) including examples of Primitive, Renaissance, Baroque, Rococo and neo-classical works. The gallery also devotes space to 19C American painting, the 20C European Romanticism and Realism movements and presents a representative selection from the Impressionnist, Post-Impressionist and Expressionist periods. The visit concludes with paintings from both the European and American Avant-garde movements.

Second floor – The visit begins with the Italian Primitives *(Gallery 1)* : **Duccio di Buonisegna's** *Christ and the Samaritan Woman*, in which concern for scenic realism – one of the predominant themes of the Renaissance – can be seen, stands out. In a display case in **Gallery 2**, a delicate 14C *Ivory Diptych with scenes from the Life of Christ* is of particular note. **Gallery 3** displays some splendid examples of 15C Dutch religious painting such as **Jan van Eyck's** *The Annunciation Diptych*, in which the artist parades his prodigious technique by giving the finely-proportioned Angel and the Virgin the appearance of high reliefs carved in stone; next to it is the small *Our Lady of the Dry Tree* by **Petrus Christus** in which the Virgin and Child symbolize the flowering of the dry tree.

The museum possesses a magnificent **portrait collection**. It is worth spending some time in **Gallery 5** containing some superb examples of the Early Renaissance which encompass its values of identity and autonomy. These come to the fore in the beautiful and well-known *Portrait of Giovanna Tornuaboni* by the Italian painter **D. Ghirlandaio**. The room also houses a further dozen portraits of exceptional quality which emanate from various schools from the period, notably *A Young Man at Prayer* by **Hans Memling**, *A Stout Man* by **Robert Campin**, *Henry VIII* by **Hans Holbein the Younger** and **Juan of Flanders'** extremely delicate *Portrait of an Infanta (Catherine of Aragón?)*.

Henri VIII of England
by Holbein the Younger, Madrid

BRIDGEMAN/GIRAUDON

Zurbarán's stunning canvas of *Santa Casilda* can be seen in the Villahermosa Gallery *(Gallery 6)* while **Gallery 7** (16C) reveals **Vittore Carpaccio's** *Young Knight in a Landscape* in which the protagonist's elegance stands out from a background heavy with symbolism. The *Portrait of Doge Francesco Vernier* by **Titian** should not be missed, with its sober, yet diverse tones. After admiring **Dürer's** *Jesus Among the Doctors (Gallery 8)*, where the characters are surprisingly portrayed given the period (1506), move on to **Gallery 9**, which contains an excellent selection of portraits from the 16C German School including *The Nymph from the Fountain*, one of several paintings by **L. Cranach**, and the *Portrait of a Woman* by **Hans Baldung Grien**, in which the original expression and the delicacy of contrasts give the portrait an attractive air. The display of 16C Dutch paintings in **Gallery 10** includes **Patinir's** *Landscape with the Rest on the Flight into Egypt* while **Gallery 11** exhibits several works by **El Greco** as well as **Titian's** *Saint Jerome in the Wilderness* (1575), with its characteristic use of flowing brush-strokes, painted the year before his death. One of the splendid early works of **Caravaggio** – the creator of tenebrism – *Saint Catherine of Alexandria*, can be admired in **Gallery 12.** In the same gallery is the only sculpture *(Saint Sebastian)* by the Baroque artist **Bernini** to be found outside Italy. Also displayed here is the *Lamentation over the Body of Christ* (1633) by **Ribera** – one of Caravaggio's followers – which captures the Virgin's suffering with great subtlety. After passing through several rooms dedicated to 17C baroque art (includind **Claude Lorrain's** *Pastoral Landscape with a Flight into Egypt* in **Gallery 13**), you reach the 18C Italian Painting section *(Galleries 16 - 18)* with its typical Venetian scenes by **Canaletto** and **Guardi**. The remaining galleries on this floor *(19 - 21)* are consecrated to Dutch and Flemish works from the 17C. **Van Dyck's** magnificent *Portrait of Jacques le Roy*, **de Vos's** *Antonia Canis*, and two memorable **Rubens**: *The Toilet of Venus* and *Portrait of a Young Woman with a Rosary* all hang from the walls of **Gallery 19** while **Gallery 21** possesses the extraordinary *Portrait of a Man Reading a Coranto* by **Gerard ter Borch**.

First floor – The first few galleries *(22 - 26)* represent Dutch paintings from the 17C with scenes of daily life and landscapes. Pay particular note to **Frans Hals'** *Family Group in a Landscape*, a fine example of a collective portrait. The century is completed by the Still Lifes in **Gallery 27**. Several interesting portraits stand out from the 18C French and British schools, such as **Gainsborough's** *Portrait of Miss Sarah Buxton* in **Gallery 28**. 19C North-American painting, virtually unknown in Europe, takes pride of place in the next two rooms *(29 and 30)*. The European Romanticism and Realism of the 19C is best expressed by **Constable's** *The Lock*, *The Water Stream* by **Courbet** and *Easter Morning* by **Friedrich**, together with the three works in the collection by **Goya** *(Gallery 31)*.

Galleries 32 and 33 are dedicated to Impressionism and Post-Impressionism. Here, admire the magnificent works by the principal masters of these movements: Monet, Manet, Renoir, Sisley, Degas, Pissarro, Gauguin, Van Gogh, Toulouse-Lautrec, Cézanne. *At the Milliner* by **Degas** is considered to be one of his major canvases. Other works which equally stand out include **Van Gogh's** *"Les Vessenots" in Auvers*, a landscape painted in the last year of his life and which displays the explosion of brushstrokes synonymous with some of his later works, *Mata Mua* by **Gauguin**, from his Polynesian period, and **Cézanne's** *Portrait of a Farmer*, in which his particular use of colour is used to build volumes, a style which opened the way to "Cubism". Expressionism is represented in **Galleries 35 - 40**, following a small display of paintings from the "Fauve" movement in **Gallery 34**. The Expressionist movement, the best represented in the entire museum, supposes the supremacy of the artist's interior vision and the predominance of colour over draughtsmanship. The works exhibited illustrate the different focal points of German Expressionism. Two highly emblematic paintings by **Grosz**, *Metropolis* and *Street Scene*, hang in **Gallery 40**. A small selection of lithographs by **Toulouse-Lautrec** can be admired in the rest area overlooking the central patio.

Ground floor – The first few galleries *(41 - 44)* contain exceptional Experimental Avant-garde works (1907-1924) from the diverse European movements: Futurism, Orphism, Suprematism, Constructivism and Cubism. *Proun 1 C* by **Lissitzky** and *New York City, New York* by **Mondrian** merit special mention. The next gallery *(44)* displays Cubist paintings by **Picasso** *(Man with a Clarinet)*, **Braque** *(Woman with a Mandolin)* and **Juan Gris** *(Woman Sitting)*.

Gallery 45 shows post-First World War European works by **Picasso** *(Harlequin with a Mirror)* and **Joan Miró** *(Catalan Peasant with a Guitar)*, a sculpture by **Giacometti** *(The Glade)* and a 1914 abstract composition by **Kandinsky** *(Picture with Three Spots)*. In the next gallery, mainly dedicated to North-American painting, can be seen *Brown and Silver I* by **Jackson Pollock** and *Green on Maroon* by **Mark Rothko**, two different examples of abstract American Expressionism. The last two galleries *(47 and 48)* are given over to Surrealism, Figurative Tradition and Pop Art. The following are worthy of particular note: *The Key to the Fields* by the Surrealist artist **Réne Magritte**, *Hotel Room* by the Realist **Edward Hopper**, *Portrait of George Dyer in a Mirror* by **Francis Bacon**, *Express* by **Robert Rauschenberg** and *A Woman in a Bath* by **Roy Lichtenstein**.

The Botanical Gardens (**Jardín Botánico** ☉) stretch alongside Paseo del Prado between the fountain of Neptune and the fine architecture of the Atocha Railway Station. They were designed by the architect Juan de Villanueva and the botanist Gómez Ortega in 1781.

★ **Museo Nacional Centro de Arte Reina Sofia** (Queen Sofia Art Centre) (**MZ**) ☉ – Opposite the station, on Glorieta de Atocha, also known as Plaza Emperador Carlos V, stands the former Hospital de San Carlos founded by Charles III, which now houses the Centro de Arte Reina Sofia. The austere, grandiose granite building has recently been modified and now has modern glass lifts running up the façade. The vast arched halls inside form an impressive setting for the programme of temporary cultural exhibitions organised by the centre.

On the second floor the modern art collection is presented around the works of Picasso, Miró, Dalí, Juan Gris and Julio González and divided into two completely different parts. The first traces the development of Spanish art from 1900 through to the Seventies. The second, under the generic title of *Propuestas* or Proposals, presents more recent works by both Spanish and foreign artists (Chillada, Gordillo, Fontana, Bacon, Schnabel, Nauman, Flavin). The collection's most important work is undoubtedly Picasso's **Guernica**★★. In angry reaction to the atrocious bombardment of Guernica *(qv)* in 1937, the artist set to work on one of his masterpieces, a vast composition in black and white *(photograph p 30)* which combines the principal art movements of the 20C: Surrealism, Cubism and Expressionism.

The painting was displayed in the Museum of Modern Art in New York until 1981. The neighbouring rooms contain preliminary sketches of the work.

Outside, the street bordering the Jardín Botánico to the south, the **Cuesta de Claudio Moyano**, is famous for its book stalls. Calle Alfonso XII leads off left towards the Museo del Ejército.

★ **Museo del Ejército** (Army Museum) (**NY**) ☉ – A wide range of weapons and equipment (some 27 000 objects) are displayed in the vast rooms of the Palacio del Buen Retiro which was built in 1631. Arms and armour (16C), flags, banners, trophies, paintings and sculptures trace Spain's military history.

Museo Naval (Maritime Museum) (**NXY M³**) ☉ – Among the displays are models of ships and Juan de la Cosa's map of 1500 on which America is shown for the first time.

★ **Puerta del Alcalá** (Alcalá Arch) (**NX**) – *Plaza de la Independencia.* The arch was built by Sabatini between 1769 and 1778 to celebrate the triumphant entrance of Charles III into Madrid.

★★ **Parque del Buen Retiro** (Retiro Park) (**NXYZ** and **CTU**) ☉ – El Retiro is popular with Madrileños as a place to meet and go for a walk. The park originally formed the grounds of a palace built in the 17C by Philip IV of which only the building containing the Museo del Ejército (Army Museum) and the Casón del Buen Retiro remain, in the same way that the nearby church is all that is still standing of a Hieronymite monastery built by the Catholic Monarchs in the 15C. The Duke of Olivares had the palace grounds developed into a park.

El Retiro (130ha - 321 acres) is a beautiful island of greenery in the middle of the city with dense clumps of trees (La Chopera at the south end), elegant, formal flower-beds (El Parterre at the north end) and a sprinkling of fountains, temples, colonnades and statues.

The Palacio de Cristal in the Retiro, Madrid

F. Bouillot/MARCO POLO

Beside the lake (Estanque) where boats may be hired, is the imposing **Monumento a Alfonso II**. Near the graceful **Palacio de Cristal**, in which exhibitions are held, are a pool and a grotto.

ADDITIONAL SIGHTS

★★ **Museo Arqueológico Nacional** (National Archaeological Museum) (**NV**) ☉ – *Entrance in Calle de Serrano.* The **Biblioteca Nacional** (National Library) is housed in the same building *(entrance in Paseo de Recoletos).*

★ **Prehistoric Art and Archaeology** – *Galleries 1-18.* The art of the Upper Palaeolithic Period is represented by the reproduction, in the garden, of the **Cuevas de Altamira** (Altamira Caves) *(qv)* and their paintings of bison. The arrival of metal in the Iberian Peninsula (around the middle of the 3rd millennium BC) coincided with the development of the Los Millares culture which has left interesting female-shaped idols. The galleries that follow are devoted to the Bronze Age (2nd millennium BC); the so-called Bell Beaker and El Argar cultures and the megalithic culture (Talayots) of the Balearic Islands – note the splendid bronze Costix **bulls★**. The remaining galleries contain objects from Nubia, Egypt, the Middle East and Greece (magnificent collection of vases).

★★ **Iberian and Classical Antiquities** – *Galleries 19-26*. Exhibits in two Iberian galleries illustrate the origin of local techniques and the artistic influence of the Phoenicians, the Greeks and the Carthagenians. The works displayed at the beginning of the section show an Eastern tendance: note the *Lady of Galera*, a 7C BC alabaster figurine flanked by sphinxes, and the terracottas from Ibiza. The second gallery, where the influence of Carthage is obvious, shows sculpture at a high peak of artistic expression: standing out from the greatest Iberian sculptures is the Lady of Elche, the **Dama de Elche★★★**, *(qv)* a stone bust, with a sumptuous head-dress and corsage, mysterious and imposing in expression *(photograph in Introduction under Art)*. In the same gallery are the **Dama de Baza★★**, a realistic goddess figure of the 4C BC, and the woman bearing an offering discovered at Cerro de los Santos. Other galleries illustrate Spain's adoption, when under Roman domination, of the invader's techniques – bronze law tablets, sculptures, mosaics, sarcophagi, ceramics and, in particular, a hydraulic pump made of bronze – and later how she developed a Hispanic palaeo-Christian art which incorporated ideas from Christian Africa and Byzantium.

★ **Medieval and Renaissance Decorative Art** – *Galleries 27-35*. In this section are the magnificent **votive crowns of Guarrazar★★** dating from the Visigothic period. Most of them were offered by the 7C Visigothic King Recceswinth and are made of embossed gold plaques decorated with pearls, revealing a mixture of Germanic and Byzantine techniques.

This section is also devoted to the incomparable art of Muslim Spain. Among other objects, ivory caskets are displayed. Gallery 31 contains some of the treasures from San Isidoro de León *(qv)*, in particular the magnificent 11C ivory **processional cross★★** of Don Fernando and Doña Sancha.

Romanesque tombs and capitals, together with Gothic sculpture in subsequent galleries, continue to show deep Moorish influence. Gallery 35 is a reconstruction of a Mudéjar interior, complete with furniture and a magnificent **artesonado★** ceiling. Finally, the Renaissance brought with it influences from Italy, as can be seen in the bronzes and furniture.

16-19C Art – *Galleries 36-40*. The building and furnishing of royal palaces under the Bourbons in the 17, 18 and 19C encouraged the decorative arts, particularly porcelain (Buen Retiro), ceramics (Talavera, *qv*) and crystal work (La Granja).

North of the Museo Arqueológico are the Jardines del Descubrimiento (Discovery Gardens), an extension to **Plaza de Colón** (**NV 44**), with massive carved stone blocks, monuments to the discovery of the New World. Madrid's Centro Cultural is below street level, beneath Plaza de Colón.

★★ **Museo Lázaro Galdiano** (**CS**) ⊘ – The museum in the neo-classical mansion is a bequest to the nation by a great art lover, José Lázaro Galdiano. The collection of **enamels and ivories★★★** *(ground floor)* traces the evolution of enamelling from Byzantium to 19C Limoges; equally outstanding are the medieval gold and silver work and the Italian Renaissance jewellery and other art objects.

The 1st floor galleries, full of precious furniture, contain paintings by Flemish Primitives and Spanish masters (Morales, Murillo, Carreño and Sánchez Coello).

The 2nd floor is entirely devoted to painting, starting with Spanish (Berruguete, the Master of Astorga) and Flemish Primitives (Hieronymus Bosch, a fine *Crucifixion* by Quentin Metsys) and Spain's Golden Age which includes works by El Greco, Zurbarán, Murillo and Carreño.

The English school is well represented with pictures by several artists including Gainsborough, Reynolds, Romney, Constable and Bonington. There are canvases by the Italians, Francesco Guardi and Tiepolo, and also paintings from Goya's Black Period.

The collections on the 3rd floor include embroideries, fabrics, fans and weapons.

★ **Real Academia de Bellas Artes de San Fernando** (San Fernando Royal Fine Arts Academy) (**LX M²**) ⊘ – The picture gallery has a rich collection of works by foreign (Correggio, Veronese, Rubens, Mengs) and Spanish artists. Of particular interest are Zurbarán's portraits of monks, canvases by Ribera, Alonso Cano and Murillo, and a room devoted to Goya which contains his *Burial of the Sardine* and a *Self-portrait*.

★ **Museo de América** (Museum of the Americas) (**AS**) ⊘ – This archaeological and ethnological museum, which provides a general overview of European ties with the American continent, has brought together historical, geographical, cultural, artistic and religious aspects of the Americas, at the same time retaining the vision of the New World held by Europe since its discovery. Over 2500 objects are on display on two floors and are accompanied by explanations, maps, models, reconstructions of dwellings, etc. Among the exhibits of great historical value on display, the following stand out: the 17C *Conquest of Mexico*, the *Stele of Madrid* (Mayan), the powerful **Treasure of Los Quimbayas**★ (Colombian) and two manuscripts, the *Tudela Manuscript* (1553) and the 13-16C **Cortesano Manuscript**★★★, one of four remaining Mayan manuscripts in existence and the museum's prized historical work.

San Antonio de la Florida (**AT**) ☉ – The chapel, built in 1798 under Charles IV, and painted by Goya, contains the remains of the famous artist. The **frescoes**★★ on the cupola illustrate a religious theme, the miracle of St Anthony of Padua – but the crowd witnessing the miracle is of a far more worldly nature as Goya used the beautiful women of 18C Madrid as models. The result is a marvellous depiction of Madrid society at the time.

★ **Museo Cerralbo** (**KV**) ☉ – The museum, installed in a late 19C mansion, displays the collection left to the Spanish state by the Marquis of Cerralbo, a man of letters and patron of the Arts, on his death in 1922. A wide range of exhibits can be seen in the mansion's rooms and galleries, including an extensive collection of mainly Spanish paintings, furniture, fans, clocks, amour and Weaponry, porcelain, archaeological finds, photographs and personal mementoes belonging to the Marquis.

★ **Museo de Cera** (**Waxworks Museum**) (**NV**) ☉ – Wax figures from Spanish history and contemporary celebrities in a realistic setting.

★ **Museo Sorolla** (**Sorolla Museum**) (**CS**) ☉ – The works of the Valencian Joaquín Sorolla (1863-1923), a member of the Luminista art movement, are exhibited in his home.

★ **Plaza Monumental de las Ventas** (**Bullring**) (**DS**) – The bullring (1931), known as the cathedral of bullfighting, is Spain's largest, with a seating capacity of 22300. Adjoining it is a **Museo Taurino** (Bullfighting Museum) ☉ in honour of the great toreadors.

Museo de la Ciudad (**City Museum**) (**CS**) ☉ – A stroll through the museum's rooms *(3rd and 4th floors)* provides the visitor with a journey through the history of Madrid, from prehistory through to the present day. Special mention should be made of the superb **models**★ of various parts of the city and of some of the city's most emblematic buildings.

MÁLAGA★

Andalucía
Population 534683
Michelin map 446 V 16 – Michelin Atlas España Portugal p 85
Plan of the conurbation in the current Michelin Red Guide España Portugal

Málaga, a vast white, sprawling city at the mouth of the Guadalmedina, is dominated by **Gibralfaro** (**DY**) or Lighthouse Hill. This is crowned by 14C ramparts which command a fine **view**★★ of the town, the harbour and surroundings.
After its founding by the Phoenicians, the town became an important Roman colony and under the Moors, the main port for the Kingdom of Granada.
Today, Málaga is the lively capital of the Costa del Sol and enjoys a particularly pleasant climate. There are ferry links with Melilla in Africa. Some of the districts have retained a distinctive character, such as **Caleta** in the east with its old houses and gardens, and **El Palo** *(7km - 4 miles east)*, a former fishermen's quarter known for its seafood restaurants.

Málaga wine – The town produces the sweet, full-bodied wine known as Málaga, made from grapes from local hillside vineyards and which can be served either as an aperitif or dessert wine. Since its popularity has fluctuated grapes are now also dried for sale as currants.

SIGHTS

★ **Alcazaba** (**DY**) ☉ – The winding approach is lined with the ruins (fortified gateways, columns and capitals) of the Roman theatre unearthed at the foot of the fortress. Inside the final gateway, Puerta del Cristo (Christ's Door) (**DY C**), where the first mass was celebrated on the town's reconquest (1487), are Moorish gardens. There is a view of the harbour from the ramparts.
The former palace, inside the inner perimeter, is now a **museum**★ of Moorish art. There are two *patios* with Arabic decoration from the 11 to the 15C and a room with an *artesonado* ceiling, along with models of the Alcazaba and part of the cathedral.

Catedral (**CZ**) ☉ – The building begun in the 16C is incomplete to this day as its south tower lacks its full elevation.

MÁLAGA

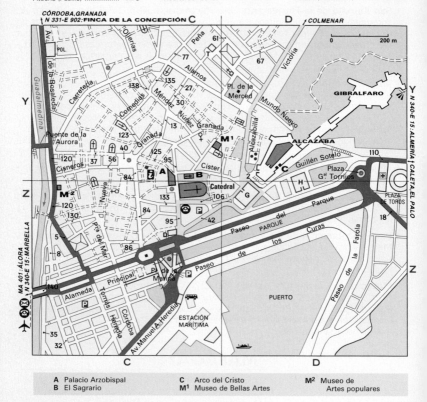

A Palacio Arzobispal	**C** Arco del Cristo
B El Sagrario	**M¹** Museo de Bellas Artes

M² Museo de Artes populares

The three aisles of the vast hall-church are covered inside with cupolas studded with palm fronds, shells and other motifs but are supported on classically ordered Corinthian columns, entablatures and cornices. The decoration includes 17C choir-stalls with figures by Pedro de Mena, pulpits of rose stone and an 18C organ.

The **Palacio Arzobispal** (Archbishop's Palace) (**CYZ A**) on the cathedral square has a baroque façade behind which are two beautiful *patios*.

El Sagrario (**CY B**) – This curious rectangular church was originally a mosque. The north portal is Isabelline Gothic in style. Inside is a mannerist **altarpiece** crowned by a *Calvary*.

Museo de Bellas Artes (Fine Arts Museum) (CDY M¹) ⊘ – The former Moorish palace serves as a setting for interesting collections by local artists. A gallery contains works by Picasso, who was born in Málaga in 1881 (no 15 Plaza de la Merced, **DY**, was his parents' home), and another one is dedicated to his very first master, Muñoz Degrain. In another *patio* are paintings by Murillo and Morales together with a great many 19C works.

Museo de Artes Populares (Museum of Popular Art) (CZ M²) ⊘ – The museum is housed in a restored 17C inn, the Mesón de la Victoria. The ground floor displays objects used in the past for work on the land or sea, such as a ploughing implements, a sardine fishing boat and tools used for wine-making.
On the first floor is a collection of statuettes in 18 and 19C costumes.

EXCURSION

★ **Finca de la Concepción** ⊘ – *7km - 4 miles north.*
The domain's gardens and shrubbery are mainly planted with tropical species. There are also some Roman remains and, amidst the cypresses, a viewpoint overlooking orange and lemon groves in an otherwise arid valley.

MARBELLA★

Andalucía (Málaga)
Population 84 410
Michelin map 446 W 15 – Michelin Atlas España Portugal p 89
Town plan in the current Michelin Red Guide España Portugal

Marbella stretches out alongside a bay sheltered by the Sierra Blanca mountains. It was the Costa del Sol's *(qv)* pioneer town and has since become one of the most famous resorts on the Andalusian coast, a holiday home to the international jet-set. Luxury hotels, elegant residential areas and golf-courses landscaped amongst pine-woods and gardens, welcome celebrities from all over the world.

Village – The village has an attractive **casco antiguo** (old quarter) of white-walled houses and narrow streets which converge on a small lively square shaded by orange trees. There are several beaches and a pleasure boat harbour.

EXCURSIONS

★ **Puerto Banús** – Puerto Banús, west of Marbella in the Nueva Andalucía district, is an elegant white-walled complex of cafés, restaurants and fashion boutiques. The superb sailing boats and yachts of the very wealthy are moored in its marina.

Monda – *18km - 11 miles north on the Coín road.*
The road passes through the picturesque mountain village of **Ojén** set in the Sierra Blanca. Monda village is typical of the Andalusian hinterland with its whitewashed houses.

Each year
the Michelin Red Guide España Portugal
presents a wealth of up-to-date information in a compact
form. It is the ideal companion for a holiday,
a long weekend or a business trip.

MEDINA DE RIOSECO

Castilla y León (Valladolid)
Population 5 037
Michelin map 441 G 14 – Michelin Atlas España Portugal p 24

Medina de Rioseco is the agricultural centre of the Tierra de Campos, the granary of Castilla. The picturesque narrow main street, **Calle de la Rúa,** is lined by porticoes supported by wooden pillars.
In the 16C, the town benefited from the work of Castilian sculptors, mainly from the Valladolid school, such as Juni, del Corral and Jordán, who have left their mark in its churches.

Iglesia de Santa María ⊙ – 15-16C. The church's central altarpiece was carved by Esteban Jordán. The **Capilla de Benavente★** (Benavente Chapel) (16C), to the left of the high altar, contains a 16C retable by Juan de Juni. The decoration on its walls and cupola by Jerónimo del Corral illustrates scenes from the Last Judgment and the Garden of Eden. The treasury contains ivories and gold and silverwork including a 16C monstrance by Antonio Arfe.

Iglesia de Santiago ⊙ – 16-17C. The altarpieces in the church's three apsidal chapels form a spectacular Churrigueresque group.

MELILLA

North Africa
Population 63 670
Michelin map 959 folds 6 and 11

In 1497, under the reign of Catholic Monarchs, the Duke of Medinaceli's troops seized this town which then became Spanish territory. In the past, like many towns along the North African coast, Melilla fell prey to the waves of navigators and conquerors in the Mediterranean (Carthaginians, Phoenicians, Romans).
The enclave is situated at the entrance to a peninsula, its rugged landscape jutting into the Mediterranean for a length of 20km-12 miles culminating in the Cabo de Tres Forcas (Three Forks headland). This almost exclusively European city is calm yet lively and exudes an opulent air with its wide avenues and large buildings. The market gardening area which surrounds the town to the south and west, the two parks in the centre of the city and the sailing and fishing vessels all hold greater interest for the visitor than the port area.

★CIUDAD ANTIGUA (OLD TOWN)

At the end of Avenida del General Macía, climb the steps which go though the ramparts.

The old town, built on a rocky peninsula and encircled by 16 and 17C fortifications, dominates the port area. The tiny **Capilla de Santiago** *(at the end of a covered passageway)*, recognisable by its Gothic vault, stands out.

Museo principal ⊘ – *In the Baluarte de la Concepción (bastion)*. Exhibits on display in this museum include pottery, vases, coins and jewels from the Carthaginian, Phoenician and Roman periods which have been discovered in the area. 17-19C Spanish weaponry hangs from the walls.

Views – From the museum's terrace there are panoramics **views**★ of the old and new towns, the port and, to the north, the Cabo de Tres Forcas.

MÉRIDA★

Extremadura (Badajoz)
Population 51 135
Michelin map 444 P 10 – Michelin Atlas España Portugal p 61
Town plan in the current Michelin Red Guide España Portugal

In 25 BC, the Roman governor of Augustus founded the township of *Emerita Augusta* in this hitherto uncolonised region. It was well situated on the Guadiana River and at the junction of major Roman roads between Salamanca and Sevilla, Toledo and Lisbon. It soon became capital of Lusitania. The Romans lavished upon it temples, a theatre, an amphitheatre and even a 400m - 437yd racecourse, now overgrown.

Two Roman bridges still span the rivers Albarregas and Guadiana (where an adjoining quay was also built). Water for the colony was brought by means of two aqueducts, San Lázaro and Los Milagros, of which a few elegant polychrome brick and stone arches remain. The water was fed from two reservoirs, the Cornalvo and Proserpina, north of the town.

★★THE ROMAN MONUMENTS *time: 3 hours*

★★ **Museo Nacional de Arte Romano (National Museum of Roman Art)** ⊘ – The modern building (1985) was designed by the architect Rafael Moneo Vallés to display Mérida's rich Roman archaeological collections. The vast construction, its sober, majestic lines reminiscent of edifices built under the Roman Empire, is made entirely of brick, an ideal material as its warm colour sets off the marble statues inside. A ramp leads up to the main hall which is separated into bays by nine semicircular arches. The skilfully designed complex also includes two upper floors of galleries and light passageways, suspended, as it were, above the hall.

Among the sculptures in the hall are statues from the Roman theatre including the strong-featured head of Augustus *(at the end of the 2nd bay)* and in the last bay, parts from the portico of Mérida's *forum*: statues of important people, caryatids and giant medallions (Medusa and Jupiter) which made up the frieze. The upper floors display jewellery, coins and pottery. Wonderful **mosaics**★ may be admired at close range from the passageways.

The basement, the excavation site around which the museum was built, contains the remains of Roman villas and tombs.

A. Abbe/VLOO

Teatro Romano, Mérida

★★ **Teatro Romano (Roman Theatre)** ⊘ – The theatre was built by Agrippa, Augustus's son-in-law, in the Classical style of the great theatres in Rome, in 24 BC. A semi-circle of stone tiers afforded seating for 6000, the front row being reserved for high dignitaries; a pit held the orchestra or crowd players; a high stage wall was decorated during Hadrian's reign (2C AD) with a covered colonnade and statues. Behind the stage, overlooking the gardens, is a portico where the audience could walk during intervals. The great blocks of granite in the vaulting of the passage-ways which lead to the tiers are secured by drystone construction alone.

★ **Anfiteatro (Amphitheatre)** ⊘ – The arena dates from the 1C BC and held, it is esti-mated, 14000 spectators. It staged chariot races and the *naumachiae* or mimic sea battles performed when the amphitheatre had been especially flooded. The steps to the audience seats and the *vomitoria*, the great covered passageways through which the crowd left, can still be seen. The tiers have disappeared apart from those reconstituted on either side of the east *vomitorium* (right coming from the theatre). Round the chariot course is a wall crowned by a cornice which protected the front row of spectators – usually notables – from wild beasts when there were gladia-torial combats. The open ditch in the centre presumably contained arena machinery and workshops.

Casa Romana del Anfiteatro (Roman Villa) ⊘ – 3C remains, including water chan-nels, pavements and bases of walls, formed part of a patrician villa built around a peristyle and dependent rooms. The pavements and mosaics are in remarkably good condition. Some show intricate geometrical motifs while others illustrate scenes from everyday life. One in particular, called *Autumn*, depicts grape-treading.

Templo de Diana – *Calle Romero Leal*. The temple with its tall fluted columns now stands free from the house into which it had been integrated.

ADDITIONAL SIGHT

Alcazaba ⊘ – The Moors built the fortress in the 9C to defend the 792m - 866yd **Puente Romano** ★ (Roman Bridge) across the islet-strewn Guadiana river. Inside the walls is an interesting **cistern** dug to the same depth as the bed of the river. To decorate the fortress, the Moors took Corinthian capitals and Visigothic marble friezes from former buildings or ruins.

MOJÁCAR★

Andalucía (Almería)
Population 4305
Michelin map 446 U24 – Michelin Atlas España Portugal p 87

The white-walled village of Mojácar stands in a splendid **site** ★ on a rocky outcrop over-looking, on one side, long beaches, and on the other, a cultivated plain out of which emerge strange rock formations. The architecture and urban planning evoke the village's Moorish past.

Mojácar to Carboneras road – *22km - 14 miles south*. The road first skirts the shore before turning inland to climb up the pyramid-shaped mountains in a series of twists and bends. There are beautiful viewpoints before it drops to Carboneras beach.

MONDOÑEDO

Galicia (Lugo)
Population 5774
Michelin map 441 B7 – Michelin Atlas España Portugal p 3

The low slate-covered houses and wide golden stone cathedral façade of Mondoñedo rise out of the hollow of a lush, well cultivated valley as you drive along the Villalba road. The streets of the old town are lined with stylish white-walled houses ornamented with armorial bearings and wrought-iron balconies. The cathedral square is particu-larly delightful with its arcades and *solanas* (glassed-in galleries).

★ **Catedral** ⊘ – The cathedral's immense façade combines the Gothic grace of the three large portal arches and the rose window, all dating from the 13C, with the grandiose baroque style of the towers added in the 18C.
The **interior**, lit by a beautiful rose window, is transitional Romanesque with the plain walls setting off the works of art. These include a series of late-14C frescoes one above the other (below the extraordinary 1710 organ) illustrating the Massacre of the Innocents and the Life of St Peter. The retable at the high altar is rococo. A polychrome wood statue of the Virgin in the south ambulatory is known as the English Virgin since the statue was brought from St Paul's, London, to Mondoñedo in the 16C. Off the south aisle is the burial niche of Bishop Juan Muñoz who gave the church its present façade.
The classical **cloisters** were added in the 17C.

Sierra de MONTSENY★

Catalunya (Barcelona, Girona)
Michelin map 443 G 36-37 – Michelin Atlas España Portugal p 33

The Sierra de Montseny, a mighty range of Pyrenean foothills in the heart of Catalunya, is a vast granite dome covered in beeches and cork oaks. The two highest peaks are Matagalls (1 700m - 5 577ft) and Turó de l'Home (1 709m - 5 607ft). Many rivers rise in the area on account of the wet climate and the impermeability of the rock face.

★★**From Sant Celoni to Santa Fé del Montseny** – *22km - 14 miles – about 3/4 hour*. This drive into the heart of the mountains is the most interesting. Beyond Campins, the road rises in hairpin bends, affording **views** of the coastal plain; it continues in a magnificent **corniche** *(2km - 1 mile)* to the lake *(embalse)* of Santa Fé (alt 1 130m - 3 707ft). The road then climbs up *(7km - 4 miles)* to the Ermita de Sant Marçal (alt 1 260m - 4 134ft), a hermitage perched on the side of the lofty Matagalls ridge.

★**From Sant Celoni to Tona via Montseny** – *43km - 27 miles – about 1 hour*. There are good views of the *sierra* from the **route**★ across the plain irrigated by the Tordera. Beyond Montseny, the road rises, reaching a wild area, before descending to Tona past the Romanesque church in **El Brull** and the tower of **Santa María de Seva**.

From Tona to Sant Celoni by the northern road – *60km - 37 miles – about 1 1/2 hours*. The road goes through pine and beechwoods and the delightful village of **Viladrau** before beginning a gradual descent with mountain views off to the right. The view opens out onto the steep Montseny slopes as the road continues its hillside descent. After the attractively sited **Arbúcies**, it runs beside the river for a distance before turning off for **Breda**, dominated by a beautiful Romanesque tower, and Sant Celoni.

Sierra de MONTSERRAT★★

Catalunya (Barcelona)
Michelin map 443 H 35 – Michelin Atlas España Portugal p 32

The Macizo de Montserrat (Montserrat Massif) has a grandiose **site**★★★ and was, in fact, used by Wagner as the setting for his opera, *Parsifal*. The range is composed of hard eocene conglomerates, which stand solidly above the more eroded surrounding rock formations. The piling up of the boulders into steep cliffs, crowned by weird pinnacles, has produced a serrated outline which has given Montserrat the nickname "sawtooth mountain". It is the principal religious and cultural centre of Catalunya, its Marian shrine attracting thousands of pilgrims.

Access – The best approach, by far, is from the west. There are excellent **views**★★ all the way along the monastery road. Access to the Montserrat cableway is best from near Monistrol de Montserrat on the Barcelona-Manresa road.

Monastery – The history of Montserrat, one of the five main hermitages on the mountain, begins in the 9C with the arrival of Benedictines from Ripoll. In 1025 Abbot Oliva founded a priory on the site which grew rapidly in importance, until by the 13C the Romanesque buildings had to be greatly enlarged. It continued to flourish and, as an abbey, declared its independence from Ripoll in 1409. It had become powerful; its monks were learned – one of the abbots, Giuliano della

Monasterio de Montserrat

Rovere, the future Pope Julius II, was a scholar, artist and patron of the Italian Renaissance – the community was rich; its pilgrims were fervent and numerous. Every century saw additions to the monastery making it an anthology of master-pieces of every architectural style.

In 1812, however, disaster struck; the monastery was sacked by the French. The present buildings, therefore, are 19 and 20C (the church façade was completed in 1968). At the end of the dark, overly ornate **basílica** ⊙ (15C), stands the shrine of the Black Madonna.

★ **La Moreneta** – La Moreneta is the Catalan name for the Black Madonna. The polychrome wood statue is said to date from the 12C; the seated figure of the Infant Jesus was restored in the 19C. According to legend, the figure, now in a niche *(camarín)* above the high altar, and venerated annually by thousands of pilgrims as the patron saint of Catalunya, was found by shepherds in a cave on the mountainside.

Access to the *camarín* for a closer view of the statue, is through the chapels in the south aisle. The church services by the monks (the Montserrat community consists of 80 members) are known for the high standard of their singing: concelebratory mass is at 11am; vespers at 6.45pm; there are special services at Christmas and in Holy Week. The **Escolanía**, one of Europe's oldest boys' choirs – its foundation dates back to the 13C – may be heard at morning mass *(Sundays and holidays at 11am)* at the Salve *(1pm)* and at the end of vespers *(7pm)*.

Hermitages and viewpoints – Access is by mountain road, cableway and funic-ular railway (**funicularse** ⊙).

Before the arrival of Napoleon's troops, there were 13 hermitages, each occupied by a hermit. Today, they are all deserted but some make interesting walks.

Sant Jeroni – *1 1/2 hour walk.* From the viewpoint (1238m - 4062ft) there is a **panorama,** on a clear day, stretching from the Pyrenees to the Balearic islands.

Ermita de Santa Cecília – Until the 16C Santa Cecília was a Benedictine monastery like Santa María of Ripoll, but lacked its influence. The 11C Romanesque church has a most attractive exterior with its east end circled by Lombard bands, its roof and its asymmetric, free standing belfry.

Santa Cova – *3/4 hour walk.* According to legend, it was in this cave that the statue of the Virgin was found. Views of the Llobregat valley.

Sant Miquel – *1/2 hour walk from the monastery; 1 hour from the upper terminal of the Sant Miquel funicular.* General view of the monastery.

Sant Joan – *20 minutes from upper terminal of Sant Joan funicular.* Beautiful pano-rama; the Ermita de San Onofre may be seen clinging to the rock face.

MORELLA

Comunidad Valenciana (Castellón)
Population 2717
Michelin map 445 K 29 – Michelin Atlas España Portugal p 44

Morella has an amazing **site**★: 14C ramparts, punctuated by towers, form a mile-long girdle round a 1004ft - 3294ft high hill on which the town has been built in tiers. Crowning the rock summit are the ruins of a medieval castle.

El Maestrazgo – Morella lies at the heart of the mountain region which was the fief *(maestrazgo)* of the Knights of Montesa, a military order founded by James II of Aragón. The order, which had its seat at San Mateo *(40km - 25 miles southeast of Morella)* as of 1317, fortified all villages in the region so as to better fight the Moors. Each community at the foot of its castle had a main porticoed square and narrow streets lined by balconied houses. Most occupy attractive sites in isolated, strongpoint positions and have retained considerable character.

★ **Basílica de Santa María la Mayor** ⊙ – The basilica is one of the most interesting Gothic churches in the Levante. It has two fine portals surmounted by gables: the 14C Apostle Doorway, and the later Virgins' Doorway with an openwork tym-panum. The unusual raised Renaissance *coro* at the nave centre has a spiral staircase magnificently carved by a local artist (Biblical scenes) and a delicate bal-ustrade with a frieze illustrating the Last Judgment. The sanctuary was sumptuously decorated in baroque style in the 17C and an elegant organ loft intro-duced in the 18C. There is a small museum with a beautiful Valencian *Descent from the Cross* and a 14C *Madonna* by Sassoferrato.

Castillo – *Access through the Convento de San Francisco. 1/4 hour climb.* On the way up there are good **views**★ of the town, the 13-14C monastery ruins, the 14-15C aqueduct and the reddish heights of the surrounding *sierras*.

EXCURSION

Mirambel – *30km - 19 miles west on the CS 840.* Bear left after 11km - 7 miles. The small *maestrazgo* village, its houses adorned with coats of arms, has retained its medieval character.

MURCIA★

Murcia
Population 338 250
Michelin map 445 S 26 – Michelin Atlas España Portugal p 79
Plan of the conurbation in the current Michelin Red Guide España Portugal

Murcia lies on either side of the Segura, at the centre of a fertile market gardening area *(huerta)*. The city, founded in the reign of Abd ar-Rahman II in 831 as Mursiya, was finally captured during the Reconquest in 1266 and was soon sufficiently secure for the pope to transfer the episcopal seat to it from Cartagena, a city always vulnerable to pirate attack. Up to the 18C, Murcia prospered from agriculture and silk weaving.

Today it is a university town and a commercial and industrial centre (fruit canning), expanding by wide avenues and walks (Paseo del Malecón) from the original kernel of medieval streets.

Two famous 18C sons of Murcia – Francisco Salzillo (1707-1783), the son of an Italian sculptor and a Spanish mother, is the last famous name in Spanish polychrome wood sculpture. *Pasos,* or processional groups, were his speciality (although he did do other types of carving); 1 800 works are attributed to the artist.

The other notable 18C Murcian was the statesman, Don José Moñino, **Count of Floridablanca** (1728-1808), minister to Charles III and IV. If Murcia owes him much, Spain owes him more, for it was by his counsel that the country's economy was put on its feet.

The Murcia Festivals – Murcia Holy Week processions are particularly solemn: on the morning of Good Friday, penitents in mauve robes bear eight Salzillo *pasos (see below)* in procession through the town. The week after the Spring Festival is the occasion for general rejoicing with processions of floats and finally the Entierro de la Sardina, or Burial of the Sardine, which symbolises the end of Lent.

SIGHTS

★ **Catedral** (**DY**) ⊙ – The original cathedral, built in the 14C, is camouflaged outside by Renaissance and baroque additions.

The **façade**★, with an arrangement of columns and curves as successful architecturally as decoratively, is a brilliant example of baroque. The impressive belfry was completed in the 18C.

The interior, however, beyond the entrance covered by a cupola matching the façade, is preponderantly Gothic, apart from the 16C **Capilla de los Junterones** *(4th south chapel)* which has rich Renaissance decoration. The **Capilla de los Vélez**★ *(off the ambulatory)* is sumptuous late Gothic with splendid star vaulting and wall decoration which clearly includes Renaissance and Mudéjar motifs.

The sacristy, approached through two successive Plateresque doors (note the beautiful panels of the first), is covered by an unusual radiating dome. The walls are richly panelled with Plateresque carving below and baroque above.

The interesting carved **stalls** (1567) in the *coro* are from an old Castilian monastery.

Museo ⊙ – At the entrance to the museum there is part of a Roman sarcophagus showing Apollo and the Muses, while the silver monstrance (1678) is the third largest in Spain. The side rooms contain Salzillo's **St Jerome**★ and a 14C altarpiece by Barnaba da Modena of St Lucy and the Virgin. The **treasure**, in the chapter house, includes monstrances and chalices as well as the crowns of Murcia's venerated Virgen de la Fuensanta.

Torre (Belfry) – A ramp leads up to the top which commands an interesting **panorama**★ of Murcia and its *huerta*.

In the cathedral square is the Italianate **Palacio Episcopal** (**DYZ**), with elegant cloisters.

Calle de la Trapería (**DY**) – In the main street (pedestrian) through the old quarter is one of the most sumptuous **Casinos** in Spain, a late-19C building with an inner Moorish *patio* and elaborate decoration.

★ **Museo Salzillo** (**CY**) ⊙ – The museum possesses many of Salzillo's masterpieces including the eight polychrome wood sculptures of **pasos** carried in the Holy Week processions. They stand in the side chapels off the rounded nave of the Church of Jesus. The deep emotion on the faces in the groups of the Last Supper and Christ's Arrest and the majesty of St John and the Angel in the Agony in the Garden are truly impressive. There are also in the museum countless numbers of the artist's vivid terracotta figurines, which form a **Nativity scene**.

EXCURSIONS

Alcantarilla – *9km - 6 miles west on the N 340.* There is the **Museo de la Huerta** ⊙ in the outskirts of the village beside the road on the approach from Murcia. In this museum, which is dedicated to local farming and irrigation, there is an ethnographic pavilion providing background information, while outside, dispersed amongst the orange trees, are white *barracas* or rustic dwellings of another age and a **noria**, the giant waterwheel devised for irrigation by the Moors.

MURCIA

Santuario de la Fuensanta (La Fuensanta Shrine) – *7km - 4 miles south. Follow the signs from Puente Viejo* (**DZ**).
From the shrine of the Virgen de la Fuensanta, patron saint of Murcia, are fine **views** of the town and the *huerta*.

Orihuela – *24km - 15 miles northeast on the N340.*
The peaceful town of Orihuela, with its many churches, lies along the banks of the Segura at the foot of a deeply scored hill. The river provides water for the fertile *huerta* and for the local **palm grove.**
In the 16C Orihuela was made an episcopal see and for two centuries was a university town. The poet and dramatist Miguel Hernández was born in the town in 1910.
At the north end of the town is the former university, the **Colegio de Santo Domingo** ⊙. The Renaissance façade of the college conceals two cloisters: one Renaissance style and the other Herreran. The 18C church has coloured frescoes and rich rococo stucco mouldings.
The Gothic **cathedral** ⊙ (14-15C) has a Renaissance style north doorway illustrating the Annunciation.
Inside, part of the vaulting is highly original as it has spiral ribs. The **museo** ⊙ houses a *Temptation of St Thomas Aquinas* by Velázquez, a *Christ* by Morales and a *Mary Magdalene* by Ribera.
The **Iglesia de Santiago** ⊙ (near the Ayuntamiento) was founded by the Catholic Monarchs whose emblems, together with a statue of St James, may be seen on the Gothic portal. In the interior, note the statues attributed to Salzillo in the side chapels.

*When driving from Britain to a destination in Spain
use the Michelin Motoring Atlas Europe.*

*In addition to the maps at a scale of 1:1 000 000 or 1:3 000 000
there is a selection of 70 town plans
and a wealth of motoring information.*

Large format in paperback or spiral bound versions.

NÁJERA

La Rioja
Population 6901
Michelin map 442 E 21 – Michelin Atlas España Portugal p 27

Nájera stands across a bridge on the pilgrim road to Santiago de Compostela *(qv)*. It was the capital of the Kingdom of Navarra until 1076 when La Rioja *(qv)* – and Nájera with it – was incorporated into Castilla.

★ **Monasterio de Santa María la Real** ⊘ – The monastery was founded by Don García III, King of Navarra, in 1032. According to legend, the site is that of a cave which the king stumbled upon (while following a vulture and a partridge) and where he found a statue of the Virgin.

★★ **Claustro** – The cloisters abut a strangely purple-coloured cliff. The bays in the lower gallery are filled with Plateresque stone tracery (1520), each to a different arabesque pattern.

Iglesia – Beneath the gallery, two soldiers bearing the colours of King García and his Queen, Estefanía of Barcelona, guard the entrance to the **Panteón Real** (Royal Pantheon) ★ of princes of Navarra, León and Castilla of the 11 and 12C. The recumbent statues were carved in the 16C. At the centre, between the kneeling figures of the founders, is the entrance to the cave where the Virgin was found. The present polychrome figure is 13C. Among the royal sarcophagi in the south aisle is the 12C **tomb of Doña Blanca de Navarra** ★. The figures have been carved in natural, graceful postures with elegant draperies.

In the *coro alto*, note the beautiful carving and infinite variety of the misericords and armrests in the **choir-stalls** ★ (1495) and particularly the central seat on which the founder king is depicted majestically in full armour beneath a delicate canopy.

EXCURSIONS

★ **Santo Domingo de la Calzada** – *19km - 12 miles west on the N 120.*
The small town owes its name to Dominic, an 11C hermit who built a bridge or causeway *(calzada*: road, causeway) on the site to help pilgrims on their way to Santiago de Compostela. This done, he also founded a hospice and a hospital. A town grew up around the halt on the Camino Francés or French Way (so named on account of the many French pilgrims who trod it) and in the 14C was considered sufficiently important to be encircled by the ramparts which are still standing. The former hospital has been converted into a *parador*.

★ **Catedral** – The church is Gothic, apart from the ambulatory and one of the apsidal chapels which are Romanesque. The saint's tomb, beneath a 1513 canopy, is in the south transept, and opposite is a sumptuous Gothic cage. This contains a live white cock and hen in memory of a miracle attributed to the saint. According to legend, a pilgrim was unjustly accused of theft and hanged. After a month on the gallows, he was still alive and, on seeing his parents, said ^ Tell the judge to let me down; St Dominic has protected me.» The judge, on hearing the news just as he was about to begin a meal of roast chicken, declared ^ He must be as alive as this bird»; whereupon the cockerel stood up and, fully feathered, crowed aloud to proclaim the pilgrim's innocence.

The **retable** ★ at the high altar (1538) is Damian Forment's last work. The artist has used the human body as a decorative element, making this an original work and by far the freest of his compositions. The second chapel off the north aisle contains a fine 15C Hispano-Flemish altarpiece.

San Millán de la Cogolla – *20km - 12 miles southwest. Leave Nájera on the C 113, then bear right after 6km - 4 miles.*
In the 5C, Millán or Emilian de Berceo and his followers settled here as hermits and when Millán died a centenarian in 574 his tomb became a place of pilgrimage. First, in the 10C, a monastery and Mozarabic church were built in the mountains (Suso) and then, in 1053, another monastery was built in the valley (Yuso). The first known manuscripts in Castilian Spanish were written here.

★ **Monasterio de Suso** ⊘ – The Mozarabic church, partly hollowed out of the rock, stands on a hillside above the Cardenas valley. It has a cubic apse with large carved corbels and two aisles separated by three horseshoe-shaped arches. The aisles were extended westwards in the Romanesque era. A cave necropolis for the burial of the monks was discovered near the church.

Monasterio de Yuso Monastery ⊘ – The monastery was built between the 16 and 18C, in Renaissance style in the case of the church, neo-classical and baroque respectively for the portals and sacristy. In the treasury are splendid **ivories** ★★ from two 11C reliquaries. These were robbed of their gold mounts and precious stones by French soldiers and are now shown as sets of ivory plaques – San Millán's (1067-1080), consisting of 14 Romanesque pieces, is carved with great human expression, while San Felices' (1090), consists of 5 pieces with a distinctly Byzantine hieratic style.

Valle del NAVIA

Asturias

Michelin map 441 BC 9 – Michelin Atlas España Portugal p 4

The Navia, which rises in Galicia in the Sierra de Cebreros, crosses several steep volcanic ridges before flowing into the Cantabrian Sea. The wild, enclosed valley is punctuated by three dams, in which the high mountains stand reflected.

FROM NAVIA TO GRANDAS DE SALIME

82km - 51 miles – allow 2 1/2 hours

Navia – A new town and fishing port on the right bank of the *ría*. A road follows the bank to a point overlooking the inlet where a **belvedere dedicated to the Great Seafaring Discoverers** gives a pleasant view.

In Navia *(qv)*, take the Grandas de Salime road with runs alongside the *ría*.

Coaña – The circular foundations of a few houses and parts of a road system remain from the Celtic village or *Castra Celta* built on a mound.

For a striking **panorama**★★ of the **Arbón dam**, built just above a giant bend in the river, pause at the viewpoint.

Shortly after Vivedro, there is a **panoramic view**★★ extending from a loop in the river in the foreground, to the Navia Ría mouth in the far distance.

The **confluence**★★ of the Navia and the Río Frío is impressive as you look down on it from a giddy height. Beyond the bridge across the Frío, the road returns to the Navia which it follows to Miñagón. The squat drying sheds or *hórreos* you see from the road are the same rectangular shape as those in nearby Galicia.

The road descends beyond Boal to the level of the Navia, where 3km - 2 miles further on, the valley is blocked by the high **Doiras dam.**

The small village of **Sarzol**, perched on a hillside on the far bank from San Esteban, is surrounded by very steep slopes, all of which are cultivated.

Grandas de Salime – This is a large agricultural town. The **Museo Etnográfico** ⊙ housed in a former presbytery, traces aspects of traditional life in Asturias through reconstructed rooms, displays of objects found in a small agricultural holding or *casería* and tools used for various crafts. One of the functions of the "living museum" is to preserve local cottage industries (craftsmen give demonstrations) as well as ancestral farming methods.

4 km - 2 miles away is the **Embalse de Salime**. There are viewpoints overlooking the dam wall and the power station.

OLITE★

Navarra

Population 3 049

Michelin map 442 E 25 – Michelin Atlas España Portugal p 15

Olite, the best-loved residence of the Kings of Navarra in the 15C, is known as the Gothic town. It still lives in the shadow of its castle which has all the appearance and size of a medieval city. The San Martín de Unx road affords a good general view.

SIGHTS

★**Castillo de los Reyes de Navarra (Fortress of the Kings of Navarra)** ⊙ – Charles III, the Noble, gave orders for the castle to be built in 1406. The French origins of the prince – he was a Count of Evreux and native of Mantes – explain the foreign style fortifications, a transition between the massive stone constructions of the 13C and the royal Gothic residences of the late 15C with galleries and small courtyards. The building was carried out by architects from north of the Pyrenees assisted by Moorish craftsmen. Behind the 15 or so towers marking the perimeter were hanging gardens; within were inner halls and chambers decorated with *azulejos*, painted stuccowork and coloured marquetry ceilings. The plan is now confused as a result of a great many alterations and devastations. Restored areas have been converted for use as a *parador*.

Iglesia de Santa María la Real ⊙ – The church is the former chapel royal. An atrium of slender multifoil arches precedes the 14C **façade★**, a beautiful example of Navarra Gothic sculpture. The only figurative carving on the portal is on the tympanum which illustrates the Lives of the Virgin and Christ. A painted 16C retable above the high altar frames a Gothic statue of Our Lady.

Iglesia de San Pedro – The church façade below the tapering octagonal spire has a somewhat disparate appearance. The portal covings are set off by tori (large convex mouldings). Eagles on either side symbolise, right and left respectively, Gentleness and Violence. Inside the church, at the beginning of the north aisle, is a stone, carved to represent the Trinity (15C).

EXCURSION

★ **Monasterio de La Oliva** ⊙ – *28km - 17 miles southeast on the NA 533 and C 124.*
La Oliva was one of the first Cistercian monasteries to be built by French monks
outside France during the lifetime of St Bernard (1090-1153). The monastery's
influence was considerable in the Middle Ages when it spread the Christian word
far beyond the confines of Spain. The buildings, now stripped of treasure and trap-
pings, retain the beauty of the pure Cistercian style.

★★ **Iglesia** – Late 12C church. Apart from a triangular coping and the turret (17C) the
church front is unadorned – a perfect setting for the interplay of lines of the portal
and two rose windows. The interior is surprisingly deep with pillars and pointed
arches lined with thick polygonal ribs in austere Cistercian style.

★★ **Claustro** – Late 15C. The cloister bays appear exceptionally light. Gothic additions
were simply grafted onto an older construction, as can be seen by the arch springs
which, in part, obscure the entrance to the 13C **Sala Capitular** (chapter house).

OLIVENZA

Extremadura (Badajoz)
Population 10004
Michelin map 444 P 8 – Michelin Atlas España Portugal p 60

Five centuries of Portuguese history have left their mark on the appearance and architecture of this quiet white-walled town set in the middle of olive groves. Olivenza is
one of the few places in Spain where the Manueline style can be seen – that specifically Portuguese architecture of the early 16C, contemporary with the reign of King
Manuel (1495-1521). This style brought to late Gothic architecture Renaissance,
Moorish and maritime features (sailors' knots, ropes and armillary spheres).

La Guerra de las Naranjes (War of Oranges) – At the end of the 13C, Olivenza was
given in dowry to King Denis of Portugal. In 1801, it was ceded to Spain to prevent
the Alentejo invasion – begun by Godoy's *(qv)* troops – becoming a major conflict
between the two nations. The skirmish, however, left no other souvenir than the story
of Godoy's futile gesture of sending oranges to Queen María Luisa from trees at the
foot of the Elvas ramparts *(see Michelin Green Guide Portugal)*.

Iglesia de Santa María Magdalena – The brothers Diego and Francisco de Arruda,
architects of the Mosteiro dos Jerónimos and the Torre de Belém in Lisbon, are
believed to have designed the church's Manueline nave. The sober elegance of the
lierne and tierceron vaulting supported on cabled pillars contrasts with the sumptuous altarpieces and *azulejos* which decorate the baroque sanctuary.

Ayuntamiento (Town Hall) – The doorway, a delightfully graceful example of
Manueline style decoration, is adorned with two armillary spheres, symbols of the
discoveries by the great Portuguese navigators of the 15 and 16C.

OÑATI / OÑATE

País Vasco (Guipúzcoa)
Population 10264
Michelin map 442 C 22 – Michelin Atlas España Portugal p 14

Oñati with its seignorial residences, monastery and old university, is content now to
sit back in its fertile valley. Twice during the First Carlist War *(qv)* the town served
as Don Carlos' headquarters.
The road 6km - 4 miles east affords a beautiful **panorama** of Oñati nestling in the valley
at the foot of Monte Aloña (1321m - 4334ft) and the distant Udala and Amboto peaks.

Antigua Universidad (Old University) ⊙ – The university, now administrative headquarters of Guipúzcoa province, was founded in 1542 by a native prelate of Oñati
and closed early this century; it was the only university in the Basque country and
enjoyed considerable cultural prestige. The gateway by the Frenchman, Pierre
Picart, is surmounted by pinnacles and crowded with statues. Among the figures
is the founding bishop (at the centre) and Sts Gregory and Jerome (right and left
respectively). The exuberant decoration reappears at the corner of each tower and
again in the exceedingly elegant *patio*.

Ayuntamiento (Town Hall) – The fine 18C baroque building was designed by the
architect Martín de Carrera. At Corpus Christi, unusual traditional dances and processions which date back to the 15C are held in the square.

Iglesia de San Miguel ⊙ – The Gothic church facing the university was modified
in the baroque period. A Renaissance chapel off the north aisle, closed by beautiful iron grilles, contains an interesting gilded wood altarpiece and the marble
tomb of the founder of the university. The golden stone cloister exterior with
gallery tracery, ogee arches, and statue niches is Isabelline Plateresque in style.

EXCURSIONS

★ **Santuario de Arantzazu** ⊘ – *9km - 6 miles south.*
The corniche **road**★ follows the course of the Río Arantzazu which flows through a narrow gorge. The **shrine** is perched at an altitude of 800m - 2 625ft in a mountain **setting**★ facing the highest peak in the province, Mount Aitzgorri (1 549m - 5 082ft). Dominating the church is an immense bell-tower 40m - 131ft high, built, like the towers framing the façade, with diamond-faceted stone symbolising the hawthorn bush (*arantzazu* in Basque) in which the Virgin appeared to a local shepherd in 1469. A hermitage was then built on the spot and occupied by Franciscans in the 16C but the present building only dates from 1955. Inside, a statue of the Virgin, patron of the province, stands at the centre of a huge wooden altarpiece painted by Lucio Muñoz.

Elorrio – *18km - 11 miles northwest on the Durango road.*
This small, ancient town in which many houses are emblasoned with coats of arms, possesses a collection of 15 and 16C crucifixes unique in the Basque country. The one at the town's west entrance is decorated with a frieze of people, the one at the east with a cabled column. The **Iglesia de la concepción** (Church of Our Lady of Holy Conception), which is a typically Basque church with its thick round pillars and star vaulting, contains an exuberant Churrigueresque altarpiece.

Parque Nacional de
ORDESA Y MONTE PERDIDO★★★

Aragón (Huesca)

Michelin map 443 E 29-30 – Michelin Atlas España Portugal p 16 – Local map under
PIRINEOS ARAGONESES

The Valle de Ordesa was declared a national park in 1918 and was expanded in 1982 to cover an area of 15 608ha - 38 569 acres, including the Monte Perdido massif and the Ordesa, Añisclo, Escuain and Pineta valleys. The purpose of the park is to safeguard its outstanding natural beauty – the massif's limestone relief of canyons, cliffs and chasms – as well as the variety and richness of its flora and fauna (Pyrenean ibex, golden eagle and izard).

The park must be visited between May and September as the snow makes it inaccessible by car in winter.

★★★VALLE DE ORDESA

The Ordesa valley is a grandiose canyon cutting through vast, layered limestone folds. The escarpments which rise nearly 1 000m - 3 280ft from the valley floor, are divided into steel grey or red ochre strata. In spring, cascades of melted snow streak the vertical rock face. Along the valley bottom, the Río Arazas, a turbulent trout stream, rushes beneath flourishing beech and maple trees. Growing up the lower slopes are pines, larches, firs – some 25m - 82ft tall – and a carpet of box, hawthorn and service trees.

WALKING TOURS

A viewpoint on the road into the park offers a general panorama of the reserve and a little further on, a second point looks over the 60m - 197ft high **Cascada de Tamborrotera** ①. As the road soon comes to an end, the rest of the park may only be visited on foot.

The best route for inexperienced walkers or families with young children is along the path that runs through the bottom of the canyon beside the Arazas river itself, which makes for a pleasant, shady walk.

Allow a day for a round tour from the car park to the end of the canyon and back.

The three walks below are feasible for experienced, well-equipped hikers.

Torla and the Parque Nacional de Ordesa

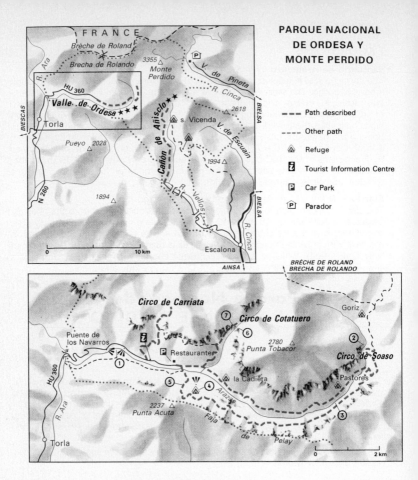

PARQUE NACIONAL DE ORDESA Y MONTE PERDIDO

- – – – Path described
- – – – Other path
- ⌂ Refuge
- 🛈 Tourist Information Centre
- 🅿 Car Park
- Ⓟ Parador

Circuito del Circo de Soaso (Tour of the Soaso Cirque) – *Start from the Cadiera refuge beyond the car park; time: 7 hours.*

The first part of the walk as far as the valley floor is easy and can be attempted by anyone. The second part, via the Cola de Caballo (Horse's tail) is more difficult, however, and is only recommended to those who are well equipped and in good physical condition (steep climbs). This walk provides the best and most complete tour of the Ordesa valley. From the Circo de Soaso path several waterfalls can be seen including the **Gradas de Soaso** ③, or Soaso Steps, followed by the impressive, 70m - 230ft high **Cola de Caballo** ②. The path continues along the **Faja de Pelay** overlooking the canyon to a depth of 2 000m - 6 562ft at the foot of the Sierra de Cutas. Continue along the **Senda de los Cazadores** (Huntsman's Path) ⑤, from where there is a wonderful view of the canyon. The best panorama can be had from the **Mirador de Calcilarruego** ④. The path back to the refuge drops sharply (almost 1 000m - 3 300ft).

Circo de Cotatuero (Cotatuero Cirque) – *Start from the restaurant; time: 4 hours.*
On the park's northern border are the **Cotatuero** ⑥ and the **Copos de Lana** (Tufts of Wool) *cascadas* (waterfalls) ⑦ with a drop of 250m - 820ft.

Circo de Carriata – *Start from the Centro de Información; time: 4 hours.*
The walk is worth doing although the *clavijas* or mountaineering peg track is difficult and not recommended for those who suffer from vertigo.
A long hike is possible to Monte Perdido via the Goriz refuge, and beyond, along paths leading to the Cirque de Gavarnie in France via the Brecha de Rolando (Roland Gap) *(ask at the Centro de Información)*.

★★ CAÑÓN DE AÑISCLO

Access from Escalona village on the Bielsa-Ainsa road – a 13km - 8 mile drive.

The Añisclo canyon, narrower than that of Ordesa, is a cool, attractive valley with pine trees clinging to the limestone walls.

Walk to Ripareta – *Start from San Urbez bridge. Time: 5 hours Rtn.* The wide, well-defined path follows the course of the enclosed Río Vellos which cascades down the valley to its confluence with the Pardina.

ORENSE / OURENSE

Galicia
Population 108 382
Michelin map 441 E, F 6 – Michelin Atlas España Portugal p 7
Plan of the conurbation in the current Michelin Red Guide España Portugal

Since Antiquity, Orense – the name is said to come from the legendary gold believed to exist in the Miño valley – has been famous for its waters which pour out from three springs, **Las Burgas,** at a temperature of 65°C - 150°F. The town has preserved an old bridge, **Puente Romano,** which dates from the 13C when it was rebuilt on Roman foundations to provide a crossing for pilgrims on their way to Santiago de Compostela. The town today is a busy commercial centre with modern buildings although there is still an old quarter around the cathedral.

OURENSE / ORENSE

M¹ Museo Arqueológico y de Bellas Artes

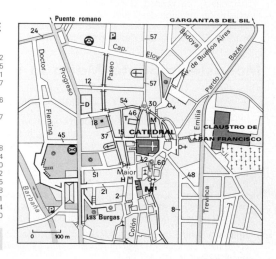

SIGHTS

★**Catedral** ○ – The cathedral, which took from the 12 to the 13C to build, has been constantly modified over the ages. The **Portada Sur** (South Door), in the Compostelan style, lacks a tympanum, but is profusely decorated with carvings on covings and capitals. The **Portada Norte** (North Door) has two statue columns and, beneath a great ornamental arch, a 15C Deposition framed by a Flight into Egypt and statues of the Holy Women.

The **interior** is noteworthy for its pure lines. At the end of the 15C, a Gothic-Renaissance transitional style **lantern** was built above the transept. The high altar has an ornate Gothic retable by Cornelius de Holanda. The 16 and 17C **Capilla del Santísimo Cristo** (Chapel of the Holy Sacrament), decorated with exuberant sculpture in the Galician baroque style, opens off the north transept. The triple-arched **Pórtico del Paraíso**★★ (Paradise Door) at the west end, with its beautiful carvings and bright medieval colouring, illustrates the same theme as the Pórtico de la Gloria in Santiago cathedral. The central arch shows the 24 Old Men of the Apocalypse; to the right is the Last Judgment. The pierced tympanum above, like the narthex vaulting, is 16C.

A door in the south aisle opens onto the 13C chapter house, now a **museum**. Among the items displayed are church plate, statues, chasubles and a 12C travelling altar.

Museo Arqueológico y de Bellas Artes (Archaeological and Fine Arts Museum) (**M¹**) ○ – The finely emblasoned façade overlooking the Plaza Mayor belongs to the former episcopal palace, now a museum. The collections inside include prehistoric specimens, *castro* cultural objects (mainly statues of warriors) and a section of fine arts with, in particular, an early-18C wood carving of the **Camino del Calvario**★ (Stations of the Cross).

★**Claustro de San Francisco** ○ – The elegant 14C cloisters consist of slightly horseshoe-shaped Gothic arches resting on slender, paired columns to which a diamond and leaf decoration adds simple sophistication. Some of the capitals illustrate scenes of the hunt or historic personages.

For a quiet place to stay
consult the annual *Michelin Red Guide España Portugal*
which gives a choice of pleasant hotels.

EXCURSION

★ Round tour of 65km - 40 miles – *2 1/2 hours plus 1/2 hour for a tour of the monastery. Leave Orense on the C536 east; turn left after 6km - 3 1/2 miles onto a road going north to Luintra; continue for 18km - 11 miles.*

Monasterio de San Estevo de Ribas de Sil – The monastery appears suddenly in a majestic **setting ★**, spread over a great spur, against a background of granite mountains deeply cut by the Sil. The church's Romanesque east end remains, as do the three cloisters, built to grandiose proportions largely in the 16C, although one still has Romanesque galleries surmounted by elegant low arches.

★ Gargantas del Sil (Gorges of the Sil river) – *Return on the downhill road on the left towards the Sil (do not take the signposted turning to the Embalse de San Esteban). Two dams, one vaulted, the other a buttressed type, control the waters of the Sil which flow through deep gorges.*
At the second dam, without leaving the left bank of the river, turn into the road marked Embalse de San Pedro which joins the N 120. Bear left for Orense.

Monasterio Santa María la Real de OSEIRA★

Galicia (Orense)
Michelin map 441 E 6 – Michelin Atlas España Portugal p 7

The grandiose Cistercian monastery, commonly known as the Escorial of Galicia, was founded by Alfonso VII in the middle of the 12C. It stands in an isolated position in the Arenteiro valley, a region that once abounded in bears *(osos)* as the monastery's name suggests.

Monasterio ⊘ – The **façade** (1708) consists of three sections. In a niche below the statue of Hope which crowns the doorway is the figure of a Nursing Madonna with St Bernard at her feet. Of note inside the monastery are an **escalera de honor** (grand staircase) and the **Claustro de los Medallones** (Medallion Cloisters) decorated with 40 busts of famous historic personages.

Iglesia – Behind the baroque façade of 1637, the 12-13C church has retained the customary Cistercian simplicity modified only by the frescoes in the transept which were painted in 1694.

★ Sala Capitular – This chapter house dates from the late 15 and early 16C and is outstanding for its beautiful vaulting of crossed ribs descending like the fronds of a palm tree onto four spiral columns.

OSUNA★

Andalucía (Sevilla)
Population 16 240
Michelin map 446 U 14 – Michelin Atlas España Portugal p 84

Osuna is an elegant Andalusian town with a beautiful **monumental centre ★** *(follow the Zona Monumental signs)*, inherited from its former status as a ducal seat. The dukedom was created in 1562 and the house of Osuna has remained one of the greatest in Spain.

Colegiata ⊘ – This C16 Renaissance style collegiate church houses five **paintings ★** by **José de Ribera "Lo Spagnoletto"** (1591-1652), including **The Crucifixion**, in the side chapel off the Nave del Evangelio. The remainder are exhibited in the sacristy.

★ Sepulcro Ducal (Ducal Sepulchre) ⊘ – The first crypt is approached through a delightful *patio* with marble arcades decorated in the Plateresque style; it is a church in miniature. The ceiling roses, once blue and gold, are now black with candle smoke. Below, a second crypt (1901) contains the coffins of the major grandees.

Walk in the town – *Mainly around the Plazas del Duque and España.* The straight lines of the streets are punctuated by the occasional noble baroque façade; massive wooden doors, darkly shining and copper nailed, reveal, when opened, fine wrought-iron grilles and cool green *patios*. Of particular note are the **Calle San Pedro ★** (Cilla del Cabildo, Palacio de los Marqueses de la Gomera), the Antigua Audencia (former Law Courts), the Palacio de los Cepeda, the former Palacio de Puente Hermoso, several fine churches (Santo Domingo, San Agustín) and, near to the Colegiata, the Monasterio de la Encarnación and the former university, both C16.

Gourmets should look in the current **Michelin Red Guide España Portugal**
for the restaurants with stars.

OVIEDO★

Asturias

Population 204 276

Michelin map 441 B 12 – Michelin Atlas España Portugal p 5

Plan of the conurbation in the current Michelin Red Guide España Portugal

Oviedo, the economic and cultural capital of Asturias, is a modern town built on a rise in the middle of a fertile, green basin, with the added attraction of a large park at its centre. It developed in the 18C with the establishment of an arsenal and expanded rapidly in the 19C as the coal basin began to be exploited. It is a university town with a College of Mining Engineering.

The old town round the cathedral with its many ancient broad-fronted seignorial mansions contrasts sharply with the modern city.

The capital of the Kingdom of Asturias (9-10C) – All that the Muslims left of the small city built by Fruela I (722-768) around a Benedictine monastery on a hill named Ovetum, was a pile of ruins. Fruela's son, Alfonso II, the Chaste (791-842), transferred the court from Cangas de Onís and Pravia where it had been previously to Oviedo. He rebuilt the town, encircling it with ramparts and embellishing it with religious buildings of which only traces remain – the Cámara Santa, the east end of San Tirso church and Santullano church. His successor Ramiro I (842-850) continued the royal patronage and built a splendid summer palace which remains, in part, on the slopes of nearby Monte Naranco *(see Excursions below)*.

But in 914, with the extension of the kingdom's boundaries southwards, the king, Don García, transferred the court to León. The Asturias-León Kingdom existed briefly from 1037 to 1157 and then in 1230 was finally incorporated into Castilla. Recognition of a sort returned to the old kingdom in 1388 when the heir apparent to the Castilian throne took the title, Prince of Asturias. The heir to the Spanish throne still carries the same title today.

The Battles of Oviedo – In 1934, following the insurrection in the Asturian mining area, the town was heavily damaged during fighting between insurgent miners and regular forces: the Cámara Santa was destroyed, the university set on fire and the cathedral damaged. In 1937, Oviedo was once more the scene of fighting, this time during the Civil War.

CIUDAD VIEJA (OLD TOWN) *time: 1 1/2 hours*

★Catedral ⊘ – The cathedral, a characteristically Flamboyant Gothic edifice, was begun in the 14C with the construction of the cloisters, and completed in the 16C with that of the porch and the massive 80m - 262ft south tower, which tapers into a delicate openwork spire (restored after the Civil War). Three Gothic portals pierce the asymmetrical façade. The doors, which are considerably later, are panelled in 18C walnut; the centre door bears a figure of Christ *(on the left)* and St Eulalia in a maize field *(on the right)*.

Interior – The triforium surmounted by tall windows, together with the façade and transept rose windows, have the wavy lines typical of Flamboyant Gothic. The open vista down the nave enhances the 16C high **altarpiece ★** of wood, carved with scenes from the Life of Christ.

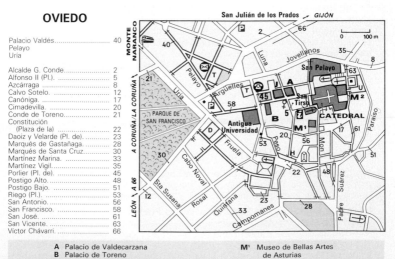

OVIEDO

A Palacio de Valdecarzana
B Palacio de Toreno
J Palacio de Camposagrado

M¹ Museo de Bellas Artes de Asturias
M² Museo Arqueológico

The side chapels were profusely ornamented during the baroque period. On the left on entering, is the overly ornate 17C Capilla de Santa Eulalia, containing the relics of the patron saint of Asturias in a massive baroque shrine.

The **Capilla de Alfonso II el Casto** – Alfonso II was known as The Chaste – off the north transept, stands on the site of the original church and is the pantheon of the Asturian kings. The decoration inside the gate is late Gothic. In the embrasures are the figures of the Pilgrim St James, Sts Peter, Paul and Andrew, in the covings, the 12 old musicians. In the chapel lie the illustrious Asturian kings.

Cámara Santa ⊙ – The Cámara Santa was built by Alfonso II early in the 9C as a shrine for a coffer containing holy relics brought from Toledo *(qv)* on the fall of the Visigothic Kingdom. It was remodelled in Romanesque times and destroyed in an explosion in 1934; the rebuilt chapel contains many of the original works of art.

Six groups of apostles in the vestibule form a series of stylised **statue columns** ★★ which are among the most masterly sculptures of 12C Spain. The head of the Christ figure over the entrance is also remarkable – the artist was obviously influenced by the Pórtico de la Gloria (Doorway of Glory) in Santiago cathedral, which is not surprising as the Cámara Santa was often a stop for pilgrims going to Santiago de Compostela. Column capitals illustrate the marriage of Joseph and Mary, the Holy Women at the Tomb and lion and wild boar hunts.

The **tesoro** (treasury) ★★ in the apse includes an outstanding collection of ancient gold and silver plate: the **Cruz de los Angeles** (Cross of the Angels), a gift from Alfonso II in 808, made of cedar wood and studded with precious gems, Roman cabochons and cameos, the **Cruz de Victoria** (908), faced with chased gold and precious stones, which was carried by Pelayo at the victory of Covadonga *(qv)*, the **Arqueta de las Ágatas** or Agate Reliquary, a gift by Fruela II in 910 and the 11C **Arca Santa**, a silver plated reliquary casket.

Claustro – The cloisters have intersecting pointed arches and delicate tracery in the bays. The **Capilla de Santa Leocadia** *(to the left on entering)* is in fact the Cámara Santa crypt. It is decorated outside *(garden)* with blind arcades and covered inside with barrel vaulting and contains an altar, tombs from the time of Alfonso II and an unusually small stone cubicle. The **sala capitular** (chapter house) contains fine stalls dating from the late 15C.

Plaza de la Catedral (Plaza de Alfonso II) (**5**) – To the left of the cathedral is a garden with low reliefs and busts carved in homage to the Asturian kings. On the north side of the cathedral square is the 17C **Palacio de Valdecarzana** (**A**). *Walk south round the cathedral.* Note the east window of the **Iglesia de San Tirso** – all that remains of the 9C church. The existence of the Moorish *alfiz* in a building of that date remains a mystery.

Museo de Bellas Artes de Asturias (**Fine Arts Museum of Asturias**) (**M**¹) ⊙ – The elegant 18C Palacio de Velarde houses a large collection of paintings in which Asturian artists are particularly well represented. Note the Flemish triptych of the **Adoration of the Magi**, painted during the reign of Emperor Charles V by the master of the *Legend of Mary Magdalene*, and the portrait of Charles II by Carreño de Miranda.

Museo Arqueológico (**Archaeological Museum**) (**M**²) ⊙ – The museum is housed in a former convent.

Two galleries opening off the 15C Plateresque cloisters at ground level contain pre-Romanesque art. Humble fragments and reproductions provide striking evidence of the delicate sophistication of monumental decoration in the Asturian period. Among the exhibits are altars such as that of Naranco surmounted by its original stone, reconstructions of chancel screens, low reliefs often showing Byzantine influence, column bases from San Miguel de Lillo and pierced bays inlaid in walls.

Local prehistoric finds, coins and carved wood objects, including old musical instruments, are on view in the upper cloister.

The façade next to the museum fronts the 17 and 18C **Monasterio de San Pelayo**.

Plaza de Porlier (**45**) – Among the fine palaces on the square are the **Toreno** (**B**), dating from 1673 (now a library) and the **Camposagrado** (**J**), a harmonious 18C edifice now the Law Courts (note the spread eaves).

Antiguo Universidad (**Former University**) – The austerely-fronted building was completed in the 17C. The classical court, although restored, retains much of its former style.

ADDITIONAL SIGHTS

Antiguo Hospital del Principado (**Former Hospital of the Principality**) – *Leave Oviedo on Calle Conde de Toreno (marked on the plan).* The façade of the hospital, which is now a hotel, is emblasoned with a fine baroque **coat of arms** ★.

Iglesia de Santullano or **San Julián de los Prados** ⊙ – The church is an outstanding example of Asturian art in the first half of the 9C with its porch, nave and twin aisles, wide transept and at the east end, three chapels vaulted in brick. The walls are covered in frescoes which, from their composition, suggest a Roman influence. There is a fine Romanesque Crucifix in the central apse. Outside, the east end is typical with a window with a triple arcade and claustra.

ENVIRONS

★**Santuarios del Monte Naranco** (Mount Naranco Church and Chapel) – *4km - 2 miles north-west.*
Of the summer palace built by Ramiro I on the south side of the mountain in the 9C, there remain the former audience chamber, now the Iglesia de Santa María, and the royal chapel, San Miguel. The **panorama** from the site includes Oviedo.

Iglesia de Santa María del Naranco, near Oviedo

★★**Iglesia de Santa María del Naranco** ⊘ – The building is attractive, with harmonious lines: it is square, two-storeyed, supported by grooved buttresses and lit by vast bays. On the upper floor two loggias open off the great chamber covered by barrel vaulting. Exterior and interior decoration have been cleverly adapted to architectural necessity and are often similar in style: clusters of slender cabled colonnettes adorn the pillars; the loggia capitals are Corinthian, those abutting the walls polygonal; the arch ribs descend to the squinches on fluted pilasters and medallions minutely decorated in Byzantine style.

★**Iglesia de San Miguel de Lillo** ⊘ – The chapel was truncated when the east end was remodelled in the 17C. The narrowness of the aisles accentuates the height of the walls in which several claustra type windows remain. The delicacy of the interior carving is a delight: on the door **jambs**★★ are identical scenes in relief of a consul, surrounded by dignitaries, presiding over contests in an arena. A cord motif is repeated on the capitals and on the vaulting in the nave and gallery.

EXCURSIONS

★**Iglesia de Santa Cristina de Lena** ⊘ – *34km - 21 miles south on the N630. At Pola de Lena, head for Vega del Rey and there take the signposted road. Park the car before the viaduct and walk up the steep path (1/4 hour).*
Santa Cristina de Lena is a well-proportioned church built of golden stone. It stands on a rocky crag from which there is a **panoramic view**★ of the green Caudal valley. The little building, which is later than those on Monte Naranco, has a Greek cross plan unusual in Asturias, but the traditional stone vaulting remains, with blind arcades, in which the columns have pyramid-shaped capitals emphasised by a cord motif, sculpted medallions extending the arch ribs and cabled columns in the choir. The nave is separated from the raised choir by an iconostasis in which the superimposed arches increase the impression of balance. The low reliefs in the chancel are Visigothic sculptures, recognizable by their geometric figures and plant motifs, which have been placed in a new setting.

Teverga – *43km - 27 miles southwest on the N634, the 0424 and the 430.*
The road follows the Río Trubia which, after Proaza, enters a narrow gorge. As you emerge, glance back for a **view**★ of the Peñas Juntas cliff face which marks the end of the gorge. Beyond the Teverga fork the road penetrates the enclosed **Desfiladero de Teverga**★ (Teverga Defile).
The **Colegiata de San Pedro de Teverga** ⊘ is just outside La Plaza village. This collegiate church, which is late 12C, has had a porch and tower added. The architecture is an obvious continuation of the pre-Romanesque Asturian style. The building includes a narthex, a tall narrow nave and a flat east end, originally three chapels. The narthex capitals are carved with stylised animal and plant motifs.

SPAIN: the Michelin Map Series at 1:400 000
When choosing a lunchtime or overnight stop
use the above maps as all towns listed in
the Red Guide España Portugal are underlined in red.

When driving into or through a town
use the map as it also indicates all places with
a town plan in the Red Guide España Portugal.
Common reference numbers make the transfer from map to plan easier.

Puerto de PAJARES★★

For many years the Puerto de Pajares, between the provinces of León and Asturias, provided the least arduous route across the western part of the Cordillera Cantábrica. The **road**★★ (N 630) approaching the pass from the south follows the course of the Bernesga to La Robla from where it continues directly upwards across several gullies. In the village of **Arbás**, 1km - 1/2 mile south of the pass, is the Romanesque **Colegiata de Santa María**. Although this collegiate church was modified during the Renaissance, it still retains interesting capitals decorated with plant motifs which show a Byzantine influence.

★★ **The Pass** – The pass at 1 379m - 4 524ft makes an excellent point from which to scan the sharply pointed Cordillera Cantábrica mountain range. Several ski-lifts provide easy access to the heights for winter sports. The *corniche* road down the north side of the mountains is steep in places (15% - 1: 6). There are opencast coalmines on the mountainsides and rocky escarpments overlooking the ravine.

PALENCIA

Castilla y León
Population 81 988
Michelin map 441 F 16 – Michelin Atlas España Portugal p 25
Town plan in the current Michelin Red Guide España Portugal

Palencia, in the fertile Tierra de Campos region, is a long narrow town built along a north-south axis hemmed in to the west by the Río Carríon and to the east by the railway. Immediately surrounding the town is a green swathe of market gardens, irrigated by the Canal de Castilla and its tributaries.
Palencia was the seat of Spain's first university, founded by Alfonso VIII in the early 13C.

★★ **Catedral** ⊙ – Palencia's "beautiful, unknown cathedral" – the townspeople believe the monument is not given sufficient recognition – is a 14-16C Gothic edifice with a good many Renaissance features. In the 7C a chapel was built on the site to enshrine the relics of a Visigothic saint, Antolín. The chapel lay forgotten during the Moorish occupation and for long after, until, according to tradition, Sancho III de Navarra came upon it while hunting wild boar. The king erected a Romanesque chapel (1034) over the ruins which survives today as the crypt to the cathedral.

★★ **Interior** – The centre of the cathedral contains an incredible concentration of works of art in all the different styles of the early 16C: Flamboyant Gothic, Isabelline, Plateresque and Renaissance. This wealth is due to Bishop Fonseca who gathered round him in the early 16C a group of highly skilled artists. The monumental high altar **retable** (early 16C), with its many compartments, was carved by Felipe Vigarny, painted by Juan of Flanders and is surmounted by a Crucifix by Juan de Valmaseda. The 16C tapestries on the sides were commissioned by Bishop Fonseca. The *coro* grille, with a delicately wrought upper section, is by Gaspar Rodríguez (1563); the choir-stalls are Gothic, the organ gallery, above, is dated 1716. The **Capilla del Sagrario** (Chapel of the Holy Sacrament) behind the high altar and closed by a fine Romanesque grille, is exuberantly Gothic with a rich altarpiece by Valmaseda (1529). To the left, and slightly higher up, is the sarcophagus of Queen Urraca of Navarra (d 1189). The sculptures in the *trascoro* are the work of Gil de Siloé and Simon of Cologne; the central **triptych**★ is a masterpiece, painted in Flanders by Jan Joest de Calcar in 1505 – the donor, Bishop Fonseca, is depicted at its centre.
A Plateresque staircase beside the *trascoro* leads to the Romanesque **crypt** which retains several vestiges (arches and capitals) of the 7C Visigothic chapel.

★ **Museo** ⊙ – The museum is to the right of the west door. The collection includes a *St Sebastian* by El Greco and four 15C Flemish **tapestries**★ of the Adoration, the Ascension, Original Sin and the Resurrection of Lazarus. They were commissioned by Bishop Fonseca who had his crest woven into the corners.

EXCURSIONS

Baños de Cerrato – *14km - 9 miles southeast; cross the railway at Venta de Baños before turning right towards Cevico de la Torre. Bear left at the first crossroads.* The Visigothic **Basílica de San Juan Bautista**★ ⊙ is the oldest church in Spain in a good state of preservation. It was built by the Visigothic King Recceswinth, while he was taking the waters in Baños de Cerrato, in 661. The date is shown beneath the apsidal arch. The church consists of three aisles covered in timber vaulting, a transept and three apses. The horseshoe arches separating the aisles are supported on marble columns. The capitals are carved with a stylised foliage motif which includes the long, ribbed leaf which later appeared widely in Asturian art. Note the decorative frieze in the central apse.

PAMPLONA / IRUÑEA★

Navarra
Population 191 197
Michelin map 442 D 25 – Michelin Atlas España Portugal p 15

Pamplona is the main town of the Spanish Pyrenees. Of the period when it was capital of the kingdom of Navarra and a fortified city, there remain, around the cathedral, a quarter of old houses lining narrow streets and ramparts to the north and east overlooking the Río Arga.

Modern quarters – wide, straight avenues, lined by luxurious buildings **(Paseo de Sarasate)** (**AY 72**), arcaded squares decorated with fountains and flowers **(Plaza del Castillo)** (**BY**) – have been developed, extending the southern periphery. Finally, a wide green belt of parks and gardens **(La Taconera)** (**AY**), rings this now prosperous looking city and its large private university.

On a lighter note, Pamplona is renowned for its coffee-flavoured caramels and its famous *feria*.

The "Sanfermines" – The *feria* of San Fermín is celebrated with joyous ardour from 6 to 14 July each year. Visitors pour in, doubling the town's population, to see the great evening bullfights and enjoy the carefree atmosphere (described by Hemingway in *Fiesta, The Sun Also Rises*). The most spectacular event, and the one most prized by "Pamplonés", however, is the **encierro** or early morning *(around 8am)* running of the bulls. The beasts selected to fight in the evening are let loose to rush through the streets along a set route, 800m - 875yds long, which leads to the bullring in a matter of minutes. Youths costumed in white with red berets, scarves and sashes, and brandishing rolled-up newspapers, run with them. The festival is broadcast live on Spanish television and eagerly watched by the entire country. The following ditty is sung in accompaniment:

"Uno de enero, dos de febrero	*1st January, 2nd February*
Tres de marzo, cuatro de abril	*3rd March, 4th April*
Cinco de mayo, seis de junio	*5th May, 6th June*
Y siete de julio, San Fermín	*and 7th July, San Fermín"*

Sanfermines, running with the bulls in Pamplona

Dibujo de una fotografía de Marín

Historical notes – Pamplona goes back to Roman times and is said to have been founded by Pompey who, tradition has it, gave the town his name. In the 8C, the Moors occupied the town briefly before being expelled with the help of Charlemagne, who, however, took advantage of the weakness of the native forces to dismantle the city walls. In revenge the people of Navarra took part in the historic massacre of Charlemagne's rearguard in the Roncesvalles pass.

In the 10C Pamplona became the capital of Navarra. Throughout the Middle Ages, the city was troubled by disputes between the citizens of the old quarter – the Navarrería – who supported an alliance with Castilla, and the freemen who lived on the city outskirts in the districts of San Cernin and San Nicolás and favoured the retention of the Navarra crown by a French line.

The disputes were settled in 1423 when Charles III, the Noble, promulgated the Union between the three municipalities. They joined to become a single city and Pamplona reached the peak of its power. Building of the citadel began during the reign of Philip II in 1571.

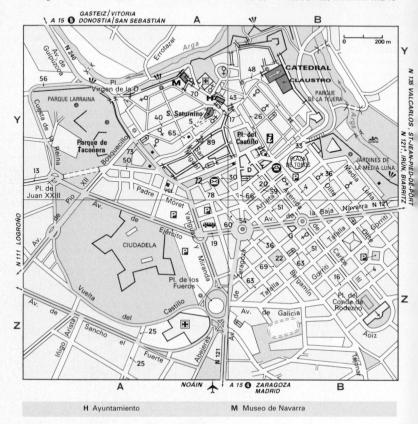

H Ayuntamiento   M Museo de Navarra

SIGHTS

★**Catedral** (**BY**) ⊙ – The present Gothic cathedral was built in the 14 and 15C over an earlier Romanesque edifice whose only remains (doorway and cloister capitals) are now in the Museo de Navarra. At the end of the 18C, Ventura Rodríguez rebuilt the west front in the baroque and neo-classical style then fashionable. The nave, only two tiers high, has wide arches and windows and, with plain ribbing and great bare walls, the unadorned appearance typical of Navarra Gothic. Before the finely wrought grille closing the sanctuary, stands the alabaster **tomb**★, commissioned in 1416 by Charles III the Noble, founder of the cathedral, for himself and his queen. The expressive reclining figures and mourners were carved by the Frenchman, Janin Lomme. Note the late-15C Hispano-Flemish altarpiece (south ambulatory chapel).

★**Claustro** – 14-15C. The cloisters have a delicate appearance, with elegant Gothic arches surmounted, in some cases, by gables. Sculptured tombs and doors add interest; note the Dormition of the Virgin on the tympanum of the cloister door which is almost baroque in expression.

Off the east gallery is the Capilla Barbazán – a chapel named after the bishop who had it built to house his tomb – which has beautiful 14C star vaulting. On the south side the doorway of the Sala Preciosa is a key piece in the sculpture of the period, with tympanum and lintel beautifully carved with scenes from the Life of the Virgin and, on either side of the door, two statues together forming a fine Annunciation.

Museo Diocesano ⊙ – The diocesan museum is in the old refectory and adjoining kitchen, which date from 1330. The refectory, a lofty hall with six pointed arches, contains a reader's rostrum decorated with an enchanting scene of a unicorn hunt. The square kitchen, with a fireplace in each corner, has a central lantern rising to a height of 24m - 79ft. The museum displays religious objects including a 13C *Reliquary of the Holy Sepulchre* donated by St Louis (Louis IX of France) and polychrome wood statues of the Virgin and Christ from all parts of the province.

On leaving the cathedral follow the narrow, picturesque Calle del Redín to the ramparts.

Murallas (Ramparts) – A small bastion, now a garden, commands a view of the fortified Puerta de Zumalacárregui (a gate which is visible below and to the left) and a stretch of the old walls and, further away, a bend in the Río Arga and Monte Cristóbal.

★ **Museo de Navarra (AY M)** ⊙ – The Navarra museum was built on the site of a 16C hospital of which the Renaissance gateway has been preserved. The Roman period is represented by lapidary exhibits such as funerary steles, inscriptions and **mosaic**★ pavements from 2 and 4C villas. The mosaics are principally geometric and often in black and white – gallery 3, however, contains an illustration of Theseus and the Minotaur.

Pride of place is given to the Romanesque period with **capitals**★ from the former 12C cathedral of Pamplona on which an unknown artist carved three Biblical scenes – the Passion, the Resurrection and the Story of Job – with a care for detail only equalled by his mastery of composition and brilliance of imagination.

Gothic and Renaissance paintings are also on display. The first three galleries, reconstituted as the interior of the Palacio de Oriz, are decorated with 16C monochrome painted panels depicting the story of Adam and Eve and the wars of Emperor Charles V. The galleries that follow contain fragments of **wall paintings**★ from different periods and all areas of the province: Artaíz (13C), Artajona and Pamplona (13 and 14C), Gallipienzo (14 and 15C) and Olleta (15C). The apparently diverse collection has common characteristics – the unobtrusive emphasis on face and feature, the crowds, the sideways stance – passed down from French miniaturists and well exemplified in Juan Olivier's refectory mural, painted in 1330 *(gallery 24)*. Among the major works exhibited in the museum are the early-11C Hispano-Arab ivory **arqueta**★ (casket) from Córdoba and the portrait of the *Marqués de San Adrián* by Goya.

Before leaving, look at the large mosaic from the Roman villa of Liédena (2C) in the courtyard.

Iglesia de San Saturnino (AY) ⊙ – This composite church at the centre of a tangle of narrow streets in the old quarter has a mingled architecture of Romanesque brick towers, 13C Gothic porch and vaulting and numerous later additions.

Ayuntamiento (Town Hall) (AY H) – This has a reconstructed baroque façade originally dating from the late 17C with statues, balustrades and pediments.

EXCURSION

★ **Valle del Bidasoa** – *Leave town to the east by the Avenida de la Baja Navarra. 100km - 62 miles north on the N 121A, NA 254 and N 121B.*

The Bidasoa has cut a course through the lower foothills of the western Pyrenees. Villages of typical Basque houses lie surrounded by lush meadows and fields of maize. The N 121 winds through hilly country over the Velate pass. The NA 254 then leads through Berroeta, Irurita and on to **Elizondo**, capital of the **Valle del Baztán** which is home to the many *Indianos* or *Americanos*, as Basques who go to Latin America to make their fortune and then return, are known. Many of the house façades are decorated with armorial bearings.

By returning to the N 121 and heading north, you enter the ancient confederation of the **Cinco Villas** or five delightful towns (off minor roads on either side of the N 121): **Etxalar, Arantza, Igantzi, Lesaka** and **Bera**. The house façades, typical of Basque architecture, have deep eaves which shelter wooden balconies with delicate balustrades. The Bidasoa enters a narrow gorge the Garganta de Endarlaza, and continues through the Basque country to the sea, marking the frontier between Spain and France.

El PARDO

Madrid

Michelin map 444 or 442 K 18 – Michelin Atlas España Portugal p 39

The town, now on the outskirts of Madrid, has grown around one of the royal residences. Its surrounding forests of holm oak, often painted by Velázquez, were the traditional hunting preserve of Spanish monarchs.

King Juan Carlos I lives 5km – 3 miles to the southwest in the **Palacio de la Zarzuela**.

★ **Palacio Real** ⊙ – The royal palace was built by Philip III (1598-1621) on the site of Philip II's palace (1556-1598) which had been destroyed in a fire in 1604, and remodelled by Sabatini in 1772. For a long time the palace was the residence of the Head of State; Franco lived here for 35 years. Today, it is used by foreign Heads of State on official visits. As you walk through the reception rooms and private apartments you will see elegant ensembles from Charles IV's collections including furniture, chandeliers and clocks. More than 200 **tapestries**★ illustrating hunting scenes and country life, hang on the walls; the majority are 18C from the Real Fábrica de Tápices (Royal Tapestry Factory) in Madrid after cartoons by Goya, Bayeu, González Ruiz and Van Loo.

Casita del Príncipe (The Prince's Pavilion) ⊙ – The pavilion, built in 1772 for the children of the future Charles IV and his wife María Luisa, was completely remodelled by Juan de Villanueva in 1784. It is a single-storeyed building of brick and stone decorated in the extremely ornate, refined taste fashionable in the late 18C with silk hangings and Pompeian style ceilings.

La Quinta ⊙ – The former residence of the Duke of Arcos became crown property in 1745. Inside, elegant early-19C wallpaper embellishes the walls.

Convento de Capuchinos (Capuchin Monastery) – A chapel contains one of the major works of Spanish sculpture, a polychrome wood figure of **Christ Recumbent ★** by Gregorio Fernández. It was commissioned by Philip III in 1605.

PEDRAZA DE LA SIERRA★★

Castilla y León (Segovia)
Population 448
Michelin map 442 or 444 I 18 – Michelin Atlas España Portugal p 39

Pedraza, perched on a knoll, has kept much of the atmosphere of a seignorial town as it stands encircled by medieval walls and surveyed by a powerful castle on the crag. A fortified gateway opens into a maze of steep, narrow alleys, bordered with country style houses, many with family crests. The **Plaza Mayor**, one of the most delightful main squares in Castilla, is framed by ancient porticoes superimposed by wide balconies, and a slender Romanesque bell tower.

EXCURSION

Sepúlveda – *25km - 16 miles north.*
By approaching Sepúlveda from Pedraza you will get a good view of its terraced **site ★** on the slopes of a deep gorge. Leave the car in the town hall square, overlooked by the old castle ruins, and walk up to the **Iglesia de San Salvador** from which there is a fine view of the town and surrounding countryside. The church itself is typical Segovia Romanesque with a multiple storeyed belfry with paired bays and an east end decorated with a carved cornice. It has one of the oldest side doors in Spain, dating from 1093.
The restaurants are renowned for their roast lamb *(cordero asado).*

PEÑAFIEL★

Castilla y León (Valladolid)
Population 5 003
Michelin map 442 H 17 – Michelin Atlas España Portugal p 25

Peñafiel was one of the strongpoints in the fortified line *(p 257)* built along the Duero during the Reconquest.

★ **Castillo** – The village of Peñafiel is dominated by its redoubtable 14C castle, built to massive proportions at the meeting point of three valleys. The fortress consists of two concentric oblong perimeters built along the ridge. Crowning it, within the second, fairly well preserved perimeter, is a characteristically Castilian square keep, reinforced at its summit by machicolated turrets.

Iglesia de San Pablo – The church (1324) has a Mudéjar east end, and inside, Renaissance vaulting over the 16C Capilla del Infante (Infante Chapel).

Plaza del Coso – The vast, typically Castilian square is almost completely ringed by houses with wide balconies which serve as galleries for viewing bullfights held below.

PEÑARANDA DE DUERO★

Castilla y León (Burgos)
Population 609
Michelin map 442 G 19 – Michelin Atlas España Portugal p 26

The small Castilian town is dominated by the ruins of its **castle**.

★ **Plaza Mayor** – The square forms an interesting architectural unit of half-timbered houses resting on robust stone pillars; at its centre is a 15C pillory.

★ **Palacio de Avellaneda** ⊙ – The palace with its noble façade and fully ornamented Renaissance entrance fronts the Plaza Mayor. The interior, designed by Francisco de Colonia, makes it one of the finest Renaissance residences in Spain. There is a *patio* surrounded by a two tier gallery, an inner *patio* arch, a grand staircase and chambers with **artesonado ceilings ★**.

PEÑÍSCOLA★★

Comunidad Valenciana (Castellón)

Population 3 677

Michelin map 443 or 445 K 31 – Michelin Atlas España Portugal p 57

Peñíscola, a rocky peninsula (from which the name derives) closely built up now with white-walled cottages to the foot of the stone castle at the summit, was the final refuge of the medieval antipope, **Benedict XIII**.

A modern resort is developing on either side of the neck of the promontory, beside the vast sand beaches. The fishing harbour below the old town comes to life in the late afternoon when the boats bring home their catch.

Pope Luna – On the death of the antipope Clement VII in 1394, the Aragonese Cardinal Pedro de Luna was elected successor by the French cardinals in conclave at Avignon. It was a dubious heritage, however, as his predecessor had never succeeded in establishing his claim. The withdrawal of the support of King Charles VI of France and of St Vincent Ferrer *(qv)*, the accusation of heresy by the Councils of Pisa (1409) and Constance (1416), in no way diminished the self-styled Benedict XIII's conviction of his right. He considered the proposal that he should abdicate and help to seal the schism inadmissible and, in the face of general hostility, sought refuge in the fortress on Peñíscola There he remained until he died in 1422, a nonagenarian, tenacious as ever, who even named his own successor! (This prelate, however, soon abdicated in favour of the Rome elected Martin V).

★CIUDAD VIEJA (OLD TOWN) *Closed to cars – time: 1 hour*

The old town huddled within the ramparts, which date from the reign of Philip II, makes for a pleasant stroll. It has narrow winding streets lined with souvenir shops.

Castillo ⊘ – The castle, built by the Templars in the 14C, was modified by Pope Luna whose coat of arms, which features a crescent moon in allusion to his name, can be seen on one of the gates. Grouped round the parade ground are the church, a vast hall with pointed vaulting and a free standing tower containing the conclave room and the study of the learned antipope who, among his many acts, confirmed in six bulls the foundation in 1411 of St Andrew's University in Scotland *(see Michelin Green Guide to Scotland)* and promulgated the Statutes of Salamanca University.

There is a **panorama**★ of the village and coastline from the castle terrace.

Peñíscola promontory

A. Muñoz de Pablos/EXPLORER

*Help us in our constant task of keeping up to date.
Send your comments and suggestions to*

Michelin Tyre PLC
Tourism Department
The Edward Hyde Building
38 Clarendon Road
WATFORD Herts WD1 15X
Fax: 01923 415250

PICOS DE EUROPA★★★

Castilla y León, Asturias, Cantábria

Michelin map 441 C 14-16 – Michelin Atlas España Portugal p 11

The Picos de Europa, the highest range in the Cordillera Cantábria (Torre Cerredo: 2648m - 8688ft), stand massed between Oviedo and Santander, some 30km - 20 miles from the sea.

Gorges, cut by torrents teaming with fish, circumscribe the Primary limestone formation and have divided it into three blocks: the western or Covadonga massif, the central or Naranjo de Bulnes massif and the eastern or Andara massif. The impressive landscape is one of deep clefts as well as high peaks, jagged with erosion and always snow-capped. The south face is less steep and looks out over a less abrupt but harsher terrain.

Besides the traditional occupations of *cabrales* making – a blue cheese made of ewes' milk – and stock raising, there is mining in the area. The Liébana region, around Potes, has a mild climate sheltered from the northwest winds and grows walnuts, cherries and medlars and even grapes halfway up the slopes.

The Picos de Europa form a restricted hunting reserve (Reserva Nacional de Los Picos de Europa) and the Parque Nacional de Covadonga which covers 17000ha - 42000 acres of the western massif. Since 1995, the park has been enlarged and is now part of the **Parque nacional de los Picos de Europa** (64660ha - 159780 acres).

★★DESFILADERO DE LA HERMIDA (LA HERMIDA DEFILE)

① From Panes to Potes
27km - 17 miles – about 1 hour – local map below

The outstanding feature of the drive is the **ravine★★**, some 20km-12 miles long in all, which extends either side of a basin containing the hamlet of La Hermida. The gorge is narrow and so lacking in sunlight as to be bare of vegetation; the Deva has sought out weaknesses in the rock wall to carve out a saw-tooth course.

Iglesia de Nuestra Señora de Lebeña ⊘ – The small 10C Mozarabic church stands surrounded by poplars at the foot of tall cliffs. The belfry and porch are later additions. The semicircular vaulting over the three aisles rests on horseshoe-shaped arches decorated with beautifully carved Corinthian style capitals.

Potes – Potes is a delightful village in a pleasing **site★** set in the hollow of a fertile basin against a background of jagged crests, the peaks of the central massif. From the bridge there is a view, reflected in the Deva, of old stone houses and the austere 15C **Torre del Infantado**, a restored tower which now serves as the town hall *(Ayuntamiento)*.

★★THE CLIMB TO FUENTE DÉ

② *30km - 19 miles – about 3 hours – local map right*

The road follows the Deva through a mixed landscape of mountain woods and meadows dotted here and there with the pink tile roofs of villages *(photograph p 12)*. Finally it reaches the wild rock cirque of Fuente Dé where the river rises.

Monasterio de Santo Toribio de Liébana ⊘ – *Approach along a signposted road on the left (heading back towards Potes from Fuente Dé).* The monastery now occupied by Franciscans, was founded in the 7C and grew to considerable importance in the following century when a fragment of the True Cross, brought from Jerusalem by Turibius, Bishop of Astorga, was placed in its safekeeping. A *camarín (access through the north aisle of the church)* now contains the fragment (the largest known piece of the True Cross) in the *lignum crucis* reliquary, a silver gilt Crucifix. The church, transitional Romanesque in style, has been restored to its original harmonious proportions. The monastery was also the house of **Beatus**, the 8C monk famous for his **Commentary on the Apocalypse** which was copied in the form of illuminated manuscripts *(photograph p 33)*.

There is a **view★** of Potes and the central range from the lookout point at the end of the road.

★★ **Fuente Dé** – The *parador* is at 1 000m - 3 300ft. Nearby is the starting point of the cableway **(teleférico ⊘)** which rises a further 800m - 2 625ft to the terminal at the top of the sheer rock face. During the **ascent** you may see wild chamois. The **Mirador del Cable★★** at the terminal commands a splendid panorama of the upper valley of the Deva and Potes, and the peaks of the central range.

A path leads to the Aliva refuge. The effect of erosion on the upper heights of karst limestone are spectacular, producing long stony plateaux and huge sink-holes known as **hoyos**.

★PUERTO DE SAN GLORIO (SAN GLORIO PASS)

③ From Potes to Oseja de Sajambre
83km - 52 miles – about 3 hours – local map below

The road crosses the green Quiviesa valley with its poplar woods, then begins to climb through mountain pastures. 10km - 6 miles beyond Bores, a series of bends affords a changing panorama on the left. The drive up to the San Glorio pass is through silent, lonely countryside.

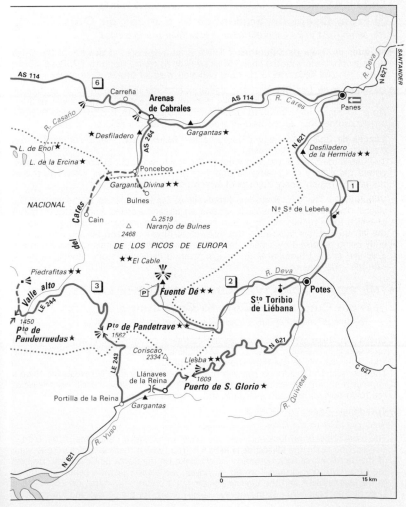

★ **Puerto de San Glorio** – Alt 1 609m - 5 279ft. A track leads north *(1 hour Rtn)* to near the Peña de Llesba, where the **Mirador de Llesba** forms a magnificent natural **viewpoint** ★★ for the highest crests: to the right is the east range and to the left the central massif with its steep south face dominating the Fuente Dé. The peak in the left foreground is the Coriscao (2 234m - 7 330ft).

The scenery remains austere until you come to the village of **Llánaves de la Reina**, tucked into the opening of the **Gargantas de Yuso** (Yuso Gorge) which is spectacular for its rock colouring.

At Portilla de la Reina, bear right into the LE 243.

★★ **Puerto de Pandetrave** – An ascent through the high mountains brings you to the pass (1 562m - 5 125ft) and a **panorama** of the three ranges with, in the right foreground, the Cabén de Remoña and Torre de Salinas, both part of the central massif, and in the distance, lying in a hollow, the village of Santa Marina de Valdeón.

The road between Santa Marina de Valdeón and Posada de Valdeón is narrow but practicable.

★ **Puerto de Panderruedas** – The road climbs to mountain pastures at an altitude of 1 450m - 4 757ft. Walk up the path to the left *(1/4 hour Rtn)* to the **Mirador de Piedrafitas** ★★ *(viewing table)* from where there is an impressive view of the immense cirque which closes off the Valdeón valley. To the northeast can be seen the Torre Cerredo (2 648m - 8 688ft), the highest peak in the range.

★ **Puerto del Pontón** – Alt 1 280m - 4 200ft. From the pass you will get a picturesque **view** ★★ of the Sajambre valley.

The descent to Oseja de Sajambre *(see below)* begins with tight hairpin bends in full view of the western range; it continues as a spectacular *corniche* (tunnels) during which you can see the formidable rock wall through which the Sella has hollowed its course.

★★★DESFILADERO DE LOS BEYOS (LOS BEYOS DEFILE)

④ From Oseja de Sajambre to Cangas de Onís
38km – 24 miles - about 1 hour – local map previous page

★★ **Mirador de Oseja de Sajambre** – There is an awe-inspiring **view** ★★ of the Oseja de Sajambre basin with the sharp Niaja peak at its centre rising to 1 732m-5 682ft, and of the Los Beyos defile opening between walls of broken rock strata.

★★★ **Desfiladero de Los Beyos** – The defile, one of the most beautiful in Europe, is 10km - 6 miles long, cut by the Sella through an exceptionally thick layer of limestone. Though wide enough to allow sunlight to penetrate, it is too precipitous for anything other than an occasional tree to have gained a hold on its sides.

Cangas de Onís – An elegant hump-backed **Roman bridge** *(puente romano)* across the Sella lies west of the town.

The Capilla de Santa Cruz, also west of the town, was built in Contranquil, to celebrate the victory of Covadonga and was rebuilt after the Civil War. The chapel houses the region's only dolmen of which one stone is engraved.

Villanueva – The 17C **Monasterio Benedictino de San Pedro** stands at the end of the village. The monastery was built around an already existing Romanesque church of which there remain the apse and an elegantly decorated side portal – note on the left the capitals illustrating the farewell of King Favila and his sad end, apparently being devoured by a bear. Inside there are further capitals to be seen in the apse and at the triumphal arch. Imaginatively ornamented stone modillions decorate the apse exterior.

★★THE ROAD TO COVADONGA AND THE LAKES

⑤ From Cangas de Onís to Covadonga
35km – 22 miles - about 3 hours – local map previous page

Cueva del Buxu ⊙ – The cave in the cliff face contains charcoal drawings and rock engravings dating back to the Magdalenian period. There are a stag, horse and bison scarcely larger than the size of a hand.

The approach to Covadonga *(from a road to the right)* gradually reveals the town's impressive mountain setting. The Covadonga and Peña Santa massifs southeast of the town now form a national park and a wildlife sanctuary.

Covadonga – See COVADONGA.

Take the CO 4 to the lakes.

The road is steep; on looking back you have an extensive panorama. After 8km – 5 miles, you reach the **Mirador de la Reina** ★★ from where there is a picturesque view of the succession of rock pyramids which make up the Sierra de Covalierda. Beyond the pass, two rock cirques formed by *hoyos (see above)*, provide beautiful settings to the **Lago de Enol** ★ and the **Lago de Ercina** ★ (alt 1 232m - 4 042ft). On 25 July, the Lago de Enol Shepherd's Festival draws large crowds for the dances and kayak races.

★★GARGANTAS DEL CARES (CARES GORGES)

6 From Covadonga to Panes *90km - 56 miles – about 1 day*

As you come out of Las Estazadas village there is a splendid **panorama**★★ of the rock wall which closes off the Río Casaño valley. From a viewpoint on the right, shortly after Carreña de Cabrales, there is a glimpse of the fang-like crest of **Naranjo de Bulnes** (2519m - 8264ft).

Arenas de Cabrales – Arenas, as its name suggests, is the main production centre for *cabrales*, a blue ewes' milk cheese. The road now, for a while, skirts the Río Cares.

Bear right into the AS264 which runs through the upper Cares valley.

Upper Cares valley – The Poncebos road leads south, through a pleasant **ravine**★. After the Embalse de Poncebos (Poncebos Reservoir) a track *(3 hours Rtn on foot)* leads to the mountain village of Bulnes. From Poncebos to Caín *(3 1/2 hours' walk one way)* a path follows the Cares and plunges down into the **defile**★★ before reaching the foot of the central massif *(here you can hire a car with a driver to take you back to Poncebos)*.

Return to the AS114.

Beyond Arenas the **gorges**★ are green with moss and even the occasional tree. Narrow hump-backed road bridges and fragile looking footbridges span the emerald waters of the river.

Monasterio de PIEDRA★★

PIEDRA MONASTERY – Aragón (Zaragoza)
Michelin map 442 or 443 I24 – Michelin Atlas España Portugal p 42

On the approach to the monastery by way of Ateca or the spa, Alhama de Aragón, the roads cross the arid, red earth countryside above the Tranquera reservoir. The village of **Nuévalos** comes into view, high up against a clay hillside.

The site – Hidden in a fold of the dried out plateau is a green oasis fed by the Río Piedra. It was discovered and settled by Cistercian monks, who generally chose pleasant surroundings for their retreats. The monks in this case came from the Abbey of Poblet in Tarragona and established a monastery on the spot in 1194. This was rebuilt several times and suffered damage in the 19C. The conventual buildings have been reconstructed as a hotel.

★★ **Parque y cascadas (Park and waterfalls)** ⊙ – Waterfalls and cascades are to be seen along the marked footpath through the heart of the forest *(follow the red signposts to go and the blue ones to return)*. The paths, steps and tunnels laid out last century by **Juan Federico Muntadas** have transformed an impenetrable forest into a popular park. The first fall is the **Cola de Caballo** (Horse's Tail), a cascade of 53m - 174ft. This you first look down on from a viewpoint and come on again at the end of your walk if you descend the steep and slippery steps into the beautiful Cueva Iris (Iris Grotto), when you will see it from the back. **Baño de Diana** (Diana's Bath) and the romantic **Lago del Espejo** (Mirror Lake), cupped between tall cliffs, are both worth a halt.

The signposted route ends outside the park at the monastery ruins. Of the Gothic building there remain the kitchen, refectory and cloisters.

PIRINEOS ARAGONESES★★

THE PYRENEES IN ARAGÓN – Aragón (Huesca)
Michelin map 443 D28-32, E29-32, F 30-31 – Michelin Atlas España Portugal pp 16-17

The central Spanish Pyrenees, in the northern part of the province of Huesca, include the highest peaks in the Pyrenean chain: Aneto (3404m - 11168ft), Posets (3371m - 11060ft) and Monte Perdido (3355m - 11007ft). The foothills are often ravined and covered only with sparse vegetation; the landscape at the heart of the massif, accessible up the river courses, is on a different scale altogether. The valleys, whether wide and lush or narrow and gullied, lead to mountain cirques well worth exploring.

Structure and relief – The geological division of the Pyrenees into vast longitudinal bands can be clearly seen in this region. The **axis of Primary terrain** and granite rocks comprises the Maladeta, Posets, Vignemale and Balaïtous massifs, where there are still remains of the Quaternary glaciers. There follows the Pre-Pyrenees or Monte Perdido region where the deep **Secondary limestone** layer has been deeply eroded to form an area of sharp relief: the canyons, gorges and cirques of the upper valleys. The limestone area, which extends in broken mountain chains as far as the Ebro Basin (Sierras de Guara and de la Peña) is divided at Jaca by a long depression through which the Río Aragón flows. Tertiary sediment has accumulated into hills, some of which remain bare of vegetation, affording an unusual blue marl landscape like that around the Yesa artificial lake.

Life in the valleys – The upper valleys of the Kingdom of Aragón developed an independent political and pastoral way of life based on self-contained communities very early in their history. In spite of improved roads, local individuality remains, folklore is still followed and native costume worn in certain valleys like the **Ansó** *(qv)*. Here no farm stands isolated from its neighbour; hamlets and villages are numerous but the inhabitants leave their slate covered cottages to work in Zaragoza, Pamplona and Barcelona. The raising of mountain sheep is declining while that of cattle is increasing. There is some industry, such as the chemical and aluminium works at **Sabiñánigo**.

Major hydroelectric undertakings are bringing life to certain areas; artificial lakes now lie in previously barren valleys: the **Yesa** in the Aragón, **La Peña** in the Gállego, **El Grado** in the Cinca, **Canelles** and **Escales** in the Noguera Ribagorçana.

Tourism is becoming one of the major economic activities in the region with the development of winter sports resorts such as Candanchú, Astún, Canfranc, Panticosa, El Formigal and Benasque.

☐1 FROM VIELHA TO BENASQUE

122km - 76 miles – about 3 hours – local map below

Vielha – *See PIRINEOS CATALANES: Vall d'Arán.*

The road cuts through the Maladeta massif by way of the Vielha tunnel which ends in the lonely upper valley of the Noguera Ribagorçana where the attractive hamlet of **Vilaller** stands huddled around a hillock. A little further south the valley opens onto the **Embalse de Escales★** (Escales Dam).

★ **Valle de Benasque** – **Benasque** (1 138m - 3 734ft) lies in an open valley, lush and green in spite of its altitude, overshadowed by the Maladeta massif. The town serves as a base for walkers, climbers (ascending the Aneto) and skiers (Cerler 5km - 3 miles away). Benasque's narrow streets are lined with old seignorial mansions.

☐2 FROM BENASQUE TO AINSA

180km - 112 miles – about 1/2 day – local map below

As the road heads south through the Esero valley, it follows the **Congosto de Ventamillo★**, a defile of 3km - 2 miles with sheer limestone rock walls.

Graus – The village huddles around its irregular shaped square, the Plaza de España, lined with old houses decorated with frescoes, carved beams and brick arcades. 25km - 16 miles northeast on the A 1605 is the picturesque village of

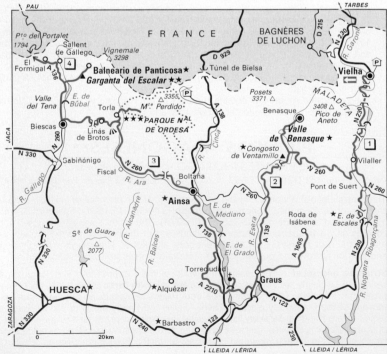

Roda de Isábena in a beautiful mountain setting ★. The **Catedral** ⊘ has an 11C east end with Lombard bands and contains, in the crypt, the **tomb of San Ramón** ★ with polychrome low reliefs. A chapel off the cloisters is adorned with 13C frescoes. The cathedral square is overlooked by the façades of ancient buildings.

The road beyond Graus runs westwards past **Torreciudad** *(qv)*, then heads north skirting the turquoise El Grado and Mediano dams set in a weird black marl landscape.

★ **Ainsa** – Ainsa stands on a promontory still girded by a wall, commanding the juncture of the Cinca and Ara rivers. In the 11C the town was the capital of a small kingdom. Today, its arcaded **Plaza Mayor** ★ in the upper part of town, dominated by the tower of a Romanesque church, is a gem of Aragonese architecture.

③ FROM AINSA TO BIESCAS

81km - 50 miles – about 3 hours – local map opposite

Between Boltaña and Fiscal, the river course has uncovered uneven earth strata which now rise out of the water curiously like dorsal fins. From Broto the great mass of the Mondarruego (alt 2 840m - 9 317ft), closing the Ordesa valley to the north, provides a backdrop for the spectacular **landscape** ★★ in which the small village of **Torla** can be seen massed against the western slope of the Ara valley.

★★★ **Parque Nacional de Ordesa y Monte Perdido** – *See Parque Nacional de ORDESA Y MONTE PERDIDO.*

Beyond **Torla** you get **views** ★ down the entire length of the Ara valley as the *corniche* road climbs to the pretty village of Linás de Broto.

④ THE PORTALET ROAD

52km - 32 miles – about 2 hours – local map opposite

The **Tena** valley beyond Biescas is at first narrow and boulder strewn but widens out majestically to be filled by the vast Búbal reservoir.

A short distance before Escarilla, bear right into the HU 610 for Panticosa.

★★ **Garganta del Escalar (Escalar Gorge)** – The gorge is so narrow that the sun seldom penetrates its depths; the stream below hollowed out a bed first through limestone and later through lamellar schists and granite. The road cuts down the west slope by long ramps and tight hairpin bends to an austere mountain cirque.

★ **Balneario de Panticosa** – The spa (alt 1 639m - 5 377ft), dominated by the Vignemale peak, is known for the curative properties of its six sulphur and radioactive springs.

Return to Escarilla and continue northwest to Portalet.

The mountain town of **Sallent de Gállego,** a little east of the A 136 at a height of 1 305m - 4 281ft., is a centre for trout fishing and mountaineering while **El Formigal** (alt 1 480m - 4 856ft) further on is a well-equipped ski resort.

Carretera del Portalet – Alt 1 794m - 5 886ft. The pass lies between the Portalet peak and the sharply pointed Aneu summit to the west. The view northwest extends towards the Aneu cirque and the Pic du Midi d'Ossau in France (alt 2 884m - 9 462ft).

Tourist Information Centres
are located on the town plans by the symbol 🖪
and the telephone number and address are listed
in the Michelin Red Guide España Portugal

PIRINEOS CATALANES★★

THE CATALAN PYRENEES – Catalunya (Girona, Lleida)

Michelin map 443 D 32, E 32-37, F 32-37 – Michelin Atlas España Portugal pp 17, 18 and 19

The mountain chain, continuing the ranges which cross Aragón, forms an almost unbroken west-east barrier from Maladeta to the Mediterranean. The last range, as the chain drops from the Pico d'Estats (3 145m - 10 318ft) in the west of Catalunya, to Puigmal (2 910m - 9 547ft) in the centre, is the Albères which plunges finally into the sea at the Cabo de Creus from a height of 700m - 2 297ft.

Advancing south from the granite axial ridge are the Cadí, Boumort and Montsec sierras. The mountains are deeply cut by valleys such as those of the Segre and Nogueras rivers and the Vallespir, Cerdaña and Vall d'Arán basins. Lacking intercommunication, each has become a region on its own with an individual tradition, evident, for instance, in the local Romanesque churches, often decorated, as at Taüll, with unique and, in this case, now well-known frescoes.

1 VALL ALTO DEL TER (UPPER VALLEY OF THE TER)
From the Collado d'Ares to Ripoll
76km - 47 miles - about 2 1/2 hours – local map below

The Ares pass road, which links the French Vallespir (Amélie-les-Bains) with central Catalunya (Ripoll) avoids the frontier post of Le Perthus, which is often crowded, and has the additional advantage of taking in the mountain region and its villages.

Molló – The 12C Romanesque church has a beautiful Catalan belfry.
Take the winding mountain road east to Beget.

Beget – Beget, lying in a small valley through which a rushing stream flows, is an attractive mountain village of stone houses with tiled roofs. Its Romanesque **church** is adorned outside, on the east end, with Lombard bands while the inside boasts a magnificent 12C **Christ in Majesty★**.

Camprodón – Camprodón stands at the confluence of the Ritort and Ter rivers, crossed by a fine **hump-backed bridge**. The village has grown around the Benedictine monastery of **Sant Pere** of which only the 12C church remains.

★**Sant Joan de les Abadesses** – *See SANT JOAN DE LES ABADESSES.*

★**Ripoll** – *See RIPOLL.*

2 LA CERDAÑA
From Ripoll to Puigcerdà
63km - 39 miles - about 2 hours – local map below

The Cerdaña basin, between the Andorran massifs and the Sierra del Cadí, was formed by subsidence. It owes its fertility to the irrigation provided by the Río Segre, a tributary of the Ebro. Since 1659 the Cerdaña has been divided, the northern part, now known as the Cerdagne, going to France under the Treaty of the Pyrenees (1659).
The *corniche* road from Ribes de Freser to Puigcerdà lies nearly always high up the mountainside far above the wooded slopes of the steeply enclosed Freser valley. Beyond the pass the road winds continuously, commanding further spectacular views.

Puigcerdà – The town overlooks the Cerdaña of which it was once the capital and remains the centre. It is an attractive place to wander around with old streets and balconied houses. Puigcerdà's turn-of-the-century mansions hidden in large parks beside the lake are a reminder that the town was, and still is, an elegant holiday resort.

Llívia – *6km - 4 miles from Puigcerdà.* The little town became a Spanish enclave in French territory in 1659. It has picturesque alleyways and a fortified church. Housed in the **museo municipal** ⊙ is an interesting **pharmacy** with pots, boxes and all the paraphernalia of an old apothecary's shop which operated from 1415 to 1926.

★ 3 VALL DEL SEGRE
From Puigcerdà to Tremp
158km - 98 miles – about 1/2 day

The Segre valley is a long depression of fertile basins like that of Urgell in which sediment suitable for cultivation has accumulated.

Bellver de Cerdanya – The town is perched on a rock overlooking the Segre valley.

★**La Seu d'Urgell** – *See under La SEU D'URGELL.*

★ **Garganta de Tresponts** (Tresponts Gorges) – The colour of the rock changes from deep red *(puzolana)* to grey as the river enters the narrow limestone gorges. The river emerges to flow gently through a small green basin of cultivated fields.

★ **Grau de la Granta** – The lake, as narrow as a river, lies enclosed between grey walled cliffs enlivened in the spring by leaping waterfalls – the effect is wonderful from the road.

Return to Coll de Nargó and continue the journey westwards.

★★ **Carretera del Collado de Bóixols** (Bóixols Pass road) – Between Coll de Nargó and Tremp. The road passing below the spur crowned by Coll de Nargó, follows a series of canyons which it dominates most of the time, either along pine and holm oak covered slopes or bare hillsides below yellow and pink limestone crests. There are a good many viewpoints over the fantastic landscape, in particular around the Collado de Bóixols.

You emerge into a wide U-shaped valley where terrace cultivation stretches to the foot of the glacial ridge on which cling the church and few surrounding houses of Bóixols. The road continues to descend the valley which finally merges into the Tremp depression.

★ 4 VALL DEL NOGUERA PALLARESA

From Tremp to the Puerto de la Bonaigua

110km - 68 miles – about 1/2 day

The road through the valley climbs first into the limestone Pre-Pyrenees, past time-worn cliffs behind La Pobla de Segur.

★★ **Desfiladero de Collegats** (Collegats Defile) – Great vertical clefts have been cut by torrents through the soft red, ochre and grey rocks.

You then enter the granite axis of the Pyrenees where the scenery becomes more mountainous and more luxuriant. Tributary valleys like the fresh, green **Llessui**★★ and **Cardós**★ valleys are inhabited by isolated communities.

Bear left into the Espot road.

★★ **Parque Nacional de Aigüestortes and Lago de San Mauricio** – *See Parque Nacional de AIGÜESTORTES and Lago de San Mauricio.*

The village of **Espot**, spread along the banks of a stream full of fish, is an entrance to the park, in particular to the area around the Lago de San Mauricio.

Beyond Esterri d'Aneu, the *corniche* road rises through impressive mountain scenery, where wild horses graze the bare slopes, to the **Puerto de la Bonaigua**, a pass giving access to the Arán valley. The **view** from the pass is of a magnificent glacial cirque.

Pyrenean countryside between Coll de Nargó and Tremp

★★ 5 VALL D'ARÁN

From the Puerto de la Bonaigua to Vielha

60km - 37 miles – about 2 hours – local map previous page

The Arán valley on the northern side of the Pyrenees has belonged to Spain since the 13C. Difficulties of communication with the world outside brought about the development of a community with its own tradition and language, Aranés. Only in 1925 was a car-worthy road made over the Puerto de la Bonaigua and in 1948 a tunnel was built to connect the valley capital to the Lleida road. These two roads and an increase in population have brought changes in the local economy: pasture is being replaced by arable land, fir and beech trees are being felled for timber and mineral and water resources (for hydro-electric power) are being exploited. But nothing alters the beauty of the mountain scenery and the brilliant green fields, blotched occasionally by a blue-grey mass which closer inspection reveals are the slate-roofed cottages of one of the valley's 39 villages, in many cases clustered round a Lombard Romanesque style church. Today the area is seeing the development of large winter sports resorts.

Baqueira Beret – A well-equipped winter sports centre which slopes from 1 520 to 2 470m - 4 987 to 8 104ft.

Salardú – Schist and granite houses and a 13C church with a tall belfry, distinguish this delightful village. In the **iglesia** (church) ☉ is a stylised but anatomically detailed wooden 12C Crucifix.

Vielha – Alt 971m - 3 186ft. The small Arán valley capital stands close to the frontier at the juncture of two Pyrenean roads and bustles with passing traffic. The parish **church** has an octagonal belfry and a 13C doorway with roughly carved copings. Inside, in a chapel to the left, is a 12C wooden sculpture (all that remains of a Descent from the Cross) of the **Mig Aran Christ ★**, a long, handsome face framed by an intricately carved head of hair and beard.

The *parador* above Vielha commands a wonderful **view:** in the distance is the cirque which closes the Arán valley to the south and on the right, the formidable foothills of the Maladeta massif.

Bossost – *16km - 10 miles north of Vielha.* Bossost has a well-preserved **Romanesque church.** A nave and two aisles are separated by rounded pillars which support the barrel vaulting for the massive roof; there are three Lombard banded apses and a north door archaically carved to show the Creator surrounded by the sun, the moon and the symbols of the Evangelists.

On your way back to Vielha, bear left into the Vilamós road.

Vilamós – This isolated village with its traditional architecture of tall schist roofs, clings to a platform 400m - 1 312ft above the valley. It commands a fine **view ★** of the green Garona valley and in the distance of the Maladeta peaks.

The length of time given in this guide
– for touring allows time to enjoy the views and the scenery
– for sightseeing is the average time required for a visit.

⑥ VALL DEL NOGUERA RIBAGORCCANA

From Vielha õ Caldes de Boí

65km - 40 miles - about 1 1/2 hours – local map pp 204-205

The road cuts through the Maladeta massif by way of the long Vielha tunnel.

Vilaller – The small attractive village, huddled around a hillock, has a church with an unusual belfry.

7km - 4 miles further on turn left into the Boí road.

★ **Vall del Noguera de Tort** – This valley contains the most beautiful Romanesque churches in the Pyrenees: built to a square plan with small, irregular stone blocks and tile-stone roofs, they can be distinguished from a distance by their tall square belfries which abut the nave. They are decorated with double or triple arcades and Lombard bands, like the church at **Erill la Vall**.

Boí – Boí has a pretty Romanesque belfry and an information centre for the Parque Nacional de Aigüestortes.

★ **Taüll** – The village, now developing rapidly, is famous for the outstanding frescoes of its two churches which feature among the masterpieces currently exhibited in the Museu d'Art de Catalunya, Barcelona *(qv)*. The **Iglesia de Sant Climent** ★ ⊙, just outside Taüll, was built in 1123. This church can be spotted from a distance by its elegant arcaded **belfry** ★ which rises six storeys high, dwarfing the Romanesque east end below. The interior walls, columns and apse were formerly covered with paintings; a copy of the famous Christ in Majesty which originally adorned the apse now stands in its place. The village, with its maze of small streets and wooden galleried houses, clusters around another church, **Santa María**, which has been restored inside.

★★ **Parque Nacional de Aigüestortes and Lago de San Mauricio** – *Access from the road between Boí and Caldes de Boí. See Parque Nacional de AIGÜESTORTES and Lago de San Mauricio.*

Caldes de Boí – The thermal spa has springs flowing at a temperature of 56°C - 133°F.

PLASENCIA★

Extremadura (Cáceres)
Population 36 826
Michelin map 444 L11 – Michelin Atlas España Portugal p 49

The regional town of Plasencia stands on a hill at the meeting point of central limestone *sierras* and the Extremaduran plateau. Below flows the Jerte river, circling the jagged mountains with their massive granite boulders. Storks come to nest in the town from February to July.

★ **Catedral** ⊙ – The cathedral is in fact two buildings from different periods. A Romanesque-Gothic edifice was built in the 13 and 14C. At the end of the 15C, its east end was demolished and a new cathedral with a bolder architectural design was begun. Only the chancel and transept were completed. Enter the cathedral by the north door which has a rich Plateresque decoration. A door left of the *coro* opens into the old cathedral (now the parish church of Santa María). The cloisters have pointed arches and Romanesque capitals while the chapter house is covered by a fine dome on squinches which is disguised outside by a pyramid shaped belfry covered in tiles. The shortened nave houses a museum of religious art.
Inside the **Catedral Nueva** (New Cathedral), the tall pillars and slender ribs extending into network vaulting, illustrate the mastery of the famous architects responsible for the design: Juan de Java, Diego de Siloé and Alonso de Covarrubias.
The **altarpiece** ★ is decorated with statues by the 17C sculptor Gregorio Fernández; the **choir-stalls** ★ were carved in 1520 by Rodrigo Alemán – look on the backs and misericords of the lower row for scenes, on the right, from the Old Testament, and on the left, of everyday life.

★ **Barrio Viejo (Old Quarter)** – The streets around the cathedral and the Plaza Mayor, well worth a walk, are lined by noble façades and houses with wrought-iron balconies.
Start from the Plaza de la Catedral and leaving on your right the **Casa del Deán** (Deanery) with its unusual corner window, and the **Casa del Dr Trujillo**, now the Law Courts (Palacio de Justicia), make for the Gothic **Iglesia de San Nicolás**, a church which faces the beautiful façade of the **Casa de las Dos Torres** (House with Two Towers).
Continue straight ahead to the **Palacio Mirabel**. This palace, flanked by a massive tower, contains a fine two-tiered *patio* and the Museo de Caza (Hunting Museum). A passage beneath the palace *(door on right-hand side)* leads to the **Calle Sancho Polo** and the more popular quarter near the ramparts where there are stepped alleys, white-walled houses and washing hanging from the windows – a scene typical of villages further south. Turn right for the **Plaza Mayor**, an asymmetrical square surrounded by porticoes, which is the bustling town centre.

EXCURSIONS

Parque Nacional de Monfragüe – *25km-16 miles to the south by the C524. Centro de Información (Information Centre) in Villareal de San Carlos. Various itineraries on foot or by car.* Some parts of the hills flanking the Tajo river at its confluence with the Tiétar are situated within the park (17842ha-44089 acres). The ecological importance of these areas is determined by their typically Mediterranean flora (rockrose, cork oak, gall oak, lavender, arbutus, etc.); and their rich and varied fauna, with, in this park, a large number of protected species (black and tawny vultures, Imperial eagles, Iberian lynx, mongooses, etc.).

La Vera – *Take the C501 to the east of Plasencia.* This fertile valley is given over to tobacco growing and market-gardening. Villages like that of **Cuacos de Yuste** where Don Juan of Austria grew up, have managed to preserve their picturesque character. The 15C castle in **Jarandilla de la Vera** has been converted into a *parador*.

★ **Monasterio de Yuste** ⊘ – *1.8km - 1 mile from Cuacos de Yuste.* In 1556, when Emperor **Charles V** had grown weary of power, he abdicated and retired to this modest Hieronymite monastery. He died on 21 September 1558. Even today, the serene atmosphere, particularly of the beautiful surrounding countryside, makes one understand why the great emperor chose this retreat in which to pass his last years.

The monastery which was devastated during the War of Independence and during the period following the passing of Mendizábal's *(qv)* decrees, has been partially restored. Of Charles V's small palace one sees the dining hall, the royal bedroom built to adjoin the chapel so that the emperor could hear mass without having to rise, the Gothic church and, lastly, the two fine cloisters, one Gothic, the other Plateresque.

Monasterio de POBLET★★★

Catalunya (Tarragona)

Michelin map 443 H33 – Michelin Atlas España Portugal p 31

Poblet, set at the foot of hills cloaked in holm oak and almond trees, is the largest and best preserved of all Cistercian monasteries. It was the Reconquest which brought Poblet into existence, for after Ramón Berenguer IV had recaptured Catalunya from the Moors he gave thanks to God by founding the monastery. By 1150 twelve Cistercians, sent from Fontfroide Abbey near Narbonne in France, had begun to construct the buildings and till the soil for the future community.

The kings of Aragón maintained a patronage of the monastery which with Santes Creus, became a favourite halt on kingly progresses between the two capitals of Zaragoza and Barcelona. It also became a place of royal religious retreat – the abbot was the royal almoner. Finally the monastery was given the supreme honour of being selected as the royal pantheon. It began to decline at the end of the 16C, suffered particularly during the Napoleonic Wars and in the so-called Constitutional Period (1820-1823), when religious orders were suppressed, and in 1835 when riches were sold and the monastery was left to ruin and pillage. A century later the buildings were restored and in 1940 a community was re-established. In spite of all its vicissitudes, the monastery remains a rare example of medieval monastic architecture.

TOUR ⊘ *time: 1 1/4 hours*

An outer perimeter 2km - 1 mile long protected the peasants and workmen employed by the abbey. A second, inner wall, incorporating the 15C Puerta Dorada (Golden Door), which owes its name to the gilded bronze plates which covered it, enclosed the conventual annexes. A third wall, 600m - 1968ft long, built by Peter the Ceremonious at the end of the 14C, surrounds the monastery proper. Inside, on the right, is the baroque entrance to the church built in about 1670 which was flanked fifty years later by two lavishly ornate windows. On the left, the Puerta Real (Royal Door), between two massive machicolated towers, opens onto the conventual buildings.

Locutorio (Parlatory) – The late-14C vaulting in the lay brothers' dormitory forms one with the walls.

★★ **Claustro** – The size of these cloisters (40 x 35m - 131 x 115ft) and their sober lines give some indication of the monastery's importance. The south gallery and huge lavabo with 30 taps are in pure Cistercian style; the other galleries, built a century later, have a floral motif tracery; beautiful scrollwork adorns the **capitals**★ throughout.

Cocina and Refectorio – The kitchen and refectory are 12C. The reader's lectern can be seen strategically placed overlooking the long refectory tables (in use to this day).

Biblioteca – Columns in the middle of the 13C library support the magnificent palm fan vaulting with its clearly defined design.

Sala Capitular – The delicacy of the slender columns and capitals in this chapter house shows them to be 13C. Tombstones of eleven of Poblet's abbots can be seen inlaid in the pavement.

★★ **Iglesia** – The light, spacious church, imbued with serenity, is typically Cistercian. It has pure architectural lines, broken barrel vaulting over the nave, two storeys in elevation, and unadorned capitals. The only decorative note lies in the windows and wide arches joined beneath an arch which dissolves into the piers of the engaged columns. In contrast to the lack of ornament, the church had to incorporate numerous altars because of the growing community; the apse was therefore ringed by an ambulatory and radiating chapels, a feature more commonly found in Benedictine churches.

★★ **Panteón Real** (Royal Pantheon) – The church's major ornament and its most original feature, are the immense shallow arches spanning the transepts on either side of the crossing, surmounted by the alabaster, royal tombs. These were constructed in about 1350 to provide a repository for the kings of Aragón, buried at Poblet between 1196 and 1479. The sepulchres were desecrated in 1835 but were restored by the sculptor Frederic Marès.

★★ **Retablo** – Damián Forment was commissioned in 1527 to carve the monumental Renaissance altarpiece. Figures in shell-shaped niches in four superimposed registers can be seen glorifying Christ and the Virgin.

A wide flight of stairs leads from the north transept to the monks' dormitory.

Dormitorio – Massive central arches support the ridge roof above the vast, 87m - 285ft long gallery. Part of the dormitory has been converted into monks' cells.

Palacio del Rey Martín el Humano (Palace of King Martín the Humane) – The sovereign had sumptuous apartments, which included carved tracery in the windows, built for his own use in the monastery around 1400.

EXCURSION

Vallbona de les Monges – *27km - 17 miles north of Poblet.*
The Cistercian **Monasterio de Santa María de Vallbona**, ⊘, in the heart of the village, completes the "Cistercian Trinity" along with the abbeys of Poblet and Santes Creus. The convent was founded in 1157 by the hermit Ramón de Vallbona and became a Cistercian community for women. In 1563, when, as a result of the Council of Trent, a decree was passed stipulating that convents could not remain isolated, the nuns of Vallbona encouraged inhabitants from the neighbouring village to settle around the abbey.
The **church** with a Greek cross plan, is striking in its simplicity. It is lit by a lantern over the transept crossing. There are several statues of the Virgin including a 14C work in the church and another dating from the 12C called the Claustro Virgin. The cloisters retain a Gothic and two Romanesque galleries. The abbesses' tombstones are inlaid in the floor in the church and chapter house.

PONFERRADA

Castilla y León (León)
Population 59 702
Michelin map 441 E 10 – Michelin Atlas España Portugal p 9

Ponferrada, centre of a mining area and capital of the fertile Bierzo, a subsided basin, owes its name to an iron bridge built at the end of the 11C across the Sil to help pilgrims on their way to Santiago de Compostela *(qv)*. The town is dominated by the ruins of the **Castillo de los Templares** (Templars' Castle).

EXCURSIONS

★ **Peñalba de Santiago** – *21km - 13 miles southeast.*
Peñalba stands isolated in the heart of the so-called Valle del Silencio (Valley of Silence). Its characteristic architecture of schist walled houses with wooden balconies and slate tile-stone roofs, remains intact. The village has grown up around the Mozarabic **Iglesia de Santiago**, a church which is all that remains of a 10C monastery. Note the portal with its paired horseshoe arch set off by an *alfiz*. There are fine views from the belfry of the village and the valley beyond.

★ **Las Médulas** – *22km - 14 miles southwest.*
The northwest slopes of the Aquilianos mountains on the left bank of the Sil have been transformed into a magic landscape of rocky crags and strangely shaped hillocks of pink and ochre by debris from a gold-mine worked in Roman times. Over the ages this has been covered by a vegetation of gnarled old chestnut trees.

Galicia

Population 75 148

Michelin map 441 E 4 – Michelin Atlas España Portugal p 6 – Local map under RÍAS BAJAS

Pontevedra was once a busy port lying sheltered at the end of its *ría;* fishermen, merchants, overseas traders lived there as did sailors and explorers such as **Pedro Sarmiento**, skilled navigator of the 16C, wise cosmographer and author of *Voyage to the Magellan Straits*. The Lérez delta, however, silted up so that by the 18C Pontevedra had begun to decline and the new port at Marín was taking its place.

★ BARRIO ANTIGUO (OLD QUARTER) *time: 1 1/2 hours*

In spite of extensive development, the new town has respected the old, a kernel tucked into the area between Calles Michelena, del Arzobispo Malvar and Cobián, and the river, where life continues peacefully in the shadow of glazed house fronts, squares occasionally adorned with a Calvary (**Plaza de la Leña Z; del Teucro Z; de Mugártegui Y 45**) and streets near the Lérez (**Pedreira Y 55, Real Y, San Nicolás Y 75**). The town comes to life in **Calle Sarmiento** (**Z**) on market days.

★ **Plaza de la Leña** (**Z**) – This is a delightful square with its asymmetrical shape, its Calvary and the beautiful façades that surround it. Two 18C mansions on the square have been converted into a museum.

Museo Provincial (**Z**) ⊘ – The first mansion housing this museum contains prehistoric collections, in particular the Celtic **treasures**★ from A Golada and Caldas de Reis which date from the Bronze Age, and that of Foxados from the 2 and 1C BC. Among the paintings on the first floor are 15C Aragonese Primitives.

The second mansion displays maritime exhibits including a reconstruction of the officers' mess from the *Numancia*, the frigate captained by Admiral Méndez Núñez during the disastrous Battle of Callao (Peru's chief sea port) in 1866. When told that it was folly to attack a port so well defended, the admiral replied "Spain prefers honour without ships to ships without honour." On the museum's upper floor are an interesting antique kitchen and 19C Sargadelos ceramics.

★ **Iglesia de Santa María la Mayor** (**Y**) ⊘ – Old alleyways and gardens surround this delightful Plateresque church which was built by the mariner's guild in the fishermen's quarter between approximately the late 15C and 1570. The **west front**★ is carved like an altarpiece, divided into separate superimposed registers on which are reliefs of the Dormition and Assumption of the Virgin and the Trinity. At the summit is the Crucifixion at the centre of an openwork coping finely carved with oarsmen and fishermen hauling in their nets.

The **interior** is a generally successful mingling of Gothic (notched arches), Isabelline (slender cabled columns) and Renaissance (ribbed vaulting) styles. The back of the west façade is covered in naïve low reliefs of scenes from Genesis (Adam and Eve, Noah's Ark) and the New Testament.

PONTEVEDRA

San Francisco (**Z**) – The church's simply styled Gothic façade looks onto the gardens of the Plaza de la Herrería. The interior features timber vaulting.

Ruinas de Santo Domingo (Santo Domingo Ruins) (**Z**) ⊙ – Only the church's Gothic east end remains, its tall bays overgrown with ivy. Arranged inside is a lapidary museum of Roman steles, Galician coats of arms and tombs, in particular, tombs of craftsmen showing the tools they used, and tombs of noblemen.

EXCURSION

★★ **Mirador Coto Redondo** – *14km - 9 miles south on the N550.* The hill climb through pine and eucalyptus woods, with occasional good views, is pleasant. The **panorama** ★★ from this viewpoint extends over both the Pontevedra and Vigo *rías*.

PRIEGO DE CÓRDOBA★

Andalucía (Córdoba)
Population 20 823
Michelin map 446 T 17 – Michelin Atlas España Portugal p 85

This lovely town is situated on a plain in the heart of the Subbética Cordobesa range. It reached its economic and artistic zenith in the 18C as a result of the silk industry.

SIGHTS

★ **Fuentes del Rey y de la Salud** (Fountains of the King and Health) – *At the end of the Calle del Río.* The sight created by these two fountains, the most well-known in the town, is a surprising one. The older, the **Fuente de la Salud**, is a Mannerist frontispiece built in the 16C. Next to it is the lavish **Fuente del Rey** which was completed at the beginning of the 19C. Both the dimensions and the richness of its design evoke the gardens of a baroque palace. It has a total of 139 jets spouting water from the mouth of the same number of masks. The central display represents Neptune's chariot and Amphitrite.

Parroquia de la Asunción (Parish Church of the Assumption) ⊙ – *At the end of the Paseo del Abad Palomino.* This 16C church was remodelled in baroque style in the 18C.

★★ **El Sagrario** – The chapel, which opens on to the Nave del Evangelio, is a masterpiece of Andalusian baroque. It is comprised of an antechamber leading into an octogonal space surrounded by an ambulatory. Light plays an important part in the effect of the scene; intensified by the whiteness of the walls and ceiling, it shimmers over the extensive and lavish **yeserías** (plasterwork decoration), creating a magical atmosphere. In spite of this excessive adornment, the overall effect is one of delicacy.

★ **Barrio de la Villa** – This charming quarter, dating back to medieval and Moorish times, has narrow, winding streets and flower-decked whitewashed houses.

El Adarve – This delightful balcony which looks out on to the Subbética mountain range encircles the Barrio de la Villa to the north.

PUEBLA DE SANABRIA

Castilla y León (Zamora)
Population 1 969
Michelin map 441 F 10 – Michelin Atlas España Portugal p 22

Puebla de Sanabria is an attractive mountain village near the Portuguese border, a short distance from Galicia and the province of León. Its white-walled houses with tile-stone roofs and the occasional emblasoned façade are dominated by the 15C castle of the Count of Benavente. The **church** is a late-12C, reddish granite construction with a west door simply outlined with a large bead motif. The view from the castle esplanade takes in the Río Tera and part of the lake.

EXCURSION

Valle de Sanabria – *19km - 12 miles northwest.*
The valley, now a nature reserve, was hollowed out northwest of Puebla by glacial erosion at the feet of the Sierras de Cabrera Baja and Segundera. It is a delightful area, well-known for its hunting and fishing, that owes much of its appeal to the many streams running through the light bush vegetation.

Lago de Sanabria – Sanabria, the largest glacial lake in Spain, lies at an altitude of 1 028m - 3 373ft. It is used for all types of water sports, and salmon-trout fishing.

San Martín de Castañeda – There are attractive **views** ★ of the rushing stream of the Tera and the mountain encircled lake all the way to this Galician looking village. The first distinguishable sight of this is the east end of its noble 11C Romanesque **church**.

PUEBLOS BLANCOS DE ANDALUCÍA

WHITE VILLAGES OF ANDALUCÍA

Michelin map 446 V 12-14 – Michelin Atlas España Portugal pp 83 and 84

The mountainous region between Ronda and Arcos de la Frontera is formed by the Sierras de Grazalema, Ubrique and Margarita. In these often weirdly shaped mountains, ranging from desolate heights to lush green valleys, are the remains of the *pinsapos* forest of native pines dating from the beginning of the Quaternary Period.

The area is well-watered on account of its proximity to the Atlantic; some years the rainfall exceeds 3m - 118 inches. This abundant precipitation is borne out by the region's many dams and reservoirs, among them Bornos, Arcos and Guadalcacín. The beauty of the countryside is set off by the delightful white villages *(pueblos blancos)* often perched on rocky crags or stretched out along escarpments, their narrow streets of whitewashed houses dominated by a ruined castle or a church. The inhabitants make a living from farming, stock raising and local crafts.

FROM RONDA TO ARCOS DE LA FRONTERA

By the southern route; 104km - 65 miles – about 3 hours

★★ **Ronda** – *See RONDA.*

★ **Grazalema** – The village, set in a mountain cirque, is one of Andalucía's most beautiful. Its natural-coloured woollen blankets woven on long looms are famous.

The lonely road between Grazalema and Ubrique cuts its way through grey and pink countryside deeply scoured by erosion into fantastic shapes.

Ubrique – The town nestling in the mountains is an industrial centre for leather goods (bags and shoes).

After climbing to El Bosque the road crosses a cultivated area of orchards and olive groves to Arcos de la Frontera.

★ **Arcos de la Frontera** – *See ARCOS DE LA FRONTERA.*

FROM ARCOS DE LA FRONTERA TO RONDA

By the northern route; 102km - 63 miles – about 3 hours

The road skirts the white village of Bornos which stands out against the vast reservoir of the same name. As you approach Algodonales, a beautiful **view**★ opens up of **Zahara** village, built on a rocky height dominated by the ruins of its castle.

Olvera – The village houses stretch out along a ridge amidst rows of olive trees. Once past **Torre-Alháquime**, look back for a fine view of the village with Olvera in the background.

Setenil – The village lies huddled in a gorge cut by the Guadalporcún river with many of its houses nestled under the overhanging rock ledge.

Setenil

H. W. Silvester / RAPHO

For a pleasant hotel in peaceful surroundings look in the current
Michelin Red Guide España Portugal.

PUENTE VIESGO★

Cantabria
Population 2 464
Michelin map 442 C 18 – Michelin Atlas España Portugal p 12

The **cuevas** (caves) – El Castillo, Las Chimeneas, Las Monedas, La Pasiega – hollowed out of the limestone mountainsides all round Puente Viesgo provide ample proof of their habitation in prehistoric times.

★ **Cueva del Castillo** ⊘ – Cave dwellers began engraving and painting the walls towards the end of the Palaeolithic Age (from the Aurignacian to the Magdalenian period). The many designs – 750 have been counted – outlines only and some-times incomplete, are widely scattered and some are difficult to get to. Many remain enigmatic, particularly the hands dipped in ochre and pressed against the wall, or outlined in red, to form negatives. They are thought, perhaps, to sym-bolise man's superiority or to possess magical powers. Of the almost 50 discovered only three are right hands.
The meaning of the parallel lines and point alignments also remains obscure. They may refer to weapons or traps for catching animals.

EXCURSION

Castañeda – 6km - 4 miles northeast.
The **Antigua Colegiata** ⊘, a former collegiate church dating from the end of the 12C, stands in the small, pleasant valley through which the Pisueña runs. The unusually deep doorway is given considerable elegance by a simple decoration of alternate convex and concave covings.
Inside, the central area has retained its original plan with semicircular arches in the nave and the cupola on squinches.

The PYRENEES

See PIRINEOS ARAGONESES and PIRINEOS CATALANES

REINOSA

Cantabria
Population 12 852
Michelin map 442 C 17 – Michelin Atlas España Portugal p 12

Reinosa, built on the southern slopes of the Montes Cantábricos, in the vast depres-sion formed by the Ebro basin, really belongs to the Castilian landscape with its vast expanses of tableland and cereals. In the 18C its position on the road linking Castilla with the port of Santander encouraged commercial development.
It is becoming a tourist centre as it is near the **Embalse del Ebro** (a reservoir which is navigable for 20km - 12 miles) and the winter sports resort of Alto Campóo.

EXCURSIONS

Retortillo – 5km - 3 miles south of the C6318.
All that remains in the small **church** of the Romanesque period are the oven-vaulted apse and the triumphal arch with two finely carved capitals illustrating warriors. A few yards away are the ruins of a villa which stood in the Roman city of **Julióbriga**.

★ **Cervatos** – 5km - 3 miles south on the N611.
The **antigua colegiata** ★ ⊘, a former collegiate church with an unusually pure Romanesque style, is remarkable for the richness and imaginativeness of its carved **decoration** ★. The portal tympanum is meticulously patterned with a tight openwork design. There is a frieze of lions back to back while varied and audacious figures decorate the cornice modillions and those beneath the capitals of the south apsidal window. Inside there are harmonious blind arcades in the apse and, again, the carving on the capitals and the consoles supporting the arch ribs is both dense and sophisticated with entangled lions, eagles with spread wings, plant motifs and strapwork. The nave was raised with intersecting ribbed vaulting in the 14C.

★★★ **Pico de Tres Mares** – 26km - 16 miles west. Take the Alto Campóo road.
On the way, paths from the village of Fontibre lead to a greenish pool, the **source of the Ebro** (Fuente del Ebro), the greatest Iberian river.
Access to the Pico de Tres Mares by chairlift. The peak (2 175m - 7 136ft), one of the summits of the Sierra de Peña Labra, got its name as the source of three rivers which flow from it to three different seas (sea: *mar* in Spanish) – the Híjar, tributary of the Ebro which flows into the Mediterranean; the Pisuerga, tributary of the Duero which flows into the Atlantic, and the Nansa, which flows directly into the Cantabrian sea. From the crest there is a splendid circular **panorama** ★★★:

to the north, of the Nansa and the Embalse de la Cohilla (Colilla dam) at the foot of Monte Cueto (1517m - 4977ft), and circling right, the Embalse del Ebro, the Sierra de Peña Labra, the Embalse de Cervera de Pisuerga and the Montes de León; due west, the central range of the Picos de Europa including the 2618m - 8589ft Peña Vieja, and linked to it by a series of high passes, the eastern range which includes the Peña Sagra (2042m - 6699ft). In the foreground is the eroded mass of the Peña Labra (2006m - 6581ft).

RÍAS ALTAS★

Galicia (Lugo, La Coruña)

Michelin map 441 A 5-7, B 4-8, C 2-5, D 2 – Michelin Atlas España Portugal pp 2 - 4

Although indented by *rías* – inlets made by the Atlantic into the coastline, like the sea lochs of Scotland or the *fjords* of Norway – the northern coast of Galicia from Ribadeo to Cabo Finisterre is generally low-lying. The rocks, bare and smooth, the granite houses with slate roofs, give the impression that the climate must be grim – yet holidaymakers arrive with the fine season, attracted by the scenery and small sandy creeks. Galicia's *rías* are described below from east to west.

Ría de Ribadeo – The Ría de Ribadeo is formed by the estuary of the Eo. After a headlong course, the Río Eo, forming the border between Galicia and Asturias, slackens its pace to wind gently between the wide green banks of its lower valley. There is a beautiful **view★** up the estuary from the bridge across the mouth of the river.

The old port of **Ribadeo** is now an important regional centre and summer resort.

Ría de Foz – **Foz**, at the mouth of its *ría*, is a small port with a coastal fishing fleet. Its two good Atlantic beaches are popular in summer.

Iglesia de San Martín de Mondoñedo ⊙ – *5km - 3 miles west*. Standing almost alone on a height is the church, once part of a monastery of ancient foundation and an episcopal seat until 1112 when this was transferred to Mondoñedo. The style of the church is archaic and, most unusually in this region, shows no sign of Compostelan influence. The east end, decorated with Lombard bands, is supported by massive buttresses; inside, the transept **capitals★** are naïvely carved and rich in anecdotal detail: the one illustrating the parable of the rich man who allows Lazarus to die of hunger, shows the table overflowing with food while a dog beneath it is licking Lazarus's feet as he lies stretched out on the ground. The capitals, believed to date from the 10C, bear Visigothic influence in the plant motifs.

★ **Ría de Viveiro** – Sea, countryside and mountain combine in a varied landscape, a coastline of white sand beaches and lofty headlands sung by **Nicomedes Pastor Díaz**, 19C politician and poet. All **Viveiro** retains of its town walls is the Puerta de Carlos V (Charles V Gateway), emblasoned with the emperor's arms. In the summer months the port is transformed into a holiday resort. On the 4th Sunday in August, visitors from all over Galicia come for the local Naseiro Romería.

Ría de Santa María de Ortigueira – The *ría* is deep and surrounded by green hills while **Ortigueira** port has quays bordered by well kept gardens.

Ría de Cedeira – A small, deeply enclosed *ría* with beautiful beaches. The road gives good **views** of **Cedeira** (summer resort) and the surrounding countryside.

Ría de Ferrol – The *ría* forms a magnificent natural harbour entered by way of a narrow 6km - 4 mile channel guarded by two forts. In the 18C, on account of its exceptional site and favourable position for trade with America, King Ferdinand VI and King Charles III decided to make the port of **Ferrol** a naval base. The symmetry of the town plan evident in the old quarter dates from the same period.
Ferrol today is one of Spain's major naval bases and is also a dockyard.

Ría de Betanzos – *See BETANZOS*.

Ría de La Coruña – *See La CORUÑA*.

Costa de la Muerte (Coast of Death) – The landscape between La Coruña and Cabo Finisterre is of a wild, harsh and majestic coast. It has long been whipped by stormy weather and owes its inhospitable name to the many ships that have run aground or been smashed to pieces against its rocks. Tucked away in its more sheltered coves, however, are small fishing villages like **Malpica de Bergantiños** which is protected by the Cabo de San Adrián (opposite the Islas Sisargas, islands on which there is a bird sanctuary) or **Camariñas** which is famous for its bobbin-lace.

★ **Cabo Finisterre** or **Fisterra** (Cape Finisterre) – **Corcubión★**, near Cabo Finisterre, is an attractive old harbour town of emblasoned houses with glassed-in balconies. The *corniche* **road★** to the cape looks down over the Bahía de Cabo Finisterre, a bay which is enclosed by three successive mountain chains. The lighthouse on the headland commands a fine **panorama★** of the Atlantic and the bay.

RÍAS BAJAS★★

Galicia (La Coruña, Pontevedra)

Michelin map 441 D 2-3, E 2-3, F 3-4 – Michelin Atlas España Portugal p 6

The Rías Bajas, a coastline well supplied by the sea (crustaceans) and with deep inlets affording safe anchorages, is Galicia's most privileged and attractive region. In the season, holidaymakers, Spanish for the most part, come to enjoy the beaches and resorts like those of A Toxa.

★★RÍA DE MUROS Y NOIA

1 From Muros to Ribeira

71km - 44 miles – about 1 1/4 hours – local map below

The *ría* is especially delightful for its wild scenery. The coastline, lower than in other *rías*, is strewn with rocks. The wooded northern bank is particularly attractive.

Muros is a seaside town with a harbour and typical local style houses, while **Noia** is notable for its main square looking out to sea, upon which stands the Gothic **Iglesia de San Martín★** with a magnificently carved portal and rose window.

RÍA DE AROUSA

2 From Ribeira to A Toxa

115km - 71 miles – about 3 hours – local map below

Ría de Arousa, at the mouth of the Río Ulla, is the largest and most indented of the inlets.

Ribeira – A large fishing port with vast warehouses.

★★★ **Mirador de la Curota** – *10km - 6 miles from Puebla del Caramiñal.*
From a height of 498m - 1 634ft there is a magnificent **panorama** of the four inlets of the Rías Bajas. On a clear day the view extends from Cabo Finisterre to the Río Miño.

Padrón – It was to this village that the legendary boat came which brought St James *(qv)* to Spain. The boat's mooring stone *(pedrón)* can be seen beneath the altar in the **iglesia parroquial** (parish church) ☉ near the bridge. The town, renowned for its green peppers, stands on the banks of the Sar and Ulla rivers beside which runs the pleasantly shaded promenade often sung in the poems of **Rosalía de Castro** (1837-1885) who lived and died here. Padrón is also the birthplace of the writer **Camilo José Cela**, winner of the Nobel Prize for Literature in 1989.

Vilagarcía de Arousa – A garden bordered promenade overlooking the sea gives the town the air of a resort. The Convento de Vista Alegre, founded in 1648, stands in the outskirts on the Cambados road. It is an old *pazo* (qv) with square towers, coats of arms and pointed merlons.

★ **Mirador de Lobeira** – *4km - 2 miles south. Take a signposted forest track at Cornazo. The view from the lookout takes in the whole* ría *and the hills inland.*

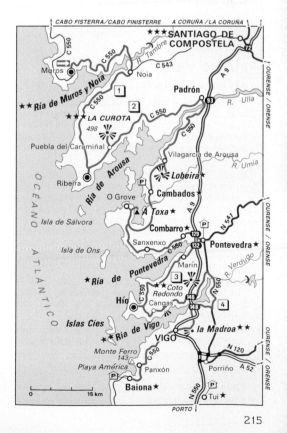

★ **Cambados** – Cambados has retained an old quarter of alleyways bordered by beautiful houses. At the town's northern entrance is the magnificent, square **Plaza de Fefiñanes★**, lined on two sides by the emblasoned Fefiñanes *pazo*, on the third by a 17C church with lines harmonising with the *pazo*, and on the fourth by a row of arcaded houses. Cambados is the place to try the local white Albariño wine which has a light fruity flavour.

★ **A Toxa** – A sick donkey abandoned on the island by its owner and later recovered cured, was the first living creature to discover the health-giving properties of the spring on A Toxa. The stream has

run dry but the pine-covered island in its wonderful **setting★★** remains an ideally restful place. It's the most elegant resort on the Galician coast with luxury villas and an early 20C palace. There is a small church covered in scallop shells.

The seaside resort and fishing harbour of **O Grove** on the other side of the causeway is renowned for its seafood.

The A Toxa-Canelas **road★** affords a succession of views of sand dunes and extensive, rock enclosed beaches like that of La Lanzada.

★RÍA DE PONTEVEDRA

③ From A Toxa to Hío

62km - 39 miles – about 3 hours – local map previous page

Sanxenxo – A very lively resort in summer with one of the best climates in Galicia.

A *hórreo* in Combarro

★ **Combarro** – This small, typical fishing village with winding alleyways has a good many Calvaries and is famed for its **hórreos★** (drying sheds) on the seafront.

★ **Pontevedra** – *See PONTEVEDRA.*

Marín – Headquarters of the Escuala Naval Militar or Naval Academy.

Hío – The village at the tip of the Morrazo headland has a famous and intricately carved **Calvary★**.

★★RÍA DE VIGO

④ From Hío to Baiona *70km - 43 miles – about 3 hours – local map p 215*

Although smaller than the Ría de Arousa, the Vigo inlet is deeper and better protected, remarkably sheltered inland by hills and out to sea by islands, the Islas Cíes. In addition, by Domaio, where the steep, wooded banks draw together and the narrow channel is covered in mussel beds, it becomes really beautiful. From Cangas and Moaña you can see the white town of Vigo covering the entire hillside on the far side of the inlet.

Vigo – *Town plan in the current Michelin Red Guide España Portugal.* Vigo, Spain's principal transatlantic port, is the country's leading fishing port and one of its most important industrial and commercial centres. Legend has it that treasure dating from the time of Philip V lies at the bottom of the inlet. Vigo's **setting★** is outstanding: built in an amphitheatre on the south bank of the *ría* and surrounded by parks and pine-woods. There are magnificent **views★★** of Vigo and its bay from El Castro hill behind the town. Berbés, Vigo's oldest quarter and home to fishermen and sailors, is a picturesque part of town. Beside it is the unusual A Pedra market where fishwives sell the oysters which may be tasted in the many bars nearby.

Islas Cíes – Boats from Vigo harbour take passengers to the islands *(about 1 hour)*. The beautiful archipelago of crystalline water and immaculate white sand guards the entrance to the Ría de Vigo. The islands, a sanctuary to birds, were decreed a Nature Reserve in 1980.

★★ **Mirador la Madroa** – *6km - 4 miles. Follow signs to the airport and then to the zoo.* The esplanade commands a fine **view★★** of Vigo and the *ría*.

The Alcabre, Samil and Canido beaches stretch down the coast south of Vigo.

Panxón – A seaside resort at the foot of Monte Ferro.

Playa América – A very popular, elegant resort in the curve of a bay.

★ **Baiona** – *See BAIONA.*

La RIOJA

La Rioja, Navarra, Álava

Michelin map 442 E 20-23, F 20-24 – Michelin Atlas España Portugal pp 11, 26 and 27

La Rioja, a fertile area in the Ebro valley called after a tributary, the Río Oja, covers an area of 5 000km² - 1 931sq miles comprising La Rioja province and parts of Álava and Navarra. **Rioja Alta** – Upper Rioja – to the west around Haro, is devoted principally to wine-growing while **Rioja Baja** – Lower Rioja – with **Logroño** and Calahorra as its main towns, has unusual tableland relief and is given over to extensive vegetable growing. La Rioja flourished culturally and economically early in its history thanks to its position on the pilgrim route to Santiago de Compostela. Since then it has become famous for its wine.

The all-important **vineyards** of La Rioja cover an area of 43 000ha - 106 260 acres. Although the vine has long held pride of place – Rioja wines are mentioned in a document as early as 1102 and they were already being exported to France, Flanders and Italy in the 16C – it really began to develop in the 19C when French wine-growers ruined by phylloxera came to try their luck in La Rioja. Today, La Rioja is Spain's leading producer of quality wines, in particular the reds (11° - 12°) which, though light and smooth, have some body. The "Rioja" mark of guaranteed origin covers wine from Rioja Alta and Álava but also includes the stronger wines from Rioja Baja. This part of the province, however, specialises more in early vegetables – asparagus, artichokes, peppers and tomatoes – for the important local canning industry.

SIGHTS

Ezcaray – This delightful holiday village at the foot of the Sierra de la Demanda range has preserved its quaint mountain style, its stone and wood porticoes, seignorial mansions, the church of **Santa María la Mayor** as well as the buildings of a former tapestry factory founded by Charles III in 1752. Today the tradition lives on in the manufacture of blankets.

★**Santo Domingo de la Calzada** – *See NÁJERA: Excursions.*

Haro – Capital of Rioja Alta, Haro is a small but prosperous farming and commercial centre famous for its wines. There are countless cellars and taverns in the old quarter where seignorial mansions with elegant 16 and 18C façades recall the town's prestigious past.

★**Laguardia** – You see the town immediately as it stands perched high, still ringed in part by ramparts, towers and fortified gateways. The townspeople in the medieval city were actively concerned with the rapid development of the Rioja wine trade. Today, cellars open directly onto the narrow streets which in autumn are heady with the smell of grape marc. The houses are characterised by strings of peppers hanging from their balconies.

The parish church of **Santa María de los Reyes** retains its late-14C **portal**★ in the late Gothic style of many church entrances in Vitoria. It was painted in the 18C. The Apostles in the embrasures are somewhat mannered and already decadent in style with over large but, nevertheless, expressive faces. Inside, the central altarpiece dates from the 17C.

The walkway around the village commands views over vast sweeps of vineyard.

The **panorama** from the **Balcón de Rioja**★ or Rioja Balcony 12km - 7 miles northwest of Laguardia near the Puerto de Herrera (Herrera Pass) (1 100m - 3 609ft), is incredibly extensive, particularly along the length of the Ebro valley, flat and arid in appearance apart from the winding silver thread of the river's own course.

Nájera – *See NÁJERA.*

San Millán de la Cogolla – *See NÁJERA: Excursions.*

★**Valle del Iregua** (Iregua Valley) – *50km - 31 miles south of Logroño on the N 111.* For 15km - 9 miles the road skirts orchards and market gardens in the Ebro plain, until, near Islallana, appear the first **rock faces**★ of the Sierra de Cameros, overlooking the Iregua from a height of more than 500m - 1 640ft. Two tunnels later, the valley narrows, squeezed between massive reddish-coloured boulders. It opens out into an island of greenery and narrows again upstream with the torrent running at the bottom of a deep ravine while the *corniche* road dominates the site of Torrecilla en Cameros. In the village of **Villanueva de Cameros** the half-timbered houses are roofed with circular tiles.

If you intend combining a tour of Spain
with a visit to one of the neighbouring countries,
remember to take the appropriate
Michelin Green Guide France *or* **Portugal.**

RIPOLL★

Catalunya (Girona)
Population 11 204
Michelin map 443 F 36 – Michelin Atlas España Portugal p 18
Local map under PIRINEOS CATALANES

While Ripoll is the capital of an industrial region (ironworks, textiles and paper-making) its main interest lies in its Benedictine monastery founded in the 9C by **Wilfred the Hairy**, Count of Barcelona. The monastery was the pantheon of the Counts of Barcelona, Besalú and Cerdaña until the 12C.

The monastery as a centre of learning – The library at Ripoll was one of the richest in Christendom: not only did it possess texts of the scriptures and theological commentaries but also works by pagan authors such as Plutarch and Virgil as well as scientific treatises. The learning of Antiquity was restored by the Arabs, who treasured and disseminated the works of the Greeks which they discovered when they captured Alexandria and, with it, its incredible library. Ripoll, previously overrun by the Moors, became, under Abbot Oliva, a link between Arab and Christian civilisations, a centre of culture, ideas and exchange to which came such men as Brother Gerbert, the future Pope **Sylvester II** (999).

Abbot Oliva – Oliva, son of a Count of Cerdaña and Besalú, a learned man and a born leader, held the appointments simultaneously from 1008 of Abbot of Ripoll and St-Michel-de-Cuxa in the French Roussillon and from 1018 also of Bishop of Vic. He lived until 1046 and thus had time to impress his mark deeply on the region both intellectually and as a great builder. He favoured the basilical type plan with prominent transepts and a dome over the crossing as in the Collegiate Church at Cardona.

★ANTIGUO MONASTERIO DE SANTA MARÍA ⊘

All that remains of the original monastery are the church portal and the cloisters.

Iglesia – The 9C monastery church soon had to be enlarged; by the end of the 10C, Count Oliva Cabreta was constructing a third church, consecrated in 1032 by his son, the famous abbot. This was a majestic edifice, a jewel of early Romanesque art. An earthquake in 1428, various remodellings over the ages and a fire in 1835, all destroyed the building. It was rebuilt at the end of the 19C according to the original plan, with a nave and four aisles cut by a great transept on which seven apses abutted. The south transept contains the 12C tomb of Ramón Berenguer III, the Great, while in the north is the funerary monument to Wilfred the Hairy.

★★ **Portada (Portal)** – The 12C portal, built a century after the church, is weather worn in spite of the late-13C overhang, and the figures are difficult to decipher. The portal design, comprising a series of horizontal registers, has been compared to that of a triumphal arch crowned by a large frieze. The carving may be seen to illustrate the glory of God and his people, victorious over his enemies (Passage of the Red Sea), a symbol of special significance at the time of the Reconquest.
The low reliefs cover not only the doorway but also the surround. The result is an exceptionally intricate series of carvings illustrating Biblical personages and events.

Claustro (Cloisters) – Only the gallery abutting the church dates back to the 12C. It was the only gallery until the 14C when the others were added, their later date being betrayed only by the carving on some of the capitals.

A – **Vision of the Apocalypse**
1) The Eternal Father enthroned
2) Angels
3) Winged Man, the symbol of St Matthew
4) An eagle, the symbol of St John
5) The 24 Old Men of the Apocalypse
6) A lion, the symbol of St Mark
7) A bull, the symbol of St Luke

B – **Exodus**
1) The crossing of the Red Sea
2) Manna descending from Heaven
3) Flight of quail guiding the People of God
4) Moses bringing forth water from the rock
5) Moses keeping his arms uplifted to ensure victory for his people
6) Foot soldiers and cavalry in combat

C – **The Book of Kings**
1) David and the musicians
2) Transporting the Ark of the Covenant
3) The plague of Zion
4) Gad (standing) speaks to David (seated) before the crowd
5) David declares Solomon his heir
6) Solomon, riding David's mule, is proclaimed by the people
7) The judgment of Solomon
8) Solomon's dream

9) Elijah rises to heaven in a chariot of fire
D – David and the musicians
E – Monsters fighting
F – St Peter
G – St Paul
H – The life and martyrdom of St Peter (left) and St Paul (right)
I – The story of Jonah (left) and Daniel (right)
J – (at the arch centre reading simultaneously right and left) - at the centre, the Creator – two angels – above, the offering of Abel and Cain – below, the killing of Abel; the death of Cain
K – (inner sides of the doorway pillars): the months of the year

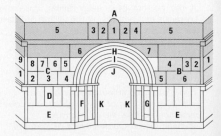

RONCESVALLES

Navarra

Michelin map 442 C 26 – Michelin Atlas España Portugal p 15

Roncesvalles has come down to us rather as a heroic epic than as the geographical pass, known to countless medieval pilgrims on their way to Santiago de Compostela *(qv)*. It is the site where, in 778, the Basques of Navarra massacred the rearguard of Charlemagne's army as Roland was leading it back through the Pyrenees to France. The late-12C early-13C **Poem of Bernardo del Carpio** describes Bernardo as a national hero who sought only with his Basque, Navarra and Asturian companions in arms to avenge the Frankish invasion of Spain; the early-12C **Song of Roland**, the first French epic poem, on the other hand, glorifies the heroic but ultimately despairing resistance of a handful of valiant Christian knights – Roland and the twelve peers of the Empire – against hordes of Saracen fanatics brought to the field by the traitor Ganelon.

Ecclesiastical buildings – This vast, grey walled mass of buildings with bluish zinc roofs, dating back to the 12C, appears hidden by dense vegetation. The buildings served formerly as an important pilgrims' hostelry with a funerary chapel, square in plan, now the Capilla del Sancti Spiritus (Chapel of the Holy Spirit), and a collegiate church rich in relics.

Iglesia de la Real Colegiata ⊙ – This Gothic collegiate church, inspired by those of the Ile-de-France, was consecrated in 1219, since when it has been repeatedly, and unfortunately, restored. Beneath the high altar canopy is the centre-piece of a pilgrimage, a **Virgin and Child** in wood, plated in silver and made in France in the 13 or 14C.

Sala Capitular (Chapter house) ⊙ – The beautiful Gothic chamber, off the cloisters, contains the tombs of the founder, Sancho VII, the Strong (1154-1234), King of Navarra and his queen.

★ **Museo** ⊙ – Housed in the old stables, the museum contains fine pieces of ancient plate: a Mudéjar casket, a Romanesque book of the Gospel, a 14C enamelled reliquary which, doubtless on account of its chequered design, is known as *Charlemagne's chessboard*, a 16C Flemish triptych, an emerald, said to have been worn by Sultan Miramamolín el Verde in his turban on the day of the Battle of Las Navas de Tolosa in 1212, and a lovely *Holy Family* by Morales.

RONDA★★

Andalucía (Málaga)

Population 35788

Michelin map 446 V 14 – Michelin Atlas España Portugal p 84

The town was built at the edge of the Serranía de Ronda on a platform **site**★★ cut by the Guadalevín ravine. The ravine (*tajo* in Castilian Spanish) actually divides Ronda into two: the **Ciudad** or old town and the Mercadillo, now extended by the modern town. There is an impressive bird's eye **view**★ from the bridge, **Puente Nuevo**, down the sheer rock face. The road (Camino de los Molinos) to the power station, which passes along the foot of the cliffs, affords another good **view**★ – this time up the ravine cut by the bridge.

Puente Nuevo and the ravine, Ronda

RONDA

E Palacio del Marqués
  de Salvatierra

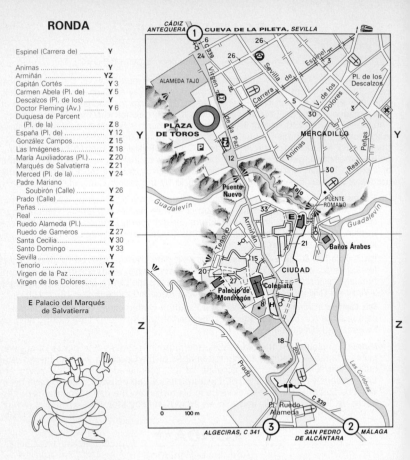

The cradle of bullfighting – Born in Ronda in 1695, **Francisco Romero** laid down the rules of bullfighting, which until then had been only a display of audacity and agility. He became the father of modern bullfighting by his introduction of the cape and the **muleta**. His son Juan introduced the *cuadrillo* or supporting team and his grandson, **Pedro Romero** (1754-1839), became one of Spain's greatest bullfighters. He founded the **Ronda School**, known still for its classicism, strict observance of the rules and *estocada a recibir*.

SIGHTS

★ **Plaza de Toros (Bullring) (Y)** – The bullring, built in 1785, is one of the oldest in Spain. It is entered through an elegant gateway and is surrounded by fine arcades inside. Traditional *Corridas Goyescas*, fights in period costumes from the time of Goya, are held annually. The bullring was used in Rosi's film *Carmen* in 1984.
The **Museo Taurino** (Bullfighting Museum) ⊘ contains sumptuous costumes and various mementoes and photographs of generations of Ronda matadors including the Romero family and Ordoñez.

★ **La Ciudad (YZ)** – The old walled town, a vestige from the Moorish occupation which lasted until 1485, is a picturesque enclave of narrow alleys and white houses with ironwork balconies.

Colegiata (Z) ⊘ – This collegiate church was built between the 15 and 16C on the site of a former mosque of which it has retained a 13C horseshoe arch and the Mudéjar minaret which was converted into a belfry in the 16C.
A two-tiered balcony on the church façade served as a gallery from which notables could watch events in the square below. Inside are three different architectural styles: Gothic in the aisles, Plateresque in the chancel and baroque in the stalls.

Palacio de Mandragón (Z) – The palace's noble Renaissance façade is surmounted by twin Mudéjar turrets. The square nearby commands a **view** over the ravine.

Palacio del Marqués de Salvatierra (Y E) – The Marquis, a great Renaissance traveller, adorned his palace with the strange figures of two Inca Indian couples holding up the triangular pediment. A wrought-iron balcony and detailed low reliefs complete the decoration.

Baños Árabes (Moorish Baths) **(Z)** ⊘ – A reminder that Ronda was once the capital of a *taifa (qv)* kingdom.

EXCURSIONS

★★ **Ronda to San Pedro de Alcántara road** – *49km - 30 miles southeast on the C339 – about 1 hour.*
For 20km - 12 miles the road travels through a bare mountain landscape; it then climbs steeply into a **corniche**★★ above the Guadalmedina valley and its smaller tributary valleys. The route is deserted, there's not a single village.

★ **Ronda to Algeciras road** – *118km - 73 miles southwest on the C341, the C3331 and the N340 – about 3 hours.*
The Ronda-Gaucín section is particularly interesting when the road climbs steeply to overlook the Genal valley. It then continues, winding around the foot of Jimena de la Frontera perched on a hill. 22km - 14 miles further on, a narrow road on the right leads to **Castellar de la Frontera**, a village of flower-filled alleyways huddled within the castle grounds.

★ **The White Villages of Andalucía** – *See PUEBLOS BLANCOS DE ANDALUCÍA.*

★ **Cueva de la Pileta** (Pileta Cave) ⊙ – *27km - 17 miles – about 1 hour plus 1 1/2 hours sightseeing. Take the northerly C339 (towards Sevilla) and turn left after 14km - 9 miles.*
There is a striking **view**★★ when you come upon the Montejaque dam. The cave is interesting archaeologically: lamplight reveals beautiful natural concretions of draperies and hangings but more importantly, rock paintings, antedating those of Altamira *(qv)* and which are believed to date back at least 25 000 years. There are figures of goats and panthers, symbolic drawings and a giant fish measuring 1.25m - 49 inches.

SAGUNTO

Comunidad Valenciana (Valencia)
Population 55 957
Michelin map 445 M 29 – Michelin Atlas España Portugal p 57

Sagunto lies surrounded by a *huerta*; the town itself is backed up against a wide hill crowned by the ruins of an ancient citadel. The port 5km - 3 miles away is also an industrial centre.

A legendary siege – Sagunto has a place in Spain's heroic history. In 218 BC the Carthaginian general, **Hannibal**, besieged Sagunto, then a small seaport allied to Rome – the harbour and surrounding countryside have since silted over. Sagunto was abandoned by Rome, and the inhabitants, seeing only one alternative, to surrender, lit a huge fire. They fed the fire until the flames were high, then women and children, the sick and the old, threw themselves into the furnace while soldiers and menfolk made a suicidal sortie against the enemy. The event marked the beginning of the Second Punic War. Five years later, Scipio Africanus Major rebuilt the city which became an important Roman town.

Ruinas ⊙ – The ruins are reached through the upper part of town, through the narrow alleyways of the old Jewish quarter.

Teatro – The ancient Roman theatre was built on the hillside.

Acrópolis – Ruins and remains can be seen superimposed and juxtaposed of ramparts, temples and houses built by Iberians, Phoenicians, Carthaginians, Romans, Visigoths and Moors. In 1811, in the War of Independence, the French general Suchet besieged the town, leaving major works on the west side to mark yet another period in Sagunto's history. A vast **panorama**★ spreads out on all sides of the Acropolis of the town, huerta, Palancia valley and the sea.

EXCURSIONS

Grutas de San José (San José Caves) ⊙ – *27km - 17 miles north. First take the N340 and then head for Vall de Uxó.*
The caves have been hollowed out by an underground river along which you go by boat for about 1 200 yds.

Segorbe – *33km - 21 miles northwest on the N234.*
The cathedral is chiefly important for its museum (**museo** ⊙) which contains a large **collection of altarpieces painted by the Valencia school**★. There are several paintings by **Juan Vicente Macip** (d 1550) who was influenced by the Italian Renaissance style. An *Ecce Homo* by his son **Juan de Juanes** bears the touch of gentleness favoured by Leonardo da Vinci. There are also works by Rodrigo de Osona and Jacomart and a 15C marble low relief of a Madonna by Donatello.

Michelin Maps, Red Guides and Green Guides
are complementary publications to be used together.

SALAMANCA★★★

Castilla y León (Salamanca)
Population 166 322
Michelin map 441 and 444 J 12-13 – Michelin Atlas España Portugal p 37

Salamanca is a lovely university city of golden stone, narrow streets, splendid buildings and exuberantly rich façades; it is a city of domes and spires with a long tradition of learning still youthfully alive.

HISTORICAL NOTES

The tumultuous past – Iberian in origin, Salamanca was conquered by Hannibal in the 3C BC, flourished under the Romans who built the **Puente Romano** (Roman bridge) **(AZ)** across the Tormes, and invaded repeatedly by the Moors. Alfonso VI took the city from the Moors in 1085. It recovered only to be troubled in the 14 and 15C by rivalry among the nobility whose younger members formed factions known as **Los Bandos.** Such was the vendetta spirit that two Monroy brothers of the Sant Tomé Bando were killed by Manzano brothers of the San Benito Bando after an argument at a game of pelota: immediate vengeance by their mother, Doña María, and the Santo Tomé faction resulted in the decapitated Manzano heads being triumphantly planted on the Monroy tomb – after which the mother was known as **María La Brava.** Her 15C house remains to this day **(AY Q).** The *bandos* remained active until 1476.

Salamanca was occupied by the French during the War of Independence; when the French evacuated the town, Wellington entered it in June 1812 but within days had moved south to the **Arapiles valley** where, on 22 July, he won the resounding Victory of Salamanca which proved to be a major turning point in the war.

La Universidad – The University was founded in 1215 (Oxford University *c*1167) and grew under the patronage of Kings of Castilla, high dignitaries and learned men such as the antipope Benedict XIII *(qv).* Its teaching was soon widely renowned (it took part in the reform of the Catholic Church) and by the 16C it numbered 70 professors of studies and 12 000 students.

Its great and famous members include the Infante Don Juan, son of the Catholic Monarchs; St John of the Cross and his teacher, the great humanist **Fray Luis de León** (1527-1591) *(qv)*; and **Miguel de Unamuno** (1864-1936) *(qv)*, Professor of Greek, University Rector and philosopher of international standing.

The red inscriptions which appear on most of the town's monuments, in particular those of the University, are part of an old tradition that dates back to the 15C: on graduating, students would take part in a bullfight and, with the blood of the bull they had killed, write the word "Victor" and the date on a wall. Today the same is done with paint.

The artistic flowering – In the late 15C and early 16C, two major painters were working in Salamanca: **Fernando Gallego**, one of the best Hispano-Flemish artists (much influenced in precision of line and realism by Dirk Bouts) and **Juan of Flanders** (*b*1465), who settled in the city in 1504 and whose elegant and gentle work is outstanding for the subtle delicacy of its colours.

The 15C also saw the evolution of the original Salamanca *patio* arch, a mixtilinear arc in which the line of the curve, inspired by Mudéjar design, is broken by counter curves and straight lines. The 16C brought decoration to an ebullient climax in Plateresque art, the purest examples of which may be seen in Salamanca.

★★★MONUMENTAL CENTRE

Time: 1 day. Follow the itinerary on the town plan p 224.

★★★**Plaza Mayor** **(ABY)** – The square, built for the city by Philip V between 1729 and 1755 in gratitude for its support in the War of Succession, is among the finest in Spain. It was designed as a homogeneous unit principally by the Churriguera brothers: four ground level arcades with rounded arches decorated by a series of portrait medallions of the Spanish kings from Alfonso XI to Ferdinand VI and famous men such as Cervantes, El Cid, Christopher Columbus and Cortés support the three storeys which rise in perfect formation to an elegant balus-

Plaza Mayor, Salamanca

Geopress /EXPLORER

trade. On the north and east sides are the pedimented fronts of the Ayuntamiento (Town Hall) and the Pabellón Real (Royal Pavilion), the latter distinguished by a bust of Philip V.

Iglesia de San Martín (**AY**) – The Romanesque church has a north door with dog-tooth covings in the Zamora style.

★ **Casa de las Conchas (House of Shells)** (**AYZ**) – *(Photograph p 323)* This 15C house with its 400 scallop shells, carved in the same golden stone as the wall, its line of highly decorative Isabelline windows and lower down, beautiful wrought-iron window grilles, composes a timelessly decorative and unique façade. The patio has delicate mixtilinear arches, openwork balustrades, carved lions' heads and coats of arms.

Clerecía (**AZ**) ⊘ – This impressive Jesuit College was begun in 1617 and was only finished with the completion of the baroque towers by Andrés García de Quiñones in 1755. There are baroque cloisters beside the church.

★★★ **Patio de las Escuelas (Schools' Square)** (**AZ**) – This small square, off the old Calle Libreros, is surrounded by the best examples of Salamanca Plateresque. A bronze statue of Fray Luis de León stands in the middle of the square.

Universidad (**U**) ⊘ – *(Illustration p 26)* The university's sumptuous **entrance**★★★ of 1534 is a brilliant piece of sculpture, composed with the utmost care for detail, as in the goldsmith's art. Above the twin doors, covered by basket arches, the carving is in ever greater relief as it rises through the three registers, to compensate for the increasing distance from the ground.

A central medallion in the first register shows the Catholic Monarchs who presented the doorway; in the second, above crowned escutcheons and medallions, are portrait heads in scallop shell niches; in the third, flanking the pope supported by cardinals, are Venus and Hercules (in square frames) and the Virtues (in roundels). The most famous motif in this outstanding ensemble is the death's head surmounted by a frog (on the right pilaster) symbolising the posthumous punishment of lust.

B. Brillon/MICHELIN

The Catholic Monarchs, Salamanca University

Off the **patio** are the lecture halls: the **Paraninfo** or Large Hall, where official functions were held, is hung with 17C Brussels tapestries and a portrait of *Charles IV* by Goya; the hall or aula of **Maestro Salinas** (1513-1590), professor of music, contains a 15C portfolio of music; the hall where Fray Luis de León lectured in theology, is as it was in the 16C with the professor's desk and sounding-board overlooking the rough-hewn students' benches – a luxury in days when students usually sat on the floor. Fray Luis' ashes are buried in the chapel (1767).

The grand staircase rises beneath star vaulting, its banister carved with foliated scrollwork and imaginary scenes and, at the third flight, a mounted bullfight.

A gallery on the first floor has its original, rich, coffered ceiling with stalactite ornaments and a delicate low relief frieze along the walls. A still Gothic style door with a fine 16C grille opens into the 18C library which contains 40 000 16-18C volumes as well as incunabula and manuscripts, some of which date back to the 11C.

Hospital del Estudio (Students' Hospice) – The hospice, completed in 1533, has an interesting Gothic entrance where a trefoil arch and escutcheons are framed by an *alfiz (qv)*.

Escuelas Menores (Minors' Schools) (**U¹**) ⊘ – Standing to the right of the hospital and crowned by the same openwork Renaissance frieze, is the entrance to the Minors' Schools – a Plateresque portal decorated with coats of arms, roundels and scrollwork. The typical Salamanca **patio**★ (1428) inside, has lovely lines. The library, on the right as you enter, has a Mudéjar ceiling; the Calderón de la Barca gallery, on the *patio* side, contains the former University Library decoration (converted into a chapel in the 18C) including a third of the so-called **Cielo de Salamanca**★ (Salamanca Sky) by Fernando Gallego illustrating constellations and signs of the zodiac. The interest of this remaining part gives an idea of what the whole must have been like in the 15C.

★★ **Catedral Nueva (New Cathedral)** (**AZ**) ⊘ – Construction, begun in 1513, was largely completed by 1560, although additions continued to be made until the 18C – hence the variety of architectural styles: Gothic, Renaissance and baroque.

The **west front**★★ is divided below the windows into four wide bays which correspond to the ground plan. The bays are outlined by pierced stonework, carved as minutely as the keystones in the arches, the friezes and pinnacled balustrades. The Gothic decoration of the central portal, which in retable style includes scenes such as a Crucifixion shown between Sts Peter and Paul, overflows the covings and tympanum.

SALAMANCA

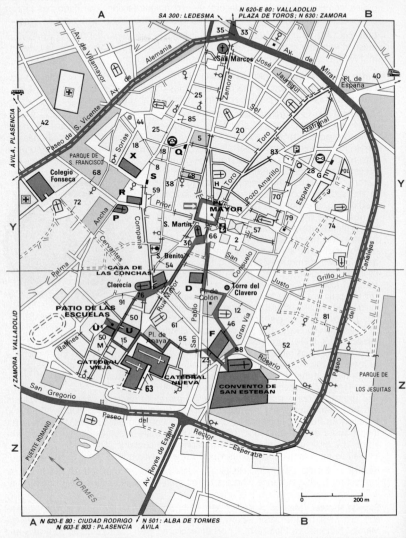

D	Palacio de Fonseca (Diputación)	R	Palacio de Monterrey	X	Convento de las Úrsulas
F	Convento de las Dueñas	S	Casa de las Muertes	U	Universidad
P	Purísima Concepción	Q	Casa de Doña María la Brava	U¹	Escuelas menores

The north doorway, facing the Colegio de Anaya, is adorned with a delicate low relief of Christ's entry into Jerusalem (Palm Sunday).

The **interior**, in particular the pattern of the vaulting, the delicacy of the cornices and the sweep of the pillars, strikes one immediately on entering. The eight windows in the lantern are given added effect by a drum on which scenes from the Life of the Virgin were painted in the 18C by the Churriguera brothers who also designed the ornate baroque stalls in the *coro*, the *trascoro* and organ loft above the stalls on the north side; the south loft is Plateresque (1558).

★★ **Catedral Vieja (Old Cathedral)** (**AZ**) ⊘ – *Enter through the first bay off the south aisle in the new cathedral.* Fortunately the builders of the new cathedral respected the fabric of the old which, nevertheless, is almost totally masked outside by its larger descendant. It was built in the 12C and is a good example of the

Romanesque, the pointed arching being a legitimate, if unusual, innovation; the **cimborrio** (lantern), or Torre del Gallo, with two tiers of windows and ribbing, is outstanding. High up beneath the vaulting, the capitals are carved with scenes of tournaments and imaginary animals.

The **altarpiece★★** in the central apsidal chapel was painted by Nicholas of Florence in 1445 and comprises 53 compartments decorated in surprisingly fresh colours in vivid detail – an interesting testimony to the architecture and dress of the times – beneath a Last Judgment in which the dark background enhances the brilliance of the Risen Christ. The Virgin of the Vega at the retable centre is a 12C wooden statue, plated in gilded and enamelled bronze.

Recesses in the south transept contain French influenced 13C recumbent figures and frescoes; the Capilla de San Martín (St Martin's Chapel) at the end of the nave is covered in 13C frescoes by Antón Sanchez de Segovia and others dating from the 14C.

Claustro – Some of the capitals from earlier Romanesque galleries destroyed during the Lisbon earthquake in 1755 remain in these cloisters, forming a surprising contrast to the Plateresque decoration. The adjoining **Capilla de Talavera** with a Mudéjar dome on carved ribs was where the ancient Mozarabic rite was celebrated – the altarpiece is in the style of Pedro Berruguete. The Capilla de Santa Barbara was formerly used for university examinations. The Museo Diocesano (Diocesan Museum) in the chapter house contains works by Fernando Gallego and his brother Francisco as well as others by Juan of Flanders on the first floor (St Michael altarpiece).

The **Capilla Anaya** contains the outstanding 15C alabaster **tomb★★** of Diego de Anaya, archbishop first of Salamanca and then of Sevilla. The sides are decorated with saints and their emblems. Surrounding the tomb is a magnificently wrought Plateresque grille. There is also a 15C organ and 16C recumbent statues of Gutierre de Monroy and Constancia de Anaya.

From the **Patio Chico (AZ 63)** you can see the old cathedral apse and the scallop tiling on the **Torre del Gallo** (Cock Tower).

★ **Convento de San Esteban (St Stephen's Monastery) (BZ)** ⊘ – Gothic and Renaissance styles are mingled in this 16 and 17C building, so that while typically Gothic pinnacles decorate the side buttresses, nothing could be more Plateresque in style than the sculpture of the impressive **façade★**. The low relief of the Martyrdom of St Stephen is by Juan Antonio Ceroni (1610).

Claustro – In these cloisters, note the prophets' heads in **medallions★** and the grand staircase (1553).

Iglesia – The large church has star vaulting in the gallery and a central altarpiece by José Churriguera with an abundance of carving and gilt decoration. Crowning it is a painting *The Martyrdom of St Stephen*, by Claudio Coello.

Convento de Las Dueñas (Las Dueñas Convent) (BZ F) ⊘ – The Renaissance **cloisters★★** have profusely carved capitals which are extraordinarily forceful in spite of their small size. Among the sculptures are the figures of symbolic animals, distorted human shapes as well as medallions decorated with the heads of majestic old men or delicately featured women.

Torre del Clavero (BZ) – The tower, all that remains of a castle built in 1450, is an octagonal keep, crowned with sentry turrets decorated underneath with Mudéjar trellis-work.

Palacio de Fonseca or **Diputación (Fonseca Palace** or **Council) (AZ D)** – The **patio★** of this Renaissance palace combines Salamanca mixtilinear arches at one end with a corbelled gallery – supported by distorted atlantes – on the right and an arcade on the left in which the capitals resemble those in the Convento de Las Dueñas.

ADDITIONAL SIGHTS

Palacio de Monterrey (AY R) – The typical Renaissance palace (1539), has an openwork balustrade crowning a long top floor gallery, between corner towers.

Barrio de San Benito (San Benito Quarter) (AY) – Surrounding the square, at the centre of which stands the **church (AY)**, are the mansions of Salamanca's old noble rival families. The church itself, dating from 1490, was the Maldonado family pantheon.

Iglesia de la Purísima Concepción (Church of the Immaculate Conception) (AY P) ⊘ – The church contains works by Ribera, including one of his most famous paintings, the **Immaculate Conception★**, which hangs above the high altar.

Casa de las Muertes (House of Death) (AY S) – The early-16C façade, one of the first examples of Plateresque, is attributed, complete with its design of medallions, foliated scrollwork and decorative putti, to Diego de Siloé.

Convento de las Úrsulas (Ursuline Convent) (AY X) ⊙ – The 16C church contains the **tomb★** of Alonso de Fonseca on which the incredibly delicate carved low reliefs are attributed to Diego de Siloé. The **museum**, with its *artesonado* and coffered ceilings, houses panels and fragments of an altarpiece by Juan de Borgoña, one of which illustrates *St Ursula and the Virgins*. There are also two noteworthy works by Morales the Divine *(qv)*, an *Ecce Homo* and a *Pietà*.

Colegio Fonseca (AY) ⊙ – The college was built to plans by Diego de Siloé for Irish students in the 16C. A beautifully carved Plateresque door leads into a Gothic **chapel★** with star vaulting. This contains a fine altarpiece by Alonso Berruguete. The **patio★** is an elegant example of the Renaissance style.

Iglesia de San Marcos (St Mark's Church) (BY) – The 12C church's round shape was no doubt originally designed as protection against possible Moorish attack. Inside are fragmentary frescoes.

EXCURSIONS

Alba de Tormes – *23km - 14 miles southeast on the N501 and C510*.
The small town stands on the banks of the wide Río Tormes. Only the massive keep remains of the castle of the Dukes of Alba. The town boasts of possessing the mortal remains of St Teresa of Ávila *(qv)* in the church of the Carmelite Convent.
The **Iglesia de San Juan**, a church with a Romanesque-Mudéjar east end, contains an outstanding 12C **sculpture★** in the apse. It illustrates Christ and the Disciples seated in a semicircle, all equally noble in expression and stance.

Castillo del Buen Amor ⊙ – *21km - 13 miles north on the N630 then bear right into a signposted private road*.
This fortified castle served as the Catholic Monarchs' base in the early years when they were fighting supporters of La Beltraneja *(qv)*. Alonso II, Archbishop of Toledo, converted it into a palace, adding a pleasant Renaissance *patio* as a suitable setting for his mistress! Inside, note a Mudéjar fireplace and *artesonado* ceilings.

SANGÜESA★

Navarra
Population 4 447
Michelin map 442 E 26 – Michelin Atlas España Portugal p 15

Sangüesa stands in arable country (mostly cereals) on the left bank of the Aragón river. It still seems to guard the bridge which in the Middle Ages brought the town prosperity.

Sangüesa and the pilgrim way – Fear of the Moors compelled Sangüesans to live until the 10C on the **Rocaforte** hillside; by the 11C, however, the citizens had moved down to defend the bridge and clear a safe passage for pilgrims. In 1122, Alfonso I of Aragón, the Battler, granted a *fuero* or charter to the town which then grew rapidly. Sangüesa reached its climax at the end of the Middle Ages when, in contrast to the austere **Palacio del Príncipe de Viana** (Palace of the Prince of Viana), residence of the Kings of Navarra, now the Ayuntamiento (Town Hall), with its façade (seen through the gateway) flanked by two imposing battlemented towers, prosperous citizens began to build elegant residential mansions. The main street, the former **Rúa Mayor** which was once part of the pilgrim road, is lined with comfortable brick houses with the classical carved wood eaves and windows with rich Gothic or Plateresque surrounds. In the second street on the right coming from the bridge can be seen the baroque front of the **Palacio de Vallesantoro**, a palace protected by monumental overhangs carved with imaginary animals.

★**Iglesia de Santa María la Real** – The church, begun in the 12C, was completed in the 13C with the construction of the splendid south portal, the octagonal tower and its spire.

★★**Portada Sur** (South Portal) – Late-12 to 13C. The portal is so crowded with sculpture that one stands amazed at the number of subjects depicted and the variety of ways in which they have been illustrated. At least two artists worked on the masterpiece: the Master of San Juan de la Peña and a certain Leodegarius.
The **statue columns**, already Gothic, derive from those at Chartres and Autun. On the **tympanum**, God the Father at the centre of a group of angel musicians receives, at his right, the chosen, but with down-pointing left arm reproves the sinners. In a corner weighing souls is St Michael.
The **covings** swarm with motifs; the second innermost shows the humbler trades: clogmaker, lutemaker and butcher.
The older **upper arches**, marked by an Aragonese severity of style, show God surrounded by the symbols of the four Evangelists, two angels and the twelve disciples.

CASTILLO DE JAVIER (JAVIER CASTLE) ⊘

7km - 4 miles northeast on the NA541.

St Francis Xavier, patron saint of Navarra, was born here in 1506. At 22, in Paris, he met his Basque compatriot, Ignatius Loyola, with whom he was later to formulate the principles of the Society of Jesus *(qv)*. Xavier was sent by the Portuguese who had considerable and well-established commercial interests with the Far East, as a missionary first to Goa and then to Japan. He died in 1552, on his way to China. He was canonised in 1622.

Castillo – The fortress, birthplace of the saint, was in part destroyed by Cardinal Cisneros in 1516. The visit includes the Patio de Armas (Parade Ground), the Oratorio (Oratory), which contains a 13C Christ in walnut and an unusual 15C fresco of the Dance of Death, the Sala Grande (Great Hall) and, among the oldest parts of the castle dating from the 10-11C, the Cuarto del Santo (Saint's bedroom).

Santuario de SAN IGNACIO DE LOYOLA

País Vasco (Guipúzcoa)
Michelin map 442 C 23 – Michelin Atlas España Portugal p 14

A sanctuary (**santuario** ⊘) was built by the Jesuits to plans by the Italian architect Carlo Fontana around the Loyola family manorhouse near Azpeitia at the end of the 17C. It has since become an important place of pilgrimage where large crowds attend the solemnities held annually on St Ignatius day (31 July).

The Soldier of God – **Ignatius de Loyola** was born in 1491 in the Castillo de Loyola to an old family of the lesser nobility. He was bred to arms. It was while recovering from wounds received at the siege of Pamplona, that he heard the call of God and eight months later, in 1522, left the Loyola manor to go on a pilgrimage to Arantzazu and Montserrat. He next withdrew to a cave near Manresa in Catalunya where he began to write his **Spiritual Exercises**. In 1523 he set off in pilgrimage to Jerusalem from where, before returning to Spain, he journeyed to Paris (1528) and London (1530). After further wanderings and attendance at various universities, he and the compatriots he had met in Paris, Diego Laínez and Francis Xavier *(qv)*, were ordained (1537) and repaired to Rome. In 1540, the pope recognised the **Society of Jesus** which Loyola had conceived and for which he had drawn up the constitution.
Ignatius of Loyola died in 1556 and was canonised in 1622 at the same time as Francis Xavier and Teresa de Ávila.

SIGHTS

Santa Casa – The basement casemates of the 15C tower are vestiges of the original Loyola manorhouse. The rooms in which Ignatius was born, convalesced and converted have been transformed into profusely decorated chapels.

Basílica – The baroque basilica is more Italian than Spanish in style. It is circular and surmounted by a vast cupola (65m – 213ft high) attributed to Churriguera.

Monasterio de SAN JUAN DE LA PEÑA★★

Aragón (Huesca)
Michelin map 443 E 27 – Michelin Atlas España Portugal p 15
Local map under JACA: Excursions

After a long climb through wild countryside in the Sierra de la Peña, the monastery appears minute, in a hollow under overhanging rocks. The **site★★** itself is spectacular. The monastery, symbol of the continued existence of the Christian faith in the Pyrenees at the time of the Muslim invasion, was chosen by the kings and nobles of Aragón-Navarra as their pantheon. The community had been founded in the secluded site in the 9C. In the 11C the order adopted the Clunaic reform. Generous royal donations attracted many monks, some foreign, to the house.
In the 17C, a second monastery was built higher up the mountainside.

TOUR ⊘ *time: about 3/4 hour*

Because of its age and extraordinary site lodged in the side of the mountain, the monastery plan is unique.

Lower storey – This is partially underground and is believed to have been built in the time of King Sancho Garcés in about 922.

Sala de Concilios – This council chamber, also known as the dormitory, has been built in a massive architectural style.

Iglesia Baja (Lower Church) – This, the original church which later served as a crypt, is one of the rare Mozarabic constructions still existing in the region. It consists of two adjoining aisles divided by wide arches and ending in twin niche-apses hollowed out of the living rock. Traces of mural painting can be seen on the walls and on the undersides of the arches.

Upper storey – On reaching the upper storey, you enter the court of the pantheon of the nobles.

Pantéon de nobles aragoneses (Pantheon of the Aragón nobility) – 11-14C. Funerary niches line the left wall in surrounds of moulded billets or pearls, each emblasoned with a coat of arms, Chi-rho (sacred monogram) or a cross with four roses, emblem of Íñigo Arista, founder of the Kingdom of Navarra. On one of the niches an angel is shown carrying the soul of the deceased. A door opposite leads into a **museum** which contains finds from the monastery excavations.

Iglesia Alta (Upper Church) – Late 11C. Rock roofs part of the single aisle, while the three apsidal chapels, decorated with blind arcades, are hollowed out of the cliff face.

The **Pantéon de Reyes** or Royal Pantheon, where the kings of Aragón and Navarra were buried for 500 years, opens off the north wall. The present décor is 18C.

★ **Claustro** – 12C. A Mozarabic door serves as an entrance. The cloisters, cornered between the precipice and the cliff face, which provides an unplanned roof, now consist of two galleries only with historiated capitals and a third gallery in a poor state of preservation.

The original column arrangement, alternating single, double or quadruple columns is reproduced in miniature between the capital abacuses and the arch billets. The mason who carved the **capitals**★★ developed a personal style and symbolism, apparent in his chronological survey of man from the Creation to the coming of the Evangelists, which was to influence sculpture throughout the region for years to come.

EXCURSION

★ **Santa Cruz de la Serós** – *5km - 3 miles north.*
This famous convent, founded late in the 10C, was richly endowed by royal princesses. The religious abandoned the convent in the 16C.
Only the **Romanesque church,** surrounded by small, typically Aragonese houses, remains. The stout belfry, crowned by an octagonal turret abuts on the lantern. The portal with its Chi-rho (sacred monogram) decorated tympanum recalls that of Jaca cathedral.
Inside, a column and capitals have been assembled to form an unusual stoup.

San Caprasio, the small church at the entrance to the village, has a nave adorned with Lombard bands and a low apse, typical of the 11C. The belfry is late-12C.

SAN MARTÍN DE VALDEIGLESIAS

Madrid
Population 5 428
Michelin map 442 or 444 K 16 – Michelin Atlas España Portugal p 52

The old market town dominated by its castle walls serves as a departure point for local excursions.

EXCURSIONS

Toros de Guisando – *6km - 4 miles northwest.*
The Bulls of Guisando, as they are called, four rudimentarily carved figures in granite, stand in an open field. Similar figures may be seen throughout the province of Ávila. They are, however, obviously ancient and remain an enigma in spite of the possible theory that they represent a commemorative monument, a Celtiberian idol. They have certain similarities to the stone sows or *porcas* that may be seen in villages in the Trás-os-Montes region of Portugal.

★ **Embalse de Burguillo** (Burgillo Reservoir) – *20km - 12 miles northwest.*
The manmade lake on the Alberche river, amidst hills covered in sparse vegetation, provides a fine setting for water sports enthusiasts.

Pantano de San Juan – *8km - 5 miles east.*
As the road descends to this artificial lake there are attractive **views**★ of the narrow part of the Alberche reservoir where the banks are deeply indented and covered in pine trees. The area is popular with Madrileños in summer on account of its water sports facilities.

Safari Madrid ⊙ – *27km - 17 miles southeast.*
This is one of Spain's largest game parks, where wild animals from the world over may be observed. The main attraction is a demonstration by birds of prey.

Santuario de SAN MIGUEL DE ARALAR★

Navarra

Michelin map 442 D 24 – MIchelin Atlas España Portugal p 14

To reach the sanctuary take the San Miguel de Aralar road from Uharte Arakil between Pamplona and Vitoria on the N240. There are good views from the road as it runs for 10km - 6 miles through attractive rocky countryside and oak forests.

The **santuario** ⊘, which dates from different periods – the apse and part of the walls are Visigothic (9C), while the rest is pre-Romanesque (10C) – encloses a small 11-12C Romanesque chapel which replaced a church built in the 8C. It was here that a magnificent gilt and enamel **altarfront★★**, now considered one of the major works of European Romanesque goldsmithery, was discovered in the 18C. It may be late-12C Limousin.

SAN SEBASTIÁN / DONOSTIA★★

País Vasco (Guipúzcoa)

Population 176 019

Michelin map 442 C 23 – Michelin Atlas España Portugal p 14

Local map under COSTA VASCA

Town plan in the current Michelin Red Guide España Portugal

The resort and its setting★★★ – San Sebastián – Donostia in Basque – long known as the Pearl of the Cantabrian coast, stretches between Monte Urgull and Monte Iguelda alongside its scallop shaped bay, the Bahía de la **Concha**. The islet of Santa Clara partly closes off the bay.

Two vast sand beaches follow the curve of the bay: La Concha, and beyond the promontory, the fashionable **Ondarreta** (A). Behind are gardens, promenades and luxury apartment blocks and beyond the Playa de Ondarreta, at the foot of Monte Igueldo, can be found the **Peine de los Vientos,** a sculpture by Eduardo Chillida.

Historically, San Sebastián's recognition as a resort began in 1889 with the construction of the **Palacio de Miramar** (A), a palace built to designs by an English architect, Selden Warnum. It was patronised by the Regent, María Cristina of Habsburg-Lorraine and thereafter by the Spanish aristocracy.

The summer calendar includes international jazz and film festivals, a Semana Grande (in August) and Basque folklore festivals, golf and tennis tournaments, racing and regattas.

A gastronomic capital – A feature of the city where one eats well and copiously, are the 30 or so gourmet clubs. The all-male members prepare excellent meals which they then consume, accompanied by cider or the local *chacolí* wine. Basque specialities include fish dishes (gilt-head, hake, sardines) and the wonderful squid or *chipirones*.

B Santa María   **M¹** Museo de San Telmo

PANORAMIC VIEWS

★★★ **Monte Igueldo** (**A**) ⊙ – *Access by funicular; by car, follow the Concha and Ondarreta beaches and then bear left.* At the top are an amusement park, hotel and restaurant. There is also a splendid **panorama** of the sea, the harbour with Santa Clara island and San Sebastián itself, set within a mountain cirque. The view is beautiful in the evening when the town lights up.

★★ **Monte Urgull** (**B**) – Monte Urgull, now a public park, is crowned by a fortress, **Castillo de Santa Cruz de la Mota**. From the summit there is a good **panorama** of the monuments of the old town directly below and the Bahía de la Concha.

OLD TOWN *time: 2 hours*

San Sebastián was founded at the foot of Monte Urgull and there, between the harbour and the mouth of the Urumea, you can still see the old city. Although, in fact, it all dates only from the last century – the original town was devastated by fire in 1813 – the narrow streets have considerable character. The area comes alive at the evening aperitif hour when locals and tourists (especially the French, many of whom cross the border for a meal) crowd the bars and small restaurants round the Plaza de la Constitución to pick at the *tapas* (reputed to be the best in Spain), shellfish, crustaceans and *chipirones*.

Plaza de la Constitución (**B 12**) – The square is lined with houses with tall arcades and numbered balconies – a reminder of the days when they served as ringside seats when bullfights were held in the square.

Iglesia de Santa María (**B B**) ⊙ – The church has a strikingly exuberant late-18C portal. The vast sober interior is highlighted by baroque altars.

Museo de San Telmo (**B M'**) ⊙ – The museum is in an old 16C monastery. The Renaissance stone cloisters contain Basque stone funerary crosses carved in the traditional Iberian style and dating for the most part from between the 15 and 17C. The former chapel was decorated by José María Sert in vigorous camaieu style painting with events from Basque history.
On the 1st floor, off the cloister gallery – where there is an interesting ethnographic display including a Basque interior – there are rooms with paintings by Zuloaga *(Torerillos de Turégano),* Ortiz Echagüe and artists of Spain's Golden Age (Ribera, El Greco, Carreño). Displayed in another gallery are headdresses worn by local women until the mid-18C. The headdresses, said to be of oriental influence, were made with bands of cloth wrapped over a framework. On the 2nd floor is a large collection of Basque paintings.

Paseo Nuevo (**B**) – The wide corniche promenade almost circles Monte Urgull and affords good **views** of the open sea and the bay. At the end is the **Palacio del Mar** (Sea Palace) (**B**) ⊙, which houses an oceanographic museum, an aquarium and a Seafaring Museum (Museo Histórico Naval) with models and different displays concerning the great Basque sailors (Churruca, Elcano).

EXCURSION

★ **Monte Ulía (view from)** – *7km - 4 miles east.*
Follow the N 1 towards Irún and before reaching the summit and descending to San Sebastián, take the first road on the right. While driving to the top via a series of hairpin bends there are good **views** of the town and its setting. A path at the top leads off to the right across a park to Monte Ulía restaurant.

Monasterio de SANTA MARÍA DE HUERTA★★

Castilla y León (Soria)
Michelin map 442 I23 – Michelin Atlas España Portugal p 41

In 1144, on the request of Emperor Alfonso VII, a Cistercian community came to settle in what was to become the Soria region on the border between Castilla and Aragón. Monks settled in Huerta in 1162 and shortly afterwards laid the foundations of the present buildings. The main initiators of the work, which continued until the late 13C, were the Abbot Martín de Finojosa and Rodrigo Jiménez de Roda. The sober Cistercian style was slightly modified by Renaissance innovations.
From 1835 to 1930 the monastery buildings stood empty before being re-inhabited and restored.

TOUR ⊙ *time: about 1 hour*

The monastery is entered through a 16C **triumphal arch**.

Claustro herreriano (Herreran Cloisters) – 16-17C. The buildings surrounding the cloisters are the monks' living quarters.

★ **Claustro de los Cabelleros (Knights' Cloisters)** − 13-16C. The cloisters owe their name to the many knights who lie buried there. The two storeys of the cloisters have very different styles: the arches at ground level are elegant, pointed and purely Gothic while above, the gallery added in the 16C has all the exuberance and imagination of the Plateresque *(it is a copy of the gallery in the Palacio de Avellaneda in Peñaranda de Duero, -qv)*. The decorative medallions are of prophets, apostles and Spanish kings.

Sala de los Conversos (Laybrothers' Hall) − 12C. This is divided down its length by stout pillars, crowned with stylised capitals.

Cocina − The kitchen has a monumental central chimney.

★★ **Refectorio** − The refectory, a masterpiece of 13C Gothic, impresses by its sheer size − it has sexpartite vaulting rising 15m - 50ft above the 35m - 115ft long hall − and the amount of light shining through the windows, in particular, the wonderful rose window in the south wall. Leading up to the **reader's lectern** is a beautiful staircase carved out of the wall with small arches supported by slender columns.

Claustro de los Caballeros,
Monasterio de Santa María de Huerta

Iglesia − The church has been restored to its original state although the royal chapel has kept its sumptuous Churrigueresque decoration. Between the narthex and the aisles there is an intricate 18C wrought-iron screen.

Coro Alto − The choir is beautifully decorated with Renaissance panelling and woodwork. The Talavera *azulejos* on the floor are very old.

SANTANDER★

Cantabria

Population 196 218
Michelin map 442 B 18 − Michelin Atlas España Portugal p 12
Town plan in the current Michelin Red Guide España Portugal

Santander has a beautiful site along the north shore of a great bay closed by the narrow Magdalena headland and the sandy Somo point. The added advantage of extensive sand beaches makes it one of Cantabria's most sophisticated resorts. Its famous International University courses held in the summer and its music and dance festival make it all the more prestigious.

The new town − A tornado struck Santander on 15 February 1941: the sea swept over the quays and a fire broke out, devastating the entire centre of the town. Reconstruction was undertaken to a street plan of blocks of no more than 4 or 5 storeys; space was allocated to gardens beside the sea and promenades such as the Paseo de Pereda which skirts the pleasure boat harbour known as Puerto Chico. The heart of the town is around the Avenida de Calvo Sotello, with its shops, and Plaza Porticada. The port developed from the natural advantage of the immense sheltered bay. Trade diversified over the centuries as local industries developed, particularly steel, chemicals and shipbuilding in **El Astillero**.

SIGHTS

Catedral ⊘ − The edifice at the top of the rise looks more like a fortress, even after the rebuilding in Gothic style following the 1941 tornado. Inside, the **font** to the right of the ambulatory is obviously a Muslim ablutionary basin.
The 12C **crypt** *(access through the south portal)* has three low aisles separated by solid cruciform pillars. The Gothic cloisters have been considerably restored.

★ **Museo Regional de Prehistoria y Arqueología** ⊘ − The archaeological museum in the basement of the Diputación consists mainly of finds excavated in prehistoric caves in Cantabria (particularly El Castillo and El Pendo). The richest period is the Upper Palaeolithic Era from which there are bones engraved with animal silhouettes and **batons**★ made of horn and finely decorated for a purpose still unknown. The best specimen, made from an antler, was discovered at El Pendo.

Among the Neolithic axeheads, note the particularly high polish on those of diorite. Four large steles are representative of the apogee of the Cantabrian culture (Bronze Age). Finally, one gallery is devoted to remains of the Roman occupation. The finds are mostly from Julióbriga *(see REINOSA: Excursions)* and Castro Urdiales and include coins, bronzes and pottery figurines.

Biblioteca Menéndez y Pelayo ⊘ – **Marcelino Menéndez y Pelayo** (1856-1912), Spanish and universal savant, amassed this fabulous collection of nearly 45 000 books, including manuscripts by great Castilian authors. The library, bequeathed by the writer to his native town and since enlarged, is opposite his house.

Museo de Bellas Artes (Fine Arts Museum) ⊘ – Works by Goya including a portrait of *Ferdinand VII*, some of his *Disasters of War*, *La Tauromaquia* and *Caprichos* etchings, are displayed along with works by regional painters.

★★ EL SARDINERO

At the end of the 19C the Spanish royal family took to sea bathing at Santander, making both pastime and town highly fashionable. The town went so far as to build the **Palacio de Magdalena** on the point of the same name for Alfonso XIII – now the International University annexe. Summer visitors have the choice of several beaches along the promontory, along the Magdalena headland and, bordering El Sardinero, three areas divided at high tide by tongues of land brilliant with flower gardens but when the tide recedes, linked by a long sand bank. Water sports, theatrical and other entertainments, the casino and golf course (at Pedreña, across the bay) are supplemented in July by further events, including the great Santiago festival of bullfighting and throughout August by a festival of drama, music and dance.

EXCURSIONS

Cabo Mayor – *7km - 4 miles north.* Good view from the lighthouse on this cape.

Muriedas – *7km - 4 miles south on the Burgos road.* The house of Pedro Velarde, hero of the War of Independence, has been restored and is now the home of the **Museo Etnográfico de Cantabria** (Cantabrian Ethnographic Museum) ⊘. A typical Cantabrian gateway opens onto grounds in which may be seen a *hórreo* (squat drying shed) from the Liébana region and a Cantabrian stele. The 17C residence contains furniture, utensils and tools from all parts of the province. Mementoes of Velarde are displayed in his former bedroom and another large room on the first floor.

Parque de la Naturaleza de Cabárceno (Cabárceno Nature Reserve) ⊘ – *17km - 11 miles south.* An old iron mine in the Sierra de Cabarga that had been worked from Roman times until 1989, is now part of an environmental rehabilitation project which includes a **game park** where animals from the world over may be seen.

SANT CUGAT DEL VALLÈS

Catalunya (Barcelona)
Population 38 834
Michelin map 443 H 36 – Michelin Atlas España Portugal p 32

The town is named after the Benedictine monastery established in the Middle Ages on the site of an earlier chapel. This had been built very early to contain the relics of St Cucufas whose throat had been cut by Diocletian's legionaries on this spot 8 Roman miles along the road from Barcelona around 304 AD.

★ **Monasterio** ⊘ – The old wall encloses the monastic chapel, cloisters, episcopal palace and conventual buildings abandoned in 1835 which now serve as the parish church and a centre for the restoration of works of art.

Iglesia – The oldest part of the church is the 11C belfry decorated with Lombard bands incorporated into the main building when the side chapels were built (15C). A chancel had already been added in the 12C. The façade was completed in 1350. The flat, crenellated wall supported by thrusting buttresses was relieved by a radiating rose window as vast as the doorway below with its smooth covings. There are three apses, polygonal outside and with engaged pillars inside; the central one was given radiating vaulting, a feature which was to mark an alteration in style, reflected in the ogival vaulting in the lantern and above the three aisles. Among the works of art, note the 14C **All Saints Altarpiece★** by Pere Serra.

★ **Claustro** – The cloisters are among the largest Romanesque cloisters in Catalunya. Early in the 13C a double row of columns (144 in all) was built around a close; in the 16C an upper gallery was added above a blind arcade decorated with sculpted modillions. The skilfully carved **Romanesque capitals★** are Corinthian (acanthus leaves), ornamental (strapwork), figurative (birds) and historiated (Biblical scenes); these last ones are grouped largely in the south gallery which abuts the church. The most interesting of all, however, is the one over the northeast corner column on which the sculptor, Arnaud Cadell, portrayed himself at work and then cut his name.

Monasterio de SANTES CREUS★★

Catalunya (Tarragona)
Michelin map 443 H34 — Michelin Atlas España Portugal p 32

Approached from the south, the Monasterio de Santes Creus appears as a vast complex of buildings set in undulating countryside. The monastery, pendant to Poblet, was founded shortly after the latter in the 12C. It was placed in the care of Cistercians from Toulouse, came under the protection of the great families of Catalunya and into the favour of the Kings of Aragón who appointed the abbot royal chaplain. The splendours of the Middle Ages were followed, as at Poblet, by the ravages of the 19C with the difference that at Santes Creus, worship never ceased in the church.

TOUR ⊘ *time: 1 hour*

The monastery plan is similar to that of Poblet in that it has three perimeter walls. A baroque gateway leads to the principal courtyard where the monastic buildings now serve as shops. To the right is the abbatial palace, with its attractive *patio*, which is now the town hall and school; at the end stands the 12-13C church. The façade is plain apart from a rounded doorway, a large Gothic window and battlements added a century later.

★★**Gran Claustro (Great Cloisters)** – The **Puerta Real** or Royal Gate on the south side of the church opens onto cloisters with Gothic bays which, although much restored, still have lively carvings – particularly the illustration of Adam and Eve on the first corner frieze where Eve is shown emerging out of Adam's rib. The tracery shows a first hint of the Flamboyant style. In contrast, the transitional style of the **lavabo**, which incorporates a marble basin, appears almost clumsy. Carved tombs of the Catalan nobility fill the gallery niches.

★**Sala capitular** – This chapter house is an elegant hall with arches supported on four pillars. Abbots' tombstones have been inlaid in the pavement.

Dormitorio – Stairs next to the chapter house lead to the dormitory, a long gallery divided by diaphragm arches supporting a timber roof.

★**Iglesia** – The church, begun in 1174, closely follows the Cistercian pattern of a flat east end and overall austerity; the square ribbed ogive vaulting, replacing the more usual broken barrel vaulting, does nothing to soften its severity. The lantern (*c*1300), the stained glass in the great west window, and the superb apsidal **rose window★**, partially hidden by the high altar retable, do, however, relieve the bareness. The ribbed vaults rest on pillars which extend back along the walls and end in unusual consoles with rich corbelling. Gothic canopies at the transept openings shelter the royal tombs: on the north side that of Peter the Great (*c*1295) and on the south, that of his son, James II, the Just, and his Queen, Blanche d'Anjou. The Plateresque decoration below the crowned recumbent figures in Cistercian habits, was added in the 16C.

Claustro viejo – The design of these old cloisters is simple with a small central fountain and four cypresses in the close, imparting a cool, contemplative atmosphere. Leading off the cloisters are the cellar *(right of the entrance)*, kitchens and refectory and beyond, the royal palace (14C *patio* and beautiful staircase).

SANTIAGO DE COMPOSTELA★★★

Galicia (La Coruña)
Population 105 851
Michelin map 441 D4 — Michelin Atlas España Portugal p 6
Plan of the conurbation in the current Michelin Red Guide España Portugal

In the Middle Ages, Santiago de Compostela, the third most important city of pilgrimage after Jerusalem and Rome, attracted pilgrims from all parts of Europe *(see The Way of Saint James below)*. It remains one of Spain's most remarkable cities with old quarters, churches, conventual buildings and an air at once ancient, mystical and, on account of the 32 000 or so students at the University, lively.

Contrary to all expectations, the style of architecture that predominates is not Romanesque but baroque and neo-classical which lends an air of solemnity to the town. This can be best appreciated from the Paseo de la Herradura *(qv)*.

Legend and history – The Apostle James the Greater, known as the Thunderer on account of his temper, crossed the seas, so the legend goes, to convert Spain to Christianity. His boat was cast ashore at the mouth of the Ulla and he preached for seven years throughout the land before returning to Judaea where he fell an early victim to Herod Agrippa. His disciples, forced to flee, returned to Spain with his body which they buried near the earlier landing place. Invasions by the Barbarians and later the Arabs caused the grave to be lost to memory.

Early in the 9C a star is believed to have pointed out the grave to some shepherds. This legend was to reinforce the theory that Compostela derived from *campus stellae* or field of stars although a more recent thesis, following the discovery of a necropolis beneath the cathedral, holds that the derivation is from *compostela*, the Latin for cemetery.

In 844 Don Ramiro I was leading a handful of Spaniards in a bold attack against the Moors grouped at **Clavijo** near Logroño, when a knight in armour mounted on a charger and bearing a white standard with a red cross upon it, is said to have appeared on the battlefield. As he beat back the infidels the Christians recognised St James, naming him from that time *Matamoros* or Slayer of the Moors. The Reconquest and Spain had found a patron saint. During the crusade the Lord of Pimentel, it is said, had to swim across a *ría*. He emerged from the sea covered in shells which were then adopted as the pilgrim symbol.

★★ THE WAY OF SAINT JAMES

The relics of St James (Santiago) discovered early in the 9C soon became the object of a local cult and then of pilgrimage. In the 11C devotion spread abroad until a journey to St James's shrine ranked equally with one to Rome or Jerusalem, particularly perilous since the invasion of the Holy Land by the Turks. St James had a particular appeal for the French who felt united with the Spanish in face of the Moorish threat but English, Germans, Italians and even Scandinavians made the long pilgrimage travelling for the most part through France along the routes organised to a considerable degree, by the Benedictines and Cistercians of Cluny and Cîteaux and the Knights Templars of the Spanish Order of the Red Sword who assured the pilgrims' safety in northern Spain, provided them with funds and flagged the route with cairns. Hospitals and hospices in the care of the Hospitallers received the sick, the weary and the stalwart alike who travelled almost all in the pilgrims' uniform of heavy cape, eight foot stave with a gourd attached to carry water, stout sandals and broad-brimmed felt hat, turned up in front and marked with three or four scallop shells. A Pilgrim Guide of 1130, the first "tourist" guide ever written, probably by Aimeri Picaud, a Poitou monk from Parthenay-le-Vieux, describes the inhabitants, climate and customs of different regions, the most interesting routes and the sights on the way – the pilgrim in those days was in no hurry and frequently made detours which took weeks or months to complete, to visit a sanctuary or shrine. Churches, therefore, both on and off the way, benefited, as did the associated towns, from the pilgrims who numbered between 500 000 and two million a year.

In 1175, Pope Alexander III recognised the statutes of the Military Order of Santiago, drawn up to ensure the protection of pilgrims.

Of those who "took the cockleshell", the English, Normans and Bretons often came part of the way by boat *(see Parson's Quay in the Michelin Green Guide England: The West Country)*, disembarking at Soulac and following the French Atlantic coast south through Bordeaux to the Pyrenees, or they landed directly in Spain at La Coruña, on the north coast or in Portugal. Mediterranean pilgrims landed in Catalunya and Valencia and crossed the peninsula. The land routes through France began at Chartres, St Denis and Paris, and joining at Tours, continued south to Bordeaux, at Vézelay and Autun to go through Limoges and Périgueux and at Le Puy and Arles.

The stopping places along the way formed a main street or Calle Mayor around which a village would develop. Farming communities grew into towns and some were settled by foreigners or minority groups (often French or Jewish), who consolidated the recovered territory and brought with them a wealth of culture.

With the passage of time, however, the faith that made people set out on pilgrimages began to diminish; those seeking gain by trickery and robbery, and known as false pilgrims, among whom was the poet Villon, increased; the Wars of Religion, when Christians fought amongst themselves, reduced the faithful even more. Finally in 1589, Drake attacked La Coruña and the bishop of Compostela removed the relics from the Cathedral to a place of safety. They were lost and for three hundred years the pilgrimage was virtually abandoned. In 1879 they were recovered, recognised by the pope and the pilgrimage recommenced. In Holy Years, when the feast day of St James (25 July) falls on a Sunday, there are jubilee indulgences and thousands of pilgrims once more visit the shrine.

THE WAY IN SPAIN - MAIN HALTS

See local map above opposite

The diverse ways through France met at Roncesvalles, Behobia and Somport to cross the Pyrenees and continued through northeastern Spain as two routes only – the Asturian, from Roncesvalles, until the 15C considered extremely dangerous because of possible attack by brigands and a more southerly route, from Somport, known as the **Camino Francés** or French Way on account of the number of French pilgrims who followed it. It became marked over the centuries by churches and monasteries in which French architectural influence is obvious. The two routes converged at Puente la Reina.

THE WAY OF ST JAMES

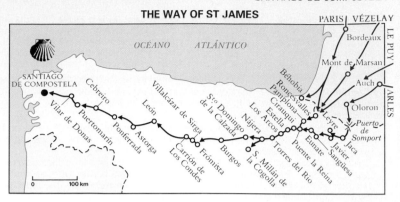

The route from **Roncesvalles** *(qv)* to Puente la Reina was the shorter of the two with only one main stop: **Pamplona** *(qv)*, while the longer Somport-Puente la Reina way stopped at **Jaca** *(qv)*, **Santa Cruz de la Serós** (qv), **San Juan de la Peña** *(qv)*, the **Monasterio de Leyre** *(qv)* and **Sangüesa** *(qv)*.

★**Puente la Reina** – The venerable hump-backed bridge which spans the Río Arga and gives the town its name, was built in the 11C for the pilgrims on their way to Santiago. Standing at the entrance to the town, on the Pamplona road, is a bronze pilgrim, marking the point at which the two caminos converged.
The wide N 111 circles the old town outside whose walls stands the **Iglesia del Crucifijo** (Church of the Crucifix) ⊘. The porch communicated with the pilgrims' hospice. A second nave was added to the existing 12C main aisle in the 14C and now contains the famous Y-shaped Cross with the profoundly expressionist **Christ**★ carved in wood and said to have been brought from Germany by a pilgrim in the 14C. Leave the church to walk along the narrow but extremely elegant main street, the Calle Mayor, fronted by houses of golden brick and carved wood eaves, to the bridge. On the way you will see the **Iglesia de Santiago** (Church of St James) ⊘ with its **doorway**★ crowded with carvings, by now almost effaced. Inside, the nave, remodelled in the 16C, was adorned with altarpieces. Note also the two statues placed facing the entrance: St James the Pilgrim in gilded wood, and St Bartholomew.

★**Eunate** – *5km - 3 miles east of Puente la Reina.* The origin of this **Romanesque chapel**, so harmonious in proportion and design, remains unknown. The finding of human bones supports the theory of the building having been a funerary chapel on the pilgrim road like that of Torres del Río *(qv)*. The outside gallery, now exposed, formerly led to adjoining buildings and was used by the pilgrims as a shelter.

★**Cirauqui** – The village's winding alleys are lined by steps and closely crowded by houses, their lower walls whitewashed, with rounded doorways, and their upper fronts adorned with iron balconies and further embellished with coats of arms and carved cornices. At the top of the village *(difficult climb)* stands the **Iglesia de San Román** with a multifoil 13C **portal**★ similar to that of San Pedro de la Rúa in Estella.

★★**Estella and the Monasterio de Irache** – *See ESTELLA.*

Los Arcos – The **Iglesia de Santa María de los Arcos** (Church of St Mary of the Arches), visible from a distance by its high tower, is Spanish baroque inside. The effect is overwhelming: stucco, sculpture and painting cover every available space. Particularly noteworthy are the transept walls decorated in imitation Córdoba leather. Above the high altar, pure baroque in style, rises a 13C polychrome wood statue of the Black Virgin of Santa María de los Arcos. The cloisters with Flamboyant bays illustrate the elegance and lightness of 15C Gothic.

Torres del Río – The **Iglesia del Santo Sepulcro** (Church of the Holy Sepulchre) ★ is an unusual Romanesque building, tall in height, octagonal in plan and dating from about 1200. Its resemblance to the chapel in Eunate has given rise to speculation that it is also a funerary chapel. Inside, vertical lines predominate; the magnificent Mudéjar inspired, star-shaped cupola is geometrical perfection. The decoration is sparse, consisting only of minute windows at the points of the star, modillions and historiated capitals.

Nájera and Santo Domingo de la Calzada – *See NÁJERA.*

★★★**Burgos** – *See BURGOS.*

★★**Iglesia de Frómista** – *See Iglesia de FRÓMISTA.*

Villalcázar de Sirga – The vast Gothic **Iglesia de Santa María la Blanca** ☉ has a fine carved **portal★** on its south front and inside, in the south transept, two out-standing Gothic **tombs★**. The recumbent statues of the brother of Alfonso X, who had him murdered in 1271, and his wife Eleanor, have been delicately carved with an eye for detail (the costumes in particular) as has the tomb of the prince showing the funeral procession.

Carrión de los Condes – The Counts of Carrión, attracted by the rich dowries pro-mised to the daughters of El Cid, married but then mistreated them, and were executed for their sins.

Monasterio de San Zoilo ☉, rebuilt during the Renaissance, has **cloisters★** designed by Juan de Badajoz with distinctive vaulting. The keystones and bosses are adorned with figurines and medallions.

The **Iglesia de Santiago** has beautiful 12C carvings on the façade including, on the portal's central coving, an architect with his compass, a barber with his scissors, a potter at his wheel, a cobbler, and so on. The high reliefs on the upper part show a Gothic influence.

★★León – See LEÓN.

Astorga – See ASTORGA.

Ponferrada – See PONFERRADA.

Cebreiro – Cebreiro, not far from the Puerto de Piedrafita (Piedrafita pass) (1 109m - 3 638ft), is one of the places where one can best imagine the hardships pilgrims underwent on their long tiring journey. The unusual drystone and thatched houses *(pallozas)*, inhabited until recently, go back in construction to ancient Celtic huts, one of which houses an **Ethnographic Museum** (Museo Etnográfico). Still offering shelter to the traveller is an inn beside the small 9C mountain church where pilgrims venerated the relics of the miracle of the Holy Eucharist which took place in c1300, when the bread was turned to flesh and the wine to blood. The holy relics are preserved in silver caskets presented by Isabel the Catholic and may be seen together with the miraculous chalice and paten.

Portomarín – The village of Portomarín had stood for centuries beside a bridge spanning the Miño when modern civilisation required the construction of a dam at Belesar. Before the old village was drowned, however, the **church★** of the Knights of St John of Jerusalem was taken down and re-erected stone by stone on the new site. It is square in shape, fortified and ornamented with massive supporting arches and Romanesque doors with delicately carved covings. The west door depicts Christ in Majesty with the 24 old musicians of the Apocalypse.

Vilar de Donas – *6.5km - 4 miles east of Palas de Rei.* The **church,** slightly off the main road, is entered through a Romanesque doorway. Lining the walls **inside,** are the tombs of the Knights of the Order of St James, slain in battle against the infi-dels. 15C **frescoes★** still decorate the apse, illustrating Christ in Majesty with St Paul and St Luke on his left and St Peter and St Mark on his right and, on the chancel walls, the faces of the elegant young women who gave the church its name – *(donas* in Galician).

★★★THE TOWN OF SANTIAGO *see town plan p 239*

★★★Praça do Obradoiro (Plaza de España) (V)
The size of the square and the architectural quality of its surrounding buildings make it a fitting setting for the cathedral.

★★★Catedral (V) ☉ – The present cathedral, built upon the same site as the first basi-lica erected over the apostle's tomb shortly after its discovery, and that of Alfonso III destroyed by Al-Mansur in 997, dates almost entirely from the 11, 12 and 13C, although from the outside it looks more like a baroque building.

★★★Obradoiro façade – This baroque masterpiece (its name means work of gold) by **Fernando Casas y Novoa** has adorned the cathedral entrance in magnificence since 1750. The central area, richly sculptured and given true baroque movement by the interplay of straight and curved lines, rises to what appears almost to be a long tongue of flame. The upward triangular lines are emphasised by high flan-king towers, slender and slightly in recess but sumptuously ornate.

★★★Pórtico de la Glória (Doorway of Glory) – Behind the baroque façade stands the narthex and the Pórtico de la Gloria, a late-12C wonder by **Maestro Mateo**, leading to the nave. The statues of the triple doorway are exceptionally beautiful both as a composition and in detail, for the master used all his artistry to give variety of expression, style and colour.
The doorway is slightly more recent than the rest of the Romanesque cathedral and shows features of the Gothic style. Mateo, who also built bridges, had the crypt be-low reinforced to bear the weight of the portico. The central portal is dedicated to the Christian Church, the one on the left to the Jews, that on the right to the

Gentiles or pagans. The central portal tympanum shows the Saviour surrounded by the four Evangelists while on the archivolt are the 24 Old Men of the Apocalypse. The engaged pillars are covered in statues of apostles and prophets. Note the figure of Daniel with the hint of a smile, a precursor to the famous Smiling Angel in Reims cathedral in France. The pillar beneath the seated figure of St James, bears finger marks upon the stone; traditionally, on entering the cathedral, exhausted pilgrims placed their hands here in token of safe arrival. On the other side of the pillar, the statue

Pórtico de la Gloria, Santiago de Compostela cathedral

known as the "saint of bumps" is believed to impart memory and wisdom to whoever bumps his forehead against it.

Interior – The immense Romanesque cathedral into which pilgrims crowded in the Middle Ages has remained intact with all the characteristics of pilgrim churches at the time: vast proportions, an ambulatory and a triforium. The nave and transept, complete with aisles, are plain but incomparably majestic. Galleries open onto the aisles through twin bays beneath a supporting arch. At major festivals a huge incense burner, the **botafumeiro** *(displayed in the library)*, is hung from the transept dome keystone and swung to the eaves by eight men pulling on a rope.

The decoration in the sanctuary is surprisingly exuberant for a Romanesque setting. The **Altar Mayor** or High Altar, surmounted by a sumptuously apparelled 13C statue of St James, is covered by a gigantic baldachin. (Pilgrims mounting the stairs behind the altar may kiss the saint's mantle).

Beneath the altar is the **cripta**, a crypt built into the foundations of the 9C church which contained St James' tomb and now enshrines the relics of the saint and his two disciples, St Theodore and St Athanasius.

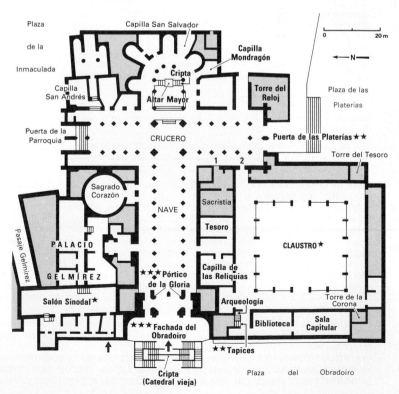

Particularly beautiful among the cathedral's many outstanding features are the wrought-iron grilles and vaulting of the **Capilla Mondragón** (1521), a chapel off the ambulatory, and the Renaissance doors to the **sacristía** (sacristy) (**1**) and claustro (cloisters) (**2**).

Tesoro and Capilla de las Reliquias ☉ – The treasury, in a Gothic chapel to the right of the nave, houses a gold and silver monstrance by Antonio de Arfe (1539-1566). Beside the treasury, the Plateresque reliquary chapel by Juan de Álava contains the head of the Apostle James the Lesser.

Museo ☉ – The **biblioteca** (library), where the *botafumeiros* are displayed, and the **sala capitular** (chapter house) hung with 17C Flemish and three 18C Madrid tapestries, are on the ground floor; on the first floor the **Museo de Tapices**★★ (tapestry museum) contains works after cartoons by Goya, Teniers and Bayeu. An **archaeological section** below ground displays finds from the excavations in the nave and south transept.

★ **Claustro** – The plain dignified cloisters with vast galleries dating from 1521 are crowned by an openwork balustrade with pinnacles.

Catedral Vieja (Old Cathedral) – A crypt which lies beneath the flight of steps before the Obradoiro façade, was built in the 11C to support the present cathedral nave on the uneven ground. The style is Romanesque with carved capitals and columns.

★★ **Puerta de las Platerías** (Goldsmiths' Doorway) – Every square inch of this beautiful Romanesque doorway, with its double arch, is carved in low relief with individual scenes closely juxtaposed as at Sangüesa and Leyre. The sculptures, dating from the 11C, show a French influence. The most famous scenes are of Adam and Eve being driven out of the Garden of Eden and, in the right hand corner of the left tympanum, the Pardoning of the Adulterous Woman.

The **Torre del Reloj** (Clock Tower), on the right, was added at the end of the 17C. To the left, stands the Torre del Tesoro (Treasury Tower).

Palacio Gelmírez (**V A**) ☉ – This is the bishops' palace, to the left of the cathedral. 12C and Gothic style apartments are open to the public, including the vast **Salón Sinodal**★ (Synod Hall) which is more than 30m – 98ft long and has sculptured ogive vaulting. Carved in high relief on the bosses are scenes from the wedding banquet of Alfonso IX de León.

★ **Hostal de los Reyes Católicos (Hostelry of the Catholic Monarchs)** (**V**) – The hostelry, founded by Ferdinand of Aragón and Isabel of Castilla as a pilgrim inn and hospital and now a *parador*, has an impressive **façade**★ adorned with a splendid Plateresque doorway. The hospital's plan of a cross within a square, which affords four elegant Plateresque *patios*, was common to hospitals of the period.

Ayuntamiento (Town Hall) (**V H**) – Opposite the cathedral is the severely classical 18C façade of the former Palacio de Roxoy by the French architect Charles Lemaur. Today, the building serves as the Town Hall and the Presidency of the Xunta de Galicia.

Colegio de San Jerónimo (**VX**) – The college, a 17C building on the square's south side, has an elegant 15C gateway with a strong Romanesque influence.

★★ Barrio Antiguo (Old Town) *time: 1 1/2 hours*

Rúa do Franco (**X**) – This is a picturesque street with old colleges (such as Fonseca), shops and cafés.

Rúa do Vilar (**X**) – The street leading to the cathedral is bordered by arcaded and ancient houses like the **Rúa Nova** (**X**) which runs parallel, although this has more shops.

★★ **Plaza de la Quintana** (**VX**) – The square surrounding the east end of the cathedral bustles with lingering students. The lower part is bordered by the former **Casa de la Canónica** (Canon's Residence) (**R**) with a plain but harmonious arcade and, at right angles, a monastery, whose windows barred by beautiful old wrought ironwork embellish an otherwise austere construction.

Opposite, the doorway in the cathedral's east end, known as the **Puerta del Perdón**★ (Door of Pardon) or Puerta Santa (Holy Door), designed by Fernández Lechuga in 1611 and opened only in Holy Years (when the feast day of St James, 25 July, falls on a Sunday), incorporates all the statues of the prophets and patriarchs carved by Maestro Mateo for the original Romanesque *coro*. At the top of a large flight of stairs is the **Casa de la Parra**, House of the Bunch of Grapes (**P**), a fine late-17C baroque mansion.

★ **Monasterio de San Martín Pinario** (**V**) ☉ – The monastery church overlooking the Plaza San Martín, preceded by a double flight of stairs, has an ornate front composed like a Plateresque altarpiece.

The interior consists of a surprisingly wide single aisle covered by coffered barrel vaulting. It is lit by a Byzantine-style lantern without a drum. The high altar retable, in the most ornate Churrigueresque manner, is by the great architect Casa y Novoa

A	Palacio Gelmírez
H	Ayuntamiento
P	Casa de la Parra
R	Casa de la Canónica

(1730). On either side are baroque pulpits canopied by cottage-loaf-shaped sounding boards. A grand staircase beneath an elegant cupola leads to three 16-18C cloisters, one of which is the Claustro de las Procesiones (Processions Cloister). The monastery façade overlooking the Plaza de la Inmaculada is colossal in style with massive Doric columns in pairs rising from the ground to the roof.

Additional Sights

Paseo da Ferradura (Herradura) (X 40) – The wooded hill rising from the old town makes a pleasant walk with a good **view**★ of the city and the cathedral.

★ **Colegiata de Santa María del Sar** ⊙ – *Calle Castron d'Ouro.* The 12C Romanesque collegiate church appears anachronistic by the addition in the 18C of its buttresses. The strength of the latter, however, is not superfluous when one looks inside at the astonishing slant of the pillars caused by the pressure of the vaulting. The only cloister gallery to remain abuts the church and is exceedingly elegant, with paired **arches**★ richly decorated with carved floral and leaf motifs.

EXCURSION

★ **Pazo de Oca** ⊙ – *25km - 16 miles south on the N 525.*
This austere Galician **manor** or *pazo,* with a crenellated tower, surrounds, on two sides, a vast square in which stands a Calvary. The romantic **park**★★ behind comes as a complete surprise. There are shady arbours, terraces covered with rust coloured lichen, pools, and a silent lake on which a stone boat floats idly.

SANTILLANA DEL MAR★★
Cantabria
Population 3 839
Michelin map 442 B 17 – Michelin Atlas España Portugal p 12

Santillana del Mar has kept almost intact its ancient buildings and traditions; at night-fall farmers still return with their beasts to stable them in age-old byres above which rise the fine stone façades of *casonas* or seignorial mansions with coats of arms. One would barely be surprised to see **Gil Blas**, the unpretentious hero of the 18C French writer, Lesage, spring into sight.
Santillana grew up around a monastery which sheltered the relics of St Juliana, who was martyred in Asia Minor – the name Santillana is a contraction of Santa Juliana. Throughout the Middle Ages, the monastery was famous as a place of pilgrimage and was particularly favoured by the Grandees of Castilla. In the 11C it became powerful as a collegiate church; in the 15C, the town, created the seat of a marquisate, was enriched by the fine mansions which still give it so much character.
The famous **Cuevas de Altamira** (Altamira Caves) *(qv)* are 2km - 1 mile from the village.

★★THE VILLAGE *time: 1 1/2 hours*

The village has two main streets, both leading to the collegiate church. Between the two lies a network of communicating alleys. Most of the noblemen's residences, with plain façades of massive rough stone, date from the 15, 16 and 17C. Almost all have wrought-iron balconies or wooden galleries *(solanas)* and the majority sport traditional crests or coats of arms.

Calle Santo Domingo – **Casa de los Villa** is distinguishable by its semicircular balconies. The device on the armorial bearings shows an eagle with spread wings pierced by an arrow and the motto "A glorious death crowns a whole life with honour."
Turn left at the fork into Calle de Juan Infante.

Plaza de Ramón Pelayo or **Plaza Mayor** – The vast triangular square is bordered on the right by the **Parador Gil Blas** and the 14C **Torre de Merino** (Merino Tower) with crenellations visible beneath the roof. The **Torre de Borja-Barreda** opposite has an elegant doorway with a pointed arch. On the left is the *Ayuntamiento* (Town Hall) in an 18C building.

Calle de las Lindas *(at the end of the square on the right)* runs between massive looking houses with austere façades to join Calle del Cantón and Calle del Río which lead to the collegiate church.
As you approach the church, you will see several noblemen's residences: on the right is the **Casa de los Hombrones**, named after the two knights supporting the Villa coat of arms. Further along, the **Cossío** and **Quevedo** houses both have magnificent coats of arms. Calle del Río is named after the stream that feeds the village drinking fountain and disappears beneath Quevedo House. On the left, the house of the Archduchess of Austria, the former **Casa de los Abades** (Abbot's House), is adorned with three coats of arms.

Plaza de las Arenas – The much restored but still impressive **Torre de los Velarde** behind the collegiate church, was originally the keep of the 15C palace.

★**Colegiata** ⊙ – The collegiate church dates from the 12 and 13C. While the design of the east end is pure Romanesque, that of the west to some extent lacks unity, although the harmonious placing of the windows and towers and the golden colour of the stone make it blend in well with the overall architecture of the square. Above the portal, which was remodelled in the 18C, is a niche with a statue of St Juliana.

★**Claustro** – Although the Romanesque east gallery has disappeared, these late-12C cloisters still have great appeal. Each pair of twin columns is covered by a capital carved by a master craftsman. Though plant and strapwork motifs predominate, the **capitals**★★ in the south gallery, which do illustrate a scene, often in allegory, are very expressive: look out for Christ and six of the disciples, Christ's baptism, the beheading of John the Baptist and Daniel in the Lions' den.

Interior – The vaulting in the aisles was rebuilt at the end of the 13C when it was given intersecting ribs, but that above the transept and apses is original. The aisles and apses are out of line and the cupola, unusually, is almost elliptical. The pillars are crowned by highly stylised capitals. St Juliana's memorial sarcophagus, carved in the 15C, stands at the centre of the nave. The chancel contains a 17C Mexican beaten silver altarfront and Romanesque stone figures of **four Apostles**★ carved in the Byzantine hieratic style. The 16C Hispano-Flemish **altarpiece**★ has the original polychrome wood predella which is carved to show the Evangelists in profile.

Convento de Regina Coeli – *On the other side of the village*. The **Museo Diocesano** ⊙ now occupies the restored 16C Convento de Clarisas (Convent of the Poor Clares). On display are popular religious art objects found in the province.
A large coat of arms adorns the fine 18C **Casa de Los Tagle** at the end of the street.

SANT JOAN DE LES ABADESSES

Catalunya (Girona)
Population 3 898
Michelin map 443 F 36 – Michelin Atlas España Portugal p 18
Local map under PIRINEOS CATALANES

If you approach the ancient Abbesses' Town from Ripoll, you will see the graceful, recently restored **medieval bridge** which spans the Río Ter.
The first abbess, in the late 9C, was Emma, daughter of Wilfred the Hairy, the founder of the monastery. The community, however, was superseded and it was for canons that the present church was consecrated in 1150.

★**Iglesia de San Juan** ⊙ – Before entering, note the east end with its three storeys. The arches and columns with carved capitals recall those of southwest France.

Interior – Originally, the single aisle led to an elaborate east end with an ambulatory and radiating chapels, again French influenced, but this disappeared when an earthquake destroyed the chancel roof. Local masons repaired the church by extending the nave, placing columns where previously the ambulatory had been.

The decoration of the apses echoes that of the east end, the motifs on the richly carved capitals those of oriental fabrics.

A magnificent **Descent from the Cross**★★, a group in polychrome wood carved in 1251, presides over the central apse. The artist departed from the traditional scene by introducing additional figures and greater realism – note St John's sad gestures and the Virgin receiving her son. In 1426 an unbroken host was discovered on the Christ figure's head, which has made the statue an object of particular veneration to this day. Among the church's other treasures are the lovely 14C Gothic altarpiece in alabaster of Santa María la Blanca and the tomb of Miró de Tagamanent.

★ **Claustro** – These cloisters are simple and elegant; the sweeping arches and slender columns with capitals decorated with plant motifs replaced those of an earlier Romanesque cloister in the 15C.

Antiguo Palacio de la Abadía (Former Abbatial Palace) – Opening off the small church square is the attractive bishop's *patio* with gracefully carved capitals.

Monasterio de SANTO DOMINGO DE SILOS★★

Castilla y León (Burgos)

Michelin map 442 G 19 – Michelin Atlas España Portugal p 26

The Monasterio de Santo Domingo de Silos ⊙ is named after an 11C monk, Dominic, who reconstructed the conventual buildings of a former 6-8C Visigothic abbey that was demolished by Al-Mansur. The new buildings were abandoned in 1835 but were reoccupied by Benedictine monks from Poitou, in France, in 1880, who planted the magnificent cypress in the cloisters and a huge sequoia in front of the portal.

★★★ **Claustro** – These are among the most beautiful cloisters in Spain. Countless poets have been inspired by the atmosphere of spirituality that emanates from the well-proportioned galleries, the lone cypress and the lovely coloured vaulting. The cloisters are very big for a Romanesque building and comprise two superimposed, architecturally similar galleries. The ground floor galleries have about sixty rounded arches supported by paired columns and, in the middle of each gallery, by a group of five columns. The eight low reliefs on the corner pillars are masterpieces of Romanesque sculpture. Careful study reveals that several major sculptors worked on the stone. The first and most original craftsman (mid to late 11C) was primarily a linear artist who favoured hieratic postures and preferred symbolism to realism – his work extends along the east, north and part of the west galleries and includes the low reliefs on the southeast, northeast and northwest corner pillars. The second artist (early 12C) was more partial to volume than line and personified his figures. The third mason, again using a completely different style, carved the southwest pillar (12C).

The **capitals**, apart from those which are historiated, illustrate a fantastic bestiary which derives from the Mudéjar use of animal and plant motifs. *The most interesting have been numbered in the description of the galleries that follows.*

Southeast pillar – Carved like an ivory diptych; Ascension *(left)*, Pentecost *(right)*.

East gallery – (**1**): strapwork, (**2**): entwined plants, (**3**): harpies defended by dogs.

Northeast pillar – This shows the Descent from the Cross and on the upper register, the earth and the moon on the point of being clouded over; on the other side is an original representation of the Entombment and the Resurrection as a single composition. Opposite the pillar is the fine doorway known as the **Puerta de las Vírgenes** (**4**) which led to the former Romanesque abbey church. Its horseshoe arch is flanked by columns with interesting capitals.

North gallery – (**5**): entwined plants, (**6**): the Old Men of the Apocalypse, (**7**): harpies attacked by eagles, (**8**): birds. The gallery also contains St Dominic's 13C tomb (**9**): three Romanesque lions bear the recumbent figure of the saint.

Northwest pillar – This pillar, concerned with the doubts on the Resurrection in the minds of some disciples, shows Christ on the road to Emmaus and before St Thomas.

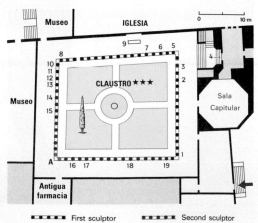

West gallery – (**10**): strapwork, (**11**): birds with necks entwined, (**12**): perfectly curved flamingoes, (**13**): birds and lions ensnared by plant tendrils. The capitals that follow are by the second sculptor. (**14**): the birth of Jesus, (**15**): scenes of the Passion. Note the well-preserved 14C *artesonado* ceiling.

Southwest pillar (**A**) – By the third artist. On the left is an admirable Annunciation in which the Virgin Mary appears crowned by two angels; on the right is a Tree of Jesse.

South gallery – (**16**) and (**17**): plant tendrils ensnaring birds in the first and stags in the second, (**18**): eagles clutching hares, (**19**): grimacing monster heads.

Museo – The museum displays some very old pieces, including an 11C chalice of St - Dominic's with filigree decoration, an enamel reliquary, a 10-11C manuscript of the Mozarabic rite and the tympanum from the portal of the original church.

Antigua Farmacia (Old Pharmacy) – Fine collection of Talavera ceramic jars.

Iglesia – The present church (1756-1816), which is agreeably proportioned, combines the rounded volume of baroque with the plain grandeur of the Herreran style.

EXCURSION

Garganta de la Yecla – *3km - 2 miles southwest; time: 20 min.*
A footpath follows a deep narrow gorge cut into a thick layer of grey limestone.

SARAGOSSA★★

See ZARAGOZA

SEGOVIA★★★

Castilla y León
Population 57 617
Michelin map 444 J 17 – Michelin Atlas España Portugal p 39
Local map under Sierra de GUADARRAMA
Plan of the conurbation in the current Red Guide España Portugal

The noble Castilian city of Segovia, former residence of King Alfonso X the Wise and King Henry IV, was an important economic and political centre in the Middle Ages and was to play a decisive role in the history of Castilla. Segovia has an extraordinary **site★★** that is best appreciated if approached from the east. The centre of the city, which is circled by ramparts, appears perched on a triangular rock at an altitude of 1 000m - 3 280ft. To the left is the Roman aqueduct, to the right are the cathedral domes and spires and further right still, at the tip of the triangle, the Alcázar, 100m - 328ft above the confluence of the Eresma and Clamores rivers. For a good overall view, drive along Cuesta de los Hoyos and Paseo de la Alameda.

Historical notes – Segovia was an important military town in Roman times; under the Moors in the Middle Ages it became a wool town and industrial centre – by the 15C it numbered 60 000 citizens and had entered its golden age.

Isabel the Catholic, Queen of Castilla – On the death of Henry IV in 1474 many grandees refused to recognise the legitimacy of his daughter, Doña Juana, known as **La Beltraneja** after her mother's favourite, Beltrán de la Cueva. In Segovia in her stead, the grandees proclaimed Henry's half-sister, Isabel, Queen of Castilla – thus preparing the way for Spain's unification since Isabel was already married to Ferdinand, heir apparent of Aragón. La Beltraneja, aided by her husband, Alfonso V of Portugal, pressed her claim, but renounced in 1479 after the defeats at Toro and Albuera.

The "Comuneros" – The Spanish were incensed at the beginning of Charles V's reign by the emperor's Flemish court and companions, his attempt to impose absolute rule and new taxes. Town forces *(comunidades)* under the leadership of the Toledan, Juan de Padilla and the Segovian, Juan Bravo, rose in revolt but were crushed finally at Villalar in 1521 and their leaders beheaded in Segovia.

The Alcázar, Segovia

B. Brillon / MICHELIN

Architecture – Picturesque streets have 15-16C Castilian type entrances surrounded by *alfiz (qv)* and plaster façades with Mudéjar geometrical designs or **esgrafiados**. Segovia's main treasures, however, are her Romanesque churches.

Romanesque churches – These beautiful churches of golden stone have common architectural features: well rounded apses, frequently a tall square belfry beside the east end and a covered gallery where weavers' or merchants' guilds used to meet.

Segovia today – Segovia is famous for its outstanding monuments as well as its gastronomic specialities like the exquisite sucking-pig *(cochinillo asado)*.

★★★ ACUEDUCTO ROMANO (BY)

This Roman aqueduct is one of the finest still in existence and it is still operating. The simple, elegant structure, was built during the reign of Trajan in the 1C to bring water from the Río Acebeda in the Sierra de Fuenfría to the upper part of the town. It is 728m - 2 388ft long, rises to a maximum height of 28m - 92ft in the Plaza del Azoguejo where the ground is lowest and consists throughout of two tiers of arches.

★★ CIUDAD VIEJA (OLD TOWN) *time: 4 hours. Follow the itinerary on the plan.*

Plaza Mayor (ABY 59) – Dominated by the impressive cathedral, the arcaded square with its terrace cafés is a popular meeting place with Segovians. Among the buildings surrounding the square are the Ayuntamiento (Town Hall) and the Teatro Juan Bravo.

★★ **Catedral (AY)** ⊘ – This was built during the reign of Emperor Charles V to replace the cathedral that had been destroyed during the Comuneros' Revolt in 1511. It is an example of the survival of the Gothic style in the 16C when Renaissance architecture was at its height. The beautiful golden stone, the stepped east end with pinnacles and delicate balustrades and the tall tower, bring considerable grace to the massive building. The width of the aisles combines with the decorative lines of the pillars and ribs in the vaulting, to make the interior both light and elegant. Among the chapels, which are closed by fine wrought-iron screens, the first off the south aisle contains as altarpiece an *Entombment* by Juan de Juni. The *coro* stalls, in the late-15C Flamboyant Gothic style, are from the earlier cathedral.

★ **Claustro** ⊘ – The 15C cloisters from the former cathedral, which stood near the Alcázar, were transported stone by stone and rebuilt on the new site. The Sala Capitular (Chapter house) has beautiful 17C Brussels **tapestries★** which illustrate the story of Queen Zenobia. The museum (**museo** ⊘) displays church plate and the Corpus Christi monstrance.

★ **Plaza de San Martín (BY 78)** – The square in the heart of the old aristocratic quarter is the most evocative of historic Segovia. It is formed of two small squares joined by a flight of steps. The statue is of Juan Bravo. Around the square stand the **Casa del Siglo XV** (15C House) (**X**), also known as Juan Bravo's house, with a gallery beneath the eaves, the 16C tower of the **Casa de los Lozoya** (**V**) as a reminder of the family's power in former times, the Plateresque façade of the **Casa de Solier** (Solier Mansion, also known as Casa de Correas) (**R**) and the ornate entrances to big houses. In the middle of the square is the 12C **Iglesia de San Martín★**, a church framed on three sides by a covered gallery on pillars with carved strapwork and animal figures on the capitals.
The 17C **Antigua Cárcel** (Old Prison) (**BY Y**) has a decorative baroque pediment.

Casa del Conde de Alpuente (BY Q) – The elegant façade of this 15C Gothic house is adorned with *esgrafiado* designs.

Casa de los Picos (BY Z) – The house, faced closely with diamond pointed stones, is the most original of Segovia's 15C mansions.

★★★ **Acueducto Romano** (Roman Aqueduct) (**BY**) – *See above.*

Iglesia de San Sebastián (BY L) – Small Romanesque church on a quiet square.

Plaza del Conde de Cheste (BY 21) – On the square stand the palaces of the Marqués de Moya (**B**), the Marqués de Lozoya (**E**), the Condes de Cheste (**F**) and the Marqués de Quintanar (**K**).

Iglesia de San Juan de los Caballeros (BY P) – This is Segovia's oldest Romanesque church (11C). Its outstanding feature is the portico (taken from the church of San Nicolás) with its carvings of portrait heads, plant motifs and animals.

Iglesia de la Trinidad (Holy Trinity Church) (**BY**) – This somewhat austere Romanesque church has a decorated apse where there is blind arcading and capitals carved with imaginary beasts and plant motifs.

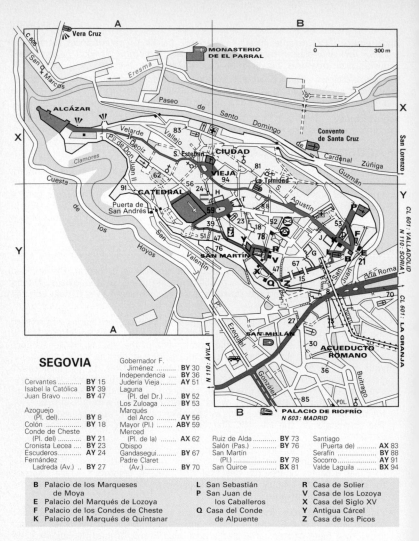

Iglesia de San Esteban (St Stephen's Church) (**AX**) ⊘ – One of the latest (13C) and most beautiful of Segovia's Romanesque churches. The porticoes running along two of its sides have finely carved capitals.

The five-storeyed **tower**★ has elegant bays and slender columns on the corners. Inside, the altar in the south transept has a 13C Gothic figure of Christ in polychrome wood.

★**Alcázar** (**AX**) ⊘ – The Alcázar, standing on a cliff overlooking the valley, was built in the early 13C and modified in the 15 and 16C. Its keep is flanked by corbelled turrets. Several rooms have retained their magnificent *artesonado* ceilings and display medieval armoury, period pictures and furnishings. The Sala del Cordón and terrace command a fine **panorama** of the fertile Eresma valley, the Monasterio de El Parral, the Capilla de la Vera Cruz and the Meseta beyond. The **views** from the keep *(152 steps)* stretch across the city to the Sierra de Guadarrama.

SIGHTS OUTSIDE THE WALLS

★**Iglesia de San Millán** (**BY**) ⊘ – The early 12C church stands in the middle of a large square which allows a full view of its pure, still primitive Romanesque lines and two porticoes with finely carved modillions and capitals. Inside, the three aisles have alternating pillars and columns as in Jaca cathedral. The apse has blind arcading and a decorative frieze which continues throughout the church. The transept has Moorish ribbed vaulting.

★**Monasterio de El Parral** (**AX**) ⊘ – The monastery was founded by Henry IV in 1445 and later entrusted to the Hieronymites. The **church**, behind its unfinished façade, has a Gothic nave with beautifully carved doors, a 16C altarpiece by Juan Rodríguez and, on either side of the chancel, the Plateresque tombs of the Marquis and Marchioness of Villena.

Capilla de la Vera Cruz (AX) ⊘ – The unusual polygonal chapel was erected in the 13C, probably by the Templars; it now belongs to the Order of Malta. A circular corridor surrounds two small chambers, one above the other, in which the order's secret ceremonies were conducted. The Capilla del Lignum Crucis contains an ornate Flamboyant Gothic altar. There is a good **view** of Segovia.

Convento de Santa Cruz (BX) – The convent pinnacles, the decorated Isabelline **entrance** with a Calvary, a *Pietà* and the emblems of the Catholic Monarchs, can be seen from the road.

Iglesia de San Lorenzo (BX) – The Romanesque church with its unusual brick belfry stands in a picturesque square surrounded by corbelled half-timbered houses.

EXCURSIONS

★ **Palacio de La Granja de San Ildefonso** – *See La Granja de San Ildefonso.*

★ **Riofrío** – *11km - 7 miles south on the N 603.*
The Palacio Real (Royal Palace) can be seen through the holm oaks where deer roam, below the Mujer Muerta (the Dead Woman), a foothill of the Sierra de Guadarrama.

Palacio ⊘ – Riofrío was planned by Isabel Farnese as the equal of La Granja which she had to vacate on the death of her husband, Philip V. Construction began in 1752 but though it was very big – it measures 84m x 84m - 276ft x 276ft – it was nothing more than a somewhat pretentious hunting lodge. A classical style grand courtyard and monumental staircase with double flights lead to sumptuously decorated apartments.
A **Museo de Caza** (Hunting Museum) illustrates the development of hunting methods since prehistoric times with the aid of paintings and display cases of animals in their natural habitat.

La SEU D'URGELL / SEO DE URGEL★

Catalunya (Lleida)
Population 11 195
Michelin map 443 E 34 – Michelin Atlas España Portugal p 18
Local map under PIRINEOS CATALANES

This onetime city of prince-archbishops, stands in peaceful countryside where the Valira, which rises in the mountains of Andorra, joins the Segre river. Since 1278 the duties of the archbishop have included those of joint ruler of Andorra with the French President, until the 1993 constitution granting Andorra full independence.
The former county capital now lives on trade and agriculture which includes stock farming and dairy produce, particularly cheese.

★★ **Catedral de Santa María** ⊘ – The cathedral, built in the 11 and 12C, shows a strong Lombard influence. The west face with two different colours of stone, is divided into three parts corresponding to the three aisles inside. The central part is typically Italian with its pediment crowned by a small campanile.
Inside, the elevation is spectacular, the nave rising on cruciform pillars, surrounded, in the French style, by engaged columns. A most effective twin arched gallery decorates the east transept wall and then reappears outside to circle the apse.

★ **Claustro** – The cloisters are 13C, although the east gallery had to be rebuilt in 1603. The granite capitals illustrating human figures and animals were carved with consummate artistry and humour by masons from the Roussillon. A door at the southeast corner opens into the 11C **Iglesia de Sant Miquel**, the only building remaining constructed by St Ermangol.

★ **Museo Diocesano** (Diocesan Museum) ⊘ – The museum has a wonderful collection of works of art from the region, dating from the 10C to the 18C. The most precious work is a beautifully illuminated 11C **Beatus★★**, one of the best preserved copies of St John's Commentary on the Apocalypse written in the 8C by the priest, Beatus of Liébana *(qv)*.
Of note also are the 13C enamelled Romanesque crucifix from the Monasterio de Silos which shows a Byzantine influence, the 14C **Abella de la Conca★** altarpiece by Pere Serra also with a Byzantine influence as well as characteristics from the Siena school, and the 14C *St Bartholomew Altarpiece* in coloured stone which illustrates scenes with great realism. The crypt contains church plate and the 18C *Funerary Urn of St Ermangol*.

The Michelin Motoring Atlas España Portugal
provides the motorist in Spain and Portugal
with the best possible information
for route-planning and choosing where to go.

SEVILLA★★★

SEVILLE – Andalucía
Population 704 857
Michelin map 446 T11-12 – Michelin Atlas España Portugal p 83 – Plan of the conurbation
on Michelin map 446 and in the current Michelin Red Guide España Portugal

Sevilla, standing in the plain of the Guadalquivir, is capital of Andalucía and Spain's fourth largest city. It has all the characteristics of a bustling metropolis but has many moods and facets which may escape the visitor in too much of a hurry. One needs to take the time to stroll along the narrow streets of old quarters like Santa Cruz or ride slowly through the city's peaceful parks and gardens in a horse-drawn carriage.

The great festivals, when vast crowds flock to the city from all over Spain and over-seas, reveal the provincial capital in many guises. During the **Semana Santa** or **Holy Week** *pasos* processions are organised nightly in each city quarter by rival brotherhoods. *Pasos* are great litters sumptuously bejewelled and garlanded with flowers on which are mounted pious, polychrome wood statues; these constructions are borne through the crowd on the shoulders of between 25 and 60 men. Accompanying the statues are penitents, hidden beneath tall pointed hoods; from time to time a voice is raised in a *saeta*, an improvised religious lament. During the **April Fair** or **Feria** (last week in April) the city becomes a fairground with horse and carriage parades. The women in flounced dresses and the men in full Andalusian costume ride up to specially erected canvas pavilions to dance the *sevillana*. Sevilla is also the great centre of *flamenco* and *tablaos* (tableaux), famous too for its bullfights held in the 18C **Plaza de la Maestranza** **(AX)**, and finally for its many little bars and cafés where the merrymaking continues around *copas* (drinks) and *tapas*.

HISTORICAL NOTES

Sevilla's history is neatly summed up by the lines carved long ago on the Puerta de Jerez (Jerez Gate): "Hercules built me; Caesar surrounded me with walls and towers; the King Saint took me." Sevilla, known as Hispalis under the Iberians, was chief city of Roman Baetica and, before Toledo, became the capital of the Visigothic Kingdom. In 712 the Moors arrived; in the 11C, on the fall of the Córdoban caliphs, the city was created capital of a kingdom which gained in prosperity a century later under the Almohads. In 1195 **Sultan Yacoub al-Mansur** (1184-1199), builder of the famous Giralda, won victory over the Christians at the Battle of Alarcos.

On 19 November 1248, **King Ferdinand III of Castilla**, the Saint, as he was known (and is referred to in the lines above) and who was cousin to St Louis of France, delivered the city from the Moors who were all expelled.

The discovery of America in 1492 brought new prosperity to Sevilla. Expeditions to the New World set out from the port: **Amerigo Vespucci** (1451-1512), the Florentine who determined to prove that Columbus's discoveries were not the Indies but a new continent to which his own name was ultimately given; **Magellan**, who set out in 1519 to circumnavigate the world. By 1503 the city's trade with ports far and near had become such that Isabel the Catholic created the *Casa de Contratación* or Exchange to encourage and also to control all trade with America. This monopoly lasted until 1717 when the silting up of the Guadalquivir brought about the transfer of the Casa concession to Cádiz.

Art and architecture in Sevilla – The ramparts on the north side of the town, the lofty Alcázar, the Torre del Oro *(Gold Tower)* **(BY)** – built in 1220 on the banks of the Guadalquivir to guard the port which could be closed by a chain stretched across the river to another tower, since vanished, on the far bank – and finally, the Giralda, are all reminders of Sevilla's Moorish occupation.

Interestingly, Sevilla was, in fact, Christian at the time the Nasrids were building the Alhambra in Granada and so the use of the **Mudéjar style**, that mixture of Moorish and Christian, long after the reconquest of the town in 1248, reflected their fascination for Arab design   as exemplified in the Alcázar built under Peter the Cruel, the Casa de Pilatos, the **Palacio de las Dueñas** **(BCV)** and the **Torre de San Marcos** (San Marcos Belfry) **(CV)**.

In Spain's Golden Age, the **Sevilla school** of painters brought renown to the city. Three generations of artists corresponded to the three reigns: under Philip III (1598-1621) **Roelas** and **Pacheco**, portraitist and Velázquez' master; under Philip IV (1621-1665) **Herrera the Elder**, whose paintings have an epic touch, and **Zurbarán** (1598-1664) *(qv)* who after having studied in the city remained here and portrayed motionless figures with rare spiritual intensity. Finally under Charles II (1665-1700) there was **Murillo** (1618-1682), a baroque artist, author of numerous gently radiant Immaculate Conceptions and, also, of brilliantly depicted everyday scenes, particularly those including young women, children and characters common to every town and village, such as the water carrier. Also of this period was **Valdés Leal** (1622-1690), who had a violent baroque technique, and whose best work can be seen in the Hospital de la Caridad (Hospital of Charity) *(qv)*. **Velázquez** (1599-1660) *(qv)* was born in Sevilla; he entered Pacheco's Academy and later became his son-in-law; on moving to Madrid he became court portraitist and, laden with honours, spent the rest of his life painting the royal family.

Sevilla's statues, many the work of the 17C sculptor, **Martínez Montañés**, are dispersed throughout the city's churches. The best known are the **Cristo del Gran Poder** (Christ of Great Power) by **Juan de Mesa** in **San Lorenzo** (**AV**), the **Cachorro** by Francisco Antonio Gijón in the **Capilla del Patrocinio**, Calle Castilla (**AX**), named after the gypsy who served as the sculptor's model, and finally, the **Macarena Virgin**, the most popular figure in Sevilla, which stands, when not in procession, in a special chapel (**CV**).

Sevilla today – Sevilla is an important industrial town (textiles, food processing, farm machinery, aeronautics) and the centre of an agricultural region (cereals, cotton, sugar beet) as well as the only river port in Spain.

The **1992 World Fair** was held on the **Isla de la Cartuja** (Island of the Carthusian Monastery) between two branches of the Guadalquivir. This great event, which has left an indelible mark on Sevilla, not only resulted in a large-scale urban modernization programme for the city (bridges, communications, etc.), but also involved the incorporation of the land on the Isla de la Cartuja into the urban structure of Sevilla. The **"Cartuja. El Parque de los Descubrimientos"** (Cartuja. The Park of the Discoveries) ⊙ complex, together with the fun fair *(Parque de Attracciones)*, offers the visitor the chance to discover several of the most important pavilions built for Expo '92 (Navigation, Universe, Environment, etc.).

• • • • • • • • • • • • • • • • Life in Sevilla • • • • • • • • • • • • • • •

Sevilla has managed to hold on to its traditions and at the same time keep pace with the times. It is a lively town with a wide variety of entertainment and culture (cinemas, theatres, museums, classical and rock music concerts, *tablaos*, etc) but what distinguishes it most are its **traditional bars** where Sevillians meet for lunchtime drinks with *tapas (p 10)* and sherry. The art of the *tapeo* reaches its height in Sevilla and in the evening, especially on Saturdays, patrons, glasses in hand, literally fill the streets. The town's many bars are concentrated in the Santa Cruz (**BCX**), El Arenal (**AX**), near the bullring, and Triana (**AY**) districts. On Sundays, it is customary to meet for a lunchtime aperitif in the Plaza del Salvador (**BX**). Young Sevillians tend to go to the Los Remedios and Triana districts across the Guadalquivir in the evenings.

Shopping – Most of the shops and department stores are in and around Calles Sierpes, O'Donnell and San Pablo. Another, more traditional shopping area, behind the church of San Salvador, is popular for clothes, shoes and books while the Calle de l'Asunción across the river in **Los Remedios** (**AZ**) is home to the city's most fashionable shops. Sevilla's antique shops are in the old quarter, especially in Santa Cruz. On Thursdays, the **Jueves** (Thursday in Spanish) flea market is held in Calle Feria, while another takes place in Alameda de Hércules on Sundays.

Arts and Crafts – Sevilla has a rich tradition of cottage industries. Potters have long set up in Santa Cruz and more particularly in **Triana** (**AY**) where one of the streets bears the name Alfarería (pottery). La Cartuja (Carthusian monastery), once a ceramics factory and now a museum, illustrates the traditional methods used first by the Romans and then the Moors. Other Sevillian specialities include lace, mantillas, fans, shawls, flamenco costumes, wrought iron, saddlery, guitars and castanets.

In the gastronomic line, Sevilla is famous for its confectionery, particularly the *yemas*, egg-yolk sweets made in the Convento de San Leandro, and its orange marmalade.

Strolling through Sevilla – One of the great pleasures of Sevilla is the wonderful variety of places to walk: the peaceful alleyways in Santa Cruz, Parque de María Luisa and the banks of the Guadalquivir along Paseo Alcalde Marqués de Contadero or Calle Betis on the other side.

★★★THE GIRALDA AND CATHEDRAL *time: 1 1/2 hours*

★★★**Giralda** (**BX**) ⊙ – The Giralda – 98m - 322ft high – was once a minaret; its name, literally weather vane, comes from the revolving bronze statue of Faith at its summit. When the Giralda was built in the 12C, it resembled its Moroccan sisters, the Koutoubia in Marrakesh and the Hassan Tower in Rabat, and was surmounted by four decorative gilded spheres. The top storey and Renaissance style lantern were added in the 16C. The delicate ornament is typical of the style of the Almohads, a dynasty of strict religious belief, opposed to ostentation, whose members created monumental grandeur in exact accordance with their ideals of utter simplicity. A gently sloping ramp, interrupted at intervals by platforms, leads to the top at 70m - 230ft from which there are excellent **views**★★ of the town.

The **Patio de los Naranjos** (Orange Tree Court) also remains from the ancient mosque; the Pardon Gate on the court's north wall (best viewed from the street), built in 1552, is a fine example of the Mudéjar style.

SEVILLA

B   Hospital de los
    Venerables
E   Archivo General
    de Indias
H   Ayuntamiento
U   Universidad

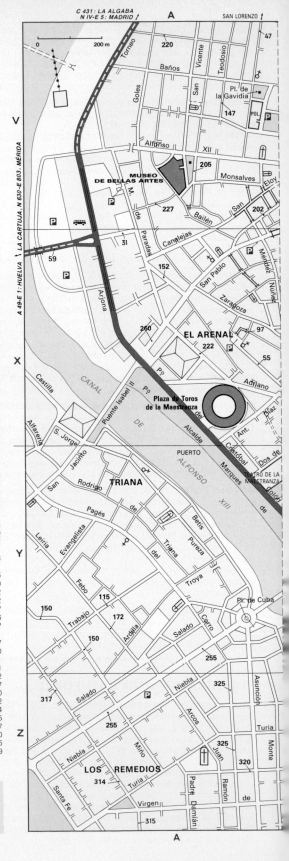

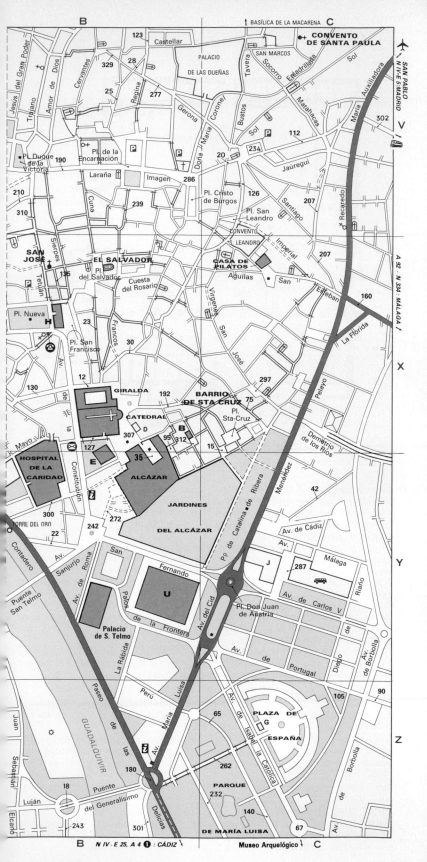

CATEDRAL

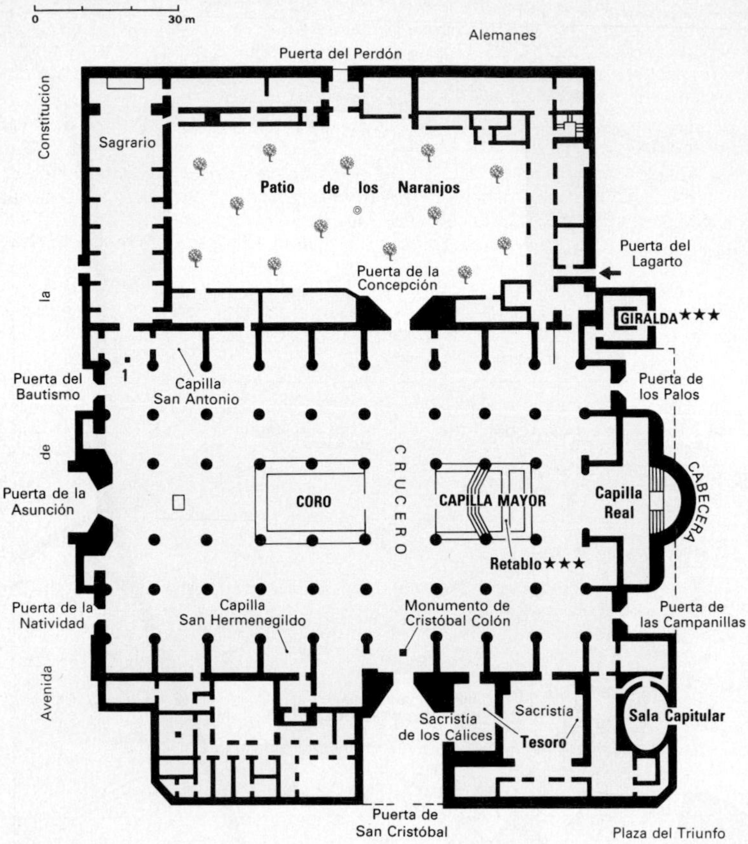

0   30 m

Floor plan labels:

Alemanes

Puerta del Perdón

Constitución

Sagrario

Patio   de   los   Naranjos

Puerta del Lagarto

Puerta de la Concepción

la

GIRALDA ★★★

Puerta del Bautismo

Capilla San Antonio

Puerta de los Palos

de

CRUCERO

CORO

CAPILLA MAYOR

Capilla Real

CABECERA

Puerta de la Asunción

Retablo ★★★

Puerta de las Campanillas

Puerta de la Natividad

Capilla San Hermenegildo

Monumento de Cristóbal Colón

Avenida

Sacristía de los Cálices

Sacristía Tesoro

Sala Capitular

Puerta de San Cristóbal

Plaza del Triunfo

★★★ **Catedral** (BX) ⊘ – "Let us build a cathedral so immense that everyone on beholding it, will take us for madmen," the chapter is said to have declared when they were knocking down the mosque. They succeeded, for Sevilla's cathedral is the third largest in Europe after St Peter's in Rome and St Paul's in London. The exterior is massive.

As one of the last to be built in the Gothic style, the cathedral shows obvious Renaissance influence. The main portals are modern though harmonising with the whole, however, the Puerta de la Natividad (Nativity Doorway) on the right and the Puerta del Bautismo (Baptism) on the left, on either side of the west door, include beautiful sculptures by Mercadente de Bretaña or Brittany (c 1460) while the Gothic Puerta de Los Palos and Puerta de las Campanillas, on either side of the rounded Capilla Real (Royal Chapel) (1575) at the east end, have Renaissance style tympana in which Maestro Miguel Perrin (1520) has made full play of perspective in true Renaissance style.

The interior is striking in size and richness. The massive column shafts, supporting huge arches, appear slender because they are so tall; the magnificent Flamboyant vaulting rises 56m – 184ft above the transept crossing.

Enter through the Lonja or Puerta de San Cristóbal in the south transept.

Columbus's tomb lies in the south transept; the 19C monument shows the discoverer's coffin being borne by four kings symbolising León, Castilla, Navarra and Aragón.

Capilla Mayor (Chancel) – The chancel is unbelievably rich. Splendid Plateresque grilles (1518-1533) precede the immense Flemish **altarpiece ★★★**, profusely but delicately carved with scenes from the Life of Christ and gleaming with gold leaf (1482-1525).

Coro – Partly hidden by a grille (1519-1523) by Brother Francisco of Salamanca, are magnificent 15 and 16C choir-stalls. The **trascoro**, a screen of multicoloured marble, jasper and bronze, is 17C.

Tesoro – The treasury is in 16C rooms; the sacristy contains the cathedral plate including a Renaissance **monstrance** (custodia) by Juan de Arfe and the Tenebrario or Plateresque candelabrum with 15 branches used in Holy Week.

The **Sacristía de los Cálices** (Chalice Sacristy) displays painting and sculpture including canvases by Goya *(Santa Justa and Santa Rufina)*, Valdés Leal and Murillo. The rooms adjoining the chapter house contain collections of chasubles, lecterns and antiphonaries. One of them displays the pages' costumes of the *Seises*, a group of choristers who dance before the high altar at Corpus Christi and on 8 December, perpetuating a secular tradition of unknown origin.

Sala Capitular – The vast 16C Renaissance chapter house has an elliptical dome and an *Immaculate Conception* by Murillo.

★★**Capilla Real** (Chapel Royal) – The Chapel Royal opens through an arch so high that the decoration can only be appreciated from a distance. It is covered by an elegant, richly ornamented Renaissance dome with carved busts decorating the cells. On either side are the tombs of Alfonso X of Castilla (d 1284) and his mother, Beatrice of Swabia.

At the centre of the high altar is the robed figure of Our Lady of the Monarchs, patron of Sevilla, given, according to legend, by St Louis of France to his cousin St Ferdinand of Spain, who lies buried in a silver gilt shrine below the altar. The chapel screen dates from 1771.

Numerous works of art are displayed in the periphery chapels: the tomb of Cardinal Juan de Cervantes in the Capilla de San Hermenegildo (St Hermenegild's Chapel) on the south side and paintings by Murillo, Jordaens and Valdés Leal in that of San Antonio (north side). Beside this last chapel is a replica of the **Estatua de la Fe** (Statue of Faith) (**1**) that crowns the Giralda.

★★★THE ALCÁZAR AND THE BARRIO SANTA CRUZ

time: 2 1/2 hours

★★★**Alcázar (Reales Alcázares) (BXY)** ☉ – All that remains of the Alcázar of the Almohads are the Patio de Yeso and the section of wall dividing the Patio de la Montería from the Patio del León. The rest of the building dates from the Christian period. The palace was built by **Peter the Cruel** (1350-1369) in 1362, 78 years after the departure of the Moors from Sevilla.

The decoration is based in detail on that of the Alhambra in Granada *(qv)* which dates from the same period, making the building, in spite of later modifications, one of the purest examples of the Mudéjar style. Moorish architects are believed to have contributed to the design.

Cuarto del Almirante (Admiral's Apartments) – *Right side of the Patio de la Montería.* It was here that Isabel the Catholic founded the Casa de Contratación. The Sala de Audiencias (Audience Chamber) contains a model of Columbus's vessel *Santa María* and an altarpiece, the **Virgin of the Navigators★** (1531-1536), painted by Alejo Fernández.

★★★**Palacio de Pedro el Cruel** (Peter the Cruel's Palace) – The narrow façade, sheltered by a carved wood overhang, is strongly reminiscent of the Patio del Cuarto Dorado (Golden Room Court) in the Alhambra.

Beyond the façade is the **Patio de las Doncellas** (Court of the Maidens), a beautifully proportioned, Moorish arched *patio* which remains exquisite in spite of the upper storey added in the 16C.

Surrounding the court, the rooms are especially attractive and interesting with carved stucco decoration, bright *azulejos* and *artesonado* ceilings. These include the **Salón del Techo** (Ceiling Saloon) with an outstanding coffered ceiling, the apartments of María de Padilla, Peter the Cruel's mistress, and the Salón de Embajadores (Ambassadors' Hall) covered by a remarkable 15C cedarwood **cupola★★**, described as a half-orange or *media naranja*. Afterwards follows the Salón de Felipe II (Philip II's Saloon), which leads first to the delicately ornamental **Patio de las Muñecas** (Dolls' Court) so named because of its small size, and then to the bedroom *(dormitorio)* of Isabel the Catholic, the Salón de los Príncipes (Princes' Saloon) and finally the Dormitorio de los Reyes Moros (Bedroom of the Moorish Kings) with its blue toned stucco.

Come out of the palace into the Patio de la Montería and through a vaulted passage on the right.

Palacio de Carlos V (Charles V's Palace) – This houses a magnificent collection of Brussels **tapestries★★** (1554) illustrating Emperor Charles V's conquest of Tunis in 1535.

★**Jardines (BCY)** – The terraced gardens, planted with exotic trees and shrubs and cooled by ornamental basins, descend from a 17C terrace to a tree-covered maze and the Pabellón de Carlos V (Charles V Pavilion), finely domed in cedarwood.

An alleyway leads to the Patio de Banderas or Flag Court.

Patio de Banderas (Flag Court) (**BX 35**) – The small enclosed square is bordered by elegant façades which stand out against the background of the cathedral and the Giralda tower.

★★ **Barrio de Santa Cruz** (Santa Cruz Quarter) (**BCX**) – This former Jewish quarter or Judería was the quarter favoured by Sevilla nobility in the 17C; it remains well worth visiting for its character, its alleys, wrought-iron grilles, flower-filled *patios* and squares shaded by orange trees and palms. It is even more delightful in the evenings when cafés and restaurants overflow into the squares like those of Doña Elvira, los Venerables Sacerdotes, Alfaro, Santa Cruz and las Cruces.

★ **Hospital de los Venerables** (**BX B**) ⊘ – *(Plaza de los Venerables)*. This recently restored building is one of the best examples of 17C Sevillian baroque art. It now serves as the headquarters for the Cultural Focus Foundation. Its fine **church** is covered with frescoes painted by Valdés Real and his son Lucas Valdés.

ADDITIONAL SIGHTS

★★ **Museo de Bellas Artes** (Fine Arts Museum) (**AV**) ⊘ – This excellent museum in the former Convento de la Merced (Merced Friary) was built in the 17C by Juan de Oviedo around three beautiful *patios*. It houses an important collection of paintings covering Spain's Golden Age. The baroque doorway was added in the 18C.

The first of the museum's 14 rooms contains examples of medieval art. **Room II**, once the refectory, is dedicated to Renaissance art, in particular a fine sculpture of *St Jerome* by Pietro Torrigiani, a contemporary of Michelangelo. Other works of note include Alejo Fernández's *Annunciation*, with its Flemish and Italian influence clearly evident, a diptych of *The Annunciation and Visitation* by Coffermans, and a *Holy Family* by Villegas. Two magnificent portraits of *A Lady and a Gentleman* by Pedro Pacheco are the highlight in **Room III** while several baroque style pictures of the Infant Jesus are on display in **Room IV**.

Room V★★★ is undoubtedly the museum's star attraction. The church, its walls decorated with paintings by the 18C artist Domingo Martínez, sets the tone, along with an extraordinary collection of work by Murillo and one of Zurbarán's masterpieces *The Apotheosis of St Thomas Aquinas* (in the nave), outstanding for its play between light and shade. **Murillo**, a master of both the pictorial technique and the use of light in his canvases, is the great painter of religious themes and children; his subjects, always so human, emanate tenderness and delicacy in a world of balance fleeing from drama and excess. His works can be found in the transept and in the apse where his monumental *Immaculate Conception*, with its energetic movement, holds pride of place. It is surrounded by several notable paintings of saints: *Santa Rufina and Santa Justa*, clutching the Giralda, and *San Leandro and San Buenaventura*. On the right-hand side of the transept a soft *Virgen de la Servietta* stands out (admire the effect of the Child moving towards you), as do a *St Francis embracing Christ on the Cross* and a further *Immaculate Conception*, also known as *The Child*. Among several paintings on its left-hand side, *St Anthony and Child*, *Dolorosa* and *St Felix of Cantalicio and Child* are all worthy of particular note. **Upper Floor: Room VI** (a gallery) displays a fine, richly decorated collection of Saints (anonymous, though some painted by followers of Zurbarán), two saints and a *Christ* by Zurbarán himself, and a powerful portrait of *St James the Apostle* by Ribera. **Room VII** contains further works by Murillo and his disciples while **Room VIII** is entirely devoted to the other great Baroque artist Valdés Real. European Baroque is represented in **Room IX** with, among others, canvases by Bruegel and the supreme *Portrait of a Lady* by Cornelis de Vos. **Room X**★★ merits special attention, with its walls mostly set aside for **Zurbarán** (1598-1664). He alone is able to paint the shades of white of the monks' habits and the pure cloth of Christ, as admired in the fine *Christ on the Cross* (in this same room), in which the body of Christ, painted against a dark background, almost appears in sculptured relief. Zurbarán's compositions are both simple and peaceful. In some of his work a lack of concern for perspective is apparent, causing him to commit inaccuracies, as can be seen in *St Hugh and Carthusian Monks at Table,* so outstanding in other respects. His preoccupation with the treatment of the canvas, as already seen in the Fathers of the church in *The Apotheosis of St Thomas Aquinas*, can equally be admired in the splendid velvet brocade in *San Ambrosio*. In addition to his paintings of saints, his *Virgin of the Caves* and *San Bruno's visit to Urbano II* are also notable. On display in the same room are various sculptures, including *San Bruno* by Martínez Montañés. The ceiling of the inner room should not be missed. **Room XI** (a gallery), with its collection of 18C works, is enlivened by Goya's *Portrait of Canon José Duato*. The following two rooms (**XII and XIII**) portray 19C art, in particular, the superb portraits by Esquivel, while the final room (**XIV**) shows several 20C canvases (Vázquez Díaz, Zuloaga).

★★ **Casa de Pilatos** (Pilate's House) (**CX**) ⊘ – The palace, built between the late 15 and early 16C by Don Fadrique, the first Marquis of Tarifa, is thought to be based on Pontius Pilate's house in Jerusalem. It is a mixture of Mudéjar, Renaissance and Flamboyant Gothic styles.

The large *patio*, in which the Mudéjar style predominates, resembles an elegant Moorish palace with finely moulded stuccowork and magnificent lustre **azulejos**★★. The statues, some Antique and the rest 16C, portray, among others, Roman

Casa de Pilatos, Sevilla

emperors and Athena. The ground floor rooms with *artesonado* ceilings, the chapel with Gothic vaulting and *azulejo* and stucco decoration on the altar, and the remarkable wood **dome**★ over the grand **staircase**★ illustrate the vitality of the Mudéjar style in civil architecture during the Renaissance. Among the painted ceilings on the first floor is that by Francisco Pacheco (1603) illustrating the Apotheosis of Hercules.

★★ **Parque de María Luisa** (**BCZ**) – The 19C park with its beautiful trees, pools and fountains, once formed the grounds of the Palacio de San Telmo. Several buildings remain from the 1929 Ibero-American Exhibition including the semicircular edifice surrounding the vast **Plaza de España**★ (**CZ**) *(photograph overleaf)*. Each of the 58 benches around the square with their *azulejo* decoration, represents a province of Spain and illustrates an episode from its particular history. There is rowing in the canals on the square.

Museo Arqueológico (**Archaeological Museum**) (**CZ**) ⊘ – The museum in the neo-Renaissance palace on Plaza de América houses interesting collections of objects from prehistoric through to Phoenician, Punic and Roman times. The 7C BC **Carambolo Treasure**★ includes gold jewellery from the ancient Tartessos civilisation, as well as a statue of Astarte with a Phoenician inscription and the Ebora Treasure dating from the period of Phoenician colonisation, the 8 to the 5C BC. The Roman section, with part of its finds from Itálica *(see below)*, consists of statues: Venus, Diana the Huntress, Trajan, a head of Alexander the Great, a beautiful Hispania, as well as mosaics and bronzes.

★ **Hospital de la Caridad** (**Hospital of Charity**) (**BY**) ⊘ – The hospital was founded in 1625 by Miguel de Mañara who called upon the great Sevillian artists of the time to decorate the church with the themes of Death and Charity. Valdés Leal illustrated the first with a striking sense of the macabre, Murillo the second in two large paintings: *The Miracle of the Loaves and Fishes* which faces *Moses Smiting Water from the Rock*, as well as in *St John of God* and *St Isabel of Hungary caring for the Sick*. Pedro Roldan's *Entombment* adorns the high altar.

★ **Convento de Santa Paula** (**CV**) ⊘ – This 15C convent is one of the most beautiful and lavish in the city. The church's breathtaking **portal**★ (1504) is adorned with ceramics. Despite the obvious mix of styles (Mudéjar, Gothic and Renaissance), the overall effect is a harmonious one. Inside, the nave is covered by a 17C roof and the chancel by a Gothic vault covered with attractive frescoes. The church also contains sculptures and paintings of interest.

Museum – *Entrance through no 11 on the plaza.* It has some fine works on display by important artists such as Ribera, Pedro de Mena, Alonso de Cana, etc.

★ **Iglesia del Salvador** (**BX**) ⊘ – This 17-18C church rises majestically on one side of the square which gives it its name. The sensation of vastness pervades the whole of the interior. It contains some of the city's most impressive 18C **baroque retables**★.

Archivo General de Indias (**The Indies Archives**) (**BXY E**) ⊘ – The building, dating from 1572, was designed by Juan de Herrera, architect of the Escorial, as an Exchange *(lonja)*. It now houses a unique collection of documents on America at the time of its discovery and conquest including maps and charts, plans of South American towns and their fortifications as well as the autographs of Columbus, Magellan, Cortés and others.

★ **Capilla de San José** (**St Joseph's Chapel**) (**BX**) ⊘ – The profusely gilded, baroque chapel, gleams at night by the lights of evening service. The overpowering altarpiece, organ and ornate galleries are typical of the period (1766).

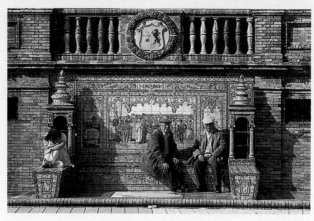

Plaza de España, Sevilla

B. Brillion/MICHELIN

Ayuntamiento (Town Hall) (**BX H**) – The hall's **east face★**, dating from 1527-1534, is attractively Renaissance in style with delicate scrollwork decoration. Star vaulting covers the vestibule.

Palacio de San Telmo (**BY**) – The palace (1682-1796), once a naval academy and residence of the Dukes of Montpensier and now a seminary, has a grand baroque **entrance**, three storeys high, by Leonardo de Figueroa. It now serves as the headquarters of the Presidencia de la Junta de Andalucía.

Universidad (**BY U**) – The University with its harmonious baroque façades and elegantly laid-out *patios*, is in the old, 18C, tobacco factory.

EXCURSION

Itálica ⊘ – *9km - 6 miles northwest on the N630 towards Mérida.*
Standing on a cypress-covered hillside overlooking the Guadalquivir plain, are the remains of a **Roman town**, the birthplace of the emperors Hadrian and Trajan and the poet Silius Italicus. The great size of the amphitheatre illustrates the importance of the town at the time. By following the network of streets covering the hillside you see mosaics, among others of birds and Neptune, in their original sites.

Anfiteatro – This amphitheatre was one of the largest in the Roman Empire with seating for twenty-five thousand spectators. Parts of both the seating area and the pit beneath the stage remain from its original elliptical design.
The Itálica theatre, on the far side of the old road leading to the N 630, has now been restored.

SIGÜENZA★

Castilla-La Mancha (Guadalajara)
Population 5 426
Michelin map 444 I 22 – Michelin Atlas España Portugal p 41

The pink and ochre coloured town of Sigüenza, descending in tiers from its hilltop, is dominated by its imposing cathedral fortress and castle *(parador)*. The old town is a maze of narrow streets bordered by stylish mansions. In the centre, the **Plaza Mayor**, which extends from the south wall of the cathedral, is a delightful square with its 16C arcaded gallery and Renaissance town hall *(Ayuntamiento)*.

★★Catedral ⊘ – The nave, begun to a Cistercian plan in the 12C, was only completed in 1495, the end of the Gothic period; the ambulatory and cloisters are slightly later. The roof and transept dome were rebuilt after the bombings of 1936.
The façade appears more like that of a fortress than a church as it stands flanked by crenellated towers and powerful buttresses until you notice its great rose and Romanesque windows with their old stained glass.

Interior – The nave with sober lines and high vaulting supported on massive pillars graced by slender engaged columns, conveys an impression of solid strength.
In the **north aisle**, the **doorway★** into the Capilla de la Anunciación (Chapel of the Annunciation) is decorated with Renaissance pilasters, Mudéjar arabesques and Gothic cusping. The 15C triptych beside it by the Castilian school is dedicated to Sts Mark and Catherine. In the **north transept** is a fine **sculptured unit★★**: a 16C **porphyry doorway** opening onto the cloisters of multicoloured marble. The 16C **Santa**

Librada altar designed by Covarrubias as a retable features a central niche containing an altar surmounted by painted panels of the martyrdom of the saint and her eight sisters, all born, according to legend, on the same day. Beside it, note the 16C **sepulchre of Dom Fadrique of Portugal**, a more ornate monument adorned with Plateresque decoration.

The **sacristy** by Covarrubias has an amazing **ceiling★** – a profusion of heads and roses between which peer thousands of cherubim; the panelling and woodwork of doors and furniture are delicately carved in ornate Plateresque. The 16C **Capilla de las Reliquias** (Reliquary Chapel) is covered with a **dome★**.

A chapel off the **ambulatory** contains a 16C wooden **Crucifix**.

The **chancel** (Presbiterio) has a beautiful 17C wrought-iron grille framed by two alabaster pulpits, one Gothic (on the right), the other Renaissance (on the left). The altarpiece is 17C.

The Capilla del Doncel in the south transept was designed for the **Doncel tomb★★** commissioned by Isabel the Catholic for her young page, Don Martín Vázquez de Arce, who died at the gates of Granada in 1486. The figure, considered a major work of sepulchral art in Spain, shows the youth reclining on one elbow and reading serenely; it is extraordinarily realistic. In the centre of the room is the mausoleum of the Doncel's parents.

Claustro – The 16C Gothic cloisters are surrounded by chapels with Plateresque doors, among them the 16-17C Puerta de Jaspe (Jasper Doorway) which communicates with the transept. The **Sala Capitular** (Chapter house) displays books, manuscripts and a collection of 17C Flemish tapestries.

Museo de Arte Antiguo (Museum of Ancient Art) ⊘ – *Opposite the cathedral.* Among the many works displayed are sculptures by Pompeo Leoni (Room C), a *Pietà* attributed to Morales, an *Immaculate Conception* by Zurbarán (Room E) and a fiery statue of the *Prophet Elijah* by Salzillo (Room N).

EXCURSION

Atienza – *31km - 19 miles northwest on the C114.*
Atienza is a typical Castilian village built at the foot of a castle of which only the keep remains proudly upright on its rock. **Plaza del Trigo**, surrounded by porticoes, is attractively medieval. The town, an important commercial enclave during the Middle Ages, was granted protection by Alfonso VIII of Castilla in recognition for the support its citizens gave him in 1162 when, as a child, he sought refuge from his uncle, Ferdinand II of León who hoped to secure the Castilian throne. The event is commemorated annually in the Whitsun **Caballada** festival. Atienza once had seven churches but since the Civil War all that remains of interest are the Churrigueresque altarpiece in the **parish church** on Plaza del Trigo and the rococo chapel in the **Iglesia de la Trinidad** (Holy Trinity Church) near the cemetery.

SITGES★

Catalunya (Barcelona)
Population 13 096
Michelin map 443 I35 – Michelin Atlas España Portugal p 32
Town plan in the current Michelin Red Guide España Portugal

Sitges, south of Barcelona, is a favourite resort with wealthy Catalan families who have built elegant houses along the Paseo Marítimo or Sea Promenade. It was an important artistic centre at the turn of the century when Art Nouveau took a hold in Catalunya and it has fine examples of Modernist architecture.

Sitges is renowned for the carpets of flowers that decorate the streets during the Corpus Christi festival.

BARRIO ANTIGUO (OLD TOWN) *time: 1 1/2 hours*

Rising from the breakwater, sheltering the fishing harbour, is the pink façade of the parish church. All around are the streets of the old town lined with white-walled houses, their balconies brilliant with flowers. Local museums housed in neo-Gothic mansions contain canvases from the late 19C, when Rusiñol and Miguel Utrillo (official father of the French painter) painted in this quarter.

Museo del Cau Ferrat ⊘ – The painter **Santiago Rusiñol** (1861-1931) converted two 16C fishermen's houses, adding some Gothic features, into a home for himself and an art centre which was inaugurated in 1884, at the same time as the Casa de la Vila opposite, a neo-Gothic mansion. The collections left to the town by Rusiñol, and which are displayed in this museum, include ceramics, drawings and paintings by himself and other artists such as Ramón Casas, Juan Llimona, Miguel Utrillo as well as two paintings by El Greco. Of particular interest is his collection of wrought-iron works (locks, hinges, candelabra, etc).

Museo Maricel del Mar ⊘ – The museum is in the house the American Charles Deering had built under the supervision of Miguel Utrillo in 1913. It is linked by a footbridge to another mansion, the Maricel de Terra. The collections displayed are of medieval and baroque works of art. At the entrance is a fine Gothic high relief of the Three Wise Men in a Spanish-Flemish style.

Casa Llopis ⊘ – A Romantic Museum has been set up in two buildings: the Casa Llopis in Sitges and the Casa Papiol in Vilanova i la Geltrú *(see below)*. The Casa Llopis, a bourgeois house built at the end of the 18C in the then new part of the town, gives a good idea of the life of the middle and upper classes during the Romantic period with frescoes on the walls, English furniture, various mechanical devices and musical boxes. Dioramas on the ground floor

Barrio Antiguo, Sitges

supplement the picture with scenes of private, social and popular activities.

The museum also houses the **Lola Anglada Collection**, an outstanding display of 17, 18 and 19C dolls from all over Europe made of wood, leather, papier mâché and china.

EXCURSION

Vilanova i la Geltrú – *7km - 4 miles west.*
Vilanova i la Geltrú, a coastal town, is home to the second building housing the Romantic Museum, the Casa Papiol.

★ **Casa Papiol** ⊘ – The large mansion built by the Papiol family between 1780 and 1801 gives a good idea of the values cherished by the devout yet well to do industrial middle classes in the 19C. A certain austerity reigns in the library with its 5000 or so 16 to 19C volumes, in the Deputy's office, the chapel with its strange relic of St Constance and in the reception rooms where the walls are covered in Biblical scenes executed in grey monochrome. On the other hand, the opulence of the house is evident in the rich furnishings, the ballroom and the Louis XVI apartment where the French General, Suchet, once stayed. The kitchen is spick and span, gleaming with ceramic tiles.

Workrooms and annexes on the entresol and ground floors contain equipment and stores: the stove, olive oil reserve, servants' kitchen and the stables.

Monasterio de SOBRADO DOS MONXES

Galicia (La Coruña)
Michelin map 441 C 5 – Michelin Atlas España Portugal p 3

Sobrado ⊘ is one of Galicia's vast monasteries, built between the Renaissance and baroque periods. It is badly weatherworn but is in process of restoration by the Cistercian community now living within its walls.

Preoccupation with size brought a certain severity in the decoration of the church façade. The interior, on the other hand, displays a wealth of imagination in the design of the **cupolas** in the transept, the sacristy and the Capilla del Rosario (Rosary Chapel) as well as in the Claustro de los Medallones (Medallion Cloisters).

Of the monastery's medieval buildings, there remain a kitchen with a monumental chimney, a chapter house and the Capilla de la Magdalena (Mary Magdalene Chapel).

The Michelin Red Guide España Portugal
which is revised annually gives a selection of
establishments offering
– carefully prepared meals at reasonable prices
– simple meals at moderate prices
– prices including or excluding service
– car parking.

SOLSONA

Catalunya (Lleida)
Population 6 601
Michelin map 443 G 34 – Michelin Atlas España Portugal p 32

Narrow winding streets with the occasional medieval house in the shadow of the castle ruins, give the town character.

Corpus Christi is the occasion for young men, dressed in ancient costumes, to parade through the streets firing salvoes from blunderbusses, for giant pasteboard figures to appear and children to dance the "Ball de Bastons" in the streets.

Catedral ⊙ – Only the apse, decorated with Lombard bands and carved modillions, remains of the Romanesque church, the rest is Gothic with baroque additions such as the portals and the Capilla de la Virgen (Lady Chapel) off the south transept. The latter was designed to shelter within its ornate marble walls the **Virgin of the Cloister ★**, a beautifully carved Romanesque figure in black stone.

★ Museo Diocesano y Comarcal (Diocesan and Regional Museum) ⊙ – The Romanesque and Gothic style **paintings ★★** in the museum housed in the Palacio Episcopal (Episcopal Palace), are excellent examples of Catalan art. The fresco collection of works from throughout the province includes a painting from Sant Quirze de Pedret, discovered beneath an overpainting done 100 years later. This fresco, executed in an archaic style, shows God, with arms outstretched, in a circle which represents heaven, surmounted by a phoenix symbolising immortality. The narrative talent of the 12C Maestro de Pedret can be seen in the theme of the Apocalypse, painted in a style obviously Byzantine influenced in a reconstituted Mozarabic apse. Totally different are the thinly outlined, elegant 13C paintings from Sant Pau de Casserres – in particular, some wonderful angels of the Last Judgment – and the already Gothic style, 14C works from Cardona.

The museum is also known for its collection of **altarfronts** which includes a frontal from Sagars, in which all decoration is omitted to heighten the symbolism of the scenes illustrated, and a realistic painting of the *Last Supper* by Jaime Ferrer (15C). The **Museo de la Sal** (Salt Museum), another department, is possibly unique. Everything displayed on the table has been carved out of rock salt from Cardona: the setting, the repast and the weird, pinnacled centrepiece.

SORIA★

Castilla y León
Population 35 540
Michelin map 442 G 22 – Michelin Atlas España Portugal p 27

Soria stands at an altitude of 1 050m - 3 445ft on the banks of the Duero, the river that waters and cools the vast, windswept, russet coloured Castilian plateau. The desolate scenery and medieval atmosphere of the old town have been sung by poets over the ages including the Sevillian **Antonio Machado** (1875-1939), who wrote *Campos de Castilla*.

"Soria pura, cabeza de Extremadura" – The motto in the city arms recalls events in the 10C when Soria and its dependent countryside marked the limits of Castile in the face of the Muslim conquered south. Gradually the Christians built a **fortified line** along the Duero reinforced by bastions such as **Soria, Berlanga, Gormaz, Peñaranda** and **Peñafiel**.

In the Middle Ages, the town grew prosperous partly through its role in the **Mesta**, a powerful association of sheep farmers that organised the seasonal migration of flocks between Extremadura, Castilla and pastures in the north of the country.

SIGHTS

★ Iglesia de Santo Domingo (A) – The attraction of this church's west front lies in its two tiers of blind arcades, its window and richly carved **portal ★★**. The overall French air is explained by the fact that the church's founders were Alfonso VIII and his queen, Eleanor Plantagenet, on either side of the portal. The carving on the tympanum is less cluttered than that of the archivolt where the figures have been carved with great attention to detail. The scenes so realistically illustrated include the early chapters of Genesis (on the capitals of the jamb shafts), the 24 Old Men of the Apocalypse playing stringed instruments, the Massacre of the Innocents, and Christ's childhood, Passion and Death (in ascending registers on the archivolt).

Palacio de los Condes de Gómara (Palace of the Counts of Gómara) (B J) – The long façade, part Renaissance, part classical, the bold upstanding tower and double *patio* are a proud example of late-16C opulence.

Iglesia de San Juan de Rabanera (A R) – The Romanesque portal taken from a ruined church dedicated to St Nicholas, recalls the events of the saint's life in the capitals on the slender columns on the right and on the tympanum. The unusual

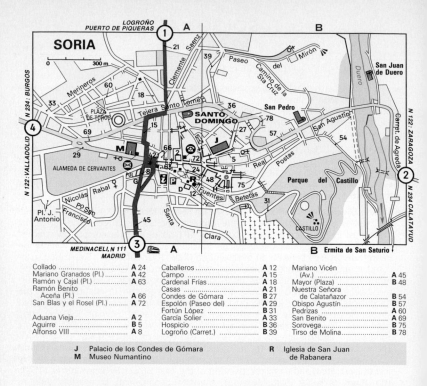

Collado	A 24	Caballeros	A 12	Mariano Vicén	
Mariano Granados (Pl.)	A 42	Campo	A 15	(Av.)	A 45
Ramón y Cajal (Pl.)	A 63	Cardenal Frías	A 18	Mayor (Plaza)	B 48
Ramón Benito		Casas	A 21	Nuestra Señora	
Aceña (Pl.)	A 66	Condes de Gómara	B 27	de Calatañazor	B 54
San Blas y el Rosel (Pl.)	A 72	Espolón (Paseo del)	B 29	Obispo Agustín	B 57
		Fortún López	B 31	Pedrizas	A 60
Aduana Vieja	A 2	García Solier	A 33	San Benito	A 69
Aguirre	B 5	Hospicio	B 36	Sorovega	B 75
Alfonso VIII	A 8	Logroño (Carret.)	B 39	Tirso de Molina	B 78

J	Palacio de los Condes de Gómara	**R**	Iglesia de San Juan
M	Museo Numantino		de Rabanera

decoration at the church's east end shows both Byzantine and Gothic influences. Inside are two interesting Crucifixes – a Romanesque one over the altar and a baroque one in the north transept.

Museo Numantino (Numantia Museum) (A M) ⊘ – The collections in the recently restored museum illustrate the historical development of Soria from the Palaeolithic Age to modern times. Most of the items displayed come from local excavations – note the artefacts from Celtiberian necropolises and the coloured pottery from Numantia *(see below)*.

Catedral de San Pedro ⊘ **(B)** – The 16C Gothic cathedral is light and spacious; the **cloisters★** are older, possessing three Romanesque galleries. The capitals have been delicately re-sculpted in a pure Romanesque style that recalls the work in Santo Domingo de Silos *(qv)*. In the gallery walls are the funerary niches in which the monks are buried.

Monasterio de San Juan de Duero (B) ⊘ – The monastery founded by the Hospitallers of St John of Jerusalem stands in a rustic setting on the far bank of the Duero. Only the graceful gallery arcading, with four different orders, remains of the 12-13C **cloisters★**. The intersecting, overlapping arches owe much to Moorish art.
The church contains a small lapidary museum. Two small chambers with beautiful historiated capitals stand at the entrance to the apse; the ciborium effect is unusual, more like in an Orthodox church.

Parque del Castillo (Castle Park) (B) – The lines of the poet, Machado *(qv)*, on the Soria countryside come alive on this hillside: "...., violet mountains, poplars beside green waters..."

Ermita de San Saturio (San Saturio Hermitage) (B) ⊘ – A shaded path beside the Duero leads to the cave where the holy man sat in meditation. The octagonal chapel built into the rock and covered with frescoes is 18C.

EXCURSIONS

Ruinas de Numancia ⊘ – *4km-3 miles north; take the N111 as far as Garray and then a little road sharp right heading south.* There are few signs of the events which took place in Numancia in 133 BC. The Romans were in Spain at the time and thought that having pacified the peninsula their legions would suffer little opposition; Numancia, however, resisted them. **Scipio Aemilianus**, who had destroyed Carthage, directed the siege against Numancia. After eight months the Numantines could resist no more but, unwilling to submit, they burned their city and perished one and all.
The present ruins are of the Numancia rebuilt by the Romans.

★★ Sierra de Urbión – *Roads are liable to be blocked by snow between November and May.* It seems surprising that this part of the Sistema Ibérico mountain range which at one point rises to 2 228m - 7 310 ft and is so close to the Soria plateau and the flat ochre coloured Ebro valley, should be hilly and green, filled with streams rushing through pine-woods and meadows. One of these streams is the source of the Duero, one of Spain's longest rivers *(910km - 565 miles).*

★★ Laguna Negra de Urbión – *53km - 33 miles northwest by ④ on the plan – about 1 hour. At Cidones bear right towards Vinuesa; continue for 18km - 11 miles before turning into the Montenegro de Cameros road. After 8km - 5 miles bear left into the Laguna road (9km - 6 miles).* The **road★★**, after skirting the Cuerdo del Pozo reservoir *(embalse),* which is ringed by tall stone cliffs, rocks and holm oaks, continues through pines to the **Laguna Negra** (alt 1 700m - 5 577ft). The lagoon is a small glacial lake at the foot of a semicircular cliff over which cascade two waterfalls.

★★ Laguna Negra de Neila – *About 86km - 53 miles northwest by ④ on the plan. At Abejar turn right towards Molinos de Duero; continue to Quintana de la Sierra where you bear right for Neila (12km - 7 miles) and then left for Huerta de Arriba; 2km - 1 mile on the left is the road to Laguna Negra.* The **road★** through green, picturesque countryside commands changing views of the valley and Sierra de la Demanda. The lake lies at an altitude of 2 000m - 6 562ft.

SOS DEL REY CATÓLICO★

Aragón (Zaragoza)
Population 974
Michelin map 443 E 26 – Michelin Atlas España Portugal p 15

It was in this town in the **Palacio de los Sada** (Sada Palace) that Ferdinand the Catholic, who was to unite Spain, was born in 1452. The houses, palaces, walls and doorways which line the narrow cobbled streets and alleys leading to the keep and the church give the town a medieval air.

On the **Plaza Mayor,** an irregularly shaped square, stand the imposing 16C Ayuntamiento (Town Hall), which like the Palacio de los Gil de Jaz has large carved wood overhangs, and the Lonja (Exchange) with wide arches.

★ Iglesia de San Esteban (St Stephen's Church) ⊘ – The church is reached through a vaulted passageway. The 11C **crypt★** beneath the church is dedicated to Our Lady of Forgiveness (Virgen del Pardón). Two of the three apses are decorated with fine 14C **frescoes.** The central apse contains outstanding capitals carved with the figures of women and birds.

The statue columns at the **main door** have the stiff and noble bearing of those at Sangüesa *(qv).* The church itself, built in the transitional style, has a beautiful Renaissance **gallery★**. A chapel contains a 12C Romanesque figure of Christ with staring eyes.

EXCURSIONS

Uncastillo – *21km - 13 miles southeast.*
The Romanesque **Iglesia de Santa María** has an unusual 14C tower adorned with machicolations and pinnacle turrets. The **south portal's★** rich and delicate carving, of imaginary beasts for the most part, makes it one of the most beautiful doorways of the late Romanesque period. The church gallery with Renaissance **stalls★** and the **cloisters★** are 16C Plateresque.

TALAVERA DE LA REINA

Castilla-La Mancha (Toledo)
Population 69 136
Michelin map 444 M 15 – Michelin Atlas España Portugal p 51

The name Talavera, like that of Manises and Paterna, has been associated since the 15C with the **ceramic tiles** used to decorate the lower walls of palaces, mansions and chapels. Talavera *azulejos* were always recognisable by their blue and yellow designs *(photograph p 33);* today tiles have been largely replaced by the manufacture of domestic and purely decorative ware such as plates, vases and bowls. Green indicates that an object was made in **El Puente del Arzobispo,** a small village *(34km - 21 miles southwest)* which now specialises in the mass production of pottery drinking jars – *cacharros.*

Basílica de la Virgen del Prado (Basilica of the Prado Virgin) ⊘ – *In a park at the entrance to the town coming from Madrid.* The church, which is virtually an *azulejos* museum, gives a good idea of the evolution of the local style. The oldest tiles, dating from the 14 to 16C, yellow coloured and with geometric designs, are in the sacristy *(access through the north door);* 16 to 18C tiles, blue coloured and with narrative designs, are in the church proper and the portal.

EXCURSION

Oropesa – *32km - 20 miles west.*
Two churches and a castle rise above the town. The **castle**★ retains its proud
bearing of 1366; the annexes were built in 1402 and are now a *parador*. A plaque
in the stairwell recalls that a Count of Oropesa, **Francisco de Toledo**, was Viceroy of
Peru from 1569 to 1581.
The village of **Lagartera**, 2km - 1 mile west of Oropesa, has been known for several
centuries for the embroidery done by its women who, during the summer months,
may be seen sitting at their front doors working. They embroider long skirts and
vivid coloured bonnets in peasant style, tablecloths and subtly toned silk hangings
with scatterings of flowers – every cottage has its own display.

The main shopping streets are printed in red
at the head of the street list accompanying town plans.

TARRAGONA★★

Catalunya
Population 112 801
Michelin map 443 I33 – Michelin Atlas España Portugal p 45
Plan of the conurbation in the current Michelin Red Guide España Portugal

Tarragona, a city rich in reminders of Antiquity and the Middle Ages, is also a modern
town with wide avenues and prosperous commercial streets. Its seafront rising in tiers
up the cliffside and brilliant with flowers, skirts the old city and circles the Palace of
Augustus, before following the line of the perimeter enclosing the cathedral.
Various industries, in particular petrochemicals, are developing in the outskirts along
with the expansion of the port.

TARRAGONA

Nova (Rambla)	**ABZ**
Sant Agustí	**BZ**
Unió	**AZ**
Baixada de Misericòrdia	**BZ** 2

Baixada de Toro	**BZ** 5
Baixada Roser	**BZ** 8
Civadería	**BZ** 10
Enginyer Cabestany	**AZ** 13
López Peláez	**AZ** 19
Pau Casals (Av.)	**AZ** 27
Plá de la Seu	**BZ** 29

Plá de Palau	**BZ** 32
Portalet	**BZ** 34
Ramon i Cajal (Av.)	**AZ** 40
Roser (Portal del)	**BZ** 43
Sant Antoni (Portal de)	**BZ** 46
Sant Hermenegild	**BZ** 49
Sant Joan (Pl.)	**BZ** 52

M	Museo Arqueológico	**R**	Ruinas del anfiteatro

Capital of Tarraconensis – Tarragona goes back a very long time. The imposing ramparts built of enormous Cyclopean blocks of stone, indicate that it was founded by peoples from the eastern Mediterranean early in the first millennium BC. In due course it suffered occupation by the Iberians. The Romans, who by 218 BC had control of the larger part of the peninsula, developed Tarraconensis into a major city and overseas capital. Although it could never equal Rome, it enjoyed many of the same privileges as the imperial capital and Augustus, Galba and Hadrian did not disdain to live in it.

Conversion to Christianity, it is said by St Paul, brought it appointment as a metropolitan seat, its dignitaries, the primacy of Spain, an honour it retained throughout the Barbarian invasions of the 5C and the devastations of the Moors in the 8C but lost finally to the ambition of Toledo in the 11C.

★ROMAN TARRAGONA *time: 2 1/2 hours*

The best preserved monuments lie outside the city limits: the Mausoleo de Centcelles (Centcelles Mausoleum) and the Acueducto de las Ferreres (Ferreres Aqueduct) *(qv)*, Scipios tower and the Arco de Triunfo de Berá (Berá Triumphal Arch).

★ **Passeig Arqueològic (Archaeological Promenade)** (BZ) ⊘ – It was the Scipios, according to Livy and Pliny, who built Tarragona's city walls in the 3C BC. They were erected on existing Cyclopean bases, the great boulders being held in position by their sheer size. They were so massive that they were for a long time thought to have been "barbaric" or pre-Roman. The medieval inhabitants extensively raised and rebuilt the ramparts; the 18C citizens remodelled them but still left us with walls bearing the marks of 2000 years of history. A pleasant walk has been laid out through the gardens at the foot of the walls.

The outer perimeter was built by the English in 1707 during the War of the Spanish Succession.

Museo Arqueológico (Archaeological Museum) (BZ M) ⊘ – The exhibits are all from Tarragona or its immediate environs; most date from the Roman period. There are beautiful mosaics, including the **Head of Medusa**★★ with its penetrating gaze, statues which once adorned public buildings and squares; friezes, carved cornices and medallions from the Temple of Jupiter (which stood on the cathedral site) and the Temple of Augustus.

Adjoining the museum is the **praetorium**, a tall square tower from the 1C BC, considerably restored in the Middle Ages. It now houses the Museo de Historia de la Ciudad (Town History Museum).

Ruinas del anfiteatro (Amphitheatre ruins) (BZ R) ⊘ – The site is reached through a park. The arena was built beside the sea, using the natural slope of the hillside for the tiers.

It was here that Bishop Fructuosus and his deacons, Augurius and Eulogius, were martyred in 259.

Traces of the commemorative basilica have been discovered within the Romanesque walls of the Iglesia de Santa María del Miracle, a church which replaced the original basilica in the 12C and is itself now in ruins.

Ruins of the Roman amphitheatre, Tarragona

F. Bouillot / MARCO POLO

Necrópolis Paleocristiana (Palaeo-Christian Necropolis) (AZ) ⊘ – *Access: Avenida Ramón i Cajal.* All the different types of tile-covered tomb and amphorae including sarcophagi and a family vault can be seen in this 3 to 6C cemetery of the early Christians of Tarragona.

Some of the sarcophagi in the museum, in the centre of the garden which contains the most interesting finds, make it evident that they had previously served as pagan tombs. One of the exhibits, the so-called **lion sarcophagus**★, is simply but powerfully carved.

CUIDAD MEDIEVAL (MEDIEVAL CITY) *time: 1 hour*

The city walls enclose a network of ancient alleys. A wide flight of steps leads up to the cathedral.

★ **Catedral** (**BZ**) ⊘ – The cathedral was built on the site of the Roman Temple of Jupiter.

The 12C apse could still be called Romanesque in style but the greater part of the edifice is Gothic, although of different periods; from the transept to the west front and in the side chapels one sees in succession Flamboyant Gothic, Plateresque and baroque ornament.

Amidst this interior richness are many works of art: the Capilla de la Virgen de Montserrat (Chapel of the Virgen of Montserrat) *(2nd chapel, north aisle)* contains a fine 15C altarpiece by Lluís Borassá; the baroque Capilla de Santa Tecla *(3rd chapel, south aisle)* is in Tarragona marble (1760-1775) and the Capilla de Santa María or "dels Sastres" has intricate Gothic vaulting.

In the place of honour in the central apse, is the **altarpiece of Santa Tecla ★★**, patron of the city; legend says she was converted by the preaching of St Paul. The unconverted, among whom was her mother, persecuted the convert cruelly but each time she was saved from death by divine intervention.

The altarpiece, carved in about 1430 by Pere Johan, completely fills the apse, two Flamboyant doors on either side allowing one to pass through to the east end. The detail and ornament become ever more intricate the nearer they are to the predella which is as finely worked as a piece of goldsmith's filigree. The scenes are wonderfully realistic, especially those with animals (note the flies shown resting on the open wound of an ox).

An earlier Romanesque style low relief, dating from the 13C on the altar before the retable, again illustrates the saint's life.

To the right of the high altar is the **tomb of the Infante Don Juan de Aragón**. The carving is 14C Italian work.

★ **Claustro** – The cloisters are very unusual and large – each gallery is 45m - 148ft long. They were built in the 12 and 13C and the arches and geometric decoration are clearly Romanesque, but the vaulting is Gothic, as are the large supporting arches which divide the bays into groups of three.

Moorish influence is evident in the claustra of geometrically patterned and pierced panels filling the oculi below the arches, the line of multifoil arches at the base of the cathedral roof and the octagonal lantern which can be seen from the northeast corner of the cloisters. Inlaid in the west gallery is a *mihrab*-like stone niche, dated 960.

Museo Diocesano (Diocesan Museum) ⊘ – The Sala (chamber) de Corpus Christi contains several works including an altarpiece and several 14C frescoes.

The museum's most interesting exhibit, however, is its collection of tapestries; the finest amongst them, a 15C Flemish work, *The Good Life*, hangs in the **Sala Capitular** (Chapter house).

EXCURSIONS

★ **Acueducto de Las Ferreres** – *Leave by Rambla Nova* (**AZ**). 4km - 2 1/2 miles from Tarragona you will see the Roman aqueduct up on your right. It is a well preserved two-tier structure, 217m - 712ft long, known as the Puente del Diablo (Devil's Bridge). You can walk *(1/2 hour)* through the pines to the base.

★ **Mausoleo de Centcelles** ⊘ – *5km - 3 miles by Ramón i Cajal Avenue* (**AZ**). *Take the Reus road; bear right after crossing the Francolí. Turn right in Constanti into the Calle de Centcelles; continue a further 500yds along an unsurfaced road. Just before the village of Centcelles make a right-angle turn to the left.*

The mausoleum, which now stands in a vineyard, takes the form of two monumental buildings faced in pink tiles. They were built in the 4C by a wealthy Roman near his summer residence which was also vast and included private thermal baths. The first chamber in the mausoleum is covered by an immense cupola (diameter: 11m - 36ft), decorated with **mosaics ★** on themes favoured by the early Christians such as hunting scenes, Daniel in the Lions' Den, etc. The adjoining chamber, which is the same size only square, has an apse on either side. The group of buildings is obviously outstanding although its symbolism remains obscure.

Port Aventura

In May 1995 Spain's first major theme park, Port Aventura, was opened near Salou, 12km - 8 miles southwest of Tarragona. The park is divided into sections reflecting different parts of the world (Mexico, China, Polynesia, Catalunya, the Far West). Visitors can explore the park on foot or in a special train, and take boat or canoe trips on the lake (3ha - 7 acres) or one of the many canals that run throught the park. There are fun rides, shows and refreshments on offer too. The park is open May to October; for further details, call ☎ +34 3 400 55 99.

TERRASSA / TARRASA

Catalunya (Barcelona)
Population 157 442
Michelin map 443 H 36 – Michelin Atlas España Portugal p 32

Terrassa is a large industrial town near Barcelona which specialises in spinning and weaving. It has, nevertheless, managed to preserve monuments from the ancient city of Egara.

★★ **Ciudad Egara (City of Egara)** ⊘ – A Roman town, then an important episcopal see under the Visigoths, Egara has preserved within a perimeter wall, three historic churches (9-12C) of exceptional archaeological importance.

  ★ **Sant Miquel** – Sant Miquel, a former baptistry of square design with a heptagonal apse, was built in the 9C using late Roman remains. The dome above the font is supported on eight pillars, each different in shape and each of a different stone; four have Roman capitals, four have Visigothic. Alabaster windows in the apse provide a filtered light by which to see the 9-10C pre-Romanesque wall paintings. Below is a crypt, abutted by three small apses with horseshoe-shaped arches.

  Santa Maria – The church is a good example of the Romanesque Lombard style. Before the façade are the remains of a 5C mosaic from the original church. The present edifice is in the shape of a Latin cross, with a *cimborrio* (lantern) and an octogonal cupola. Inside, the 11C paintings on the apsidal vaulting have been effaced but a 13C wall painting in the south transept, illustrating the martyrdom of Thomas Becket of Canterbury, has preserved its bright colours. Among the superb 15C altarpieces, note the one in the north transept by Jaime Huguet *(qv)* of **Sts Abdon and Sennen** ★★.

  Sant Pere – This ancient country church which probably dates from the 6C, has an unusual stone altarpiece in the apse.

  ★ **Museo Textil (Textile Museum)** ⊘ – Oriental materials, including rare Coptic fabrics from the 4 and 5C, Merovingian fabrics and brocades provide an excellent panoramic history of textile and manufacture.

TERUEL★

Aragón
Population 31 068
Michelin map 443 K 26 – Michelin Atlas España Portugal p 56

The capital of Bajo (Lower) Aragón, at an altitude of 916m - 3 005ft, occupies a table-land separated from the surrounding plateau by a wide divide through which flows the Turia. A landscape of ravined brown ochre heights provides a unique **setting**★.

A Mudéjar town – Old Mudéjar towers rise above the tawny brick of the town. The great richness of Mudéjar architecture *(qv)* in Teruel arises because Christians, Jews and Muslims all lived peacefully together in the town until the 15C – the last mosque was closed only in 1502.

The legend of the Lovers of Teruel – In the 13C, **Diego de Marcilla** and **Isabel de Segura** were in love and wished to marry but Isabel's father had set his sights on a richer suitor. Diego thereupon went to the wars to win honour and riches. The day of his return, five years later, was Isabel's wedding day to his rival. He died before her in despair and the following day Isabel was overcome with grief and died in her turn. This drama inspired many 16C poets and dramatists including **Tirso de Molina** *(qv)*.

SIGHTS

Plaza del Torico, in the heart of the town, is the traditional local meeting place. The square lined with rococo style houses, gets it name from the small statue of a bull calf on a pillar at its centre.

★ **The Mudéjar Towers** – There are five in all. They were built between the 12 and 16C, in each case to a three-storey plan: at the base an arch provided access to the street; the centre, pierced only by

The Mudéjar Torre de San Martín, Teruel

F. Bouillot / MARCO POLO

263

TERUEL

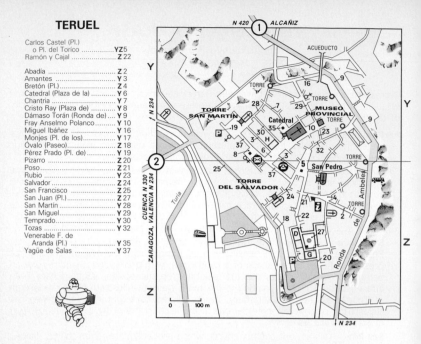

narrow Romanesque openings, was decorated with Moorish influenced ornamental brickwork and ceramics, while at the top was a belfry, pierced by bays in pairs below and quadruples above. The two best examples, the **Torre de San Martín** and the **Torre del Salvador**, are both 13C.

★ **Museo Provincial** ⊘ – The museum, housed in a mansion with an elegant Renaissance façade crowned by a gallery, displays ethnological and archaeological collections. The former stables in the basement house tools and other everyday objects from the region; note the reconstitution of a forge and the 15C Gothic door knocker.

The first floor is given over to ceramics, an industry for which Teruel has been renowned since the 13C. Green and purple designs adorn the oldest pieces, blue those produced in the 18C (as is the case for pots and jars from a pharmacy in Alcalá).

The upper floors contain archaeological collections from different periods: prehistoric (an Iron Age sword from Alcorisa), Iberian, Roman (a catapult) and Arab (an 11C censer).

Catedral ⊘ – The cathedral, originating in the 13C with the tower, was enlarged in the 16C and further increased by a lantern and ambulatory in the 17C. The late-13C **artesonado ceiling ★**, hidden in the 17C beneath star vaulting and so preserved, has now once more been revealed and is a precious example of Mudéjar painting. Its cells, beams and consoles are painted with decorative motifs, people at court and hunting scenes.

The cathedral possesses a 15C **altarpiece** of the Coronation of the Virgin (north transept) in which the scenes depicted along the second band are shown in perspective suggesting Flemish influence. The **retable at the high altar**, carved in the 16C, is by **Gabriel Joli**. Joli was known for his powerful portraits and his skilful way of illustrating movement by a marked turn of the body.

Iglesia de San Pedro ⊘ – In spite of 18C reconstruction, the church has kept its original Mudéjar style in its tower and east end.

The **Mausoleo de los Amantes de Teruel** (The Teruel Lovers' Mausoleum) ⊘ adjoins the church. They are shown in an alabaster relief by Juan de Ávalos (20C). Through the glass walls of the tomb, also in the chapel, the lovers' actual skeletons can be seen.

TOLEDO★

Castilla-La Mancha
Population 63 561
Michelin map 444 M 17 – Michelin Atlas España Portugal p 52

Toledo stands out dramatically against the often luminously blue Castilian sky: a golden city rising from a granite eminence, encircled by a steep ravine filled by the green waters of the Tajo (Tagus). It is as spectacular as it is rich in history, buildings, art; every corner has a tale to be told, every aspect reflects a brilliant period of Spanish history when the cultures of east and west flourished and fused: one is constantly aware of this imprint of Christian, Jewish and Moorish cultures which, as in Granada, productively co-existed during the Middle Ages. Within its **walls**, the city shelters beautiful sights amidst old winding alleys which provide a splendid setting for the **Corpus Christi** procession, held on the first Sunday following Corpus Christi.

Toledo is renowned for its **damascene** ware (black steel inlaid with gold, silver and copper thread) as well as its culinary specialities including braised partridge and marzipan.

★★ **The site** – The city's incomparable site can be seen particularly well from the Carretera de Circunvalación, a road which, for 3.5km - 2 miles, parallels, on the far bank, the almost circular loop of the Tajo which flows all the way round from the Puente de Alcántara (Alcántara Bridge) to the Puente de San Martín. For truly memorable views of the city, couched between the Alcázar and the Monasterio de San Juan de los Reyes (Monastery of St John of the Kings), it is worth going to the **lookout points** on the surrounding heights. These are covered by extensive olive groves *(cigarrales)* in which white houses stand half concealed. The **Parador** terrace (**BZ P**) set above the Carretera de Circunvalación commands a good panorama.

HISTORICAL NOTES

Roman town to Holy Roman city – The Romans, appreciating the site's advantage strategically and geographically at the centre of the peninsula, fortified and built up the settlement into a town they named Toletum. It passed, in due course, into the hands of the Barbarians, and in the 6C to the Visigoths who ultimately made it a monarchial seat. The Visigoths, defeated at Guadelete in 711, abandoned the town to the Moors who incorporated it in the Córdoba Emirate, until the successful revolt of the *taifas* in 1012 raised it to the position of capital of an independent kingdom. In 1085 Toledo was conquered by Alfonso VI de León. Two years later, the king moved his capital to it from León. It is to Alfonso VII, crowned emperor there, that Toledo owes its title of imperial city. Toledo, with its mixed Moorish, Jewish and Christian communities, began to prosper richly. The Catholic Monarchs gave it the Monastery of St John and only found the city pall when compared to Granada, reconquered under their own aegis in 1492. Emperor Charles V had the Alcázar rebuilt. Also during his reign the city took part in the Comuneros' Revolt *(qv)* led by **Juan de Padilla**, a Toledan.

Progress was halted in 1561 when Philip II named Madrid as Spain's capital, leaving Toledo as the spiritual centre, the seat of the primacy. The events of 1936 within and without the Alcázar, brought it briefly into the limelight of history.

Toledo and the Visigoths – Toledo played a key role during the Visigothic supremacy in the peninsula which began in 507. By 554 they had made it their capital and Councils of State, which had met in Toledo as early as 400, were resumed; that of 589, following upon the conversion of King Reccared two years previously, established Visigothic hegemony and the religious unification of Spain. The Visigoths, torn by internal strife, however, were unable to resist the Moors and abandoned Toledo in 711; it took Pelayo *(qv)* and a small band of Christians to reinstate the dynasty.

Toledo and the Jews – Toledo would appear to have been by far the most important Jewish town in Spain: in the 12C the community numbered 12 000.

Under **Ferdinand III** (1217-1252), a tolerant monarch who encouraged the intermingling of the races which brought about a cultural flowering, the city developed into a great intellectual forum. This well-being reached its climax under his son, **Alfonso X, the Wise** (1252-1284), who gathered round him a court of learned Jews and established the *School of Translation*. Jewish prosperity and immunity suddenly and brutally ceased in 1355 with a pogrom instigated by the supporters of Henry IV of Trastamara; at the same time many conversions followed the preaching of the Dominican, **San Vicente Ferrer**. The final blow came in 1492 with the Catholic Monarch's decree of expulsion.

Mudéjar art in Toledo – Toledo, which for centuries had numbered citizens of different races and religions, became the ideal setting under Christian rule for the development of the Mudéjar style *(qv)* which appears not only in palaces (Taller del Moro), but also in synagogues (Transitó, Sta María la Blanca) and churches. Thus in the 13 and 14C most Toledan churches were given Romanesque semicircular **east ends** but blind arcades with variations unknown elsewhere; bricks were used in place of stone and **belfries** squared and decorated until they appeared strongly reminiscent of minarets. The edifices often have a nave and two aisles – a Visigothic influence – tripartite apses – a Romanesque souvenir – and wood vaulting carved in the Moorish style.

Detail of The Burial of the Count of Orgaz, by El Greco
(in the Iglesia de Santo Tomé, Toledo)

El Greco – Domenikos Theotokopoulos, the Greek – El Greco – one of the great figures in Spanish painting, was born in Crete in 1541. After an apprenticeship painting icons, he went to Italy where he worked under Titian and studied Michelangelo before journeying to Spain in 1577 and settling in Toledo where he remained until he died in 1614. Although he didn't always succeed in pleasing Philip II he found favour and fortune with Toledans. His work, with its acquired Italian techniques, retained considerable Byzantine influence which appeared as a lengthening of forms – a mannerism which increased as the painter aged. A recurring feature in illustrated scenes was the division of the canvas into two – earth and heaven – demonstrating El Greco's belief that this life was but preparation for an exalted hereafter. The supernatural is a constant preoccupation, figures convey an intense spiritual inner power – all is seen with the eye of the visionary and portrayed sometimes by means of apparent distortion, by brilliant, occasionally crude colours, often by violent, swirling movement so that some pictures have the aspect of hallucinations. But the portraits by contrast are still, the colours deep, expressions meditative in religious, watchful in the worldly.

★★★TOLEDO ANTIGUO (OLD TOLEDO) *time: 1 day*

There is something to see and enjoy at every step in Toledo. Walking along the maze of narrow, winding lanes you pass churches, old houses and palaces.

★★★**Catedral (BY)** ☉ – Construction began in the reign of Ferdinand III (St Ferdinand) in 1227, under Archbishop Rodrigo Jiménez de Rada. Unlike other churches in the vicinity, the design was French Gothic but as building continued until the end of the 15C, plans were modified and the completed edifice presents a conspectus of Spanish Gothic, although considerably masked by additions. The church, nevertheless, remains of outstanding interest for its sculptured decoration and numerous works of religious art.

Exterior

The **Puerta del Reloj** (Clock Doorway), in the north wall, is the old entrance, dating from the 13C although modified in the 19C. The west front is pierced by three tall 15C portals of which the upper registers were completed in the 16 and 17C. At the centre is the **Puerta del Perdón** (Pardon Doorway), crowded with statues and crowned with a tympanum illustrating the legend according to which the Virgin, wishing to reward San Ildefonso, Bishop of Toledo in the 7C, for his devotion, appears, at Assumption, in the episcopal chair, to present him with a magnificent embroidered chasuble.

The harmonious tower is 15C; the dome, which replaces the second tower, was designed by El Greco's son in the 17C. In the south wall, the 15C **Puerta de los Leones** (Lion Doorway) designed by Master Hanequin of Brussels *(qv)* and decorated by Juan Alemán was flanked in 1800 by a neo-classical portal.

Enter through the Puerta del Mollete, left of the west front, which opens onto the cloisters.

Interior

The size and sturdy character of the cathedral rather than its elevation are what strike one as one gazes up over the five unequal aisles and the great supporting pillars. A wonderful collection of stained glass (1418-1561) colours the windows; magnificent wrought-iron grilles enclose the chancel, *coro* and chapels.

Capilla Mayor – The chancel, the most sumptuous part of the cathedral, was enlarged in the 16C by Cardinal Cisneros.

The immense polychrome **retable**★★, carved in Flamboyant style with the Life of Christ depicted in detail on five registers, is awe inspiring. The silver statue of the Virgin at the predella dates from 1418. The marble tomb of Cardinal Mendoza in Plateresque style on the left is by Covarrubias *(qv)*. The recumbent figure is the work of an Italian artist.

Coro – A series of 14C high reliefs and wrought-iron enclosed chapels form the perimeter of the choir which is itself closed by an elegant iron screen (1547). Within are magnificent 15 and 16C **choir-stalls**★★★ of which the lower parts, in wood, were carved by Rodrigo Alemán to recall, in 54 beautifully detailed and picturesque scenes, the conquest of Granada; the 16C upper parts, in alabaster, portraying Old Testament figures, are by Berruguete *(qv)* (left) and Felipe Vigarny *(qv)* (right). The central low relief, the Transfiguration, is also by Berruguete. The style of his work creates the impression of movement while that of Vigarny is more static. The pipes of a sonorous organ dominate the central area, occupied by two bronze lecterns and a Gothic eagle lectern. The 14C marble White Virgin is French.

Girola – The double ambulatory, surmounted by an elegant triforium with multifoil arches, is bordered by seven apsidal chapels separated by small square chapels. The vaulting is a geometrical wonder.

There is little room to step back for a good look at the **Transparente**, the contentious but famous work by Narciso Tomé *(qv)* which forms a baroque island in the Gothic church. Illuminated by the sun's rays which pour through an opening in the ambulatory roof (made to allow light to fall on the tabernacle), the Transparente appears as an ornamental framework of angels and swirling clouds and rays surrounding the Virgin and the Last Supper. The **Capilla de San Ildefonso** (Chapel of San Ildefonso) contains tombs, of which the one in the centre of Cardinal Gil de Albornoz (14C) is the most notable. The **Capilla de Santiago** (St James) is a mausoleum for Don Alvara de Luna, Constable of Castilla, and his family.

Sala Capitular (Chapter house) – The antechamber is adorned with an impressive Mudéjar ceiling and two Plateresque carved walnut wardrobes. Remarkable Mudéjar stucco doorways and carved Plateresque panels precede the chapter house where there is a particularly beautiful multicoloured **Mudéjar ceiling**★. Below the frescoes by Juan de Borgoña *(qv)*, are portraits of former archbishops including two by Goya painted in 1804 and 1823.

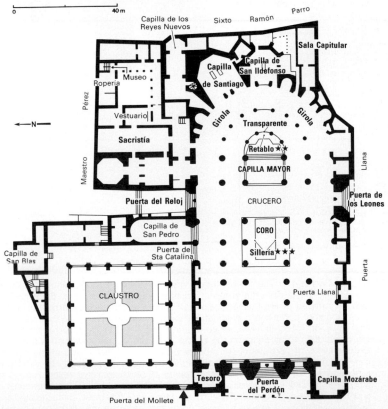

TOLEDO

A Posada de la Hermandad
B Palacio Arzobispal
H Ayuntamiento
K Portada de S. Clemente
M¹ Casa y Museo de El Greco
P Parador
V Puerta antigua de Bisagra

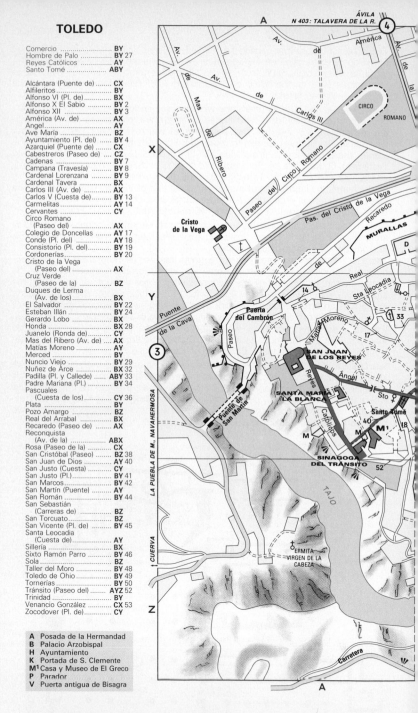

Sacristía (Sacristy) – The first gallery, with its vaulted ceiling painted by Lucas Jordán, includes a powerful group of **paintings by El Greco★** of which **El Expolio** (the Saviour stripped of His Raiment), painted soon after the artist's arrival in Spain, is outstanding. It conveys a dominating, exalted personality, set against the swirling folds of robes in vivid, often acidic tones, which establish a rhythmical movement akin to baroque, on the canvas. Also among the collection is one of El Greco's series of portraits of the Apostles. Works by other artists in the sacristy include a remarkable portrait of *Pope Paul III* by Titian, a *Holy Family* by Van Dyck, a *Mater Dolorosa* by Morales and the *Taking of Christ* by Goya which displays to advantage his skill in composition, in the use of light and portraying individuals in a crowd. There is also one of Pedro de Mena's (17C) most characteristic and famous sculptures, *St Francis of Assisi* (in a glass case). In the vestry are portraits by Velázquez *(Cardinal Borja)*, Van Dyck *(Pope Innocent XI)* and Ribera.

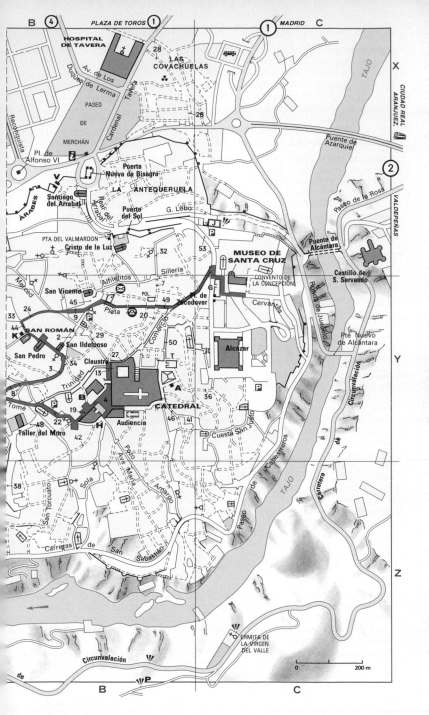

The old laundry *(ropería)* contains liturgical objects dating back to the 15C. Continuing on from the sacristy you reach the **Nuevas Salas del Museo Catedralicio** (Cathedral Museum's New Galleries), installed in the Casa del Tesorero (Treasurer's House). The rooms display works by Caravaggio, El Greco, Bellini and Morales.

Tesoro (Treasury) – A Plateresque doorway by Covarrubias *(qv)* opens into the chapel under the tower. Beneath a Granada style Mudéjar ceiling note the splendid 16C silver-gilt **monstrance★★** by Enrique de Arfe, which, although it weighs 180kg and is 3m high – just under 400lbs and 10ft high, is paraded through the streets at Corpus Christi. The pyx at its centre is fashioned from gold brought from America by Christopher Columbus.

There is also a 13C Bible given by St Louis of France to St Ferdinand (Ferdinand III of Castilla).

Capilla Mozarabic (Mozarabic Chapel) – The chapel beneath the dome was built by Cardinal Cisneros (16C) to celebrate mass according to the Visigothic or Mozarabic ritual which had been threatened with abolition in the 11C.

Claustro (Cloisters) – The architectural simplicity of the 14C lower gallery contrasts with the bold mural decoration by Bayeu of the Lives of Toledan saints (Santa Eugenia and San Ildefonso).

Ringing the square before the cathedral are the 18C **Palacio Arzobispal** (Archbishop's Palace) (**BY B**), the 17C **Ayuntamiento** (Town Hall) (**BY H**) with its classical façade and the 14C **Audiencia** (Law Courts) (**BY**).

Iglesia de Santo Tomé (**AY**) ⊘ – The church, like that of San Román *(qv)*, has a distinctive 14C Mudéjar tower. Inside is El Greco's famous painting **The Burial of the Count of Orgaz**★★★ executed for the church in about 1586 *(photograph p 266)*. The interment is transformed by the miraculous appearance of St Augustine and St Stephen waiting to welcome the figure from earth, symbolised by a frieze of figures in which, as he highlighted faces and hands and painted vestments with detailed biblical references, El Greco made every man an individual portrait – he is said to have painted a self-portrait in the sixth figure from the left.

★**Casa y Museo de El Greco** (**El Greco House and Museum**) (**AY M¹**) ⊘ – In 1585, El Greco moved into a house similar to this attractive 16C Toledan **house**. In the first floor studio hang a *St Peter Repentant*, a version of the painting in the cathedral and, in what would have been the artist's workroom, a signed *St Francis and Brother León*.

Museo – On the first floor of the museum are an interesting View and Plan of Toledo (including a likeness of his son, one of various differences from the version in the Prado) and the complete series of individual portraits of the Apostles and Christ (a later, more mature series than that in the cathedral). The **capilla** on the ground floor, with a multicoloured Mudéjar ceiling, has a picture in the altarpiece of *St Bernadino of Siena* by El Greco. *The Crowning of Thorns* is Hispano-Flemish.

★★**Sinagoga del Tránsito** (**AYZ**) ⊘ – Of the ten synagogues of the old Jewish quarter (Judería), this and Santa María la Blanca are the only ones to remain. Money for its construction was provided in the 14C by Samuel Ha-Levi, treasurer to King Peter the Cruel. In 1492 it was converted into a church and dedicated soon afterwards to the Dormition (Tránsito) from which it gets its name.

It appears from the outside as a small unpretentious building but inside an amazing **Mudéjar decoration**★★ covers the upper part of the walls and all the east end. Above the rectangular hall is an *artesonado* ceiling of cedarwood; just below, are 54 multifoil arches, some blind, others pierced with delicate stone tracery. Below again runs a frieze, decorated at the east end with *mocárabes (qv)* and on the walls, bearing the arms of Castilla, with inscriptions in Hebrew to the glory of Peter the Cruel, Samuel Ha-Levi and the God of Israel. The three arches at the centre of the east wall are surmounted by a panel in relief of roses surrounded by magnificent strapwork and, at either side, by inscriptions describing the synagogue's foundation. The women's balcony opens from the south wall.

The adjoining rooms, at one period a Calatrava monastery, have been converted into a **Museo Sefardí** (Sephardic Museum) displaying tombs, robes, costumes and books. Several are presents from Sephardim *(qv)* or descendants of the Jews expelled from Spain in 1492.

★**Sinagoga de Santa María la Blanca** (**AY**) ⊘ – This was the principal synagogue in Toledo in the late 12C; in 1405, however, it was given to the Knights of Calatrava who converted it into a church and gave it its present name. Subsequent vicissitudes, including modification of the east end in the 16C, left the Almohad-style mosque incredibly unharmed so that the hall appears as before with five tiered aisles, separated by 24 octagonal pillars supporting horseshoe-shaped arches. The plain white of the pillars and arches is relieved by the intricately carved **capitals**★ adorned with pine cones and strapwork. Above, the decoration is equally outstanding. The polychrome wood altarpiece is 16C.

★**Monasterio de San Juan de los Reyes** (**St John of the Kings Monastery**) (**AY**) ⊘ – The monastery was built by the Catholic Monarchs in thanksgiving to God for their decisive victory over the Portuguese at Toro in 1476. It was entrusted to the Franciscans. The overall architecture is typically Isabelline, that style which includes in the Flamboyant Gothic style, touches of Mudéjar and even Renaissance art, particularly in this case since construction continued until the early 17C. The exterior is somewhat austere despite the ornamental pinnacles and stone balustrade which crown the edifice and, in the latter instance, circles the octagonal lantern. Covarrubias designed the north portal during the later stages of construction, including in the decoration, the figure of John the Baptist flanked by Franciscan saints. The fetters from the façade were taken from Christian prisoners freed from the Muslims in Andalucía.

Claustro – Although restored, the cloisters remain extremely attractive with Flamboyant bays and the original Plateresque upper galleries (1504) crowned with a pinnacled balustrade. The upper gallery has Mudéjar *artesonado* vaulting.

Iglesia – The church, rebuilt after being fired by the French in 1808, has the single wide aisle typical of Isabelline churches; at the crossing are a dome and a lantern. The **sculptured decoration★** by the church's Flemish architect, Juan Guas, provides a delicate stone tracery *(crestería)* which at the transept forms twin tribunes for Ferdinand and Isabel. The transept walls are faced with a wonderful frieze of royal escutcheons, supported by an eagle, the symbol of St John. Other decoration includes Mudéjar *mocárabes* (qv) on the bosses in the transept vaulting and heads in picturesque high relief on the triumphal arches. The original altarpiece has been replaced by a 16C Plateresque retable.

Not far away are a Visigothic palace and gateway, which were once part of the town perimeter. The gateway was rebuilt in the 16C. The **Puerta del Cambrón (AY)** is named after the *cambroneras* or hawthorns which once grew around it.

Turn left out of Calle Santo Tomé into the picturesque Travesía del Campana alley.

Before you, in the small shaded Plaza del Padre Mariana, stands the monumental baroque façade of the **Iglesia de San Ildefonso (BY)** and higher up, that of the **Iglesia de San Pedro (BY)**.

★ **Iglesia de San Román: Museo de los Concilios de Toledo y de la Cultura Visigoda (Museum of the Councils of Toledo and Visigothic Culture) (BY)** ⊘ – The 13C Mudéjar church, at the highest point in the town, has a fine upstanding tower closely resembling that of Santo Tomé. Inside, the three aisles divided by horse-shoe-shaped arches are reminiscent of Santa María la Blanca. The walls are covered in 13C frescoes of the raising of the dead, the Evangelists and, on the far wall, one of the Councils of Toledo. The apse was modified in the 16C when a cupola was built over it by Covarrubias *(qv)*. Note the 18C altarpiece.

The Visigothic collections include, in glass cases, fine bronze jewellery and copies of votive crowns decorated with cabochon stones from Guarrazar (originals in the Museo Arqueológico, Madrid). On the walls are steles, fragments from capitals, balustrades from the choir and pilasters decorated with geometric motifs or scrollwork. The Plateresque **doorway** *(portada)* opposite the church belongs to the Convento de San Clemente **(BY K)**.

In the Plaza de San Vicente, note the Mudéjar east end of the **Iglesia de San Vicente (BY)** before continuing up Calle de la Plata with its houses with carved entrances.

Plaza de Zocodover (BCY) – This bustling triangular square is the heart of Toledo. It was rebuilt after the Civil War as was the Arco de la Sangre (Arch of Blood) which opens onto Calle de Cervantes.

★★ **Museo de Santa Cruz (Santa Cruz Museum) (CXY)** ⊘ – Cardinal Pedro González de Mendoza, Archbishop of Toledo, died before fully realising his ambition to build a hospital for the sick and orphaned, but his project was completed by Queen Isabel. The result is a fine group of Plateresque buildings begun by Enrique Egas *(qv)* and completed by Covarrubias *(qv)* who was responsible for the **façade★**. On the gateway tympanum Cardinal Mendoza kneels before the Cross supported by St Helena, St Peter, St Paul and two pages; on the arches are the cardinal virtues while above two windows frame a high relief of St Joachim and St Anne.

Inside, the architecture is outstanding for the size of the nave and transept – forming a two-tiered Greek cross – and for the beautiful coffered ceilings.

The museum which is large but well arranged, is known for its **collection of 16C and 17C pictures★** which includes **18 paintings by El Greco★**.

Ground floor – The first part of the nave contains 16C Flemish tapestries, **Primitive paintings★**, and the *Astrolabios* or *Zodiac* tapestry, woven in Flanders in the mid-15C for Toledo cathedral, which fascinates still by its originality and modern colouring. Note, in the south transept, the *Ascension* and the *Presentation in the Temple* by the Maestro de Sigena. In the second part of the nave hangs the immense pennant flown by Don Juan of Austria at the Battle of Lepanto *(qv)*. Before it is a 17C Crucifix, recalling the one believed to have been present at the battle and which is now in Barcelona cathedral *(qv)*. The north transept contains a *Christ at the Column* by Morales.

First floor – A staircase leads to the upper gallery of the north transept which displays the **paintings by El Greco★**. There are gentle portraits of the *Virgin* and *St Veronica* as well as a version of the *Expolio (original in the Cathedral Sacristy)*, later than that in the cathedral. The most famous painting in the collection is the **Altarpiece of the Assumption★**, which dates from 1613, the artist's final period. The figures are particularly elongated, the colours rasping.

The south transept contains a *Holy Family at Nazareth* by Ribera, the specialist in tenebrism (term applied to paintings in dark tones) who here showed himself to be a master of light and delicacy.

In the first part of the nave are 16C Brussels tapestries illustrating the life of Alexander the Great. There are also 17C statues by Pedro de Mena of a *Mater Dolorosa* and an *Ecce Homo*. The next room along contains a *Crucifixion* by Goya. The **Plateresque patio★** has bays with elegant lines complemented by the openwork of the balustrade and enhanced by beautiful Mudéjar vaulting and, even more, by the magnificent **staircase★** by Covarrubias. Adjoining rooms house a museum of archaeology and decorative arts.

ADDITIONAL SIGHTS

Within the city walls

Alcázar (**CY**) ⊘ – The Alcázar, destroyed and rebuilt so many times, stands, massive and proud as ever, dominating all other buildings. It was Charles V who decided to convert the 13C fortress of which El Cid had been the first governor, into an imperial residence. The conversion was entrusted first to Covarrubias *(qv)* (1538-1551) and subsequently to Herrera *(qv)*, who designed the austere south front.

The siege and shelling of 1936 left the fortress in ruins. From 21 July for eight weeks, infantry cadets under Colonel Moscardó, resisted the Republicans. Their families, about 600 women and children, took refuge in the underground galleries.

Reconstruction has restored the Alcázar to its appearance at the time of Charles V – an innovation is the Victory Monument by Ávalos in the forecourt. Inside, you see the underground galleries which sheltered the cadets' families, and the office above in which Colonel Moscardó was ordered by phone to surrender or see his son shot. His son died on 23 August; the Alcázar was relieved on 27 September. Weapons and uniforms are displayed in museum rooms off the *patio*.

Posada de la Hermandad (**House of Brotherhood**) (**BY A**) – A 15C building which was formerly a prison.

Puerta del Sol (**BX**) – The Sun Gate in the town's second perimeter, rebuilt in the 14C, is a fine Mudéjar construction with two circumscribing horseshoe arches. At the centre a later low relief shows the Virgin presenting San Ildefonso with a chasuble. At the top, the brick decoration of blind arcading incorporates an extraordinary sculpture of two girls bearing on a charger the head of the chief alguazil (officer of justice) of the town, who was condemned for their violation.

Cristo de la Luz (**Christ of the Light**) (**BX**) – In 1000 AD the Moors built a mosque on the site of a ruined Visigothic church; in the 12C this mosque was converted into a Mudéjar church. Legend has it that the church was named Christ of the Light because when Alfonso VI was making his entry into Toledo, El Cid's horse in the royal train suddenly knelt before the mosque in which, inside a wall, a Visigothic lamp was discovered lighting up a Crucifix. Three series of arches of different periods, intersecting blind arcades and a line of horizontal brickwork surmounted by Cufic characters, make up the façade. Inside, pillars, for the most part Visigothic, support superimposed arches, similar in design to those in the mosque in Córdoba. Nine domes, each different, rise from square bays.

The adjoining gardens lead to the top of the Puerta del Sol from which there is an interesting view of the city.

Taller del Moro (**BY**) ⊘ – This workshop *(taller)*, used by a Muslim as a collecting yard for building material for the cathedral is, in fact, an old palace. The Mudéjar decoration can still be seen in rooms lit by small openwork windows, interconnected through horseshoe-shaped openings ornamented with *atauriques* or Almohad style stucco.

Iglesia de Santiago del Arrabal (**St James on the Outskirts**) (**BX**) – This beautifully restored Mudéjar church contains the ornate Gothic Mudéjar pulpit from which San Vincente Ferrer *(qv)* is said to have preached. The altarpiece is 16C.

Beyond the city walls

★ **Hospital de Tavera** (**BX**) ⊘ – The hospital, founded in the 16C by Cardinal Tavera, was begun by Bustamante in 1541 and completed by González de Lara and the Vergaras in the 17C.

After the Civil War, the Duchess of Lerma rearranged certain **apartments**★ in 17C style, where paintings of great artistic value may be seen.

Ground floor – In the vast library, the hospital archives contain volumes bound in leather by Moorish craftsmen. Among the paintings displayed, El Greco's *Holy Family* is arresting, the portrait of the *Virgin* perhaps the most beautiful the artist ever painted. Note also the *Birth of the Messiah* by Tintoretto, the *Philosopher* by Ribera and, in an adjoining room, his strange portrait of the *Bearded Woman*.

First floor – The reception hall contains another El Greco, the portrait of *Cardinal Tavera*, painted from a death mask. Beside it are *Samson and Delilah* by Caravaggio and the *Marquis de las Navas* by Antonio Moro. In the duchess' bedroom is a precious Gothic style ivory Crucifix.

A gallery to the **church** leads off from the elegant twin *patio*. The Carrara marble portal is by Alonso Berruguete who also carved the tomb of Cardinal Tavera. The retable at the high altar was designed by El Greco whose last work, a **Baptism of Christ** ★, is displayed in the church. It is an outstanding painting in which the artist's use of brilliant colours and elongated figures is at its most magnificent.

Standing off the *patio*, the hospital's former pharmacy is now restored.

Puerta Antigua de Bisagra (Old Bisagra Gate) (BX V) – This gate in the former Moorish ramparts, is the one through which Alfonso VI entered the city in 1085.

Puerta Nueva de Bisagra (New Bisagra Gate) (BX) – The gate was rebuilt by Covarrubias in 1550 and enlarged during the reign of Philip II. Massive round crenellated towers, facing the Madrid road, flank a giant imperial crest.

Puente de Alcántara (CX) – The 13C bridge ends respectively to west and east in a Mudéjar tower and a baroque arch. On the far side of the Tajo, behind battlemented ramparts, the restored 14C **Castillo de San Servando** (San Servando Castle), an advanced strongpoint in medieval times, can be seen.
A plaque on the town wall by the bridge recalls how **St John of the Cross** (1542-1591) escaped through a window from his monastery prison nearby.

Puente de San Martín (AY) – The medieval bridge, rebuilt in the 14C following damage by floodwaters, is marked at its south end by an octagonal crenellated tower; the north end is 16C.

Cristo de la Vega (AX) – The Church of Christ of the Vega, formerly St Leocadia, stands on the site of a 7C Visigothic temple, the setting of early church councils and, according to legend, the apparition of St Ildefonso before San Ildefonso and the king. Although considerably modified in the 18C, it still has a fine Mudéjar apse. Inside, a modern Crucifix now stands in place of the one around which many legends had gathered including one in which the figure offered an arm to a jilted girl who had come to seek comfort.

EXCURSION

Guadamur ⊙ – *15km - 9 miles southwest. Leave Toledo by* ③ *on the map, bearing left into the Naverhermosa road.*
The **castillo** (castle) overlooking the village was built in the 15C and restored in the late 19C. The apartments, occupied for a period by Queen Juana the Mad and her son, the future Emperor Charles V, have been furnished with Spanish period furniture.

TORDESILLAS

Castilla y León (Valladolid)
Population 7 637
Michelin map 442 H14-15 – Michelin Atlas España Portugal p 24

The historic town, massed upon the steep bank of the Duero, gave its name to the famous **Treaty of Tordesillas**. In 1494, the kings of Spain and Portugal, under the arbitration of the Borgia Pope Alexander VI, signed the treaty dividing the New World between them. All lands west of a line of longitude 370 leagues west of Cape Verde were to be Spanish, all to the east, Portuguese – a decision which gave Spain all Latin America except Brazil.

Juana the Mad locked herself away here on the death of Philip the Fair in 1506 *(qv)*. On her death 46 years later, she was buried in the Convento de Santa Clara. Her body was later removed to Granada.

★ **Convento de Santa Clara** ⊙ – The former palace, built by Alfonso XI in 1350 in commemoration of his victory at the Battle of Salado, was converted into a convent by his son, Peter the Cruel *(qv)* where he installed María de Padilla, to whom he may have secretly been married, in spite of Blanche de Bourbon being his queen. For María, who in this distant heart of Castilla was homesick for the beauty of Sevilla, he commissioned Mudéjar decoration.
The **patio★**, with multifoil and horseshoe-shaped arches, has strapwork decoration and multicoloured ceramic tiles. The **Capilla Dorada** (Gilded Chapel) with a fine Mudéjar cupola, exhibits mementoes and works of art including Juana's organ, Charles V's virginal, Philip II's clavichord and a 13C altarfront.
The **church** is on the site of the former throne room; the choir has a particularly intricate **artesonado ceiling★★**. In the Flamboyant Gothic **Capilla de los Saldaña** (Saldaña Chapel) are the founders' tombs and a 15C retable, originally a travelling altar.

EXCURSIONS

Medina del Campo – *24km - 15 miles southeast on the N 6.*
The town was famous for its fairs in the Middle Ages. Isabel the Catholic died here in 1504. Today, Medina del Campo is a major railway junction and busy agricultural centre where a large market is held on Sundays *(shops close on Thursdays to open on Sundays)*.

★ **Castillo de la Mota** – The impressive brick castle overlooking the town is flanked on one side by a massive keep. Juana the Mad often stayed here and Cesare Borgia was imprisoned in the keep for two years.

TORO

Castilla y León (Zamora)
Population 9 649
Michelin map 441 or 442 H 13 – Michelin Atlas España Portugal p 23

Toro stands beside the Duero at the centre of a vast clay soil plain. Wheat is grown north of the river (Tierra del Pan), vines to the south (Tierra del Vino).
Most of the town's Romanesque churches, built in brick with interesting Mudéjar decoration, have sadly deteriorated with age. The collegiate church, on the other hand, is built of limestone and has survived better.

★ **Colegiata** ⊙ – Construction of the collegiate church began in 1160 with the elegant transept lantern and ended in 1240 with completion of the west portal.

Exterior – The Romanesque **north portal** illustrates typical themes: above, the Old Men of the Apocalypse and below, angels linked together by a rope symbolising the unity of Faith.
The Gothic **west portal** ★★, repainted in the 18C, is the church's great treasure. It is dedicated to the Virgin; the Celestial Court is shown on the archivolt, an expressive Last Judgment on the coving. The statues on the jambs of the pier and tympanum, although a little stiff, have very youthful faces.

Interior – Start beneath the **cupola** ★, one of the first of its kind in Spain, with two tiers of windows in the drum. Polychrome wood statues stand against the pillars at the end of the nave on consoles, one of which is carved with an amusing version of the birth of Eve (below the angel). In the sacristy is the **Virgin and the Fly** ★, a magnificent Flemish painting by either Gerard David or Hans Memling.

Iglesia de San Lorenzo ⊙ – This is the best preserved of Toro's Romanesque churches made of local brick. With its stone base, blind arcading and dog-tooth decoration on the upper cornice, it has much of the Mudéjar style of Castilla and León. Inside, the Gothic **altarpiece** flanked by Plateresque tombs, was painted by Fernando Gallego *(qv)*.

EXCURSIONS

San Cebrián de Mazote – *30km - 19 miles northeast.*
The 10C **Iglesia de San Cebrián de Mazote** ⊙, built to a cruciform plan with three aisles divided by horseshoe-shaped arches, is a rare Mozarabic church. The modillions are typical but some of the capitals and low reliefs bear traces of an earlier, Visigothic style.

TORTOSA

Catalunya (Tarragona)
Population 29 717
Michelin map 443 J 31 – Michelin Atlas España Portugal p 45

Tortosa, for centuries the last town before the sea, was charged in those times with guarding, from the heights overlooking the Ebro, the region's only river bridge. Today it is an agricultural town prospering from the olives planted on the hillsides, terraced and divided by low drystone walls, and, lower down, from the early vegetables, the maize, oranges and peaches sheltered from the sea wind by lines of cypresses and flourishing in the rich alluvial soil brought down by the Ebro. From the Castillo de la Zuda, a castle which has been converted into a *parador*, there is a fine **view** of the town, the Ebro and the valley.

Historical notes – Tortosa was first Roman then Visigothic; in 714 it was seized by the Moors who built the Fortaleza de la Zuda (fortress). It was reconquered by Ramón Berenguer IV in 1148. For several centuries Catalans, Moors and Jews lived peacefully together, providing a wonderful setting in which different cultures flourished side by side.
During the Battle of the Ebro in July 1938, the Republicans lost 150 000 men at Tortosa.

CIUDAD ANTIGUA (OLD TOWN) *time: 1 hour*

★ **Catedral** ⊙ – The never completed baroque façade conceals a cathedral built in pure Gothic style even though construction, begun in 1347, continued for 200 years. In Catalan tradition the lines are plain, the arches high and divided into two tiers only in the nave. The chancel is framed by radiating chapels which, as was originally planned, should be divided by fenestration like that at the north entrance to the ambulatory.
The retable at the high altar has a large wood **triptych** ★ painted in the 14C, illustrating the Life of Christ.
The two stone 15C **pulpits** ★ in the nave are beautifully carved with low reliefs: those on the left illustrate the Evangelists and their symbols, those on the right the Doctors of the Roman church, Saints Gregory, Jerome, Ambrose and Augustine.

Capilla de Nuestra Señora de la Cinta (Chapel of Our Lady of the Belt) – *2nd chapel off the south aisle*. This was built in the baroque style of the 18C and is decorated with paintings and local jasper and marble; at its centre is the relic, the belt of Our Lady *(services of special veneration: first two weeks in September)*.

Font – *1st chapel off the south aisle*. The stone basin is said to have stood in the garden of the antipope Benedict XIII, Pedro de Luna *(qv)* and bears his arms. The 14C **cloisters** *(claustro)* are most attractive with their simple arches and cypress trees.

Palacio Episcopal (Bishop's Palace) ⊘ – The 14C Catalan *patio* is memorable for the straight flight of steps which completely occupies one side and the arcaded gallery, lined with slender columns. On the upper floor, the Gothic chapel, entered through a carved doorway from a well-proportioned ante-room, has ogive vaulting in which the ribs descend on to figured bosses. The final decorative touch is given by the false relief windows built into the walls on either side.

EXCURSION

Parque Natural del Delta del Ebro (Ebro Delta Nature Reserve) ⊘ – *25km - 16 miles east*.

There are boat trips between Deltebre and the river mouth *(45 mins Rtn)*. The reserve, covering an area of 7 736ha - 19 116 acres, was created in 1983 to protect the birds that shelter there and to encourage local economic development. The vast delta, closed by the Isla de Buda (Buda Island), is a swampy stretch of alluvium deposits collected by the Ebro from the Montes Cantábricos range, the Pyrenees and the Aragón plateaux. Three quarters of the land is given over to the growing of rice and early fruit and vegetables.

TRUJILLO★★

Extremadura (Cáceres)
Population 8 919
Michelin map 444 N 12 – Michelin Atlas España Portugal p 50

The modern town gives little idea of the originality and charm of the old town, built on a granite ledge higher up the hillside. This was hastily fortified by the Moors in the 13C against attack by the Christians and, as the centuries passed, had superimposed on its Arabic appearance, noble mansions built in the 16 and 17C by the Indianos – those who had journeyed across the Atlantic and returned with a fortune.

The land of the Conquistadores – "Twenty American nations", it is said, "were conceived in Trujillo". Accurate or not, it is certainly true that the city can claim to have fathered numbers of conquerors and colonisers of the New World: **Francisco de Orellana** who left in 1542 to explore the legendary country of the Amazons; **Diego García de Paredes**, nicknamed on account of his Herculean strength, the Samson of Extremadura, and the most famous of all, **Francisco Pizarro** (1475-1541), the conqueror of Peru. This swineherd, who married an Inca princess, followed what had been Cortés' policy in Mexico of seizing and executing the ruler, in this case the Emperor Atahualpa, plundering his riches and occupying his capital, Cuzco (1533). The early discovery of the Potosí silver mines made Peru the most important colony in the Spanish Empire but an implacable rivalry between Pizarro and his companion in arms, Almagro, brought the death first of Almagro in 1538 and then of Pizarro, murdered amidst untold riches in his own palace.

Statue of Pizarro in the Plaza Mayor, Trujillo

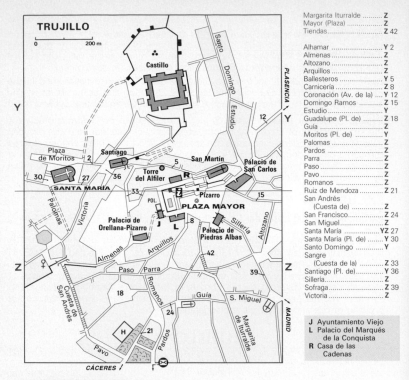

TRUJILLO

0 — 200 m

★★PLAZA MAYOR (Z)

The Plaza Mayor, like all the old quarter of Trujillo, is less austere than Cáceres, the mansions generally having been built later in the 16 and 17C, and decorated with arcades, loggias and corner windows. The widespread use of whitewash on house fronts and the more steeply inclined alleys bring additional interest to the town. Those visiting Trujillo in late spring or at any time throughout the summer will hear the flapping wings and see the outline of many a high perched stork.

The square is unusual for its irregular shape and different levels linked by wide flights of steps and the great variety of seignorial mansions overlooking it. Worth examining in detail, it evokes a way of life long gone and at night is positively theatrical.

Equestrian statue of Pizarro (YZ) – 1927 bronze by the American sculptors, Charles Runse and Mary Harriman.

Iglesia de San Martín (Y) – 16C. The rubble and freestone walls of the church enclose a vast nave chequered with funerary paving stones. The south parvis served in the past as a public meeting ground.

★**Palacio de los Duques de San Carlos** (Palace of the Dukes San Carlos) (Y) – 17C. Now an enclosed convent. The tall granite façade, decorated in the transitional classical-baroque style has a corner window surmounted by the double-headed eagle crest of the Vargas. One may see the **patio** with two tiers of rounded arches and a fine staircase of four flights.

Palacio del Marqués de Piedras Albas (Palace of the Marquis of Piedras Albas) (Z) – The Renaissance loggia has been accommodated into the original Gothic wall.

Palacio des Marqués de la Conquista (Palace of the Marquis de la Conquista) (Z L) – The palace was built by Hernando Pizarro, the conquistador's brother. It has an exceptional number of windows with iron grilles and a Plateresque **corner window★**, added in the 17C with, on the left, the busts of Francisco Pizarro and his wife, and on the right Hernando and his niece, whom he married. Above is the family crest. Crowning the façade is a series of statues representing the months of the year.

Ayuntamiento Viejo (Former Town Hall) (Z J) – 16C. Three tiers of Renaissance arcades from a nearby *patio* have been reconstructed to form the façade of what is now the Palacio de Justicia (Law Courts).

Casa de las Cadenas (House of Chains) (Y R) – The chains are said to have been brought by Christians freed from Moorish serfdom.

Torre del Alfiler (Alfiler Tower) (Y) – The so-called needle tower is a Mudéjar belfry and a favourite spot with storks.

ADDITIONAL SIGHTS

Palacio de Orellana-Pizarro (Z) – 16C. This palace has a beautiful Plateresque upper gallery.

Iglesia de Santiago (Y) – The church's 13C Romanesque belfry and the tall seignorial tower belonging to the Palacio de los Chaves (Chaves Palace) stand on either side of the Arco de Santiago (St James' Arch), one of the town's seven original gateways. The nave was modified in the 17C.

★ **Iglesia de Santa María** (Y) ⊘ – 13C. This Gothic church, in which the network vaulting was reconstructed in the 15C, is the pantheon of Trujillo's great men. In the *coro alto*, lit by a wide rose window, are the two stone seats in which the Catholic Monarchs sat during mass when in residence in the city. The 24 panels of the Gothic **retable**★ at the high altar are attributed to Fernando Gallego *(qv)*. From the top of the belfry there is a delightful **view** of brown tile roofs, the Plaza Mayor arcades and the castle.

Castillo (Y) – The castle stands out prominently from the granite ledge from which the blocks were hewn for its construction. The massive crenellated curtain wall is reinforced by numerous heavy square towers. Above the keep the patron of Trujillo, Our Lady of Victory, can still be seen in vigil. The view from the walls takes in the town and its Plaza Mayor.

TUDELA★

Navarra
Population 26 163
Michelin map 442 F 25 – Michelin Atlas España Portugal p 28

Tudela is the centre of the Ribera, a well irrigated, prosperous horticultural region growing and canning asparagus, haricot beans, artichokes and peppers.
In the 9C, the town was a dependency of the Córdoba Caliphate. From that time and later periods, it has preserved a large Moorish quarter, the Morería, and old Mudéjar style houses.
St Anne's feast day (26 July) is celebrated annually, as at Pamplona *(qv)*, with several days of great rejoicing including *encierros* and bullfights. During Holy Week, an event known as the "Descent of the Angel", takes place on the picturesque Plaza de los Fueros, which served as a bullring in the 18C.

SIGHTS

★ **Catedral** ⊘ – The 12-13C cathedral is an excellent example of the transitional Romanesque-Gothic style. The **Last Judgment Doorway** ★ (Portada del Juicio Final) difficult to see through lack of space, is an incredibly carved unit with nearly 120 groups of figures illustrating the Last Judgment.
The **interior**, Romanesque in the elevation of the nave, is Gothic in its vaulting and clerestory. Excepting the *coro* enclosure and several side chapels, which are baroque, the church is rich in Gothic works of art including early 16C choir-stalls, the retable at the high altar and the stone reliquary statue of Byzantine appearance dating from about 1200 of the *White Virgin*. Just beside it, the **Capilla de Nuestra Señora de la Esperanza**★ (Chapel of our Lady of Hope) has several 15C masterpieces including the sepulchre of a chancellor of Navarra and the central altarpiece.
The 12-13C **cloisters**★★ (claustro) are exceedingly harmonious with Romanesque arches resting alternately on groups of two or three columns with historiated capitals. Most of them relate scenes from the New Testament and the lives of the saints in a style inspired by the carvings of Aragón. A door of the mosque which once stood on the site has been preserved in one of the gallery walls.

Iglesia de San Nicolás – When the church in Calle Rua in the old quarter was rebuilt in the 18C a tympanum of Romanesque origin was placed in the façade built of brick in the Mudéjar style. God the Father is shown seated, holding his Son and surrounded by the symbols of the Evangelists.

EXCURSIONS

Tarazona – *21km - 13 miles southwest on the N 121.* Population 11 195. (Aragón). In the Middle Ages, Tarazona was for a time, the residence of the Aragón kings. Round the former royal mansion, now the **Palacio Episcopal** (Episcopal Palace), an old quarter still remains with narrow streets overlooking the quays of the Río Queiles.
Catedral ⊘ – The cathedral was largely rebuilt in the 15 and 16C. Several architectural styles may be seen: Aragón Mudéjar in the belfry tower and lantern, Renaissance in the portal and, in the **2nd chapel**★ as you walk left round the ambulatory, delicately carved Gothic **tombs** of the two Calvillos cardinals from Avignon. The **Mudéjar cloisters** have bays filled with 16C Moorish plasterwork tracery.

Not far away, a small enclosed square surrounded by houses, the 18C **Plaza de Toros Vieja**, was once a bullring.

★★**Monasterio de Veruela** ⊘ – *39km - 24 miles south from Tudela and 17km - 11 miles from Tarazona. From Tarazona, take the N 122 then bear right.*
Cistercian monks from southern France came in the middle of the 12C to this spot where they founded a monastery and surrounded it with a fortified perimeter wall. Seven centuries later the Sevillian poet **Bécquer** was to stay while writing his *Letters from my Cell* in which he described the Aragón countryside much in the manner of later guide books!

★★**Iglesia** – The church, built in the transitional period between Romanesque and Gothic, has a sober but attractive façade with a single oculus, a narrow band of blind arcades strangely lacking a base line and a doorway decorated with friezes, billets and capitals.
The interior, with pointed vaulting, is an amazing size. The vault groins are pointed over the nave and horseshoe-shaped over the aisles and ambulatory. A Plateresque chapel with a multicoloured carved door was built onto the north transept in the 16C. Opposite, the sacristy door is in a surprising rococo style.

★**Claustro** – The cloisters are ornate Gothic. At ground level the brackets are carved with the heads of men and beasts; above are three galleries with Plateresque decoration. The **Sala Capitalar**★ (Chapter house), in pure Cistercian style, contains the tombs of the monastery's first fifteen abbots.

TUI / TUY★

Galicia (Pontevedra)
Population 15 346
Michelin map 441 F 4 – Michelin Atlas España Portugal p 20

Tui (Tuy in Galician) stands just across the border from Portugal in a striking **setting**★. Its old quarter, facing the Portuguese fortress of Valença, stretches down the rocky hillside to the right bank of the Río Miño. The **Parque de Santo Domingo** (Santo Domingo Park), in which stands a Gothic church of the same name, commands a good view of the site.
Discoveries on Monte Alhoya confirm that a settlement existed on the site in ancient times. The town was then occupied successively by Romans, Arabs and Northmen and grew rapidly in the Middle Ages.
Since 1884, when a bridge was built by Gustave Eiffel across the Miño, Tui has served as a gateway to Portugal.

SIGHTS

The historic town is one of the oldest of Galicia's four provinces; its emblasoned houses and narrow stepped alleys climbing towards the cathedral testify to its rich past.

★**Catedral** ⊘ – The low-lying cathedral, fringed with crenellations and flanked by towers, still resembles the fortress it was for so long. It was consecrated in 1232 having been built, for the most part, in Romanesque Gothic, a style perfectly suited in its simplicity to its military role. The Romanesque north door, marked only by arches cut into the wall stone, is almost austere. In contrast the west front is adorned with a 14C porch which, while remaining defensive in character, is highly decorative with equilateral arches preceding a richly sculptured **portal**★. The tympanum, beneath the carved covings, glorifies the Mother of God; above the Adoration of the Magi and Shepherds are the towers of heavenly Jerusalem rendered ethereal by the interplay of mass and void.
Inside are the impressive reinforcing beams the cathedral was given in the 15 and 18C to compensate for the slant of the pillars. The transept plan of three aisles is Compostelan and, in Spain, is found only in this church and that of Santiago de Compostela. Modifications were made to the chapels from the 16 to the 18C.
The choir-stall carvings recount the life and miracles of San Telmo, patron of Tui. The sentry path over the wide **cloister** galleries, soberly decorated in Cistercian style, commands good views of the river valley.

Capilla de San Telmo (San Telmo Chapel) – A Portuguese style reliquary shrine has been built below the cathedral on the site of the house of **San Pedro González Telmo**, a Dominican who lived in Tui and died in 1240. Pilgrims visit the alcove in the crypt where the saint died *(entrance: Rúa do Corpo Santo).*

*Book well in advance as it may be difficult
to find accommodation during high season.*

ÚBEDA★★

Andalucía (Jaén)
Population 31 962
Michelin map 446 R 19 – Michelin Atlas España Portugal p 76

Úbeda was, at one time, very prosperous. It was recaptured from the Moors in 1234 and became a base in the Reconquest campaign. It is now one of the best examples in Spain of homogeneous construction, dating principally from the time of the Renaissance.

Traditional craftsmen, chiefly potters, are to be found in Calle Valencia (**BY**).

The Good Friday evening procession, in Holy Week, is deeply fervent.

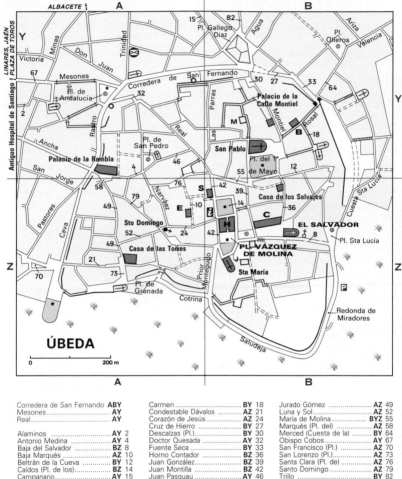

ÚBEDA

Corredera de San Fernando **ABY**		Carmen	**BY** 18	Jurado Gómez	**AZ** 49
Mesones	**AY**	Condestable Dávalos	**AZ** 21	Luna y Sol	**AZ** 52
Real	**AY**	Corazón de Jesús	**AZ** 24	María de Molina	**BYZ** 55
		Cruz de Hierro	**BY** 27	Marqués (Pl. del)	**AZ** 58
Alaminos	**AY** 2	Descalzas (Pl.)	**BY** 30	Merced (Cuesta de la)	**BY** 64
Antonio Medina	**AY** 4	Doctor Quesada	**AY** 32	Obispo Cobos	**AY** 67
Baja del Salvador	**BZ** 8	Fuente Seca	**BY** 33	San Francisco (Pl.)	**AZ** 70
Baja Marqués	**AZ** 10	Horno Contador	**BZ** 36	San Lorenzo (Pl.)	**AZ** 73
Beltrán de la Cueva	**BY** 12	Juan González	**BZ** 39	Santa Clara (Pl. de)	**AZ** 76
Caídos (Pl. de los)	**BZ** 14	Juan Montilla	**BZ** 42	Santo Domingo	**AZ** 79
Campanario	**AY** 15	Juan Pasquau	**AY** 46	Trillo	**BY** 82

B Casa del Obispo Canastero	**E** Palacio del Marqués del Contador	**S** Palacio de la Vela
C Palacio del Deán Ortega	**H** Casa de las Cadenas	de los Cobos

★★BARRIO ANTIGUO (OLD QUARTER) time: 1 1/2 hours

★★**Plaza Vázquez de Molina** (**BZ**) – The square, the monumental centre of Úbeda, is lined with old, historic buildings like the **Palacio del Deán Ortega** (Dean Ortega's Palace) (**BZ C**), which has been converted into a *parador*.

Casa de las Cadenas (House of Chains) (**BZ H**) – The mansion, now the Ayuntamiento (Town Hall), named after the chains round the forecourt, was designed in 1562 by Vandelvira *(qv)*, who was also responsible for the construction of Jaén cathedral.

The majestic but not overly ornate façade is relieved by alternating bays and pilasters and decorated above with caryatids and atlantes.

The *patio*, bordered by delicate arcades, opens onto the Plaza del Ayuntamiento. The archives room on the 2nd floor, covered by *artesonado* decoration the entire length of the façade, commands fine views of the square and the town.

Iglesia de Santa María (BZ) – The church's architecture is varied: the main door and that of Consolada *(left side)* are 17C, the cloisters 16C. The **chapels★**, set in sculptured surrounds, are closed by beautiful **grilles★**, most of which were wrought by Maestro Bartolomé.

★★ Iglesia de El Salvador (BZ) ⊘ – *If visiting outside service times, enter by the north door.* Diego de Siloé *(qv)* designed this homogeneous and sumptuous church in 1536. Its massive façade combines the most characteristic ornamental motifs of the Renaissance.
The **interior★** is frankly theatrical: the nave has vaulting outlined in blue and gold and is closed by a monumental wrought-iron grille. Beyond, the Capilla Mayor (chancel) forms a kind of rotunda in which an immense 16C altarpiece includes a baldachin with a sculpture by Berruguete *(qv)* of the Transfiguration (only the figure of Christ remains).
The **sacristy★★**, by Vandelvira, is ornamented with coffered decoration, medallions, caryatids and atlantes with all the splendour of the Italian Renaissance style.

Casa de los Salvajes (House of the Savages) (BZ) – Two very odd "savages", dressed in animal skins held together with belts of blackberry branches, may be seen on the façade, supporting a bishop's crest.

★ Iglesia de San Pablo (BY) – The church is a harmonious mixture of Gothic architecture, as seen in the west door, and the Isabelline style, to be seen in the **south door★** (1511). The **chapels★**, adorned in several instances with fine wrought-iron grilles, are the church's chief interior feature: the Capilla de las Calaveras (Chapel of the Skulls) was designed by Vandelvira; the Capilla de las Mercedes is in Isabelline style and richly carved.

Palacio de la Calle Montiel (BY) – This palace was one of the town's first Renaissance buildings and has a monumental gate flanked by twisted columns.

Casa del Obispo Canastero (Bishop Canastero's Mansion) (**BY B**) – Among the figures decorating the mansion's diamond pointed stone façade are two soldiers bearing the owner's coats of arms.

Palacio del Marqués del Contadero (Palace of the Marquis of Contadero) (AZ E) – The late-18C façade, crowned by a gallery, is Renaissance, a testimony to the long survival of the style in Úbeda.

Palacio de la Vela de los Cobos (ABZ S) – The palace's distinguished façade, surmounted by an arcaded gallery, is most unusually L-shaped.

ADDITIONAL SIGHTS

Casa de las Torres (Tower Mansion) (AZ) – The mansion front, closely flanked by two square towers, is profusely decorated in the Plateresque style, with delicately carved sculpture.

Antiguo Hospital de Santiago (Former St James' Hospital) – *Take Calle Obispo Cobos* **(AY)**. A high relief of St James Matamoros stands over the entrance to the former hospital, now a cultural centre. Inside are an arcaded *patio* and a grand staircase with multicoloured vaulting (1562-1575).

Palacio de la Rambla (AY) – The portal includes the figures of soldiers bearing the palace's coat of arms.

Iglesia de Santo Domingo (AZ) – The church's south door, overlooking a small picturesque square, is a delicate Renaissance work decorated with foliage motifs and roses.

UCLÉS

Castilla-La Mancha (Cuenca)
Population 297
Michelin map 444 M 21 – Michelin Atlas España Portugal p 54

The massive castle-monastery *(castillo-monasterio)* of Uclés stands impressively on a hill overlooking the village. From 1174 to 1499 it was the headquarters of the Order of Santiago.
Because of its strategic value, the little village was the scene of a good deal of fighting, including the Battle of Uclés in 1108 when the Almoravids defeated the army of Alfonso VI of Castilla.

Castillo-monasterio ⊘ – The present building was begun in 1529 in the Plateresque style, but the greater part of the work was undertaken by Herrera's disciple, **Francisco de Mora** (1560-1610) who tried to build his own Escorial – the building is, in fact, known as the Little Escorial. Two successful baroque sculptures are immediately evident: the courtyard fountain and the main gate.
The ramparts command an extensive panorama.

UJUÉ★

Navarra
Population 209
Michelin map 442 E 25 – Michelin Atlas España Portugal p 15

Ujué, perched on a summit overlooking the Ribera region, remains, with its tortuous streets and picturesque façades, much as it was in the Middle Ages.

Its **romería** (pilgrimage) is famous: the procession, dating back to the 14C, sets out annually on the Sunday after St Mark's Day (25 April), when penitents dressed in black capes and hoods and bearing a Cross gather from far and wide to implore the mercy of the Virgin of Ujué.

Iglesia de Santa María – A Romanesque church was built on the site at the end of the 11C. In the 14C, Charles II, the Bad, undertook the building of a Gothic church but work must have been interrupted for the Romanesque chancel remains to this day. The central chapel contains the venerated **Santa María la Blanca**, a wooden Romanesque statue, plated in silver.

Fortaleza (Fortress) – The church towers, invariably used for military purposes, command a view which extends to Olite, the Montejurra and the Pyrenees. Of the medieval palace there remain lofty walls and a covered watch path circling the church.

VALDEPEÑAS

Castilla-La Mancha (Ciudad Real)
Population 25 067
Michelin map 444 P 19 – Michelin Atlas España Portugal p 65

Valdepeñas, which stands at the southern tip of the vast wine-growing area of La Mancha, is the production centre of a well-known table wine.

Life in the town centres around the Plaza de España where blue and white coloured houses rise above shady porticoes. On one side stands the Late Gothic façade of the **Iglesia de la Asunción** (Church of the Assumption), with a harmonious tower and a Plateresque upper gallery.

EXCURSIONS

★**San Carlos del Valle** – *22km - 14 miles northeast.*
The small village of San Carlos has a delightful 18C **Plaza Mayor**★ set off by the warm colour of its brick houses. A former hospice, at no 5, has a stone entrance and a typical *patio*. Overlooking all is the baroque village church, crowned by a dome and four lantern turrets.

Las Virtudes – *24km - 15 miles south.*
The village claims that its **bullring** *(plaza de toros)* is the oldest in Spain (1641). It is square and is blocked along one side by the wall of the 14C **Santuario de Nuestra Señora de las Virtudes** (Sanctuary of Our Lady of Holy Virtue) ⊙ which inside has a Mudéjar ceiling over the nave and a Churrigueresque altarpiece.

VALENCIA★★

Comunidad Valenciana
Population 777 427
Michelin map 445 N 28 – Michelin Atlas España Portugal p 57
Plan of the conurbation in the current Michelin Red Guide España Portugal

Valencia, Spain's third largest city, has all the character of a large Mediterranean town and is notable for its pleasant, mild climate and the quality of its light. Its wide avenues (Grandes Vías), lined with palms and fig trees, encircle the old quarter with its fortified gateways, churches and narrow streets with quaint, old-fashioned shop fronts and Gothic houses, of which some have attractive *patios*.

Valencia is the capital of a fertile agricultural province as well as a prosperous industrial centre with shipyards, metallurgical and chemical plants, furniture, paper and textile factories. Its produce for export, including the citrus fruit, early vegetables and wine from the surrounding *huerta*, is handled by its busy port, **El Grao**.

Tourism has developed rapidly along the poetically named **Costa del Azahar** (Orange Blossom Coast) which stretches in a wide fringe of sand to the north and south of Valencia. The coast, on account of its sunshine and the fact that it is sheltered from Meseta winds by nearby *sierras*, has become one of Spain's major summer tourist centres with resorts such as **Benicasim, Oropesa, Peñíscola** *(qv)*, **Benicarló** and **Vinarós** to the north and **El Saler, Cullera, Gandía** *(qv)* and **Oliva** to the south. Apartment blocks have sprung up to form an unusual urban landscape between the long sandy beaches and the orange groves inland.

2000 years of history – The city, founded by the Greeks in 138 BC, passed succes-sively into the hands of the Carthaginians, Romans, Visigoths and Arabs. In 1094 it was reconquered by **El Cid** *(qv)*, who was titled Duke of Valencia but lived only five years in the city before dying there in 1099. The Moors recaptured it three years later and held it until 1238 when it was repossessed, this time by James the Conqueror, who declared it the capital of a kingdom which he allied to Aragón. Valencia then enjoyed a long period of prosperity until the end of the 15C when, following the discovery of America and the development of ports in Andalucía, it began to decline. A silk renaissance in the 17C renewed its fortunes.

Over the past two centuries, Valencia has been involved in every war and insurrection in Spain. During the War of the Spanish Succession (1701-1714), the city sided with the Archduke Charles of Austria but found itself stripped of its privileges; in 1808, it rebelled against the French and was then taken by Suchet in 1812; in 1843 it rose under **General Narváez** to restore the regency of María Cristina of Naples; finally in the Civil War the city became in March 1939 after the fall of Catalunya, the last refuge of the Republican forces.

Art in Valencia – Valencia enjoyed a brilliant period, both economically and artisti-cally, in the 15C. Examples of Gothic architectural flowering are to be seen in the old city's palaces, mansions, city gates, the cathedral and the Lonja (Exchange). In painting, several artists won renown: **Luis Dalmau,** influenced by Flemish painting, who developed a Hispano-Flemish style; **Jaime Baço,** known as **Jacomart,** and his fellow artist **Juan Reixach** who were both influenced by Flanders and Italy; and the **Osonas,** father and son, who also showed Flemish austerity in their work.

Valencia craftsmen of the 15C were also outstanding in the decorative arts: wrought ironwork, gold and silversmithing, embroidery and particularly ceramics, for which special centres were established at Paterna and Manises *(see the Museo de Cerámica below)*.

The Valencia huerta and Albufera – The city lies along the banks of the Turia at the heart of fertile countryside known locally as **La Huerta.** On this expanse, watered by an irrigation system laid down by the Romans and improved by the Moors, are the count-less citrus trees and market gardens which produce the fruit and early vegetables exported throughout Europe.

South of Valencia, a vast lagoon, **La Albufera** (from the Arabic meaning Small Sea), sep-arated from the Mediterranean by an offshore bar, the Dehesa, has, since the 13C, been planted with paddy fields. It is also a fishing area; its eels appear on typical menus in restaurants in **El Palmar** *(18km - 11 miles south)* which also serve Valencia's famous dish, **paella.**

Tribunal de las Aguas (Water Tribunal) – Since the Middle Ages disputes in the *huerta* have been settled by the Tribunal de las Aguas: every Thursday at 1200, representa-tives of the areas irrigated by the eight canals, accompanied by an alguazil (officer of justice), meet in front of the Portada de los Apóstoles (Apostle's Door) of the cathe-dral; the offence is declared, judged (the judges all in black) and the sentence pronounced immediately (a fine, deprivation of water) by the most senior judge. The proceedings are oral and there is no appeal.

The *huerta* has found its place in literature in the realistic, dramatic novels of **Vicente Blasco Ibáñez** (1867-1928) including *La Barraca (The Cabin)* and *Entre Naranjos* (Amongst the Orange Trees).

Las Fallas – Valencia holds a week-long carnival every year during the week pre-ceding 19 March. The custom goes back to the Middle Ages when on St Joseph's Day, the carpenters' brotherhood, one of the town's traditional crafts, burned their accu-mulated wood shavings in bonfires known as *Fallas* (from the Latin *fax:* torch). The name became synonymous with a festival for which, in time, objects were made solely for burning – particularly effigies of less popular members of the community! In the 17C single effigies were replaced by pasteboard groups or floats produced by quar-ters of the town – rivalry is such that the figures today are fantastic in size, artistry and satirical implication. Prizes are awarded during the general festivities which include fireworks, processions, bullfights etc., before everything goes up in the fires or *cremá* on the evening of 19 March. Those figures spared from the bonfires are on display in the small **Museo Fallero** (Fallas Museum) ⊘.

★CIUDAD VIEJA **(OLD TOWN)** *time: 2 hours*

★ **Catedral (EX)** ⊘ – The cathedral stands on the site of a former mosque. Although work began in 1262, the major part of the building dates from the 14 and 15C. The Gothic style was completely masked in the late 18C by a neo-classical reno-vation which has since been removed.

★ **El Miguelete** ⊘ – Abutting the façade, El Miguelete, or El Micalet as the Valencians call it, an octagonal tower, owes its name to the large bell consecrated on St Michael's Day. From the top there is a bird's eye view of the cathedral roofs and the town with its countless glazed ceramic domes.

Dibujo de una fotografía de N. Thibaut/EXPLORER

The cathedral, Valencia

Exterior – The early-18C west face, which is elegant in spite of being narrowly confined, is in imitation of the Italian baroque style, after plans by a German architect. The Assumption on the pediment is by Ignacio Vergara and Esteve.

The south door, the Puerta del Palau (Palace Door), is Romanesque, the north, the **Portada de los Apóstoles** (Apostles' Door), Gothic, decorated with numerous, but time-worn sculptures. The Virgin and Child statue, which once stood against the pier, is now on the tympanum surrounded by angel musicians.

Interior – Although the elevation of the Gothic vaulting is not very great, a great deal of light filters in through the alabaster windows in the beautiful Flamboyant Gothic **lantern**.

The high altar retable, painted early in the 16C by Fernando de Llanos and Yáñez de la Almedina, illustrates the Lives of Christ and the Virgin in a style markedly influenced by Leonardo da Vinci.

In the ambulatory, beneath a beautiful balustrade behind the high altar, there is an alabaster relief of the Resurrection (1510). Opposite is the 15C Virgen del Coro (Chancel Virgin) in polychrome alabaster and, in a chapel, a Crucifixion known as the Cristo de la Buena Muerte (Christ of Good Death).

Capilla del Santo Cáliz or Sala Capitular (Chapel of the Holy Grail or Chapter house) – The chamber, which in the 14C served as a reading room, has elegant star vaulting. Behind the altar, twelve alabaster low reliefs by the Florentine sculptor, Poggibonsi, frame a magnificent purple agate cup, said to be the Holy Grail (the vessel traditionally used by Our Lord at the Last Supper and in which a few drops of his blood are said to have fallen). The cup, according to legend, was brought to Spain in the 3C and belonged first to the Monasterio de San Juan de la Peña *(qv)* then to the crown of Aragón which, in the 15C, presented it to the cathedral.

Museo ⊙ – *Access through the Capilla del Santo Cáliz.* Among the treasures contained in this museum are two large paintings by Goya of San Francisco de Borja and a monumental monstrance made after the Civil War.

Iglesia de Nuestra Señora de los Desamparados (**EX B**) ⊙ – Beneath the church's painted cupola stands the venerated statue of the patron of Valencia: the Virgin of the Abandoned *(desamparados)*.

★**Palacio de la Generalidad** (**EX**) ⊙ – This fine 15C Gothic palace to which one tower was added in the 17C and a second identical one added in the 20C, was until 1707 the meeting place of the Valencia Cortes charged with the collection of tax.

You enter an attractive Gothic *patio* decorated with a sculpture by Benlliure of Dante's *Inferno* (1900). You then see a golden saloon with a wonderful gilt and multicolour **artesonado ceiling**★ and a large painting of the Tribunal de las Aguas or Water Tribunal *(see above)*. On the first floor are the Sala de los Reyes (Royal Hall) displaying portraits of the Valencian kings, the Oratorio (Oratory) with its altarpiece by the local 16C painter, Juan Sariñena and the Gran Salón de las Cortes Valencianas (Valencian Government Grand Council Chamber). The *azulejos* frieze and the coffered ceiling are 16C. Members of the Cortes are portrayed in several 16C canvases.

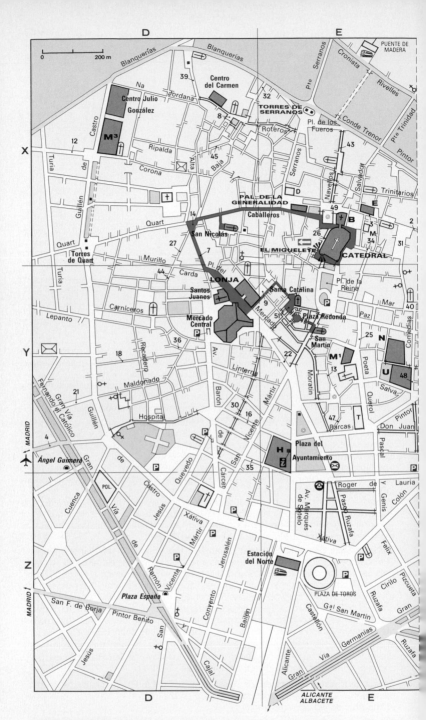

Calle de Caballeros (**DX**) – Some of the houses along the main street of the old town have kept their Gothic *patios* (no 22).

Iglesia de San Nicolás (**DX**) ⏱ – This, one of the town's oldest churches, has been completely renovated in the Churrigueresque style. Among the 16C paintings are an altarpiece by Juan de Juanes *(chapel to the left on entering)* and a *Calvary* by Osona the Elder *(by the font)*.

★ **Lonja (Silk Exchange)** (**DY**) – The present building was erected on the request of the Valencia silk merchants in the 15C to replace an earlier commodities exchange similar to those of Barcelona and Palma. The prosperity which required a larger building was well reflected in the style of the new edifice: Flamboyant Gothic. The Lonja, topped by a crenellated roof ridge, has an impressive Gothic entrance. The left wing, separated from the entrance by a tower, is crowned by a gallery

decorated with a medallion frieze. The old commercial silk **hall**★★ is lofty, with ogival arches supported on elegantly cabled columns; the bays in the walls are filled with delicate tracery.

A staircase from the Jardín de los Naranjos (Orange Tree Court) leads up to the Sala del Consulado del Mar (Maritime Consulate Law Court). The late-15C **ceiling**★, from the old Ayuntamiento or Town Hall, is made up of carved and gilded beams supported by consoles sculpted with human and imaginary animal figures.

Today, now that its commercial activity has ceased, the Lonja serves as a centre for cultural events including concerts and exhibitions.

Iglesia de los Santos Juanes (**DY**) ⊘ – This is a vast church with a baroque façade. The single aisle, originally Gothic, was modified in the 17 and 18C by the addition of exuberant baroque stuccowork.

Mercado Central (Central Market) (DY) – The enormous metal and glass construction, built in 1928, is a good example of Modernist architecture. Try going there in the mornings when it is at its busiest with stalls of glistening fish and great piles of fruit and vegetables fresh from the *huerta*.

Iglesia de Santa Catalina (EY) – The church is notable for its 17C baroque belfry which is best seen from Plaza de Zaragoza.

Plaza Redonda (EY) – A passageway leads to this unusual little round square, more like a *patio*, surrounded by stalls selling lace and haberdashery.

Iglesia de San Martín (EY) – The west door is decorated with a group of bronze figures by the Flemish Gothic school, which illustrates San Martín on horseback dividing his cloak.

ADDITIONAL SIGHTS

★★ **Museo de Cerámica (Ceramics Museum) (EY M¹)** ⊘ – The former **Palacio del Marqués de Dos Aguas** (Palace of the Marquis de Dos Aguas)★ has an amazing Churrigueresque façade: the alabaster doorway, carved in the 18C by Ignacio Vergara after a cartoon by the painter, Hipólito Rovira, shows two atlantes pouring water from amphorae in illustration of the marquis' name. The painter covered the façade with frescoes which were destroyed in the 19C. The marquis' impressive carriage may be seen on the ground floor.

The **museo** (museum), housed in the exuberantly decorated palace rooms, contains over 5 000 ceramic exhibits dating from the Iberian period to the present day. The collection was donated in large part by González Martí. Most of the pieces on display were made locally. The oldest, going back to the 13C, are from **Paterna** *(6km - 4 miles northwest of Valencia)*. The green and white ware, in which brown manganese streaks can be seen, and the alternative blue and white, were supplanted in popularity in the 14C by lustreware from **Manises** *(8km - 5 miles west)*. This, in turn, fell from favour in the 17C, when the colours of Talavera ceramics *(qv)* were found more pleasing. In the 18C potteries were set up in **Alcora** and the craft was revived locally in Valencia and the surrounding area. Manises has resumed production and is now manufacturing on a fairly large scale. Paterna ware is displayed in a gallery on the ground floor. On the 1st floor are galleries showing Alcora ceramics, 17 and 18C Manises lustreware, Oriental porcelain from China and Japan and *socarrats* or the tiles which, in the 14 and 15C, were used to face the areas between beams in ceilings. On the second floor a **Valencian kitchen** *(cocina)* has been reconstituted.

★ **Museo San Pío V (FX)** ⊘ – This Fine Arts museum near the Jardines del Real (Royal Gardens) is especially interesting for its **collection of Valencia Primitives★★**. Countless altarpieces prove the vitality of the Valencia school of the 15C.

Among the many artists are Jacomart, Reixach and the Elder and Younger Osonas. Some of the retables are by less well-known artists such as Gonzalo Pérez, the author of the Flemish influenced altarpiece of San Martín, or by anonymous artists like that of Fray Bonifacio Ferrer. The triptych of the *Passion* by Hieronymous Bosch is an extraordinarily expressive work; the central panel is a copy of *Los Improperios* – the Mocking of Christ – in El Escorial.

Representing the Renaissance are Macip, Juan de Juanes, Yáñez de la Almedina and Fernando de Llanos whose use of colour recalls that of Leonardo da Vinci. Tenebrism (term applied to paintings in dark tones) made its first appearance in Spain at the beginning of the 17C in the works of Ribalta and came to full fruition in those of Ribera *(St Sebastian)*. One gallery is devoted to Goya.

Most of the works on the 2nd and 3rd floors are by 19 and 20C Valencian artists.

★ **Colegio del Patriarca (Patriarch or Corpus Christi College) (EY N)** ⊘ – This former seminary, founded by the Blessed Juan de Ribera, Archbishop of Valencia and Patriarch of Antioch, dates back to the 16C.

The *patio*, which is architecturally harmonious and decorated with *azulejos* friezes, has, at the centre, a statue of the founder by the modern sculptor Benlliure. In the chapel hang four 15C Flemish tapestries.

The **museum** is in the Rectorial saloon and adjoining rooms on the 1st floor. The interesting collection of 15 to 17C pictures includes paintings by Juan de Juanes, a precious **triptych of the Passion★** by Dirk Bouts, a portrait (on pasteboard) of the founder, Ribera, by Ribalta, and other works by Ribalta, Morales and El Greco (one of the many versions of the *Adoration of the Shepherds*). There is also an admirable 14C Byzantine Cross from the Monasterio de Athos.

Facing the college is the **Universidad** (University) **(EY U)**, its buildings grouped round a vast Ionic quadrangle.

★ **Torres de Serranos (EX)** ⊘ – The towers, now considerably restored, are, nevertheless, a good example of late-14C military architecture; they guarded one of the entrances to the medieval city. The defensive features all face outwards. Note the flowing lines of the battlements and the delicate tracery above the gateway.

Torres de Quart (**DX**) – 15C towers, again a fine example of military architecture, guard another entrance to the city.

Almudín (**EX E**) – This is a 14 to 16C granary with popular style frescoes covering the walls and two 19C *azulejos* altars.

Instituto Valenciano de Arte Moderno (**Valencian Institute of Modern Art**) – The institute comprises two separate buildings standing at some distance from each other:
– the **Centro Julio González** (**DX**), a vast modern building, displays works by two Valencian artists, the sculptor Julio González and the painter Pinazo. Most of its galleries, however, are used for temporary exhibitions, often featuring the institute's own collection of paintings by Tàpies, Saura, Millares, Chillida and the Equipo Crónica group.
– the **Centro del Carmen** (**DX**), a former Carmelite convent, architecturally a mixture of the Gothic, Renaissance and classical styles, provides a wonderful setting for works by contemporary artists.

Plaza del Ayuntamiento (**EY**) – This bustling square in the centre of modern Valencia, with the Ayuntamiento (Town Hall) overlooking it on one side, holds a brilliantly spectacular flower market.

Museo Paleontológico (Palaeontology Museum) (**EY H**) ⊘ – Beneath the *Ayuntamiento*. It has an interesting collection of antediluvian fossils and skeletons on display.

Estación del Norte (**Railway Station**) (**EZ**) – The station, built between 1909 and 1917, was designed by an admirer of Austrian Modernist *(Sezession)* architecture. It is an interesting example of early-20C architecture and decoration with its wood counters and *azulejos* panels decorated with scenes of the *huerta* and *Albufera (in the cafeteria).*

Convento de Santo Domingo (**FY**) – The monastery's classical style entrance, with statue niches for saints, was designed by Philip II (1527-1598).

Jardines del Real (**FX**) – The royal gardens have become Valencia's major park. The **Puente del Real**, Royal Bridge, is 16C.

Museo de Prehistoria (**Prehistory Museum**) (**DX M³**) ⊘ – Exhibits of archaeological finds from excavations throughout the province of Valencia include reproductions of Parpalló cave paintings and a fine collection of Neolithic ceramics fashioned with shells.

EXCURSION

Puig – *18km - 11 miles north on the N340* (**FX**).
The **Monasterio de la Virgen del Puig** ⊘, occupied by the Order of Mercy, overlooks the village. The monastery's foundation in the 13C was prompted by the discovery, in 1237, of a 6C Byzantine style marble low relief of the Virgin which had lain hidden in the earth beneath a bell since the barbarian invasion. James the Conqueror chose the Virgin as patron of the Kingdom of Valencia and ordered the building of a convent in her honour.
In the church, the Gothic vaulting has been freed of its 18C stucco overlay. The Byzantine Virgin is to be seen at the high altar. The present monastery was built between the 16 and 18C; paintings from the Valencia school are displayed in the upper 18C cloisters.

VALLADOLID★

Castilla y León
Population 345 891
Michelin map 441 H15 – Michelin Atlas España Portugal p 24
Plan of the conurbation in the current Michelin Red Guide España Portugal

Valladolid, one of the former capitals of Castilla, is rich in decorated buildings, and in art. It is also a modern industrial (engineering, automobiles, food production) and commercial (trade fairs) centre. The Holy Week *(Semana Santa)* ceremonies are splendid.

Historical notes – As from the 12C, Castilla's kings frequently resided at Valladolid and the Cortes (Parliament) often assembled there. Peter the Cruel married there in the 14C, Ferdinand and Isabel in 1469; it was the birthplace of Philip IV and his sister Anne of Austria, mother of Louis XIV.
The city was also deeply involved in the 16C Comuneros Revolt *(qv)* during the reign of Emperor Charles V.

Castillo de Simancas *(11km - 7 miles southwest)* – This castle was converted by Emperor Charles V into a repository for state archives. The collection represents a complete history of Spanish administration from the 15 to the 19C.

The Isabelline style – The Isabelline style, which emerged in the late 15C, is a mixture of Flamboyant Gothic and Mudéjar tradition, the ultimate stage before Plateresque. The decorative focus on entrances produced rectangular panels which eventually extended from ground level to cornice and were compartmented like an altarpiece.

The most characteristic examples of the style in Valladolid are the Colegio de San Gregorio and the façade of the Iglesia de San Pablo.

Whereas the Salamanca Plateresque fronts, abundantly and delicately decorated with a hint of the Renaissance, are outstanding, those of Valladolid, being earlier, demonstrate a less sophisticated but more vigorous art.

★ISABELLINE VALLADOLID *time: 1 1/2 hours*

★★★ **Museo Nacional de Escultura Policromada** (National Museum of Polychrome Sculpture) (**CX**) ⊙ – The museum is housed in the **Colegio de San Gregorio**, the city's greatest Isabelline monument, founded in the 15C by Fray Alonso de Burgos, confessor to Isabel the Catholic.

Ch. Sappa / CEDRI

The entrance to the Colegio de San Gregorio, Valladolid

The **entrance★★**, attributed to Gil de Siloé and Simon of Cologne, is one of the marvels of Spanish art. The decoration is unbelievably rich; every fantasy from savages to interwoven branches of thorns, is somehow felicitous in its inclusion in the strongly hierarchical composition which focuses first on the doorway and then rises to the magnificent heraldic motif above.

Museo – From the 16 to the 17C Valladolid was one of Spain's major centres for sculpture. This museum is a reflection of this with its wonderful collection of religious statues in polychrome wood, a material which, because both carved and painted, was particularly well suited to the expression of the dramatic. On the ground floor are the remarkable altarpiece designed by Alonso Berruguete *(qv)* for the church of San Benito but shown here dismantled and the *Martyrdom of St Sebastian*, one of his major works. Some of the galleries on the first floor have kept their *artesonado* ceilings. The walnut stalls from San Benito (1525-1529) are the combined work of Andrés de Najera, Diego de Siloé, Felipe Vigarny and Juan de Valmaseda.

A door opens into an extraordinary **patio★★**. At ground level, tall cabled columns support basket arches; above the theme is repeated but with an infinitely delicate, dense decoration: twin bays, their arches and tympanums adorned with lacework tracery, rise above a magnificent balustrade. A cornice frieze, evenly interspersed with escutcheons, completes the stonework fantasy. Exhibits in the remaining rooms include the *Entombment* by Pedro de Juni, in which the figures display a certain mannerism, and works by Pompeo Leoni and Pedro de Mena *(Mary Magdalene)*.

A Plateresque staircase leads down to the ground floor where the outstandingly natural **Christ Recumbent** by Gregorio Fernández and a painting by Zurbarán of the *Holy Shroud* are displayed.

A **chapel★**, designed by Juan Guas, contains an altarpiece by Berruguete, a tomb by Felipe Vigarny and carved choir-stalls.

Iglesia de San Pablo (St Paul's Church) (**CX**) – The lower **façade★★**, by Simon of Cologne *(qv)*, consists of a portal with an ogee arch all framed within a segmental arch, and above, a large rose window and two coats of arms supported by angels.

The upper façade, from a later date, is a less exuberant composition in the Plateresque style, divided into panels adorned with inset statues and armorial bearings.

VALLADOLID

Duque de la Victoria .... BY 17
Fuente Dorada (Pl. de) .... BY 20
Miguel Iscar .... BY 29
Santiago .... BY 41
Teresa Gil .... BY

Arco de Ladrillo (Paseo del) .... BZ 2
Arzobispo Gandásegui .... CY 3
Bailarín Vicente Escudero .... CY 5
Bajada de la Libertad .... BCY 6
Cadenas de San Gregorio .... CX 8
Cánovas del Castillo .... BCY 9
Cardenal Mendoza .... CY 10
Chancillería .... CX 13
Claudio Moyano .... BY 14
Doctrinos .... BY 16
España (Pl. de) .... BY 18
Gondomar .... CX 21
Industrias .... CY 24
Maldonado .... CY 25
Marqués del Duero .... CXY 26
Pasión .... BY 30
Portillo de Balboa .... CX 32
San Agustín .... BXY 35
San Ildefonso .... BY 36
San Pablo (Pl. de) .... BX 37
Santa Cruz (Pl. de) .... CY 40
Santuario .... CY 42
Sanz y Forés .... CXY 45
Zorrilla (Paseo de) .... BZ 47

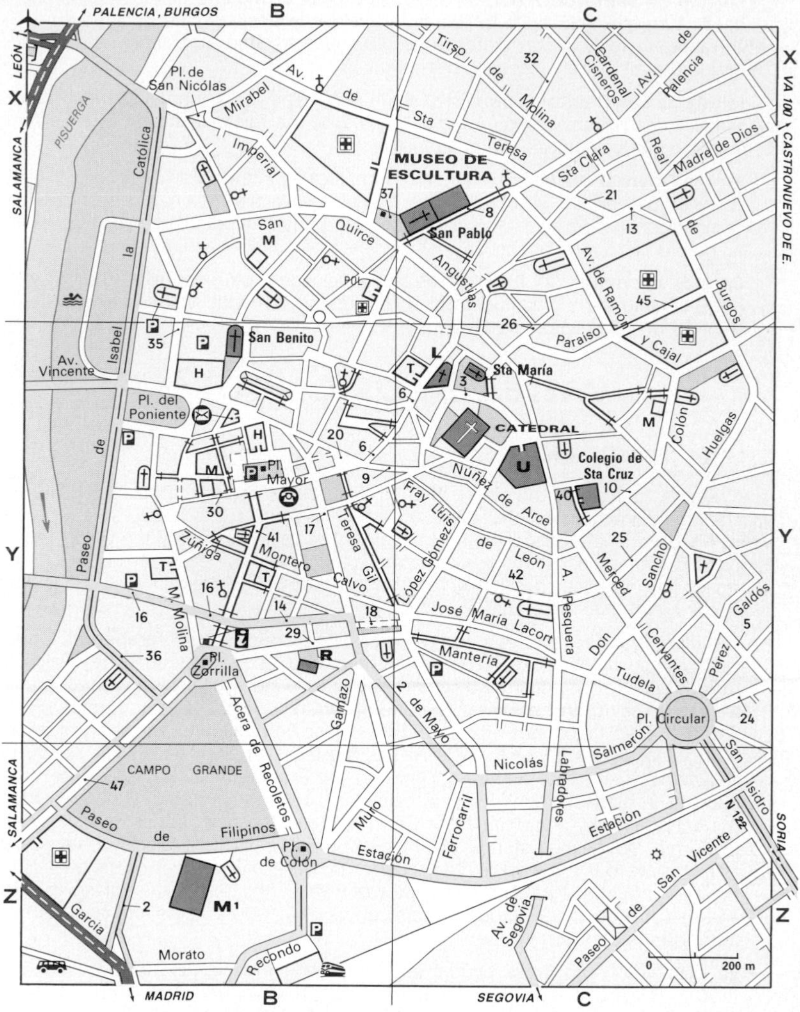

L Iglesia de las Angustias
M¹ Museo Oriental
R Casa de Cervantes
U Universidad

ADDITIONAL SIGHTS

★ **Catedral** (**CY**) ⊙ – The cathedral project, commissioned in about 1580 by Philip II from Herrera *(qv)*, was only realised very slowly and was distorted to some degree by the architect's 17 and 19C successors – as in the upper part of the façade, filled with baroque ornament by Alberto Churriguera, and in the octagonal section of the tower.

Although never completed, the **interior** remains one of Herrera's major successes. The altarpiece (1551) in the central apsidal chapel, where the interplay of perspective and relief makes the figures come to life, is by Juan de Juni *(qv)*.

Museo (Museum) (**CY**) ⊙ – In the old Gothic Iglesia de Santa María la Mayor at the east end of the cathedral, are a 15C altarpiece, two paintings by the Ribera school, two portraits attributed to Velázquez and a silver monstrance by Juan de Arfe (16C).

Iglesia de Santa María la Antigua (**CY**) ⊙ – The only Romanesque features in this otherwise Gothic church, are its tall slender Lombard tower and its portico with triple columns along the north wall.

Iglesia de las Angustias (CY L) ⊘ – The church, built by one of Herrera's disciples, contains in its south transept, Juan de Juni's masterpiece, the **Virgen de los Siete Cuchillos** (Virgin of the Seven Knives).

Universidad (CY U) – The university's baroque façade is by Narciso and Antonio Tomé.

Colegio de Santa Cruz (CY) – The college, built at the end of the 15C, is one of the first truly Renaissance buildings in Spain; the finely carved decoration at the entrance, in fact, is still Plateresque but the rusticated stonework and window design are of entirely classical inspiration.

Iglesia de San Benito (St Benedict's Church) (BY) – The 15C church's generally robust simplicity and massive, monumental porch, give it a fortress-like air. The Herreran style *patio* is magnificent in its simplicity.

Museo Oriental (BZ M¹) ⊘ – The museum, located in a neo-classical college (18C) designed by Ventura Rodríguez *(qv)*, houses a collection of Chinese (bronze, porcelain, lacquerware, coins and silk embroidery) and Philippine art (ivory pieces and numerous reminders of the Spanish presence on these islands).

Casa de Cervantes (BY R) ⊘ – The house belonged to Cervantes in the last years of his life and looks much as it did at that time (17C) with whitewashed walls and some of his own simple furnishings.

VALLE DE LOS CAÍDOS★★

Madrid

Michelin map 444 K 17 – Michelin Atlas España Portugal p 39

The Valle de los Caídos, the Valley of the Fallen, built between 1940 and 1958, is a spectacular monument to the dead of the Civil War (1936-1939) in a beautiful **setting★★** deep in the Guadarrama Mountains. The valley, formerly the Cuelgamuros, is splendid with granite outcrops and pine trees. The road leads to the foot of the esplanade in front of the basilica which was hollowed out of the rock face and is dominated by a monumental Cross.

★★Basílica ⊘ – The basilica's west door in its austere granite façade is a bronze work carved by Fernando Cruz Solís, crowned by a *Pietà* by Juan de Ávalos. At the entrance to the immense interior, is a fine wrought-iron screen with 40 statues of Spanish saints and soldiers. The 262m - 860ft nave (St Peter's, Rome: 186m - 610ft; St Paul's, London: 152m - 500ft) is lined with chapels between which have been hung eight copies of 16C Brussels tapestries of the Apocalypse. Above the chapels' entrances are alabaster copies of the most famous statues of the Virgin in Spain. A **cupola★**, 42m -138ft in diameter, above the crossing, shows in mosaic the heroes, martyrs and saints of Spain approaching both Christ in Majesty and the Virgin. On the altar stands a painted wood figure of Christ Crucified, set against a tree trunk; it is the work of the sculptor Beovides. At the foot of the altar is the funerary stone of José Antonio Primo de Rivera, founder of the Falangist Party, and that of Franco. Ossuaries contain coffins of 40 000 soldiers and civilians from both sides in the Civil War.

★La Cruz ⊘ – The Cross by the architect Diego Mendez, is 125m - 410ft high (150m -492ft including the base), the width from fingertip to fingertip, 46m - 150ft. The immense statues of the Evangelists around the plinth and the four cardinal virtues above are by Juan de Ávalos. There is a good **view** from the base *(access by funicular)*. The great building showing Herreran influence on the far side of the valley from the basilica is a Benedictine monastery, seminary and social studies centre.

VERÍN

Galicia (Orense)
Population 11 018
Michelin map 441 G7 – Michelin Atlas España Portugal p 21

Verín, built between the wide vine-covered slopes of the Támega valley (viñedos del Valle), was already well known in the Middle Ages; today it lies off the main road and is lively and picturesque with narrow paved streets, houses with glassed-in balconies, arcades and carved coats of arms.

Thermal springs with curative qualities rise in the neighbourhood, notably those of Fontenova and, further on, Cabreiroa, Sousas and Villaza.

Castillo de Monterrei – *6km - 4 miles west.* There is a *parador* next to the castle. It played an important role throughout the Portuguese-Spanish wars, having been strategically built on the frontier for the purpose. It was more than a castle since included within the perimeter were a monastery, a hospital and a town which was abandoned in the 19C.

The approach is up an avenue of lime-trees which commands a full **panorama★** of the valley below. To enter the castle you pass through three defence walls, the outermost dating from the 17C. Inside, at the centre, stand the square 15C Torre del Hamenaje (Keep) and the 14C Torre de las Damas (Lady's Tower); the palace courtyard is lined by a three-storey arcade and is less austere. The 13C church has a **portal★** delicately carved with a notched design and a tympanum showing Christ in Majesty between the symbols of the Evangelists.

VICH / VIC

Catalunya (Barcelona)
Population 29 113
Michelin map 443 G36 – Michelin Atlas España Portugal p 32

Since ancient times there has always been a village on the site now occupied by the commercially and industrially thriving town of Vich (leather goods, food processing and textiles). Vich sausages have long been well-known in Catalunya.

SIGHTS

Catedral ⊙ – The elegant Romanesque belfry and the crypt, both built in the 11C, are all that remain of the present church's forerunners.

The cathedral was built in the neo-classical style between 1781 and 1803. In 1930 the famous Catalan artist **José María Sert** decorated it with wall paintings which were lost when the church was set on fire at the beginning of the Civil War in 1936. Sert took up his brushes again and by 1945, when he died, the walls were once more covered with vast murals.

The **paintings★** have an intensity, a power reminiscent of Michelangelo and also a profound symbolism. They evoke the mystery of the Redemption *(chancel)* awaited from the time of Adam's original sin *(transept)* and prophesied by the martyrs *(nave)*. Three scenes on the back of the west door illustrate the triumph of human injustice in the Life of Christ and in the history of Catalunya: against an architectural background which includes the cathedral in ruins after the fire, Jesus chases the moneylenders from the temple *(right)* but is himself condemned to crucifixion *(left)*, while *(in the centre)* Pilate washes his hands and the crowd hails Barabbas, symbol of the vandals of revolution. The monochrome golds and browns in the murals tone with the fluted pillars, the scale of the murals with the vastness of the nave.

The former high altar **retable★★**, at the end of the ambulatory, is a 15C alabaster work which escaped the cathedral's many restorers. Its twelve panels, divided by statues of the saints and by mouldings, are devoted to the glorification of Christ, the Virgin and St Peter. Opposite, lies the canon who commissioned the retable in a Gothic tomb by the same sculptor.

Claustro (Cloister) – Wide, tracery filled 14C arches surround the small close in which stands the monumental tomb of the philosopher, Jaime Balmes (1810-1848), native of Vich. In a cloister gallery one can see the tomb of the painter J.M. Sert, surmounted by his last and unfinished work, a *Crucifixion*, intended by the artist to replace the one in the cathedral.

★★Museo Episcopal ⊙ – The museum next to the cathedral contains works from local churches. Its rich collections, particularly of Romanesque altarfronts painted on wood and Gothic altarpieces, provide a comprehensive survey of the development of Catalan art.

Room 1 (11, 12, 13C) – The exhibits include statues, often of the Virgin, in polychrome wood, frescoes – notably a *Last Supper* from the Seu d'Urgell – and a remarkable series of altarfronts which show a clear evolution in style from the hieratic Byzantine manner to a more personal, narrative approach.

Room 2 (14 and 15C) – Sculpture became more lifelike as perspective and detail increased after the Romanesque period (c1300). Besides the beautiful French and Italian influenced statues of the Virgin, the outstanding object in this room is the alabaster altarfront of the Life of Christ carved by B. Saulet in 1341 for the Sant Joan de les Abadesses parish.

Remaining Rooms – The remaining rooms are devoted to Gothic painting and include works by several great artists: Ferrer Bassá *(qv)* and Pedro Serra (1356-1405) *(qv)* who introduced the Italian style; Ramón de Mur (1402-1435) who added a personal note and a sense of the picturesque. After canvases by the Maestro de Cardona and Jaime Ferrer I (15C), there is a room with paintings by Luis Borrassá *(qv)*, a clever colourist who introduced the International Gothic style and another with those of Bernat Martorell *(qv)*, his successor, and Jaime Huguet *(qv)*, who reveals the first signs of the Renaissance spirit which was to appear clearly in Juan Gascó's *Holy Visage* (late 15, early 16C), displayed in the last room.

EXCURSION

L'Estany – *24km - 15 miles southwest.*
The village grew up around the Augustinian **Monasterio de Santa María** ⊘ of which the 12C church and adjoining cloisters remain. Surmounting the double row of columns in the cloisters are 72 unusual **capitals★★**. The north gallery is Romanesque and narrative in style (New Testament); the west, decorative with palm fronds and gaunt griffons; the south, geometrical and interlaced although the sophisticated execution and heraldic positions of the animals indicate a later date; the east is profane with wedding scenes and musicians after ceramics from Paterna which drew on Moorish motifs for their design.

VILLAFAMÉS

Comunidad Valenciana (Castellón)
Population 1 399
Michelin map 445 L29 – Michelin Atlas España Portugal p 57

There is a lovely view of this charming town with its cobblestone streets from the castle ruins. A good many artists have made Villafamés their home.

Museo Popular de Arte Contemporáneo (Contemporary Art Museum) ⊘ – The museum, housed in a 15C palace, is the centre of a very active cultural scene. Many of the works it displays are by famous artists including Miró, Barjola, Serrano and Genovés.

VILLENA

Comunidad Valenciana (Alicante)
Population 31 141
Michelin map 445 Q27 – Michelin Atlas España Portugal p 68

In the Middle Ages the region of Villena was a powerful feudal domain guarded by outpost strongholds, invariably perched on rocky heights: Chinchilla, Almansa, Biar, Sax and La Mola. The **castillo** (castle) with its majestic keep, had several owners, among them two well-known men of letters: **Don Juan Manuel** *(qv)* in the 14C, and, in the 15C, **Enrique de Aragón** (1384-1434).

Museo Arqueológico (Archaeological Museum) ⊘ – The museum is in the Town Hall *(Ayuntamiento)* which has a fine Renaissance façade. It displays two solid gold collections dating from the Bronze Age (1500-1000 BC) of which one is the outstanding **Villena Treasure★★** with gold jewellery and gourds decorated with sea urchin shell patterns.

Iglesia de Santiago ⊘ – The vaulting in this 15-16C church is supported in an unusual way upon spiral pillars which continue above the carved imposts as turned engaged columns. The overall effect gives the nave great elegance.

EXCURSION

Bocairent – *26km - 16 miles northeast.* The church in this small market town where **Juan de Juanes** *(qv)* died (1523-1579) has an interesting **Museo Parroquial** (Parish Museum) ⊘ with several paintings by the artist – known as the Spanish Raphael – and his school (a 14C *Last Supper* by Marcial de Sax), as well as a collection of church plate.

The Michelin Maps which accompany this Guide are shown on the back cover.

Vitoria (Gasteiz in Basque), capital of the largest of the Basque provinces, is the seat of the Autonomous Basque (Euskadi) Community government. It lies at the centre of the *Llanada alavesa*, a vast cereal covered plateau far closer in appearance to the plains of Castilla than the green hills of the Cantabrian coast. The town has developed rapidly this century around the hill on which in 1181, Sancho the Wise, King of Navarra, founded a walled city.

Today it is a city of business, trade and industry – food processing, chemicals, engineering and farm machinery. It is also the capital of the manufacturing of playing cards (the Fournier factory was founded in 1868) and has been famous since the 18C for its chocolate truffles. The modern quarters around Calle Dato provide a lively contrast to the quiet, serene atmosphere of the old town.

Among the local amenities are water sports at two vast reservoirs, Urrunaga and Ullívarri, north of the town.

The August Virgen Blanca festival is colourful and perpetuates a strange tradition: everyone lights a cigar as the "angel" descends from the Torre de San Miguel (St Michael's Belfry).

CIUDAD VIEJA (OLD TOWN) *time: 1 1/2 hours*

Seignorial houses with balconies and fronts bearing family coats of arms stand in concentric streets – each named after a trade – around the cathedral.

Plaza de la Virgen Blanca (BZ 55) – The square, dominated by the Iglesia de San Miguel (St Michael's Church), is surrounded by house fronts with glassed-in balconies or *miradores*, framing the massive monument at the square's centre which commemorates Wellington's decisive victory at the Battle of Vitoria on 21 June 1813, after which King Joseph and 55 000 of his men fled north of the Pyrenees. The square communicates with the nobly ordered 18C **Plaza de España** also known as **Plaza Nueva (BZ 18)**.

Iglesia de San Miguel (BZ) – A jasper niche in the church porch exterior contains the polychrome statue in late Gothic style of the Virgen Blanca, patron of the city. The church is entered through a late-14C portal. Its tympanum illustrates the Life of St Michael as does the 17C chancel altarpiece carved by Gregorio Fernández *(qv)*.

Plaza del Machete (BZ 30) – The square lies at the back of the **Arquillos**, a tall arcade which links the upper and lower towns. A niche in the east end of San Miguel church formerly contained the *machete* or cutlass, on which the procurator general had to swear to uphold the town's privileges *(fueros)*.

Museo "Fournier" de Naipes (Playing Cards Museum) (BY M⁴) – Housed in the Palacio de Bendaña. Félix Alfaro Fournier, grandson of the founder of the playing cards factory, has assembled a valuable collection of playing cards which was acquired by the City Council of Álava in 1986. The present collection, from all over the world, numbers over 15 000 packs, dating from the late 14C to the present day illustrating history (wars, battles, revolutions), geography, politics (caricatures of personalities) and local customs (traditional dress and pastimes). There is also a display of a variety of materials (paper, parchment, cloth, metal, etc.) demonstrating printing and engraving techniques.

Catedral de Santa María (BY) ⊘ – 14C. The north wall of the cathedral still has a fortified appearance. The west door is covered by Gothic vaulting in which the ribs radiate with a sunburst effect from behind large statues. A polychrome *Virgin and Child* stands at the central pier. The tympana over the 14C Gothic doorways illustrate the lives of the saints most venerated in Spain, namely Lawrence, Ildefonso, James (right portal) and Nicholas and Peter (left portal).

Inside, in a chapel off the south aisle, there is a striking portrayal of the Martyrdom of St Bartholomew. One of the pillar capitals between the nave and the south aisle shows a bullfighting scene – a carving unique in a church even in Spain! In the south transept are a Plateresque altarpiece in polychrome wood and a painting by the 17C artist, Carreño *(qv)*, the *Immaculate Conception;* in the north arm are an interesting *Descent from the Cross* by Gaspar de Crayer (17C) and a polychrome stone tympanum from the original church. A decorative Plateresque funerary stone can be seen inlaid into the wall of a chapel near the entrance.

Museo de Arqueología (Archaeological Museum) (BY M¹) ⊘ – The museum in a 16C half-timbered and brick house, displays finds from excavations in Álava province, covering the period from the Palaeolithic to the Middle Ages. Note the dolmen collections, particularly that of Eguilaz *(30km - 19 miles east on the N 1)* and the Roman steles and sculptures including the **Estela del Jinete★** (Knight's stele) from Iruña. The **Portalón restaurant (BY L)** facing the museum, installed in a 15C house, displays, in a shop, stables and a cellar, all manner of old country instruments and utensils.

CIUDAD NUEVA (MODERN TOWN)

As Vitoria grew in the 18C, neo-classical constructions began to appear such as the **Arquillos** arcade *(see above)* and **Plaza Nueva**. In the 19C, the town expanded southwards with the **Parque de la Florida** (Florida Park) (**AZ**) – near to which the **Catedral Nueva** (New Cathedral) (**AZ N**) was built in 1907 – and two wide avenues: the Paseo de la Senda and the Paseo de Fray Francisco. The latter was built up in the late 19C-early 20C with mansions and large town houses, one of which, the Palacio de Ajuria Enea, is now the seat of the Lehendakari or Basque government.

Museo de Bellas Artes (Fine Arts Museum) (**AZ M²**) ⊘ – The museum, housed in the neo-Renaissance Palacio de Agustí, displays painting and sculpture from the 14C to the present day.

On the first floor landing are interesting wood reliefs from Erenchun and a 16C collection of Flemish triptychs and reliquaries. In the galleries to the left are a *Descent from the Cross* by a painter of the Flemish school, a series of five 16C reliquary busts influenced by the Rhenish school and, in rooms devoted to the baroque period, canvases by Ribera *(qv)*, Alonso Cano *(qv)* and Carreño de Miranda *(qv)*.

The museum also has a comprehensive section on **Basque painting** with works by Iturrino, Regoyos *(qv)*, Zubiaurre and Zuloaga *(qv)* and a rich collection of **contemporary Spanish art** since 1950 (Miró, Tàpies, Millares and Serrano).

★ **Museo de Armería (Museum of Arms and Armour)** (**AZ M³**) ⊘ – The well-presented collection housed in a modern building traces the evolution of weaponry from prehistoric axes to early-20C pistols. Note the 15 to 17C **armour**, including suits of 17C Japanese armour, and a model of the Battle of Vitoria.

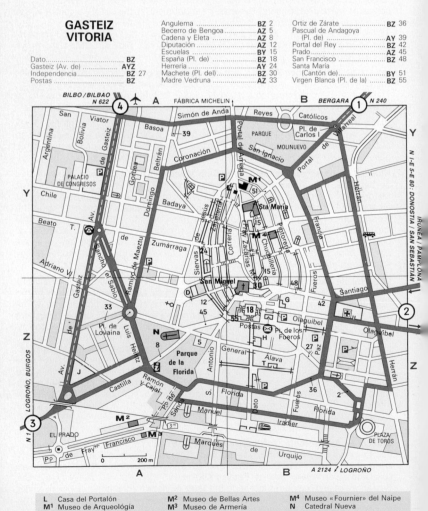

L Casa del Portalón
M¹ Museo de Arqueología
M² Museo de Bellas Artes
M³ Museo de Armería
M⁴ Museo «Fournier» del Naipe
N Catedral Nueva

EXCURSIONS

Tour east of Vitoria – *25km - 16 miles. Leave Vitoria by ② on the town plan.*

★ **Gaceo** – Superb 14C **Gothic frescoes** ★ decorate the chancel of the church **(iglesia** ⊘**)**. The south wall shows hell in the form of a whale's gullet, the north, the Life of the Virgin with the Crucifixion at the centre and Christ in Majesty above. On the roof are scenes from the Life of Christ.

Alaiza – In 1982 obscure paintings were discovered on the walls and roof of the church **(iglesia** ⊘**)** apse. The paintings, which probably date from the late 14C, consist of a series of rough red outlines representing castles, churches, soldiers and many other personages. They remain an enigma.

Santuario de Estíbaliz – *10km - 6 miles east. Leave Vitoria by ② on the town plan and then take the C 132. Bear left after 4km - 2 1/2 miles.*
The shrine, a popular pilgrimage with the Basques, comprises a late Romanesque sanctuary **(santuario** ⊘**)**. The south front has an attractive wall belfry. Inside, the Romanesque statue of the Virgin has been restored.

Tour west of Vitoria – *105km - 65 miles. Leave Vitoria by Calle Tomás de Zumárraga* (**AY**) *then bear left into the L 621.*

Mendoza – In the heart of the village stands the Castillo de Mendoza, a fortress with embrasures, a stout outer wall lacking battlements but flanked by four towers. This former residence of the Duke of Infantado is now the **Museo de Heráldica Alavesa** (Álava Heraldry Museum) ⊘ with a collection of the coats of arms of all the nobility of the region. The castle commands a view of the plateau.

Head back to the N1 and bear right into the L 622 towards Pobes.

Salinas de Añana – The salt-pans rising in tiers up the hillside in the form of an amphitheatre next to the village produce a most unusual effect – water from several local springs is channelled between the ridges. The **church** contains a Flemish picture of the *Annunciation* with sensitively painted faces. At Easter all the salt makers walk in a procession known traditionally as the "Quema de Judas."

Tuesta – The **Romanesque church**, dating from the 13C and later modified, has an interesting portal with a pointed arch and a decoration of archivolts and historiated capitals, one of which shows a man hunting a boar (left). Above is the Epiphany. Inside, note the naïve wood sculpture of St Sebastian *(north wall of the nave)* and a 14C figure of the Virgin.

Take the N 625 north towards Orduña.

Once over the **Puerto de Orduña** (Orduña Pass) (900m - 2953ft), a beautiful **panorama** ★ opens up of the lush hollow in which Orduña town nestles; in the distance are Amurrio and the Basque mountains *(viewpoint)*. The descent to the plain is down a series of hairpin bends.

Take the C 6210 and return to Vitoria via Murguia.

ZAFRA

Extremadura (Badajoz)
Population 14065
Michelin map 444 Q 10 – Michelin Atlas España Portugal p 61

A 15C *alcázar* (now a *parador*) stands guard at the entrance to this white-walled town, one of the oldest in Extremadura. It was built by the Dukes of Feria with nine round towers crowned by pyramid shaped merlons. The white marble *patio* is Renaissance and the delightful gilded saloon, Mudéjar.
Zafra's cattle fairs are famous locally, especially the Feria de San Miguel (St Michael's Fair) during the week of 5 October.

★ **The squares** – The town's two squares, the large 18C **Plaza Grande** and the adjoining and much smaller 16C **Plaza Chica**, with their fine arcaded houses, form an attractive precinct.

Iglesia de la Candelaria ⊘ – The 16C church in transitional Gothic-Renaissance style can be identified by its massive red brick belfry. In the shallow south transept there stands an **altarpiece** by Zurbarán *(qv)* painted in 1644.

EXCURSION

Llerena – *42km - 26 miles southeast.*
The **Plaza Mayor** of this modest country town is one of the most monumental in all Extremadura. On one side stands the **Iglesia de Nuestra Señora de Granada** (Church of Our Lady of Granada) in which the composite façade is harmonised by the colourful interplay of white limestone and brick; the delicacy of two superimposed arcades contrasts with the mass of a great baroque belfry. A pomegranate – *granada* in Spanish – decorates the escutcheon on the tympanum over the main door.

ZAMORA★

Castilla y León
Population 68 202
Michelin map 441 H12 – Michelin Atlas España Portugal p 23

Only traces remain of the walls which made Zamora the westerly bastion of the fortified Duero line during the Reconquest. The town played its part in the repeated struggles for the throne of Castilla: in the 11C when Sancho III's sons fought for his kingdom, and in the 15C, when La Beltraneja unsuccessfully disputed the rights of Isabel the Catholic.

Semana Santa (Holy Week) – Zamora's Holy Week solemn celebrations are renowned for the numbers who attend and for the spectacular *pasos* street processions. On Palm Sunday a children's procession escorts a *paso* of Christ's entry into Jerusalem; on Maundy Thursday evening a totally silent, torchlight procession follows the poignant *Dead Christ*, a sculpture by Gregorio Fernández *(qv)*, borne by white-robed penitents through the streets in imitation of the walk to Golgotha. Most of these *pasos* may be seen in the **Museo de la Semana Santa (B M¹)** ⊘.

SIGHTS

★**Catedral (A)** ⊘ – The cathedral was built between 1151 and 1174 and was subsequently given additions and alterations.

The north front is neo-classical in keeping with the square it overlooks; it contrasts, however, with the Romanesque **bell-tower** and the graceful cupola covered in scallop tiling which recalls the Torre del Gallo in Salamanca *(qv)*. The south front, the only original part of the building, has blind arcades and a Romanesque portal with unusual covings featuring openwork festoons.

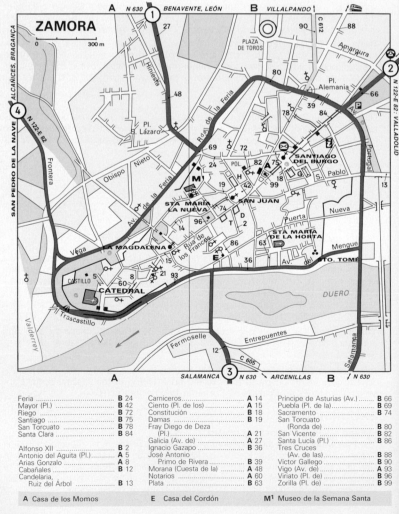

Cupola with scallop tiling, Catedral de Zamora

The aisles are transitional Romanesque-Gothic, the vaulting ranging from broken barrel to pointed ogive. Slender painted ribs support the luminous **dome★** on squinches above the transept. At the end of the Gothic period, master wood carvers and wrought-iron smiths worked in the church – there are fine **grilles** enclosing the *coro*, two 15C Mudéjar pulpits and **choir-stalls★★**, decorated with Biblical figures on their backs and with allegorical and burlesque scenes on armrests and misericords.

Museo Catedralicio (Cathedral Museum) ⊘ – The museum, off the Herreran-style cathedral cloisters, displays a collection of 15C Flemish **tapestries★★** illustrating the life of Tarquin and the Trojan War; others, dating from the 17C, are of Hannibal's campaigns.

The **Jardín del Castillo** (Castle Garden) (**A**) behind the cathedral, commands fine **views** of the Duero river below.

★**Romanesque churches** – The 12C saw a series of originally designed Romanesque churches built in Zamora province. Particular features included portals without tympana, surrounded by multifoil arches and often possessing heavily carved archivolts; the larger churches also had domes on squinches over the transept crossing. The best examples of the style in Zamora are the **Magdalena** (**A**), **Santa María la Nueva** (**B**), **San Juan** (**B**), **Santa María de la Orta** (**B**), **Santo Tomé** (**B**) and **Santiago del Burgo** (**B**).

Seignorial mansions – **Casa del Cordón** (**B E**) and **Casa de los Momos** (**B A**) have elegant Isabelline windows.

EXCURSIONS

★**San Pedro de la Nave** – *19km - 12 miles northwest. Leave Zamora by* ④ *on the town plan. Follow the N 122 for 12km - 7 miles then turn right.*
The Visigothic church (**iglesia** ⊘), in danger of being submerged on account of the damming of the Esla, has been rebuilt at El Campillo. It is late 7C and is artistically remarkable for the carving on the transept **capitals** with its a strong sense of composition: Daniel in the Lions' Den, the Sacrifice of Isaac, etc. The frieze, halfway up the wall, presents Christian symbols including grapes and doves.

Arcenillas – *7km - 4 miles southeast on the C 605* (**B**).
Fifteen **panels★** of the life, death and resurrection of Christ from the great Gothic altarpiece designed for Zamora cathedral by the late-15C artist **Fernando Gallego** *(qv)*, one of the greatest painters to adopt the Hispano-Flemish style, have been reassembled in the village church (**iglesia** ⊘).

Benavente – *66km - 41 miles north. Leave Zamora by* ① *on the town map and take the N 630.*
During the Middle Ages the town was a prosperous commercial centre. Several fine monuments from that period remain.
The Renaissance style **Castillo de los Condes de Pimentel** (Castle of the Counts of Pimentel), now a *parador*, has preserved its 16C Torre del Caracol (snail-shell tower). From the terrace are **views** of the valley.
The transitional **Iglesia de Santa María del Azogue** is a church with a wide east end with five apses and two Romanesque portals typical of the local Zamora style. Inside, a beautiful 13C *Annunciation* stands at the transept crossing.
The **Iglesia de San Juan del Mercado** has a 12C carving on the south portal illustrating the journey of the Magi.

ZARAGOZA★★

SARAGOSSA – Aragón
Population 622 371
Michelin map 443 H 27 – Michelin Atlas España Portugal p 29
Plan of the conurbation in the current Michelin Red Guide España Portugal

Zaragoza is a warm brick agglomeration lying between its two cathedrals and spreading down into the Ebro basin of which it is the capital. It occupies a privileged position at the centre of the vast depression, once an arid desert and now a fertile plain, watered by the three rivers which meet in it and the nearby imperial canal now used for irrigation. Sugar refining and textiles are staple industries in the local economy which is being developed and diversified.

The city was largely rebuilt in the 19C after the War of Independence and although not especially striking, pleases on account of its historic monuments and the bustling life along its modern boulevards.

Zaragoza is both a major university and religious centre, veneration of the Virgen del Pilar (Virgin of the Pillar) making it the leading Marian shrine in Spain.

The Pilar festivals – In the week of 12 October, Zaragozans extol "their" Virgin with incredible pomp and fervour: on the 13th at about 7pm the **Rosario de Cristal** procession moves off by the light of 350 carriage-borne lanterns. Other festivals during the week include the **Gigantes y Cabezudos** procession (cardboard giants and dwarfs with massive heads), jota dancing and the famous bullfights.

HISTORICAL NOTES

Caesaraugusta-Sarakusta – Salduba, well situated at the confluence of the Ebro and its tributaries, the Gállego and the Huerva, became, in the year 25 BC, a Roman colony named Caesaraugusta after the Emperor Caesar Augustus. On 2 January in AD 40, according to tradition, the Virgin appeared miraculously to St James, leaving as proof of her apparition the pillar around which the **Basílica de Nuestra Señora del Pilar** was later built. In the 3C the city is said to have suffered persecution at the hands of Diocletian – it still honours from that time the memory of the Uncounted Martyrs, interred in the crypt of **Santa Engracia** (**Z**).

Four centuries of Muslim occupation would appear to have left the city, renamed Sarakusta, with but a single major heirloom. From the brilliant but shortlived *taifa* kingdom *(qv)* established under the Benihud dynasty in the 11C, there remains the **Aljafería**, a palace, built by the first monarch of the line and a unique and very precious example of Hispano-Muslim art.

Zaragoza, capital city – The Aragón kings, after freeing the city from the Moors, proclaimed Zaragoza, the great agricultural town on the Ebro, as capital. The city, however, jealous of its autonomy, voted itself the most democratic *Fueros* in the whole of Spain and increased its prosperity through wise administration and the establishment of the **Lonja** (Commodities Exchange). Tolerant by tradition, it protected its Muslim masons, so that the Mudéjar style could be used to embellish its churches: the apse of **La Seo** (Cathedral), **San Pablo** (**Y**) and **Magdalena** (**Z**) towers. Houses in the old town with elegant *patios* and *artesonado* ceilings give a good idea of the city's prosperity in the 16C.

Two heroic sieges – Zaragoza's resistance before Napoleon's army in the terrible years 1808-9 shows the Spanish people's desire for independence and the determination of those of Aragón in particular.

In June 1808 the city was invested for the first time by the French, the siege only being lifted on 14 August. The exultant Zaragozans sang "The Virgin of Pilar will never be French." Alas! On 21 December General Lannes appeared with his men who remained until the town capitulated on 20 February. By the end, half the inhabitants, some 54 000, had died. From that appalling siege there remains the shrapnel pitted **Puerta del Carmen** (Carmen Gate) (**Z**).

SIGHTS

★★ **La Seo** (**Y**) ⊘ – The Cathedral of Zaragoza, La Seo, remarkable for its size, includes all the decorative styles from the Mudéjar to the Churrigueresque, although it is basically Gothic in design. In the 17C, the tall belfry which harmonises with those on the Pilar cathedral nearby, was added; in the 18C the Seo was given a baroque façade. Walk into Calle del Sepulcro to see the Mudéjar decoration on the **east end**.

The interior is impressive with its five aisles of equal height. Above the high altar is a Gothic **retable**★ with a predella carved by the Catalan, Pere Johan, and the three central panels of the Ascension, Epiphany and the Transfiguration sculpted by Hans of Swabia (the stance of the figures and the modelling of the faces and robes strike a German note).

The **surrounding wall of the chancel** (trascoro) and some of the side chapels were adorned in the 16C with groups of carved figures, clear evidence of the vitality of Spanish sculpture during the Renaissance. Other chapels, ornamented in the 18C,

ZARAGOZA

Alfonso I .... **YZ**
Alonso V .... **Z** 6
Conde de Aranda .... **YZ**
Coso .... **Z**

Don Jaime I .... **YZ**
Independencia (Av.) .... **Z**
San Vicente de Paúl .... **YZ**

Candalija .... **Z** 10
Capitán Portolés .... **Z** 13
César Augusto (Av.) .... **Z** 15

Cinco de Marzo .... **Z** 18
Magdalena .... **Z** 42
Manifestación .... **V** 43
Sancho y Gil .... **Z** 58
San Pedro Nolasco (Pl. de)...... **Z** 63
Teniente Coronel
   Valenzuela.......................... **Z** 67

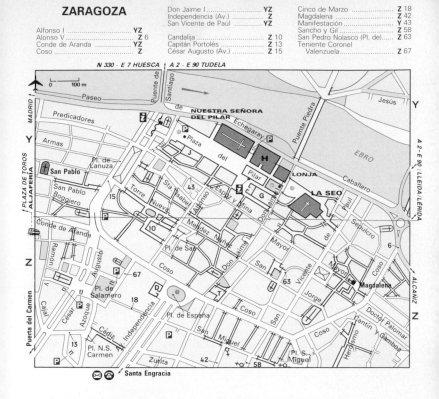

show the all too excessive exuberance of the Churrigueresque style; one exception
is the **Parroquieta**, a Gothic chapel containing a 14C tomb influenced by the
Burgundian style and, in particular, a **cupola**★ in the Moorish style, in polychrome
wood with stalactites and strapwork (15C).

★ **Museo Capitular** (Chapter Museum) – *In the sacristy.* Exhibited are paintings, an
enamel triptych, religious objects and a large amount of church plate including
silver reliquaries, chalices and an enormous processional monstrance made up of
24000 pieces.

★★ **Museo de Tapices** (Tapistry Museum) – An outstanding collection of Gothic hangings.
All were woven in Arras or Brussels; titles include the *Sailing Ships*, the *Crucifixion*
and the *Passion*.

★ **Lonja (Exchange)** (**Y**) ⊘ – Zaragoza, like the other major trading towns of Valencia,
Barcelona and Palma de Mallorca in the Kingdom of Aragón, founded a commercial exchange as early as the 16C. These buildings, in a transitional style between
Gothic and Plateresque, include some of the finest examples of civil architecture
in Spain. In this instance the vast hall is divided into three by tall columns, their
shafts ornamented with a carved band of grotesques. Coats of arms supported by
cherubim mark the start of the ribs which open out into star **vaulting**.
The **Ayuntamiento** (Town Hall) (**Y H**) has been rebuilt in traditional Aragón style with
ornate eaves. Two modern bronzes stand at the entrance.

★ **Basílica de Nuestra Señora del Pilar** (Our Lady of the Pillar Basilica) (**Y**) ⊘ – Several
sanctuaries have been built successively on this site to enshrine the miraculous
pillar. The present building, Zaragoza's second cathedral, was designed by
Francisco Herrera the Younger in about 1677. It takes the form of a buttressed
quadrilateral lit by a central dome. The cupolas, with small lantern towers, whose
ornamental tiles may be seen reflected in the waters of the Ebro, were added by
Ventura Rodríguez in the 18C.
The interior is divided into three aisles by giant pillars with fluted pilasters. Some
of the frescoes decorating the cupolas were painted by Goya as a young man.
The **Capilla de la Virgen** (Lady Chapel) by Ventura Rodríguez is, in fact, virtually a
miniature church on its own. It contains in a niche on the right, the pillar and a
Gothic wood statue of the Virgin. The Virgin's mantle is changed every day except
on the 2nd of the month, the anniversary of the apparition (2 January) and the
12th of the month, that of the Hispanidad (12 October). Pilgrims go to kiss the
pillar through an opening behind.
The **high altar** in the centre of the church is surmounted by a **retable**★ carved by
Damián Forment of which the predella is outstanding. The **coro** is closed by a high
grille and adorned with Plateresque stalls.

★ **Museo Pilarista** ("Pilar" Museum) ⊘ – Displayed are the sketches made by Goya, González Velázquez and Bayeu for the cupolas of Our Lady of the Pillar, a model by Ventura Rodríguez and some of the jewels which adorn the Virgin during the "Pilar" festivals. Among the very old ivory pieces are an 11C hunting horn and a Moorish jewellery box.

★ **Aljafería** ⊘ – *Access by Calle Conde de Aranda* (**Z**). The Aljafería, a Moorish palace built in the 11C by the Benihud family, was rearranged to serve as a palace for the Aragón kings and Catholic Monarchs before being taken over by the Inquisition and later converted into a barracks. The enormous building, so closely resembling the Muslim-style mansions of Andalucía, comes as a surprise so far north.

The Moorish palace is centred around a rectangular *patio* bordered by porticoes with delicate tracery and carved capitals. The **musallah**, a form of private mosque for the emirs, has been restored complete with *mihrab (qv)* and all the accustomed Moorish fantasy of multifoil arches and floral decoration. The stuccowork is brightly painted.

The first floor and the staircase transport the visitor 400 years ahead to the sumptuous style of the Catholic Monarchs when Flamboyant Gothic reigned supreme. Only the ornate **ceiling**★, its cells divided by geometric interlacing and decorated with fir cones, remains, however, of the throne room. Another *artesonado* ceiling can be seen in the room in which **Santa Isabel**, daughter of Pedro III of Aragón and future Queen of Portugal, was born in 1271.

EXCURSION

Fuendetodos – *45km - 28 miles southwest. Take the N 330 and after 21km – 13 miles bear left into the Z 100.*
It was in a modest house (**Casa de Goya** ⊘ – *open to the public*) in this village that the great painter **Francisco Goya y Lucientes** was born in 1746. The **Museo de Grabados** (Engravings Museum) ⊘ next door displays a collection of his work in this field.

National parks

Areas are designated national parks with a view to protecting particularly beautiful or unusual, but often also fragile, natural environments, whilst contributing to the local economy by encouraging tourism. Visitors are able to learn about nature and also how to show their appreciation of it by treating it with respect.

Spain has ten national parks, of which
– five are in mainland Spain:

Los Picos de Europa, founded in 1995, with an area of 64 660ha - 159 780 acres (incorporating the old Montaña de Covadonga national park in the west of the Picos de Europa, founded in 1918, with an area of 17 000ha - 42 000 acres);

Ordesa y Monte Perdido (Spanish central Pyrenees), founded in 1918, with an area of 15 608ha - 38 569 acres;

Aigüestortes y Lago Sant Maurici (Catalan Pyrenees), with an area of 10 230ha - 25 279 acres;

Tablas de Daimiel (La Mancha), with an area of 1 928ha - 4 764 acres;

Doñana (Andalucía), with an area of 50 720ha - 125 332 acres;

– four are in the Canaries:

Teide (Tenerife);

Caldera de Taburiente (La Palma);

Timanfaya (Lanzarote);

Garajonay (Gomera);

– and one is in the Balearics:

Cabrera (small island south of Mallorca).

West coast, Mallorca

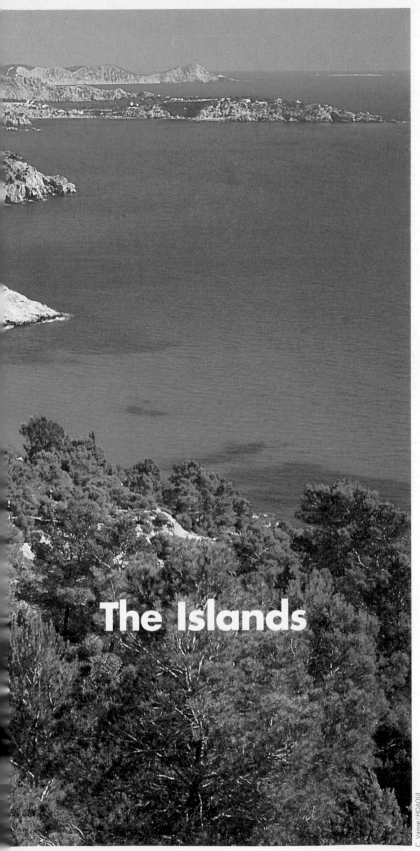

The Islands

Islas Baleares
Balearic Islands

The Balearic Archipelago covers a land area of 5 000km² - 1 900sq miles and is made up of three large islands – Mallorca, Menorca and Ibiza, – two small ones – Formentera and Cabrera – as well as many islets. The Comunidad Autónoma Balear (Balearic Autonomous Community) is one of Spain's 50 provinces, with Palma de Mallorca as administrative capital. The language, Balearic, is derived from Catalan but has kept ancient roots (such as the articles *Se*, *Sa* and *Ses* from the Latin *Ipse*).

The three larger islands differ considerably in landscape, history and lifestyle, a fact borne out by, among other things, the different architectural traditions on each island. *(See Regions and Landscape in the Introduction and the detailed description of each island below).*

Mallorca★★★
ISLAND OF MAJORCA

Michelin map 443 M, N, O 36-40 – Michelin Atlas España Portugal pp 90-91

Mallorca, the largest of the Islas Baleares, has an area of 3 640km² - 1 405sq miles and measures some 75km - 47 miles from north to south and 100km - 62 miles from east to west. It has a population of 602 074.

The scenery, the mild climate and the hotel infrastructure, make the island a major European tourist centre.

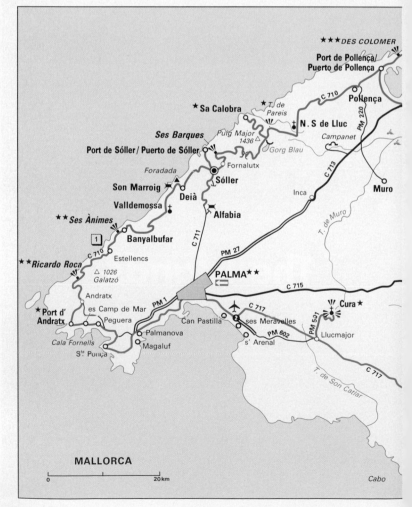

MALLORCA

Landscape – A relief map of Mallorca shows three different zones:

The **Sierra de Tramuntana** in the northwest rises in limestone crests – the highest is **Puig Major** (1 436m - 4 711ft) – running parallel to the coast. In spite of its low altitude, the chain, its cliffs plunging spectacularly into the sea, forms a solid rock barrier against offshore winds from the mainland. Pines, junipers and holm oaks cover the slopes, interspersed here and there by the gnarled and twisted trunks of Mallorca's famous olive trees. Villages, perched halfway up hillsides, are surrounded by terraces planted with vegetables and fruit trees.

The central plain, **El Pla**, is divided by low walls into arable fields and fig and almond orchards; the market towns, with outlying windmills to pump water, retain the regular plan of medieval fortress towns.

The **Sierras de Levante** to the east have been scoured by erosion, hollowed out into wonderful caves. The coast is rocky and indented with sheltered, sand-carpeted coves.

The short-lived Kingdom of Mallorca (1262-1349) – On 5 September 1229, James (Jaime) I of Aragón set sail from Salou to recapture Mallorca, an important commercial bastion in the Mediterranean, from the Muslims, hoping to quell unrest among his nobles by offering them land. The decisive battle took place in the Bay of Palma on 31 December 1229.

Thirty years later the Conqueror united Mallorca-Baleares, Roussillon and Montpellier in a single independent kingdom which he presented to his son, James II. He and his successor, Sancho, brought prosperity to the island, founding new towns, building strongpoints and peopling the territory with Catalan immigrants. Nor did it apparently suffer when Pedro IV seized the archipelago in 1343, killing the young prince at Llucmajor, to reunite it to the crown of Aragón.

Churches were built, a merchant navy was established which brought local prosperity and a school of cartography founded which rapidly became famous.

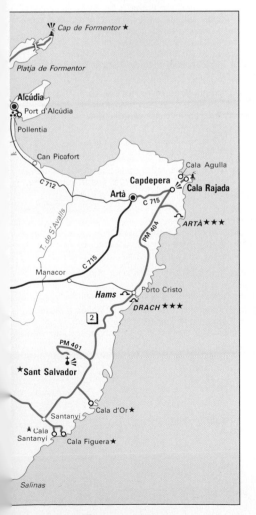

The Mallorcan Primitives (14-15C) – Gothic Mallorcan painting, characterised by a marked gentleness of expression, was wide open to external influences: the so-called **Master of Privileges** (Maestro de los Privilegios) showed, even in the 14C, a Sienese preference for miniaturisation and warm colours; later, both **Joan Daurer** and the talented **Maestro de Obispo Galiana** became inspired by Catalan painting; the end of the century saw the assertion of personal characteristics in **Francesch Comes**, whose mannerism was to portray figures with full lips.

In the 15C, artists on the island included some who had studied in Valencia such as **Gabriel Moger**, the suave **Miguel de Alcanyis** and **Martí Torner**. The **Maestro de Predellas** is distinguishable by his attention to detail, **Rafael Moger** by his realism. There were also two master painters, both from abroad, **Pedro (Pere) Nisart** and **Alonso de Sedano**, who introduced the Flemish style which was to dominate Mallorcan painting in the 16C (see the Museo de Mallorca in Palma).

Famous Mallorcans and illustrious visitors – **Ramón Llull** (1232-1316) is a good example of the cosmopolitan outlook of Mallorca in the 13C. A reformed libertine, he became a great humanist, learning foreign languages and studying philosophy, theology and alchemy. A defender of the Christian faith, he travelled widely and was later beatified.

Fray Junípero Serra (1713-1783) left to do missionary work in California, where he founded a number of missions including those of San Francisco and San Diego. He was beatified in 1988.

Among the foreign writers, poets and savants to visit the island in the 19C, were **Frédéric Chopin** and **George Sand** who spent the winter of 1838 in the Cartuja de Valldemossa (Valldemosa Carthusian Monastery) *(qv)*.

Robert Graves (1895-1985), the strongly individualistic English poet, novelist and critic whose works include *I, Claudius, Good-bye to All That* and *The White Goddess*, lived (as of 1929) and died here.

The Austrian Archduke, **Ludwig Salvator** (1847-1915), spent most of his 53 years' stay on the west coast where he compiled the most detailed study ever made of the archipelago. He was patron to the French speleologist, E.A. Martel, who explored many of the island's caves in 1896.

Economy – Tourism is the major force in the economy, with shoe manufacturing second and an artificial pearl industry at Manacor now finding foreign outlets. Horticulture supplies the fresh fruit canning and dried fruit industries (figs and apricots) while the almond crop is largely exported.

Ensaimada, a light spiral roll dusted with sugar, and **sobrasada,** a hot pork sausage, are the tasty, local specialities.

ALCÚDIA

Population 8 004
Local map under MALLORCA

Alcúdia, still encircled by 14C ramparts, guards access to the promontory which divides the Bahía de Pollença (Pollença Bay) from that of Alcúdia. The **Puerta del Muelle** or **Xara** (Quai Gate), which led to the harbour, and the **Puerta de San Sebastián** or **Puerta de Mallorca** on the other side of town, remain of the early fortified walls and were reconstructed and incorporated into the ramparts when they were strengthened in the 14C. The streets in the shadow of the walls have a distinctive medieval air as have the town's houses, brightened by Renaissance surrounds to their windows.

1.5km - 1 mile south is the site of the ancient Roman town of **Pollentia** founded in the 2C BC. All that remains of the city are the theatre ruins.

Museo monográfico de Pollentia (Pollentia Monographic Museum) ⊘ – A chapel in Alcúdia's old quarter houses the museum with its collections of statues, oil lamps, bronzes and jewellery from the site of the ancient city of Pollentia.

EXCURSIONS

Port de Alcudia – *2km - 1 mile east.*
The port of Alcúdia overlooks a vast bay built up with hotels and tower blocks. A long beach stretches away to the south as far as Can Picafort. The marshy hinterland of La Albufera is a nature reserve.

Cuevas de Campanet (Campanet Caves) ⊘ – *17km - 11 miles southwest along the C 713 and a secondary, signposted road.*
The caves were discovered in 1947. About half the caves along the 1 300m - 1 500yds long path have ceased formation, their massive concretions now totally dry. In the area still waterlogged, straight and delicate stalactites predominate.

Muro – *Take the C 713 southwest for 11km - 7 miles and then bear left for another 7km - 4 miles via Sa Pobla.*
The road crosses countryside bristling with windmills.

Sección etnológica del Museo de Mallorca (Ethnological Section of the Mallorca Museum) ⊘ – The museum, in a large 17C nobleman's residence, displays collections of traditional furniture, dress and farm implements as well as an old pharmacy and island ceramics including *Xiurels* whistles.
An annexe houses exhibitions on various craftsmen: a blacksmith, cabinetmaker, gilder, engraver, welder, goldsmith and cobbler.

Help us in our constant task of keeping up to date.
Send your comments and suggestions to

Michelin Tyre PLC
Tourism Department
The Edward Hyde Building
38 Clarendon Road
WATFORD Herts WD1 1SX
Fax: 01923 415250

PALMA DE MALLORCA★★

Population 308 616
Local map under MALLORCA
Plan of the conurbation in the current Michelin Red Guide España Portugal

The visitor who has the good fortune to arrive in Palma by boat, discovers a city spread across the curve of a wide bay, its proud cathedral standing guard as in foregone days of maritime glory. The town's many ancient buildings testify to its former heyday. The city's residential quarters with their hotels stretch out on either side of the historic centre and along the seafront, in Avinguda Gabriel Roca, shaded by palms, which leads to the harbours. The old harbour, bordered by Passeig Sagrera, serves both passenger and merchant ships.The new harbour, at the southern tip of Terreno quarter, accommodates the largest liners.

The Bahía de Palma – The bay, protected from north and west winds by the Puig Major range, has a mild climate all the year round. Hotels and tourist apartment blocks stretch along the seafront for 20km - 12 miles. To the west, the hotels stand along the indented Bendinat coastline where there is little sand, except at the two beach areas of **Palmanova** and **Magaluf.** The coast to the east is less sheltered, being straight, but has mile upon mile of fine sand with a series of resorts – **Can Pastilla, ses Meravelles** and **s'Arenal** whose beaches are known collectively as the Platjas de Palma.

The "Ciutat de Mallorca" – This was the name by which the city was known after its liberation on 31 December 1229 and during its most prosperous period when trade links were forged with Barcelona, Valencia, the countries of Africa and the kingdoms of northern Europe; Jews and Genoese established colonies in the town, the latter even founding an exchange, and James II (Jaime II) and his successors endowed the city with beautiful Gothic buildings. Finally, the Aragón policy of expansion in Naples and Sicily, enabled Palma to extend her commercial interests also.

PALMA DE MALLORCA

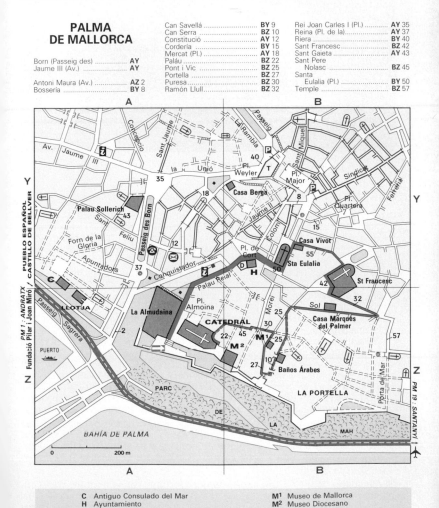

C Antiguo Consulado del Mar	**M¹** Museo de Mallorca
H Ayuntamiento	**M²** Museo Diocesano

Palma's old mansions – In the 15 and 16C, the great families of Palma, descended from rich merchants and members of the aristocracy, favoured the Italian style. They built elegant residences with stone façades, relieved by windows with Renaissance style decoration. It was only in the 18C that a characteristic Mallorcan *casa* (house) appeared with an inner court of massive marble columns, wide shallow arches and incorporating stone steps to a high and graceful loggia. Balustrades of stone or wrought-iron completed the decoration. The same families built themselves luxurious summer villas in the mountains to the north of Palma.

Palma today – The city in which more than half of the island's population lives, has the greatest number of visitors of any town in Spain (more than 4.5 million in 1994). Tourists congregate in and around the **Terreno** – especially in Plaza Gomila – and **Cala Major** quarters in the west of town, but the native heart of the city, remains the Passeig des Born. This wide *rambla*, known as **El Born** (**AY**), followed the course of the Riera river before this was diverted in the 16C to run outside the walls on account of its devastating floodwaters. The shops selling pearls, glassware, leather goods, clothes and local craftwork are in the old town east of El Born in pedestrian streets around Plaça Major and in Avinguda Jaime III.

The cathedral, Palma de Mallorca

★BARRIO DE LA CATEDRAL (CATHEDRAL QUARTER) *time: 3 hours*

★★**Catedral** (**AZ**) ⊙ – The bold yet elegant cathedral, its tall buttresses surmounted by pinnacles, rises above the seafront. The Santany limestone of its walls changes colour according to the time of day: ochre, golden or pink. The cathedral, which was begun in the early 14C on the site of a former mosque, is one of the greatest constructions of the late Gothic period.

The west face was rebuilt in neo-Gothic style in the 19C after an earthquake but its 16C Renaissance portal has remained intact. The south door, known as the **Portada del Mirador** (Viewpoint Doorway), overlooks the sea, the delicate Gothic decoration dating from the 15C preserved beneath a porch. On the tympanum is a scene of the Last Supper while the statues of Saints Peter and Paul on either side prove that Sagrera, architect of the Llotja (Exchange), was also a talented sculptor. The **interior** is both large and light, measuring 121m x 55m - 397ft x 180ft with a height of 44m - 144ft to the top of the vaulting above the nave. 14 tall, incredibly slender octagonal pillars divide the nave from the aisles. The lack of adornment increases the impression of spaciousness. The Capilla Mayor or Real (Royal Chapel), itself the size of a church, contains at its centre an enormous wrought-iron baldachin by Gaudí (1912) with Renaissance choir-stalls on either side. The tombs of the Kings of Mallorca, Jaime II and Jaime III, lie in the Capilla de la Trinidad (Trinity Chapel).

Museo-Tesoro (Treasury Museum) ⊙ – The Gothic chapter house contains the Santa Eulalia altarpiece by the Maestro de los Privilegios *(qv)* (1335). In the oval, baroque chapter house are a number of reliquaries including that of the True Cross, decorated with precious stones. There are also two baroque candelabra in embossed silver by Joan Matons.

La Almudaina (**AZ**) ⊙ – This ancient Moorish fortress, dating from the Walis' caliphate, was converted in the 14 and 15C by the Kings of Mallorca into a royal palace. Today, as one of the official residences of the King of Spain, several rooms have recently been restored and elegantly furnished with Flemish tapestries, clocks and paintings. In the courtyard, note the carved overhanging eaves and the doorway of the Iglesia de Santa Ana (St Anne's Church), one of the rare examples of Romanesque architecture in the Balearics. There is a 15C altarpiece inside.

Ayuntamiento (Town Hall) (BY H) ⊙ – Carved wood eaves overhang the 17C façade.

Iglesia de Santa Eulalia (BY) ⊙ – 13-15C. The tall nave is unusually bare for a Gothic church. The first chapel off the south aisle contains a 15C altarpiece.
Between the churches of Santa Eulalia and Sant Francesc, at no 2 Carrer Savellá, is the 18C **Casa Vivot**, its beautiful *patio* decorated with marble columns.

Iglesia de Sant Francesc (BY) ⊙ – 13-14C. The church's façade, rebuilt in the late 17C, has an immense Plateresque rose window and a baroque portal with a beautifully carved tympanum by Francisco Herrera *(qv)*. The interior consists of a vast single aisle. The first apsidal chapel on the left contains the tomb of Ramón Llull: a recumbent statue of the philosopher lies upon a frieze of imaginary beasts supported by seven Gothic niches.
The **cloisters★** *(claustro)*, begun in 1286 and completed in the 14C, are extremely elegant. Apart from one side of trefoil openings, the architect divided the remaining galleries into multifoil bays supported on groups of slender columns which he varied in diameter together with the decoration on the capitals, to achieve diversity and grace. The ceiling throughout is painted.
A statue of Brother Junípero Serra *(qv)* stands before the church.

Casa Marqués del Palmer (BZ) – In the middle of the aristocratic Calle del Sol stands the impressive Casa Marqués del Palmer, a mansion built in 1556 in stone and now blackened by age. Renaissance decoration around the upper floor windows mellows the austerity of its Gothic wall. The upper gallery, protected by the traditional deep eaves, is a replica of the one adorning the Llotja.
The former old Jewish quarter, **La Portella**, lies close against the town wall.

Baños Árabes (Moorish Baths) (BZ) ⊙ – The baths are the only relic to have remained intact from the time of the caliphate in Palma. The baths, beneath their small circular windows, and classical dome, supported on twelve columns with rudimentary capitals, were used after the Reconquest by Jews and Christians alike.

Museo de Mallorca (BZ M¹) ⊙ – The museum consists of three sections: Archaeological, Fine Arts (Bellas Artes) and Ethnographical *(this last section is in Muro, see ALCÚDIA: Excursions)*.

★★ **Muslim Archaeology** – Palma was occupied by the Muslims from the 8C to 1229 when it was known as Madina Mayurqa. The only architectural vestiges from the 12C, when it was one of the most important towns in all *Al-Andalus*, are the Almudaina, Arco de la Almudaina (Almudaina Arch) and the Baños Árabes. The ground floor displays capitals, *artesonado* ceilings and ceramics from this period.

★ **Fine Arts** – *(See the Mallorcan Primitives under MALLORCA.)* This section of the museum has an excellent collection of Mallorcan Gothic paintings from the 14 and 15C. Works from the early 14C show a clear Italian influence: among them is the Santa Quiteria altarpiece by the Maestro de los Privilegios. Catalan works begin to appear after 1349 when Mallorca was annexed by Aragón: the *Crucifixion* by Ramón Destorrents *(qv)*, interesting for its composition and expression, was to influence other paintings. In Room 2 are the *Annunciation, St Lucy* and *Mary Magdalene* by Maestro del Obispo Galiana (late 14C). Room 3: Francesch Comes, one of the most prestigious of the early-15C painters, is represented here by his **St George★**, remarkable for the depth and detail of the landscape. There is also a 15C *San Onofre Altarpiece* by the Maestro de Predellas. In the rooms devoted to 16, 17 and 18C art, note the paintings of St Michael and St John by Juan de Juanes *(qv)*.

Museo Diocesano (Diocesan Museum) (BZ M²) ⊙ – *On the square behind the cathedral*. Among the many Gothic works displayed is Pere Nisart's outstanding **St George★** (1568) which shows him slaying the dragon with the town of Palma, as it was in the 16C, in the background.

A WALK WEST OF EL BORN *time: 1 hour*

★ **Llotja (AZ)** ⊙ – The designer of this 15C commodities exchange was **Guillermo Sagrera**, a famous architect who was a native of Mallorca. The Llotja's military features are only for the sake of appearances: the openwork gallery made to look like a sentry path never served as one; the merlons and turrets are not for defence but decoration. But such devices distract the eye from the inevitable buttresses and the austerity of the outer walls which were further modified by Gothic windows with delicate tracery. The interior, in which cross vaults outline the pointed arches which descend onto six beautiful, spirally fluted columns, is unbelievably elegant.

Antiguo Consulado del Mar (Former Maritime Consulate) (**AY C**) – The early-17C building adorned with a Renaissance balcony was the meeting place of the Tribunal de Comercio Marítimo (Merchant Shipping Tribunal). Today it is the presidential seat of the Comunidad Autónoma de las Islas Baleares (Autonomous Community of the Balearic Islands).

Walk up the Passeig des Born.

Palau Sollerich (Sollerich Palace) (**AY**) ⊙ – The decoration of the front of this 18C residence overlooking the Born, is completed by an elegant loggia; behind this front *(follow the narrow covered way round the building)* is the most perfect **patio** ★ in Palma, complete with a beautifully proportioned double flighted staircase set off by delicate wrought-ironwork. Exhibitions are held the palace rooms.

ADDITIONAL SIGHTS

Casa Berga (**BY**) – The mansion dating from 1712 now houses the Palacio de Justicia (Law Courts). The façade is encumbered uncharacteristically with stone balconies but the inner courtyard, although vast, is a typical Mallorcan *patio*.

★ **Pueblo Español (Spanish Village)** ⊙ – *Off the town plan, along Passeig Sagrera* (**AZ**). This model village, where the most typical houses of every region of Spain have been reconstructed, differs from the village built in Barcelona *(qv)*, in that here the buildings are exact reproductions of actual famous houses or monuments: the Patio de los Arrayanes (Myrtle Court) from Granada, the Casa de El Greco in Toledo, the Plaza Mayor in Salamanca, etc. Craftsmen at work in the alleys and folk dancing and singing in the streets bring the village to life.
Features of all the major Roman constructions in Spain have been incorporated in the monumental **Palacio de Congresos** (Congressional Hall) facing the village.

★ **Castillo de Bellver** ⊙ – *Leave Palma by Passeig Sagrera* (**AZ**). The castle, built by the Mallorcan kings of the 14C as a summer residence, was converted not long afterwards into a prison, which it remained until 1915.
Among those incarcerated was the poet, dramatist and politician **Jovellanos** *(qv)*, known also, at the time, for his progressive system of education. He was released in 1808, just as French officers captured by the Spanish at the Battle of Bailén, arrived. The castle's circular perimeter, round buildings and circular inner court are highly original; a free-standing keep dominates all. The arcade on the ground floor is set off by a series of tall Roman statues. These were donated by Cardinal Despuig together with his Italian collections, and belong to the Museo Municipal de Historia (Municipal History Museum). Also displayed in the museum are finds from excavations in Pollentia.
A full **panorama** ★★ of the Bahía de Palma can be seen from the terrace.

Fundació Pilar i Joan Miró (Pilar and Joan Miró Foundation) ⊙ – *Leave the town centre via the Passeig Sagrera* (**AZ**). The museum was born from the desire of the artist and his wife to provide the city of Palma with a lively cultural and artistic centre. In the shadow of Son Abrines, Miró's private residence since 1956, the works donated by the artist are displayed in a part of the building called the "Espacio Estrella", a satellite section of Moneo, an amalgam of the Museo de Arte Romano, Mérida, and the Museo Thyssen-Bornemisza in Madrid. Visitors to the foundation are also provided with an introduction to one of the most complete and personal artists in contemporary art. The large studio provided for him by his friend J. L. Sert and the San Boter studio are also shown.

COSTA ROCOSA★★★
THE ROCKY COAST
Local map under MALLORCA – itinerary **1**

Mallorca's west coast, known as the "Rocky Coast", is dominated by the limestone barrier of the Sierra de Tramuntana which reaches an altitude of 1 436m - 4 711ft at Puig Major. The mountain range, its wild terrain softened only by the occasional pinewood, drops dramatically to the deep, translucent sea. In the south, around the villages of Estellencs and Banyalbufar, the slopes have been terraced into *marjades* where olives, almonds and vines are grown. In the more fertile valleys further inland, *fincas* or large estates with seignorial mansions such as Granja and Alfabia were established from the 17 to 19C.

FROM PALMA TO SÓLLER *125km - 78 miles – allow 1 day*

The indented coast between Palma and Port d'Andratx with its wide sandy creeks and coves has been built up into a series of resorts: **Palmanova, Santa Ponça** where a Cross commemorates the landing of James I of Aragón in 1229, **Peguera, Cala Fornells** and **es camp de Mar.**

★ **Port d'Andratx** – The small fishing port now also used by pleasure craft, lies well sheltered in the curve of a narrow harbour. The town of Andratx surrounded by almond plantations some distance behind the harbour, is scarcely distinguishable against the grey mountain background, dominated by the 1026m - 3366ft high Galatzó peak.

The C710 between Andratx and Sóller is an extremely winding **corniche road** ★★★, mostly along the cliff edge that extends all the way to the indented northwest coast. It commands outstanding views and is shaded along its length by pine trees.

★★ **Mirador Ricardo Roca** – The view from this lookout point drops sheer to tiny coves below, lapped by the wonderfully limpid sea.

Estellencs – The village is surrounded by terraces of almond and apricot trees.

Banyalbufar – The tall stone village houses stand in terraces surrounded by fields of tomatoes and vines. There is swimming in the harbour.

★★ **Mirador de Ses Ánimes** – The panorama from the watch-tower stretches along the coast from the Isla de Dragonera to the south and as far as Port de Sóller.

Real Cartuja de Valldemossa (Valldemossa Carthusian Monastery) ⊘ – The monastery, set in the heart of Valldemossa village, was made famous by the visit George Sand and Chopin paid in the winter of 1838-1839. The bad weather and local hostility to their unorthodox way of life left George Sand disenchanted, although the beauty of the countryside did evoke enthusiastic passages in her book, *A Winter in Majorca* and Chopin regained his inspiration during the stay. There are pleasant views of the village's surrounding olive groves, carob trees and almond orchards from their cells.

An 18C **pharmacy**, built into one of the cloister galleries, has a fine collection of jars and boxes. A small **museum** displays xylographs (wood engravings).

The road beyond Valldemossa runs along cliffs more than 400m - 1300ft high.

Son Marroig ⊘ – The former residence of Archduke Ludwig Salvator includes an exhibition of archaeological finds and Mallorcan furniture collected by the author and his volumes on the Balearic Islands. A small marble belvedere in the garden affords a view of the locally famous, pierced rock rising out of the sea, the **Foradada**.

Deià – The village of reddish-brown houses perched on a hillside amidst olive and almond trees has attracted a number of writers and painters. All around are higher hills, covered in holm oaks and conifers giving it almost a mountain setting. There is a pleasant walk from the village down to a creek with a small beach.

Sóller – The town lies spread out in a wide basin where market gardens, oranges and olives grow.

Port de Sóller – Port de Sóller lies in the curve of an almost circular bay, its sheltered harbour ideal for pleasure boats. With the advantages of a sand beach and low mountain hinterland, it is now the major seaside resort of the west coast. A small train runs between Port de Sóller and Sóller. Boat trips along the coast set off from the harbour.

Take the C711 from Sóller to Alfabia.

The road twists steeply up the hillside commanding views westwards of Sóller, the harbour and the sea before descending the range's southern slopes towards the plain.

Jardines de Alfabia (Alfabia Gardens) ⊘ – The domain was originally a Moorish residence although all that now remains of the 14C period is the *artesonado* ceiling over the porch.

Follow the signposted path through the gardens with their bowers, fountains and luxuriant palms, bougainvillaeas and clumps of bamboo.

A visit to the **library** and grand saloon conveys the atmosphere of a traditional seignorial residence.

Return to Sóller.

FROM SÓLLER TO ALCÚDIA 130km - 80 miles – allow 1 day

Take the narrow mountain road from Sóller via the picturesque villages of Biniaraix and Fornalutx, their ochre-coloured stone houses set off by green shutters, to join the C710.

Mirador de Ses Barques – From this viewpoint there is an interesting panorama of Port de Sóller.

The road leaves the coast to head inland through mountainous countryside. It runs through a long tunnel before following the upper valley of the Pareis. All the while the landscape is dominated to the west by the impressive **Puig Major** *(military base on the summit)*.

After skirting Gorg Blau reservoir (embalse), take the Sa Calobra road.

★★★**Sa Calobra road** – The magnificently-planned road plunges towards the Mediterranean, dropping 900m - 2 953ft in 14km - 9 miles. It descends vertiginously through a weird and desolate landscape of steep, jagged rocks, dominated by the Puig Major.

★**Sa Calobra** – Pleasure boats from Port de Sóller are often to be seen moored in the rocky creek beside which stand the few houses of Sa Calobra village. Nearby is the mouth of the **Pareis river**★, its clear water pouring over the beach of round white shingle which lies in its path to the sea. The river bed is accessible along a track (200m - 220yds) which passes through two underground galleries; a 2-3km - 1 1/2-2 mile walk along the course gives an idea of how enclosed the stream is.

Return to the C 710.

1km - 1/2 mile north of the Sa Calobra fork, a small **mirador**★ *(lookout)* (alt 664m - 2 178ft) gives a good view over a length of the cleft hollowed out by the Pareis. The road then passes through a lovely forest of holm oaks.

Monasterio de Nuestra Señora de Lluc ⊘ – The origin of the monastery dates back to the 13C when a young shepherd found a statue of the Virgin on the site and a shrine was subsequently built. The present buildings date from the 17C (church) and early 20C (hostelry). *"La Moreneta"*, as the dark stone Gothic statue of the Virgin is known, is patron of Mallorca and venerated by a great many pilgrims.

From a pass 5km - 3 miles north of Lluc, you can see right across to the Bahía de Pollença.

Pollença – The town stands between two hills, the Puig (333m - 1 092ft) to the east, and a hill to the west crowned by a Calvary *(access up a long flight of steps bordered by cypresses)*. The streets are picturesque, lined with low ochre-coloured houses with rounded arches over the entrances.

Port de Pollença – This large resort has a perfect **setting**★ in a sheltered bay between the Cabo Formentor headland to the north and the Cabo del Pinar to the south, and provides a vast expanse of calm water for water-skiing and sailing. There are moorings in the harbour for pleasure craft and a pleasant promenade skirts the beach.

★**Cabo de Formentor road** – The road commands spectacular views as it twists and turns, rises several times to a high *corniche* and, at one point, follows a narrow jagged crest. The **Mirador des Colomer viewpoint**★★★ *(access by a stepped path)* overlooks, in an impressive, vertical drop, what is known as Mallorca's Costa Brava where great rock promontories plunge to the sea.

The **Platja de Formentor** is a well sheltered beach facing Pollença bay. It is further enhanced by the flowered terraces of the grand Hotel Formentor, built in 1928, and once famous for its casino and millionaire guests. The road continues towards the cape and once through the tunnel which temporarily hides the Cala Figuera to the north, it passes through a steep and arid landscape. The **Cap de Formentor**★, dominated by a lighthouse, is the most northerly point of the island. It drops sheer to the sea, 200m - 650ft, in a formidable rock wall.

Return to Port de Pollença, then skirt the bay until you reach Alcúdia.

Alcudia – See ALCÚDIA.

The EAST COAST and its CAVES★★

Local map under MALLORCA – itinerary ②

FROM ARTÀ TO PALMA

165km - 103 miles – allow 1 day

Artà – The town of Artà with its narrow streets may be distinguished from a distance by its high rock site crowned by the Iglesia de San Salvador (San Salvador Church) and the ruins of an ancient fortress. The Artà region is rich in **megalithic remains** *(see MENORCA)*, particularly *talayots* which sometimes can be seen over the low walls dividing the fields.

Take the C 715 east.

Capdepera – *Access to the fortress: by car, along narrow streets; on foot, up steps.* The remains of a 14C fortress still girding the hilltop give Capdepera an angular silhouette of crenellated walls and square towers. The buttressed ramparts now enclose only a restored **chapel**, but it is still possible to walk the old sentry path, **viewing**★ the sea and the nearby *calas*.

Cala Rajada – Cala Rajada with its delightful fishing village and pleasure boat harbour, has grown into a seaside resort on account of the creeks which lie on either side of it.

Casa March ⊘ – The gardens of this vast residence on the hillside facing the port, have become an outdoor museum of modern sculpture. Over 40 sculptures, blending in perfectly with the vegetation, are the works of famous artists such as Henry Moore, Sempere, Otero Besteiro, Berrocal, Barbara Hepworth, Eduardo Chillida and Arman.

By crossing the pine-wood towards the lighthouse, you come to two rocky inlets, so far relatively wild, but 2km - 1 mile further north, is **Cala Agulla**, well known for its sandy beach.

Return to Capdepera and follow the signs to the Coves d'Artà.

★★★ **Coves d'Artà** ⊘ – The caves, magnificently sited in the cape closing Canyamel bay to the north and accessible by a corniche road, were largely hollowed out by the sea – the giant mouth overlooks the sea from a height of 35m - 115ft. The chambers themselves are impressively lofty and contain massive concretions. The vestibule is blackened by smoke from 19C visitors' torches but the caves that follow are varied and equally impressive, containing the **Reina de las Columnas** (Queen of Columns) 22m - 72ft tall, Dantesque surroundings cleverly highlighted in the **Sala del Infierno** (Inferno Chamber) and a fabulous decoration of concretions in the **Sala de las Banderas** (Hall of Flags), 45m - 148ft high.

Return to the PM404 and bear left. At Porto Cristo, take the Manacor road off which you soon turn for the Coves dels Hams.

Coves dels Hams ⊘ – The caves, following the course of a former underground river, communicate directly with the sea, so that the water level in several of the small clear pools rises and falls with the slight Mediterranean tide. The concretions are delicate and some, such as the stalactites in the **Sala de los Anzuelos** (Fish-hook Chamber) ★ are as white as snow.

Return to Porto Cristo and bear right.

★★★ **Coves del Drach** ⊘ – Four chambers succeed one another over a distance of 2km - 1 mile, their transparent pools reflecting richly decorative concretions. The marine origins of the caves seem unquestionable in spite of their size: the French speleologist, **E.A. Martel,** who first explored them in 1896, believed that infiltration through the limestone subsidence and faults had caused the cavities in which several pools are slightly salty. Rainfall dissolved the soft Miocene limestone, forming as it did so, countless concretions. In the words of Martel: "On all sides, everywhere, in front and behind, as far as the eye can see, marble cascades, organ pipes, lace draperies, pendants of brilliants hang suspended from the walls and roof." It is the **roofs,** above all, which are amazing, glittering with countless, sharply pointed icicles. The tour ends with a look at the limpidly translucent **Lago Martel** (Martel Lake). Its vast chamber has been converted into a kind of concert hall; musicians in boats rise up as it were, from the depths, and, in a dreamlike atmosphere, glide across the water as they play.

Continue along the road towards Santanyí and turn right into the PM401.

★ **Monasterio de Sant Salvador** ⊘ – The monastery perched on a rise 500m - 1 640ft above the plain *(tight hairpin bends),* commands a wide **panorama**★★ of the eastern part of the island.

It was founded in the 14C although the **church** and buildings, now used for pilgrims, were rebuilt in the 18C. In the church behind the baroque high altar is a deeply venerated **Virgin and Child,** while in the south chapels are three **cribs** set in dioramas and a multi-coloured stone **altarpiece** carved in the 14C in low relief with scenes of the Passion.

Return to the C717 and head south to Santanyí.

Secondary roads lead off the C 717 to a series of resorts built up in the creeks along the coast, namely **Cala d'Or**★, with fully developed tourist facilities, **Cala Figuera**★, which is still a delightful little fishing village, and **Cala Santanyí**★.

Take the Palma road from Santanyí. At Llucmajor, bear right into the PM501.

★ **Santuario de Cura** ⊘ – The road climbs from Randa by tight hairpin bends to the monastery high on the hillside. The buildings have been restored and modernised by the Franciscans who have occupied them since 1913. You may visit the 17C **church,** the Sala de Gramática (Grammar Room) and a small **museum.**

From the terrace on the west side of the monastery there is a **panorama** ★★ of Palma, the bay, the Puig Major chain and, in the northeast, Cabo Formentor headland, the northernmost point on the island.

Return to Llucmajor and continue west along the C717 to Palma.

★★ **Palma de Mallorca** – *See PALMA DE MALLORCA.*

A number of Touring Programmes is given on pp 7-9
Plan a trip with the help of the Principal Sights Map on pp 4-6.

Menorca★★
ISLAND OF MINORCA
Michelin map 443, M41-42 – Michelin Atlas España Portugal p 91
Local map below

Menorca, the most northerly of the Islas Baleares, ranks second in terms of size, 669km² - 258sq miles (48km - 30 miles long and 15km - 9 miles wide), and population, 65 109. The island has, so far, remained out of the tourist mainstream, its 189km - 117 miles of coastline escaping, for the most part, overdevelopment. Nevertheless, the windswept plateau, the heaths more akin to a mist enveloped Atlantic countryside, have a certain, if somewhat melancholy, charm.

Menorca divides into two distinct zones, determined by relief and geological origin. The island's highest point, Monte Toro, 358m - 1 174ft, is in the northern part of the island, known as the Tramuntana, where there are outcrops of dark slate rock from the Primary and Secondary periods. Along the coast, these ancient, eroded cliffs have been cut into a saw's edge of *rías* and deep coves. The second zone, south of the Ciutadella-Maó dividing line, is the Migjorn limestone platform of light-coloured rock which forms tall cliffs along the coast cut by creeks.

The vegetation is typically Mediterranean with pine-woods, wild olives battered into gnarled and twisted shapes by the north wind, together with mastic trees, heather and aromatic herbs such as rosemary, camomile, and thyme.

Throughout the island, fields are divided by drystone walls punctuated by gates made from twisted olive branches.

Historical notes – After settlement by prehistoric peoples, whose monuments may be seen throughout the island, Menorca was colonised by the Romans, conquered by Vandals in 427 and then came under Muslim control. In the 13C, Alfonso III de Aragón invaded the island, made Ciutadella capital and encouraged settlers from Catalunya and Aragón. In the 16C, Barbary pirates attacked first Maó and then Ciutadella, leaving both cities in virtual ruin.

In 1713, Menorca, which had begun to prosper through sea trade in the late 17C, was ceded to the English crown by the Treaty of Utrecht. Maó became England's economic stronghold in the Mediterranean. Apart from a short period of French rule from 1756 to 1763, the island remained throughout the 18C under the British who built houses and, under an enlightened governor, Kane, roads. The island's first road, between Maó and Ciutadella, still exists (north of the C 721) and is known as Camino Kane. At the beginning of the 19C, Menorca was restored definitively to Spain.

The island's economy has gradually been oriented towards the leather industry and jewellery making while cattle raising provides the island with dairy products, particularly its well-known cheeses.

The Megalithic monuments – In the second millennium BC, at the end of the Bronze Age, the Balearics were populated by settlers similar to those who inhabited Sardinia during the same period. The cavernous nature of the Minorcan countryside offered natural shelter both for the living and the dead; some of the caves, such as **Cala Coves**, they even decorated. At the same time, **talayots** began to appear (over 200

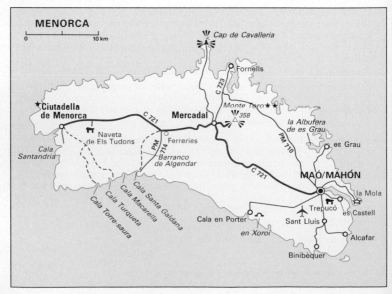

have been identified). They take the form of great cones of stones possibly covering a funeral chamber and forming, it is believed, the base for a superimposed wooden house. Other characteristic monuments of the civilisation include **taulas**, consisting of two huge stone blocks placed one on top of the other in the shape of a T, possibly serving as altars, and **navetas**, single monuments which take the form of upturned boats and contain funeral chambers.

Naveta de Els Tudons, Menorca

For more detailed information on local archaeology, a map may be bought on the island showing the sites of the monuments: "Mapa Arqueológico de Menorca", by J. Mascaró Pasarius.

Minorcan architecture – The walls and even the roofs of Minorcan houses are brightly whitewashed; the low dividing walls so typical of the island also have a white band along the top. Tiles are used for roofing, chimneys and guttering. Houses are built facing south, their fronts characterised by wide, open bays while the northern walls, exposed to fierce *tramontana* winds, have very small windows.

English influence on architecture is evident in the towns where many of the houses have sash windows and some of the seignorial mansions are in the Palladian style fashionable in Britain in the 18C.

The fields around Ciutadella are scattered with curious stone constructions shaped like ziggurats (the pyramidal stepped towers of ancient Mesopotamia); these *barracas*, vaulted inside with false ceilings, served as shelters for shepherds.

CIUTADELLA/CIUDADELA★

Population 20 707
Local map under MENORCA

In the Middle Ages, Ciutadella, the citadel, and capital of Menorca, was ringed with walls. The ramparts were demolished in 1873 but their layout can still be distinguished in the circle of avenues around the old quarter. The fortified aspect of the city becomes evident when viewed from the harbour.

After being sacked by Turkish pirates in the 16C, Ciutadella was partly rebuilt in the late-17 and 18C. Today, the atmosphere in the alleys of the old quarter and in the harbour, give the town a calm and indefinable charm.

Each year the **Midsummer's Day** or **Fiestas de San Juan**, are celebrated with traditional rejoicing. On the preceding Sunday, a man representing John the Baptist, dressed in animal skins and carrying a lamb, runs through the town to the sound of fabiols (small flutes) and tambourins. On 24 and 25 June, over a hundred horsemen take part in jousting tournaments and processions.

TOUR *time: about 1 hour*

Barrio antiguo (Old quarter) – **Plaza del Born**, the former parade ground, is flanked by the eclectic 19C façade of the **Ayuntamiento** (Town Hall) and the early-19C **Palacio de Torre-saura**, a palace with its side loggias. In the centre of the square is an obelisk commemorating the townspeople's heroic stand against the Turks in the 16C.

Catedral ⊘ – The late-14C fortified church has kept part of the minaret of the mosque which once stood on the site. Inside, the single aisle is ogival and the apse pentagonal. You will be able to see the church's baroque doorway from Calle del Rosario facing the cathedral.

At the end of the street, turn left into Calle del Santísimo where two fine late-17C mansions may be seen on opposite sides of the street: **Palacio Saura** has a baroque façade adorned with a cornice, while **Palacio Martorell** is of a more sober design.

By way of Calle del Obispo Vila, in which stand the Claustro de Socorro (Socorro Cloisters) and the Iglesia de Santo Cristo (Santo Cristo Church), you come to the main street which leads to **Plaza de España** and the arcaded **Carrer de Ses Voltes**.

Puerto (Harbour) – The ramp approach to the harbour, which is well sheltered and serves mainly pleasure craft, is along a former counterscarp. The buildings along the quays are bustling with cafés and restaurants. The esplanade beyond, Pla de Sant Joan, the centre for Midsummer's Day festivities, is bordered by boat shelters hollowed out of the living rock. The whole area comes alive at night.

EXCURSIONS

Nau or **Naveta de Els Tudons** – *5km - 3 miles east of Ciutadella.*
This funerary monument, shaped like an upturned ship, is notable for the vast size of the stones in the walls and more particularly, those lining the floor inside.

Cala Santandria – *3km - 2 miles south.*
This is a small sheltered beach in a creek.

Cala Torre-saura, Cala Turqueta, Cala Macarella – *Ask on the spot for directions.*
The three beaches are set in small, beautifully unspoilt creeks fringed by sweet smelling pines.

MAÓ / MAHÓN

Population 21 814
Local map under MENORCA

Maó's **site★** is most striking when approached from the sea: it appears high atop a cliff in the curve of a deep, 5km - 3 mile long roadstead or natural harbour.
Mahón reached its height during the English occupation from 1713 to 1782 *(qv)* when it was endowed with Palladian style mansions.
On the north side of the harbour is the Finca de San Antonio – the Golden Farm – where Admiral Nelson lived during a brief stay on the island, and where he put the finishing touches to his book, *Sketches of My Life* (October 1799).
The town gave its name to the famous *mahonnaise* sauce which we now know as mayonnaise.
Most of the town's shops are in the network of streets between **Plaza del Ejército**, a large, lively square lined with cafés and restaurants, and the quieter **Plaza de España** with its two churches: **Santa María**, with a beautiful baroque organ, and **Carmen**, whose cloisters have been converted to hold the municipal market.

Museo Arqueológico (Archaeological Museum) ⊙ – Prehistoric objects, many from local *talayots (qv)*, provide the major displays in the museum in the Palacio de los Archivos in Plaza de la Conquista.

Puerto (Harbour) – Walk down the steep ramp from Carrer de Ses Voltes, cut by a majestic flight of steps, and follow the quay to the north side of the roadstead. Look across the water for a view of the town at its most characteristic, with its larger buildings lining the top of the cliff and below, the open-air dance halls, the restaurants, shops and coloured fishermen's cottages, snug against the foot.

EXCURSIONS

★La Rada (Roadstead) – The south side consists of a series of coves and villages, among them Cala Figuera with its fishing harbour and restaurants. **Es Castell,** further along, was built as a garrison town by the English when it was called Georgetown. It has a grid plan, with the parade ground at its centre. The islands in the natural harbour include Lazareto and, beside it, Cuarentena, which, as its name suggests, was a quarantine hospital for sailors. A road follows the northern shore to the Faro de la Mola (Mola Fort) affording views of Maó.

Talayot de Trepucó – *1km - 1/2 mile south of Maó.*
This megalithic site is famous for its *taula* which is 4.80m - 16ft high.

Sant Lluís – *4km - 2 miles south.*
The town with its narrow streets was founded by the French during their occupation of the island.
Small resorts have grown up nearby, at **Alcafar** where the houses stand a little distance inland beside a creek between two rocky promontories, and **Binibèquer,** a small, completely new village which, with its alleyways, small squares, and dazzling white houses, has been made to look like a fishing hamlet.

Es Grao – *8km - 5 miles north.*
Beside the attractive white village with its long beach is a vast lagoon, **Albufera de es Grau,** 2km - 1 mile long and 400m - 437yds wide. It is an ideal spot to watch the rich migrant bird life (rails, ducks and herons).

Cala en Porter – *12km - 7 miles west.*
High promontories protect a narrow estuary inlet, lined by a sandy beach. Houses stand perched upon the left cliff. From their lofty position, ancient troglodyte dwellings, the **Coves d'en Xoroi,** overlook the sea. A bar has been installed in one of them.

The maps to use with this Guide are: 441, 442, 443, 444, 445 and 446

MERCADAL

Population 2601
Local map under MENORCA

Mercadal, a small town of brilliantly whitewashed houses halfway between Maó and Ciutadella, is the point where roads to the coast meet on the north-south axis.

EXCURSIONS

★★ **Monte Toro (view)** – *3.5km - 2 miles along a narrow road.*
On a clear day, the **view** from the church crowned summit (358m - 1175ft), is of the entire island. You can see the indented Bahía de Fornells (Fornells Bay) to the north, the straight line of the coastal cliffs to the south and Maó to the southeast.

Fornells – *8.5km - 5 miles north on the C723.*
Fornells, a small fishing village of whitewashed houses with green shutters, lies at the mouth of a deep inlet, surrounded on all sides by bare moorland. The village lives off crawfish fishing, as can be seen from the single-sail craft moored in the harbour. The local speciality, crawfish soup or *caldereta*, is a food-lover's delight.

Cap de Cavalleria – *12km - 7 miles north along narrow signposted roads.*
The drive to the cape, the northernmost point on the island, is through windswept moorland, battered by the *tramontana* from the north, while the country houses, like that at Finca Santa Teresa, are large and beautifully white. The **view** from the lighthouse is of a rocky, indented coast, more Atlantic than Mediterranean.

Cala Santa Galdana – *16km - 10 miles southwest via Ferreries.*
The beauty of this magnificent cove set in a limpid bay flanked by tall cliffs, has been somewhat marred by large hotels.
One may also walk to the cove from **Barranco de Algendar** *(as you leave Ferreries, take the track left towards Ciutadella)*. The path *(3 hrs Rtn)* winds through a ravine beside a stream which is enclosed in places by cliffs 50m - 160ft tall.

Ibiza★

Michelin map 443 O, P 33-34 – Michelin Atlas España Portugal p 91
Local map below

Ibiza, the **Isla Blanca** or White Island, as it has been called, is the largest of the Pityuses Islands (the name given to Ibiza and Formentera by the ancient Greeks). It lies 52 nautical miles from the peninsula and 45 southwest of Mallorca, has an area of 572km^2 - 221sq miles, a length of 41km - 25 miles and a population of 74001.

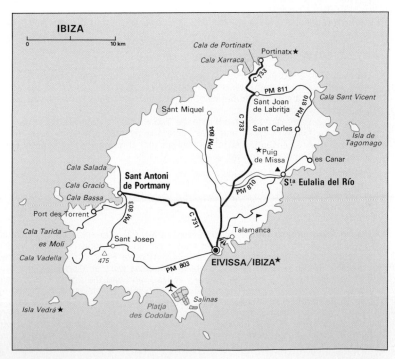

Brilliantly white house walls, flat roof terraces, tortuous alleys and an atmosphere similar to that of a Greek island, give Ibiza a unique personality within the Balearics. Ibiza's history dates from the beginnings of trade development throughout the Mediterranean: in the 10C BC, Phoenicians made the island a staging post for ships loaded with Spanish metal ores returning to Africa; in the 7C BC, Carthage grew all powerful and founded a colony on the island; under the Romans the capital grew in size and prosperity to judge from the necropolis discovered at Puig des Molins.

Landscape – Ibiza is a mountainous island where the muddled lines of relief leave little space for cultivation between the limestone hills. Among pines and junipers on the hillsides stand the cube-shaped houses of many small villages. The shore appears wild and indented, guarded by high cliffs; promontories are marked by rocks out to sea, some standing as high as the amazing limestone needle known as **Vedrá**★ (almost 400m - 1 300ft).

Traditional architecture – While the architecture inland has managed to preserve its traditions, that on the coast tends to have suffered from overdevelopment.
The cottage, or **casament**, is made up of several white cubes with few windows; each represents a single room and opens off a central common room. The arched porches provide shade and a sheltered area for storing crops.
Country churches are equally plain with gleaming white exteriors and dark interiors. The façades are square, surmounted by narrow bell gables and pierced by wide porches. In the days of pirate attacks, the island's inhabitants took refuge in the fortified churches of villages such as San Carlos, San Juan, San Jorge and Puig de Missa.

Folklore and traditional costume – Ibiza has a living folklore which is uncomplicated and authentic. Women may still be seen wearing the long gathered skirt and dark shawl. At festivals the costume is brightened with fine gold filigree necklaces or *emprendades*. The island dances are performed to the accompaniment of flute, tambourine and castanets, by groups whose skill is demonstrated by the gathering speed at which they can accomplish the steps.

Economy – Ibiza's main resource is its tourism, an industry that has unfortunately marred some of the sites. The **salt-pans** *(salinas)* in the south, exploited since Carthaginian times, produce about 50 000 tonnes of salt a year.

EIVISSA / IBIZA★

Population 30 376
Local map previous page

Eivissa's colourful beauty and impressive **site**★★ should be seen, if possible, for the first time from the sea; alternatively take the **Talamanca** road out of town and look back *(3km - 2 miles northeast)*. The town, built on a hill overlooking the sea, consists of an old quarter ringed by walls, the lively Marina district near the harbour, and, further out, residential and shopping areas. The *corniche* skirting the shoreline is bordered by large hotels.

★DALT VILA (UPPER TOWN) (Z) *time: 1 1/2 hours*

The Dalt Vila, enclosed by the 16C walls built under Emperor Charles V, is the heart of the old city and retains even today a certain rustic, medieval character. There remain many noble houses worth looking at particularly for their vast *patios* and Gothic windows.
Enter the quarter through the Puerta de **Tablas** (**YZ**), a gateway which is surmounted by Philip II's crest, and either continue by car up a steep slope to the cathedral square or wander there leisurely on foot through the quiet meandering streets with their shops and art galleries.

Catedral (**Z**) ⊙ – The cathedral's massive 13C belfry, which closely resembles a keep but for its two storeys of Gothic bays, totally dominates the town. The nave was rebuilt in the 17C. An ancient bastion behind the east end has been converted into a lookout point from which you can get a good **panoramic view**★ of the town and harbour.

★ **Museo Arqueológico (Archaeological Museum)** (**Z M¹**) ⊙ – The museum provides the visitor with an introduction to a lesser known period of art which had little outside influence and left few remains – the art of Carthage or Punic Art which flourished from the 7C BC to the 3C AD. The items exhibited were all discovered on Ibiza and Formentera; most from excavations at Illa Plana and the Cove de es Cuiram (Es Cuiram Cove). The latter contained hollow, bell-shaped terracottas formed by two curved parts, like folded wings, crowned by a cylindrical tiara. The cave is believed to have been a temple to the goddess Tanit, who was venerated there from the 5 to the 2C BC. The remaining rooms contain items from Punic necropolises in the country and, displayed in a chapel, artefacts from the Roman, Muslim and Christian eras.

Dalt Vila (Upper town), Eivissa

D. Clément/EXPLORER

ADDITIONAL SIGHTS

★ **Museo Monográfico de Puig des Molins** (Puig des Molins Monographic Museum) (**Z**)
⊘ – The Puig des Molins hillside necropolis was a burial-ground for the Phoenicians from the 7C BC and then for the Romans until the 1C AD. There is a model of the site in Room IV and some of the hypogea or underground funerary chambers, of which over 3 000 have been discovered, may be visited.

The objects displayed were found in the tombs and include articles from everyday life (oil lamps, dishes, Iberian ceramics) as well as items used in rituals such as finely decorated ostrich eggs, which were a symbol of resurrection.

Room III contains terracottas and religious clay figurines which today throw light on the way people dressed at the time. The outstanding, partly coloured, 5C BC **bust of the goddess Tanit★**, a Punic version of the Phoenician Astarte, is a perfect example of Greek beauty. A second bust is more Carthaginian.

The museum also contains jewellery of moulded glass, necklaces, coins and Greek and Roman ceramics.

La Marina (**Y**) – The Marina district near the municipal market and the harbour, with its restaurants, bars and shops, stands in lively contrast to the quieter Dalt Vila.

★ **Sa Penya** (**Y**) – The former fishermen's quarter, now the centre of Ibiza's night life, is built on a narrow rock promontory at the harbour mouth and is quite different from the rest of the town. Within the limited space available, white cubic houses overlap and superimpose on one another in picturesque chaos, completely blocking streets in places and compelling them to continue by means of steps cut out of the rock.

SANT ANTONI DE PORTMANY / SAN ANTONIO ABAD

Population 14 663
Local map under IBIZA

Sant Antoni with its vast, curved bay has been fully developed by the tourist industry. The old quarter, hidden behind modern apartment blocks, centres around a fortified 14C church rebuilt in the 16C. There is a large pleasure boat harbour. Several coves and creeks are within easy distance of the town.

EXCURSIONS

Cala Gració – *2km - 1 mile north.*
A lovely, easily accessible, sheltered creek.

Cala Salada – *5km - 3 miles north.*
The road descends through pines to a well sheltered beach in a cove.

Port des Torrents and Cala Bassa – *5km - 3 miles southwest.*
Port des Torrents is all rocks; Cala Bassa a long, pine fringed beach. In this part of the coast the rocks are smooth and separate and just above or just below the water line, providing perfect underwater swimming conditions.

Cala Vadella – *15km - 9 miles south.*
A road skirts the shoreline through pine trees between the beaches of Cala Tarida (rather built-up), Es Moli (unspoiled) and Cala Vadella in its enclosed creek.
You can return to Sant Antoni along a mountain road that rises in a *corniche* to Sant Josep.

SANTA EULÀRIA DES RIU / SANTA EULALIA DEL RÍO

Population 15 545
Local map under IBIZA

Santa Eulària, standing in a fertile plain watered by Ibiza's only river, has grown into a large seaside resort with modern buildings. Beaches in the vicinity, like that at **Es Canar**, have also been developed.

★ **Puig de Missa** – *Bear right off the Ibiza road 50m after the petrol station (on the left).* The minute, fortified town crowning the hilltop is a remarkable conspectus of the island's traditional peasant architecture; the town is a surviving example, in fact, of those easily defended religious hills, where, in case of danger, the church (16C), served as a refuge.

EXCURSION

★ **Portinatx** – *27km - 17 miles north on the PM 810, PM 811 and C 733.*
The road passes through **Sant Carles** which has a fine church and is a departure point for quiet local beaches. It then descends to the vast **Sant Vicent** creek *(cala)* with a beautiful sandy beach and opposite, the Isla de Togomago, before crossing an almost mountainous landscape covered in pines. The last section of the approach road is picturesque as it threads its way between holm oaks and almond trees and you look down on **Cala Xarraca**. Creeks sheltered by narrow cliffs with pine trees fringing the sandy beaches, make **Cala de Portinatx** one of the island's most attractive areas.

The Michelin Red Guide España Portugal
lists hotels and restaurants
which offer good meals at moderate prices;
consult the latest edition.

Formentera

Formentera, the Wheat Island of the Romans (*frumentum:* wheat in Latin) lies barely 7km - 3 1/2 nautical miles south of Ibiza, the sea between them being dotted with small islets. It is the fourth largest of the Islas Baleares with an area of 115km² - 44sq miles and an overall west to east length of 14km - 9 miles although it is in fact really two islets joined by a sandy isthmus. The "capital" Sant Francesc (St Francis Xavier), the passenger port, Cala Sabina, the salt-pans, Cap Berbería and the dry open expanse on which cereals, figs, almonds and a few vines are grown, are on the western islet; the island's 192m - 630ft high "mountain", its slopes covered in low pines, rises from the **Mola** promontory on the eastern islet. Rock cliffs and sand dunes alternately line the shore.

4760 people live on Formentera. The inhabitants arrived comparatively recently, the island having been abandoned in the Middle Ages in the face of marauding Barbary pirates and only repopulated at the end of the 17C. Most of the present population are fishermen and peasant farmers, shipping figs and fish to Ibiza and salt to Barcelona.

The beaches (Playas or **Platjas)** – The white sandy beaches with their clear water are the island's main attraction. Long beaches stretch along either side of the isthmus, the rocky Tramontana to the north and the sheltered, sandy Mitjorn to the south. Other, smaller beaches around the island include Es Pujos (the most developed), Illetas and Cala Saona.

Cala Sabina – Your landing point on the island is in the main harbour: a few white houses stand between two big lagoons, salt-marshes glisten in the distance on the left.

Sant Francesc (San Francisco Javier) – Chief and only town on the island. Its houses are clustered around the 18C church-fortress.

El Pilar de la Mala – The hamlet at the centre of the Mola promontory has this geometrically designed church which is similar to those on Ibiza only smaller.

Faro de la Mola – The lighthouse overlooks an impressive cliff. There is a monument to Jules Verne who mentioned this spot in one of his books.

Islas Canarias
Canary Islands

The Canary Islands lie in the Atlantic, ten times nearer to the coast of Africa than they are to Spain – 115 to 1150km respectively (70 and 700 miles). The archipelago slightly to the north of the Tropic of Cancer – average latitude 28° – consists of 7 islands covering an area of 7273km² - 2808sq miles with a population of 1637641. It is divided into eastern and western administrative provinces namely, **Las Palmas**, comprising the islands of Gran Canaria, Fuerteventura and Lanzarote, and that of **Santa Cruz de Tenerife** with the four islands of Tenerife, La Palma, Gomera and Hierro.

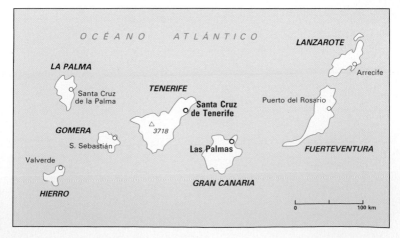

A volcanic archipelago – Volcanic eruptions would appear to have thrust the islands from the bottom of the Atlantic seabed well prior to the Tertiary era. Two, Gomera and Gran Canaria, have the true volcanic cone shape and most, with the exception of Fuerteventura and Lanzarote, have hills inland and cliff-lined shores.

The Fortunate Islands – The islands make their first appearance in history when they are referred to in Greek literature. Plutarch mentions them and they are described in some detail by Pliny the Elder who named them the Isles of the Blessed or the Fortunate Islands. However, the island conquerors did not arrive until the 15C – the first true expedition to the archipelago took place in 1402 – when they found a native population, the **Guanches**, who, lacking all outside contact, were still living in the Stone Age. Resistance to the newcomers was strong and it took until the end of the century to bring the entire archipelago under Spanish control.

THE ISLANDS

Tenerife – 2053km² - 793sq miles. Tenerife, the largest of the islands, gets its name from the Guanche word meaning snow-capped mountain. It is dominated by the Pico del Teide, a gigantic volcanic cone of 3718m - 12198ft, the highest Spanish summit, and nearly always snow-capped. The cone is ringed by the ancient collapsed Las Cañadas crater which is now the **Parque Nacional del Teide** (Teide National Park). The northern coast is lush with banana trees, the shore edged by high cliffs, while the south is arid. Seaside resorts have developed along the western coast.

Gran Canaria (Grand Canary) – 1532km² - 592sq miles. The capital, **Las Palmas,** is the largest town in the archipelago with a population of 360 483. The north, wet and fertile and the kingdom of the banana tree, contrasts with the wide expanse of desert in the south. The north and west coasts are edged by steep cliffs while the south is swathed in long beaches rapidly being developed for tourism.

Fuerteventura – 1 688km² - 652sq miles. This is an arid land, a skeletal island scattered with countless bare crests. The island's attraction lies in the beauty of the desert landscape and in a shore lined by immense beaches of white sand or rocks which provide good underwater swimming.

Lanzarote – 813km² - 314sq miles. This is the most unusual of the Canary Islands. Seaside resorts are being developed along its fine white sand beaches but its greater attraction lies in its quite outstanding volcanic features: in the **Parque Nacional de Timanfaya** there are about a hundred craters lying in fields of lava and thick black layers of cinder. The island has another curiosity: dromedaries.

La Palma – 728km² - 281sq miles. A beautifully green island with crops grown in terraces and a peak 2 433m - 7 982ft high. A gigantic volcanic crater, **Caldera de Taburiente,** now a national park, stands in the centre of the island.

Gomera – 535km² - 207sq miles. This small round island forms a mountain mass which rises to a height of 1 487m - 4 879ft on Monte Garajonay **(Parque Nacional de Garajonay)**. The coast is edged by steep cliffs. The fertile red soil is carefully terraced and there are numerous date palms.

Hierro – 278km² - 107sq miles. In shape it resembles a half crater and is surrounded by a rocky coast ideal for underwater swimming.

Practical
Information

Travelling to Spain

Optimum seasons for travelling, depending on the region

Spring and Autumn are the best seasons for a general tour but there is a region in Spain for every season:

Spring – Andalucía, Extremadura, Castilla, the Islas Baleares (Balearic Islands) and the Mediterranean coast.

Summer – By the sea: País Vasco (Basque Country), Cantabrian coast and Galicia; in the mountains: Pyrenees, Picos de Europa, Sierra Nevada, Sierra de Gredos and Sierra de Guadarrama.

Autumn – The whole of Spain.

Winter – Mediterranean and the Islas Baleares; winter sports: Pyrenees and Sierra Nevada.

Temperature chart:

	1	2	3	4	5	6	7	8	9	10	11	12
Barcelona	13 6	14 7	16 9	18 11	21 14	25 18	28 21	28 21	25 19	21 15	16 11	13 7
Madrid	9 1	11 2	15 5	18 7	21 10	27 14	31 17	30 17	26 14	19 9	13 5	9 2
Santander	12 7	12 6	15 8	15 9	17 11	20 14	22 16	22 16	21 15	18 12	15 9	12 7
Sevilla	15 6	17 6	20 9	23 11	26 13	32 17	36 20	36 20	32 18	26 14	20 10	16 7
Valencia	15 5	16 6	8 8	20 10	23 13	26 16	29 19	29 20	27 17	23 13	19 9	16 6

Maximum temperatures in red; minimum temperatures in black.

Formalities – Despite the law which came into force on 1 January 1993 authorising the free flow of goods and people within the EU, it is nonetheless advisable that travellers should be equipped with some valid piece of identification such as a **passport**. Holders of British, Irish and US passports do not need a visa for a visit to Spain of less than 90 days. Visitors from some Commonwealth countries or those planning to stay longer than 90 days should enquire about visa requirements at their local Spanish consulate. US citizens should obtain the booklet *Your Trip Abroad* (US$ 1.25) which provides useful information on visa requirements, customs regulations, medical care etc for international travellers. Apply to the Superintendent of Documents, PO Box 371954, Pittsburgh, PA 15250-7954, ☎ 202-783-3238.

Customs regulations – Tax-free allowances for various commodities within the EU have increased with the birth of the single European market. The HM Customs and Excise Notice 1 *A Guide for Travellers* explains how recent changes affect travellers within the EU. The US Customs Service (PO Box 7407, Washington DC 20044, ☎ 202-927-5580) offers a publication *Know Before You Go* for US citizens.

Pets (cats and dogs) – A general health certificate and proof of rabies vaccination should be obtained from your local vet before departure.

By air – The various national and other independent airlines operate services to Spain's international airports (Madrid, Alicante, Barcelona, Bilbao, Málaga, Palma, Sevilla and Valencia). Information, brochures and timetables are available from the airlines and from travel agents.
Iberia Airlines: 29 Glass House St., London, W1R6JU, ☎(0171) 830 0011.
JKF airport, New York, ☎ 212-656-2555.

By sea – Brittany Ferries operates a ferry service between Plymouth and Santander (leaves Plymouth on Mondays and Wednesdays, returns from Santander on Tuesdays and Thursdays; *journey time: 24 hours*). Contact:
Millbay Docks, Plymouth PL1 3EW, Devon, ☎ (01752) 22 1321.
Estación marítima, Santander, Spain, ☎ 00 34 4 222 0000.

By sea then on through France – There are also numerous cross-Channel services (passenger and car ferries, hovercraft, SeaCat) from the United Kingdom and Eire to France.
The two major frontier posts on the French-Spanish border are at either end of the Pyrenees – Irún in the west and La Jonquera in the east. You may also cross (from west to east) at Bera de Bidasoa, Echalar, Dancharia, Erratzu, Ochagavía, Valcarlos, Isaba, Canfranc, Sallent de Gállego, Bielsa, Les Puente del Rey, Bossòst, Andorra, Puigcerdà, Collado d'Ares and Cerbère.

Under the Channel then on through France – An alternative to the cross-Channel ferry services is the **Channel Tunnel**. The high-speed undersea rail link carries passengers (without cars) from London to Paris, from where it is possible to travel on by train *(see below)*. It also ferries motorists and their cars through the tunnel (35 min) on specially designed double-decker wagons. The Calais terminal is linked by slip-roads to the French motorway network (the distance to Madrid by road is about 1 600km - just under 1 000 miles; a possible route is via Bordeaux, Biarritz, San Sebastián, either Bilbao or Vitoria, and Burgos).
For information, contact Le Shuttle passenger enquiries: ☎ 01 303 271100.

By rail – British Rail offers a wide range of services to the Channel ports and French Railways (SNCF) operates an extensive network of lines including many high-speed passenger trains and motorail services throughout France. Information and bookings from:
British Rail International, Ticket and Information Office, PO Box 303, Victoria Station, London SW1V 1JY, ☎ (0171) 834 2345 (enquiries only).
French Railways, 179 Piccadilly, London W1V 0BA, ☎ (0171) 409 3518.
For local Spanish services apply to Spanish Railways (RENFE) European Office, 8 Boulevard Poissonnière, 75009 Paris, ☎ 00 331 48 01 97 80.
The Madrid Talgo, a night train, runs between Paris and Madrid via Bordeaux in 12 1/2 hours (8 hours from Bordeaux). Alternatively, the Puerta del Sol takes 16 hours. (There are other possibilities with the French TGV or high-speed train which connects with other trains south). The Barcelona Talgo, a night train, takes 11 1/2 hours from Paris to Barcelona. The same trip may be done in less than 10 hours by taking a TGV from Paris to Montpellier and changing trains. For further information enquire at Spanish Railways (RENFE) or French Railways (SNCF).

By coach – Regular coach departures are operated from London to Madrid and to larger provincial towns.
Eurolines, 52 Grosvenor Gardens, Victoria, London SW1W 0AU, ☎ (0171) 730 8235.

Travelling in Spain

Documents – An **international driving licence** (obtainable in the UK from the AA or the RAC or in the US from the American Automobile Association for US$ 10) is required when driving in Spain.
For the vehicle it is necessary to have the **registration papers** (log-book) and a **nationality plate** of the approved size.

Insurance – An International Insurance Certificate (Green Card) is compulsory. Third party insurance is also compulsory in Spain. Certain UK motoring organisations (AA, RAC) run accident insurance and breakdown service schemes for members. Europ-Assistance (25 High Street, Croydon CRO 1NF) has special policies for motorists. Bail bonds are no longer necessary, although travellers may wish still to take this precaution (consult your insurance company). Members of the American Automobile Association should obtain the free brochure "Offices to Serve You Abroad" (which gives details of affiliated organisations in Spain).
If the driver of the vehicle is not accompanied by the owner, he or she should have written permission from the owner to drive in Spain.

Driving regulations and general information – The minimum driving age is 18. Traffic drives on the right. It is compulsory for passengers in both front and rear seats to wear **seat belts**. Motorcyclists (on all sizes of machine) must wear safety helmets. The **maximum speed** permitted is:
      50km/h - 31mph in built-up areas;
      90km/h - 56mph on the open road (without a hard shoulder);
      100km/h - 62mph on the open road with a hard shoulder of at least 1.5m - 5ft;
      120km/h - 75mph on dual carriageways/motorways *(autovía/autopista)*.
In 1991 the Spanish road network included over 2 000km - 1 250 miles of motorways. Most of the Spanish motorways have **tolls** *(peajes)*.
Super (97-96 octanes), normal (92-90 octanes) and diesel are generally available but not all petrol stations sell unleaded petrol *(sin plomo)*.

Road maps – Michelin map 990 at a 1: 1 000 000 scale covers the whole of Spain, while the 441 - 446 series at 1: 400 000 covers the different regions. See the back cover of this guide for the map numbers and their corresponding regions.

Car hire – The major car hire firms have offices in all large towns. Cars may be hired from branches at airports, main stations and large hotels. The minimum age to qualify for car hire is 21. Tourists driving vehicles with rental plates are advised to leave no valuables in the car. The US Bureau of Consular Affairs publishes a pamphlet *A Safe Trip Abroad* which is available from the Superintendent of Documents, US Government Printing Office, Washington DC, 20402-9328. Fly-drive schemes are operated by major airlines.

By train – Spanish Railways, RENFE *(see above for the address)* have a 13 000km - 8 080 mile rail network offering first and second class travel. They have a variety of special rates and tourist fares including discounts for travel on 'Blue Days' *(días azules)*, or for Youthpass and non-resident Eurailpass holders. Mention should be made of two particularly comfortable trains, the Al-Andalus Express in Andalucía and the Transcantábrico in the north, designed to give the traveller a cultural, scenic introduction to the country. Lastly, in 1992 (to coincide with Expo '92), RENFE inaugurated the AVE (Alta Velocidad Española - Spanish High Speed Train) on the Madrid - Córdoba - Sevilla route. This train (similar to the French TGV) has reduced travel time between Madrid and Córdoba to under 2 1/2 hours and Madrid and Sevilla to 3 hours. Trains leave Madrid from Atocha station and Sevilla from the newly opened Santa Justa station.

By boat – For information on boat travel to the Islas Baleares, the Islas Canarias or to Africa, contact the state-owned shipping company Transmediterránea at: c/o Southern Ferries, 1st floor, 179 Piccadilly Street, London W1.
☎ 0171 491 4968/3502.

General information

Currency – The unit of currency in Spain is the peseta, written as pts. Coins come in the following denominations: 1, 5, 10, 25, 50, 100, 200 and 500 pts, with notes in 1 000, 2 000, 5 000 and 10 000 values. Visitors should be aware of the increasing variety of Spanish coins (over 15 different ones) and that several denominations (5, 25, 100 and 200 pts) are represented by several different coins. There are no restrictions on the amount of currency (Spanish or other) that foreigners may bring with them into Spain. They may leave Spain with the currency equivalent of up to 500 000 pesetas.

Changing money, credit cards – Banks, airports and some stations have exchange offices. International credit cards are accepted in most shops, hotels and restaurants. An increasing number of *cambios* (bureaux de change) are also available throughout the country.

Banks – Banks are generally open Mondays to Fridays 9am to 2pm and on Saturdays from 9am to 12.30pm. These times are subject to change, especially in summer. Most banks have cash dispensers which accept international credit cards.

Differences in time – Spain is one hour ahead of GMT.
The Spanish keep very different hours from either British or Americans *(see p 10)*. As a general rule, restaurants serve lunch from 1.30 to 3.30pm and dinner from 9 to 11pm.

Post Offices (Correos) – Post Offices are open weekdays from 9am to 2pm. The main post offices in large towns and those in international airports have a 24-hour service. Stamps *(sellos)* are sold in post offices and tobacco shops *(estancos)*. The **Michelin Red Guide España Portugal** gives the post code for every town covered.
The National **Girobank's** postcheque allows British customers to withdraw cash on their UK accounts from main post offices in Spain. Check with your local Girobank Office.

Telephone (Telefónica) – Telephones in new public booths take 5, 25, 50, 100 and 500 peseta coins (older booths only take 5, 25 and 100 peseta coins). For **international calls**, dial 07, wait for the dialling tone and then dial the country code (44 for the United Kingdom, 353 for Ireland, 071 for the United States), the area code and the number. Card phones are widespread throughout Spain. Telephone cards *(tarjeta telefónica)* in 1 000 and 2 000 pts denominations can be purchased in *tabacos* and are particulary recommended for international dialling.
For **internal calls**, from one province to another, dial 9 then the area code (Madrid 1, Barcelona 3, Valencia 6, Sevilla 54, Granada 58), followed by the number. The **Michelin Red Guide España Portugal** gives the area code for each town covered.
Dial 003 for telephone enquiries, 009 for area codes.
To call Spain from the United Kingdom, dial 00 (Ireland, 16) + 34 + area code + number. (Do not dial 9 before the area code; this is only necessary for inter-provincial calls within Spain).

Shops – These are generally open weekdays 10am to 1.30pm and 5 to 8pm (some department stores stay open during the lunch hour). Some shops are closed on Saturday afternoons and most all day Sunday.

Monuments, museums and churches – Monuments and museums are generally open 10am to 1.30pm and 4 to 7pm. Some churches are only open during services early in the morning or in the evening.

Entertainment – When there are two performances scheduled, matinées begin at 7pm (4.30pm on Sundays and holidays) and the evening performances at 10 or 10.30pm.

Public Holidays – The dates in italics are holidays in some, but not all, Autonomous Communities.

1 January	*25 July*
6 January	15 August
19 March	12 October
Maundy Thursday	1 November
Good Friday	6 December
1 May	8 December
Corpus Christi	25 December
(2nd Thursday after Whitsun)	

In addition each town celebrates the feast day of its patron saint. For local holidays contact the Tourist Information Centres (*Oficina de Turismo* or simply *Turismo*).

Medical treatment – British citizens should apply to the Department of Health and Social Security for **Form E 111**, which entitles the holder to urgent treatment for accident or unexpected illness in EU countries. On arrival in Spain, exchange the form at the Dirección Provincial del Instituto Nacional de la Seguridad Social for a booklet of health coupons.

Since medical insurance is not always valid out of the United States, travellers are advised to check with their insurance companies about taking out supplementary medical insurance with specific overseas coverage.

Electric current – 220 volts AC (some of the older establishments may still have 110 V). Plugs are two-pin.

Water – Water is generally safe to drink although it may be a little salty along the Mediterranean coast – this is true of Barcelona – in which case you may prefer mineral water *(agua mineral)*.

Accommodation

Hotels and restaurants – The **Michelin Red Guide España Portugal** is revised annually and is an indispensable complement to this Green Guide with information on hotels and restaurants including category, price, degree of comfort and setting. Towns underlined in red on Michelin maps 441 - 446 are listed in the current Red Guide with a choice of hotels and restaurants.

The Spanish Tourist Board also publishes a hotel guide with hotel categories ranging from one-star to five-star establishments.

Bear in mind that hotel prices do not include the 7% VAT and that they may vary according to the season.

Special mention should made of Spanish **paradors**, most of which are extremely comfortable, restored historic monuments (castles, palaces and monasteries) in beautiful sites. For further information, contact Paradores de Turismo, Carreterra Requena 3, 28013, Madrid, ☎ (91) 559 00 69. The official UK representative is Keytel International, 402 Edgware Road, London W2 1ED, ☎ (0171) 402 8182. Paradors are indicated on Michelin maps 990 and 441 - 446 *(see Key on p 2 for symbol)*.

Tipping – Bar, restaurant and café bills always include service in the total charge. Nevertheless, it is customary to leave an extra 10%. Porters, doormen, taxi drivers and cinema usherettes will also generally appreciate a tip.

Youth Hostels (Albergues Juveniles) – Spain's 160 youth hostels are open to travellers with an International Card. For further information, contact the Instituto de la Juventud, Calle Ortega y Gasset 71, 28006 Madrid, ☎ (91) 347 77 00. Information about facilities for students may be obtained from TIVE Jose Ortega y Gasset 71, 28006 Madrid.

Camping – Details on camping and caravanning are supplied by the Federación Española de Campings, Calle San Bernardo no 97-99, Edificio Colomina 28015 Madrid, ☎ (91) 448 1234. It is advisable to book in advance for popular resorts during summer.

Useful addresses

Spanish Embassies and Consulates
Spanish Embassy, Portland House, 16th floor, Stag Place, London SW1E 5SE, ☎ (0171) 235 5555.
Spanish Consulate, 20 Draycott Place, London SW3 2RZ, ☎ (0171) 581 5921, consulates also in Manchester and Edinburgh.
Embassy of Spain, 2700 15th Street NW, Washington DC 20009, ☎ 202-265-0190, consulates in Boston, Chicago, Houston, Los Angeles, Miami, New Orleans, New York and San Francisco.

Foreign Embassies and Consulates in Spain

American Embassy: Serrano 75, 28006 Madrid, ☎ (91) 577 4000.

American Consulates: Paseo Reina Elisenda de Montcada 23, 08034 Barcelona, ☎ (93) 280 2227
Avda Lehendakari Agirre 11-3, Deusto, 48014 Bilbao, ☎ (94) 475 8300.
In addition there are consular agencies in Málaga (☎ 952 47 48 91), Sevilla (☎ 95 423 18 85), Valencia (☎ 96 351 69 73), Las Palmas (☎ 928 27 12 59), La Coruña (☎ 981 21 32 33) and Palma de Mallorca (☎ 971 72 50 51).

Australian Embassy: Paseo de la Castellana 143, 28046 Madrid, ☎ 579 04 28.

Consulates: Barcelona (☎ 330 94 96); **Sevilla** (☎ 422 02 40).

British Embassy: Calle Fernando el Santo 16, 28010 Madrid, ☎ (91) 319 02 00.

British Consulate-General: Centro Colon, Marques de la Ensenada 16, 2a, 28004 Madrid, ☎ 91 308 52 01.

Consular offices: Alicante (☎ 965 21 60 22); **Barcelona** (☎ 93 419 90 44); **Bilbao** (☎ 94 415 76 00); **Ibiza** (☎ 971 30 18 18); **Las Palmas**, Islas Canarias (☎ 928 26 25 08); **Málaga** (☎ 952 21 75 71); **Menorca**, Menorca (☎ 971 36 33 73); **Palma de Mallorca**, Mallorca (☎ 971 71 24 45); **Santa Cruz de Tenerife**, Islas Canarias (☎ 922 28 68 63); **Santander** (☎ 942 22 00 00); **Sevilla** (☎ 954 22 88 75); **Tarragona** (☎ 977 22 08 12); and **Vigo** (☎ 986 43 71 33).

Canadian Embassy: Calle Núñez de Balboa 35, 28001 Madrid, ☎ (91) 431 43 00.

Consulates: Barcelona (☎ 93 209 06 34); **Málaga** (☎ 952 22 33 46) and **Sevilla** (☎ 954 22 94 13).

Embassy of Ireland: Claudio Coello 73-1°, 28001 Madrid, ☎ (91) 576 35 00.
Honorary Consulates: Barcelona (☎ 93 491 50 21); **Málaga** (☎ 95 247 51 08); **Palma de Mallorca**, Mallorca (☎ 971 722 504); **Sevilla** (☎ 95 421 63 61); and **Santa Cruz de Tenerife**, Islas Canarias (☎ 922 245 671).

Tourist information

Spanish National Tourist Offices:

London: 57-58 St James's Street, London SW1A 1LD, ☎ (0171) 499 0901.

New York: 665 Fifth Avenue, New York, NY 10022, ☎ 212-759-8822.

Chicago: Water Tower Place, Suite 915 East, 845 North Michigan Avenue, Chicago, IL 60611, ☎ 312-642-1992.

Los Angeles: 8383 Wilshire Blvd, Suite 960, Beverly Hills, CA 90211, ☎ 213-658-7192.

Miami: 1221 Brickell Avenue, Miami, FL 33131, ☎ 305-358-1992.

Toronto: 102 Bloor St West, 14th Floor, Toronto, Ontario M5S 1M8, ☎ 416-961-3131.

Madrid: Secretaría General de Turismo, Calle Castelló 115-117, 28006 Madrid, ☎ (91) 564 65 75.

Tourist Information Centres – All Spanish towns have a Tourist Information Centre, known as the Oficina de Turismo or simply Turismo, marked on Michelin town plans with an 🛈. The Michelin Red Guide España Portugal gives the addresses and telephone numbers of the centres in each town.

901 300 600 – Tourist Information – This service operates daily from 10am to 8pm and provides tourist information in English. Reduced rate call.

To choose a hotel or restaurant use the annual
Michelin Red Guide España Portugal.

Sports

Winter sports – There are at least 30 ski resorts in Spain including 17 in the Pyrenees, 6 in the Cordillera Cantábrica, 4 in the Cordillera Central, 2 in the Cordillera Ibérica and 1 in the Sierra Nevada. Details may be obtained from the Federación Española de Deportes de Invierno, Calle Claudio Coello 32, 28001 Madrid, ☎ (91) 575 05 76 or from ATUDEM (Asociación Turística de Estaciones de Esquí y Montaña) at Calle Juan Ramón Jiménez, No 8 Ed. Eurobuilding, 28036 Madrid, ☎ (91) 458 15 57. A map showing the major resorts, their altitude and facilities (ski-lifts, downhill and cross-country runs) is available from the Spanish Tourist Office.

Sailing – There are over 350 pleasure boat harbours and sailing clubs in Spain. In season it is possible to hire boats with or without crew. Apply to the Federación Española de Vela, Calle Luis de Salazar 12, 28002 Madrid, ☎ (91) 519 50 08.

Scuba-diving – Foreigners should either obtain a diving permit from the head office of the Spanish Merchant Navy or have an equivalent document from their own country.

Windsurfing – Although this sport can be practised all around the coast the most important areas are Punta de Tarifa (Cádiz), the Islas Canarias, Mundaka and Sopelama beaches (Vizcaya). Boards can be hired on all major beaches.

Water skiing – Spain's east coast and inland lakes and reservoirs provide good conditions for water-skiing. Enquire at the local Oficina de Turismo or at the resort. Federación Española de Esquí Náutico, Calle Sabino de Arana 30, 08028 Barcelona, ☎ (93) 330 89 03.

Hunting and Fishing – Hunting and fishing permits may be obtained from local Autonomous Community authorities. However, to hunt in a National Park, apply to ICONA (Instituto Nacional para la Conservación de la Naturaleza), Gran Vía San Francisco 35, 28005 Madrid, ☎ (91) 266 82 00.

Mountaineering – For lists of qualified instructors and local guides apply to the Oficina de Turismo or the Federación Española de Montañismo, Calle Alberto Aguilera 3, 28015 Madrid, ☎ (91) 445 13 82.

Golf – Spain is now recognised as one of Europe's foremost golfing nations with world-class players such as Seve Ballesteros and José-María Olazabal and a wide selection of golf courses to choose from. Several of the 167 golf courses are of championship standard. Details may be obtained from the Federación Española de Golf, Calle Capitán Haya 9, 5°, 28020 Madrid, ☎ (91) 555 26 82.

Golf courses and their telephone numbers are listed in the current **Michelin Red Guide España Portugal** under the nearest town. A map showing the golf courses, the number of holes, addresses and telephone numbers is available from the Spanish Tourist Office.

Books to read

General

The Spaniards – John Hooper (Viking)
Imperial Spain (1469-1716) – J.H. Elliott (Pelican; Penguin)
Spain and the Jews – edited by Elie Kedourie (Thames & Hudson)
The Sephardim – Lucien Gubbay and Abraham Levy (Carnell Ltd.)
Spain: Change of a Nation – Robert Graham (1984)
Fire in the Blood – Ian Gibson (Faber)
Moorish Spain – Richard Fletcher (Weidenfeld and Nicolson)
The Basques – Collins (Blackwell Publishers)
Living in Spain in the Eighties – John Reay Smith (Robert Hale Ltd)
The Spanish Civil War – Alun Kenwood (O Wolff Publishers Ltd)
Spanish History – S Ortiz-Carboneres (O Wolff Publishers Ltd)
Contest of Christian and Muslim Spain – Reilly (Blackwell Publishers)
Hispanic World in Crisis and Change – Lynch (Blackwell Publishers)
Roman Spain – S J Keay (British Museum)

Christopher Columbus

Admiral of the Ocean Sea – Samuel Eliot Morison (Little, Brown)
The Spanish Seaborne Empire – J.H. Parry (University of California Press)
Columbus, His Enterprise – Hans Koning (Latin American Bureau)
The Mysterious History of Columbus – John Noble Wilford (Knopf)
In Search of Columbus – Hunter Davies (Sinclair-Stevenson)
The Columbus Myth – Ian Wilson (Simon and Schuster)
Columbus: For Gold, God and Glory – John Dyson (Hodder & Stoughton)

Travel

Spanish Journeys: A Portrait of Spain – Adam Hopkins (Viking)
A Stranger in Spain – H. V. Morton (Methuen)
Cities of Spain – David Gilmour (John Murray)
Barcelona – Robert Hughes (Harvill)
Barcelonas – Manuel Vázquez Montalbán (Verso)
Contrasting Spain – Charles Moore (Venton Educational Ltd)
Charm of Majorca – Charles Moore (Venton Educational Ltd)
Madrid and Southern Spain – A. Launay and M. Pendered (B.T. Batsford)
South from Granada – Gerard Brenan (Cambridge University Press)
A Visit to Spain – Hans Christian Anderson (Peter Owen)
Iberia – Spanish Travels and Reflections – James A. Michener (Secker & Warburg)
Spain – Jan Morris (Penguin Travel Library)
Andalusia – Michael Jacobs (Penguin)
Castile – J Bentley (George Philip)
Madrid – M Jacobs (George Philip)
Guide to the Wines of Spain – Jan Read (Mitchell Beazley; Reed Int)

Art - Literature

Spanish Short Stories 1 – edited by Jean Franco (Penguin)
Fiesta, The Sun Also Rises – Ernest Hemingway (Grafton Books)
Homage to Catalonia – George Orwell (Penguin)
A Moment of War – Laurie Lee (Viking)
As I Walked Out One Midsummer Morning – Laurie Lee (Penguin)
A Rose for Winter – Laurie Lee (Penguin)
The House of Bernardo – Frederico Garcia Lorca
The Prado – Sánchez Cantón (Thames & Hudson)
Velasquez – Joseph Emile Muller (Thames & Hudson)
Picasso – Timothy Hilton (Thames & Hudson)
Goya – José Gudiol (Thames & Hudson)
Miró – R Penrose (Thames & Hudson)
Salvador Dalí – Dawn Ades (Thames & Hudson)
Spanish Design and Architecture – Emma Dent Coad (Cassell Plc)

Vocabulary

GENERAL WORDS

For words and expressions used in hotels and restaurants see the current Michelin Red Guide España Portugal

Terms of address

yes, no	sí, no
good morning	buenos días
good afternoon	buenas tardes
goodbye	hasta luego, adiós
please	por favor
How are you?	¿qué tal?
thank you (very much)	(muchas) gracias
excuse me	perdone
I don't understand	no entiendo
sir, Mr., you	señor, Usted
madam, Mrs.	señora
miss	señorita

Correspondence

post box	buzón
post office	Correos
telephone	Telégrafos, Teléfonos
letter	carta
post card	(tarjeta) postal
poste restante	lista (de Correos)
stamp	sello
telephone call	conferencia
tobacco shop	estanco, tabacos

Time

when?	¿cuándo?
what time?	¿a qué hora?
today	hoy
yesterday	ayer
tomorrow morning	mañana por la mañana
tomorrow afternoon	mañana por la tarde

Shopping

how much?	¿cuánto (vale)?
(too) expensive	(demasiado) caro
a lot, little	mucho, poco
more, less	más, menos
big, small	grande, pequeño
credit card	tarjeta de crédito

On the road, in town

coche	car
gasolina	petrol
a la derecha	on the right
a la izquierda	on the left
obras	road works
peligroso	danger, dangerous
cuidado	beware, take care
dar la vuelta a	to go round, tour
después de	after, beyond
girar	to go round, to circle

SITES AND SIGHTS

See also architectural terms p 31
Words in italics are in Catalan

where is?	¿dónde está?	gargantas	gorges
may one visit?	¿se puede visitar?	gruta	cavern, grotto
key	llave	hoz	defile, narrow pass, gorge
light	luz		
sacristan	sacristán	huerto, huerta	vegetable/market garden
guide	guía		
porter, caretaker	guarda, conserje	iglesia	church *(p 29)*
open, closed	abierto, cerrado	imagen	religious statue/sculpture
no entry, not allowed	prohibido	isla	island, isle
entrance, exit	entrada, salida	lago, *estany*	lake
apply to	dirigirse a	mezquita	mosque
wait	esperar	monasterio, *monestir*	monastery
beautiful	bello, hermoso	monte	mount, mountain
storey, stairs, steps	piso, escalera	mirador	belvedere, viewpoint, lookout point
alcazaba	Muslim fortress		
alcázar	Muslim palace		
alrededores	environs, outskirts	museo, *museu*	museum
alto	pass, high pass	nacimiento	source, birthplace
ayuntamiento		palacio (real), *palau*	(royal) palace
ajuntament	town hall	pantano	artificial lake
audiencia	audience, court	paseo, *passeig*	avenue, esplanade, promenade
balneario	spa		
barranco	gully, ravine	paso	sculptured figures: the Passion
barrio, *barri*	quarter		
bodega	wine cellar/store	pazo	manor-house (Galicia)
cabo, *cap*	cape, headland		
calle, *carrer*	street	plaza, *plaça*	square
calle mayor	main street	plaza mayor	main square
camino	road, track	plaza de toros	bullring
campanario	belfry	portada	portal, west door
capilla	chapel	pórtico	portal, porch
capitel	capital	presa	dam
carretera	main road	pueblo, *poble*	village, market town
cartuja	Carthusian monastery	puente, *pont*	bridge
		puerta	door, gate, entrance
casa	house	puerto	pass, harbour, port
casa consistorial	town hall	ría	estuary
castillo	castle	río	river, stream
castro	Celtic village	romano; románico	Roman; Romanesque
ciudad, *ciutat*	town, city		
claustro	cloister	santuario	church
colegio, colegiata	college, collegiate church	siglo	century
		talla	carved wood
collado, *coll*	pass, high pass	tapices	tapestries
convento	monastery, convent	techo	ceiling
cruz	cross, Calvary	tesoro	treasury, treasure
cuadro	picture	torre	tower, belfry
cueva, gruta, cava	cave, grotto	torre del homenaje	keep
desfiladero	defile, cleft	torrente	mountain stream, torrent
embalse	reservoir, dam		
ermita	hermitage, chapel	valle, *vall*	valley
estación	station	vega	fertile plain
excavaciones	excavations	vidriera	window: plain or stained glass
finca	property, domain		
fuente	fountain	vista	view, panorama

Calendar of events

Spain's major festivals are mentioned in the list below. For smaller events, apply to the local Spanish Tourist Centre *(Oficina de Turismo)* which will have a revised calendar with details of places and times.

Week before Ash Wednesday
Cádiz - Santa Cruz de Tenerife....   Carnival festivities; processions

Carnival Sunday
Sitges ....   International Vintage Car Rally

3rd Sunday in Lent
Castellón de la Plana ....   Feast of the Magdalen; bullfights, processions

12-19 March
Valencia............................   St Joseph's Day "Fallas"

Holy Week
Cartagena, Cuenca, Málaga, Murcia, Sevilla, Valladodid, Zamora ....   Solemn processions

First week after Easter
Murcia.........................   Spring Festival

April
Sevilla ....   Feria

22-24 or 24-26 April
Alcoy ....   St George's Festival: "Moros y Cristianos"

Alcoy — Fiesta de San Jorge

Last Sunday in April
Andújar (Jaén)..........................   Romería (pilgrimage) to the Virgen de la Cabeza

Early May
Jerez de la Frontera ....   Feria del Caballo (Horse show)

Mid-May
Córdoba...........................   Patios festival and national flamenco competitions

15 May
Madrid...........................   San Isidro Festival: several days of bullfights

Whitsun
El Rocío (Huelva) ....   Gypsy pilgrimage to the Nuestra Señora del Rocío shrine

Atienza (Guadalajara) ....   Caballada festival

2nd Thursday after Whitsun: Corpus Christi
Puenteareas (Pontevedra) .... Streets carpeted with flowers
Sitges .... Streets carpeted with flowers; competitions
Toledo .... Solemn processions

24 June
Alicante .... "Hogueras" Midsummer's Day (St John) Festival

Ciutadella (Menorca) .... Midsummer's Day (St John) Festival

7-14 July
Pamplona .... "Sanfermines"

1st or 2nd Saturday in August
Arriondas-Ribadesella (Asturias) .. Kayak races down the Río Sella

15 August
Elche .... Elche Mystery Play

7-17 September
Albacete.. Feria

19 September
Oviedo .... America Day in Asturias

21 September
Oviedo .... St Matthew's (San Mateo) Festival

20-26 September
Logroño... La Rioja Wine Harvest Festival

24-28 September
Barcelona .... Festival of Our Lady of Mercy (Virgen de la Merced)

12 October
Guadalupe .... Hispanidad Festival: solemn processions

Week of 12 October
Zaragoza .... Pilar Festival

Windmills at Consuegra in La Mancha

Admission times and charges

As admission times and charges are liable to alteration, the information below is given only as a general guideline.

The following list details the opening times and charges (if any) and other relevant information concerning all sights in the descriptive part of this Guide accompanied by the symbol ⊙. The entries below are given in the same order as in the alphabetical section of the Guide.

The prices quoted apply to individual adults with no reduction. Special conditions for both times and charges are generally granted to groups if arranged beforehand.

Charges for admission are given in pesetas: pts.

Given the great wealth of Spanish painting and sculpture, museums are often re-arranging their exhibitions or undergoing restoration so it is always worth your while to telephone ahead of time to confirm admission times.

Opening times for churches are only given if the interior is of special interest. As a general rule, avoid visiting a church during a service; however, some are only open at these times in which case you are expected to be as discreet as possible.

For information on public holidays see p 327. Details on local feast days and festivals may be obtained from the Tourist Information Centre.

Telephone: telephone numbers listed below are for use within Spain; they are preceded by 9 (the inter-provincial code) and the area code. Drop the 9 if you are phoning from abroad.

A

AGUILAR DE CAMPÓO
🛈 pl. Mayor 32, 34800 ☎ (979) 12 20 24

Monasterio de Santa María la Real – Open Mondays to Saturdays 1000 to 1400 and 1600 to 2000; Sundays and public holidays 1100 to 1400 and 1700 to 2000; closed 1 January and 25 December; ☎ (979) 12 33 53.

Colegiata de San Miguel – Guided tours daily July, August and September 0900 to 2000; the rest of the year by prior arrangement; ☎ (979) 12 26 88, or ask for key at Tourist Office opposite.

AIGÜESTORTES and LAGO DE SANT MAURICI

Parque Nacional – Apply to the Centro del Parque Nacional, Calle L'estudi at Boí; ☎ (973) 69 61 89 or Calle Prado del Guarda 2 at Espot; ☎ (973) 62 40 36.

ALBACETE
🛈 Del Tinte 2. 02071. ☎ (967) 21 56 11

Museo de Albacete – Open Tuesdays to Saturdays 1000 to 1400 and 1630 to 1900; Sundays and public holidays 0900 to 1400; 1 July to 17 September 1000 to 1400; Sundays and public holidays 0900 to 1400; closed Mondays, Maundy Thursday, Good Friday, 24 December and 1 January; 200 pts; ☎ (967) 22 83 07.

ALBARRACÍN
🛈 Plaza Mayor 1. 44100. ☎ (978) 71 02 51

Catedral – Open in July and August 1030 to 1400 and 1630 to 2200; rest of the year, generally open in the morning though no fixed timetable; 100 pts (museum); ☎ (978) 71 00 84.

ALCALÁ DE HENARES
🛈 Callejón de Santa María 1. 28801. ☎ (91) 889 26 94

Antigua Universidad or Colegio de San Ildefonso – Guided tours (40 mins) daily except Mondays 1100 to 1400 and 1600 to 1900; closed on Mondays, in August, 1 January and 25 December; 200 pts (combined ticket including Capilla de San Ildefonso); ☎ (91) 889 26 94.

Capilla de San Ildefonso – See Antigua Universidad.

ALCÁNTARA
🛈 Av. de Mérida 21. 10980. ☎ (927) 39 08 63

Convento de San Benito – Guided tours (1/2 hour) Mondays to Saturdays 1000 to 1400; in the summer from 1000 to 1400 and 1800 to 2000; closed Sundays, local and public holidays, Holy Week and September; ☎ (927) 39 00 80.

ALCAÑIZ

Colegiata – Open daily 1000 to 1300 and 1700 to 2000; ☎ (978) 83 12 13.

ALICANTE
🖪 Explanada de España 2. 03002. 📞 (96) 520 00 00

Catedral de San Nicolás – Open daily 0930 to 1230 and 1800 to 1930; 📞 (96) 521 26 62.

Ayuntamiento: Capilla – Open 0900 to 1300 except Sundays and public holidays; 📞 (96) 514 91 01.

Iglesia de Santa María – Closed temporarily for restoration.

Museo de la Asegurada – Open Tuesdays to Saturdays 1000 to 1300 and 1700 to 2000; 1 May to 31 September 1030 to 1330 and 1800 to 2100; Sundays and public holidays 1000 to 1330; closed Mondays, 1 January, 1 May, 24 June and 25 December; 📞 (96) 514 94 68.

Castillo de Santa Bárbara – Open daily (museum closed on Mondays); 1 October to 31 March 0900 to 1900; 1 April to 30 September 1000 to 2000; 200 pts for use of the lift, free of charge otherwise; 📞 (96) 514 94 68.

Excursion

Cuevas de Canalobre – Guided tours (40 mins) 1 April to 30 September 1030 to 1950; 1 October to 31 March 1100 to 1750; closed 1 January and 25 December; 425 pts; 📞 (96) 569 92 50.

ALMAGRO
🖪 Mayor de Carnicerías 5. 13270. 📞 (926) 86 07 17

Corral de Comedias – Daily except Mondays 1000 to 1400 and 1600 to 1900; 1 July to 30 September 1000 to 1400 and 1800 to 2100; Sundays 1000 to 1400; closed Mondays; 400 pts; 📞 (926) 88 22 44.

Convento de la Asunción (or Padres Dominicos) – Open daily 0900 to 1400 and 1600 to 1800; in summer 0900 to 1400 and 1700 to 1900; Saturdays, Sundays and public holidays 0900 to 1400; cloisters closed during services; 📞 (926) 86 03 50.

ALMANSA

Excursion

Cueva de la Vieja – Guided visits (1 hour) 0800 to 1500; Saturdays 1000 to 1200; closed Sundays and public holidays; 500 pts; 📞 (967) 33 00 01.

ALMERíA
🖪 Hermanos Machado 4. 04004. 📞 (950) 23 08 58

Alcazaba – Open daily 0930 to 1330 and 1530 to 1900; 16 June to 30 September 1000 to 1400 and 1700 to 2000; closed 1 January and 25 December; 400 pts; 📞 (950) 27 16 17.

Catedral – Open daily 0830 to 1200 and 1730 to 2000; 📞 (950) 23 48 48.

ALQUÉZAR

Colegiata – Guided tours daily except Tuesdays 1100 to 1300 and 1600 to 1800 (1100 to 1300 and 1630 to 1930 in summer); 200 pts.

Cuevas de ALTAMIRA

The number of visitors is restricted in order to preserve the paintings in the caves. Write well in advance (a year) for permission to: Centro de Investigacíon y Museo de Altamira, 39330 Santillana del Mar, (Cantabria); 📞 (942) 81 80 05.

Museo – Open daily except Mondays 0930 to 1430 (1345 on Sundays and public holidays); closed Mondays, 1 January, 1 May, 28 June, 16 August, 24, 25 and 31 December; 400 pts.

ANTEQUERA
🖪 Infante Don Fernando – edificio San Luis. 29200. 📞 (95) 270 04 05

Museo municipal – Guided tours (3/4 hour) Tuesdays to Fridays 1000 to 1330; Saturdays 1000 to 1300; Sundays 1100 to 1300; closed Mondays and public holidays; 200 pts; 📞 (952) 84 18 27.

Iglesia del Carmen – Open during services.

Excursion

Los Dólmenes – Open Tuesdays to Saturdays 1000 to 1400 and 1500 to 1730 (1000 to 1400 and 1600 to 1800 in summer; Sundays and public holidays 1000 to 1400; closed Mondays, 1 January, Maundy Thursday, Good Friday and 25 December; 📞 (952) 70 04 05.

ARACENA
🖪 Pl. de San Pedro. s/n. 21200. 📞 (959) 11 03 55

Gruta de las Maravillas – Guided tours (3/4 hour) daily except Monday 1030 to 1330 and 1500 to 1800 (every hour); every half hour on Saturdays, Sundays and public holidays; 750 pts; 📞 (959) 11 03 55.

ARANJUEZ

🛈 Pl. Puente de Barcas s/n. 28300. **☎** (91) 891 04 27

Palacio Real – Guided tours (25 mins) daily except Mondays 1000 to 1730 (1000 to 1830 1 April to 30 September); closed Mondays, 1 and 6 January, 2 and 30 May, 25 July, 15 August, 5 September, 25 and 26 December; may also close during official ceremonies; 600 pts; **☎** (91) 891 13 44.

Parterre and Jardín de la Isla – Same details as Palacio Real.

Jardín del Príncipe – Same times of opening and closing as the Palacio Real.

Casa del Labrador – Guided tours (20 mins); same times as the Palacio Real; 400 pts (600 pts for combined ticket including the Casa de Marinos).

Casa de Marinos – Guided tours (15 mins); same times and charges as the Casa del Labrador; 300 pts (600 pts for combined ticket including the Casa del Labrador).

ARCOS DE LA FRONTERA

🛈 Cuesta de Belén s/n. 11630. **☎** (956) 70 22 64

Iglesia de Santa María – Open Mondays to Saturdays 1000 to 1300 and 1600 to 1900 (1030 to 1300 and 1630 to 1900 1 July to 31 October); closed Sundays and public holidays; 150 pts; **☎** (956) 70 00 06.

ASTORGA

🛈 Pl. Eduardo de Castro (iglesia Sant Marta). 24700. **☎** (987) 61 68 38

Catedral – Open 1 April to 30 September 0900 to 1200 (1300 on Sundays and public holidays) and 1700 to 1830 (1700 to 2030 on days before public holidays); 1 October to 31 March 0900 to 1200 (1300 on Sundays and public holidays) and 1600 to 1730 (1700 to 2030 on days before public holidays); **☎** (987) 61 58 20.

Museo de la Catedral – Open daily 1000 to 1400 and 1600 to 2000; 1 November to 31 March 1100 to 1400 and 1530 to 1830; closed January; 200 pts; **☎** (987) 61 58 20.

Palacio Episcopal – Open Mondays to Saturdays 1100 to 1400 and 1530 to 1830; summer 1000 to 1400 and 1600 to 2000; closed Sundays (except August), 1 and 6 January and 25 December; 200 pts (350 pts including museum); **☎** (987) 61 68 82.

Museo de los Caminos – Same times as the Palacio Episcopal.

ÁVILA

🛈 Pl. Catedral 4. 05001. **☎** (920) 21 13 87

Catedral – Open daily 1000 to 1300 and 1500 to 1900; 1 November to 30 April 1000 (1100 Sundays and public holidays) to 1400; closed 1 and 6 January, 15 October and 15 December; closed during Holy Week and for services during religious festivals; 200 pts; **☎** (920) 21 16 41.

Museo de la Catedral – Open daily 1 April to 31 October 1000 to 1300 and 1500 to 1900; 1 November to 31 March daily except Mondays 1000 to 1400 (1100 to 1400 Sundays and public holidays); closed 1 and 6 January, 15 October and 25 December; 200 pts; **☎** (920) 21 16 41.

Basílica de San Vicente – Open daily except Mondays 1000 to 1400 and 1600 to 2000; 50 pts; **☎** (920) 25 52 30.

Monasterio de Santo Tomás – Open daily 1000 to 1300 and 1600 to 2000; entrance to cloisters and chancel 50 pts (free on Mondays); **☎** (920) 22 04 00.

Iglesia de San Pedro – Open daily 0900 to 1230 and 1700 to 2030; **☎** (920) 22 19 04.

B

BADAJOZ

🛈 Pl. Libertad 3. 06005. **☎** (924) 22 27 63

Catedral – Under restoration; open daily 1100 to 1330; **☎** (924) 22 39 99.

Museo arqueológico provincial – Open daily except Mondays 1000 to 1500; closed 1 January, Good Friday and 25 December; 400 pts; **☎** (924) 22 23 14.

BAEZA

🛈 Pl. del Pópulo s/n. 23440. **☎** (953) 74 04 44

Catedral – Open daily 1030 to 1330 and 1730 to 1930; 500 pts; **☎** (953) 74 04 74.

Iglesia de San Andrés – Open 1800 to 2100 (during services only); **☎** (953) 74 04 74.

BAIONA

Excolegiata – Open daily 0900 to 1300 and 1600 to 2000; **☎** (986) 35 50 03.

Monterreal – Open until 2200; 100 pts and 500 pts per car; **☎** (986) 35 50 00.

BARBASTRO 　　　　　　　🄸 Pl. de España s/n, 22300. 🕾 (974) 31 01 50

Catedral – Open daily 0900 to 1300; 100 pts.

Excursion

Torreciudad – Open 1 May to 15 June 1000 to 1400 and 1600 to 1900 (2030 Sundays and public holidays); 16 June to 15 September 1000 (0900 Sundays and public holidays) to 1400 and 1600 to 2030; 16 September to 30 April 1000 to 1400 and 1600 to 1900; 🕾 (974) 30 40 25.

BARCELONA 　　　　　🄸 Gran Vía de les Corts Catalanes 658. 08010. 🕾 (93) 301 74 43

Catedral – Open daily 0900 to 1300 and 1600 to 1900 (according to services); 50 pts (chancel); 🕾 (93) 315 15 54.

Museu de la Catedral – Open daily 1100 to 1300; 50 pts.

Palau de la Generalitat – Guided tours (1/2 hour) by appointment only, weekends and public holidays; 🕾 (93) 402 46 17.

Museu d'Història de la Ciutat – Open Tuesdays to Saturdays 1000 to 1400 and 1600 to 2000; Sundays and public holidays 1000 to 1400; closed Mondays, 1 January, Good Friday, 1 May, 24 June and 25 and 26 December; 300 pts; 🕾 (93) 315 11 11.

Museu Frederic Marès – Open Tuesdays to Saturdays 1000 to 1700; Sundays and public holidays 0900 to 1400; closed Mondays, 1 January, Good Friday, Easter Monday, 1 May, 24 June, 25 and 26 December; 300 pts; 🕾 (93) 310 58 00.

Drassanes and Museu Marítim – Open Tuesdays to Saturdays 0930 to 1300 and 1600 to 1900; Sundays and public holidays 1000 to 1400; closed Mondays, 1 and 6 January, Good Friday, 1 May, 24 June, 15 August, 25 and 26 December; 300 pts; 🕾 (93) 418 32 45.

Palau Güell – Open 1000 to 1400 and 1600 to 2000 except Sundays and public holidays; 300 pts; 🕾 (93) 317 39 74.

Iglesia de Santa María del Pi – Open Mondays to Saturdays 0830 to 1330 and 1630 to 2030; Sundays and public holidays 0900 to 1400 and 1730 to 2100; 🕾 (93) 318 47 43.

Museu Picasso – Open Tuesdays to Saturdays 1000 to 2000; Sundays 1000 to 1500, closed Mondays, 1 January, Good Friday, 1 May, 24 June, 25 and 26 December; 500 pts; 🕾 (93) 319 63 10.

Iglesia de Santa María del Mar – Open daily 0845 to 1230 and 1630 to 2015; (Monday to Friday: entrance through rear of church; 🕾 (93) 310 23 90.

Museu d'Art de Catalunya – Closed for renovation; for information call (93) 423 18 24.

Poble Espanyol – Open Mondays 0900 to 1700; Tuesdays, Wednesdays, Thursdays and Sundays 0900 to 0200; Fridays, Saturdays and eves of public holidays 0900 to 0400; closed 25 December and 1 January at midday; 650 pts; 🕾 (93) 426 62 68.

Fundació Joan Miró – Open Tuesdays to Saturdays 1100 to 1900 (2130 Thursdays); Sundays and public holidays 1030 to 1430; closed Mondays, 1 and 6 January, Good Friday, 11 September, 25 and 26 December; 500 pts; 🕾 (93) 329 19 08.

Museu Arqueològic – Open Tuesdays to Saturdays 0930 to 1330 and 1530 to 1900; Sundays 0930 to 1400; closed Mondays and public holidays; 200 pts; (free on Sundays); 🕾 (93) 423 56 01.

La Sagrada Familia – Open daily 1 November to 28 February 0900 to 1800; March, April and October 0900 to 1900; May and September 0900 to 2000; 1 June to 31 August 0900 to 2100; 1 January, Good Friday and 25 December 0900 to 1400; 700 pts; 🕾 (93) 455 02 47.

La Pedrera or Casa Milá – Guided tours (1/2 hour) Tuesdays to Saturdays at 1000, 1100, 1200 and 1300 (reservation needed); closed Sundays, Mondays and public holidays; 🕾 (93) 487 36 13.

Casa Quadras: Museu de la Mùsica – Open daily except Mondays 1000 to 1400 (Wednesdays 1000 to 1400 and 1700 to 2000); closed Mondays, 1 January, Good Friday, 1 May, 24 June, 25 and 26 December; 300 pts; 🕾 (93) 416 11 57.

Parc Güell – Open daily 1 November to 28 February 1000 to 1800 (1900 in March and October, 2000 in April and September, 2100 from 1 May to 31 August); 🕾 (93) 424 38 09.

Palau de la Mùsica Catalana – Guided tours (1 hour) by appointment in Catalan, Spanish, English, French and Italian; 200 pts; 🕾 (93) 268 10 00.

Fundació Antoni Tàpies – Open daily except Mondays 1100 to 2000; 400 pts; 🕾 (93) 487 03 15.

BARCELONA

Monastir de Pedralbes – Open Sundays, Tuesdays to Fridays 1000 to 1400; Saturdays 1000 to 1700; closed Mondays; 300 pts; ☎ (93) 203 99 08.

Palau de Pedralbes – Open daily except Mondays 1000 to 1400; closed 1 January, Good Friday and 25 December; 300 pts; ☎ (93) 280 50 24.

Museu de Cerámica – Open daily except Mondays 1000 to 1400; closed 1 January, Good Friday, 1 May, 24 June, 25 and 26 December; 300 pts; ☎ (93) 280 16 21.

La Ciutadella – Open daily 0800 to 2000 (2100 1 April to 30 September); ☎ (93) 424 38 09.

Parc Zoològic – Open daily 1000 to 1700; in summer 0930 to 1930; 25 December 1000 to 1400; 900 pts; ☎ (93) 221 25 06.

Museu d'Art Modern – Open daily except Tuesdays 0900 to 2100; closed 1 January and 25 December; 300 pts; ☎ (93) 319 57 28.

BELMONTE

Castillo – Open daily 0900 to 1300 and 1530 to 1900; 150 pts; ☎ (967) 17 00 08.

BETANZOS

Iglesia de Santa María del Azogue – Open daily 0900 to 1300 and 1700 to 2000; ☎ (981) 77 07 02.

Iglesia de San Francisco – Open daily 0830 to 1300 and 1400 to 2100 (if locked knock on door); ☎ (981) 77 01 10.

BILBAO   🖪 Pl. Arriaga s/n 48005. ☎ (94) 416 02 88

Museo de Bellas Artes – Open Tuesdays to Saturdays 1000 to 1330 and 1600 to 1930; Sundays 1000 to 1400; closed Mondays and public holidays; ☎ (94) 441 01 54 or 441 95 36.

Museo Arqueológico, Etnográfico e Histórico Vasco – Open Tuesdays to Saturdays 1030 to 1330 and 1600 to 1900; Sundays 1030 to 1330; closed Mondays and public holidays; ☎ (94) 415 54 23.

Santuario de Begoña – Open daily 0800 (Sundays and public holidays 0930) to 1400 and 1700 to 2100; closed during services; ☎ (94) 412 70 91.

El BURGO DE OSMA

Catedral and Museo – Open Mondays to Saturdays in summer 1030 to 1300 and 1600 to 1830 (in winter 1100 to 1300 and 1530 to 1830); Sundays and public holidays 1200 to 1330 and 1600 (1530 in winter) to 1830; closed Mondays to Fridays 3 November to 1 March; 200 pts; ☎ (975) 34 01 96.

Excursions

Berlanga de Duero: Colegiata – Open daily in summer 1100 to 1300 and 1700 to 2000; outside summer and public holidays 1000 to 1400; closed Mondays throughout year; If closed, apply to the priest (house abutting the church); ☎ (975) 34 30 49.

Casillas de Berlanga: Iglesia de San Baudelio de Berlanga – Open Wednesdays to Saturdays 1030 to 1400 and 1600 to 1800 (1900 from 1 April to 30 June and 1 September to 31 October); 1030 to 1400 and 1700 to 2100 in July and August; Sundays and public holidays 1030 to 1400; closed Mondays and Tuesdays; ☎ (975) 34 34 19.

BURGOS   🖪 Pl. Alonso Martínez 7. 09003. ☎ (947) 20 31 25

Catedral – Open daily 0930 to 1330 and 1600 to 1900 (except during services); 350 pts; ☎ (947) 20 47 12.

Real Monasterio de Las Huelgas – Guided tours (50 mins) Tuesdays to Saturdays 1100 to 1315 and 1600 to 1715 (Saturdays 1745); 1 April to 30 September Tuesdays to Saturdays 1030 to 1315 and 1600 to 1745; Sundays and public holidays 1030 to 1415 throughout year; closed Mondays, 1 and 6 January, Good Friday, 2 June, Fiesta del Curpillo (date varies), 29 June, 25 July, 15 August and 25 December; 600 pts; ☎ (947) 20 16 30 or (91) 547 53 50 extension 417.

Cartuja de Miraflores – Open daily 1015 to 1500 and 1600 to 1800.

Museo de Burgos – Open Tuesdays to Fridays 0945 to 1400 and 1615 to 1900; Saturdays and Sundays 1000 to 1400; closed Mondays and public holidays ; 200 pts; ☎ (947) 26 58 75.

Iglesia de San Nicolás – Open daily 15 June to 15 September 0900 to 1400 and 1600 to 2000; 1 October to 31 May 1830 to 2000; Mondays open all day throughout year; public holidays 0900 to 1400 and 1700 to 1800; closed during services; ☎ (947) 20 70 95.

Museo Marceliano Santa María – Open Tuesdays to Saturdays 1000 to 1350 and 1700 to 1950; Sundays 1000 to 1350; closed Mondays and public holidays; 25 pts; ☎ (947) 20 56 87.

C

CÁCERES   🛈 Pl. Mayor 33. 10003. ☎ (927) 24 63 47

Iglesia de Santa María – Open daily 1000 to 1400 and 1700 to 2000 (1800 to 2100 1 May to 30 September); ☎ (927) 21 53 13.

Palacio de Carvajal – Guided tours (20 mins) Mondays to Saturdays 0800 to 1500 and 1530 to 2200; Sundays and public holidays 1000 to 1400; ☎ (927) 25 55 97.

Casa de las Veletas: Museo de Cáceres – Open Tuesdays to Saturdays 0930 to 1500; Sundays 1015 to 1515; closed Mondays and public holidays (except Sundays); 400 pts; ☎ (927) 24 72 34.

Iglesia de Santiago – Open Mondays to Thursdays 1900 to 2100 (2000 in summer); Fridays 1000 to 1330 and 1700 to 2100; Saturdays 1100 to 1330 and 1900 to 2100; Sundays and public holidays 1000 to 1330; ☎ (927) 24 49 06.

Excursion

Santuario de la Virgen de la Montaña – Open daily 0830 to 1400 and 1600 to 2000; in summer 0730 to 1400 and 1600 to 2200; ☎ (927) 22 00 49.

CÁDIZ   🛈 Calderón de la Barca 1. 11003. ☎ (956) 21 13 13

Museo de Cádiz – Open Tuesdays to Sundays 0930 to 1400; closed Mondays and public holidays (except Sundays), 7 October. 24 and 25 December; 400 pts; ☎ (956) 21 43 00.

Museo Histórico – Open Tuesdays to Fridays 0900 to 1300 and 1600 to 1900 (1700 to 2000 1 June to 30 September); weekends 0900 to 1300; closed Mondays, 1 and 6 January, 28 February, 1 May, 15 August, 7 and 12 October, 1 November, 6, 8, 24, 25 and 31 December; ☎ (956) 22 17 88.

Iglesia de San Felipe Neri – Open Mondays to Saturdays 0830 to 1000 and 1930 to 2130; Sundays and public holidays 1030 to 1145, 1300 to 1415 and 1930 to 2130; ☎ (956) 21 16 12.

Catedral and Museo – Open Mondays to Saturdays 1000 to 1230; closed Sundays, public holidays, 7 October. 28 December and Monday during Carnival; 250 pts; ☎ (956) 28 61 54.

Excursion

Medina Sidonia: Iglesia de Santa María – Open daily 1000 to 1400 and 1600 to 2000.

CALATRAVA

Castillo-convento – Open daily except Mondays 1000 to 1400 and 1600 to 1800 (1700 to 2000 from 1 April to 30 September); 400 pts; ☎ (908) 62 35 48.

CANGAS DE NARCEA

Excursion

Corias: Monasterio – Open daily 1000 to 1230 and 1600 to 1930; it is advisable to make an appointment beforehand; ☎ (98) 581 01 50.

CARAVACA DE LA CRUZ

Castillo-iglesia de la Santa Cruz – Open Mondays to Saturdays 1 April to 30 September 1100 to 1330 and 1700 to 2030 (1600 to 1930 rest of year); Sundays and public holidays 1100 to 1330 throughout year; 250 pts; ☎ (968) 70 77 43.

CARDONA   🛈 Av. del Rastrillo s/n. 08261. ☎ (93) 869 27 98

Colegiata – Open Tuesdays to Saturdays 1000 to 1330 and 1500 to 1730 (1830 from 1 June to 30 September); Sundays and public holidays 1000 to 1330; closed Mondays, 1 January and 25 and 31 December; 200 pts; ☎ (93) 869 27 98.

CARMONA
El Pl. de las Descalzas s/n. 41410. ☏ (95) 414 22 00

Iglesia de Santa María – Open daily 0900 to 1200 and 1830 to 2100; ☏ (95) 419 02 26.

Necrópolis Romana – Open Tuesdays to Fridays 1000 to 1400 and 1600 to 1800; 15 June to 15 September 0900 to 1400; weekends 1000 to 1400; closed Mondays and public holidays; 400 pts; ☏ (95) 414 08 11.

CARTAGENA
El Pl. Ayuntamiento. 30202. ☏ (968) 50 64 83

Museo Nacional de Aqueología Marítima – Open daily except Mondays 1000 to 1500; closed 1 January, 1 May, 24, 25 and 31 December; 400 pts; ☏ (968) 50 84 15.

CELANOVA

Monasterio – Guided tours (1/2 hour) 1 June to 30 September daily 1100 to 1300 and 1700 to 1900; rest of the year 1200 to 1300 and 1600 to 1700; if closed, go to door and ask for key; closed on public holidays; 200 pts; ☏ (988) 43 14 81.

Excursion

Bande: Iglesia de Santa Comba – Ask for keys next to the Iglesia Nueva.

CEUTA
El Alcalde José Victori Goñalons s/n. 11701. ☏ (956) 51 40 92

Museo Municipal – Open Mondays to Saturdays 1000 to 1330 and 1700 to 2030; closed Sundays and public holidays; ☏ (956) 51 73 98.

CIUDAD RODRIGO
El Pl. de las Amayuelas 1. 37500. ☏ (923) 46 05 61

Catedral – Open daily 1000 to 1330 and 1600 to 1930 (1830 on Sundays and public holidays); 200 pts charge for the cloisters and museum; ☏ (923) 48 14 24.

COCA

Castillo – Open Tuesdays to Saturdays 1030 to 1330 and 1630 to 1800; Sundays and public holidays 1100 to 1330 and 1630 to 1800; closed Mondays; ☏ (921) 58 60 38.

CÓRDOBA
El Torrijos 10. 14003. ☏ (957) 47 12 35

Mezquita-Catedral – Open 1 October to 31 March daily 1000 to 1330 and 1530 to 1730; Sundays 1530 to 1730; 1 April to 30 September 1000 to 1900; Sundays and public holidays 1330 to 1900; closed on 24 and 31 December (afternoon only), and three days of May feria; 700 pts; free admission every day 0900 to 1000 and on Sundays and public holidays 0900 to 1330; ☏ (957) 47 05 12.

Sinagoga – Open daily except Mondays 1000 to 1400 and 1530 to 1730; 50 pts; ☏ (957) 20 29 28.

Palacio de Viana – Guided visits (1 hour) Mondays, Tuesdays, Thursdays, Fridays and Saturdays 1000 to 1300 and 1600 to 1800 (1 June to 30 September 0900 to 1400); Sundays and public holidays 1000 to 1400; closed Wednesdays, 1 January, Good Friday, 1 May, 1st fortnight in June, 24 October and 25 December; 400 pts; free admission on Thursdays; ☏ (957) 48 01 34.

Museo Arqueológico Provincial – Open Tuesdays to Saturdays 1000 to 1400 and 1700 to 1900; 15 June to 15 September 1000 to 1330 and 1800 to 2000; Sundays and public holidays 1000 to 1330 all year; closed Mondays, 1 January, Good Friday, 24, 25 and 31 December; 400 pts; ☏ (957) 47 40 11.

Alcázar – Open Tuesdays to Saturdays 0930 to 1300 and 1600 to 1900; (1700 to 2000 1 May to 30 September); Sundays and public holidays 0930 to 1300; closed Mondays; 300 pts (free on Tuesdays); ☏ (957) 42 01 51.

Museo Municipal Taurino – Same admission times and charges as the Alcázar; ☏ (957) 20 10 56.

Museo Julio Romero de Torres – Open daily except Mondays 0930 to 1330 and 1600 to 1900 (1700 to 2000 1 May to 30 September); 0930 to 1330 Sundays and holidays; free; ☏ (957) 49 19 09.

Posada del Potro – Open during exhibitions 0900 to 1400 and 1800 to 2100; ☏ (957) 20 05 22.

Museo de Bellas Artes – Open weekdays 1000 to 1400 and 1700 to 1900; Saturdays 0930 to 1330; closed Sundays and public holidays; ☏ (957) 47 33 45.

Torre de la Calahorra – Open daily 1000 to 1800; 1 May to 30 September 1000 to 1400 and 1730 to 2030; 350 pts; multivision show 500 pts; ☏ (957) 29 39 29.

Excursion

Medina Azahara – Open Tuesdays to Saturdays 1000 to 1400 and 1600 to 1830 (1800 to 2030 1 May to 30 September); Sundays and public holidays 1000 to 1400; closed Mondays; 400 pts; ☏ (957) 32 91 30.

CORIA

Catedral – Open daily 1000 to 1300 and 1500 to 1830; ☎ (927) 50 39 60.

La CORUÑA
🄳 Dársena de la Marina s/n, 15001. ☎ (981) 22 18 22

Colegiata de Santa María del Campo – Open daily 0830 to 1300 and 1700 to 1900; ☎ (981) 20 31 86.

Iglesia de Santiago – Open daily 0830 to 1300 and 1800 to 2030; ☎ (981) 20 56 96.

Excursion

Cambre: Iglesia de Santa María – Open daily 0930 to 1930 (2130 in summer); ☎ (981) 67 51 57.

COSTA BRAVA

Sant Pere de Rodes: Monasterio – Open daily 1000 to 1330 and 1500 to 1730; 1 June to 30 September 1000 to 1900; closed Mondays and 1 January; 300 pts; ☎ (972) 38 75 59.

Castelló d'Empúries: Iglesia de Santa María – Open daily 1 June to 30 September 1100 to 1300 and 1700 to 2000; at other times of year on request; ☎ (972) 25 05 19.

Calella de Palafrugell: Jardín Botánico de Cap Roig – Open daily 0800 to 1800 (2000 1 April to 30 September); 200 pts; ☎ (972) 61 45 82.

Blanes: Jardín Botánico de Marimurtra – Open daily March to November 0900 to 1800; December, January and February Mondays to Fridays 1000 to 1700 and weekends 1000 to 1400; 200 pts; ☎ (972) 33 03 48.

COSTA DE CANTÁBRIA

Santoña: Iglesia de Nuestra Señora del Puerto – Open Mondays to Saturdays 0730 to 1100 and 1700 to 2030; Sundays and public holidays 0800 to 1330 and 1700 to 1930; if closed apply to priest (house abutting the church); ☎ (942) 66 01 55.

Bareyo: Iglesia de Santa María – Open daily (subject to prior request); ☎ (942) 62 10 61.

COSTA DE LA LUZ

La Rábida: Monasterio – Guided visits (35 mins) daily except Mondays at 1000, 1045, 1130, 1245, 1300, 1600, 1645, 1730, 1815 (1900 and 2000 in summer); ☎ (959) 35 04 11.

Moguer: Convento de Santa Clara – Guided tours (3/4 hour) Tuesdays to Saturdays 1100 to 1300 and 1630 to 1830; Sundays and public holidays 1100 to 1300; closed Mondays; 250 pts; ☎ (959) 37 01 07.

Sanlúcar de Barrameda: Iglesia de Santo Domingo – Open daily 0900 to 1100 (1300 on Sundays and public holidays) and 1900 to 2100; closed during services; ☎ (956) 36 04 91.

COSTA DEL SOL

Cueva de Nerja – Open daily 1030 to 1400 and 1530 to 1800; 400 pts; ☎ (95) 252 95 20.

COSTA VASCA

Zumaia: Museo de Ignacio Zuloaga – Open 15 January to 15 September Wednesdays to Saturdays 1600 to 2000; Sundays and public holidays 1100 to 1400 and 1600 to 2000; closed Mondays and Tuesdays; 400 pts; ☎ (943) 86 10 15.

Cuevas de Santimamiñe – Guided tours (1 hr) weekdays 1000, 1115, 1230, 1630 and 1800; closed Saturdays, Sundays and public holidays; ☎ (94) 625 29 75.

COSTA VERDE

Ribadesella: Cuevas de Tito Bustillo – Open 1 April to 15 September; guided tours (3/4 hour) 1000 to 1300 and 1530 to 1715; closed Mondays April to June and in September, Sundays in July and August and first Saturday in August; 235 pts (60 pts for children), free on Tuesdays; (98) 586 11 20.

Valdediós: Iglesia de San Salvador – Open daily except Mondays; guided tours (1/2 hour) 1100 to 1300 and 1600 to 1800; ☎ (985) 89 23 25 or 21 33 85.

Valdediós: Monasterio – Open Mondays to Saturdays; guided tours (1/2 hour) 0830 to 1600; closed Sundays and public holidays; ☎ (985) 89 03 70.

COVADONGA

La Santa Cueva – Open daily 0800 to 2000;   (985) 84 61 15.

Basílica – Same opening times as above;   (985) 84 60 16.

Museo de la Vírgen – Open daily 1 April to 31 October 1130 to 1400 and 1600 to 1800; rest of year only open Saturdays, Sundays and public holidays 1130 to 1400 and 1600 to 1900; 50 pts;   (985) 84 60 11.

COVARRUBIAS

Colegiata, Museo-Tesoro – 1 April to 30 September guided tours (45 mins) at 1030, 1200, 1315, 1630, 1800 and 1915 Mondays, Wednesdays to Saturdays; Sundays and public holidays open 1030 to 1400 and 1630 to 2000; rest of year guided visits Mondays, Wednesdays to Saturdays at 1030, 1315, 1630 and 1830; Sundays and public holidays open 1030 to 1400 and 1630 to 1900; closed Tuesdays; 200 pts;   (947) 40 63 11.

Excursion

Quintanilla de las Viñas: Iglesia – Open Wednesdays to Sundays 1 April to 30 September 0930 to 1400 and 1600 to 1900 (0900 to 1400 and 1530 to 1800 rest of year); closed Mondays, Tuesdays, one weekend a month, public holidays and holidays;   (947) 38 40 75.

Lerma: Colegiata – Guided tours (1hr 30 mins); open daily 21 September to 30 April 1200 to 1615; 1 May to 30 June 1000 to 1200; 1 July to 7 September 1000 to 1200 and 1600 to 1800; closed 7 to 21 September; 300 pts;   (947) 17 01 43.

CUENCA

Catedral – Open daily except Mondays 1100 to 1400 and 1600 to 1800; 200 pts;   (969) 21 24 63.

Museo Diocesano – Open Tuesdays to Saturdays 1100 to 1400 and 1600 to 1800; Sundays and public holidays 1100 to 1400; closed Mondays, 1 January, 25 December and for local festivals; 200 pts;   (969) 22 42 10.

Museo de Arte Abstracto Español – Open Tuesdays to Fridays 1100 to 1400 and 1600 to 1800; Saturdays 1100 to 1400 and 1600 to 2000; Sundays 1100 to 1430; closed Mondays; 300 pts;   (969) 21 29 83.

Museo de Cuenca – Open Tuesdays to Saturdays 1000 to 1400 and 1600 to 1900; Sundays and public holidays 1000 to 1400; closed Mondays; 200 pts;   (969) 21 30 69.

D

DAROCA

Colegiata de Santa María – Open Tuesdays to Saturdays 1000 to 1200 and 1630 to 2000; Sundays and public holidays 1100 to 1200; closed Mondays; 300 pts;   (976) 80 07 61.

Museo Parroquial – Same as above;   (976) 80 07 61.

Iglesia de San Miguel – Same as above.

Iglesia de Santo Domingo – Same as above.

Parque Nacional de DOÑANA

Visitors' centres are open 1 March to 31 May 0800 to 1900 (2000 1 June to 14 October, 2100 15 October to end February); guided tours daily except Mondays in winter and Sundays in summer 0830 to 1500 (1700 1 May to 30 September); closed 1 and 6 January, during the Romería del Rocío at Whitsun and 24, 25 and 31 December;   (959) 43 04 32.

E

ÉCIJA

Iglesia de Santiago – Open daily 1030 to 1230 and 1730 to 2000;   (954) 83 05 88.

ELCHE

Huerta del Cura – Open daily 0900 to 1800 (2030 in summer); 250 pts;   (965) 45 19 36.

Museo Arqueológico – Open Tuesdays to Saturdays 1000 to 1300 and 1600 to 1900; Sundays and public holidays 1000 to 1300; closed Mondays and certain holidays; 400 pts;   (965) 45 36 03.

EMPURIES

Neápolis – Open daily 1 October to 31 March 1000 to 1700; 1 April to 30 September 1000 to 1900; closed 1 January and 25 December; 400 pts; ☎ (972) 77 02 08.

Monasterio de El ESCORIAL

🛈 Floridablanca 10. 28200. ☎ (91) 890 15 54

Palacios, panteones, salas capitulares, basílica and biblioteca – Open daily except Mondays 1000 to 1700 (1800 1 April to 30 September); closed 1 and 6 January, 1 May, 10 August, 11 September and 25 December; 800 pts ; ☎ (91) 547 53 50 extension 417.

Casita del Príncipe – Open Saturdays and Sundays 1000 to 1745 (1845 1 April to 30 September); daily except Mondays during Holy Week and August 1000 to 1845; closed rest of year; 300 pts; ☎ (91) 547 53 50 extension 417.

Casita del Infante – Open daily except Mondays 1000 to 1845 during Holy Week and August; closed rest of year; 300 pts; ☎ (91) 890 59 03 or 890 59 05.

ESTELLA

🛈 San Nicolás 1. 31200. ☎ (948) 55 40 11 (Holy Week to October)

Iglesia de San Pedro de la Rúa – By prior arrangement; in spring and summer daily except Sundays 1000 to 1400 and 1600 to 1900; closed in winter except by prior arrangement and Sundays throughout year; 200 pts; ☎ (948) 55 40 11.

Excursions

Monasterio de Irache – Open Tuesdays 1000 to 1400; Wednesdays to Saturdays 1000 to 1400 and 1700 to 1900; Sundays and public holidays 0900 to 1400 and 1600 to 1900; closed Mondays; 400 pts; ☎ (948) 55 44 64.

Monasterio de Iranzu – Open daily 0900 to 1300 and 1600 to 2000 (closes earlier in winter according to daylight); ☎ (948) 52 00 12.

F

FIGUERES

🛈 Pl. del Sol. 17600. ☎ (972) 50 31 55

Teatre-Museu Dalí – Open 1 October to 30 June daily 1030 to 1715; 1 July to 30 September daily 0900 to 1915; closed Mondays (except public holidays or day before), 1 January and 25 December; 600 pts (900 pts 1 July to 30 September); ☎ (972) 51 18 00.

FRÓMISTA

Iglesia de San Martín – Open daily 1000 to 1400 and 1600 to 2000; ☎ (979) 81 01 44.

G

GANDÍA

🛈 Marqués de Campo. 46700. ☎ (96) 287 77 88

Palacio Ducal – Guided tours (3/4 hour) Mondays to Saturdays January to March 1100, 1200, 1630 and 1730; April to June 1100, 1200, 1700 and 1800; July to October 1100, 1200, 1800 and 1900; closed Sundays and public holidays; 225 pts; ☎ (96) 287 12 03.

GIBRALTAR

🛈 Cathedral Square. ☎ (9567) 764 00

British Dependent Territory. The border is open 24 hours a day. Visitors must be in possesion of a valid passport or other acceptable travel documents although nationals of some countries also require a visa.
Besides United Kingdom coinage, Gibraltar Government notes and Spanish pesetas are legal tender in Gibraltar.
The international telephone code for Gibraltar is 350. Further tourist information is available from the Gibraltar Information Bureau, Arundel Great Court, 179 Strand, London WC2R 1EH. ☎ 0171 836 0777.

St Michael's Cave – Open daily 1000 to 1800 (Saturdays 1000 to 1400); closed 1 January, Good Friday, 25 and 26 December; £1.50; ☎ (9567) 769 50.

GIRONA

🖪 Rambla de la Llibertad 1. 17004. ☎ (972) 22 65 75

Catedral – Open Tuesdays to Saturdays 1000 to 1300 and 1600 to 1800 (1 May to 30 September 1000 to 1400 and 1600 to 1900); Sundays and public holidays 1000 to 1400; closed Mondays and in January; ☎ (972) 21 44 26.

Tesoro – Same opening times as the Catedral; 300 pts; ☎ (972) 21 44 26;

Museu d'Art – Open Tuesdays to Saturdays 1000 to 1800 (1900 1 March to 30 September); Sundays and public holidays 1000 to 1400; closed Mondays, 1 and 6 January, Easter Sunday, 25 and 26 December; 100 pts (free on Sundays and public holidays); ☎ (972) 20 38 34.

Banys Arabs – Open daily except Mondays 1000 to 1400; 1 April to 30 September 1000 to 1900; closed Mondays, 1 and 6 January, Good Friday and 25 December; 100 pts; ☎ (972) 21 32 62.

Iglesia de Sant Pere de Galligants: Museu Arqueològic – Open Tuesdays to Saturdays 1000 to 1300 and 1630 to 1900; Sundays and public holidays 1000 to 1300; closed Mondays, 1 and 6 January, Easter Sunday, 25 and 26 December; 100 pts (free the 1st and 3rd Sundays of the month); ☎ (972) 20 26 32.

Excursion

Banyoles: Iglesia de Porqueres – To visit, contact the parish priest; ☎ (972) 57 32 17.

GRANADA

🖪 Pl. Mariana Pineda 10. 18009. ☎ (958) 22 66 88

Alhambra and Generalife – Open winter, spring and autumn daily 0900 to 1800 and Saturday evenings 2000 to 2200; summer daily 0900 to 2000 (1800 Sundays) and Tuesday, Thursday and Saturday evenings 2200 to midnight; 625 pts; ☎ (958) 22 75 25.

Capilla Real – Open daily 1030 to 1300 and 1530 to 1800 (1600 to 1900 is summer); 200 pts; ☎ (958) 22 92 39.

Catedral – Open Mondays to Saturdays 1030 to 1300 and 1530 to 1800 (1600 to 1900 April to September); Sundays 1600 to 1900; 200 pts; ☎ (958) 22 66 88.

Cartuja – Open daily October to March 1000 to 1200 and 1530 to 1830; April to September daily 1000 to 1300 (1200 Sundays and public holidays) and 1600 to 1900; ☎ (958) 20 19 32.

Iglesia de San Juan de Dios – Only open during services.

Monasterio de San Jerónimo – Open daily 1000 to 1330 and 1500 to 1930 (1600 to 1930 from April to September); 200 pts; ☎ (958) 27 93 37.

Baños árabes – Open Tuesdays to Saturdays 1000 to 1400; closed Sundays, Mondays and public holidays.

Hospital Real – Open weekdays 0900 to 2000; Saturdays 0900 to 1300; closed Sundays and public holidays; ☎ (958) 24 30 25.

Museu Arqueológico – Open daily except Mondays 1000 to 1400; closed on public holidays (except Sundays); 400 pts; ☎ (958) 22 56 40.

La GRANJA DE SAN ILDEFONSO

Palacio – Guided tours (50 mins) Tuesdays to Saturdays 1000 to 1330 and 1500 to 1700; Sundays and public holidays 1000 to 1400; 1 June to 30 September 1000 to 1800; Saturdays, Sundays and public holidays in April and May 1000 to 1800; closed Mondays throughout year, 1 and 6 January, 25 August and 25 December; 600 pts; ☎ (921) 47 00 19 or (91) 547 53 50 extension 417.

Jardines – Open daily 1000 to 1800 (2100 in summer); fountain display 1730 Wednesdays, Saturdays, Sundays and public holidays (except during periods of drought); same closing times as the Palacio; 300 pts; ☎ (911) 47 00 19.

Sierra de GREDOS

Cuevas del Águila – Open daily 1030 to 1300 and 1500 to 1800 (1900 in spring and summer); 450 pts; ☎ (920) 37 04 97 or 37 01 48.

GUADALAJARA

🖪 Pl. Mayor 7. 19001. ☎ (949) 22 06 98

Palacio del Infantado – Open Mondays to Saturdays 1030 to 1400 and 1600 to 1900; Sundays and public holidays 1030 to 1400; closed 1 January, Good Friday, 8 September and 25 December; museum closed on Mondays; 200 pts; ☎ (949) 21 33 01.

Excursion

Pastrana: Colegiata – Guided tours (1 hour) Mondays to Saturdays 1100 to 1400 and 1600 to 1900; Sundays and public holidays 1300 to 1430 and 1600 to 1900; November to March 1100 to 1300 and 1630 to 1800; Sundays and public holidays 1300 to 1430 and 1630 to 1800; 300 pts; ☎ (949) 37 00 27.

GUADALUPE

Monasterio – Guided tours daily 0930 to 1300 and 1530 to 1900; 300 pts, free on Friday mornings; 📷 (927) 36 70 00.

Sierra de GUADARRAMA

Real Monasterio de Santa María de El Paular – Guided tours (3/4 hour) Mondays to Saturdays (except Thursday afternoons) at 1200, 1300 and 1700 (also at 1800 in spring and summer); Sundays and public holidays at 1300 and 1600 to 1830; closed in the afternoons during Easter; 📷 (91) 869 14 25.

GUADIX
🅱 Carret. de Granada. 18500. 📷 (958) 66 26 65

Catedral – Open daily except Sundays and public holidays 1100 to 1300 and 1600 to 1800 (1700 to 1900 22 March to 20 December); 📷 (958) 66 08 00.

Alcazaba – Open daily except Sundays 0900 to 1400 and 1500 to 1900; if closed ask for key at porter's lodge; 100 pts; 📷 (958) 66 01 60.

Excursion

La Calahorra: Castillo – Open Wednesdays 0900 to 1800 by prior appointment; 📷 (958) 67 70 98.

H

HUESCA
🅱 Coso Alto 23. 22003. 📷 (974) 22 57 78

Catedral – Open daily 0845 to 1300 and 1600 to 1830; closed during services; 📷 (974) 22 06 76.

Museo Arqueológico Provincial – Closed temporarily for restoration.

Iglesia de San Pedro el Viejo – Open daily 0900 to 1100 and 1800 to 2000; 📷 (974) 22 23 87.

J

JACA
🅱 Av. Regimento de Galicia 2. 22700. 📷 (974) 36 00 89

Cathedral – Open daily 0745 to 1400 and 1600 to 1900 (2100 in summer); 📷 (974) 35 51 30.

Museo Episcopal – Open daily 1100 to 1330 and 1600 to 1830; 200 pts; 📷 (974) 35 51 30.

Excursions

Castillo de Loarre – Open Wednesdays to Sundays 1000 to 1330 and 1600 to 1800 (2000 in July and August); 1 September to 30 June 1000 to 1330; closed Mondays (except between 1 to 15 September) and Tuesdays; 400 pts; 📷 (974) 38 26 27.

Ansó: Museo Etnológico – Open daily from June to September 1100 to 1300 and 1600 to 1900; rest of the year by prior arrangement; 200 pts (children free); 📷 (974) 37 00 22.

JAÉN
🅱 Arquitecto Bergés 3. 23007. 📷 (953) 22 27 37

Museo Provincial – Open Tuesdays to Fridays 1000 to 1400 and 1600 to 1930; Saturdays and Sundays 1000 to 1400; 15 June to 14 September 0900 to 1400; closed Mondays and public holidays; 📷 (953) 25 03 20.

Catedral – Open Mondays to Saturdays 0830 to 1300 and 1600 to 1900 (1700 to 2000) in summer; Sundays and public holidays 0830 to 1300; 📷 (953) 22 27 37.

Museo de la Catedral – Open daily in summer 1000 to 1300 and 1700 to 2000; Saturdays and Sundays in winter 1100 to 1300; 100 pts; 📷 (953) 22 27 37.

Baños árabes and Museo de Artes y Tradiciones Populares – Open Tuesdays to Fridays 1000 to 1400 and 1600 to 1900 (1700 to 2000 1 April to 1 October); weekends 1030 to 1400; closed Mondays and public holidays; 📷 (953) 22 33 92.

JÁTIVA

☑ Noguera 1. 46800. ☎ (96) 227 33 46

Museo – Open 15 September to 14 June Tuesdays to Fridays 1000 to 1400 and 1600 to 1800; weekends and public holidays 1000 to 1400; 15 June to 14 September 1000 to 1400; closed Mondays, 1 January and 24, 25 and 31 December; ☎ (96) 227 65 97.

Ermita de Sant Feliu – Open Mondays to Saturdays 1 May to 30 September 1000 to 1300 and 1600 to 1900; the rest of the year 1000 to 1300 and 1500 to 1800; Sundays and public holidays 1000 to 1300; ☎ (96) 227 33 46.

Castillo – Open Tuesdays to Sundays 1 May to 30 September 1000 to 1400 and 1630 to 1900; the rest of the year 1000 to 1400 and 1530 to 1800; closed Mondays, the day after public holidays, 1 January and 24, 25 and 31 December; ☎ (96) 227 33 46.

JEREZ DE LA FRONTERA

☑ Alameda Cristina 7. 11403. ☎ (956) 33 11 50

Museo de los Relojes – Open daily 1000 to 1400 except Sundays and public holidays; 300 pts; ☎ (956) 18 21 00.

Real Escuela Andaluza de Arte Ecuestre – Guided tours including facilities and training session 1100 to 1300 Mondays, Tuesdays, Wednesdays and Fridays; shows 1200 Thursdays; guided tours 425 pts; shows 1 425 - 2 250 pts; ☎ (956) 31 11 10 or 31 11 11.

Colegiata – Open Mondays to Fridays 1800 to 2000; Saturdays 1100 to 1400 and 1800 to 2000; Sundays and public holidays 1100 to 1400 and 1900 to 2030.

Casa del Cabildo: Museo Arqueológico – Open Tuesdays to Saturdays 1000 to 1400 and 1600 to 1900; Sundays and public holidays 1000 to 1400; closed Mondays; 250 pts; ☎ (956) 33 33 16.

Alcázar – Closed temporarily for restoration; ☎ (956) 33 11 50.

Iglesia de San Miguel – Open mornings and afternoons (no specific times); for information, call (956) 34 33 47.

L

LEÓN

☑ Pl. de la Regla 4. 24003. ☎ (987) 23 70 83

Catedral – Open Mondays to Saturdays 0830 to 1330 and 1600 to 1900; 1 June to 31 August 0830 to 1400 and 1600 to 2000; Sundays and public holidays 0830 to 1430 and 1700 to 2000.

Museo de la Catedral – Guided tours (3/4 hour) Mondays to Fridays 0930 to 1330 and 1600 to 1900 (1930 1 June to 30 September); Saturdays 0930 to 1330; closed Sundays and public holidays; 300 pts; ☎ (987) 23 00 60.

Panteón Real de San Isidoro and Tesoro – Open Tuesdays to Saturdays 1000 to 1330 and 1600 to 1830, Sundays and public holidays 1000 to 1330; 1 July to 31 August Mondays to Saturdays 0900 to 1400 and 1500 to 2000, Sundays and public holidays 0900 to 1400; closed Mondays (except in July and August), 1 January, first fortnight in February and 25 December; 300 pts (free on Thursday afternoons); ☎ (987) 22 96 08.

Museo de León – Open Tuesdays to Saturdays 1000 to 1400 and 1630 to 2000 (1700 to 2030 1 May to 30 September); Sundays and public holidays 1000 to 1400; closed Mondays; 200 pts (free on Saturdays and Sundays); ☎ (987) 23 64 05.

Excursions

San Miguel de Escalada: Monasterio – Open Tuesdays to Saturdays 1030 to 1330 and 1600 to 1900; Sundays 1030 to 1330; closed Mondays.

Cuevas de Valporquero – Open daily from Holy Week to 1 November; opening times may vary; 525 pts; ☎ (987) 29 22 43.

Monasterio de LEYRE

Iglesia – Guided visits Mondays to Saturdays 1015 to 1330 and 1530 to 1830; Sundays and public holidays 1015 to 1400 and 1600 to 1830; in summer daily 1045 to 1400 and 1600 to 1900; 150 pts; ☎ (948) 88 40 11.

LLEIDA

☑ Av. Blondel 3. 25002. ☎ (973) 24 81 20

Seu Vella – Open Tuesdays to Saturdays 1000 to 1330 and 1500 to 1730 (1830 1 June to 30 September), Sundays and public holidays 1000 to 1330; closed Mondays, 1 January, 25 December; 300 pts (free on Tuesdays); ☎ (973) 23 06 53.

LUGO   Pl. de España 27-29. 27001. ☏ (982) 23 13 61

Museo Provincial – Open 1 September to 31 May Mondays to Fridays 1030 to 1400 and 1630 to 2030 (2000 on Saturdays), Sundays 1100 to 1400; 1 June to 31 August Mondays to Fridays 1000 to 1300 and 1600 to 1900, Saturdays 1000 to 1400, closed Sundays; ☏ (982) 24 21 12.

Excursion

Santa Eulalia de Bóveda: Monumento Paleocristiano – Open Tuesdays to Saturdays 1100 to 1700 (1900 1 June to 30 September); Sundays and public holidays 1100 to 1400; closed Mondays; ☏ (982) 22 54 51.

M

MADRID   Princesa 1. 28008. ☏ (91) 541 23 25. Pl. Mayor 3. 28012. ☏ 266 54 77

Basílica Pontificia de San Miguel – Open daily 1030 to 1400 and 1730 to 2100; closed during services; ☏ (91) 548 40 11.

Iglesia de San Francisco el Grande – Guided tours Tuesdays to Saturdays 1100 to 1300 and 1600 to 1900 (1700 to 2000 in summer); Sundays and Mondays open only for worship; daily service 0800 to 1100; 50 pts; ☏ (91) 365 38 00.

Iglesia de San Isidro – Open only during services; ☏ (91) 462 13 04.

Palacio Real – Unaccompanied or guided tours (40 mins) Mondays to Saturdays 0930 to 1700, Sundays and public holidays 0900 to 1400; 1 April to 30 September 0900 to 1800, Sundays and public holidays 0900 to 1500; closed 1 and 6 January, 1, 2 and 15 May, 9 September, 9 November, 25 December and during state receptions; 800 pts : ☏ (91) 542 00 59.

Museo de Carruajes Reales – Closed temporarily for repairs; ☏ (91) 542 00 59.

Monasterio de las Descalzas Reales – Guided tours (3/4 hour) daily except Mondays. Tuesdays, Wednesdays, Thursdays and Saturdays 1030 to 1230 and 1600 to 1730; Fridays 1030 to 1230; Sundays 1100 to 1330; closed Mondays, 1 and 6 January, Holy Week from Wednesday to Saturday, 1, 2, 11 and 15 May, 11 August, 9 September, 9 November and 25 December; 600 pts; ☏ (91) 542 00 59.

Real Monasterio de la Encarnación – Open Wednesdays and Saturdays 1030 to 1230 and 1600 to 1730; Sundays 1100 to 1330; closed Mondays, 1 and 6 January, Holy Week from Wednesday to Saturday, 1, 2, 11 and 15 May, 11 August, 9 September, 9 November and 25 December; 400 pts; ☏ (91) 542 0 59.

Parque del Oeste: Teleférico – Consult timetables for times of operation; 445 pts Rtn, 315 pts single; ☏ (91) 541 11 18 or 541 74 50.

Zoo – Open daily 1000 to sunset; 875 pts; ☏ (91) 711 99 50.

Museo del Prado and Casón del Buen Retiro – Open Tuesdays to Saturdays 0900 to 1900; Sundays and public holidays 0900 to 1400; closed Mondays, Good Friday, 1 May and 25 December; 400 pts; ☏ (91) 420 28 36.

Museo Thyssen-Bornemisza – Open daily except Mondays 1000 to 1900; closed Mondays, 1 January, 1 May and 25 December; 600 pts (free for children); ☏ (91) 369 01 51.

Jardín Botánico – Open daily 1000 to 1800, 1900, 2000 or 2100 depending on the season; closed 1 January and 25 December; 200 pts; ☏ (91) 585 47 00.

Museo Nacional Centro de Arte Reina Sofia – Open Mondays, Wednesdays to Saturdays and public holidays 1000 to 2100; Sundays 1000 to 1400; closed Tuesdays, 1 and 6 January, 1 and 16 May, 9 November and 24, 25 and 31 December; 400 pts; ☏ (91) 468 30 02.

Museo del Ejército – Open daily except Mondays 1000 to 1400; closed 1 and 6 January, Maundy Thursday, Good Friday, 1 May, 24, 25 and 31 December; 400 pts; ☏ (91) 522 89 77.

Museo Naval – Open daily except Mondays 1030 to 1330; closed 1 January, Maundy Thursday and Good Friday, all August and 25 December; ☏ (91) 379 52 99.

Parque del Buen Retiro – Open daily; ☏ (91) 573 60 82 or 573 98 59.

Museo Arqueológico Nacional – Open Tuesdays to Saturdays 0930 to 2030; Sundays and public holidays 0930 to 1430; closed Mondays, 1 and 6 January, 2 May, 25 July, 15 August, 8 September and 26 December; 400 pts; ☏ (91) 577 79 12.

Museo Lázaro Galdiano – Open daily except Mondays 1000 to 1400; closed 1 January, Maundy Thursday, Good Friday, all August, 1 November and 25 December; 300 pts; ☏ (91) 561 60 84.

Real Academia de Bellas Artes de San Fernando – Open Mondays to Saturdays 0900 to 1900. Sundays and public holidays 0900 to 1430; ☎ (91) 522 14 91.

Museo de América – Open Tuesdays to Saturdays 1000 to 1500; Sundays and public holidays 1000 to 1430; closed Mondays; 400 pts; ☎ (91) 549 26 41 or 543 94 37.

San Antonio de la Florida – Open Tuesdays to Fridays 1000 to 1400 and 1600 to 1800; weekends 1000 to 1400; closed Mondays and public holidays; 200 pts; ☎ (91) 547 79 37.

Museo Cerralbo – Open daily 0930 to 1430 (Sundays 1000 to 1400); closed Mondays and public holidays, 1 and 6 January, Maundy Thursday, Good Friday, 2 May, 25 July, all August, 9 September, 12 October, 1 November and 6, 8, 26 and 31 December; 400 pts; ☎ (91) 547 36 46.

Museo de Cera – Open daily 1000 to 1400 and 1600 to 2030; 750 pts; ☎ (91) 319 46 81.

Museo Sorolla – Open daily except Mondays and public holidays 1000 to 1500; 400 pts; ☎ (91) 310 15 84.

Museo Taurino – Open daily except Mondays and Saturdays 0930 to 1430; ☎ (91) 725 18 57.

Museo de la Ciudad – Open daily except Mondays 1000 to 1400 and 1600 to 1800 (1700 to 1900 July to September); Sundays and public holidays 1000 to 1400; closed 1 and 6 January, Holy Week, 1, 2 and 15 May, 9 November and 25 December; ☎ (91) 588 65 99.

MÁLAGA
🛈 Pasaje de Chinitas 4. 29015. ☎ (95) 221 34 45

Alcazaba – Open Tuesdays to Fridays 0930 to 1330 and 1600 to 1900 1 November to 31 May (1700 to 2000 June to October); Saturdays 1000 to 1330; Sundays 1000 to 1400; closed Mondays, 1 January, 28 February, 1 May and 25 December; 20 pts; ☎ (95) 222 04 43.

Catedral – Open Mondays to Saturdays 1000 to 1300 and 1600 to 1900; Sundays and public holidays 0900 to 1400 and 1800 to 1900; 200 pts; ☎ (95) 221 59 17 or 221 34 45.

Museo de Bellas Artes – Open Tuesdays to Fridays 1000 to 1330 and 1700 to 2000; weekends and public holidays 1000 to 1330; closed Mondays, 1 January, Maundy Thursday, Good Friday, 24, 25 and 31 December; 400 pts; ☎ (95) 221 83 82.

Museo de Artes Populares – Open Mondays to Fridays 1000 to 1330 and 1600 to 1900 (1700 to 2000 1 July to 30 September); Saturdays 1000 to 1330; closed Sundays and public holidays; 200 pts; ☎ (95) 221 71 37.

Excursion
Finca de la Concepción – Open daily except Mondays 0930 to 1630 (1900 in summer); 400 pts; ☎ (95) 221 34 45.

MEDINA DE RIOSECO

Iglesia de Santa María – Guided tours (1 1/2 hours) Mondays to Saturdays 1100 to 1300 and 1600 to 1900; Sundays and public holidays 1100 to 1400; 250 pts. ☎ (983) 70 03 27.

Iglesia de Santiago – Same admission times as above.

MELILLA
🛈 Av. General Aizpuru 20. 29804. ☎ (95) 267 40 13

Museo Municipal – Open Mondays to Saturdays 14 May to 30 September 1030 to 1400 and 1800 to 1930; rest of year 1000 to 1400; closed Sundays and public holidays; ☎ (95) 269 91 58.

MÉRIDA
🛈 Pedro María Plano s/n. 06800. ☎ (924) 31 53 53

Museo Nacional de Arte Romano – Open Tuesdays to Saturdays 1000 to 1400 and 1600 to 1800 (1700 to 1900 1 June to 30 September); Sundays and public holidays 1000 to 1400; closed Mondays, 1 January, Tuesday of Carnival, 1 May, 10, 24, 25 and 31 December; 400 pts; ☎ (924) 31 16 90 or 31 19 12.

Teatro Romano and Anfiteatro – Open daily 0900 to 1345 and 1600 to 1815 (1700 to 1915 1 April to 30 September); closed 1 January and 25 December; 300 pts combined ticket including Teatro, Anfiteatro, Casa Romana and Alcazaba; 200 pts; ☎ (924) 31 25 30.

Casa Romana and Alcazaba – Same as Teatro Romano and Anfiteatro; ☎ (924) 31 73 09.

MONDOÑEDO

Catedral – Open daily 0900 to 1400 and 1600 to 2000. Avoid visiting during services (other than to worship). ☏ (982) 52 10 06.

Sierra de MONTSERRAT
🛈 Monestir. 08199. ☏ (93) 835 02 51 Ext. 186

Basílica – Open daily 0700 to 1930; ☏ (93) 835 02 51.

Funiculares – **Sant Joan and Santa Cova:** Daily every 20 mins; 1 November to 31 March 1000 to 1620; April, May and October 1000 to 1720; 1 June to 30 September 1000 to 1850; ☏ (93) 302 48 16.
Vallvidrera: Daily 0645 to 2245; ☏ (93) 302 48 16.

MORELLA
🛈 Torres de San Miguel. 12300. ☏ (964) 17 30 02

Basílica de Santa María la Mayor – Open daily 1100 to 1400 and 1600 to 1800 (avoid visiting during services); 100 pts (museum); ☏ (964) 16 03 79.

MURCIA
🛈 Alejandro Seiquer 4. 30001. ☏ (968) 21 37 16

Catedral and Museo – Cathedral open daily 0700 to 1300 and 1700 to 2000. Museum open daily 1000 to 1300 and 1700 to 1900 (2000 in summer). Both closed during the Romería of the Virgen de la Fuensanta (dates vary); 200 pts (museo); ☏ (968) 21 63 44.

Museo Salzillo – Open Tuesdays to Saturdays 0930 to 1300 and 1500 to 1800 (1600 to 1900 in summer); Sundays and public holidays 1130 to 1300; closed Mondays, 1 January, Maundy Thursday to Easter Monday and 9 June; 200 pts; ☏ (968) 29 18 93.

Excursion

Alcantarilla: Museo de la Huerta – Open daily except Mondays 1030 to 1800 (1000 to 2000 1 June to 31 July; 1000 to 1900 in September); closed Mondays, 1 January, Good Friday, 1 May, in August and 25 December; ☏ (968) 80 03 40.

Orihuela:

Colegio de Santo Domingo – Open Mondays to Fridays 0900 to 1300 and 1600 to 1800; in summer 0900 to 1300; closed weekends and public holidays; ☏ (965) 30 27 47.

Catedral – Open Mondays to Fridays 1030 to 1330 and 1600 to 1830; Saturdays 1030 to 1330; closed Sundays and public holidays (except Maundy Thursday and Good Friday); 100 pts; ☏ (965) 30 06 38.

Museo de la Catedral – Open Mondays to Fridays 1000 to 1330 and 1600 to 1830 (1700 to 1900 in summer); Saturdays 1000 to 1330; closed Sundays and public holidays; 100 pts; ☏ (965) 30 27 47.

Iglesia de Santiago – Open daily 1000 to 1200 and 1700 to 1900; ☏ (965) 30 27 47.

N

NÁJERA
🛈 El Carmen s/n, 26300. ☏ (941) 36 16 25

Monasterio de Santa María la Real – Open autumn, winter and spring daily 1000 to 1230 (1215 on Sundays and public holidays) and 1600 to 1800; summer daily 0930 to 1230 and 1600 to 1930 (1845 on Sundays and public holidays); closed Mondays; 200 pts; ☏ (941) 36 36 50.

Excursions

San Millán de la Cogolla:

Monasterio de Suso – Open daily except Mondays 1000 to 1400 and 1600 to 1800 (1900 in summer); ☏ (941) 37 31 73.

Monasterio de Yuso – Guided tours (50 mins) daily except Mondays 1030 to 1300 and 1600 to 1800 (1 May to 30 September 1030 to 1315 and 1600 to 1815); 300 pts; ☏ (941) 37 30 49.

Valle del NAVIA

Grandas de Salime: Museo Etnográfico – Open daily except Mondays 1130 to 1400 and 1600 to 1830; closed Mondays and Sunday afternoons in winter; 200 pts; ☏ (985) 62 70 21.

OLITE   🏛 Pl. Carlos III El Noble. 31390.   ☎ (948) 74 00 35 (Holy Week to October)

Castillo de los Reyes de Navarra – Open daily 1000 to 1400 and 1700 to 2000;
300 pts; ☎ (948) 74 00 35.

Iglesia de Santa María la Real – Only open during services (1000 to 1845);
☎ (948) 71 24 34.

Excursion

Monasterio de la Oliva – Open daily 0830 to 1830 (0930 to 1930 in summer);
☎ (948) 72 50 06.

OÑATI   🏛 Foru Esparantza 11. 20560.   ☎ (943) 78 34 53

Antigua Universidad – Closed temporarily for repairs; ☎ (943) 78 34 53.

Iglesia de San Miguel – Only open during services; ☎ (943) 78 34 53.

Excursion

Santuario de Arantzazu – Open daily 0900 to 2000; ☎ (943) 78 09 51.

ORENSE   🏛 Curros Enríquez 1. 32003.   ☎ (988) 37 20 20

Catedral and Museo – Open Mondays to Saturdays 1200 to 1300 and 1630 to 1900;
Sundays and public holidays 1630 to 1900; Catedral 100 pts; Museo 150 pts;
☎ (988) 22 09 92.

Museo Arqueológico y de Bellas Artes – Open daily 0930 to 1430 except Mondays,
public holidays, 1 and 6 January, 19 March, 1 May, 25 July, 12 October, 6, 8, 24,
25 and 31 December; 400 pts; ☎ (988) 22 38 84.

Claustro de San Francisco – Closed temporarily; ☎ (988) 37 20 20.

OSEIRA

Monasteio de Santa María la Real – Guided tours (45 mins) Mondays to Saturdays
0930 to 1200 and 1530 to 1745 (1530 to 1845 in spring and 1530 to 1915 in
summer); Sundays and public holidays 1230 to 1330 and 1530 to 1745 (1530 to
1845 in spring and 1530 to 1915 in summer); ☎ (988) 28 20 04.

OSUNA

Sepulcro Ducal – Guided tours (35 mins) daily except Mondays 1000 to 1330 and
1530 to 1830 (1600 to 1900 1 May to 30 September); closed 1 and 6 January,
Maundy Thursday, Good Friday and 25 December; 200 pts; ☎ (95) 481 04 44.

OVIEDO   🏛 Pl. Alfonso II El Casto 6. 33003.   ☎ (98) 521 33 85

Catedral – Open daily 0900 to 1300 and 1600 to 1900; ☎ (98) 522 10 33.

Cámara Santa – Closed temporarily; ☎ (985) 522 10 33.

Museo de Bellas Artes – Open 16 September to 14 June Tuesdays to Fridays 1000
to 1330 and 1630 to 1900; Saturdays 1100 to 1400 and 1630 to 1900; Sundays
and public holidays 1100 to 1400; 15 June to 15 September Tuesdays to Fridays
1100 to 1330 and 1630 to 2000. Saturdays 1100 to 1400; closed Mondays, Sundays
15 June to 15 September, 1 January, Maundy Thursday, Good Friday, 1 May, Tuesday
of local festival in May, 8 and 21 September, 6 and 25 December; ☎ (98) 521 30 61.

Museo Arqueológico – Open Tuesdays to Saturdays 1000 to 1330 and 1600 to 1800;
Sundays and public holidays 1100 to 1300; closed Mondays; ☎ (98) 521 54 05.

Iglesia de Santullano or San Julián de los Prados – Open daily except Mondays;
1 May to 31 October 1100 to 1300 and 1600 to 1800; the rest of the year 1200 to
1300 and 1600 to 1700. ☎ (98) 528 55 82.

Environs

Iglesia de Santa María del Naranco – Open Mondays to Saturdays 1000 to 1300
and 1500 to 1700 (1900 1 April to 1 October); Sundays 1000 to 1300; 200 pts
(free on Mondays); ☎ (98) 529 67 55.

Iglesia de San Miguel de Lillo – Same times and charges as Santa María del Naranco.

Excursions

Iglesia de Santa Cristina de Lena – Open daily except Mondays 1200 to 1300 and
1600 to 1700 (1100 to 1300 and 1600 to 1800 in summer); ☎ (985) 49 05 25.

Teverga: Colegiata de San Pedro – Visits by prior arrangement; ☎ (985) 76 42 75.

P

PALENCIA

☒ Mayor 105. 34001. ☎ (979) 74 00 68

Catedral – Open Mondays to Saturdays 0930 to 1330 and 1630 to 1900; Sundays and public holidays 0930 to 1330; ☎ (979) 70 13 47.

Museo de la Catedral – Guided tours (1 hour) Mondays to Saturdays 1000 to 1330 and 1600 to 1830; Sundays and public holidays 0930 to 1330; 200 pts; ☎ (979) 70 13 47.

Excursion

Baños de Cerrato:

Basílica de San Juan Bautista – Guided visits (20 mins) 1000 to 1300 and 1600 to 1900; closed Mondays; ☎ (988) 77 03 38.

PAMPLONA

☒ Duque de Ahumada 3. 31002. ☎ (948) 22 07 41

Catedral – Open 16 October to 15 May Mondays to Saturdays 0900 to 1100 and 1900 to 2030; Sundays and public holidays 0900 to 1300 and 1900 to 2030; 16 May to 15 October 0900 to 1400 and 1900 to 2030; ☎ (948) 22 56 79.

Museo Diocesano – Open daily except Mondays 15 May to 15 October 0900 to 1400; 200 pts; ☎ (948) 22 74 00.

Museo de Navarra – Open Tuesdays to Saturdays 1000 to 1400 and 1700 to 1900; Sundays and public holidays 1100 to 1400; closed Mondays, 7 July, afternoons of 6 July and 24 and 31 December; ☎ (948) 22 78 31.

Iglesia de San Saturnino – Open daily 0815 to 1200 and 1830 to 1930; ☎ (948) 22 07 41.

El PARDO

Palacio Real – Guided tours (35 mins) 1 October to 31 March Mondays to Saturdays 1030 to 1700; Sundays and public holidays 1000 to 1340; 1 April to 30 September Mondays to Saturdays 1030 to 1800; Sundays and public holidays 0925 to 1340; closed during state receptions; 600 pts; ☎ (91) 376 15 00.

Casita del Príncipe – Closed temporarily for restoration; ☎ (91) 376 03 29 or 376 15 00.

La Quinta – Closed temporarily for restoration; ☎ (91) 376 03 29 or 376 15 00.

PEÑARANDA DE DUERO

Palacio de Avellaneda – Guided tours daily except Mondays 1000 to 1330 and 1600 to 1900; ☎ (947) 55 20 13.

PEÑISCOLA

☒ Paseo Marítimo. 12598. ☎ (964) 48 02 08

Castillo – Open daily 1 October to 29 March 1000 to 1300 and 1515 to 1730; 30 March to 30 September 1000 to 2100; closed 1 January, 20 May, 9 September and 25 December; 150 pts; ☎ (964) 48 00 21.

PICOS DE EUROPA

Lebeña: Iglesia de Nuestra Señora – Guided tours (1/2 hour) daily 1100 to 1300 and 1600 to 1900 (2030 in summer); ☎ (942) 73 09 43 (Señora María Luisa García Viejo).

Monasterio de Santo Toribio de Liébana – Open daily 0900 to 1300 and 1530 to 1930; ☎ (942) 73 05 50.

Fuente Dé: Teleférico – Open daily 1000 to 1800 (0900 to 2000 in summer); closed 10 January to 20 February; 1 000 pts; ☎ (942) 73 66 10.

Cueva de El Buxu – Guided visits (1/2 hour) 1000 to 1300 and 1600 to 1830; closed Mondays and in November; 175 pts (free on Tuesdays); ☎ (985) 10 67 27.

PIEDRA

Parque y Cascadas – Open daily 0900 to an hour and a half before nightfall; 800 pts; ☎ (976) 84 90 11.

PIRINEOS ARAGONESES

Graus: Catedral – Open daily 0900 to 1700 (1800 1 April to 30 September); ☎ (974) 54 07 28.

PIRINEOS CATALANES

Llívia: Museo Municipal – Open daily except Mondays 1000 to 1300 and 1500 to 1800, 1900 1 April to 15 September; closed over Christmas; ☎ (972) 89 63 13.

Salardú: Iglesia – Open daily April to September 0900 to 2000; October to March 0900 to 2200; ☎ (973) 64 50 42.

Taüll: Iglesia de Sant Climent – Open daily 1 July to 30 September 1030 to 1400 and 1600 to 2000; 50 pts; ☎ (973) 69 40 00.

PLASENCIA

Catedral – Open daily 0930 to 1230 and 1600 to 1730 (1700 to 1830 in summer); 100 pts; ☎ (927) 41 27 66.

Excursion

Monasterio de Yuste – Open daily 0930 to 1230 and 1530 to 1845; 100 pts; ☎ (927) 17 21 30.

POBLET

Monasterio – Guided tours (1 hour) daily 1000 to 1230 and 1500 to 1800 (1730 1 November to 28 February); closed 25 December; 400 pts; ☎ (977) 87 02 54.

Excursion

Monasterio de Santa María de Vallbona de les Monges – Open daily March to October 1030 (1200 Sundays and public holidays) to 1330 and 1630 to 1830; November to February daily 1030 (1200 Sundays and public holidays) to 1330 and 1630 to 1730; closed Good Friday (afternoon only) and 25 December; 150 pts; ☎ (973) 33 02 66.

PONTEVEDRA
🛈 General Mola 1 bajo, 36002 ☎ (986) 85 08 14

Museo Provincial – Open Tuesdays to Saturdays 1000 to 1330 and 1630 to 2000; Sundays and public holidays 1100 to 1300; closed Mondays, 1 and 6 January and 25 December; 400 pts; ☎ (986) 85 14 55.

Iglesia de Santa María la Mayor – Open Mondays to Saturdays 1000 to 1230 and 1700 to 1930; Sundays and public holidays 1700 to 1930 (avoid visiting during services); ☎ (986) 85 22 19.

Ruinas de Santo Domingo – Open 1 June to 30 September 1000 to 1400; closed rest of year; 400 pts; ☎ (986) 85 14 55.

PRIEGO DE CÓRDOBA

Parroquia de la Asunción – Open daily 1000 to 1300 and 2000 to 2200; if closed, ask for key at priest's house opposite; ☎ (957) 54 07 96.

PUENTE VIESGO

Cueva del Castillo – Guided tours (3/4 hour) daily except Mondays 1 November to 31 March 1000 to 1415; 1 April to 31 October 1000 to 1215 and 1500 to 1815; closed 1 January, 1 and 22 May and 25 December; 400 pts ; ☎ (942) 59 84 25.

Excursions

Castañeda: Antigua Colegiata – To visit, ask for Doña Carmen Castanedo; ☎ (942) 59 82 80.

R

REINOSA

Excursion

Cervatos: Antigua Colegiata – Ask for key at house next door (Señorita Esther or Don Julio); ☎ (942) 75 10 36.

RÍAS ALTAS

Iglesia de San Martín de Mondoñedo – Open daily by prior arrangement 1700 to 2000; ☎ (982) 14 00 27 (ask for Señora Aurora).

RÍAS BAJAS

Padrón: Iglesia Parroquial – Open afternoons daily 1 June to 30 September; closed Sundays and during services; ☎ (981) 81 03 50.

RIPOLL Pl. de l'Abat Oliba. 17500. (972) 70 23 51

Antiguo Monasterio de Santa María – Open daily 0800 to 1300 and 1500 to 2000; cloisters (claustro) open daily except Mondays 1000 to 1300 and 1500 to 1900; 50 pts for the cloisters; (972) 70 02 43.

RONCESVALLES Antiguo Molino. 31650. (948) 76 01 93

Ecclesiastical buildings

Iglesia de la Real Colegiata – Open daily except Mondays 0800 to 2000; (948) 76 00 00.

Sala Capitular – Same as above.

Museo – Guided visits (1 hour) daily during Holy Week and in summer 1100 to 1330 and 1600 to 1800; 400 pts; (948) 76 00 00.

RONDA Pl. de España 1. 29400. (95) 287 12 72

Museo Taurino – Open daily 1000 to 1800 (1930 in summer); closed day before and day of bullfights; 200 pts; (95) 287 41 32.

Colegiata – Open Tuesdays to Saturdays 1000 to 2000; Sundays and Mondays 1000 to 1215, 1315 to 1430 and 1500 to 2000; 150 pts; (95) 287 21 42.

Baños árabes – Open Tuesdays to Saturdays 0900 to 1330 and 1600 to 1800; Sundays and public holidays 1030 to 1300; closed Mondays; (95) 287 21 42.

Excursion

Cueva de la Pileta – Guided tours (1 hour) daily 0900 to 1300 and 1600 to 1800; 500 pts; (95) 216 72 02.

S

SAGUNTO Cronista Chabret. 46500. (96) 266 22 13

Ruins (Teatro and Acrópolis) – Open Tuesdays to Saturdays 1000 to 1400 and 1600 to 1800; Sundays and public holidays 1000 to 1400; 1 June to 30 September 1000 to 2000; closed Mondays. 1 January. Good Friday and 25 December; (96) 266 255 81.

Excursions

Grutas de San José – Open daily except Mondays 1 March to 31 May 1050 to 1300 and 1510 to 1800; 1 June to 30 September 1010 to 2110; rest of year 1050 to 1300 and 1520 to 1730; closed 1 January and 25 December; 800 pts; (964) 69 05 76.

Segorbe: Catedral and Museo – Guided tours (45 mins) Tuesdays, Thursdays and Saturdays 1100 to 1300; closed on other days; 200 pts (free on Tuesdays); (964) 11 02 76.

SALAMANCA Gran Vía 39-41. 37001. (923) 26 85 71

Clerecía – Open during services.

Universidad and Escuelas Menores – Open Mondays to Saturdays 0930 to 1330 and 1600 to 2000; Sundays and public holidays 0930 to 1330; 200 pts; (923) 29 44 00.

Catedral Nueva – Open daily 1 April to 31 October 1000 to 1400 and 1600 to 2000; 1 November to 31 March 1000 to 1400 and 1600 to 1800; (923) 21 74 76.

Catedral Vieja – Same opening times as Catedral Nueva above; 200 pts; (923) 21 74 76.

Convento de San Esteban – Open daily 0900 to 1300 and 1600 to 2000; 150 pts; (923) 21 50 00.

Convento de Las Dueñas – Open daily 1030 to 1300 and 1615 to 1900; 100 pts; (923) 21 54 42.

Iglesia de la Purísima Concepción – Open Mondays to Saturdays 1900 to 2030; Sundays 1130 to 1500.

Convento de las Ursulas and Museo – Open daily 1000 to 1300 and 1630 to 1900 (1800 in December and January); 100 pts; (923) 21 98 77.

Colegio Fonseca – Open daily except Mondays 1000 to 1400 and 1600 to 1800; 100 pts.

Excursion

Castillo de Buen Amor – Open daily 1000 to 1400 and 1500 to 1830 (2030 in summer); 200 pts; (923) 35 50 27.

SANGÜESA

Castillo de Javier – Guided tours (1/2 hour) daily 0900 to 1300 and 1600 to 1900 (until nightfall in winter); ☎ (948) 88 40 00.

Santuario de SAN IGNACIO DE LOYOLA

Santuario – Open daily 1000 to 1300 and 1500 to 1900; ☎ (943) 81 65 08.

Monasterio de SAN JUAN DE LA PEÑA

Monasterio – Open Wednesdays to Sundays 1 April to 14 October 1000 to 1330 and 1600 to 1900 (2000 in summer); rest of year 1100 to 1430; closed Mondays and Tuesdays; ☎ (974) 36 25 21.

SAN MARTíN DE VALDEIGLESIAS

Excursion

Safari Madrid – Opening times vary according to daylight and may be obtained by telephone. 1 300 pts (children 600 pts); ☎ (91) 862 23 14.

Santuario de SAN MIGUEL DE ARALAR

Santuario – Open daily throughout year 0930 to 1400 and 1600 until dusk; ☎ (948) 46 80 66.

SAN SEBASTIÁN

🛈 Reina Regente. 20003. ☎ (943) 48 11 66

Monte Igueldo: Funicular – Open daily 1100 to 2000 (2200 on public holidays); 80 pts single, 150 pts Rtn; ☎ (943) 21 05 64.

Iglesia de Santa María – Open daily 0830 to 1400 and 1600 to 2000; ☎ (943) 42 19 94.

Museo de San Telmo – Open Mondays to Saturdays 0930 to 1330 and 1600 to 1900; Sundays and public holidays 1000 to 1400; closed Mondays, 1, 6 and 20 January, Easter Monday, 1 May, 1 November, 6, 24 (afternoon), 25 and 31 (afternoon) December.

Palacio del Mar – Open 1000 to 1330 and 1530 to 1930 (2000 1 July to 15 September); closed Mondays from 15 September to 15 May, also 1 January and 25 December; 400 pts; ☎ (943) 42 49 77.

Monasterio de SANTA MARÍA DE HUERTA

Monasterio – Open Mondays to Saturdays 0900 to 1300 and 1500 to 1830; Sundays and public holidays 0900 to 1130, 1230 to 1300 and 1500 to 1830; 200 pts (free on Tuesdays); ☎ (975) 32 70 02.

SANTANDER

🛈 Estación Marítima, 39001 ☎ (942) 31 07 08

Catedral – Open daily 1100 to 1300 and 1600 to 2000; avoid visiting during services (other than to worship); ☎ (942) 22 60 24.

Museo Regional de Prehistoría y Arqueología – Open Tuesdays to Saturdays 0900 to 1300 and 1600 to 1900; Sundays and public holidays 1100 to 1400; closed Mondays, 1 January, Good Friday, 1 May and 25 December; ☎ (942) 20 71 05.

Biblioteca Menéndez Pelayo – Guided tours (20 mins) Mondays to Fridays 0930 to 1130 (every 1/2 hour); closed weekends and public holidays; ☎ (942) 23 45 34.

Museo de Bellas Artes – Open Mondays to Fridays 1000 to 1300 and 1700 to 2000 (1030 to 1300 and 1730 to 2000 15 June to 15 September); Saturdays 1000 to 1300; closed Saturday afternoons, Sundays and public holidays; ☎ (942) 23 94 85.

Excursions

Muriedas: Museo Etnográfico de Cantabria – Open Tuesdays to Saturdays 1000 to 1300 and 1600 to 1800 (16 June to 14 September 1100 to 1300 and 1600 to 1900); Sundays and public holidays 1100 to 1330; closed Mondays, 1 January, Good Friday, 1 May and 25 December; ☎ (942) 25 13 47.

Parque de la Naturaleza de Cabárceno – Open daily 0900 to 2100, 1 000 pts (cars); ☎ (942) 56 37 36.

SANT CUGAT DEL VALLÈS

Monasterio – Church: open daily 0800 to 1200 and 1800 to 2000; cloisters: open daily except Mondays 1000 to 1330 and 1500 to 1730 (1800 in summer); cloister closed on Mondays and afternoons of public holidays; 200 pts cloisters (free on Tuesdays); ☎ (93) 674 69 93.

Monasterio de SANTES CREUS

Monasterio – Open daily except Mondays 1000 to 1310 and 1500 to 1740 (1840 1 June to 30 September); closed 1 January and 25 December; 300 pts; 👁 (977) 63 83 29.

SANTIAGO DE COMPOSTELA 🛈 Vilar 43. 15705. 👁 (981) 58 40 81

The Way of St James

Puente la Reina:

Iglesia del Crucifijio – Open daily 0900 to 2100 (2200 in spring and summer); 👁 (948) 34 00 50.

Iglesia de Santiago – Open daily 1000 to 1400 and 1700 to 2000; 👁 (948) 34 01 32.

Villalcázar de Sirga:

Iglesia de Santa María la Blanca – Open daily 1000 to 1430 and 1630 to 2100; 👁 (979) 88 80 76 or 88 80 41.

Carrión de los Condes: Monasterio de San Zoilo – Open daily in summer 1000 to 1330 and 1600 to 2000; rest of year daily except Mondays 1100 to 1300 and 1600 to 1900; 👁 (979) 88 00 50.

Santiago de Compostela

Catedral – Open daily 0700 to 2100; 👁 (981) 58 35 48.

Tesoro, Capilla de las Reliquias and Museo – Open Mondays to Saturdays 1030 to 1330 and 1600 to 1800 (1900 in summer); Sundays and public holidays 1030 to 1330; 350 pts; 👁 (981) 58 35 48.

Palacio de Gelmírez – Open 1 April to 30 October only, 1000 to 1330 and 1600 to 1900; 150 pts.

Monasterio de San Martín Pinario – Open 1 June to 30 September only, 1000 to 1330 and 1600 to 1930; 200 pts.

Colegiata de Santa María del Sar – Open Mondays to Saturdays 1000 to 1300 and 1600 to 1900; closed on Sundays and public holidays; 100 pts; 👁 (981) 56 28 91.

Excursion

Pazo de Oca – Open daily 1000 to 1400 and 1600 to 2000; 500 pts (free on Mondays until 1230); 👁 (908) 98 50 19.

SANTILLANA DEL MAR 🛈 Pl. Ramón Pelayo. 39330. 👁 (942) 81 82 51

Colegiata and Claustro – Open daily except Wednesdays 1000 to 1300 and 1600 to 1800 (2000 15 June to 15 September); closed 27 June; 200 pts (combined ticket including the Museo Diocesano); 👁 (942) 81 80 04.

Museo Diocesano: Convento de Regina Coeli – Same as above.

SANT JOAN DE LES ABADESSES 🛈 Rambla Comte Guifré 5. 17860. 👁 (972) 72 05 99

Iglesia de San Juan – Open daily 16 September to 15 March 1100 to 1430 and public holidays 1100 to 1430 and 1600 to 1800; 16 March to 14 June 1100 to 1400 and 1600 to 1800; 15 to 30 June and 1 to 15 September 1000 to 1400 and 1600 to 1900. July and August 1000 to 1900; closed 1 and 6 January and Christmas; 200 pts; 👁 (972) 72 00 13.

SANTO DOMINGO DE SILOS

Monasterio – Open Tuesdays to Sundays 1000 to 1300 and 1630 to 1800; Mondays and public holidays 1630 to 1800; closed Maundy Thursday afternoon to Easter Monday morning; 150 pts (free on Mondays); 👁 (947) 39 00 68.

SEGOVIA 🛈 Plaza Mayor 10. 40001. 👁 (921) 43 03 28

Catedral – Open 1 November to end of February Mondays to Saturdays 0930 to 1300 and 1500 to 1800; 1 March to 31 October 0900 to 1900; Sundays and public holidays 0900 to 1900; 👁 (921) 42 53 25.

Claustro and Museo – Same opening times as above; 200 pts; 👁 (921) 42 53 25.

Iglesia de San Esteban – Open evenings weekdays, 1830 to 2000; 👁 (921) 42 22 37.

Alcázar – Open daily 1000 to 1800 (1900 May to September); closed 1 January and 25 December ; 350 pts; 👁 (921) 46 07 59.

Iglesia de San Millán – Open daily in summer 1100 to 1400; rest of the year during services only; ☎ (921) 46 03 34.

Monasterio de El Parral – Open daily 0930 to 1230 and 1500 to 1830 (avoid visiting during services); ☎ (921) 43 12 98.

Capilla de la Vera Cruz – Open daily except Mondays 1030 to 1330 and 1530 to 1900; closed in November; 150 pts; ☎ (921) 43 14 75.

Excursion

Palacio de Riofrío – Guided tours (50 mins) Tuesdays to Saturdays 1000 to 1330 and 1500 to 1700; Sundays and public holidays 1000 to 1400; closed Mondays, 1 and 6 January, 25 August and 25 December; 600 pts; ☎ (921) 47 00 19.

La SEU D'URGELL
🛈 Av. Valira s/n, 25700. ☎ (973) 35 15 11

Catedral de Santa María – Open Mondays to Saturdays 0930 to 1300 and 1600 to 1800; Sundays and public holidays 0930 to 1300; 250 pts (cloisters); ☎ (973) 35 15 11.

Museo Diocesano – Open 1 June to 30 September Mondays to Saturdays 1000 to 1300 and 1600 to 1900; Sundays and public holidays 1000 to 1300; the rest of the year Mondays to Saturdays 1200 to 1300; Sundays and public holidays 1100 to 1300; 250 pts; ☎ (973) 35 32 42.

SEVILLA
🛈 Av. Constitución 21. 41004. ☎ (95) 422 14 04

Giralda, Catedral and Tesoro – Open Mondays to Saturdays 1100 to 1700; Sundays and public holidays 1000 to 1600; closed 1 and 6 January, 30 May, 2 June, 15 August, 8 and 25 December; restricted times on Tuesdays, Maundy Thursday and Good Friday; 550 pts (300 pts on Sundays and public holidays if Giralda only is visited); ☎ (95) 456 33 21.

Alcázar – Open Tuesdays to Saturdays 1030 to 1700; 1 June to 30 September 1000 to 1330 and 1700 to 1900. Sundays and public holidays 1000 to 1300; closed Mondays, 1 and 6 January, Good Friday, 25 December; 600 pts; ☎ (95) 422 71 63.

Hospital de los Venerables – Guided tours (1/2 hour) daily 1000 to 1400 and 1600 to 2000; closed Good Friday and 25 December; 500 pts; ☎ (95) 456 26 96.

Museo de Bellas Artes – Open Tuesdays to Sundays 0900 to 1500; closed Mondays and public holidays; 400 pts ; ☎ (95) 422 07 90.

Casa de Pilatos – Open daily 0900 to 1400 and 1600 to 1800 (1900 in summer); 500 pts for each floor; ☎ (95) 422 52 98.

Museo Arqueológico – Open daily except Mondays and public holidays 0900 to 1400; 400 pts ; ☎ (95) 423 24 01.

Hospital de la Caridad – Open Mondays to Saturdays 1000 to 1300 and 1530 to 1800; closed Sundays and public holidays; 200 pts; ☎ (95) 422 32 32.

Convento de Santa Paula – Open daily 1000 to 1230 and 1630 to 1830; ☎ (95) 442 13 07.

Iglesia del Salvador – Open daily 0830 to 1300 (after 1000, entrance through patio); ☎ (95) 421 16 79.

Archivo General de Indias – Open weekdays 1000 to 1300; closed weekends and public holidays; ☎ (95) 422 51 58.

Excursion

Itálica – Open Tuesdays to Saturdays 0900 to 1700; Sundays 1000 to 1600; 1 April to 30 September 0900 to 1830, Sundays 0900 to 1500; closed Mondays and public holidays; 250 pts; ☎ (95) 599 73 76.

SIGÜENZA

Catedral – Open daily 0830 to 1330 and 1400 to 1830; 300 pts; ☎ (911) 39 14 19.

Museo de Arte Antiguo – Open daily in spring, summer and autumn 1130 to 1400 and 1700 to 1930; during winter open weekends only; 200 pts; ☎ (911) 39 10 23.

SITGES
🛈 Sinia Morera (Oasis). 08870. ☎ (93) 811 76 30

Museu del Cau Ferrat – Open Tuesdays to Saturdays 0930 to 1400 and 1600 to 1800; Sundays 0930 to 1400; closed Mondays and public holidays; 200 pts (free on Sundays); ☎ (93) 894 03 64.

Museo Maricel del Mar – Same as above.

Casa Llopis – Same as above.

Excursion

Vilanova i la Geltrú: Casa Papiol – Open Tuesdays to Saturdays 0930 to 1400 and 1600 to 1800; Sundays 0930 to 1400; closed Mondays; 200 pts (free on Sundays); ☏ (93) 893 03 82.

Monasterio de SOBRADO DOS MONXES

Open daily 1030 to 1315 and 1630 to 1830; 100 pts; ☏ (981) 78 75 09.

SOLSONA
⊞ Av. del Pont s/n, Ed. Piscis baixos. 25280. ☏ (973) 48 23 10

Catedral – Open daily 0900 to 1300 and 1600 to 2100; avoid visiting during services on Sundays and public holidays; ☏ (973) 48 01 23.

Museo Diocesano y Comarcal – Open daily except Mondays 1000 to 1300 and 1600 to 1800 (1630 to 1900 1 May to 30 September); closed Mondays (except public holidays), 1 January and 25 December; 200 pts; ☏ (973) 48 21 01.

SORIA
⊞ Pl. Ramón y Cajal s/n, 42002. ☏ (975) 21 20 52

Museo Numantino – Open Tuesdays to Saturdays 1000 to 1400 and 1700 to 2100; 1 October to 20 April 0930 to 1930. Sundays and public holidays 1000 to 1400; closed Mondays, 1 January, 2 October, 24, 25 and 31 December and during local festivals; 200 pts; ☏ (975) 22 13 97.

Catedral de San Pedro – Open daily 1100 to 1300 and 1700 to 1900; 50 pts; ☏ (975) 21 20 52.

Monasterio de San Juan de Duero – Open Tuesdays to Saturdays 1 November to 31 March 1000 to 1400 and 1530 to 1800; 1 April to 31 May and 1 September to 31 October 1000 to 1400 and 1600 to 1900; I June to 31 August 1000 to 1400 and 1700 to 2100; Sundays and public holidays 1000 to 1400; closed Mondays; ☏ (975) 23 02 18.

Ermita de San Saturio – Open daily 1 May to 30 September 1030 to 1400 and 1600 to 1900; rest of year 1030 to 1430 and 1700 to 2100; ☏ (975) 21 20 52.

Excursion

Ruinas de Numancia – Open Tuesdays to Saturdays 1 November to 31 March 1000 to 1400 and 1530 to 1800 (1600 to 1900 1 April to 30 June and 1 September to 31 October, 1700 to 2100 1 July to 31 August); Sundays and public holidays 1000 to 1400; closed Mondays; ☏ (975) 21 20 52.

SOS DEL REY CATÓLICO

Iglesia de San Esteban – Open Tuesdays to Saturdays 1000 to 1300 and 1600 to 1800; Sundays and public holidays 1000 to 1200 and 1600 to 1800; avoid visiting during services; closed occasionally on Mondays; 100 pts; ☏ (948) 88 82 03.

T

TALAVERA DE LA REINA

Basílica de la Virgen del Prado – Open daily 1 May to 30 September 0700 to 1400 and 1600 to 2200; rest of year 0830 to 1400 and 1600 to 1900; avoid visiting during services; ☏ (925) 80 53 00.

TARRAGONA
⊞ Fortuny 4. 43001. ☏ (977) 23 34 15

Passeig Arqueològic – Open daily except Mondays 1000 to 1730 (2000 April to June, midnight July to September); public holidays 1000 to 1300; closed 1 and 6 January, 1 May and 24, 25, 26 and 31 December; 400 pts; ☏ (977) 23 34 15.

Museo Arqueológico – Open daily except Mondays 16 June to 15 September 1000 to 1300 and 1630 to 2000; rest of year 1000 to 1330 and 1600 to 1900; public holidays 1000 to 1400; closed 1 and 6 January, 1 May, 24 June, 11 and 23 September and 25 December; 400 pts; ☏ (977) 23 62 09 or 23 62 06.

Ruinas del anfiteatro – Open daily except Mondays 1000 to 1730 (2000 April to September); public holidays 1000 to 1500; closed 1 and 6 January, 1 May and 24, 25, 26 and 31 December; 400 pts; ☏ (977) 23 21 43.

Necrópolis Paleocristiana – Same admission times and charges as the Museo Arqueológico; ☏ (977) 21 11 75.

Catedral and Museo Diocesano – Open daily except Sundays and public holidays; 16 March to 30 June 1000 to 1900; 1 July to 15 September 1000 to 1230 and 1600 to 1845; 16 September to 15 November 1000 to 1230 and 1500 to 1800; 16 November to 15 March 1000 to 1400; 300 pts; ☏ (977) 23 86 85.

Excursion

Mausoleo de Centcelles – Open daily except Mondays 1000 to 1330 and 1500 to 1730 (1830 June to September); public holidays 1000 to 1330; closed 1 January and 25 December; 200 pts (free on Tuesdays); ☏ (93) 412 11 40.

TERRASSA

🔲 Raval de Montserrat 14. 08221. ☏ (93) 733 21 62

Cuidad de Egara – Open Tuesdays to Saturdays 0930 to 1330 and 1500 to 1800; 1 May to 30 September 0930 to 1330 and 1530 to 1930; Sundays and public holidays 0930 to 1330; closed Mondays and local festivals; ☏ (93) 783 27 11.

Museo Textil – Open Tuesdays to Saturdays 0900 to 1800 (2100 Thursdays); Sundays and public holidays 1000 to 1400; closed Mondays and public holidays (except on Sundays); 200 pts (free on Sundays); ☏ (93) 785 72 98.

TERUEL

🔲 Tomás Nougués 1. 44001. ☏ (978) 60 22 79

Museo Provincial – Open Tuesdays to Fridays 1000 to 1400 and 1600 to 1900; weekends 1000 to 1400; closed Mondays, public holidays and 24 and 31 December; ☏ (978) 60 01 50.

Catedral – Open daily 0900 to 1400 and 1700 to 2100; ☏ (978) 60 22 75.

Mausoleo de los Amantes de Teruel – Open daily except Mondays 1000 to 1400 and 1700 to 1930; Sundays and public holidays 1030 to 1400; 50 pts; ☏ (978) 60 21 67.

TOLEDO

🔲 Puerta de Bisagra s/n. 45003. ☏ (925) 22 08 43

Catedral – Open daily 1030 to 1300 (1330 on public holidays) and 1530 to 1800 (1900 in summer); closed all day on Good Friday and 25 December, mornings of 1 January, Palm Sunday, Wednesday before Easter, Easter Sunday, Corpus Christi, 15 August, 8 December and afternoon of 31 December; 350 pts; ☏ (925) 22 22 41.

Iglesia de Santo Tomé – Open daily 1000 to 1345 and 1530 to 1745 (1845 in summer); closed 1 January and 25 December; 100 pts; ☏ (925) 22 08 43 or 21 02 09.

Casa y Museo de El Greco – Open Tuesdays to Saturdays 1000 to 1400 and 1600 to 1800; Sundays 1000 to 1400; closed Mondays, 1 January and 25 December; 400 pts; ☏ (925) 22 08 43 or 22 40 46.

Sinagoga del Tránsito – Same as above; 400 pts; ☏ (925) 22 08 43 or 22 36 65.

Sinagoga de Santa María la Blanca – Open daily 1000 to 1400 and 1530 to 1800 (1900 in summer); closed 1 January and 25 December; 100 pts; ☏ (925) 22 08 43 or 22 72 57.

Monasterio de San Juan de los Reyes – Open daily 1000 to 1345 and 1530 to 1800 (1900 in summer); closed 1 January and 25 December; 100 pts; ☏ (925) 22 08 43 or 22 38 02.

Iglesia de San Román: Museo de los Concilios de Toledo y Cultura Visigoda – Open Tuesdays to Saturdays 1000 to 1400 and 1600 to 1830; Sundays 1000 to 1400; closed Mondays, 1 January and 25 December; 100 pts; ☏ (925) 22 08 43 or 22 78 72.

Museo de Santa Cruz – Open Mondays 1000 to 1400 and 1600 to 1830; Tuesdays to Saturdays 1000 to 1830; Sundays 1000 to 1400; closed 1 January and 25 December; 200 pts; ☏ (925) 22 08 43 or 22 10 36.

Alcázar – Open Tuesdays to Saturdays 0930 to 1330 and 1600 to 1730; Sundays 1000 to 1330 and 1600 to 1730 (1830 in summer); closed Mondays, 1 January and 25 December; 125 pts; ☏ (925) 22 08 43 or 22 30 38.

Taller del Moro – Open Tuesdays to Saturdays 1000 to 1400 and 1600 to 1830; Sundays 1000 to 1400; closed Mondays, 1 January and 25 December; 100 pts; ☏ (925) 22 08 43 or 22 71 15.

Hospital de Tavera – Open daily 1030 to 1330 and 1530 to 1800; 500 pts; ☏ (925) 22 08 43 or 22 04 52.

Excursion

Guadamur: Castillo – Only open on 10th, 20th and 30th of every month; ☏ (925) 22 08 43.

TORDESILLAS

Convento de Santa Clara – Guided tours (1 hour) daily except Mondays 1030 to 1300 and 1600 to 1730 (1000 to 1300 and 1530 to 1830 1 April to 30 September); closed 1 and 6 January, Good Friday, 1 May, 2 fiestas in September (variable dates) and 25 December; 400 pts; ☎ (983) 77 00 71.

TORO

Colegiata – Guided tours daily 1130 to 1300 (1100 to 1300 and 1700 to 1900 1 June to 1 September); closed afternoons Sundays, Mondays and public holidays; ☎ (980) 69 03 88.

Iglesia de San Lorenzo – Same as above; ☎ (980) 69 03 88.

San Cebrián de Mazote: Iglesia – No fixed opening times; ☎ (983) 78 00 77.

TORTOSA
🚺 Av. de Generalitat s/n. 43500. ☎ (977) 44 25 67

Catedral – Open daily 0800 to 1300 and 1700 to 2000; ☎ (977) 44 17 52.

Palacio Episcopal – Open daily 1000 to 1400 except Sundays and public holidays; ☎ (977) 44 07 00.

Excursion

Parque Natural del Delta del Ebro – Open all year round; details from Delta Tourist Information Centres Mondays to Fridays 1000 to 1400 and 1500 to 1800; Saturdays 1000 to 1300 and 1530 to 1800; Sundays and public holidays 1000 to 1300; closed 1 January and 25 December; ☎ (977) 48 96 79.

TRUJILLO
🚺 Pl. Mayor s/n, 10200. ☎ (927) 32 26 77

Iglesia de Santa María – Open daily 1000 to 1400 and 1630 to 1900 (1700 to 2000 in summer); if closed, ask for Señor Fermín (caretaker) in the same square); 50 pts.

TUDELA
🚺 Carrera de Gaztambide 11. 31500. ☎ (948) 82 15 39 (Holy Week to October)

Catedral – Open Tuesdays to Saturdays 0900 to 1300 and 1600 to 1900; Sundays morning only; closed Mondays; 100 pts; ☎ (948) 41 17 93.

Excursion

Catedral de Tarazona – Closed temporarily for restoration.

Monasterio de Veruela – Open daily except Mondays; 1 October to 31 March 1000 to 1300 and 1500 to 1800; 1 April to 30 September 1000 to 1400 and 1600 to 1900; 400 pts; ☎ (976) 64 90 25.

TUI
🚺 Puente Tripes s/n, 36700. ☎ (986) 60 17 89

Catedral – Open Mondays to Saturdays 0930 to 1330 and 1630 to 2000; Sundays and public holidays 0930 to 1330; ☎ (986) 60 08 79.

U – V

ÚBEDA
🚺 Pl. del Ayuntamiento s/n, 23400. ☎ (953) 75 08 97

Iglesia de El Salvador – Enter through the Sacristy; ☎ (953) 75 08 97.

UCLÉS

Castillo-monasterio – Open daily 0900 to 2100; 200 pts; ☎ (969) 13 50 58.

VALDEPEÑAS

Excursion

Las Virtudes: Santuario de Nuestra Señora de las Virtudes – Open daily except Tuesdays 0900 to 1430 and 1730 to 2130; apply for key from caretaker at the sanctuary; ☎ (926) 34 23 41.

VALENCIA
🚺 Pl. del Ayuntamiento 1. 46002. ☎ (96) 351 04 17

Museo Fallero – Closed temporarily for restoration; ☎ (96) 347 65 85.

Catedral – Open daily 1030 to 1300 and 1630 to 1800 (1000 to 1300 and 1630 to 1900 1 May to 30 September); ☎ (96) 391 81 27.

Museo – Same opening times as the Catedral except closed Sundays and public holidays; 100 pts.

El Miguelete – Same opening times as the Catedral; 100 pts.

Iglesia de Nuestra Señora de los Desamparados – Open daily 0700 to 1400 and 1600 to 2100; closed Easter Saturday; ☏ (96) 391 92 14.

Palacio de la Generalidad – Guided tours by appointment Mondays to Fridays 0900 to 1400; 14 to 19 March 1000 to 1300; closed during official engagements; ☏ (96) 386 34 61.

Iglesia de San Nicolás – Open Mondays 0730 to 1300 and 1700 to 2030; Tuesdays to Saturdays 1000 to 1045 and 1845 to 2000; Sundays 1000 to 1300; best to avoid visitng during services; ☏ (96) 391 33 17.

Lonja – Open daily except Mondays 0830 to 1345 and 1615 to 1745; closed on public holidays; ☏ (96) 352 54 78.

Iglesia de los Santos Juanes – Open daily 1 October to 30 June 0800 to 1300 and 1800 to 2000; Sundays and public holidays 0930 to 1400 and 1700 to 1900. 1 July to 30 September 0800 to 1030; ☏ (96) 392 18 85.

Museo de Cerámica – Closed temporarily for restoration; ☏ (96) 351 63 92.

Museo San Pío V – Open Tuesdays to Saturdays 1000 to 1400 and 1600 to 1800; 1 July to 31 August 0900 to 1400; Sundays and public holidays 1000 to 1400; closed Mondays, 1 January, Good Friday and 25 December; ☏ (96) 360 57 93.

Colegio del Patriarca – Open daily 1100 to 1330; closed 1 January, during Holy Week, the week of Corpus Christi and 25 December; 150 pts; ☏ (96) 351 41 76.

Torres de Serranos – Open Mondays to Saturdays 0845 to 1315 and 1615 to 1745; closed Sundays, Mondays and public holidays; ☏ (96) 391 90 70.

Instituto Valenciano de Arte Moderno (IVAM) – Open daily except Mondays 1100 to 2000; closed 1 January, Good Friday and 25 December; 250 pts (free on Sundays); ☏ (96) 386 30 00.

Museo Paleontológico – Open Tuesdays to Fridays 0830 to 1330 and 1630 to 1815; Saturdays 0830 to 1330; closed Sundays, Mondays and public holidays; ☏ (96) 352 54 78.

Museo de Prehistoria – Closed temporarily for repairs. To reopen shortly. ☏ (96) 391 99 00.

Excursion

Puig: Monasterio de la Virgen del Puig – Open daily 1 April to 30 September 1000 to 1300 and 1600 to 1900 (1800 1 October to 31 March); 300 pts; ☏ (96) 147 02 00.

VALLADOLID   🅱 Pl. de Zorrilla 3. 47001. ☏ (983) 35 18 01

Museo Nacional de Escultura Policromada – Open Tuesdays to Saturdays 1000 to 1400 and 1600 to 1800; Sundays and public holidays 1000 to 1400; closed Mondays, 1 January and 25 December; 400 pts; ☏ (983) 26 79 67.

Catedral – Open Tuesdays to Saturdays 1000 to 1330 and 1630 to 1900; Sundays and public holidays 1000 to 1400; closed Mondays; ☏ (983) 30 43 62.

Museo – Same opening times as above; 250 pts; ☏ (983) 30 43 62.

Iglesia de Santa María la Antigua – Open Mondays to Saturdays 0900 to 1100 and 1900 to 2000; Sundays and public holidays 1000 to 1400 and 1900 to 2000.

Iglesia de las Angustias – Open during services Monday to Saturday 1200 to 1300 and 1600 to 1900; Sundays and public holidays 1200 to 1400.

Museo Oriental – Open Mondays to Saturdays 1600 to 1900; Sundays and public holidays 1000 to 1400; 300 pts; ☏ (983) 30 68 00 or 30 69 00.

Casa de Cervantes – Open Tuesdays to Saturdays 1000 to 1530; Sundays 1000 to 1500; closed Mondays, public holidays, 1 and 6 January, 23 April, 13 May, 8 September, 24, 25, 30 and 31 December; 400 pts; ☏ (983) 30 88 10.

VALLE DE LOS CAÍDOS

Basílica and La Cruz – Open Tuesdays to Sundays 1 April to 30 September 0930 to 1945; 1 October to 31 March 1000 to 1815; closed Mondays, 1 and 6 January, 2 May, 17 July, 10 August and 25 December; 600 pts (300 pts ascent by funicular railway); ☏ (91) 890 55 44.

VICH Pl. Major 1. 08500. ☏ (93) 886 20 91

Catedral – Open daily except Mondays 1000 to 1300; closed Maundy Thursday, Good Friday, Fiesta Mayor and 5 July; 200 pts; ☏ (93) 886 01 18.

Museo Episcopal – Open Mondays to Saturdays 1000 to 1300; 15 May to 14 October 1000 to 1300 and 1600 to 1800; Sundays and public holidays 1000 to 1300; closed 25 December; 200 pts (free the first Sunday of the month); ☏ (93) 886 22 14.

Excursion

L'Estany: Monasterio de Santa María – Open daily 1000 to 1300 and 1600 to 1900 (1800 in winter); 150 pts; ☏ (93) 830 08 25.

VILLAFAMÉS

Museo Popular de Arte Contemporáneo – Open Mondays to Saturdays 1100 to 1300 and 1700 to 1900; weekends 1100 to 1400 and 1600 to 1900; 1 July to 30 September 1100 to 1300 and 1700 to 2000; weekends 1100 to 1400 and 1700 to 2000; 200 pts; ☏ (964) 32 91 52.

VILLENA

Museo Arqueológico – Open weekdays 0900 to 1400; closed weekends and public holidays (except by prior arrangement), August and 4 to 9 September ; ☏ (96) 580 11 50.

Iglesia de Santiago – Open daily 1000 to 1300 and 1700 to 2100; ☏ (965) 81 39 19.

Excursion

Bocairent: Museo Parroquial – Open Mondays to Saturdays with prior arrangement; Sundays and public holidays guided visit (1 hour) at 1230; 100 pts; ☏ (96) 235 00 62.

VITORIA ☷ Parque de la Florida s/n, 01008. ☏ (945) 13 13 21

Catedral de Santa María – Open during services only; ☏ (945) 16 12 79.

Museo de Arqueología – Open Tuesdays to Fridays 1000 to 1400 and 1600 to 1830; Saturdays 1000 to 1400; Sundays and public holidays 1100 to 1400; closed Mondays, 1 January and Good Friday; ☏ (945) 23 17 77 or 23 21 98.

Museo de Bellas Artes – Same as Museo de Arqueología.

Museo « Fournier » de Naipes – Same as Museo de Arqueología.

Museo de Armería – Same as Museo de Arqueología.

Excursions

Gaceo: Iglesia – Apply to house no 10 in Gaceo for the key; ☏ (945) 30 02 37.

Alaiza: Iglesia – Ask for the key at house no 26 in Alaiza; ☏ (945) 30 02 37.

Estíbaliz: Santuario – Open daily 0930 to 1830 (2000 in summer); avoid visiting during services; ☏ (945) 29 30 88.

Mendoza: Museo de Heráldica Alavesa – Open Tuesdays to Fridays 1 May to 15 October 1100 to 1400 and 1600 to 2000; Saturdays 1100 to 1500; Sundays and public holidays 1000 to 1400; rest of year open Tuesdays to Saturdays 1100 to 1500 (1400 on Sundays); closed Mondays, 1 January and Good Friday; ☏ (945) 23 17 77.

Z

ZAFRA ☷ Pl. de España s/n, 06300. ☏ (924) 55 10 36

Iglesia de la Candelaria – Open daily 1030 to 1300 and during afternoon and evening services; ☏ (924) 55 01 28.

ZAMORA ☷ Santa Clara 20. 49014. ☏ (980) 53 18 45

Museo de la Semana Santa – Open Mondays to Saturdays 1000 to 1400 and 1600 to 1900; closed Sundays and public holidays; 200 pts; ☏ (980) 53 22 95.

Catedral and Museo Catedralicio – Open daily except Mondays 0900 to 1400 and 1600 to 1930; 200 pts; ☏ (980) 53 18 02.

Excursion

San Pedro de la Nave: Iglesia – Open daily 30 March to 30 September 1000 to 1300 and 1700 to 2000; rest of year apply to the custodian; ☏ (980) 55 57 09.

Arcenillas: Iglesia – Open daily 1000 to 1400 and 1600 to 1800; ☏ (980) 57 12 15.

ZARAGOZA

2 Torreón de la Zuda – Glorieta Pio XII. 50003. ☎ (976) 39 35 37

La Seo – Closed temporarily for restoration; ☎ (976) 39 03 86.

Lonja – Temporary exhibitions; open Tuesdays to Saturdays 1000 to 1400 and 1800 to 2100; Sundays and public holidays 1100 to 1400; closed Mondays and during non-exhibition periods; ☎ (976) 39 72 39.

Basílica de Nuestra Señora del Pilar – Open daily 1000 to 1300; ☎ (976) 39 03 86.

Museo Pilarista – Open daily 0900 to 1400 and 1600 to 1800; 150 pts; ☎ (976) 39 74 97.

Aljafería – Open Tuesdays to Saturdays 1000 to 1400 and 1630 to 1830 (1600 to 2000 in summer); Sundays and public holidays 1000 to 1400; closed Mondays; ☎ (976) 43 56 18.

Excursion

Fuendetodos: Casa de Goya – Open daily except Mondays 1100 to 1400 and 1600 to 1900; closed 1 January and 24, 25 and 31 December; 150 pts; ☎ (976) 14 38 30.

Museo de Grabados – Same opening times as above; 150 pts; ☎ (976) 14 38 30.

Islas Baleares

Mallorca

ALCÚDIA

2 Av. Rey Juan Carlos I 68. 07400. ☎ (971) 89 26 15

Museo monográfico de Pollentia – Open daily except Mondays 1 April to 31 October 1000 to 1330 and 1700 to 1900; rest of year by prior arrangement only; 200 pts; ☎ (971) 54 64 13.

Excursions

Cuevas de Campanet – Guided tours (40 mins) daily 1000 to 1800 (1900 in summer); closed 1 January and 25 December; 800 pts; ☎ (971) 51 61 30.

Muro: Sección Etnológica del Museo de Mallorca – Open Tuesdays to Saturdays 1000 to 1400 and 1600 to 1900; Sundays and public holidays 1000 to 1400; closed Mondays; 400 pts; ☎ (971) 71 75 40.

PALMA DE MALLORCA

2 Av. de Jaume III 10. 07012. ☎ (971) 71 22 16

Catedral and Museo-Tesoro – Open Mondays to Fridays 1000 to 1600 (1800 in summer); Saturdays 1000 to 1400; closed Sundays and public holidays; 300 pts; ☎ (971) 72 31 30.

La Almudaina – Guided tours (35 mins) Mondays to Fridays 1 May to 31 October 1000 to 1900; 1 November to 30 April 1000 to 1400 and 1600 to 1800; Saturdays and public holidays 1000 to 1400; closed Sundays, 1, 6 and 20 January, 4 April and 25 and 26 December; 600 pts; ☎ (971) 72 71 45.

Iglesia de Santa Eulalia – Open Mondays to Saturdays 0700 to 1300 and 1700 to 2000; Sundays and public holidays 0800 to 1300 and 1800 to 2200; avoid visiting during services; ☎ (971) 71 46 25.

Iglesia de Sant Francesc – Open Mondays to Saturdays 0930 to 1200 and 1530 to 1800; Sundays and public holidays 0930 to 1300; 75 pts; ☎ (971) 71 26 95.

Baños árabes – Open daily 0930 to 2000; 100 pts; ☎ (971) 72 15 49.

Museo de Mallorca – Open Tuesdays to Saturdays 1000 to 1400 and 1600 to 1900; Sundays 1000 to 1400; closed Mondays and public holidays; 400 pts; ☎ (971) 71 75 40.

Museo Diocesano – Open Mondays to Fridays 1000 to 1330 and 1500 to 1800 (2000 in summer); weekends and public holidays 1000 to 1330; 200 pts; ☎ (971) 71 40 63.

Llotja – Only open for exhibitions; Tuesdays to Saturdays 1100 to 1400 and 1700 to 2100; Sundays and public holidays 1100 to 1400; closed Mondays; ☎ (971) 71 22 16.

Palacio Sollerich – Closed temporarily for repairs; ☎ (971) 71 22 16.

Pueblo Español – Open daily 0900 to 1900; 375 pts; ☎ (971) 73 70 75.

Castillo de Bellver – Open daily 0800 to 1800 (2000 1 April to 30 September); museum closed Sundays and public holidays; castle and museum closed 1 January and 25 December; 225 pts; ☎ (971) 73 06 57.

Fundació Pilar i Joan Miró – Open Tuesdays to Saturdays 1000 to 1800 (1900 in summer); Sundays and public holidays 1100 (1000 in summer) to 1500; closed Mondays; 500 pts; (971) 70 14 20.

COSTA ROCOSA

Real Cartuja de Valldemosa – Open daily except Sundays; 1 April to 30 September 0930 to 1300 and 1500 to 1830 (1730 November to February and 1800 March and October); closed 1 January and 25 December; 900 pts; ☎ (971) 61 21 06.

Son Marroig – Open daily except Sundays; 1 April to 31 October 0930 to 1430 and 1500 to 2000 ; 1 November to 31 March 0930 to 1400 and 1500 to 1800; closed 1 January and 25 December; 250 pts; ☎ (971) 63 91 58.

Jardines de Alfabia – Open Mondays to Fridays 0930 to 1730 (1900 1 April to 31 October); Saturdays 0930 to 1730; closed Sundays; 300 pts; ☎ (971) 61 31 23.

Monasterio de Nuestra Señora de Lluc – Open all year except 25 December; ☎ (971) 51 70 25.

The EAST COAST and its CAVES

Cala Ratjada: Casa March – Guided tours (2 hours) Mondays to Fridays by prior arrangement; closed weekends and public holidays; 350 pts; ☎ (971) 56 30 33.

Coves d'Artà – Guided tours (40 mins) daily 1000 to 1700 (1900 1 April to 31 October); closed on public holidays; 750 pts; ☎ (971) 56 32 93.

Coves dels Hams – Guided tours (40 mins) daily 1030 to 1315 and 1415 to 1700 (1730 1 April to 30 September); closed 1 January and 25 December; 1 000 pts; ☎ (971) 82 09 88.

Coves del Drac – Guided tours (1 hour 10 mins) daily at 1045, 1200, 1400 and 1530 (with concert); 1 April to 31 October guided tours at 1000, 1100, 1200, 1400, 1500, 1600 and 1700 (with concert); closed 1 January and 25 December; 800 pts; ☎ (971) 82 16 17.

Monasterio de Sant Salvador – Open all day every day; ☎ (971) 58 00 56.

Santuario de Cura – Open daily 1000 to 1315 and 1530 to 1800 (1600 to 1900 in summer); ☎ (971) 66 09 94.

Menorca

CIUTADELLA

Catedral – Open daily 0930 to 1300 and 1700 to 2000; ☎ (971) 38 07 39.

MAÓ
🛈 Pl. Explanada 40. ☎ (971) 36 37 90

Museo Arqueológico – Closed temporarily for restoration.

Ibiza

EIVISSA / IBIZA
🛈 Vara de Rey 13. 07800. ☎ (971) 30 19 00

Catedral – Open daily except Sundays 1 April to 31 October 1000 to 1300; rest of year only open Fridays; ☎ (971) 31 27 73.

Museo Arqueológico – Closed temporarily for restoration. ☎ (971) 30 17 71.

Museo Monógrafico de Puig des Molins – Open Mondays to Saturdays 1000 to 1300 and 1600 to 1900 (1700 to 2000 1 July to 30 September); closed Sundays and public holidays; 400 pts; ☎ (971) 30 17 71.

Index

X - Y - Z